Computer and Information Sciences

Lecture Notes in Electrical Engineering

Volume 62

For other titles published in this series, go to
www.springer.com/series/7818

Erol Gelenbe • Ricardo Lent • Georgia Sakellari
Ahmet Sacan • Hakki Toroslu • Adnan Yazici

Editors

Computer and Information Sciences

Proceedings of the 25th International
Symposium on Computer and Information
Sciences

 Springer

Editors

Prof. Erol Gelenbe
Imperial College
EEE Dept.
Exhibition Road
SW72BT London
United Kingdom
e.gelenbe@imperial.ac.uk

Dr. Ricardo Lent
Imperial College
EEE Dept.
South Kensington Campus
Exhibition Road
SW72AZ London
United Kingdom
r.lent@imperial.ac.uk

Dr. Georgia Sakellari
Imperial College
EEE Dept.
South Kensington Campus
Exhibition Road
SW72AZ London
United Kingdom
g.sakellari@imperial.ac.uk

Dr. Ahmet Sacan
Drexel University
School of Biomedical Eng., Sci.
and Heal
Bossone 702, 3120 Market Street
19104 Philadelphia Pennsylvania
USA
ahmet.sacan@drexel.edu

Prof. Hakki Toroslu
Middle East Technical University
Dept. of Computer Engineering
06531 Ankara
Turkey
toroslu@ceng.metu.edu.tr

Prof. Adnan Yazici
Middle East Technical University - METU
Fac. Engineering
Dept. Computer Engineering
06531 Ankara
Turkey
yazici@ceng.metu.edu.tr

ISSN 1876-1100   e-ISSN 1876-1119
ISBN 978-94-007-3320-6   ISBN 978-90-481-9794-1 (eBook)
DOI 10.1007/978-90-481-9794-1
Springer Dordrecht Heidelberg London New York

Cover design: SPI Publisher Services

Printed on acid-free paper

Springer is part of Springer Science+Business Media (www.springer.com)

25th International Symposium on Computer and Information Sciences

Symposium Chair's Foreword

This conference that is held on 22nd to 24th September 2010 at the Royal Society in London and is organised by Imperial College, is the 25th of an annual series of meetings that started at Bilkent University in Ankara, Turkey, in 1986, with subsequent conferences annual held in various cities including Istanbul, Izmir, Antalya, Çesme, Belek and other sites in Turkey, as well as in the USA (Orlando) and at the Middle East Technical University campus in North Cyprus. Such a long history can only continue with the active support of Computer Scientists from Turkey, France, Greece, Italy, the UK and other countries. This conference series is inclusive as to topics, but selective in matters of quality. This year's programme benefits from the contributions of very distinguished keynote speakers, and was established by the programme committee with the help of numerous referees. I take the opportunity here to thank them all, as well as all the other Programme Co-Chairs, the Technical Area Leaders. I would like to acknowledge in particular the organisational support of Dr Ricardo Lent, Dr Georgia Sakellari, Gökçe Görbil, Mrs Shahareen Hilmy and Mrs Fabienne Paul. All those who submitted papers have my gratitude for their very valuable effort and contributions, and I am very grateful to our distinguished keynote speakers Prof. Samson Abramsky, Prof. Steve Furber, Prof. Tony Hoare, Prof. Richard Karp, Prof. Raudy Katz and Prof Aurel Lazar.

Erol Gelenbe, Imperial College

ISCIS 2010 Conference Organisers

- Conference Chair: Erol Gelenbe (Imperial College)
- Program Co-Chairs: Erol Gelenbe (Imperial College), Ahmet Sacan (Drexel University), Hakki Toroslu (METU), Adnan Yazıcı (METU)
- Publication Chair: Dr Ricardo Lent
- Publicity Chair: Dr Georgia Sakellari
- Organization Chairs: Gökce Görbil & Mrs Shahareen Hilmy

Programme Committee Technical Area Leaders

- Prof Ethem Alpaydın, Bogaziçi University (Machine Learning and Computational Intelligence)
- Prof Cevdet Aykanat, Bilkent University (Parallel and Distributed Systems)
- Dr Javier Barria, Imperial College (Computer Networks)
- Prof Manfred Broy, Technical University of Munich (Software Engineering)
- Prof Paolo Camici, Imperial College (Medical Imaging)
- Prof Reuven Cohen, Technion, (Wireless Networks)
- Prof Ilyas Çiçekli, Bilkent University (Natural Language Processing)
- Prof Mariangiola Dezani, University of Torino (Theory)
- Prof Jean-Michel Fourneau, University of Versailles (Stochastic Networks)
- Prof Steve Furber, University of Manchester (Digital Systems)
- Prof Muhittin Gökmen, Istanbul Technical University, & Prof Fatos Yarman-Vural, METU (Computer Vision and Applications)
- Prof Peter Harrison & Dr Will Knottenbelt, Imperial College (Performance Evaluation)
- Prof Volkan Atalay, METU, & Prof Jane Hillston, University of Edinburgh (Bioinformatics)
- Prof Chris Mitchell, Royal Holloway University of London (Cybersecurity)
- Prof Yves Robert, ENS Lyon (Scheduling, Load Balancing, and Resource Management Algorithms)
- Prof Hakki Toroslu, METU (Data Mining and Web Discovery)
- Prof Andreas Stafylopatis, National Technical University Athens (Neural Networks)
- Prof Adnan Yazıcı, METU (Database Systems)

Members

- Dr Niall M. Adams (Imperial College)
- Dr Baltazar Aguda (Ohio State University)
- Dr Yasemin Altun (Max Planck Institute, Tuebingen)

- Dr Francois Baccelli (Ecole Normale Superieure)
- Dr Olivier Beaumont (INRIA/LABRI, Bordeaux)
- Prof Monique Becker (INT, Evry, France)
- Dr Jeremy Bradley (Imperial College)
- Prof Fazli Can (Bilkent University, Ankara)
- Dr Zehra Çataltepe (Istanbul Technical University)
- Dr Hakan Çevikalp (Osmangazi University, Eskisehir, Turkey)
- Dr Sophie Chabridon (INT, Evry, France)
- Dr Chi-Kin Chau (University of Cambridge and University College London)
- Dr Nihan Çiçekli (METU)
- Dr Tadeusz Czachorski (Polish Academy of Science)
- Dr Gökhan Dalkılıç (Dokuz Eylul University)
- Dr T. H. Dao Thi (PRiSM, University of Versailles)
- Prof Nadia Erdogan (Istanbul Technical University)
- Dr Seyda Ertekin (The Pennsylvania State University)
- Dr Engin Erzin (Koç University, Istanbul)
- Dr Taner Eskil, Isik University, Istanbul
- Dr Guy Fayolle (INRIA)
- Dr Yutao Feng (Ambarella Laboratories, Shanghai)
- Dr Robert Ghanea-Hercock (BT)
- Dr Stephen Gilmore (University of Edinburgh)
- Dr Sezer Goren, Bahcesehir University, Istanbul
- Dr Dilan Görür (Gatsby Computational Neuroscience Unit, University College London)
- Dr Lin Guan (University of Loughborough)
- Dr Ugur Güdükbay (Bilkent University, Ankara)
- Dr Hatice Gunes (Imperial College)
- Dr Attila Gursoy (Koç University, Istanbul)
- Prof Ugur Halici (METU)
- Prof Yorgo Istefanopulos (Isik University, Istanbul)
- Dr Alain Jean-Marie (LIRMM University of Montpellier)
- Dr H. Emre Kankaya (Zirve University, Gaziantep, Turkey)
- Dr İbrahim Körpeoğlu (Bilkent University, Ankara)
- Dr Peter Key (Microsoft Research, Cambridge, UK)
- Prof Stefanos Kollias (NTUA Athens)
- Dr Alain Kurinckx (Thales Group)
- Dr Taskin Kocak (Bahcesehir University, Istanbul)
- Dr Olcay Kursun (Istanbul University)
- Prof Doron Lancet (Weizmann Institute of Science, Rehovot)
- Dr Ricardo Lent (Imperial College)
- Dr Albert Levi (Sabanci University)
- Prof Aristides Likas (NTUA Athens)
- Dr Peixiang Liu (Nova Southeastern University)
- Dr George Loukas (London Technology Network)
- Prof Pedro Mendes (University of Manchester)

- Prof Rosa Meo (University of Torino)
- Dr Philippe Nain (INRIA)
- Prof Selma Oktug (Istanbul Technical University)
- Dr Ender Ozcan (University of Nottingham)
- Dr Öznur Özkasap (Koç University, Istanbul)
- Dr Ferhan Pekergin (University of Paris-Nord)
- Prof Nihal Pekergin (LACL, Université Paris-Est Val de Marne, France)
- Dr Georgia Sakellari (Imperial College)
- Dr. Huseyin Seker (De Montfort University, UK)
- Dr Ercan Solak (Isik University, Istanbul)
- Prof Boleslaw Szymanski (Rensselaer Poytechnic Institute)
- Dr Halina Tarasiuk (Technical University of Warsaw)
- Dr Nigel Thomas (University of Newcastle upon Tyne)
- Prof Salvatore Tucci (University of Roma II - Tor Vergata)
- Dr Elif Uysal-Biyikoglu (METU, Ankara)
- Prof Ozgur Ulusoy (Bilkent University, Ankara)
- Dr Özlem Uzuner (METU NCC and University at Albany, SUNY)
- Prof. Frank Wang (Cranfield University, UK)
- Dr Zhiguang Xu (Valdosta State University)
- Dr Berrin Yanikoglu (Sabanci University, Istanbul)
- Dr Husnu Yenigün (Sabanci University)
- Dr Emine Yilmaz (Microsoft Research, Cambridge, UK)
- Dr Arda Yurdakul (Bogaziçi University, Istanbul)
- Prof Tom Ziemke (University of Skovde)
- Dr Qi Zhu (University of Houston)

Table of Contents

3   Bioinformatics & Bioengineering

4   Data Engineering

5   Learning and Clustering Methods

6   Computer and Wireless Networks

7   Computer Vision and Image Processing

8   Web Systems

9   Discovery Science

10   Distributed and Parallel Algorithms

11   Hardware Design

1 Algorithms

Partially Persistent B-trees with Constant Worst Case Update Time

George Lagogiannis[1], Nikos Lorentzos[1]

[1] Agricultural University of Athens, Dept. of Science, Informatics Laboratory, 75 Iera Odos str., Botanikos, GR-118 55, Athens, Greece

{lagogian, lorentzos}@aua.gr

Abstract: A partially persistent B-tree is presented, with a worst case constant update time, in the case that the position of the update is given. This is achieved by the use of the fat node method, which enables the transformation of an ephemeral (a, b) tree with constant update time into a partially persistent tree. Such a structure can be usZeful in persistent databases for applications in which the update time is critical. The model of computation is the external memory model.

Keywords: Data structures, Indexing structures, Algorithms, Persistence

1. Introduction

In this paper we are adding partial persistence to a balanced search tree with a worst case constant update time [6] (in the case that the position of the update is given), via the node-copying method [5].

The idea in [6] is to organize the leaves of an (a, b) tree into buckets, with each bucket containing $O(h)$ leaves, where h is the height of tree. A brief description of the structure is as follows: In every bucket, a pointer (called *r_pointer*) is stored, that points to an ancestor (or to a node "near" an ancestor) of the bucket. When an update occurs inside the bucket, we follow the r_pointer, rebalance the pointed ancestor and set the r_pointer to point one level upwards. After each such step, the bucket is split incrementally and, when the r_pointer reaches the root of the tree, the incremental process completes. Let u be the node pointed by the r_pointer of a bucket. To rebalance u, the following actions are performed: If u has more than b children (we call such a node *big*), u is split into two small nodes otherwise u is left intact (we call such a node *small*). In either case, the r_pointer is moved up one level. It is proved in [6] that, starting from an (a, b)-tree, this algorithm produces an $(a, 2b)$-tree.

To achieve partial persistence, two general methods have been presented in [5], namely the *fat-node* and the *node-copying* method. It has also been proved that only a constant number of nodes need to be updated in the amortized sense, for each ephemeral update step. Thus, both time and space overheads are $O(1)$ amortized. For the RAM model of computation, this amortization was eliminated by Dietz and Raman [4]. In the pointer machine model, Brodal [2] eliminated the amortization for

E. Gelenbe et al. (eds.), *Computer and Information Sciences*, Lecture Notes
in Electrical Engineering 62, DOI 10.1007/978-90-481-9794-1_1,
© Springer Science+Business Media B.V. 2010

partially persistent data structures of bounded in-degree. According to the solution of Brodal, the maximum number of fields stored in a node is M=$2bd$+1, where b is the bound of the in-degree and d is the bound of the out-degree (b and d are constants).

On a first glance, the feeling is that the solution by Brodal is also a solution to our problem. However, this is not true. Indeed, assuming that we can reach the exact point (leaf of the B-tree) of the update in constant time, we need to store in each node a pointer to its father, so that we can move towards the root. Thus, the in-degree and the out-degree of the internal nodes is O(B), where B is the number of records that fit into a disk block. As a consequence M, the maximum number of records in each internal node, becomes O(B^2), according to the solution by Brodal. This means that each internal node needs O(B) I/Os in order to be accessed. Contrary to this, we need a solution that produces nodes that fit into a constant number of disk blocks. Such a solution is presented in this paper.

In our new indexing structure, the time complexity, to search old versions, is O($(\log_B m/B)^2$), where m is the total number of updates and B is the number of records that fit into a block of secondary memory. For the current version, the time complexity, to search, is O($\log_B m/B$). For the current version, the time complexity for searching is O($\log_B m/B$). The space occupied by the data structure is O(m/B) blocks.

2   The new Indexing Structure

The data structure is a two-level tree. The upper level is a tree, and each node of this tree is a *fat node*. Each fat node is composed of *persistent* nodes. According to the fat-node method, each *ephemeral node* corresponds to a fat node that contains all the versions of the ephemeral node. In our data structure, each fat node is a separate tree, and all the versions of the corresponding ephemeral node are contained in the leaves of the fat node. When a node (or bucket) is rebalanced, a new right sibling is added to that node (or bucket). This means that the rightmost leaf of a fat node contains the current version of the corresponding ephemeral node. Persistent nodes and buckets that belong to the current version are called *active*, otherwise they are called *inactive*.

The general idea is to transform the leaves of the fat nodes of level 0 into buckets, with each bucket containing O(h) elements (as in [6]), where h is the height of the two-level tree. Thus, the fat nodes of level 0 are slightly different from the fat nodes of the above levels, whose leaves are persistent nodes (they are not buckets). Each bucket is rebalanced incrementally, and we can afford to split it into two new buckets and rebalance all the ancestors of the new buckets, by paying O(1) I/Os per insertion (note that we handle only insertions) while, at the same time, we are able to keep the bucket-size under control (i.e., O(h)).

Our starting point is an (a, b) tree. The only rebalancing action is a split and we organize the leaves of the tree in buckets. The height of the persistent structure is O($(\log_a m)^2$), where m is the number of updates. This is because each root-to-leaf path contains O($\log_a m/a$) fat nodes, and each fat node has O($\log_a m/a$) height. Each bucket has a capacity of O($(\log_a m)^2$) elements, i.e. O(h) elements. Each element inside a bucket corresponds to a *data record* whereas persistent nodes contain *index records* (for a detailed description of the data and the index rerecords, see [1]).

A rebalancing operation on a bucket may cause the rebalancing of all the internal persistent nodes on the path, from the bucket to the root of the tree. This rebalancing is performed incrementally, and is divided into two stages, each of them requiring $O((\log_a m)^2)$ time. During the first stage, an incremental split of the bucket is performed, and two new buckets are created. Each incremental step manipulates a constant number of records (elements). When the first stage completes, a pointer (called $r\_pointer$ in [6]) is stored in the pair of the new buckets and is initially set to point to the father of the initial bucket. This pointer is used during the second stage, during which the ancestors of the new buckets are updated. Again, the second stage is incremental, and rebalances, if needed, a constant number of ancestors at a time. Each internal node is rebalanced by using the ideas of [6].

The exact algorithm as well as its analysis and proofs are omitted due to space limitations, however it can be found in [8]. In brief, we mention the following: By using the proof methodology of [6], it is proved that the maximum number of records inside an internal node is $2b$. This means that, starting from an (a, b) tree, our algorithm produces an $(a, 2b)$ tree. Since the maximum number of records in a persistent node is $2b$, by setting $B=2b$, each persistent node fits into 1 disk block, therefore the requirement set in Section 2 is met. The space required by our indexing structure is proved to be $O(m/B)$ disk blocks. It is also shown that the time complexity for searching a key x at time t is $O((\log_B m/B)^2)$. The time complexity for updates is $O(1)$, since each update step accesses a constant number of disk blocks.

3   Enhancement of the Indexing Structure

In this section we enhance our indexing structure, thus achieving an $O(\log_B m/B)$ time for searching in the current version. For this purpose, we first need to spare $O(1)$ I/Os per fat node, as we move towards the buckets. This can easily be achieved by storing a new pointer into the root of every fat node, which points to the rightmost leaf of the fat node. Starting now from the root of the tree, we can reach the leaf-level, by sparing $O(\log_B m/B)$ I/Os. However, we additionally need to reduce the size of the buckets to $O(\log_B m/B)$ elements.

By reducing the size of the buckets to $O(\log_B m/B)$ elements, our challenge is to revise the second stage of our algorithm, so as it to complete in $O(\log_B m/B)$ updates rather than $O((\log_B m/B)^2)$ updates. To achieve this, we make use of a redundant counter (see [3], [7]), on every fat node.

Each node of the rightmost path of a fat node corresponds to a digit of a redundant counter. Also, the father of the rightmost leaf corresponds to the least-significant digit. Note that we only need to increase by one the least-significant digit of the counter. Let d_z be the digit of the counter that corresponds to node z of the path. Then d_z is equal with the number of records of z. Also, a digit is *fixed* when its value becomes equal to B. Once a digit is fixed, it becomes equal to 1. (Note that for the redundant counter to work properly, it is necessary for $B-2>1$. Clearly, it holds for realistic values of B). In particular, when we fix the digit corresponding to node z, we split z into two new nodes, z_1 and z_2. Node z_2 takes the place of z at the rightmost path. Since z_2 has only one record, as already mentioned, the digit that corresponds to z_2

becomes 1. Assume now that the rightmost leaf of a fat node is split. This action increases by 1 the least significant digit of the counter. Then, according to the algorithm that increments the least significant digit of a redundant counter, we only need to fix at most two digits of the counter (see [7]), which means that at most two nodes of the rightmost path of the fat node will be rebalanced.

We can now spare $O(1)$ I/Os per fat node, during the second stage. Since the number of fat nodes between the root and any leaf is $O(\log_B m/B)$, it follows that the second stage completes within $O(\log_B m/B)$ updates. The time complexity to search for a key at the current version has now become $O(\log_B m/B)$ I/Os.

4. A Final Remark

So far, our structure supports only insertions. To also support deletions, we use the solution given in [6], i.e. the global rebuilding technique. This way, the time complexity for searching the current version becomes optimal (i.e. $O(\log_B N/B)$ I/Os, where N is the number of valid elements in the current version). The details are omitted.

One interesting observation is that the idea of adding redundant counters to the fat nodes can easily by used in the framework of [5] (i.e., it can be used in a class of data structures, called *linked structures*), in order to reduce the logarithmic ($O\log m$) time overhead per update, to $O(1)$, for the fat node method. The details are trivial.

References

1. Becker B., Gschwind S., Ohler T., Seeger B., Widmayer P.: An asymptotically optimal multiversion B-tree. The VLDB Journal. 5, 264-275 (1996).
2. Brodal G.S.: Partially Persistent Data Structures of Bounded Degree with Constant Update Time. Nordic Journal of Computing, Vol. 3, No. 3, 238-255 (1996).
3. Clancy M. J. and Knuth D. E.: A programming and problem-solving seminar. Technical Report STAN- CS-77-606, Department of Computer Science, Stanford University, Palo Alto (1977).
4. Dietz P. And Raman R.: Persistence, amortization and randomization. In: 2nd ACM-SIAM Symposium on Discrete Algorithms (SODA), 78-88, (1991).
5. Driscoll R., Sarnak N., Sleator D. and Tarjan R.E.: Making Data Structures Persistent. JCSS, 38, 86-124 (1989).
6. Fleischer R.: A simple balanced search tree with $O(1)$ worst-case update time. International Journal of Foundations of Computer Science. 7, 137-149 (1996).
7. Kaplan H. and Tarjan R. E.: New heap data structures. Technical Report TR-597-99, Princeton University (1999).
8. Lagogiannis G., Lorentzos N.: Partially Persistent B-trees with Constant Worst Case Update Time. TR-184, Informatics Laboratory, Department of Science, Agricultural University of Athens (http://infolab.aua.gr/people.php?lang=en&id=14).

Using Mixture of Experts Method in Combining Search-Guiding Heuristics for Theorem Proving

C. Acar Erkek[1] and Tunga Güngör[2]

Boğaziçi University
Bebek, 34342 Istanbul, Turkey
[1] acarerkek@gmail.com
[2] gungort@boun.edu.tr

Abstract. The main challenge of automated theorem proving is to find a way to shorten the search process. Therefore using a good heuristic method is essential. Instead of constructing a heuristic from scratch, we propose to use the mixture of experts learning to combine the existing heuristics to construct a heuristic from similar problems. The results show that the combined heuristic is better than each individual heuristic used in combination.

1 Introduction

The resolution principle reduces proof procedures into a series of simpler, unintelligent operations, which computers perform very fast. Although the resolution principle is useful and fast, it has no predefined clause choosing mechanism and it expands the search space quickly. So, it is essential to use a heuristic method to narrow (or direct) the search path.

In automated theorem proving (ATP) systems, usually static evaluation functions are used as heuristics. These functions are dependent on the features of the clauses (e.g. the number of symbols in a clause). Usually problems have different characteristics and require different approaches. We do not have "the best" heuristic which is successful for each problem. Machine learning methods can be used for inventing good heuristics, improving existing ones, adapting methods for the given problem [1], or choosing a suitable heuristic from a given set [2].

Mixture of experts (MOE) is a variant of artificial neural networks, and it can be used to combine multiple learning or non-learning experts. Its main purpose is to learn the regions where each expert is successful. In this paper, we propose a novel method for automated theorem proving, based on the MOE approach to combine different heuristics, and to construct a new heuristic. This heuristic is shown to be more successful than each individual heuristic used independently.

2 Previous Work

A neural network can be used to learn the search-guiding heuristics [3]. The training data of the neural network are the proofs of non-heuristic version. The

E. Gelenbe et al. (eds.), *Computer and Information Sciences*, Lecture Notes
in Electrical Engineering 62, DOI 10.1007/978-90-481-9794-1_2,
© Springer Science+Business Media B.V. 2010

steps that contribute to the proof are taken as positive training data. Branches that do not contribute but are close to the positive training data are taken as negative examples.

The similarity between problem definitions is used in [4]. Solutions of solved (similar) problems are used to configure the parameters of the heuristic, to be used in the current problem. Machine learning is used to suggest a sequence of heuristics according to their similarity with the current problem [2]. Numeric features of the problem descriptions (axioms and the conclusion) are used to define the similarity. Also, two different heuristics can be learned and then combined. The success of the combination is better than both of the heuristics in some of the tests [5].

Although converting a clause into numeric representation causes some loss of information, numeric representations are usually used since they are suitable for inexact knowledge, we can define similarity and distance concepts easily, and there are powerful learning methods with numeric representations [1]. Numeric features of clauses are used to convert them into numeric representations. Number of literals (in a clause), number of distinct predicates, number of variables, number of functions and term depth of the clauses are examples.

3   Proposed Method

The given-clause algorithm is a popular and efficient algorithm used in ATP systems [6]. A good heuristic function is essential for this algorithm since after some time, the number of inferences explodes.

MOE can be seen as a general architecture for combining multiple experts, where the experts may not be linear or learning and the gating may not be linear [7],[8]. The idea is to achieve success rates better than each individual expert. MOEs are trained with the back-propagation algorithm. We prefer the cooperative learning model, since it is shown that cooperative model is more accurate than the competitive model [7].

We use clause heuristics as the experts of the system. The flexibility of MOE allows us to use different types of heuristics together (non-learning heuristics and learning heuristics). Different experts may give output in different scales, which affects the learning process negatively in early stages. We propose to filter the outputs of experts with perceptrons (which are trained separately for each expert), therefore we do not use the outputs of experts directly, but posterior probabilities, which are calculated by perceptron, are used in mixture of experts. This method also ensures that outputs of experts are in $[0, 1]$ interval.

In applying machine learning, our training data will be the output of the system, which indicates that we will use the proof steps of previous problems to solve new problems. Initially, since there is no training, we must use the outputs of problems solved with conventional heuristics. We choose clauses that contribute to the solution as positive examples, that do not contribute to the solution as negative examples. a proof has much more negative examples than positive examples. It is better to take negative examples which are close to positive examples [1]. We only include negative examples which are two steps away from positive examples in the proof tree.

The positive and negative examples are converted into their numeric representations. This numeric data are used to train the MOE network. We train the network until the coefficients are stable. In our examples, all training sessions are very fast (takes less than 1 s.), so compared to the proof sessions, the total time of the training sessions is negligible. Some of the clause features used in numerical representation are number of literals, predicates, constants, functions, variables, maximum nesting of the clause and maximum weight of literals.

The problem definition of the new problem is compared with the previously solved problems and the knowledge of the most similar problem is applied to the new problem. This concept, which is called instance-based learning, is successfully used in [2]. To determine the similarity, each problem is converted into numerical representations. Then, similarity is calculated as the euclidean distance between these feature vectors. Some of the features used in the application are term depth of the axioms, number of distinct predicates and function arities. In the future, a mechanism should be implemented for dealing with the problems that do not have applicable knowledge in their close neighborhood.

The MOE is initialized with the coefficients taken from the most similar problem. And the output of this MOE network is used as the heuristic function in the given-clause algorithm.

4   Experiments and Discussion

In our experiments, we implemented the proposed method on top of the Otter ATP system [6], by modifying the clause selection mechanism of Otter to use the mixture of experts. The other mechanisms of Otter were kept the same so that we can isolate the effect of the clause selection mechanism in the results.

The experiments were done on an Intel Pentium 4 1.7 Ghz Ubuntu Linux computer. In all of the tests, a moderate time limit (3 min.) was given to the prover to prevent running indefinitely if it does not find a solution. We used the TPTP (Thousands of Problems for Theorem Provers) library in the tests [9]. We used problems without equality, which are defined in clause normal form.

In the experiments, we combined three simple heuristics. For comparison, we used two hypothetical heuristics: For a given problem, one of these hypothetical heuristics acts as the best (H_{best}), the other acts as the worst (H_{worst}) among other heuristics (H_1, H_2, H_3). And our learned heuristic is H_{comb}. Other experts can be added to the system (learning or non-learning). The system will easily be integrated with experts which use back-propagation without any modification.

The results of experiments for the FLD domain are given in Figure 1. Results show that in 35% of the problems, H_{comb} is at least as fast as the hypothetical heuristic H_{best}. So, we can conclude that the system has gained abilities beyond the combined heuristics for these problems. Also we should consider that constructing the perfect H_{best} heuristics is impossible and all heuristics will be subject to the problems of similarity and numerical representations.

For some problems (10%), we see that, our proposed system is worse than combined heuristics. There are two possibilites for these negative results: the loss of information due to numerical representations and the similarity approach we used. An analysis of negative results should help us to improve our similarity approach. An alternative for numerical representations is symbolic representation approach, which can be combined with the current work in the future with a slight modification in the gating structure [10].

Both H_{comb} and H_{best} succeeded	82	51%
Both H_{comb} and H_{best} failed	72	45%
H_{comb} succeeded but H_{best} failed	5	3%
H_{comb} failed but H_{best} succeeded	2	1%
H_{comb} is faster than H_{best}	23	14%
H_{comb} is as fast as H_{best}	35	21%
H_{comb} is faster than H_{worst} but slower than H_{best}	10	6%
H_{comb} is slower than H_{worst}	14	9%
Total number of problems	161	100%

Fig. 1. Number of solved problems from FLD domain

References

1. J. Denzinger, M. Fuchs, C. Goller, and S. Schulz.: Learning from Previous Proof Experience: A Survey. Technical Report AR-99-4, Fakultät für Informatik der Technischen Universität München, 1999.
2. M. Fuchs.: Automatic Selection of Search-Guiding Heuristics. Proc. of FLAIRS, pages 1–5, 1997.
3. C. Suttner and W. Ertel.: Automatic Acquisition of Search Guiding Heuristics. Proc. of International Conference on Automated Deduction, pages 470–484, 1990.
4. M. Fuchs and M. Fuchs.: Applying Case-Based Reasoning to Automated Deduction. Proc. of International Conference on Case-Based Reasoning, pages 23–32, 1997.
5. M. Fuchs.: Experiments in the Heuristic Use of Past Proof Experience. Proc. of CADE-13, New Brunswick, LNAI, 1104:523–537, 1996.
6. W. McCune: OTTER 3.3 Reference Manual. Argonne National Laboratory, Technical Memorandum No.263, 2003.
7. E. Alpaydin.: Introduction To Machine Learning. MIT, 2004.
8. S.J. Russell, P. Norvig, J.F. Canny, J. Malik, and D.D. Edwards.: Artificial Intelligence: A Modern Approach. Prentice Hall, NJ, 1995.
9. G. Sutcliffe.: The TPTP Problem Library and Associated Infrastructure: The FOF and CNF Parts, v3.5.0. Journal of Automated Reasoning, 43(4):337–362, 2009.
10. C. Goller.: A Connectionist Approach for Learning Search-Control Heuristics for Automated Deduction Systems. PhD Dissertation, Technical University of Munich, 1999.

This article was processed using the LaTeX macro package with LLNCS style

Univariate Margin Tree

Olcay Taner Yıldız

Department of Computer Engineering, Işık University, TR-34980, Şile, Istanbul, Turkey, olcaytaner@isikun.edu.tr

Abstract. In many pattern recognition applications, first decision trees are used due to their simplicity and easily interpretable nature. In this paper, we propose a new decision tree learning algorithm called univariate margin tree, where for each continuous attribute, the best split is found using convex optimization. Our simulation results on 47 datasets show that the novel margin tree classifier performs at least as good as C4.5 and LDT with a similar time complexity. For two class datasets it generates smaller trees than C4.5 and LDT without sacrificing from accuracy, and generates significantly more accurate trees than C4.5 and LDT for multiclass datasets with one-vs-rest methodology.

1 Introduction

Machine learning aims to determine a description of a given concept from a set of examples provided by teacher and from the background knowledge. Learning examples can be defined as positive or negative for a two class problem. Background knowledge contains the information about the language used to describe the examples and concepts. For instance, it can include possible values of variables and their hierarchies or predicates. The learning algorithm then builds on the type of examples, on the size and relevance of the background knowledge, and on the representational issues [1], [2].

Decision trees are one of the well-known learning algorithms in Machine learning. They are tree-based structures which consist of internal nodes having one or more attributes to test and leaves to show the decision made. The type of the split determines the type of the decision tree. In univariate decision trees, the split is based on one attribute. If that attribute is continuous, there will be two children of each internal node (C4.5) [3], if that attribute is discrete, there will be L children of each internal node corresponding to the L different outcomes of the test (ID3) [4].

Linear discriminant tree (LDT) [5] is another univariate decision tree technique which uses a statistical approach to quickly determine the best split. Finding the best split with Fisher's Linear Discriminant Analysis (LDA) [6] is done as a nested optimization problem. In the inner optimization problem, Fisher's linear discriminant is used for finding a good split for the given two distinct groups of classes. In the outer optimization problem, at each node m, one searches for the best separation of K classes into two groups, C_m^L and C_m^R [7].

E. Gelenbe et al. (eds.), *Computer and Information Sciences*, Lecture Notes in Electrical Engineering 62, DOI 10.1007/978-90-481-9794-1_3, © Springer Science+Business Media B.V. 2010

Maximum margin classifiers [8], especially support vector machines (SVM), became popular in the recent years for solving problems in classification, regression, and one class classification. Maximum margin classifiers (i) approach the classification problem through the concept of *margin*, which is defined to be the smallest distance between the decision boundary and the closest data points (called support vectors) (ii) determine the model parameters by setting up a convex optimization problem, (iii) use hinge loss instead of misclassification error, and (iv) usually work for two-class problems.

In this paper we propose a novel decision tree classifier which finds the best split for each attribute at each decision node using convex optimization. Our simulation results on 47 datasets from UCI repository [9] show that our univariate margin tree classifier performs better than C4.5 and LDT in terms of accuracy and tree size.

The paper is organized as follows: In Section 2 we present and discuss our proposed Univariate Margin Tree algorithm. We present the experimental setup and results in Section 3 where we compare in detail our proposed algorithm with C4.5 and LDT. Section 4 gives the conclusions and discusses possible future directions.

2   Univariate Margin Tree

We consider the well-known supervised learning setting where the learning algorithm uses a sample of N labeled points $S = ((\boldsymbol{x}^1, y^1), \ldots, (\boldsymbol{x}^N, y^N)) \in (X \times Y)^N$, where X is the input space and Y the label set, which is $\{-1, +1\}$. The input space X is a continuous vectorial space of dimension d, the number of features. The data pairs $(\boldsymbol{x}^i, y^i)$ are independently and identically distributed according to an unknown but fixed distribution.

In training a univariate test, one tries to find the best feature x_j and the threshold w_0, namely the split $x_j + w_0 \geq 0$ that best separates two (or K) classes. To separate K classes as good as possible, C4.5 tries to minimize the impurity or maximize the information gain, LDT assumes the two class groups are normally distributed and tries to maximize the ratio of between class distance to within class distance. In this paper, we take the wide margin approach and express finding best split as a minimization problem. To find the best threshold for feature j, we require

$$y^t(x_j^t + w_0) \geq C - \epsilon^t \tag{1}$$

for each data point x_j^t with output y^t, where $|C|$ is the length of the margin. If $\epsilon^t = 0$, the instance is on the separating line. If $0 < \epsilon^t < |C|$, the instance is correctly classified but it is in the margin. If $\epsilon^t > |C|$, it is misclassified. Since there is only single variable, and its weight is 1, we only need the penalty term $(\sum \epsilon^t)$ in the objective function. So we get the following formulation:

$$
\begin{aligned}
Min \quad & \sum_t \epsilon^t \\
s.t. \ & y^t(x_j^t + w_0) \geq C - \epsilon^t \\
& \epsilon^t \geq 0
\end{aligned}
\tag{2}
$$

This is a linear programming problem in which ϵ^t and w_0 are variables. By adding Langrange multipliers ($\alpha^t \geq 0$ and $\mu^t \geq 0$), the problem can be converted to

$$L(w_0, \epsilon^t, \alpha^t, \mu^t) = \sum_t \epsilon^t - \sum_t \alpha^t [y^t (x_j^t + w_0) - C + \epsilon^t] - \sum_t \mu^t \epsilon^t \qquad (3)$$

We can remove the primal variables ϵ^t and w_0 by maximization, i.e. set the following derivatives to zero:

$$\frac{\partial L}{\partial w_0} = 0 \Rightarrow \sum_t \alpha^t y^t = 0$$

$$\frac{\partial L}{\partial \epsilon^t} = 0 \Rightarrow \alpha^t + \mu^t = 1 \qquad (4)$$

Plugging the equations 4 in the equation 3, we get the dual form:

$$D(\alpha^t, \mu^t) = \sum_t \alpha^t (C - y^t x_j^t) \qquad (5)$$

Since we have $\alpha^t \geq 0$, $\mu^t \geq 0$, and $\alpha^t + \mu^t = 1$, it follows $0 \leq \alpha^t \leq 1$. Now the dual optimization problem becomes

$$Max \sum_t \alpha^t (C - y^t x_j^t)$$

$$s.t. \quad \sum_t \alpha^t y^t = 0 \qquad (6)$$

$$0 \leq \alpha^t \leq 1$$

Neither the primal (Equation 2) nor the dual (Equation 6) is easily solvable. To solve the problem, we search all possible solutions in terms of the split point w_0 exhaustively. The inequality $y^t (x_j^t + w_0) \geq C - \epsilon^t$ can be written as

$$\epsilon^t \geq C - x_j^t y^t - w_0 y^t \qquad (7)$$

According to the convex optimization theory, the solution to a convex optimization problem (if there is a solution) lies in one of the vertices of the convex polytope and each vertex is specified by a set of $n + 1$ inequalities tight, where $n + 1$ represents the number of distinct variables. Setting the left side of the Equation 7 to zero ($\epsilon^i = 0$) gives us all possible values for $w_0 = \dfrac{C - x_j^t y^t}{y^t}$. Then the only remaining thing is to calculate other ϵ^j's and check for the maximum value of the objective function $\sum_t \epsilon^t$.

The pseudocode for finding the best split at each decision node of the univariate margin tree is given in Figure 1. For each feature i we search for the optimal w_0 exhaustively (Line 2). Given the feature i, there exists at most N different w_0's corresponding to N different inequalities shown in Equation 7, where each time a different ϵ^t is zero (Line 4). To get the minimum value of the penalty

---

Split UnivariateMarginTreeBestSplit(N, d, S, V)
1   **for** C = -2.0 **to** 2.0 **step** 0.1
2   **for** $i = 1$ **to** d
3   **for** $j = 1$ **to** N
4 $w_0 = \dfrac{C - x_i^j y^j}{y^j}$; sumepsilon = 0.0
5   **for** $k = 1$ **to** N
6 $\epsilon^k = C - x_i^k y^k - w_0 y^k$
7   **if** $\epsilon^k > 0$ **then** sumepsilon $+= \epsilon^k$
8   **if** sumepsilon < minepsilon **then** $bestw_0 = w_0$
9   error = ErrorOfSplit($x_i + bestw_0 \geq 0$, V)
10   **if** error < bestErr **then** bestErr = error; bestSplit = $x_i + bestw_0 \geq 0$
11 **return** bestSplit

Fig. 1. The pseudocode of the search algorithm for finding the best split at each decision node of the univariate margin tree: N: Number of examples at the decision node, d: Number of inputs in the dataset, $S = ((\boldsymbol{x}^1, y^1), \ldots, (\boldsymbol{x}^N, y^N))$: Sample of N labeled data points at the decision node, V: Validation data used to optimize C value

term $\sum_t \epsilon^t$ for a specific w_0, we set ϵ^k to zero if $C - x_i^k y^k - w_0 y^k < 0$ and to $C - x_i^k y^k - w_0 y^k$ if $C - x_i^k y^k - w_0 y^k > 0$ (Line 7). The threshold w_0 corresponding to the minimum overall penalty will be selected as a best split candidate (Line 8). Similar to the support vector machines, to optimize the length of the margin C, we need a separate validation set. The instances are normalized in order to use the same C value for each feature. We calculate the error rate of the current best split candidate on the validation set and compare it with the best error so far (Line 10). We return the split with minimum error as the best split.

For a given data size N and dimension d, the computational complexity of the algorithm is $\mathcal{O}(dN^2)$. But like C4.5, one can sort w_0's ($\mathcal{O}(N \log N)$) and calculate the minimum overall penalty in $\mathcal{O}(N)$ time resulting in a lower computational complexity of $\mathcal{O}(dN \log N)$, which is the same as C4.5's complexity.

3   Experiments

In this section, we compare the performance of our proposed univariate margin tree algorithm (UMT) with C4.5 and LDT in terms of generalization error and model complexity as measured by the number of nodes in the decision tree. We use a total of 47 data sets where 36 of them are from UCI repository [9] and 11 are bioinformatics cancer datasets [10].

Our methodology in generating train, validation and test sets is as follows: A data set is first divided into two parts, with 1/3 as the test set, *test*, and 2/3 as the training set. The training set is then resampled using 2×5 cross-validation to generate ten training and validation folds, tra_i, val_i, $i = 1, \ldots, 10$. tra_i are used to train the decision trees and val_i are used to prune the decision trees using

Table 1. The average and standard deviations of error rates (tree size) of decision trees generated using C4.5, LDT, and UMT for $K = 2$ class datasets

Dataset	C4.5		LDT		UMT	
	Error Rate	Tree Size	Error Rate	Tree Size	Error Rate	Tree Size
ads	**3.4±0.4**	38.8±19.8	3.7±0.4	50.2±21.6	3.9±0.3	**31.0±11.8**
breast	6.9±1.2	11.5±7.7	6.5±0.5	10.0±5.7	**6.3±1.5**	**7.6±3.4**
bupa	**38.5±4.4**	18.7±15.1	40.8±4.4	13.3±16.3	42.0±5.2	**8.2±7.0**
dlbcl	23.3±8.9	3.4±1.9	25.6±5.4	2.5±2.1	**21.5±7.2**	**1.9±1.5**
german	29.4±1.2	**4.3±7.0**	29.3±1.4	10.9±20.9	**28.2±1.6**	9.1±8.7
haberman	26.4±0.3	4.6±8.7	27.3±2.8	4.6±8.7	**26.2±0.9**	**2.2±3.8**
heart	30.9±4.0	9.4±5.4	**29.0±4.8**	8.2±5.1	32.4±2.8	**4.9±2.9**
hepatitis	22.3±4.0	10.9±9.7	21.7±1.3	**2.5±3.2**	**19.6±2.5**	4.9±4.5
ironosphere	14.2±4.4	**11.8±6.7**	14.9±4.5	12.4±9.0	**11.3±5.9**	12.1±5.8
magic	**17.1±0.4**	86.8±28.5	17.7±0.3	121.3±44.4	19.2±0.4	**63.4±13.3**
musk2	**4.7±0.6**	114.1±25.2	5.3±0.6	131.5±28.4	12.7±1.2	**24.4±11.1**
parkinsons	15.4±4.5	9.1±5.8	15.5±5.4	8.8±4.1	**14.9±3.6**	**5.8±3.5**
pima	28.9±2.7	15.1±13.3	28.4±4.3	23.8±24.8	**26.3±1.3**	**7.6±5.1**
p.adenylation	30.6±2.1	38.5±20.1	**29.6±1.7**	**54.7±37.4**	29.7±1.3	81.7±28.4
p.tumor	**15.7±2.4**	5.2±2.1	20.3±10.6	4.9±2.0	22.0±11.4	**3.7±1.0**
ringnorm	**12.0±0.7**	157.0±44.7	23.1±1.2	261.1±67.4	15.1±2.0	**70.9±11.0**
satellite47	14.6±1.3	40.6±16.4	15.2±1.2	27.4±20.3	**14.6±0.8**	**26.5±9.7**
spambase	9.3±1.2	79.9±31.8	**9.2±0.8**	106.6±38.9	10.1±0.6	**54.7±17.7**
transfusion	24.0±0.0	**1.0±0.0**	**23.8±0.8**	1.9±2.9	24.0±0.0	**1.0±0.0**
twonorm	**17.5±0.6**	225.1±45.0	17.7±0.7	248.8±51.3	19.1±0.7	**171.7±23.6**

cross-validation based postpruning. *test* is used to estimate the generalization error of the decision trees.

Table 1 shows average and standard deviations of error rates (tree size in terms of number of nodes) of decision trees generated using C4.5, LDT, and UMT for $K = 2$ class datasets. We see from the results that, UMT is as good as C4.5 and LDT in terms of error rate. In 9 (10) datasets out of 20 UMT has smaller error rate than C4.5 (LDT). On the other hand, C4.5 (LDT) has smaller error rate than UMT in 10 (10) datasets out of 20.

Better than the results above, UMT is significantly better than both C4.5 and LDT in terms of tree complexity. In 16 (18) datasets out of 20 UMT generates smaller trees than C4.5 (LDT). Whereas, C4.5 (LDT) generates smaller trees than UMT in only 3 (2) datasets out of 20. We can conclude that for two class datasets, UMT generates smaller trees than C4.5 and LDT without sacrificing from accuracy.

In UMT, for $K > 2$ class problems, we take the most commonly used approach and reduce the single multiclass problem into multiple binary classification problems. UMT uses two well-known methods to build binary classifiers where each classifier distinguishes between (i) one of the labels to the rest (one-versus-rest) or (ii) between every pair of classes (one-versus-one). The results show that, UMT (one-vs-one) is as good as C4.5 and LDT in terms of error rate.

In 13 (12) datasets out of 27 UMT (one-vs-one) has smaller error rate than C4.5 (LDT), whereas C4.5 (LDT) has smaller error rate than UMT (one-vs-one) in 14 (15) datasets out of 27. On the other hand, UMT (one-vs-rest) is significantly better than C4.5 and LDT in terms of error rate. In 19 datasets out of 27 UMT (one-vs-rest) has smaller error rate than C4.5 and LDT, whereas C4.5 and LDT have smaller error rate than UMT (one-vs-rest) only in 8 datasets out of 27.

4   Conclusion

In this paper, we propose a new decision tree learning algorithm called univariate margin tree, where the best split is found using convex optimization at each decision node. The main idea comes from simplifying the formulation of multivariate linear support vector machines. Simplification is done by (i) replacing the multivariate discriminant w with the univariate axis-orthogonal split $x_j + w_0 \geq 0$, (ii) removing the $||w||^2$ factor from the objective function since there is only single variable x_j, and (iii) redefining the margin in the one-dimensional space. None of the resulting primal and dual formulations are easily solvable, therefore we resort searching for the optimal w_0 exhaustively. Although the first-come to mind exhaustive search is expensive, with the same trick applied in C4.5, one can get a computational complexity of $\mathcal{O}(dN \log N)$, which is much better than the usual time complexity of the traditional support vector machines.

Experimental results show that for two class problems our proposed univariate margin tree not only performs as good as C4.5 and LDT in terms of accuracy, but it produces significantly smaller trees to do that. For multiclass problems, we tried two well-known reduction techniques, namely, one-vs-one and one-vs-rest. In terms of generalization error, one-vs-rest is significantly better than one-vs-one technique, which is also as good as C4.5 and LDT.

References

1. Mitchell, T.: Machine Learning. McGraw-Hill (1997)
2. Alpaydın, E.: Introduction to Machine Learning. The MIT Press (2010)
3. Quinlan, J.R.: C4.5: Programs for Machine Learning. Morgan Kaufmann, San Meteo, CA (1993)
4. Quinlan, J.R.: Induction of decision trees. Machine Learning **1** (1986) 81–106
5. Yıldız, O.T., Alpaydın, E.: Linear discriminant trees. International Journal of Pattern Recognition and Artificial Intelligence **19**(3) (2005) 323–353
6. Duda, R.O., Hart, P.E., Stork, D.G.: Pattern Classification. John Wiley and Sons (2001)
7. Guo, H., Gelfand, S.B.: Classification trees with neural network feature extraction. IEEE Transactions on Neural Networks **3** (1992) 923–933
8. Vapnik, V.: The Nature of Statistical Learning Theory. Springer Verlag, New York (1995)
9. Asuncion, A., Newman, D.J.: UCI machine learning repository (2007)
10. Statnikov, A., Aliferis, C., Tsamardinos, I., Hardin, D., Levy, S.: A comprehensive evaluation of multicategory classification methods for microarray gene expression cancer diagnosis. Bioinformatics **21** (2005) 631–643

Transformational Programming and the Derivation of Algorithms

Martin Ward and Hussein Zedan
Software Technology Research Lab
De Montfort University
Bede Island Building,
Leicester LE1 9BH, UK
martin@gkc.org.uk and zedan@dmu.ac.uk

Abstract. The transformational programming, method of algorithm derivation starts with a formal specification of the result to be achieved (which provides no indication of how the result is to be achieved), plus some informal ideas as to what techniques will be used in the implementation. The formal specification is then transformed into an implementation, by means of correctness-preserving refinement and transformation steps. The informal ideas are used to guide the selection of transformations to apply: since they only guide the selection of valid transformations, the ideas do not themselves have to be formalised.

1 Introduction

The *waterfall model* of software development sees progress as flowing steadily downwards (like a waterfall) through the following states:

1. Requirements Elicitation: analysing the problem domain and determinining from the users what the program is required to do;
2. Design: developing the overall structure of the program;
3. Implementation: writing source code to implement the design in a particular programming language;
4. Verification: running tests and debugging;
5. Maintenance: any modifications required after delivery to correct faults, improve performance, or adapt the product to a modified environment.

In theory, one proceeds from one phase to the next in a purely sequential manner. But in practice, at each stage in the process, information may be uncovered which affects previous stages. So the process described in Figure 1(a) includes feedback loops from each stage to preceding stages.

To prove that a program is correct we need a precise mathematical specification which defines what the program is supposed to do, and a mathematical proof that the program satisfies the specification. In the case of a simple loop, the proof using the method of "loop invariants" takes the following steps:

1. Determine the loop termination condition;

E. Gelenbe et al. (eds.), *Computer and Information Sciences*, Lecture Notes
in Electrical Engineering 62, DOI 10.1007/978-90-481-9794-1_4,
© Springer Science+Business Media B.V. 2010

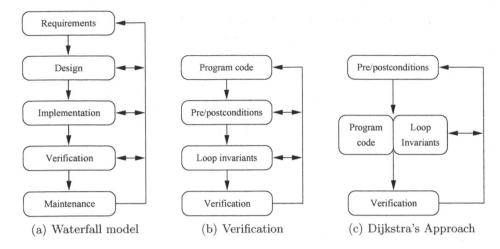

(a) Waterfall model   (b) Verification   (c) Dijkstra's Approach

Fig. 1. Program Development Methods

2. Determine the loop body;
3. Determine a suitable loop invariant;
4. Prove that the loop invariant is preserved by the loop body;
5. Determine a variant function for the loop;
6. Prove that the variant function is reduced by the loop body (thereby proving termination of the loop);
7. Prove that the combination of the invariant plus the termination condition satisfies the specification for the loop.

This process is summarised in Figure 1(b).

Loop invariants and postconditions can be difficult to determine with sufficient precision, and computing verification conditions can be tedious and proving them can be difficult. Even with the aid of an automated proof assistant, there may still be several hundred remaining "proof obligations" to discharge. In addition, should the implementation happen to be incorrect (i.e. the program has a bug), then the attempt at a proof is doomed to failure.

An alternative to the *a posteriori* method, which was originally proposed by Dijkstra [2], is to control the process of program generation by constructing loop invariants in parallel with the construction of the code. This process is summarised in Figure 1(c).

A further refinement of this approach is to develop loop invariants *before* the code itself is written. The idea has been proposed from the late 70's by several researchers in different forms. Figure 2(a) summarises this approach.

Notice that in Figures 1(b), 1(c) and 2(a), developing the loop invariant is moved to earlier and earlier phases in the process.

In all the development methods we have seen so far, *verification* is the final step in development. Up until the point where verification has been completed, the programmer cannot be sure that the program is correct. Indeed, Back [1]

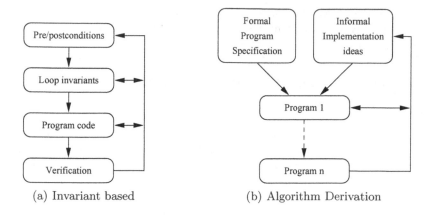

Fig. 2. Program Development Methods

makes it clear that the program under development does not have to terminate or be free from deadlocks, and that the initial invariant is usually both incomplete and partially wrong. He stresses that it is essential to carefully check the consistency of each transition when it is introduced.

In this paper we present a different method of programming, called *transformational programming* or *algorithm derivation*.

2   Transformational Programming

The transformational programming method starts with a formal specification plus some informal ideas for implementation techniques which might be useful. The formal specification is *refined* into a complete program by applying a sequence of correctness-preseving refinement steps. The choice of which transformation to apply at each stage is guided by the implementation ideas. These ideas do not have to be formalised to any particular extent, since they are only used to select between different transformations. The correstness of the transformation guarantees that the transformed program is equivalent to the original. The method is summarised in Figure 2(b).

In contrast with the refinement calculus [3], the method presented here does not require loop invariants. We have transformations to introduce, manipulate and remove loops which do not depend on the existence of loop invariants. Another key difference between Figure 2(b) and the other methods is that there is no Verification step. This is because at each stage in the derivation process we are working with a correct program. The program is always guaranteed to be equivalent to the original specification, because it was derived from the specification via a sequence of proven transformations and refinements.

Over the last twenty-five years we have developed a powerful wide-spectrum specification and programming language, called WSL, together with a large catalogue of proven program transformations and refinements which can be used in algorithm derivations and reverse engineering. The method has been applied to the derivation of many complex algorithms from specifications.

2.1 Outline of the Algorithm Derivation method

A typical algorithm derivation takes the following steps:

1. **Formal Specification:** Develop a formal specification of the program, in the form of a WSL specification statement. This defines precisely what the program is required to accomplish, without necessarily giving any indication as to how the task is to be accomplished.
2. **Elaboration:** Elaborate the specification statement by taking out simple cases: for example, boundary values on the input or cases where there is no input data. These are applied by transforming the specification statement, typically using the Splitting a Tautology transformation followed by inserting assertions and then using the assertions to refine the appropriate copy of the specification to the trivial implementation.
3. **Divide and Conquer:** The general case is usually tackled via some form of "divide and conquer" strategy: this is where the informal implementation ideas come into play to direct the selection of transformations. At this point we still have a non-recursive program: so there are no induction proofs or invariants required for the transformations.
4. **Recursion Introduction:** The next step is to apply the Recursive Implementation Theorem to produce a recursive program with no remaining copies of the specification.
5. **Recursion Removal:** We now have an executable implementation of the specification. If an iterative implementation is required, we can apply the Generic Recursion Removal Theorem (or an appropriate special case of the theorem) to produce an iterative program.
6. **Optimisation:** Apply further optimising transformations as required.

It should be noted that stages 1–3 involve analysing programs which contain no recursion or iteration. This makes the analysis particularly straightforward: for example, induction arguments are not needed. This is fortunate, as it is these stages which require the most input from the informal implementation ideas. Stages 4–6 involve standard transformations for recursion introduction, recursion removal and optimisation. As the derivation progresses, the transformations involved become more generic and less domain-specific. At some point, an optimising compiler will take over and generate executable code, or the code will be directly executed by an interpreter, as appropriate.

3 An Example of Transformational Programming

Our example illustrates multiple applications of the recursion introduction and recursion removal transformations. Recursion introduction does not have to be applied simultaneously to *every* copy of the specification: we can work on copies of the specification one (or more) at a time.

Given two character strings a and b, it required to determine whether they are equal "apart from blanks" (the space character being regarded as non-significant). We represent the strings as arrays of characters, with the special symbol end denoting the end of the string.

Define the function $\mathsf{strip}(s, i)$ to return the sequence of all non-space characters in s from the ith character to the end of the string:

$$\mathsf{strip}(s, i) = \begin{cases} \langle\rangle & \text{if } s[i] = \mathsf{end} \\ \mathsf{strip}(s, i + 1) & \text{if } s[i] = \mathsf{space} \\ \langle s[i]\rangle \mathbin{+\!\!+} \mathsf{strip}(s, i + 1) & \text{otherwise} \end{cases}$$

Formal Specification With this definition of strip our formal specification is:

$$\mathsf{COMP} =_{\mathrm{DF}} \textbf{if } \mathsf{strip}(a, 1) = \mathsf{strip}(b, 1) \textbf{ then } R := 1 \textbf{ else } R := 0 \textbf{ fi}$$

Informal Ideas Our informal idea is to step through both arrays a character at a time until we reach the end, or find a significant difference. This suggests generalising the specification to compare the strings from a given index onwards:

$$\mathsf{COMP}(i, j) =_{\mathrm{DF}} \textbf{if } \mathsf{strip}(a, i) = \mathsf{strip}(b, j) \textbf{ then } R := 1 \textbf{ else } R := 0 \textbf{ fi}$$

Program Derivation The obvious special cases to consider are the values of $a[i]$ and $b[j]$. First we consider the case where $a[i] = \mathsf{space}$:

if $a[i] = \mathsf{space}$ **then** $\mathsf{COMP}(i, j)$
                        else $\mathsf{COMP}(i, j)$ **fi**

By definition, if $a[i] = \mathsf{space}$ then $\mathsf{strip}(a, i) = \mathsf{strip}(a, i + 1)$ so $\mathsf{COMP}(i, j) \approx \mathsf{COMP}(i + 1, j)$. We have:

if $a[i] = \mathsf{space}$ **then** $\mathsf{COMP}(i + 1, j)$
                        else $\mathsf{COMP}(i, j)$ **fi**

By the precondition for the program, there is an array element $a[i] = \mathsf{end}$ for some i. Let i' be the first such element. Then the variant function $i' - i$ is reduced before the first copy of the specification, but (obviously) not before the second copy. We can still apply Recursive_Implementation, provided we only apply it to the *first* copy of the specification:

proc comp $\equiv$
    if $a[i] = \mathsf{space}$ **then** $i := i + 1$; comp
                        else $\mathsf{COMP}(i, j)$ **fi**

This simple tail-recursion is transformed to a **while** loop:

while $a[i] =$ space **do** $i := i + 1$ **od**;
COMP(i, j)

A similar argument for $b[j]$ produces:

while $a[i] =$ space **do** $i := i + 1$ **od**;
while $b[j] =$ space **do** $j := j + 1$ **od**;
COMP(i, j)

Consideration of the cases where $a[i] =$ end and/or $b[j] =$ end gives:

while $a[i] =$ space **do** $i := i + 1$ **od**;
while $b[j] =$ space **do** $j := j + 1$ **od**;
if $a[i] =$ end $\wedge$ $b[j] =$ end **then** $R := 1$
elsif $a[i] \neq a[j]$ **then** $R := 0$
                    else $i := i + 1$; $j := j + 1$; COMP(i, j) **fi**

We can now apply Recursive_Implementation, and Recursion_Removal, to get the final iterative program:

do while $a[i] =$ space **do** $i := i + 1$ **od**;
    while $b[j] =$ space **do** $j := j + 1$ **od**;
    if $a[i] =$ end $\wedge$ $b[j] =$ end **then** $R := 1$; **exit**(1)
    elsif $a[i] \neq a[j]$ **then** $R := 0$; **exit**(1) **fi**;
    $i := i + 1$; $j := j + 1$ **od**

4   Conclusion

This paper presents a brief introduction to the Transformational Programming method of software development. The method starts with a formal specification of the result to be achievedtogether with some informal ideas as to what techniques will be used in the implementation. The formal specification is then transformed into an implementation, by means of correctness-preserving refinement and transformation steps. A key advantage of this approach is that loops can be introduced and manipulated while maintaining program correctness and with no need to derive loop invariants. Another advantage is that at every stage in the process we are working with a correct program: there is never any need for a separate "verification" step. These factors help to ensure that the method is capable of scaling up to the dvelopment of large and complex software systems.

References

[1] Ralph-Johan Back, "Invariant Based Programming: Basic Approach and Teaching Experiences," *Formal Aspects of Computing* 21 #3 (May, 2009), 227–244.

[2] E. W. Dijkstra, "A Constructive Approach to the Problem of Program Correctness.," Technische Hogeschool Eindhoven, EWD209, http://www.cs.utexas.edu/users/EWD/ewd02xx/EWD209.PDF.

[3] C. C. Morgan, *Programming from Specifications*, Prentice-Hall, Englewood Cliffs, NJ, 1994, Second Edition.

Factorizing three-way binary data*

Radim Belohlavek, Vilem Vychodil

Dept. Computer Science, Palacky University, Olomouc
17. listopadu 12, CZ-771 46 Olomouc, Czech Republic
radim.belohlavek@upol.cz, vilem.vychodil@upol.cz

Abstract. We present a problem of factor analysis of three-way binary data, i.e. data described by a 3-dimensional binary matrix I, describing a relationship between objects, attributes, and conditions. The problem consists in finding a small number of factors which explain the data. In terms of matrix decompositon, we look for a decomposition of I into three binary matrices, an object-factor matrix A, an attribute-factor matrix B, and a condition-factor matrix C, with the number of factors as small as possible. Compared to other decomposition-based methods, the difference consists in the composition operator and the constraint on A, B, and C to be binary. Due to the space limit, we present the problem statement, a non-technical description of our approach, and, as the main part, an illustrative example.

1 Problem Description

Recently, there has been a growing interest in matrix-decomposition-based methods for analysis of three-way and generally N-way data. [4] provides an up-to-date survey with 244 references. We are concerned with the following problem. Let matrix I represent three-way binary data. That is, I is a 3-dimensional binary matrix of dimension $n \times m \times p$ with entries I_{ijt} interpreted as follows:

$$I_{ijt} = \begin{cases} 1 \text{ if object } i \text{ has attribute } j \text{ under condition } t, \\ 0 \text{ if object } i \text{ does not have attribute } j \text{ under condition } t. \end{cases} \quad (1)$$

Our aim is to decompose I in a way similar to the one employed in Boolean factor analysis. In particular, our approach is inspired by [1]. We look for a decompositions of I into three binary matrices, an $n \times k$ object-factor matrix A with entries A_{ik}, an $m \times k$ attribute-factor matrix B with entries B_{jk}, an $p \times k$ condition-factor matrix A with entries C_{tk}, with respect to a ternary composition $\circ$ defined by

$$\circ(A, B, C)_{ijt} = \max_{l=1}^{k} A_{il} \cdot B_{jl} \cdot C_{tl}. \quad (2)$$

Our aim is to find a decomposition $I = \circ(A, B, C)$ with the smallest number k of factors possible.

* Supported by grant no. P202/10/0262 of the Czech Science Foundation and by grant no. MSM 6198959214.

2 Factors for Decomposition

In our approach, we use so-caled triadic concepts of I [?,6], which come from fomal concept analysis [2], as factors. The role of triadic concepts is crucial because, as we show in a forthcoming paper, triadic concepts are optimal factors in that they provide us with decompositions with the smallest number of factors. A triadic concept of I is a particular triplet $\langle D_1, D_2, D_3 \rangle$ where D_1, D_2, and D_3 are subsets of the sets of all objects, attributes, and conditions, respectively. To conceptually describe our method, we omit the question of how we compute good factors, i.e. triadic concepts. For a set

$$\mathcal{F} = \{\langle D_{11}, D_{12}, D_{13} \rangle, \ldots, \langle D_{k1}, D_{k2}, D_{k3} \rangle\}$$

of triadic concepts of I, we denote by $A_{\mathcal{F}}$, $B_{\mathcal{F}}$, and $C_{\mathcal{F}}$, the $n \times k$, $m \times k$, and $p \times k$ matrices defined by

$$(A_{\mathcal{F}})_{il} = \begin{cases} 1 \text{ if } i \in (D_{l1}), \\ 0 \text{ if } i \notin (D_{l1}), \end{cases} \quad (B_{\mathcal{F}})_{jl} = \begin{cases} 1 \text{ if } j \in (D_{l2}), \\ 0 \text{ if } j \notin (D_{l2}), \end{cases} \quad (C_{\mathcal{F}})_{tl} = \begin{cases} 1 \text{ if } t \in (D_{l3}), \\ 0 \text{ if } t \notin (D_{l3}). \end{cases}$$

If $I = \circ(A_{\mathcal{F}}, B_{\mathcal{F}}, C_{\mathcal{F}})$, $\mathcal{F}$ can be seen as a set of factors which fully explain the data. In such a case, we call the triadic concepts from $\mathcal{F}$ *factor concepts*. Given I, our aim is to find a small set $\mathcal{F}$ of factor concepts.

3 Illustrative Example

Let $X = \{a, b, \ldots, h\}$ be a set of students (objects); $Y = \{co, cr, di, fo, in, mo\}$ be a set of student qualities (attributes): communicative, creative, diligent, focused, independent, motivated; and $Z = \{AL, CA, CI, DA, NE\}$ be a set of courses passed by the students (conditions): algorithms, calculus, circuits, databases, and networking. Matrix I, with $I_{xyz} = 1$ meaning "student x showed quality y in course z", is represented by the following table:

	AL co	cr	di	fo	in	mo	CA co	cr	di	fo	in	mo	CI co	cr	di	fo	in	mo	DA co	cr	di	fo	in	mo	NE co	cr	di	fo	in	mo
a	1	1	1	1	1	1	0	0	1	1	0	1	1	1	0	0	1	1	0	0	1	1	0	1	1	1	0	0	1	1
b	1	1	0	0	1	1	0	0	0	0	0	0	1	1	0	0	1	1	1	1	0	0	0	0	1	1	0	0	1	1
c	1	1	1	1	0	1	0	0	1	1	0	1	1	1	0	0	0	0	1	1	1	1	0	1	1	1	0	0	0	0
d	1	1	1	1	1	1	0	0	1	1	0	1	1	1	0	0	1	1	0	0	1	1	0	1	1	1	0	0	1	1
e	1	1	0	0	1	1	0	0	0	0	0	0	1	1	0	0	1	1	1	1	0	0	0	0	1	1	0	0	1	1
f	1	1	1	1	1	1	0	0	1	1	0	1	1	1	0	0	1	1	1	1	1	1	0	1	1	1	0	0	1	1
g	1	1	0	0	1	1	0	0	0	0	0	0	1	1	0	0	1	1	0	0	0	0	0	0	1	1	0	0	1	1
h	0	0	1	1	0	1	0	0	1	1	0	1	0	0	0	0	0	0	0	0	1	1	0	1	0	0	0	0	0	0

One may show that there exist the following 14 triadic concepts of I:

$$D_1 = \langle \emptyset, \{co, cr, di, fo, in, mo\}, \{AL, CA, CI, DA, NE\} \rangle,$$
$$D_2 = \langle \{f\}, \{co, cr, mo\}, \{AL, CI, DA, NE\} \rangle,$$
$$D_3 = \langle \{c, f\}, \{co, cr, di, fo, mo\}, \{AL, DA\} \rangle,$$
$$D_4 = \langle \{b, c, e, f\}, \{co, cr\}, \{AL, CI, DA, NE\} \rangle,$$

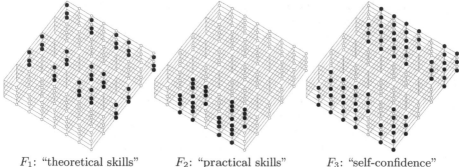

F_1: "theoretical skills" F_2: "practical skills" F_3: "self-confidence"

Fig. 1. Geometric meaning of factors as maximal cuboids.

$$D_5 = \langle \{a, d, f\}, \{mo\}, \{AL, CA, CI, DA, NE\} \rangle,$$
$$D_6 = \langle \{a, d, f\}, \{co, cr, di, fo, in, mo\}, \{AL\} \rangle,$$
$$D_7 = \langle \{a, c, d, f\}, \{co, cr, di, fo, mo\}, \{AL\} \rangle,$$
$$D_8 = \langle \{a, c, d, f, h\}, \{di, fo, mo\}, \{AL, CA, DA\} \rangle,$$
$$D_9 = \langle \{a, b, d, e, f, g\}, \{co, cr, in, mo\}, \{AL, CI, NE\} \rangle,$$
$$D_{10} = \langle \{a, b, c, d, e, f, g\}, \{co, cr\}, \{AL, CI, NE\} \rangle,$$
$$D_{11} = \langle \{a, b, c, d, e, f, g\}, \{co, cr, mo\}, \{AL\} \rangle,$$
$$D_{12} = \langle \{a, b, c, d, e, f, g, h\}, \emptyset, \{AL, CA, CI, DA, NE\} \rangle,$$
$$D_{13} = \langle \{a, b, c, d, e, f, g, h\}, \{mo\}, \{AL\} \rangle,$$
$$D_{14} = \langle \{a, b, c, d, e, f, g, h\}, \{co, cr, di, fo, in, mo\}, \emptyset \rangle.$$

Among these concepts, there exists a three-element set of factor concepts consisting of

$$F_1 = D_8 = \langle \{a, c, d, f, h\}, \{di, fo, mo\}, \{AL, CA, DA\} \rangle,$$
$$F_2 = D_4 = \langle \{b, c, e, f\}, \{co, cr\}, \{AL, CI, DA, NE\} \rangle,$$
$$F_3 = D_9 = \langle \{a, b, d, e, f, g\}, \{co, cr, in, mo\}, \{AL, CI, NE\} \rangle.$$

If we fix the order of objects, attributes, and conditions according to the above listing, and represent sets by their characteristic vectors, we get

$$F_1 = \langle 10110101, 001101, 11010 \rangle,$$
$$F_2 = \langle 01101100, 110000, 10111 \rangle,$$
$$F_3 = \langle 11011110, 110011, 10101 \rangle.$$

Using $\mathcal{F} = \{F_1, F_2, F_3\}$, we obtain the following 8×3 object-factor matrix $A_\mathcal{F}$, 6×3 attribute-factor matrix $B_\mathcal{F}$, and 5×3 conditions-factor matrix $C_\mathcal{F}$:

$$A_\mathcal{F} = \begin{pmatrix} 1 & 0 & 1 \\ 0 & 1 & 1 \\ 1 & 1 & 0 \\ 1 & 0 & 1 \\ 0 & 1 & 1 \\ 1 & 1 & 1 \\ 0 & 0 & 1 \\ 1 & 0 & 0 \end{pmatrix}, \quad B_\mathcal{F} = \begin{pmatrix} 0 & 1 & 1 \\ 0 & 1 & 1 \\ 1 & 0 & 0 \\ 1 & 0 & 0 \\ 0 & 0 & 1 \\ 1 & 0 & 1 \end{pmatrix}, \quad C_\mathcal{F} = \begin{pmatrix} 1 & 1 & 1 \\ 1 & 0 & 0 \\ 0 & 1 & 1 \\ 1 & 1 & 0 \\ 0 & 1 & 1 \end{pmatrix}.$$

One can check that $I = \circ(A_{\mathcal{F}}, B_{\mathcal{F}}, C_{\mathcal{F}})$. The meaning of the factor-concepts can be seen from the extents, intents, and modi of F_1, F_2, and F_3. For instance, F_1 applies to students $\mathsf{a, c, d, f, h}$ who are diligent, focused, and motivated in algorithms, calculus, and databases. This suggests that F_1 can be interpreted as "having good background in theory / formal methods". In addition, F_2 applies to students who are communicative and creative in algorithms, circuits, databases, and networking. This may indicate interests and skills in "practical subjects". Finally, F_3 can be interpreted as a factor close to "self-confidence" because it is manifestated by being communicative, creative, independent, and motivated. As a result, we have explained the structure of the input data set I using three factors which describe the abilities of student applicants in terms of their skills in various subjects.

The factor concepts $\mathcal{F} = \{F_1, F_2, F_3\}$ can be seen as maximal cuboids in I. Indeed, I itself can be depicted as three-dimensional box where the axes correspond to students, their qualities, and courses. Fig. 1 shows the three factors depicted as cuboids.

4   Further Issues

Further issues, to be presented in a forthcoming paper, include:

- theoretical results proving optimality of triadic concepts as factors,
- an efficient greedy approximation algorithm,
- results on complexity and experimental evaluation of the algorithm,
- extension of the presented approach to ordinal data using triadic concepts of data with graded attributes.

References

1. Belohlavek R., Vychodil V.: Discovery of optimal factors in binary data via a novel method of matrix decomposition. *J. Computer and System Sci.* **76**(1)(2010), 3–20.
2. Ganter B., Wille R.: *Formal Concept Analysis. Mathematical Foundations.* Springer, Berlin, 1999.
3. Jäschke R., Hotho A., Schmitz C., Ganter B., Stumme G.: TRIAS – An Algorithm for Mining Iceberg Tri-Lattices. *Proc. ICDM 2006*, pp. 907–911.
4. Kolda T. G., Bader B. W.: Tensor decompositions and applications. *SIAM Review* **51**(3)(2009), 455–500.
5. Kroonenberg P. M.: *Applied Multiway Data Analysis.* J. Wiley, 2008.
6. Lehmann F., Wille R.: A triadic approach to formal concept analysis. *Lecture Notes in Computer Science* **954**(1995), 32–43.
7. Wille R.: The basic theorem of triadic concept analysis. *Order* **12**(1995), 149–158.

Boosting Pattern Matching Performance via *k*-bit Filtering

M. Oğuzhan Külekci , Jeffrey Scott Vitter, and Bojian Xu

Texas A&M University
Department of Computer Science & Engineering
College Station, TX, USA

{kulekci,jsv,bojianxu}@cse.tamu.edu

Abstract. This study explores an alternative way of storing text files in a different format that will speed up the searching process. The input file is decomposed into two parts as filter and payload. Filter part is composed of most informative k-bits of each byte from the original file. Remaining bits form the payload. Selection of the most informative bits are achieved according to their entropy. When an input pattern is to be searched on the new file structure, same decomposition is performed on the pattern. The filter part of the pattern is queried in the filter part of the file following by a verification process of the payload for the matching positions. Experiments conducted on natural language texts, plain ascii DNA sequences, and random byte sequences showed that the search performance with the proposed scheme is on the average two times faster than the tested exact pattern matching algorithms.

1 Introduction

A file is a sequence of bytes stored in digital media, such as hard disks, DVDs, or flash memories. Currently text is stored on digital media as it would be written to an ordinary paper notebook. This study explores an alternative way of storing text files in a different format that will result in a boost in search performance, with the restriction that the size of the converted file will not exceed the original one.

Exact string matching, which is simply finding all occurrences of a given pattern on a text, is one of the deeply studied problems in computer science. The topic may be investigated in two classes as *online* and *offline* pattern matching [1]. Online methods create an index over the target data beforehand, while the offline methods [2] preprocess the input pattern for fast scanning over the text. The building blocks of indexing are subword graphs, suffix trees, and suffix arrays [3]. The cost of the gain via indexing is the large space consumption [4] of those structures in addition to the heavy procedure of their constructions in practice.

This study attempts to enhance the offline pattern matching performance via storing files in a different structure, given name *k-bit filter* file format. The conversion of an ordinary file into *k*-bit filter format is a light operation when

E. Gelenbe et al. (eds.), *Computer and Information Sciences*, Lecture Notes
in Electrical Engineering 62, DOI 10.1007/978-90-481-9794-1_6,
© Springer Science+Business Media B.V. 2010

compared with the constructions of index structures and the resultant file is exactly of the *same size* as the original one.

In offline pattern matching, filtering is a powerful tool. While scanning the text, filtering algorithms such as *agrep* [5] and *q-hash* [6] compute the hash of the investigated window and compare against that of the pattern. Since hash collision does not necessarily require an exact match, a complete verification is to be done on those text positions reporting a match in the filtering phase.

The bits of bytes in a file have different entropies. For example, in an English text, the most significant bit of all characters is always zero as the printable characters are the first 128 characters in the ASCII table. This indicates that no information is carried out on that bit according to the information theory [7]. Thus, any time spent on comparing these bits is not much of use. The main idea of this study is to move the most informative bits of the bytes to the beginning of the file and than use those bits as a filter. Since that filter part will compromise a great portion of the file's information content, it acts as an effective filter and reduces the number of verification calls.

The work presented in this paper is bit-oriented rather than the classical byte-oriented approaches. Hence, bit vector matching is crucial throughout the study. A variant of the Külekci's BLIM [8] algorithm is used within this study to fulfill the requirements of the proposed filtering scheme in a fast and flexible manner. Some other recent bitvector matching algorithms can be found in [9–12].

2 k-bit Filtered File Format

Let file F of size n be a sequence of bytes denoted by $F = s_1 s_2 s_3 \ldots s_n$, where each byte s_i, $1 \le i \le n$, is composed of eight bits shown by $s_i = b_1^i b_2^i \ldots b_8^i$.

The number of bits that will be extracted from each byte is denoted by k. Let set R contain the indices of the most informative k bits. The bits corresponding to the indices given in R are extracted from each byte s_i and are stored as a bit vector preserving the order of the bytes. This bit stream is placed at the beginning of the new file, and the remaining bits of each s_i are concatenated to this stream. Figure 1 denotes a sample k-bit filter file structure, assuming $k = 2$, and the indices of the most informative k bits are $R = \{3, 5\}$.

Filter Part	Payload Part		
$b_3^1\ b_5^1$ $\|$ $b_3^2\ b_5^2$ $\|\ldots\|$ $b_3^n\ b_5^n$	$b_1^1\ b_2^1\ b_4^1\ b_6^1\ b_7^1\ b_8^1$ $\|$ $b_1^2\ b_2^2\ b_4^2\ b_6^2\ b_7^2\ b_8^2$ $\|\ldots\|$ $b_1^n\ b_2^n\ b_4^n\ b_6^n\ b_7^n\ b_8^n$		
$k.n$ bits	$(8-k).n$ bits		

Fig. 1. Sample file F converted to k-bit filtered file structure, assuming $k = 2$ and $R = \{3, 5\}$.

The first step while converting a file into k-bit filter structure is to find out the indices of the most informative k bits among the bytes of that file. It is a known fact from the information theory [7] that the information carried by a sequence is inversely proportional to its compression ratio. With that in mind, let us assume eight sequences, each of which is composed of the bits appearing at positions 1 to 8 of each byte. Formally, let $B_x = b_x^1 b_x^2 b_x^3 \ldots b_x^n$, for $1 \leq x \leq 8$. When these eight sequences are individually compressed and are sorted according to their sizes in descending order, this order also represents the amount of information content of the corresponding bits. For example, if the descending order of the sizes of the eight compressed B_x sequences is obtained as $\{5, 3, 1, 6, 8, 7, 2, 4\}$, then the most informative bit in each byte is the fifth, and the next most informative one is the third. If $k = 2$ is given, then the third and fifth bits of each byte is moved to the beginning of the file according to the scheme shown in Figure 1.

3   Searching patterns on k-bit Filtered Files

An input pattern P of length m can be viewed as a sequence of bytes $p_1 p_1 \ldots p_m$, where each p_i, $1 \leq i \leq m$, is a sequence of eight bits. Given the pattern P and the set R of k indices, the search process begins with decomposing the pattern into two parts as the pattern filter PF and pattern payload PL by using the same scheme performed previously on the file.

PF is searched on the filter part of the file, which occupies the initial $k \cdot n$ bits. In case of possible matches at some bit positions 1 to $k \cdot n - m + 1$, PL is verified against the corresponding location in the payload part of the file. If PF is found to begin at a bit position $f = k \cdot h + 1$ on the k-bit filtered file, which means there may be a possible match with the $(h + 1)^{th}$ character of the original file, then PL should to be verified on the corresponding bit position $l = k \cdot n + h \cdot (8 - k) + 1$. The calculation of l comes from the fact that the payload part of the file begins after $k \cdot n$ bit filter part, and to reach the payload of the $(h + 1)^{th}$ byte, one needs to pass over the payloads of the previous h characters, which makes a total of $h \cdot (8 - k)$ bits.

4   Experimental Results

Tests have been conducted on natural language texts, plain ASCII DNA sequences, and random sequences with uniform probability distribution. The *enwik8*[1] corpus and Manzini's DNA corpus[2] are the sources of natural language and DNA sequences used in the experiments. Random files are generated via the standard *rand()* command of C with *srand(time())* seeds.

During the experiments an input file is saved in the proposed k-bit filtered format for $k = 1, 2, 4$. Sample patterns of length 5 to 50 are randomly selected from the original file. Each pattern is scanned on the input file by the Boyer-Moore [13] (BM), Sunday's quick search[14] (QS), Lecroq's q-hash [6] (LecN),

---

[1] The enwik8.txt file is the subject of the Hutter Prize compression competition, and can be downloaded from http://prize.hutter1.net.
[2] http://web.unipmn.it/manzini/danacorpus

Pattern Length	Ordinary Files						k-bit filtered files		
	LecN	BLIM	BOM2	BSOM2	BM	QS	1-bit	2-bit	4-bit
5	0.590	0.265	0.329	0.462	0.256	0.217	0.372	**0.143**	0.148
10	0.524	0.154	0.211	0.291	0.144	0.137	0.093	**0.076**	0.092
15	0.202	0.122	0.150	0.202	0.109	0.101	0.062	**0.059**	0.069
20	0.128	0.101	0.126	0.170	0.094	0.093	**0.044**	0.049	0.056
25	0.094	0.100	0.107	0.142	0.088	0.087	**0.042**	0.050	0.049
30	0.077	0.092	0.091	0.117	0.079	0.076	**0.033**	0.036	0.041
35	0.065	0.056	0.080	0.102	0.070	0.070	0.032	**0.031**	0.039
40	0.057	0.056	0.074	0.095	0.071	0.072	**0.028**	**0.028**	0.035
45	0.052	0.056	0.069	0.085	0.066	0.066	**0.024**	0.033	0.033
50	0.050	0.057	0.064	0.078	0.068	0.064	0.032	**0.025**	0.031

(a) Average user times on natural language text of 20 MB

5	0.866	0.689	0.947	1.346	0.973	0.940	0.576	**0.210**	0.360
10	0.753	0.404	0.497	0.712	0.674	0.753	0.139	**0.109**	0.198
15	0.289	0.331	0.369	0.512	0.558	0.662	**0.085**	**0.085**	0.193
20	0.183	0.253	0.286	0.405	0.536	0.647	**0.063**	0.070	0.144
25	0.136	0.250	0.240	0.335	0.461	0.589	**0.059**	0.070	0.146
30	0.110	0.241	0.204	0.280	0.449	0.537	**0.048**	0.052	0.113
35	0.093	0.177	0.187	0.257	0.524	0.809	0.046	**0.045**	0.142
40	0.082	0.172	0.169	0.224	0.454	0.618	**0.038**	0.041	0.109
45	0.076	0.167	0.153	0.206	0.441	0.651	**0.035**	0.049	0.121
50	0.071	0.166	0.143	0.190	0.432	0.690	0.043	**0.036**	0.107

(b) Average user times on plain ascii DNA sequence of 30 MB

5	0.883	0.213	0.249	0.392	0.289	0.239	0.524	0.209	**0.207**
10	0.782	0.125	0.140	0.215	0.156	0.138	0.143	**0.113**	0.134
15	0.301	0.096	0.106	0.155	0.111	0.101	0.088	**0.087**	0.099
20	0.190	0.077	0.087	0.124	0.090	0.082	**0.067**	0.071	0.079
25	0.141	0.074	0.079	0.107	0.080	0.074	**0.061**	0.072	0.068
30	0.113	0.070	0.072	0.095	0.072	0.069	**0.050**	0.052	0.058
35	0.096	0.064	0.069	0.088	0.069	0.067	0.049	**0.046**	0.054
40	0.085	0.064	0.066	0.081	0.067	0.067	**0.040**	0.042	0.049
45	0.078	0.065	0.064	0.078	0.066	0.065	**0.036**	0.048	0.046
50	0.074	0.065	0.063	0.074	0.065	0.064	0.046	**0.037**	0.042

(c) Average user times on random byte sequences of 30 MB

Fig. 2. Comparison of pattern matching performance between ordinary files and k-bit filtered files via average user times measured in milliseconds during the experiments.

backward oracle/suffix oracle matching [15] (BOM2/BSOM2), and Külekci's bit-parallel BLIM [8] algorithms.

Same patterns are scanned on the *1-bit*, *2-bit* and *4-bit* filtered files of the source files with the proposed scheme. Each sample pattern is searched on files five times, and for each length twenty random patterns are used. The experiment is repeated several times on several same length ordinary files. The user times are measured via the *getrusage* command.

Tests were run on a machine having a 64-bit Intel Xeon processor with 3 GB of memory, and best effort was deployed for the implementation of the algorithms. The compiler used was gcc 4.3.1 on Linux core 2.6.25.9-101.

Figure 2 lists the average of the measurements. Best performances are marked in bold.

Search speed is approximately doubled on k-bit filtered files for all lengths. It is observed that the gain is more significant on DNA sequences, as on short patterns up to length 20, matching via k-bit filtering is more than 3 times faster when compared with the best performing classical algorithm included in this study.

Note that as the filtered bit length k increases, so does the distinguishing power. On the other side, using more bits enlarges the length of the file filter part $(k \cdot n$ bits), which in turn slows down the pattern filter matching. In this trade-off, the results indicate that $k = 4$ is a bad choice, and up to length 15, selection of $k = 2$ seems better. Just one bit filter $(k = 1)$ is in general more speedy than the best resulting algorithm, except the very short pattern cases on natural language and random texts.

5   Conclusion and Future Work

This study focused on exploring an alternative way of storing files for fast offline pattern matching. The proposed k-bit filter file format aims to create an effective filter over a file from the most informative k bits of each character occurring in the file. Searching of a pattern in the file is performed by first extracting the filter of the pattern and locating it in the filter part of the target file followed by the verification process on matching positions.

Experiments conducted on natural language, plain ASCII DNA sequence, and random byte texts indicated that exact matching performance is doubled when files are stored in the k-bit filtered format, even for $k = 1$. Selecting $k = 2$ causes an improvement on short patterns as expected since the distinguishing power is incremented by more bits, but setting $k = 4$ worsens the performance. It is also observed that highest gain is obtained on 1-bit filtered DNA sequences, especially on patterns shorter than 20 bases.

Selection of the most informative bits is done according to compression ratios of individual bit streams. However, it is also possible to select the indices of the k bits via some other techniques, such as simply counting the 0/1 ratio, or measuring the variances of the B_x sequences, or even choosing k random indices. Another dimension is to define bit indices for each character individually instead of fixing these positions for all the characters. Further studies on the topic is planned to include these opportunities.

References

1. Apostolico, A., Galil, Z., eds.: Pattern Matching Algorithms. Oxford University Press (1997)
2. Charras, C., Lecroq, T.: Handbook of exact string matching algorithms. King's Collage Publications (2004)
3. Crochemore, M., Rytter, W.: Jewels of stringology. World Scientific Publishing (2003)
4. Grossi, R., Vitter, J.: Compressed suffix arrays and suffix trees with applications to text indexing and string matching. SIAM Journal on Computing **35** (2005) 378–407
5. Wu, S., Manber, U.: Agrep – a fast approximate pattern-matching tool. In: USENIX Winter 1992 Technical Conference. (1992) 153–162
6. Lecroq, T.: Fast exact string matching algorithms. Information Processing Letters **102** (2007) 229–235
7. Shannon, C.E.: A mathematical theory of communication. Bell System Technical Journal (1948)
8. Külekci, M.O.: A method to overcome computer word size limitation in bit-parallel pattern matching. In: Proceedings of ISAAC'2008. Volume 5369 of Lecture Notes in Computer Science., Gold Coast, Australia, Springer Verlag (2008) 496–506
9. Klein, S.T., Ben-Nissan, M.: Accelerating boyer moore searches on binary texts. In: Proceedings of CIAA. Volume 4783 of LNCS., Springer Verlag (2007) 130–143
10. Kim, J., Kim, E., Park, K.: Fast matching method for dna sequences. In: Proceedings of Combinatorics, Algorithms, Probablistic and Experimental Methodologies. Volume 4614 of LNCS., Springer Verlag (2007) 271–281
11. Faro, S., Lecroq, T.: Efficient pattern matching on binary strings. In: Current Trends in Theory and Practice of Computer Science. (2009) Poster.
12. Faro, S., Lecroq, T.: An efficient matching algorithm for encoded dna sequences and binary strings. In: Proceedings of CPM'09. LNCS (2009)
13. Boyer, R., Moore, J.: A fast string searching algorithm. Communications of the ACM **20** (1977) 762–772
14. Sunday, D.: A very fast substring search algorithm. Communications of the ACM **33** (1990) 132–142
15. Allauzen, C., Crochemore, M., Raffinot, M.: Factor oracle: A new structure for pattern matching. In: Proceedings of SOFSEM'99. Volume 1725 of LNCS., Springer Verlag (1999) 291–306

Network flow approaches for an asset-task assignment problem with execution uncertainty *

Stelios Timotheou

Intelligent Systems and Networks Group
Department of Electrical and Electronic Engineering
Imperial College London
{stelios.timotheou05}@imperial.ac.uk

Abstract. We investigate the assignment of assets to tasks where each
asset can potentially execute any of the tasks, but assets execute tasks
with a probabilistic outcome of success. There is a cost associated with
each possible assignment of an asset to a task, and if a task is not executed there is also a cost associated with the non-execution of the task.
The objective is to make asset-task assignments to minimise the total
expected cost. In [1], we showed that this is a nonlinear combinatorial
optimisation problem and proposed a Random Neural Network (RNN)
algorithm for its solution. In this paper we propose network flow algorithms which are based on solving a sequence of minimum cost flow problems on appropriately constructed networks with estimated arc costs. We
introduce three different scheme for the estimation of the arc costs and we
investigate their performance compared to RNN and greedy algorithms.

1 Introduction

Consider a set of tasks $\mathcal{T}$ that need to be executed by a set of assets $\mathcal{A}$. Task t
carries a penalty $U(t)$ if it is not executed by an asset, while there is also a cost
$C_a(a,t)$ for assigning asset a to task t. We assume that any task can be executed
by any asset and that any one of the assets suffices to execute any one of the
tasks. It is also possible that the task execution may fail despite the fact that
an asset has been assigned to it, and this will be represented by the probability
$0 \le p_f(a,t) \le 1$ that asset a will fail in executing task t when it is assigned
to it. To compensate task execution failures and to account for the fact that
the incurred assignment cost can increase the overall cost, any number of assets
$(0\text{-}|\mathcal{A}|)$ can be assigned to one task. Another important assumption is that the
assets assigned to a particular task have an independent effect, so that the total
failure probability for the particular task is given by the product of the failure
probabilities of the assets assigned to it. The problem can be formulated as:

$$\min C = \sum_{t\in\mathcal{T}}\sum_{a\in\mathcal{A}} C_a(a,t)X(a,t) + \sum_{t\in\mathcal{T}} U(t)\prod_{a\in\mathcal{A}} p_f(a,t)^{X(a,t)} \quad (1)$$
$$s.t. \quad \sum_{t\in\mathcal{T}}X(a,t) \le 1, \quad a \in \mathcal{A} \text{ and } X(a,t) \in \{0,1\} \ \forall a,t$$

* This research was undertaken as part of the ALADDIN (Autonomous Learning
  Agents for Decentralised Data and Information Networks) project and is jointly
  funded by a BAE Systems and EPSRC strategic partnership (EP/C548051/1).

where the decision variables $X(a,t)$ shows whether asset a is assigned to task t.

The problem under investigation belongs to the general class of nonlinear assignment problems. A related problem with a product of terms having the decision variables in their exponent is the Weapon Target Assignment (WTA) problem. WTA is NP-complete and hence exact algorithms have been proposed only for solving special problem cases. For the solution of the general WTA problem, much research has focused on heuristic techniques such as greedy heuristics [2], very large scale neighbourhoods [3] and genetic algorithms [4].

2   Network flow algorithms

In this section we propose three different schemes for the approximate solution of problem (1), which are based on solving a sequence of Minimum Cost Flow (MCF) problems with arc costs associated with the examined problem.

The MCF problem is the most fundamental problem in network flows; most other network flow problems are either special cases or generalisations of it [5]. The MCF problem considers a directed graph or network $G = (\mathcal{N}, \mathcal{E})$ which consists of a set of vertices or nodes $\mathcal{N}$ and a set of directed edges or arcs $\mathcal{E}$ connecting the nodes. Each arc $(i,j) \in \mathcal{E}$ is characterised by two parameters: the capacity $u(i,j)$ of the particular arc which is the upper bound of flow $X_f(i,j)$ allowed through (i,j) and an associated cost per unit of flow $C_f(i,j)$. Each node $i \in \mathcal{N}$ has a supply $s(i)$ that is interpreted as the amount of flow that enters the node from the outside. Node i is a source or supply node if $s(i) > 0$, a sink or demand node if $s(i) < 0$ and a transshipment node if $s(i) = 0$. Flow networks are governed by the flow conservation constraint which states that at each node the incoming and outgoing flows are equal. Note that the conservation constraint can hold only if $\sum_i s(i) = 0$. The objective is to find the cheapest flows that satisfy the nodes' supply, under the flow conservation and capacity constraints:

$$\min \quad \sum_{(i,j)\in\mathcal{E}} C_f(i,j)X_f(i,j) \tag{2a}$$

$$\text{s.t.} \ s(i) + \sum_{j:(j,i)\in\mathcal{E}} X_f(j,i) = \sum_{j:(i,j)\in\mathcal{E}} X_f(i,j), \forall i \in \mathcal{N} \tag{2b}$$

$$0 \leq X_f(i,j) \leq u(i,j), \qquad (i,j) \in \mathcal{E} \tag{2c}$$

Fig. 1 depicts the network used for the solution of problem (1). The network is comprised of three layers of nodes: the first layer contains the source nodes, the second layer contains the transshipment nodes and the third layer the demand node that aggregates the flows send by the source nodes. Each source node a has supply $s(a) = 1$ and corresponds to asset a. Each transshipment node $t^{(m_t)}$ denotes the m_tth asset assignment to task t, while node 0 corresponds to the case that an asset is not assigned to any task. At most M_t assets can be assigned to task t. The role of the demand node d is to aggregate the flows send in the network and its demand is equal to the total supply of the assets, $s(d) = -|\mathcal{A}|$.

A source node a is connected to all transshipment nodes $t^{(m_t)}$ and the capacity of all arcs is equal to 1, so that the associated flows $X_f(a, t^{(m_t)})$ represent the fact that asset a is the m_tth assignment to task t. Even though there are

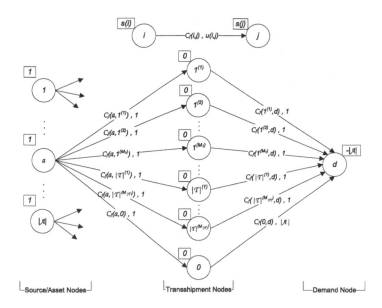

Fig. 1. Flow network for the solution of problem (1)

$|\mathcal{A}|$ arcs arriving at each transshipment node there is only one arc leaving each such node towards the demand node d. These arcs also have capacity 1 except from the arc $(0, d)$ whose capacity is equal to $|\mathcal{A}|$ so that even if no assignments are made the source nodes' supply reaches the demand node via node 0. Thus, flow $X_f(t^{(m_t)}, d), t \in \mathcal{T}$ denotes whether the m_tth assignment for task t has been made. The resulting configuration guarantees that at most one asset can be assigned to a particular transshipment node. Moreover, as all arc capacities and supplies/demands of the nodes are 0 or 1, the integrality property guarantees that in the MCF solution all flows $X_f(a, t^{(m_t)})$ will be binary (see. p.318 of [5]). We also need to ensure that the assignment of assets to a particular task t is contiguous. This ensures that $X_f(a, t^{(m_t)})$ can only be equal to 1 if $X_f(a, t^{(m)}) = 1$ for all $m = 1, ..., m_t - 1$. The contiguous property will be established after we discuss about the costs of the arcs.

The arc costs represent the net reduction in the cost function from assigning a particular asset to a task so our aim is to maximise the net reduction in the objective function. Thus, to solve the problem as a MCF problem we need to negate all the costs associated with the network.

Approximation of the arc costs is necessary because only the ones corresponding to first assignments $C_f(a, t^{(1)})$ are known and equal to $\max\{0, U(t)p_s(a, t) - C_a(a, t)\}$ for all a, t. To correctly determine the arc costs of the $(m_t + 1)$th assignment, $m_t \geq 1$, the first m_t assigned assets to task t $a_{t^{(1)}}, ..., a_{t^{(m_t)}}$ must be known. If an oracle provides this information $C_f(a, t^{(m_t+1)})$ would be:

$$C_f(a, t^{(m_t+1)}) = \max\{0, U(t) \prod^{m_t}_{m=1} p_f(a_{t^{(m)}}, t)p_s(a, t) - C_a(a, t)\} \quad (3)$$

Concerning the cost of the arcs towards node 0 we take $C_f(a,0) = \epsilon > 0$, $\forall a$. As $\epsilon > 0$, we can avoid unbounded solutions due to possible zero arc costs. At the same time the value of ϵ should be small enough so that it is never considered as a beneficial assignment. The arc costs from the transshipment nodes to the demand node are all equal to zero; the role of those flows is only to ensure that at most one asset is related to one task.

In practice, the asset assignments are not known beforehand and hence we cannot determine the cost values $C_f(a, t^{(m_t)})$, $m_t > 1$; for this reason we develop approximation schemes. A conservative approach, which we call MCF-max, is to always assume that the previously assigned asset to a particular task is the least effective one i.e. the one with the largest execution failure probability $p_{f,max}(t) = \max_{a \in \mathcal{A}} p_f(a,t)$. Hence, every term $p_f(a_{t(m)}, t)$, $m = 1, ..., m_t$ in Eq. (3) will be replaced by $p_{f,max}(t)$. An optimistic approach, called MCFmin, is to always consider the most effective asset for previous assignments. If $p_{f,min}(t) = \min_{a \in \mathcal{A}} p_f(a,t)$ then we set $p_f(a_{t(m)}, t) \equiv p_{f,min}(t)$. A third approximation scheme, called MCFrnn, is based on the RNN [6]. The approach is to solve the problem using an RNN algorithm [1], and then use the derived allocations to obtain the arc costs for the MCF network. Hence, the terms $p_f(a_{t(m)}, t)$ are changed to $p_{f,rnn}(t^{(m)})$ which denote the execution failure probabilities for the mth asset assigned to task t. As the RNN algorithm is of low time complexity the overall execution time of the MCF approach is not significantly affected.

An important property of the described flow network is that because $0 < p_f(a,t) < 1$, it is true that: $C_f(a, t^{(1)}) > ... > C_f(a, t^{(m_t)}) > C_f(a, 0) > 0$. The fact that this inequality does not include $C_f(a, t^{(M_t)})$ implies that $C_f(a, t^{(m)}) = 0$, $m = m_t + 1, ..., M_t$, so that after the m_tth assignment asset a cannot be assigned to task t. This inequality also guarantees the contiguous property as the most beneficial assignment for every asset-task pair is always the first available.

The MCF approach for the solution of problem (1) is outlined below:
1. Initialise $\mathcal{A}_{rem} \leftarrow \mathcal{A}$, $S \leftarrow \emptyset$ and $U_{cur}(t) \leftarrow U(t)$, $t \in \mathcal{T}$.
2. Compute $C_f(a, t^{(m_t)})$, $a \in \mathcal{A}_{rem}$, $t \in \mathcal{T}$ and $m_t = 1, ..., M_t$ according to Eq. (3) and the desired cost approximation scheme.
3. Construct the flow network for $a \in \mathcal{A}_{rem}$ and $t \in \mathcal{T}$ as in Fig. 1.
4. Solve the MCF problem with negated arc costs to obtain $X_f(a, t^{(k)})$.
5. Set $\mathcal{A}_{ass} \leftarrow \{a : X_f(a, t^{(1)}) = 1, a \in \mathcal{A}_{rem}, t \in \mathcal{T}\}$.
6. Set $S_{cur} \leftarrow \{(a,t) : X_f(a, t^{(1)}) = 1, a \in \mathcal{A}_{rem}, t \in \mathcal{T}\}$ and $S \leftarrow S \cup S_{cur}$.
7. Set $\mathcal{A}_{rem} \leftarrow \mathcal{A}_{rem} \backslash \mathcal{A}_{ass}$ and $U_{cur}(t) \leftarrow U_{cur}(t) \prod_{a:(a,t) \in S_{cur}} p_f(a,t)$, $t \in \mathcal{T}$
8. If $\mathcal{A}_{ass} \neq \emptyset$ and $\mathcal{A}_{rem} \neq \emptyset$ go to step (2) otherwise stop.
In the above procedure, S is the solution set where we store the assignments made, $\mathcal{A}_{rem}$ denotes the set of the assets remaining to be assigned and $U_{cur}(t)$ is the cost of task t at the particular iteration.

The approach proposed in this section is a modified version of the MCF construction based heuristic that was proposed for the solution of the WTA problem in [3]. However, our approach is different in terms of the arc cost expressions and the network structure. Furthermore, we have introduced the MCFrnn approximation scheme which has the best overall performance.

3   Evaluation

The effectiveness of the proposed MCF algorithms is compared against the RNN parameter association approach proposed in [1], and a Maximum Marginal Return (MMR) greedy heuristic [2] on two data families. In data family 1, the problem parameters are independently generated, while in data family 2 there is positive correlation between the cost of an asset and its associated execution success probabilities, so that "better" assets are more expensive. More details on the generation of the problem instances can be found in [1].

We have performed experiments for several $(|\mathcal{A}|, |\mathcal{T}|)$ pairs with up to 200 assets and 100 tasks. Due to the large size of the problems, the algorithms' performance is compared against tight lower bounds obtained by modifying an algorithm proposed for the WTA problem [7]. The performance measure that we use is the average relative percentage deviation from the lower bound, σ_{LB}:

$$\sigma_{LB} = 100(N_{PI})^{-1}\sum\nolimits_{i=1}^{N_{PI}}(C_{alg,i} - C_{LB,i})(C_{LB,i})^{-1}$$

where $C_{LB,i}$ is the cost obtained from the lower bounding algorithm and N_{PI} is the total number of problem instances considered in each case.

We report σ_{LB} for the various algorithms in Tables 1 and 2. Column LBA corresponds to the cost of the original problem (1), computed using the solution obtained from the lower bounding algorithm. LBA is only considered to demonstrate the tightness of the lower bounds and is not compared with the other methods, as it is not of polynomial complexity.

For data family 1 the most effective algorithms are the network flow approaches MCFmin and MCFrnn for all $(|\mathcal{A}|, |\mathcal{T}|)$ pairs, which have almost the same efficiency and achieve $\sigma_{LB} < 1.3\%$ in all cases. In addition, these algorithms even outperform the LBA approach for the cases that $|\mathcal{A}|/|\mathcal{T}| \leq 1$. Additionally, MCFmax only performs well when $|\mathcal{A}|/|\mathcal{T}| \leq 1$. Interestingly, for data family 2 the best overall performing algorithm is the RNN. RNN performs better than the other approaches for large problem instances when $|\mathcal{A}| = |\mathcal{T}|$ and $2|\mathcal{A}| = |\mathcal{T}|$, while for the other problems its performance is highly competitive. MCFrnn achieves better results than the MCFmin approach, especially for the problem sets with equal number of assets and tasks. The performance of the MMR approach is well improved compared to data family 1 while, the MCFmax is again the least effective approach.

4   Conclusions

In this paper we have studied an asset-task allocation problem when an asset may fail to execute an assigned task. For its solution, we have proposed three different approximation schemes based on network flows. The results indicate that the proposed network flow algorithms MCFmin and MCFrnn have better overall performance than the MMR and RNN heuristics, with the MCFrnn being the most successful; it performs equally well with the MCFmin for data family 1 and it is more effective on data family 2.

$|\mathcal{A}|$	$|\mathcal{T}|$	$|\mathcal{A}|/|\mathcal{T}|$	RNN	MMR	MCFmax	MCFmin	MCFrnn	LBA
20	40	0.5	1.954	4.068	0.611	**0.607**	**0.607**	0.626
40	80	0.5	2.366	4.162	0.921	**0.920**	**0.920**	0.977
80	160	0.5	2.542	3.908	**1.243**	1.243	1.243	1.367
20	20	1.0	3.321	8.995	2.067	**0.098**	0.101	0.098
40	40	1.0	2.419	8.556	2.042	**0.110**	**0.110**	0.112
80	80	1.0	2.204	7.469	1.815	**0.119**	**0.119**	0.124
40	20	2.0	2.683	6.717	14.802	**0.243**	0.284	0.074
100	50	2.0	2.930	7.251	18.271	**0.088**	0.105	0.088
200	100	2.0	2.866	6.550	20.056	**0.088**	**0.088**	0.101
Overall Perf.			2.588	6.408	6.870	**0.391**	0.397	0.396

Table 1. Average relative percentage deviation from the lower bound in data family 1

$|\mathcal{A}|$	$|\mathcal{T}|$	$|\mathcal{A}|/|\mathcal{T}|$	RNN	MMR	MCFmax	MCFmin	MCFrnn	LBA
20	40	0.5	**0.486**	0.540	**0.486**	**0.486**	**0.486**	0.527
40	80	0.5	**0.505**	0.561	0.509	0.508	0.508	0.553
80	160	0.5	0.684	0.740	**0.683**	**0.683**	**0.683**	0.751
20	20	1.0	0.708	3.031	0.765	1.577	**0.589**	0.094
40	40	1.0	0.673	3.384	0.822	1.710	**0.652**	0.140
80	80	1.0	**0.777**	3.719	1.007	1.826	0.806	0.518
40	20	2.0	**2.619**	3.428	5.980	3.149	3.039	0.077
100	50	2.0	**2.382**	3.393	6.441	3.429	3.307	0.580
200	100	2.0	**2.115**	3.298	6.333	3.533	3.320	1.213
Overall Perf.			**1.217**	2.455	2.558	1.878	1.488	0.4948

Table 2. Average relative percentage deviation from the lower bound in data family 2

References

1. Gelenbe, E., Timotheou, S., Nicholson, D.: Fast distributed near optimum assignment of assets to tasks. The Computer Journal (2010) doi:10.1093/comjnl/bxq010.
2. Kolitz, S.E.: Analysis of a maximum marginal return assignment algorithm. In: Proceedings of the 27th IEEE Conference on Decision and Control, Austin, Texas, USA, 7-9 December, IEEE, New York, NY (1988) 2431–2436
3. Ahuja, R.K., Kumar, A., Jha, K.C., Orlin, J.B.: Exact and Heuristic Algorithms for the Weapon-Target Assignment Problem. OPERATIONS RESEARCH 55(6) (2007) 1136–1146
4. Lee, Z.J., Su, S.F., Lee, C.Y.: Efficiently solving general weapon-target assignment problem by genetic algorithms with greedy eugenics. IEEE Transactions on Systems, Man, and Cybernetics, Part B: Cybernetics 33(1) (Feb 2003) 113–121
5. Ahuja, R.K., Magnanti, T.L., Orlin, J.B.: Network Flows: Theory, Algorithms, and Applications. Prentice Hall, United States (1993)
6. Timotheou, S.: The Random Neural Network: A Survey. The Computer Journal 53(3) (2010) 251–267
7. Manne, A.: A Target-Assignment Problem. Operations Research 6(3) (1958) 346–351

A Genetic Algorithm Approach to the Artillery Target Assignment Problem

Burçin Sapaz, İsmail Hakkı Toroslu, Göktürk Üçoluk

Middle East Technical University, Ankara, Turkey

Abstract. In this work a new assignment problem with the name "Artillery Target Assignment Problem (ATAP)" is defined. ATAP is about assigning artillery guns to targets at different time instances while some objective functions are to be optimized. Since an assignment made for any time instance effect the value of the shooting ATAP is harder than the classical assignment problem. For two variations of ATAP genetic algorithm solutions with customized representations and genetic operators are developed and presented.

1 Introduction

In military, assignment of artillery guns for targets is a complex decision process which includes many different parameters to be considered [3, 4]. Mainly at each discrete time instance, available guns are assigned to proper targets with the best possible assignment in order to perform shooting to these targets. Although, it is already difficult to determine the best assignment for a single time instance, the main challenge is that the decisions for a time instance usually affects the shooting value.

In this problem, there are three main kinds of elements, namely targets, guns and time. ATAP is about assigning n guns to m targets in p discrete time instances with best possible cost by means of required optimization parameters. Different military tactics will result in different cost functions.

In our model, we will assume that each shot of a gun to each target for each time instance is represented by a cost value, which we will aim to maximize. In ATAP each single gun that belongs to the same battery hierarchy is assumed to be identical. Furthermore, every battery has the same hierarchy structure: So batteries are sectionwise and gunwise identical. Targets though, can differ in their target values, shot values and target sizes. In military domain various firing techniques are adopted which corresponds to variations of the basic form.

In this study we investigate two important variations, namely joining targets to treat as a single target, and firing guns of a battery or a section together for large targets.

ATAP is structurally a complex problem making its GA representation complex too [1]. The main contribution of this work is modeling ATAP as a GA problem with suitable and efficient representation of its instances and algorithms to handle GA operators. We also show that our modeling produces quite successful results.

E. Gelenbe et al. (eds.), *Computer and Information Sciences*, Lecture Notes
in Electrical Engineering 62, DOI 10.1007/978-90-481-9794-1_8,

2   Handled Cases and GA Implementations

For both cases handled the chromosome structure is a 3-Dimensional binary array with dimensions in guns, targets and the discrete time. Firing a gun, to a target at a time instance is represented by a 1 in the corresponding entry in the chromosome. Otherwise the entry is 0.

Also the objective function for both cases is defined as

$$\max \sum_{i \in guns} \sum_{j \in targets} \sum_{k \in times} Chromosome_{ijk} \times ShootingCost(i,j,k) \qquad (1)$$

In equation 1 we assume all $ShootingCosts(i,j,k)$ values are provided for all i,j,k values, namely the targets, guns and time dimensions.

Solution that maximize the objective function is searched by means of GA. The GA employed is of one-point crossover and 2-point gene-swap mutation type and uses elitist selection. The selection replaces the worst 5% of the new population with the best 5% of the previous. Mutation is %1.0 mutation/gene-crossover. Population size is 100.

The crossover produces invalid chromosomes. How this is fixed is explained below. Mutation is implemented as a gun assignment swap among two random chosen genes that belong to the same time dimension. This ensures that no invalid chromosomes are produced due to mutation.

2.1   Target Joining

In order to represent target joins we will allow more than one entries to be 1 in the target dimension. We implement the single point crossover to be perfomed in all dimensions. In particular, the crossover in the time dimension is trivial and does not cause any invalid chromosomal formation. On the other hand this is not so for guns and targets dimensions. Here a repairing algorithm is needed for conducting an efficient GA search. Furthermore, the initial pool is formed to contain only valid chromosomes.

There are three possible kinds of violations that has to be dealt with:

1. A single target get more than one shot (two entry in a row). This can occur in a gun dimension crossover.
2. Two unjoinable targets got joined (a invalid two entry in a column). This can occur in a target dimension crossover.
3. Targets that must got shot in this time instance (due to their parents) might remain unshot after the crossover. (no value in row though parent had it)

For case (1) and (2) the repair phase will cancel randomly one of the two columns or rows. After the cancelation it is possible that additional cases of (3) might get generated. For case (3) the repair is done at last by randomly assigning remaining guns to remaining targets.

2.2   Hierarchical Formation of Guns

In order to represent hierarchial formations of guns, each gun, as well as each hierarchial formation is represented by a gene in the guns dimension. Only a single one of these genes will be allowed to be 1.

In a valid structure, at a time instance, no two targets can be shot by two gun formations which are hierarchically related. The forms of violations are as follows:

1. A single target might receive more than one (two) shots. This can occur for the crossovers in the guns dimension.
2. Two targets might be shot by the same gun system. This case can occur for the crossovers in the target dimension.
3. An invalid case might be generated by assigning two hierarchically related guns to targets in the single time instance. This case may occur in both forms of the crossovers.
4. A target that must be shot in the given time instance might not be shot at all. This case may occur in both forms of the crossovers also.

The first two cases are handled by randomly canceling one of the two shots in in these dimensions. This might generate more cases of (4) also. Case (3) is also handled by canceling out one of the shots of the hierarchically related guns. At this point again notice that since parents are assumed to be valid not more than two guns can be hierarchically related can shoot at a time instance. Therefore, in resolving this violations one of these two shots should be cancelled and this can be done by choosing either higher or lower gun in the hierarchy. This may also generate more cases of (4). The last case is handled by randomly assigning remaining valid guns to remaining targets. Notice that not all idle guns are valid, since no two guns in the same hierarchical path can be utilized at the same time.

3   Experimental Results and Conclusions

As part of the experimental work a an artillery weapon simulator has been implemented. GA solver is based on GAlib [2]. The screenshot of the UI is displayed in Figure 1. This simulator has been used for two purposes:

1. Realistic data generation for experiment.
2. Visual display of events of the experimentation on the timeline.

Inputs to data generation (gun and target specifications and their movements, terrain obstacles) are taken directly from real military domain. The movements of the targets are inputted through an timeline based scenario editor. Using this simulator datasets, properties of which are given in Table 1, are generated. Furthermore, for each gun-target pair the followings are assigned as a function of time.

- Cost value (value of gained by hitting the target),
- effectiveness (of the gun on that target),
- distance (between the gun and the target),
- availability of the target (hitting as early as possible of the target is desired)

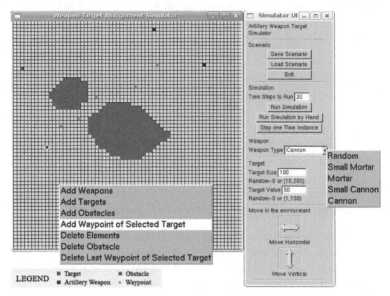

Fig. 1. Artillery Weapon Target Simulator

Table 1. Number of Elements in Datasets

	Dataset 1	Dataset 2	Dataset 3
Number of Weapons for target joining	5	10	10
Number of Weapons for hierarchial formation	45	90	90
Number of Targets	10	100	100
Number of Time Instances	50	50	100
Number of Total Joins for target joining	32	396	943

The convergence speed is very satisfying, which exhibits a linear relation with the size of the dataset. The manual verification of the solutions proved that the results are very close to the real optimal.

References

1. C.A. Coello. Theoretical and Numerical Constraint-Handling Techniques Used with Evolutionary Algorithms: a Survey of the State of the Art. Computer Methods in Applied Mechanics and Engineering, 191(11-12):1245-1287, 2002.
2. GAlib: Matthew's Genetic Algorithms Library. http://lancet.mit.edu/ga/
3. C. Huaiping, L. Jingxu, C. Yingwu, W. Hao. Survey of the research on dynamic weapon-target assignment problem. J of Sys. Eng. & Elec., 17(3):559-565, 2006
4. Z. Lee, S. Su, C. Lee. Efficiently Solving General Weapon-Target Assignment Problem by Genetic Algorithms With Greedy Eugenics. IEEE T. on Sys. Man and Cyb., Part B, 33(1):113-121, 2003.

2 Modeling and Performance Evaluation of Systems and Networks

Scheduling services in a queuing system with impatience and setup costs

Alain Jean-Marie[1] and Emmanuel Hyon[2]

[1] INRIA and LIRMM, CNRS/Université Montpellier 2, 161 Rue Ada, F-34392 Montpellier, ajm@lirmm.fr
[2] Université Paris Ouest Nanterre la Défense, LIP6, UPMC 4 place Jussieu, F-75252 Paris Cedex, Emmanuel.Hyon@u-paris10.fr.

Abstract. We consider a single server queue in discrete time, in which customers must be served before some limit sojourn time of geometrical distribution. A customer who is not served before this limit leaves the system. The fact of serving customers, holding them in queue or losing them induce costs. The purpose is to decide when to serve the customers so as to minimize these costs. We use a Markov Decision Process with infinite horizon and discounted criterion. We establish the structural properties of the stochastic dynamic programming operator, and we deduce that the optimal policy is of threshold type, and we compute the threshold explicitly.
Keywords: Scheduling, queuing system, impatience, deadline, optimal control, Markov decision processes

1 Introduction

In this paper we are interested in the optimal control of a queuing system with impatient customers (or, equivalently said, customers with deadlines). The set-up of customer services, the storage of the customers in the queue as well as their "loss" (departure from the queue due to impatience) induce some costs and it has to be decided when to begin the service in order to minimize these costs.

Controlled queuing models, deterministic as well as stochastic, have been largely studied in the literature since their application fields are numerous. Nevertheless most of these works do not consider impatient customers but rather losses due to overflow. Yet, the phenomenon of impatience, associated with deadlines or "timeouts", has become non negligible in several fields of engineering.

The literature features papers on the performance evaluation of queues with impatience, but none of them seem to address the case of choosing whether to serve or not, in the presence of setup costs. The problem of optimally controlling a batch server in a queue (without impatience) has been addressed in [1, 3] (see also the references therein, and see [2] for further references). Its resolution is based on the Markov Decision Process formalism, and goes through establishing some structural properties of the value function and the dynamic programming operator. This then allows to deduce that the solution is a threshold policy. It appears that extending the techniques developed in [3] to queues with impatience is not straightforward, because impatience tends to destroy the structural properties that are commonly used for proving the optimality of threshold policies. In this paper, we show that structural properties exist despite the occurrence of losses and present the solution for service batches of unit size. For this purpose, we use some tools which, in our opinion, will be useful for solving more complex cases.

More precisely: we adapt the framework of structural analysis of Markov Decision Processes, as described for instance in [4]. The model and the cost structure are described in Section 2. We establish in Section 3, the structural properties of the stochastic dynamic programming operator and we show that the optimal policy is a threshold policy. Furthermore, we explicitly compute the threshold value as a function of the parameters. We discuss in our conclusion some problems encountered with general batch sizes. Details are provided in [2].

2   Model

We proceed with introducing the model, and formulating the optimal control problem in the framework of Markov Decision Processes, using the notation of Puterman [4]. Due to space limitations, some notations and concepts are quoted from this reference, to which the reader is directed for formal definitions.

2.1   System Dynamics

We consider a discrete time (or slotted) model, where the slot is the time unit. Customers arrive at the beginning of each slot. They are stored in an infinite buffer in which they wait for to be admitted in the server to be processed. This admission decision is made by a controller. The service duration is one time slot.

Denote with A_n the number of arrivals at the beginning of slot n. The sequence $\{A_n\}_{n \in \mathbb{N}}$ is assumed to be an i.i.d. sequence of random variables. With the usual abuse of notation, we denote generically this common distribution with A. We furthermore assume that A is of mean λ.

The admission decision of the controller takes place just after arriving customers have been taken into account. We call $x_n \in \mathbb{N}$ the number of waiting customers at that epoch in slot n. The set of decisions, or action space, is denoted with $\mathcal{Q} = \{0, 1\}$, where $q_n = 1$ if one customer is admitted and 0 otherwise. We assume that the controller may choose $q_n = 1$ even if $x_n = 0$, which has no effect. The number of customers remaining in the buffer just after the decision is then $y_n = (x_n - q_n)^+$, with $x^+ = \max(0, x)$.

During a slot, losses can occur because customers become impatient and leave. It is assumed that each customer in the buffer has a constant probability $\alpha \in [0, 1]$ of leaving in each slot, independently from the past and from other customers. This is equivalent to assuming that the patience of each customer is geometrically distributed on $\mathbb{N}$ with parameter α. Customers in service are not impatient. For notational convenience, we introduce the stochastic operators $I(y)$ and $S(y)$ which count, respectively, the number of customers lost (impatient) and remaining (survivors), out of y present at the beginning of a slot. Conditioned on the value of $y_n = y$, $I(y)$ and $S(y)$ are Binomial random variables with respective means αy, and $\overline{\alpha} y$, where $\overline{\alpha} = 1 - \alpha$, and $I(y) + S(y) = y$. With this notation, the evolution of the state from slot n to slot $n + 1$ is given by the recurrence equation:

$$x_{n+1} = R(x_n, q_n) := S\left((x_n - q_n)^+\right) + A_{n+1} , \tag{1}$$

whereas the number of customers lost in slot n is equal to $I((x_n - q_n)^+)$.

We shall use the following property, in which $\geq_{st}$ refers to the usual (strong) stochastic ordering between random variables.

Proposition 1. *For any $x \geq y \in \mathbb{N}$ we have $S(x) \geq_{st} S(y)$. If $X \geq_{st} Y$, then $S(X) \geq_{st} S(Y)$.*

2.2 Elements of the Markov Decision Process

Transition probabilities. The dynamics of the controlled process are characterized by the probabilities to move in state z, given that the state is y and the action is $q \in \mathcal{Q}$: $\mathbb{P}\left(z|(y, q)\right) = \mathbb{P}\left(x_{n+1} = z | x_n = y, q_n = q\right)$. These probabilities do not depend on n. Their exact expression is not relevant to our analysis, which is based on the recurrence (1).

Rewards/Costs. The costs associated with decisions and transitions are the following. First, there is a setup cost c_B which is incurred when the controller chooses to admit one customer into service. Second, there is a cost associated to each customer leaving the queue due to impatience: at slot n, it is $c_L I(y_n)$, where c_L is the cost of a single loss. Finally, there is a holding cost c_H per remaining customer. We assume that it applies to all customers present after the service admission decision, so that the cost for slot n is $c_H y_n$. The total average cost incurred by taking decision q when the state is x, is then the function of (x, q):

$$c(x, q) = q c_B + (c_L \alpha + c_H)(x - q)^+ = q c_B + c_C (x - q)^+ , \tag{2}$$

where $c_C = \alpha c_L + c_H$ is the *per-capita* cost for customers. Observe that this cost function is *not* bounded, unless $c_C = 0$.

Dynamic programming. We consider a discounted cost criterion and the discount factor is denoted by θ. We make this choice in order to avoid the complexities associated with the average cost criterion. Under each policy π, the evolution of the system generates a random sequence of states x_n and decisions q_n. The value function of policy π is then defined as:

$$v_\theta^\pi(x) = \mathbb{E}_x^\pi \left[\sum_{n=0}^\infty \theta^n c(x_n, q_n) \right] ,$$

where $x_0 = x$. Our aim is to find the optimal policy π^* (in some adequate set of policies) such that $\forall x \in \mathbb{N}$, $v_\theta^{\pi^*}(x) = v_\theta^*(x) = \min_\pi v_\theta^\pi(x)$. This policy is provided by any solution to the *dynamic programming equation* $v_\theta = \min_q (Tv_\theta)$, where the operator T, acting on functions v, is:

$$(Tv)(x, q) = c(x, q) + \theta \, \mathbb{E}\left[v\left(R(x, q)\right)\right] . \tag{3}$$

3   The Optimal Policy

In this part we study the structural properties of value functions in order to get qualitative results on the optimal policy. Specifically, we prove that the optimal policy is of threshold type.

The framework is that of property propagation through the Dynamic Programming operator. It consists in three steps: first identify two related sets of "structured" value functions, V^σ and policies D^σ: if the value function belongs to V^σ, then the optimal policy belongs to D^σ. Then show that the properties of v are conserved (or "propagated") by the operator T. At last, check that these properties are kept when passing to the limit. A *structure theorem* then allows to ensure that there exists an optimal policy and states, at the same time, that this optimal policy can be chosen in the set of structured policies. In the present case, the properties involved are increasingness, convexity and submodularity. The structured policies are the monotone ones. For easier reference, the methodological framework useful to our analysis is gathered in [2]. This includes the notion of *submodularity*: a real-valued function g defined on two partially ordered sets $\mathcal{X} \times \mathcal{Q}$ is called submodular if, for any $\overline{x} \geq \underline{x} \in \mathcal{X}$ and any $\overline{q} \geq \underline{q} \in \mathcal{Q}$:

$$g(\overline{x}, \overline{q}) - g(\underline{x}, \overline{q}) \leq g(\overline{x}, \underline{q}) - g(\underline{x}, \underline{q}).$$

To submodular operators will correspond monotone decision functions.

3.1   Structural Properties of the Dynamic Programming Operator

In this part we establish structural results of the dynamic programming operator for our system: propagation of monotonicity, submodularity and convexity.

Lemma 1. *Let $\tilde{v}$ be the function defined by $\tilde{v}(x) = \min_q Tv(x, q)$ for any $x \in \mathbb{N}$. Then $\tilde{v}$ is nondecreasing in x if v is nondecreasing in x.*

Proof. The definition of Tv in (3) involves two terms given in Eqs. (2) and (1). We show first that the costs $c(x, q)$ are nondecreasing for a given decision q. Indeed, from Equation (2) the cost is either equal to $(x - 1)c_C + c_B$ or xc_C which are nondecreasing in x. Then, from Proposition 1, it follows that $S((x + 1 - q)^+) \geq_{st} S((x - q)^+)$. Therefore we have that $R(x+1, q) \geq_{st} R(x, q)$, which implies $\mathbb{E}v(R(x + 1, q)) \geq \mathbb{E}v(R(x, q))$ since v is increasing. As a consequence, the function $Tv(x, q)$ is the sum of two increasing functions of x for every q. The minimum over q is therefore also increasing.

Lemma 2 (Submodularity). *For any nondecreasing convex function v, the function $Tv(x, q)$ is submodular on $\mathbb{N} \times \mathcal{Q}$.*

Proof. We shall show that $\Delta_q Tv(x) := Tv(x, 1) - Tv(x, 0)$ is nonincreasing in x: by Lemma 4.7.6 of [4], $Tv(x, q)$ will be submodular. We have the decomposition:

$$\Delta_q Tv(x) = c(x, 1) - c(x, 0) + \theta \Delta_q \hat{T}v(x), \tag{4}$$

$$\text{where: } \Delta_q \hat{T}v(x) = \mathbb{E}v(S((x - 1)^+) + A) - \mathbb{E}v(S(x) + A). \tag{5}$$

Using (2), the difference $c(x, 1) - c(x, 0)$ is seen to be nonincreasing in $x \geq 0$. We then prove the nonincreasingness of $x \mapsto \Delta_q \hat{T} v(x)$ for any $x > 0$. In that case, we use the stochastic decomposition $S(x) = S(1) + S(x - 1)$ (where the random variables in the right-hand side are independent), in (5) to get:

$$\Delta_q \hat{T} v(x) = \mathbb{E} v(S(x - 1) + A) \; - \; \mathbb{E} v(S(x - 1) + S(1) + A)$$
$$= \; - \; \sum_{a,s} \mathbb{P}(A = a, S(1) = s) \, \mathbb{E}\left[u_{a,s}(S(x - 1))\right] , \qquad (6)$$

where we have defined: $u_{a,s}(y) := v(y + s + a) - v(y + a)$. Since v is increasing and convex, the function $u_{a,s}(y)$ is nonnegative and increasing for all nonnegative values of a and s. The stochastic increasingness of the $S(x)$ (Proposition 1), implies that $\mathbb{E} u_{a,s}(S(x)) \geq \mathbb{E} u_{a,s}(S(x - 1))$, for all $x \geq 1$ and all $s, a \geq 0$. This last inequality is conserved by convex combinations. As a result, the expression (6) is a nonincreasing function of $x > 0$. It is also negative, so that when $x = 1$:

$$\Delta_q T v(1) \; = \; c_B - c_C + \theta \Delta_q \hat{T} v(1) \; \leq \; c_B \; = \; \Delta_q T v(0) .$$

The function is therefore nonincreasing at $x = 0$ as well.

Lemma 3. *Let $\tilde{v}$ be the function defined by $\tilde{v}(x) = \min_q T v(x, q)$ for any $x \in \mathbb{N}$. Then $\tilde{v}$ is nondecreasing convex in x if v is nondecreasing convex in x.*

The proof involves a case-by-case analysis, based on the fact that the function $q_y^* := \arg\min_q T v(y, q)$ is decreasing, a consequence of Lemma 2 and 4.7.1 of [4].

3.2   Structural Properties of the Optimal Policy

One calls a threshold policy (sometimes, "control limit policy") a policy such that $q(x) = q_1$ if $x < \nu$ and $q(x) = q_2$ if $x \geq \nu$, where q_1 and q_2 are in $\mathcal{Q}$ and ν is called the threshold. For our problem, $q_1 = 0$, $q_2 = 1$ and an infinite threshold means that it is never optimal to accept customers.

Theorem 1. *The optimal policy is increasing in x (it is a monotone control) and is a threshold policy.*

The proof is based on Theorem 6.11.3 of [4]. First of all, technical issues related to the unboundedness of the cost function have to be checked. Next, the theorem is applied with V^σ the set of nondecreasing convex functions, and $\mathcal{D}^\sigma$ the set of monotone controls. Lemmas 1–3 combined with Lemma 4.7.1 of [4] prove that the class of functions V^σ is preserved by the stochastic programming operator. Therefore, there exists an optimal policy which is a monotone control. Given that the action space has two elements, this is actually a threshold policy.

3.3   The Optimal Threshold

The optimal threshold can actually be computed explicitly:

Theorem 2. *Let $\psi = c_B - c_C/(1 - \overline{\alpha}\theta)$. Then: a) if $\psi > 0$, the optimal threshold is $\nu = +\infty$; b) if $\psi < 0$, the optimal threshold is $\nu = 1$; c) $\psi = 0$, any threshold policy $\nu \geq 1$ gives the same value.*

As a first step in the proof, a direct computation provides the following expression for the value of the threshold policy with parameter ν:

$$V_\nu(x) = \frac{c_C}{1 - \theta\overline{\alpha}} \left(x + \frac{\theta \mathbb{E}(A)}{1 - \theta} \right) + \psi \left(\sum_{n=0}^{\infty} \theta^n \mathbb{P}(R_\nu^{(n)}(x) \geq \nu) \right).$$

Then the function $\Phi_\nu(x, \theta)$, defined as the series in the above equation, is shown to be positive, increasing with respect to x for every fixed ν and decreasing with respect to ν for fixed x. The proof of this relies on a sample path comparison argument. The dependence on ν being concentrated in the function Φ_ν, the minimum is either at $\nu = 1$ or $\nu = +\infty$, depending on the sign of ψ.

4   Conclusions

In this paper we show that the optimal control of service in a single-server queue with impatience is a threshold policy and we give the value of this threshold. If the framework used is not original, its application here requires some additional concepts which do not appear in previous works. For example, proving here the monotonicity of the control requires a convex value function contrarily to the usual cases where only monotonicity of the value function is required (see [4]). On the other hand, the simplicity of the result raises the idea that a proof not using the "structural" framework should exist. We discuss this issue in more detail in [2]. In particular, we explain why the exchange arguments usually invoked to compare policies, do not apply to our case.

The extension of the problem to the case where the server may serve more than one customer at a time, does not work in a straightforward manner. Actually, starting with $B = 2$, the value function of the problem ceases, in general, to have the submodularity property required in Lemma 2. On the other hand, no experimental evidence has contradicted, so far, the possibility that the optimal control still be of threshold type. The challenge of further research on the topic will therefore be to find the appropriate properties that can be propagated by the dynamic programming operator in this case.

References

1. Deb, R.K., Serfozo, R.F.: Optimal control of batch service queues. Adv. App. Prob. 5(2), 340–361 (1973)
2. Hyon, E., Jean-Marie, A.: Scheduling in a queuing system with impatience and setup costs. Tech. Rep. RR-6881, version 2, INRIA (Feb 2010)
3. Papadaki, K.P., Powell, W.B.: Exploiting structure in adaptive dynamic programming algorithms for a stochastic batch service problem. EJOR 142, 108–127 (2002)
4. Puterman, M.: Markov Decision Processes Discrete Stochastic Dynamic Programming. Wiley (2005)

Multiple Class Symmetric G-networks with Phase Type

Thu-Ha DAO-THI[1]*, Jean-Michel FOURNEAU[1], and Minh-Anh TRAN[2]
thu-ha.dao-thi@prism.uvsq.fr, jmf@prism.uvsq.fr,
minh-anh.tran@univ-paris12.fr *

[1] PRiSM, Université de Versailles St-Quentin, CNRS, UniverSud, Versailles, France
[2] Université de Paris Est Créteil, France

Abstract. We consider a queueing network of symmetric Gqueues with customers and signals. Since the seminal papers by Gelenbe in the early nineties [7, 9, 10], Generalized networks of queues have received considerable attention. But most papers assume to obtain product form that the service times follow exponential distributions. Here we propose a new generalisation of this model with Phase type service times. We also assume a new type of signal. When the signal enters a queue, it changes the phase of the customer in service when there is any. As usual after its service completion, a customer moves to another queue and may become a signal. The steady-state distribution for such a network of queues has a product form solution.

1 Introduction

G-networks of queues with customers and signals represent an important step towards the analysis of stochastic interacting components. Usual queueing networks model systems with customers. These customers wait for service, and at the completion of their service, move among a finite set of servers according to a stochastic routing matrix. These queueing models typically do not have provisions for some customers having direct control on other customers or queues. G-network models overcome some of the limitations of conventional queueing network models and still preserve the computationally attractive product form property of some Markovian queueing networks. They contain unusual signals which act upon the queue or customers present in the queue they visit. The first type of signal introduced by Gelenbe was described as a negative customer [7]. A negative customer deletes a positive customer in a queue at its arrival if it is possible. Positive customers are usual customers in classical queueing networks. A negative customer is never queued. Under typical assumptions (Poisson arrival for both types of customers, exponential service time for positive customers, Markovian routing, independence, open topology, infinite capacity queue) Gelenbe proved that such a network has a product form solution for its steady-state

---

* *Corresponding author

E. Gelenbe et al. (eds.), *Computer and Information Sciences*, Lecture Notes in Electrical Engineering 62, DOI 10.1007/978-90-481-9794-1_10,
© Springer Science+Business Media B.V. 2010

behaviour. The flow equation for these networks exhibits some uncommon properties: it is neither linear as in closed queueing networks nor contracting as in open queueing networks like Jackson networks. Therefore the existence of a solution had to be proved [8] and a numerical algorithm had to be developed [4]. Network of positive and negative customers were introduced to model neural networks where neurones exchange inhibitory and exciting signals [6, 11]. New types of signals have also been added to develop a more general theory: batch deletion [10], triggers [9] and resets [13]. G-networks and Random Neural Networks were also used in the design of the learning process for Cognitive Packet Networks [12, 14]. Multiple class versions of these models have also been derived [5] to generalize BCMP theorem [1]. Currently there are several hundred references devoted to the subject and a book [3] provide insight into some of the research issues, developments and applications in the area of networks of queues with customers and signals. Most of the results presented are based on exponential service time, the only exception is [2] where the service times follow a Cox distribution.

Here we study G-networks with Phase type service time and we also introduce a new type of *signal*. Indeed, the effect of a signal takes into account the PH representation of the service. Assume that the service is in phase ph and assume that the matrix representation of the PH distribution is H, a new type signal has the following effect : the signal change the phase of the customer in service, if there are any, according to matrix H. Furthermore the queues are assumed to be symmetric according to Kelly's definition [15]. This new extension of G-networks still has a product form for its stationary regime. The proof is based on a representation of Phase type service as visits on a set of queues and the Chao's extension of quasi-reversibility [3].

The remaining of the paper is as follows. In Section 2 we study symmetric queues with a PH service time and signals, while Section 3 describes the model assumptions and the result of product form for the steady-state distribution.

2   The model with one queue

The goal is to model a generalized network of multiple classes of (positive) customers with Phase type service times for each class and two types of signal. In [16], Bonald and Tran modelled the Phase type service by allowing a customer to change class after service. More precisely, each phase demands an exponential service time. After phase p, a customer can change to some phase q with some probability. We will use this presentation to model the network. A multi-class network of with Phase type services is equivalent to a multi-class network with exponential services and class transitions inside the queue.

First, let us consider the model of one queue. The set of classes is denoted by $\mathcal{C}$, and a special class index 0 ($0 \notin \mathcal{C}$) denote the "absorbing state". There are two types of signals: negative signal and class changing signal.

Customers of class c arrive according to a Poisson process of rate $\lambda^{(c)}$, require exponential service times of mean $1/\mu^{(c)}$, for $c \in \mathcal{C}$. A customer of class c after service will change to class k (demand another service) with probability $H[c, k]$ or reach the state 0 (service completion, quit the queue) with probability $H[c, 0]$. The following condition is satisfied: $H[c, 0] + \sum_{k \in C} H[c, k] = 1$.

The service discipline is a symmetric discipline considered by Kelly in [15] with the service effort supposed bounded by B. The total service effort is provided at rate $\phi(n)$ when there are n customers in the queue, and:

- A proportion $\gamma(l, n)$ of the total service effort is directed to customer in position l $(1 \le l \le n)$. When its service is completed, customer in positions $l+1, l+2, \ldots, n$ move to positions $l, l+1, \ldots, n-1$, respectively.

- When a customer arrive to queue i, it moves to position l $(1 \le l \le n+1)$ with probability $\gamma(l, n+1)$. Customer previously in positions $l, l+1, \ldots, n$ move to positions $l+1, l+2, \ldots, n+1$, respectively.

The function γ will be called the "proportional function" determined the service discipline. The function γ verifies: $\sum_{l \le n} \gamma(l, n) = 1$ or $\sum_{l \le n} \gamma(l, n) = 0$.

We modify the proportional function to simplify the problem of finite buffer. In the case of finite buffer, the proportional function's value is 0 for n is greater enough. The total service effort is not defined when the value of γ is 0. From now on, when writing $\phi(n)$, we will suppose that we will take into account the term $\phi(n)$ when it is well defined, otherwise, we will omit the term $\phi(n)$.

Negative signal arrives according to a Poisson process of rate $B\lambda^-$. The arrival of a negative signal finding n customers in the queue will choose a "target" in position l with probability $\phi(n)\gamma(l, n)/B$ (with probability $(B - \phi(n))/B$, the signal has no "target"). The "target" of class c is forced to reach state 0 (quit the queue) with successful probability $P^-(c)$.

Class changing signal arrives according to a Poisson process of rate $B\lambda^s$. The arrival of a changing signal finding n customers in the queue will choose a "target" in position l with probability $\phi(n)\gamma(l, n)/B$. The "target" of class c is forced to change to another class according to matrix H (change to next phase) with successful probability $P^s(c)$.

If the queue length is n, then the state of queue is: $\boldsymbol{x} = (x(1), x(2), \cdots, x(n))$, where $x(l)$ is the class of customer in position l.

Stationary distribution.

Lemma 1. *There exists a unique solution to the system of equations*

$$\rho^{(c)} = \frac{\lambda^{(c)} + \sum_{k \in C} \left(\mu^{(k)} + \lambda^s P^s(k)\right) H[k, c] \rho^{(k)}}{\mu^{(c)} + \lambda^- P^-(c) + \lambda^s P^s(c)}. \tag{1}$$

Theorem 1. *Assume that the queue is stable. If ρ is the unique solution of (1), then the stationary distribution will be given by:*

$$\pi(\boldsymbol{x}) = \pi(x(1), x(2), \cdots, x(n)) = C \frac{\rho^{(x(1))}}{\phi(1)} \frac{\rho^{(x(2))}}{\phi(2)} \cdots \frac{\rho^{(x(n))}}{\phi(n)}, \tag{2}$$

where C is the normalization constant.

In case where $\phi(n) > b (> 0)$, one has $\sum_x \pi(\boldsymbol{x}) < \infty \iff \sum_c \rho^{(c)} < 1$. Hence, the queue is stable iff $\sum_c \rho^{(c)} < 1$. This is the case for LIFO and PS queue.

Quasi-reversibility.

In [3], Chao, Miyazawa and Pinedo give a definition of quasi-reversibility in Chapter 3. This definition is so more convenient while connected to build a network. We have that the queue described above is quasi-reversible in sense of Chao, Miyazawa and Pinedo. Due to the length of this short version, we do not show the proof. You can find all the proof in the long version.

Consider 2 cases:

Case 1: Infinite buffer - ($\phi(n)$) is well defined for all n. ($\sum \gamma(l,n) = 1, \forall n$).

Corollary 1. *The queue with infinite buffer described above is quasi-reversible with respect to the set of classes $T = \mathcal{C} \cup \{-, s\}$.*

Case 2: Finite buffer - ($\phi(n)$) is well defined for $n \leq K$. ($\sum_l \gamma(l,n) = 0$ if $n > K$). In this case, we do not have the quasi-reversibility for each "class", but for the union of all classes in T.

Corollary 2. *The queue with finite buffer described above is quasi-reversible with respect to one class equal to the union of all classes in T.*

3   The network model

Description of the model.

In this section, we connect the queues in the previous section to have a network. Consider a network of N queues and $\mathcal{C}$ is the set of customers' classes, with a special class index 0 denote for the "absorbing state", and 2 types of signals: negative signal and changing signal. Note that we may have for each queue i a set of classes $\mathcal{C}_i$. However, to simplify, we consider one set $\mathcal{C}$ ($\mathcal{C} = \cup_i \mathcal{C}_i$).

Consider 2 types of queues: queue with infinite buffer and queue with finite buffer. In queue i, the total service effort is bounded by B_i. Without loss of generality, suppose that for all $i \leq N_1$, queue i is of type 1, infinite buffer. And for all $N_1 < i \leq N$, queue i is of type 2, finite buffer.

Queue i is a queue described in Section 2, with the new parameter: arrive rate $\lambda_i^{(c)}$, service rate $\mu_i^{(c)}$, matrix H_i, proportional function γ_i, negative signal's rate λ_i^- and successful probability $P_i^-(c)$, changing signal 's rate λ_i^s and successful probability $P_i^s(c)$.

If queue i is of type 1 (infinite buffer) then:

- A customer of class c reaching state 0 at the end of service leaves to queue j as a customer of class k with probability $P_{i,j}^{(c,k)}$, as a negative signal with probability $P_{i,j}^{(c)-}$, as a changing signal with probability $P_{i,j}^{(c)s}$, or quits the network with probability $d_i^{(c)}$, where: $\sum_{j,k}(P_{i,j}^{(c,k)} + P_{i,j}^{(c)-} + P_{i,j}^{(c)s}) + d_i^{(c)} = 1$.
- If the process of negative signal is successful, the "target" leaves to another queue j as a customer of class k with probability $P_{i,j}^{-(k)}$, as a negative signal with probability $P_{i,j}^{--}$, as a changing signal with probability $P_{i,j}^{-s}$, or quits the network with probability d_i^-, where: $\sum_{j,k}(P_{i,j}^{-(k)} + P_{i,j}^{--} + P_{i,j}^{-s}) + d_i^- = 1$.

– If the process of signal changing phase is successful in changing to phase 0, the "target" leaves to another queue j as a customer of class k with probability $P_{i,j}^{s(k)}$, as a negative signal with probability $P_{i,j}^{s-}$, as a changing signal with probability $P_{i,j}^{ss}$, or quits the network with probability d_i^s, where:
$\sum_{j,k}(P_{i,j}^{s(k)} + P_{i,j}^{s-} + P_{i,j}^{ss}) + d_i^s = 1$.

If the queue i is of type 2, the queue-length is bounded by K_i, then: A customer of class c reaching state 0 at the end of service; A "target" is successful eliminated by a negative signal; A "target" is successful changed phase to phase 0 by a signal changing phase; A customer of class a arriving and have no more place will leave queue i to queue j as a customer of class k with probability $P_{i,j}^{(k)}$, as a negative signal with probability $P_{i,j}^-$, as a changing signal with probability $P_{i,j}^s$, or quits the network with probability d_i, where: $\sum_{j,k}(P_{i,j}^{(k)} + P_{i,j}^- + P_{i,j}^{(s)}) + d_i = 1$.

The state of the network is represented by the vector: $\boldsymbol{x} = (\boldsymbol{x}_1, \boldsymbol{x}_2, \cdots, \boldsymbol{x}_N)$, where the component $\boldsymbol{x}_i$ denotes the state of queue i. If the queue length of queue i is n_i, then $\boldsymbol{x}_i = (x_i(1), x_i(2), \cdots, x_i(n_i))$, where $x_i(l)$ is the class of customer in position l.

Product form solution.
Consider the traffic equations:

$$\Delta_i^{(c)} = \lambda_i^{(c)} + \sum_{j \leq N_1, k} \mu_j^{(k)} \rho_j^{(k)} H_j[k, 0] P_{j,i}^{(k,c)} + \sum_{j \leq N_1, k} \Delta_j^- P_j^-(k) \rho_j^{(k)} P_{j,i}^{-(c)}/B_j$$
$$+ \sum_{j \leq N_1, k} \Delta_j^s P_j^s(k) \rho_j^{(k)} H_j[k, 0] P_{j,i}^{s(c)}/B_j + \sum_{j > N_1, k} \Delta_j^{(k)} P_{j,i}^{(c)}, \qquad (3)$$

$$\Delta_i^s = \lambda_i^s + \sum_{j \leq N_1, k} \mu_j^{(k)} \rho_j^{(k)} H_j[k, 0] P_{j,i}^{(k)s} + \sum_{j \leq N_1, k} \Delta_j^- P_j^-(k) \rho_j^{(k)} P_{j,i}^{-s}/B_j$$
$$+ \sum_{j \leq N_1, k} \Delta_j^s P_j^s(k) \rho_j^{(k)} H_j[k, 0] P_{j,i}^{ss}/B_j + \sum_{j > N_1, k} \Delta_j^{(k)} P_{j,i}^s, \qquad (4)$$

$$\Delta_i^- = \lambda_i^- + \sum_{j \leq N_1, k} \mu_j^{(k)} \rho_j^{(k)} H_j[k, 0] P_{j,i}^{(k)-} + \sum_{j \leq N_1, k} \Delta_j^- P_j^-(k) \rho_j^{(k)} P_{j,i}^{--}/B_j$$
$$+ \sum_{j \leq N_1, k} \Delta_j^s P_j^s(k) \rho_j^{(k)} H_j[k, 0] P_{j,i}^{s-}/B_j + \sum_{j > N_1, k} \Delta_j^{(k)} P_{j,i}^-, \qquad (5)$$

where

$$\rho_i^{(c)} = \frac{\Delta_i^{(c)} + \sum_k [\mu_i^{(k)} + \Delta_i^s P_i^s(k)/B_i] \rho_i^{(k)} H_i[k, c]}{\mu_i^{(c)} + \Delta_i^- P_i^-(c)/B_i + \Delta_i^s P_i^s(c)/B_i}.$$

We have the following theorem which is obtain by applying Theorem 4.9 of network of quasi-reversible queues in [3].

Theorem 2. *If the solution of the traffic equations satisfies $\sum_c \rho_i^{(c)} < 1$ for all $i \leq N_1$, then the network is stable and has a product form:*

$$\pi(\boldsymbol{x}) = C \prod_{i=1}^N \pi_i(\boldsymbol{x}_i), \qquad (6)$$

where C is a normalization constant and

$$\pi_i(\boldsymbol{x}_i) = \prod \frac{\rho_i^{(x_i(1))}}{\phi_i(1)} \frac{\rho_i^{(x_i(2))}}{\phi_i(2)} \cdots \frac{\rho_i^{(x_i(n_i))}}{\phi_i(n_i)}.$$

Conclusion

This paper considers a new type of signal and a new assumption on service distribution and we prove that the G-network still has product form steady-state distribution. We hope that this result will allow new approaches and new applications of G-networks.

Acknowledgment: This work was supported by ANR research project (SETIN Checkbound 2006).

References

1. F. Baskett, K. Chandy, R.R. Muntz, and F.G. Palacios, *Open, closed and mixed networks of queues with different classes of customers.* Journal ACM, Vol. 22, No 2, pp 248-260, 1975.
2. X. Chao, *Networks of Queues with customers, signals and arbitrary service.* Operation Research, V 43, 1995, N3, pp 537-544.
3. X. Chao, M. Miyazawa M. Pinedo, *Queueing Networks: Customers, Signals and Product Form Solutions.* J. Wiley, 1999.
4. J.M. Fourneau, *Computing the steady-state distribution of networks with positive and negative customers.* $13^t h$ IMACS World Congress on Computation and Applied Mathematics, Dublin, 1991.
5. J.M. Fourneau, E. Gelenbe, and R. Suros *G-networks with multiple classes of positive and negative customers.* Theoretical Computer Science, Vol. 155, pp 141-156, 1996.
6. E. Gelenbe, *Random neural Networks with Negative and Positive Signals and Product Form Solution.* Neural Computation, Vol. 1, No 4, pp 502-510, 1990.
7. E. Gelenbe, *Product form queueing networks with negative and positive customers.* Journal of Applied Probability, Vol. 28, pp 656-663, 1991.
8. E. Gelenbe, and R. Schassberger, *Stability of G-Networks.* Probability in the Engineering and Informational Sciences, Vol. 6, pp 271-276, 1992.
9. E. Gelenbe *G-networks with instantaneous customer movement.* Journal of Applied Probability, Vol. 30, No 3, pp 742-748, 1993.
10. E. Gelenbe *G-Networks with signals and batch removal.* Probability in the Engineering and Informational Sciences, Vol. 7, pp 335-342, 1993.
11. E. Gelenbe *G-networks: An unifying model for queueing networks and neural networks.* Annals of Operations Research, Vol. 48, No. 1-4, pp 433-461, 1994.
12. E. Gelenbe, R. Lent and Z. Xu, *Design and performance of cognitive packet networks.* Performance Evaluation, Vol. 46, No 2-3, pp 155-176, 2001.
13. E. Gelenbe and J.M. Fourneau, *G-networks with resets.* Performance Evaluation, Vol. 49, No 1/4, pp 179-191, 2002.
14. E. Gelenbe and R. Lent, *Power-aware ad hoc cognitive packet networks.* Ad Hoc Networks, Vol. 2,No 3, pp 205-216, 2004.
15. F. Kelly. *Reversibility and Stochastic Networks.* Wiley, New-York, 1979.
16. M.A. Tran and T. Bonald, *On Kelly Networks with Shuffling.* Queueing Systems , Vol. 59, pp 53-61, 2008.

Stochastic comparisons applied to G-Networks with catastrophes *

H. Castel-Taleb[1], J-M. Fourneau[2], and N. Pekergin[3]

[1] INSTITUT TELECOM, TELECOM SudParis
9,rue Charles Fourier, 91011 Evry Cedex, France
[2] PRiSM, Université de Versailles-Saint-Quentin
CNRS, UniverSud, Versailles, France
[3] LACL, Université Paris-Est, Val de Marne
61, av. du Général de Gaulle, 94010 Créteil Cedex, France

Abstract. We study the transient distribution of some G-networks of queues with customers and signals. After its service completion a customer moves to another queue and may become a signal. We consider catastrophes where the signal deletes all customers in a queue. Both networks with negative customers and with catastrophes belong to well-known Gelenbe's networks with product form steady-state distribution. As the transient distribution is impossible to obtain, we derive stochastic upper and lower bounds on the marginal distribution for each queue following Massey's approach.

1 Introduction

Since the seminal papers by Gelenbe in the early nineties [2–4], Generalized networks of queues with customers and signals have received considerable attention. G-network models overcome some of the limitations of conventional queueing network models with the addition of signals between queues. They still preserve the computationally attractive product form property of some Markovian queueing networks. The first type of signal introduced by Gelenbe was described as a negative customer [2]. A negative customer deletes a positive customer in a queue at its arrival if it is possible. Positive customers are usual customers in classical queueing networks. A negative customer is never queued. Under typical assumptions Gelenbe proved that such a network has a product form solution for its steady-state behavior. G-networks have been generalized to deal with signals such as negative customers, resets [5] catastrophes which flush all the customers out of a queue and triggers which move other customers from one queue to another [3, 4]. Like with Jackson queueing networks, it is quite impossible to derive a closed form expression of the transient distribution. Massey has introduced in [8] some stochastic bounds for the transient distribution of the size of any queue in a Jackson network. We use here the same arguments to derive stochastic upper and lower bounds for G-networks with catastrophes that we now describe. We

---

* partially supported by French research project ANR-SETI06-02

consider an open networks of n queues with infinite capacity. We assume that the arrivals of new customers (resp. signals) follow independent Poisson Processes with rate λ_i (resp. λ_i^-) at queue i. Customers wait in the queue and eventually receive service if they are not deleted by a signal. The service times are exponential with rate μ_i at queue i. Signals are not queued. When they enter a queue, they flush all the customers out the queue. At the completion of its service at queue i, a customer moves to queue j either as a customer or as signal depending of a Markovian routing described by matrices P^+ and P^-. Finally, d_i is the probability that a customer leaves the system at the completion of its service in queue i. As usual with G-networks we assume that there is no self-loops in the routing matrices: i.e. for all i, $P^+(i,i) = 0$ and $P^-(i,i) = 0$. Finally the total probability law gives that for all queue i: $\sum_{j=1}^n P^+(i,j)+\sum_{j=1}^n P^-(i,j)+d_i = 1$. Under these assumptions, it is proved in [4] that the G-networks have a product form steady-state distribution. The model in [4] is more general as it is based on destruction of batches of customer by signals. Note that the networks of PS queues with catastrophes and several classes of customers is proved in [1] to also have a product form steady-state distribution. We give here a simple version of the theorem for G-networks with catastrophes for the sake of completeness.

Theorem 1 *Consider an open network of n G-queues with signals flushing out the queue. Assume that there exists a solution to the system:*

$$\rho_i = \frac{\lambda_i + \sum_{j=1}^n P^+(j,i)\rho_j\mu_j}{\mu_i + (\lambda_i^- + \sum_j P^-(j,i)\rho_j\mu_j)\frac{1}{1-\rho_i}},$$

such that $\rho_i < 1$, then the network has a product form steady-state distribution.

Stochastic comparisons are more complex on multidimensional state spaces than on totally ordered state spaces. Several stochastic orderings can be defined, corresponding to different comparison relations of the distributions [10, 7]. Different methods can be also used to compare processes: increasing sets, and the coupling theory. Increasing sets method is a general formalism, allowing the definition of the strong stochastic ordering ($\preceq_{st}$), and also weak ordering ($\preceq_{wk}$), and weak* ordering ($\preceq_{wk^*}$). The strong ordering yields to comparisons of increasing functionals (the expectations of all increasing functions of the probability distributions) while the weak ordering is equivalent to tail probability distribution comparisons, and weak* leads to compare cumulative distributions. In this paper, we focus on the increasing set formalism in order to define the weak ordering. We propose upper and lower bounding systems in order to evaluate the transient probability distribution.

2   Stochastic comparisons for transient behavior

Massey [8] has proposed a family of bounds to study transient behaviors of Jackson networks. The upper bounding process is composed of independent $M/M/1$ queues, obtained by removing the links between queues. In [9], we use similar ideas in order to propose bounding systems for G-Networks with negative customers. In the present paper, we propose bounding systems for G-Networks with catastrophes. Note that these systems are defined on the state space $E = \mathbb{N}^n$, and we use the component-wise partial ordering denoted by $\preceq$ on this state space: $\forall x, y \in \mathbb{N}^n$, $x \preceq y \Leftrightarrow x_i \leq y_i, \forall i = 1, \ldots, n$.

Upper bound: it is represented by n independent queues, and in each queue i three kind of events happen: 1- increasing by one due to a positive customer arrival, called *up*, 2- decreasing by one due to a service completion, called *down*, 3- flushing a queue due to a signal, called *flush*. Each queue i has the following rates:

$$up : \lambda_i^+ + \sum_{j \neq i} P^+(j, i)\mu_j, \quad down : \mu_i, \quad flush : \lambda_i^-.$$

We denote by by $\{X^u(t),\ t \geq 0\}$ this system, with infinitesimal generator Q^u. We have the following proposition:

Proposition 1 $\{X(t), t \geq 0\} \preceq_{wk} \{X^u(t), t \geq 0\}$.

We apply Theorem 3.4 in [7] for the proof. It is easy to verify that $\{X^u(t),\ t \geq 0\}$ is $\preceq_{st}$-monotone using the coupling of the process with itself [6]: for every pair of states $x \preceq y$, and all kinds of transitions occurring in the system, the order between states is preserved. For the comparison of the generators, we define the increasing sets from events occurring in $\{X(t), t \geq 0\}$. In [7], the $\preceq_{wk}$ ordering is defined from the family of increasing sets $\Phi_{wk}(E) = \{\{x\} \uparrow, x \in E\}$, where $\{x\} \uparrow = \{y \in E, y \succeq x\}$. As the transitions are triggered from events, then we define the family $S_{wk}(E) \subset \Phi_{wk}(E)$ using events happening from state x. Let e_i be a vector from N^n such that all components are null except component i which equals to 1. Consider the arrival event in the queue i: from state x, we can have a transition to the state $x + e_i$, so we define the increasing set $\{x + e_i\} \uparrow = \{x + e_i, \ldots\}$. Thus we obtain:

$$S_{wk}(E) = \{\{x+e_i\} \uparrow, \{x-e_i+e_j\} \uparrow, \{x\} \uparrow, \{x-e_i\} \uparrow, \{x-e_j-x_ie_j\} \uparrow, \{x-x_ie_i\} \uparrow\}.$$

In Table 1, we give the transition rates for each increasing set of $S_{wk}(E)$ in order to compare the original system with the upper and lower bounding processes. From the third and the fourth column of Table 1, we can see that: $\forall x \in E, \forall \Gamma \in S_{wk}(E), \sum_{z \in \Gamma} Q(x, z) \leq \sum_{z \in \Gamma} Q^u(x, z)$. Hence it follows from Theorem 3.4 in [7] that proposition 1 is verified, and we derive the following inequality among the tail probability distributions:

$$Prob(X_1(t) \geq m_1, ..., X_n(t) \geq m_n) \leq \prod_{i=1}^{n} Prob(X_i^u(t) \geq m_i).$$

Lower bound: it is given by n queues and each queue i has the following transition rates:

$$up : \lambda_i^+, down : \mu_i, flush : \sum_{j \neq i} P^-(j, i)\mu_j + \lambda_i^-.$$

We denote by $X^l(t)$ the lower bound with infinitesimal generator Q^l. Similar to the upper bounding case we prove that $\{X^l(t), t \geq 0\} \preceq_{wk} \{X(t), t \geq 0\}$. We

Γ	$\sum_{z\in\Gamma} Q^l(x,z)$	$\sum_{z\in\Gamma} Q(x,z)$	$\sum_{z\in\Gamma} Q^u(x,z)$
$\{x+e_i\}\uparrow$	λ_i^+	λ_i^+	$\lambda_i^+ + \sum_{j\neq i}\mu_j P^+(j,i)$
$\{x-e_i+e_j\}\uparrow$	λ_j^+	$\lambda_j^+ + \mu_i P^+(i,j)$	$\lambda_j^+ + \sum_{i\neq j}\mu_i P^+(i,j)$
$\{x\}\uparrow$	$-\sum_{k=1}^n(\mu_k+\lambda_k^-)1_{x_k>0}$ $-\sum_{k=1}^n(\sum_{l\neq k}\mu_l P^-(l,k))1_{x_k>0}$	$-\sum_{k=1}^n(\mu_k+\lambda_k^-)1_{x_k>0}$	$-\sum_{k=1}^n(\mu_k+\lambda_k^-)1_{x_k>0}$
$\{x-e_i\}\uparrow$	$-\sum_{k\neq i}(\mu_k+\lambda_k^-)1_{x_k>0}$ $-\sum_{k\neq i}(\sum_{l\neq k}\mu_l P^-(l,k))1_{x_k>0}$ $-\sum_{k\neq i}\mu_k P^-(k,i)-\lambda_i^-$	$-\sum_{k\neq i}(\mu_k+\lambda_k^-)1_{x_k>0}$ $-\sum_{k\neq i}\mu_i P^-(i,k)1_{x_k>0}$ $-\lambda_i^-$	$-\sum_{k\neq i}(\mu_k+\lambda_k^-)1_{x_k>0}$ $-\lambda_i^-$
$\{x-e_j-x_ie_i\}\uparrow$	$-\sum_{k\neq i,j}(\mu_k+\lambda_k^-)1_{x_k>0}$ $-\sum_{k\neq j,i}\sum_{l\neq k}\mu_l P^-(l,k)1_{x_k>0}$ $-\sum_{l\neq j}\mu_l P^-(l,j)$ $-\lambda_j^-$	$-\sum_{k\neq i,j}(\mu_k+\lambda_k^-)1_{x_k>0}$ $-\sum_{k\neq i}\mu_i P^-(i,k)1_{x_k>0}$ $-\sum_{k\neq i,j}\mu_j P^-(j,k)1_{x_k>0}$ $-\lambda_j^-$	$-\sum_{k\neq i,j}(\mu_k+\lambda_k^-)1_{x_k>0}$ $-\lambda_j^-$
$\{x-x_ie_i\}\uparrow$	$-\sum_{k\neq i}(\mu_k+\lambda_k^-)1_{x_k>0}$ $-\sum_{k\neq i}(\sum_{l\neq k}\mu_l P^-(l,k))1_{x_k>0}$	$-\sum_{k\neq i}(\mu_k+\lambda_k^-)1_{x_k>0}$ $-\sum_{k\neq i}\mu_i P^-(i,k)$	$-\sum_{k\neq i}(\mu_k+\lambda_k^-)1_{x_k>0}$

Table 1. Comparison of Q^l, Q and Q^u, $\forall\Gamma\in S_{wk}(E)$.

deduce from the second and the third column of Table 1 that: $\forall x\in E$, $\forall\Gamma\in S_{wk}(E)$, $\sum_{z\in\Gamma} Q(x,z)\geq\sum_{z\in\Gamma} Q^l(x,z)$. From the $\preceq_{wk}$-comparison of the processes, we derive the following inequality for the tail probability distributions:

$$Prob(X_1(t)\geq m_1,...,X_n(t)\geq m_n)\geq\prod_{i=1}^n \Pr ob(X_i^l(t)\geq m_i).$$

References

1. J.-M. Fourneau and L. Kloul and F. Quessette, "Multiple Class G-Networks with Jumps back to Zero", IEEE MASCOTS 95, USA,1995.
2. E. Gelenbe, "Product form queueing networks with negative and positive customers", Journal of Applied Probability, Vol. 28, pp 656-663, 1991.
3. E. Gelenbe, "G-networks with instantaneous customer movement", Journal of Applied Probability, Vol. 30, No 3, pp 742-748, 1993.
4. E. Gelenbe, "G-Networks with signals and batch removal", Probability in the Engineering and Informational Sciences, Vol. 7, pp 335-342, 1993.
5. E. Gelenbe and J.M. Fourneau, "G-networks with resets" Performance Evaluation, Vol. 49, No 1/4, pp 179-191, 2002.
6. T. Lindvall, "Stochastic monotonicities in Jackson queueing networks", Prob. in the Engineering and Informational Sciences 11, 1-9, 1997.
7. W. A. Massey, "Stochastic orderings for Markov processes on partially ordered spaces", Mathematics of Operations Research, V12, N2, pp 350–367, 1987.
8. W. A. Massey, "A family of bounds for the transient behavior of a Jackson Network", Journal of App. Prob., V23, pp 543-549, 1986.
9. N.Pekergin, H. Taleb-Castel, "Stochastic bounds on the transient behaviors of the G-Network", Studia Informatica, Vol 23, 2002
10. A.Muller, D. Stoyan, "Comparison methods for Stochastic Models and Risks", J. Wiley and son in Probability and Statistics, 2002.

Measures for Evaluating the Software Agent Pro-Activity

Fernando Alonso[1], José L. Fuertes[1], Loïc Martínez[1], and Héctor Soza[2]

[1] Facultad de Informática
Universidad Politécnica de Madrid, Madrid – Spain
{falonso, jfuertes, loic}@fi.upm.es

[2] Escuela de Ingeniería
Universidad Católica del Norte, Coquimbo – Chile
hsoza@ucn.cl

Abstract. This paper is part of research aimed at determining and evaluating software agent quality considering an agent's distinctive characteristics, like social ability, autonomy, pro-activity, etc. We present a study of the pro-activity characteristic, regarded as the software agent's goal-driven behavioral ability to take the initiative and satisfy its design goals. We establish attributes associated with this characteristic and set out measures enabling its global evaluation.

Keywords: Agents quality, pro-activity, software quality.

1 Introduction

Few studies in the literature focus on the development of measures to evaluate the software agent. Those that do exist are generally measures borrowed from the procedural and object-oriented paradigms, and there are few measures created ex professo to evaluate particular characteristics of software agents [1], [2], [3].

Agent pro-activity is one of the more relevant characteristics and defines an agent's ability to exhibit goal-directed behavior by taking the initiative to achieve its goals [4]. It also refers to an agent's ability to take the initiative rather than acting simply in response to its dynamic and unpredictable environment [3] or agents being able to act in anticipation of future goals by taking the initiative [5].

Several studies have analyzed software agent pro-activity, but they are not very related to measures for evaluating this feature. For example, Cernuzzi and Rossi [5] evaluated pro-activity by assigning a value of between 0 and 1 depending on whether or not the agent dynamically assumes the different goals and whether it is possible to model goals. Shin [3] proposed the frequency of knowledge discovery as a measure, the result of calculating the number of messages that the agent uses to discover knowledge, to evaluate agent pro-activity in updating its internal states. None of the above studies provides specific quality measures for evaluating the pro-activity characteristic of agent software. This research aims to advance in the measurement of this feature.

2 Measures for Pro-activity Attributes

From the existing research [4], [6] and based on our experience [7], [8], we propose the following attributes to identify agent pro-activity: **initiative** (an agent's ability to satisfy its design goals through a goal-directed behavior [4], and to take an action with the aim of achieving its goal [9], [10]), **interaction** (an agent's ability to interact with other agents and its environment [9]) and **reaction** (an agent's ability to react to a stimulus from the underlying environment according to stimulus/response behavior, depending on the current state of the software agent [11]).

Each measure is stated by means of a formula that expresses this measure as a function of one or more parameters. The results of each measure are normalized in the interval [0, 1] (where 0 is a poor result and 1 is a good result for the measure).

Figure 1 shows the types of formula used to normalize the pro-activity measures.

$$\text{(a)} \begin{cases} 1 & 0 \le x \le k \\ e^{-\frac{(x-k)^2}{k^2}} & x > k \end{cases} \qquad \text{(b)} \begin{cases} \frac{2x}{k} - (\frac{x}{k})^2 & 0 \le x \le k \\ 1 & x > k \end{cases} \qquad \text{(c)} \left\{ 1 - \frac{1}{x} \quad x \ge 1 \right. \qquad \begin{array}{l} \text{(d)} \log_{k+1}(x+1) \\ 0 \le x \le k \end{array}$$

Fig. 1. Formula types used to normalize the measures

The constant k is a parameter that the software engineer can configure to fine tune formula performance for each particular case. The formulae depend on the argument x, where x is a value defined for each measure. Next, we present the proposed measures for evaluating the attributes defined for the characteristic of pro-activity.

The **initiative** attribute can be measured using the following measures:

- *Number of roles* measures the number of potential roles that agents are to perform. Agent roles are defined in the system design phase [3]. This measure uses curve (a) in Fig. 1, where x is the number of agent roles.
- *Number of goals* measures the number of goals achieved by the agent during execution with respect to the number of allocated goals. This measure uses curve (d) in Fig. 1, where x is the number of goals achieved by the agent during execution and k is the number of goals to be achieved by the agent.
- *Messages to achieve goals* measures agent initiative to achieve its goals by communicating with other system agents. This measure uses curve (b) in Fig. 1, where x is the average percentage of executive messages that are sent during agent execution for the goals to be accomplished.

The **interaction** attribute can be measured using the following measures:

- *Services per agent* measures the impact on agent interaction of the number of the services implemented within the agent (not including internal services) enabling it to achieve its goals [3]. This measure uses curve (c) in Fig. 1, where x is the number of services implemented within the agent.
- *Number of message types* measures the impact on agent interaction of the number of different types of messages that the agent can process. This measure uses curve (b) in Fig. 1, where x is the total of unique incoming and outgoing message types. We comply with FIPA standards for the agent message type [12].

The **reaction** attribute can be measured using the following measures:

- *Number of processed requests* measures the agent's ability to react to the number of received and resolved requests during execution. This measure uses the curve

(a) in Fig. 1, where x is the number of received requests (requiring an action to be taken in response) during execution.

- *Agent operations complexity* measures the mean complexity of the operations to be performed by the agent to achieve its goals. The software engineer could use any complexity measure regarded as suitable for achieving a good result (for example, cyclomatic complexity [13]). This measure uses the curve (a) of Fig. 1, where x is the mean complexity per goal.

3   Case Study

As an application of this research we have conducted a pro-activity study on the agents of an intelligent agent marketplace. This marketplace includes several kinds of Buyer and Seller agents that cooperate and compete to process sales transactions for their owners. In this system, a Facilitator agent acts as a manager for the marketplace [14]. The names "basic", "better" and "best" refer to the global evaluation of the software agent strategy to perform its tasks, not to their pro-activeness.

Table 1. Pro-activity attribute values

	Basic Buyer	Better Buyer	Best Buyer	Basic Seller	Better Seller	Best Seller	System
Initiative	0.81	0.88	0.78	0.81	0.79	0.85	0.82
Interaction	0.88	0.92	0.95	0.92	0.88	0.86	0.90
Reaction	0.93	0.97	1.00	1.00	1.00	1.00	0.98
Pro-Activity	0.88	0.93	0.91	0.91	0.90	0.91	**0.90**

Table 1 shows the values of the measure for each attribute calculated from the associated measures. The last row of Table 1 contains the value of the pro-activity characteristic calculated from the measures for all the attributes. Finally, the last column shows the value of the system measures calculated from the values of the attribute measures for all the agents. The bottom, right-hand cell contains the pro-activity value for the entire system. In this study, the above values are aggregated in each case using the arithmetic mean. The results could be refined using a weighted mean, with weights provided by experts using any existing weighting technique.

We find that Basic Buyer agents are less pro-active (88%) than the Best Buyer (91%) and even less than the Better Buyer (93%) agents, because they have different buying strategies. Also, their ability to react is greater than their ability to interact and their initiative. All Seller agents have almost the same pro-activity value because their strategies for achieving their goals are indistinguishable, although, like the Buyer agents, the evaluated measures indicate that their ability to react is greater than their ability to interact and their initiative.

From the above, we conclude, with respect to the attributes, that the system scores highest on Reaction (98%), followed by Interaction (90%), and Initiative (83%). Initiative is influenced by the fact that the agents do not achieve all their goals through cooperation due to the rules that they each apply to achieve their objectives.

Finally, the system's pro-activity value is 90%, that is, the pro-activity of the system agents as a whole is quite high.

4 Conclusions and Future Work

We have presented a first approximation to a set of measures of agent-oriented software considering the pro-activity characteristic, which has been decomposed into different attributes, and we show the measures considered for its evaluation.

In the future we intend to conduct a comprehensive study of an agent-based system, analyzing the measures of each characteristic of each agent type existing in the system and their contribution to the measure of system quality. To do this, we propose to build a quality evaluation model, and evaluate this model on several software agent applications, considering the different characteristics, and their attributes, present in agents.

References

1. Dumke, R., Koeppe, R., Wille, C.: Software Agent Measurement and Self-Measuring Agent-Based Systems, Preprint No 11. Fakultät für Informatik, Otto-von-Guericke-Universität, Magdeburg (2000)
2. Far, B., Wanyama, T.: Metrics for Agent-Based Software Development. In: Canadian Conf. on Electrical and Computer Engineering, pp. 1297–1300. Montréal, Canada (2003)
3. Shin, K.: Software Agents Metrics. A Preliminary Study & Development of a Metric Analyzer, Project Report No. H98010. Dept. Computer Science, School of Computing, National University of Singapore (2003/2004)
4. Wooldridge, M.: An Introduction to Multiagent Systems. John Wiley, Chichester (2002)
5. Cernuzzi, L., Rossi, G.: On the Evaluation of Agent Oriented Methodologies. In: OOPSLA 02-Workshop on Agent-Oriented Methodologies, pp. 21–30. Seattle (2002)
6. Covey, S.: The Seven Habits of Highly Effective People, 15th anniversary edition. Free Press, Old Tappan, NJ (2004)
7. Alonso, F., Fuertes, J. L., Martínez, L., Soza, H.: Measuring the Social Ability of Software Agents. In: Sixth International Conference on Software Engineering Research, Management and Applications, SERA 2008, pp. 3–10. Prague, Czech Republic, (2008)
8. Alonso, F., Fuertes, J. L., Martínez, L., Soza H.: Towards a Set of Measures for Evaluating Software Agent Autonomy. In: Seventh Joint Meeting of the European Software Engineering Conference and ACM SIGSOFT Symposium on the Foundations of Software Engineering, ESEC/FSE 2009, Amsterdam, Netherlands (2009)
9. Covey, S.: The Seven Habits of Highly Effective People, 15th anniversary edition. Free Press, Old Tappan, NJ (2004)
10. Rousseau, D., Moulin, B.: Mixed initiative in interactions between software agents. In: 1997 Spring Symposium on Computer Models for Mixed Initiative Interaction. AAAI Press, Menlo Park (1997)
11. Orro, A., Saba, M., Vargiu, E.: Using a Personalized, Adaptive and Cooperative Multi Agent System to Predict Protein Secondary Structure. In: First International Workshop on Multi-Agent Systems for Medicine, Computational Biology, and Bioinformatics, BIOMED'05, pp. 170-183, Utrecht, The Netherlands (2005)
12. Foundation for Intelligent Physical Agents: FIPA Communicative Act Library Specification. Geneva, Switzerland (2002)
13. McCabe, T. J.: A Complexity Measure. IEEE T. Software Eng. SE-2, 308–320 (1976)
14. Bigus, J., Bigus, J.: Constructing Intelligent Agents Using Java, 2nd edition. John Wiley & Sons, Inc., New York, NY (2001)

On product-form approximations of cooperating stochastic models

Andrea Marin[1] and Maria Grazia Vigliotti[2]

[1] Università Ca' Foscari di Venezia Dipartimento di Informatica
[2] Imperial College London, Department of Computing

Abstract. The main focus of this paper is to enlarge the applicability of product-form solutions by regarding models that yield this property as approximations of models that do not. To achieve this, we make use of Reversed Compound Agent Theorem (RCAT)[2, 3] and devise a useful and practical method to modify non-product form models into product-form ones. Our technique provides meaningful approximations of the original models.

1 Introduction

Stochastic models provide a very useful way to describe and derive interesting performance indices of complex systems. In particular, Markovian models have been widely applied for the quantitative analysis of software and hardware computer architectures. The main problem of this approach is that when a model is described in terms of interactions of a set of sub-models, its state space tends to be very large mainly because each state of each sub-model may be observed in combination with all the possible configurations of the states of the other sub-models. In these cases, numerical techniques for the solution of the underlying Markov process may result computationally unfeasible. Product-form solutions for steady-state distributions are useful for different purposes. Computationally, they provide a more efficient way of calculating the steady-state probabilities because each sub-model is opportunely parametrised and then studied in isolation. The joint stationary distribution is then derived as normalised product of the stationary distributions of the parametrised sub-models. Results on product-form solutions may result hard to apply in practice since only a very limited subset of models enjoys this property. In this paper we focus on making product-form solutions more applicable to the practice by regarding models that have product-form solutions as approximations of models that do not. To clarify this point we consider a network that comprises of a tandem of exponential queues with constant service rate. It is well-known that, if the external arrival rate depends on the state of the first queue, then the network has no product-form solution. One simple and effective way to obtain a product-form solution by approximation, is to change the external arrival rate to make it constant. The main disadvantage is this approach is that it will have an impact on the performance measures of the whole network. The question arises whether we can modify some parameters in the second queue to obtain a product-form solution that will leave the performance measures of the first queue unchanged. To achieve this, we resort to RCAT[2, 3], which provides specific structural conditions on queues in the network to guarantee product-form solution. Although this work gives a general technique to approximate a non-product-form model composition by a product-form one, we shall take a very practical approach to compare the correct values with the approximated ones, as shown the example in Section 2. The technique adopted in this paper to achieve approximations for non product-form solutions in Markovian models is novel. Similar work has been carried out by van Dijk [5]. using the *local balance* property [1]. However, local balance is a principle applicable to queuing networks only, while our method could be applied to a wider class of Markovian model cooperations.

2   Approximations by mean of product-form models

In this section we illustrate an algorithmic technique to approximate a non-product-form model by means of a product-form one. The proposal is based on RCAT result in the formulation given in [3]. RCAT provides sufficient conditions to guarantee product-form solutions in CTMCs. In this paper we shall use the terminology given in [3] which will be not reported here due to lack of space. In what follows we presents two ways to modify a given model to satisfy RCAT conditions, i.e., every passive action is enabled in every state of a given automaton for all actions in the cooperating set and the sum of the reversed rates of the incoming actions in the cooperating set are constant in every state of a given automaton. Given two CTMCs that cooperate, RCAT is not satisfied due at least to one of the following reasons: 1) **Missing passive transitions**, i.e., for a synchronising passive label a there exists a subset of states in which there is not an outgoing passive transition;2) **Different incoming flow into states**, i.e, the incoming flow to the states due to a synchronising active label a is not constant, i.e., Equations (1) or (2) in in Theorem 1 in [3] cannot be satisfied.

Dealing with missing passive transitions. Consider two LMA $\mathbf{M}_1$ and $\mathbf{M}_2$ synchronising on label a, with $a \in \mathcal{A}_1 \cap \mathcal{P}_2$ i.e. a is active in $\mathbf{M}_1$ and passive in $\mathbf{M}_2$. Let $\mathcal{S}_2$ be the state space of $\mathbf{M}_2$ and let $\mathcal{S}_2^{\neg a} = \{s \in \mathcal{S}_2 | \forall s' \in \mathcal{S}_2, s \xrightarrow{a} s' \notin \mathcal{T}_2\}$, i.e., the set of all the states without an outgoing transition labelled by a. $\mathbf{M}_2$ has the property that for all $s \in \mathcal{S}_2^{\neg a}$ there is a new transition (self-loop) from s to itself labelled by a. Moreover, $\tilde{\mathbf{M}}_1$ is modified by replacing all the rates of the transitions $s \xrightarrow{a} s'$ with $\tilde{q}_1(s \xrightarrow{a} s')$ which is defined as follows:

$$\tilde{q}_1(s \xrightarrow{a} s') = \left(1 - \sum_{s_2 \in \mathcal{S}_2^{\neg a}} \tilde{\pi}_2(s_2)\right) q_1(s \xrightarrow{a} s'). \tag{1}$$

In the original model $\mathbf{M}_1 \oplus_{\{a\}} \mathbf{M}_2$ there are some states that cannot be reached since $\mathbf{M}_1$ cannot carry on a transition labelled by a because a is not (passively) enabled in $\mathbf{M}_2$. Since we add a passive self loops in the modified version $\tilde{\mathbf{M}}_1 \oplus_{\{a\}} \tilde{\mathbf{M}}_2$ all active transition labelled a can be carried on. As a consequence of introduction of self loops, the synchronising transitions labelled by a are observed more often with the respect to the original model. We balance this in $\mathbf{M}_1$ with Equation (1). Note that, if the self-loops are added to states with low equilibrium probabilities, then we have $\tilde{q}_1(s \xrightarrow{a} s') \simeq q_1(s \xrightarrow{a} s')$.

Dealing with different incoming flow into states. Consider two LMA $\mathbf{M}_1$ and $\mathbf{M}_2$ synchronising only on label a, with $a \in \mathcal{A}_1 \cap \mathcal{P}_2$. Let $\mathcal{S}_1$ be the state space of $\mathbf{M}_1$, then we define for all $s \in \mathcal{S}_1$:

$$K_a(s) = \sum_{s' \in \mathcal{S}_1} \frac{\pi_1(s')}{\pi_1(s)} q_1(s' \xrightarrow{a} s). \tag{2}$$

If $K_a(s)$ is independent of $s \in \mathcal{S}_1$, then RCAT condition would be satisfied. We define:

$$\tilde{K}_a = \sum_{s \in \mathcal{S}_1} K_a(s)\pi_1(s) = \sum_{s \in \mathcal{S}_1} \sum_{s' \in \mathcal{S}_1} \pi_1(s')q_1(s' \xrightarrow{a} s). \tag{3}$$

We can see $\tilde{K}_a$ as the weighted average flux incoming to the states of $\mathbf{M}_1$ due to transitions labelled by a. We aim to obtain $\tilde{\mathbf{M}}_1$ in a way such that $\tilde{\pi}_1 = \pi_1$ but the sum of the reversed rates incoming to every state due to an active transition labelled by a is $\tilde{K}_a$. Let us define the following sets:

- $\mathcal{S}_1^{a,<\tilde{K}_a} = \{s \in \mathcal{S}_1 \mid K_a(s) < \tilde{K}_a\}$, i.e., the set of states of $\mathbf{M}_1$ whose incoming flux due to active transitions labelled by a is lower than the average;
- $\mathcal{S}_1^{a,>\tilde{K}_a} = \{s \in \mathcal{S}_1 \mid K_a(s) > \tilde{K}_a\}$, i.e., the set of states of $\mathbf{M}_1$ whose incoming flux due to active transitions labelled by a is higher that the average;
- $\mathcal{S}_1^{a,=\tilde{K}_a} = \{s \in \mathcal{S}_1 \mid K_a(s) = \tilde{K}_a\}$, i.e., the set of states of $\mathbf{M}_1$ whose incoming flux due to active transitions labelled by a is exactly $\tilde{K}_a$.

$\tilde{\mathbf{M}}_1$ is obtained from $\mathbf{M}_1$ as follows. For all $s \in \mathcal{S}_1^{a,<\tilde{K}_a}$ a self-loop labelled by a is added with rate:

$$\tilde{q}(s \xrightarrow{a} s) = \tilde{K}_a - K_a(s)$$

For all $s \in \mathcal{S}_1^{a,>\tilde{K}_a}$, rate $q(s' \xrightarrow{a} s)$ is replaced by:

$$\tilde{q}(s' \xrightarrow{a} s) = \underbrace{\frac{\tilde{K}_a}{K_a(s)}}_{\text{prop. tot. rate}} \underbrace{\frac{\pi_1(s')}{\pi_1(s)} q(s' \xrightarrow{a} s)}_{\text{rev. rate}}$$

and a new non-synchronising transition $s' \to s$ is added whose rate is:

$$\tilde{q}(s' \to s) = q(s' \xrightarrow{a} s) - \tilde{q}(s' \xrightarrow{a} s).$$

Finally, transitions in $\mathcal{S}_1^{a,=\tilde{K}_a}$ are not modified. Note that the underlying chain of $\tilde{\mathbf{M}}_1$ is identical to that of $\mathbf{M}_1$. However, the key-idea of the previous modifications is to make constant the sum of the reversed rates incoming into each state of $\tilde{\mathbf{M}}_1$ in order to satisfy the conditions (1),(2) in theorem (1) in [3]. Informally, this is achieved by augmenting the sum by self-loops when the states have an incoming flow which is lower than the expected. Conversely, when the sum of the reversed rates of the incoming transitions is higher than $\hat{K}_a$, the desired value is achieved by splitting the transitions into a synchronising one and a non-synchronising one. The rates are opportunely assigned so that the sum of the forward rates remain unchanged.

3   Network with multiple servers

In this section we illustrate an application of the proposed technique to a service station with multi servers. The key-idea is that after a job completion a server spends some time in an idle status before being ready for use again.

Model description. The queueing station consists of N identical servers that can be in one of the following two states: *idle* or *operating*. The former state denotes that the server is not available, while the latter that it can be used to serve a customer. Servers pass from the *idle* state to the *operating* after an exponentially distributed random time with rate μ_2. Customers arrive to the station according to a Poisson process with rate λ. If any of the servers is in the *operating* state, a customer is served in an exponential distributed random time with rate μ_1. After a service completion, the served customer departs and the server enters in the *idle* state. At a given time, at most one customer is being served and at most one server is being recharged (hence there may be spare servers or servers waiting for passing from the *idle* to the *operating* state). For those who are familiar with Petri net formalism, Figure 1-(A) depicts the model, where the rate of T_0, T_1 and T_2 are λ, μ_1 and μ_2, respectively. Tokens in P_1 represent the *operating* servers and those in P_2 the *idle* ones.

Model analysis. Figure 1-(B) defines a model whose underlying process is identical to that of the corresponding Petri net using two interacting stochastic automata (non-synchronising labels are omitted). The state of Process 1 represents the number of *operating* servers (the number of *idle* ones can be obtained by difference knowing N), while the state of Process 2 represents the number of customers in the station. Note that RCAT conditions are not satisfied since state 0 of Process 1 has not an outgoing passive transition. In order to obtain the product-form approximation we add a self-loop labelled by a in state 0 of Process 1 and, consequently, we adapt the rate of the corresponding active transitions in Process 2 to be $\tilde{\mu}_1$, which is defined as follows:

$$\tilde{\mu}_1 = (1 - \pi_1(0))\mu_1, \quad \text{with } \pi_1(0) = \frac{1 - (\mu_2/x_a)}{1 - (\mu_2/x_a)^{N+1}}.$$

The analysis of Process 2 gives $x_a = \lambda$ straightforwardly. Then the approximate solutions can be written as:

$$\tilde{\pi}(i,j) = \tilde{\pi}_1(i)\tilde{\pi}_2(j) = \frac{1 - (\mu_2/\lambda)}{1 - (\mu_2/\lambda)^{N+1}} \left(\frac{\mu_2}{\lambda}\right)^i (1 - \lambda/\tilde{\mu}_1) \left(\frac{\lambda}{\tilde{\mu}_1}\right)^j,$$

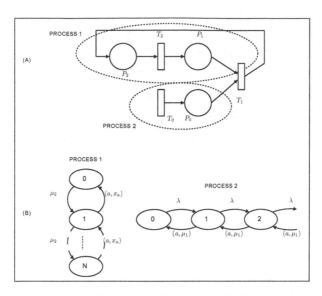

Fig. 1. Petri net of the model studied in Section 3 (A). Process decomposition (B).

with $0 \le i \le N$ and $j \ge 0$. It is worthwhile pointing out that the reversed rates of the transitions that take the model from state (i, j) to state $(i - 1, j - 1)$ are equal, in fact:

$$\frac{\tilde{\pi}(i,j)}{\tilde{\pi}(i-1,j-1)}\tilde{\mu}_1 = \frac{\mu_2}{\lambda}\frac{\lambda}{\tilde{\mu}_1}\tilde{\mu}_1 = \mu_2.$$

This is important because it allows the approximated joint model to be composed with other models in product-form by RCAT.

Comparison of the approximated and original models. In Figure 2 and Table 1 we show a significant subset of the tests we have carried out. We chose to compare the distribution of the number of customers in steady-state under different hypothesis. The exact results are obtained by applying Neut's matrix geometrics technique [4]. The approximated model performs well when $\mu_2 > \mu_1$ or when N is large enough. Note that if $\mu_1 >> \mu_2$ and N is low a different approximating strategy can be adopted, e.g., switching the passive and active model. In this example, it can be shown that making Process 1 active with respect to synchronising label a (and Process 2 passive) gives better results when $\mu_1 >> \mu_2$.

4   Conclusion

In this paper we have investigated approximations of non-product-form models with product-form ones. As future research efforts are concerned, we shall investigate the problem of the analytical definition of bounds for the errors on the performance measures introduced by the proposed approach.

Parameters	Exact	Approximate
$\lambda = 2.5,\ N = 2,\ \mu_1 = 3.5,\ \mu_2 = 6.0$	5.2802	4.0459
$\lambda = 2.5,\ N = 3,\ \mu_1 = 3.5,\ \mu_2 = 6.0$	3.1587	2.9491
$\lambda = 2.5,\ N = 4,\ \mu_1 = 3.5,\ \mu_2 = 6.0$	2.7299	2.6662
$\lambda = 2.5,\ N = 5,\ \mu_1 = 3.5,\ \mu_2 = 6.0$	2.5661	2.5893
$\lambda = 2.5,\ N = 7,\ \mu_1 = 3.5,\ \mu_2 = 6.0$	2.5148	2.5112
$\lambda = 2.5,\ N = 8,\ \mu_1 = 6.0,\ \mu_2 = 4.0$	0.77271	0.72530
$*\lambda = 2.5,\ N = 8,\ \mu_1 = 6.0,\ \mu_2 = 3.2$	1.3206	0.75856
$\lambda = 2.5,\ N = 5,\ \mu_1 = 4.0,\ \mu_2 = 4.0$	2.1447	1.8548
$\lambda = 2.5,\ N = 8,\ \mu_1 = 4.0,\ \mu_2 = 4.0$	1.7674	1.7070

Table 1. Comparison of average number of customers in the original station and in the approximated one.

Steady-state probabilities of observing j customers $\lambda = 2.4$, $\mu_1 = 3.5$, $\mu_2 = 6.0$

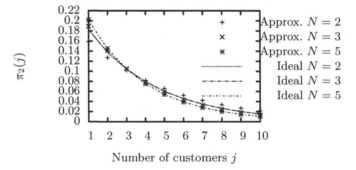

Fig. 2. Stationary distribution of the number of customers in the original model (*Ideal*) and in the approximated (*Approx.*).

References

1. K. M. Chandy and A. J. Martin. A characterization of product-form queuing networks. *J. ACM*, 30(2):286–299, 1983.
2. P. G. Harrison. Turning back time in Markovian process algebra. *Theoretical Computer Science*, 290(3):1947–1986, January 2003.
3. A. Marin and M. G. Vigliotti. A general result for deriving product-form solutions of markovian models. In *Proc. of First Joint WOSP/SIPEW Int. Conf. on Perf. Eng.*, pages 165–176, San Josè, CA, USA, 2010.
4. M. F. Neuts. *Matrix Geometric Solutions in Stochastic Models*. John Hopkins, Baltimore, Md, 1981.
5. N. van Dijk. *Queueing networks and product forms*. John Wiley, 1993.

Queue with limited volume, a diffusion approximation approach

Tadeusz Czachórski[1,2], Tomasz Nycz[2], and Ferhan Pekergin[3]

[1] Institute of Theoretical and Applied Informatics
Polish Academy of Sciences
Baltycka 5, 44–100 Gliwice, Poland
tadek@iitis.pl
[2] Silesian University of Technology
Akademicka 16, 44-100 Gliwice, Poland
Tomasz.Nycz@polsl.pl
[3] LIPN, Université Paris-Nord, 93430 Villetaneuse, France
pekergin@lipn.univ-paris13.fr

Abstract. The article presents a diffusion approximation model applied to investigate queues with finite capacity. Usually it is assumed that the size of a queue is limited by the maximum number of customers allowed to the system. Here, we assume that the size of customers is random (i.e. we consider batch arrivals with an arbitrary batch size distribution) and the constraint is given by the total volume of the queue. It is more adequate if we consider the queues of packets in e.g. IP routers where the volume of a buffer where packets are stored is limited and the size of packets is variable.

1 Introduction

The paper adapts the traditional and well known diffusion approximation model of G/G/1/N queue as proposed by Gelenbe [3] to the case where the size of the queue is limited in another way: each customer has a certain random size determined by a discrete distribution and the maximum capacity of the queue is given. Such model suits better in our opinion to the description of queues of packets observed in IP routers, as the length of IP packets is variable, and may refine their analysis, especially when the buffers are small or the utilisation of the link is high and the buffers are almost saturated. We use our semi-analytical, semi-numerical method previously applied in G/G/1/N and G/G/N/N diffusion models [1, 2] to obtain transient solution, i.e. time-dependent distribution of the queue size and time-dependent loss probabilities.

Let $A(x)$, $B(x)$ denote the interarrival and service time distributions at a service station. The distributions are general, it is assumed that their two first moments are known: $E[A] = 1/\lambda$, $E[B] = 1/\mu$, $\text{Var}[A] = \sigma_A^2$, $\text{Var}[B] = \sigma_B^2$. Denote also the squared coefficients of variation $C_A^2 = \sigma_A^2 \lambda^2$, $C_B^2 = \sigma_B^2 \mu^2$. Let $N(t)$ be the number of customers present in the system at time t. For a single class FIFO queue, the changes $N(t + \Delta t) - N(t)$ have approximately normal

E. Gelenbe et al. (eds.), *Computer and Information Sciences*, Lecture Notes
in Electrical Engineering 62, DOI 10.1007/978-90-481-9794-1_14,

distribution with mean $(\lambda - \mu)\Delta t$ and variance $(\sigma_A^2 \lambda^3 + \sigma_B^2 \mu^3)\Delta t$, provided that the time Δt is sufficiently long and the station is working without interruption. Diffusion approximation, e.g. [3] replaces the process $N(t)$ by a continuous diffusion process $X(t)$ whose incremental changes $dX(t) = X(t + dt) - X(t)$ are normally distributed with the mean βdt and variance αdt, where β, α are the coefficients of the diffusion equation

$$\frac{\partial f(x,t;x_0)}{\partial t} = \frac{\alpha}{2}\frac{\partial^2 f(x,t;x_0)}{\partial x^2} - \beta\frac{\partial f(x,t;x_0)}{\partial x} \tag{1}$$

which defines the conditional pdf $f(x,t;x_0)dx = P[x \leq X(t) < x+dx \mid X(0) = x_0]$ of $X(t)$. The choice $\beta = \lambda - \mu$, $\alpha = \sigma_A^2 \lambda^3 + \sigma_B^2 \mu^3 = C_A^2 \lambda + C_B^2 \mu$ ensures the same ratio of time-growth of mean and variance of these distributions. Function $f(n,t;n_0)$ approximates the distribution $p(n,t;n_0)$ of customers of all classes present in the queue. This approach is also extended to the case of multiple classes [4].

Boundary conditions for Eq. (1) should be also defined. In [3] diffusion approximation of a G/G/1/N station was studied as a process $X(t)$ which is defined on the closed interval $x \in [0, N]$. When the process comes to $x = 0$, it remains there for a time exponentially distributed with the parameter λ and then it returns to $x = 1$; when it comes to $x = N$, it remains there for a time which is exponentially distributed with the parameter μ and then it starts at $x = N - 1$.

2   A queue with limited volume

Here, we assume that the distribution of the size of incoming packets is discretised: a packet has the size of m blocks, $m = 1, 2, \ldots M$ with probability p_m. The total input rate is λ, the input rate of packets containing m blocks is $\lambda^{(m)}$, $p_m = \lambda^{(m)}/\lambda$.

Let V be the total size of the buffer expressed in blocks. The content of the buffer is measured in number of occupied blocks. The size of blocks is constant and the speed of service is μ_b blocks per time unit, $C_B^2 = 0$.

We distinguish $M + 1$ diffusion subintervals. The first one is $x \in [0, V - M]$ where the packets of all sizes are allowed. The input stream is composed of M streams (M classes of customers) each corresponding to packets of a fixed size m. The diffusion parameter β is here defined as $\beta_1 = \sum_{m=1}^{M} \lambda^{(m)} m - \mu_b$.

The case of butch arrivals in diffusion approximation was studied e.g. in [5]: if the distribution of groups interarrival time has mean $1/\lambda$ and variance σ_A^2, the size of the groups has mean m and variance σ_m^2, and service time distribution for one customer in the group has mean $1/\mu$ and variance σ_B^2 then the parameter $\alpha = \lambda \sigma_m^2 + m^2 \lambda^3 \sigma_A^2 + \mu \sigma_B^2$. Here, as a service time of one block is constant $\sigma_B^2 = 0$, and, as we treat customers of a specified constant size m as a separate class of customers, denoted by the upper index m, then $\sigma_m^{(m)^2} = 0$ and $\alpha^{(m)} = m^2 \lambda^{(m)^3} \sigma_A^{(m)^2} = m^2 \lambda^{(m)} C_A^{(m)^2}$. Hence, in the interval $x \in [0, V - M]$ we have $\alpha_1 = \sum_{m=1}^{M} \lambda^{(m)} m^2 C_A^{(m)^2}$.

In the next interval $x \in [V - M, V - M + 1]$, the packets of size M do not find enough space in buffer to join the queue, hence they are excluded from the input stream, and $\beta_2 = \sum_{m=1}^{M-1} \lambda^{(m)} \cdot m - \mu_b$, $\alpha_2 = \sum_{m=1}^{M-1} \lambda^{(m)} m^2 C_A^{(m)^2}$, and so on, up to the last interval $x \in [V - 1, V]$ where only one-block packets may be considered: $\beta_{M+1} = \lambda^{(1)} - \mu_b$, $\alpha_{M+1} = \lambda^{(1)} C_A^{(1)^2}$.

In transient state we should balance the probability flows between neighbouring intervals with different diffusion parameters. We put imaginary barriers at the borders of these intervals and suppose that the diffusion process entering the barrier at $x = n$, from its left side (the process is growing) is absorbed and immediately reappears at $x = n + \varepsilon$. Similarly, a process which is diminishing and enters the barrier from its right side reappears at its other side at $x = n - \varepsilon$.

Jumps from the barrier correspond to the arrivals of packets of particular sizes, hence, for the first interval, assuming that $V - M > M$, we express the density function $f_i(x, t; \psi_i)$ for an interval $i, i = 1, \ldots, M + 1$ as

$$f_1(x, t; \psi_1) = \phi_1(x, t; \psi_1) + \sum_{m=1}^{M} \int_0^t g_m(\tau) \phi_1(x, t - \tau; m) d\tau \qquad (2)$$

$$+ \int_0^t g_{V-M-\varepsilon}(\tau) \phi_1(x, t - \tau; V - M - \varepsilon) d\tau$$

where $g_m(\tau)$ are the probability mass flows coming from the barrier at $x = 0$ to $x = m$ and having density $p_0(\tau) \lambda^{(m)}$. Function $\phi_1(x, t; \psi_i)$ is the density of diffusion process inside first interval having absorbing barriers on both sides (the process is finished when it reaches either of the barriers). This function is relatively easy to obtain analytically, and the function $f_1(x, t; \psi_1)$ is represented as a superposition of functions $\phi_1(x, t; \psi_i)$ started at all possible regeneration points [1]. We proceed similarily in all other intervals.

The relationships between the probability mass flows entering the barriers and reappearing at regeneration points include the jumps from the barrier at $x = V$ to points $x = V - m$ when a m-block packet is dispatched. The density $g_{V-M-\varepsilon}(t)$ is probability flow coming from this barrier to the point $V - M - \varepsilon$ and corresponding to the departure of M-block packets plus the flow coming through the barrier from the second interval. As the service time of packets is constant, we assume $l_V(t) = \sum_{m=1}^{M} p_m \delta(t - m/\mu_b)$ or $\bar{l}_V(s) = \sum_{m=1}^{M} p_m e^{-sm/\mu_b}$.

The system of equations is transformed with the use of Laplace transform and solved numerically to obtain the values of $\bar{f}_n(x, s; \psi_n)$. Then we use the Stehfest inversion algorithm. The time-dependent loss probability of packets of size m is estimated as $p_V(t)$ plus the integral from $x = V - m$ to $x = V$ over the appropriate functions $f_i(x, t; \psi_i)$.

Numerical example

Let the packet length be $1, 2, \ldots 5$ blocks with probabilities $p_1 = 9/20$, $p_2 = 5/20$, $p_3 = 9/20$, $p_4 = 2/20$, $p_5 = 1/20$, and the overall input stream of packets be $\lambda = 0.4390$ packets per time unit. The volume of the buffer is $M = 50$ blocks. At the time $t = 0$ the buffer is empty. The time of sending one block from the buffer $1/\mu_{bl}$ is equal one time unit. An exemplary result, the probability that the buffer is saturated is given in Fig. 1.

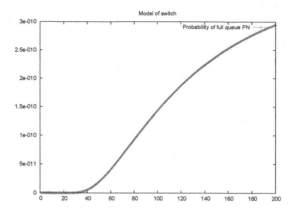

Fig. 1. The probability $p_V(t)$ that the buffer is saturated as a function of time.

3   Conclusions

The proposed model allows us to investigate the behaviour of a buffer content when the input rate of packets is changing with time. The assumptions of the model: general distribution of batch size and general distribution of interarrival times allow us to assume realistic parameters of IP packets flows transmitted in networks. We are able to predict the distribution of the size of occupied memory and the probability that the buffer is full and incoming packets are lost. The programming effort needed to assure numerical stability of computations is not negligible.

References

1. Czachórski, T.: A method to solve diffusion equation with instantaneous return processes acting as boundary conditions. Bulletin of Polish Academy of Sciences, Technical Sciences **41** (1993) 417–451
2. Czachórski, T., Fourneau, J.-M., Nycz, T., Pekergin, F.: Diffusion approximation model of multiserver stations with losses. Electronic Notes in Theoretical Computer Science **232** (2009) 125–143
3. Gelenbe, E.: On Approximate Computer Systems Models. Journal of ACM, **22** (1975), 261–269
4. Gelenbe, E., Pujolle, G.: The Behaviour of a Single Queue in a General Queueing Network. Acta Informatica, **7** (1976) 123–136
5. Gelenbe E.: Diffusion approximations: waiting times and batch arrival. Acta Informatica **12** (1979) 285–303

Exactly Solvable Stochastic Processes for Traffic Modelling

Maxim Samsonov[1], Cyril Furtlehner[1], and Jean-Marc Lasgouttes[2]

[1] INRIA-Saclay, France. e-mail: `firstname.lastname@inria.fr`
[2] INRIA Paris-Rocquencourt, France. e-mail: `jean-marc.lasgouttes@inria.fr`

Abstract. We analyze different available methods in the study of the exactly solvable stochastic models and their application to construction and modeling the road traffic with acceleration/deceleration dynamics.

1 Introduction

In the study of models for traffic, a fundamental role is played by the the fundamental diagram (FD) of traffic flow, which gives a relation between the traffic flux (cars per unit of time) and the traffic density (cars per unit of length). In the three phases traffic theory of Kerner [6], the FD on highways consists of the free flow phase, the synchronized flow phase and the congested phase. It is not clear however whether these phases, and especially the synchronized one, are genuine dynamical or thermodynamical phases, or are intricate transient features of a slowly relaxing system. In fact there is still controversy about the reality of the synchronized phase of Kerner at the moment [10].

There have been many successful applications of exactly solvable models to problems of non-equilibrium statistical physics. Applying those methods to traffic could help to clarify this kind of questions, and in particular if we find a stochastic model (exclusion process, zero range process) able to account for some empirical features of the FD, like the braking/acceleration asymmetry [8], and suitable for exact computation. Having such a model could allow to study the emergence of non-trivial collective behaviors at macroscopic level, caused for example by some spontaneous symmetry breaking among identical vehicles that can be seen experimentally on a ring [12]. The purpose of this paper is to describe briefly one such model and two different approaches for solving it. The reader is referred to [9] for more details.

2 A Multi-speed exclusion processes

We study an exclusion process with two types of particles (A=fast, B=slow, O=empty), defined by the following set of reactions, involving pairs of neighbouring sites (with periodic boundary conditions):

$$AO \xrightarrow{\lambda_a} OA; \quad BO \xrightarrow{\lambda_b} OB; \quad BO \xrightarrow{\gamma_{bo}} AO; \quad AO \xrightarrow{\delta_{ao}} BO$$

$$AB \xrightarrow{\lambda_{ab}} BA; \quad AA \xrightarrow{\delta_{aa}} BA; \quad AB \xrightarrow{\delta_{ab}} BB; \quad BA \xrightarrow{\delta_{ba}} BB$$

$$AB \xrightarrow{\gamma_{ab}} AA; \quad BB \xrightarrow{\gamma_{bb}^1} BA; \quad BA \xrightarrow{\gamma_{ba}} AA; \quad BB \xrightarrow{\gamma_{bb}^2} AB,$$

E. Gelenbe et al. (eds.), *Computer and Information Sciences*, Lecture Notes in Electrical Engineering 62, DOI 10.1007/978-90-481-9794-1_15,
© Springer Science+Business Media B.V. 2010

where the λ's, γ's and δ's denote the transition rates, each transition corresponding to a Poisson event. The model itself can be seen as a two particle exclusion
hopping model with coagulation/decoagulation dynamics including overtaking.
It generalizes several integrable sub-models. The hopping part of the model is
just the totally asymmetric exclusion process [11, 7] (TASEP) when $\lambda_a = \lambda_b$,
which is integrable, while the multi-types version with overtaking is the so-called
Karimipour model [2, 4] when $\lambda_{ab} = \lambda_a - \lambda_b$, which turns out to be integrable
as well. In some cases, the model can be exactly reformulated in terms of generalized queueing processes, where service rates of each queue follows as well
a stochastic dynamics [3]. The mapping works by identifying empty sites with
queues containing as clients the vehicles in front of them.

Based on numerical simulations, Figure 1 illustrates some observations of
a simplified form of the model, where non-zero rates are λ_a and λ_b, $\gamma_{bo} = \gamma$,
$\delta_{aa} = \delta_{ab} = \delta$; in particular overtaking is excluded ($\lambda_{ab} = 0$). The asymmetry
between braking and accelerating ($\gamma \neq \delta$) is crucial to observe a condensation
mechanism, which occurs if the apparition of slow vehicles is a sufficiently rare
event, resulting e.g. from a cascade of braking events. We remark that Figure 1(a)
is very reminiscent of coagulation-decoagulation process.

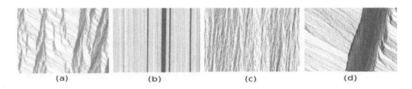

Fig. 1. Space-time plots for process with 2 speed levels (a) (b) and (c) and with 3
speed levels (d). Time is going downward and particles to the right. red, green and blue
represent different speeds in increasing order. The size of the system is 3000 except for
(b) where it is 100000. Setting are $\lambda_a = 100$, $\lambda_b = 10$, $\gamma_a = 100$, $\delta_b = 2$ for (a) and (b)
and $\delta_b = 10$ for (c), all with density $\rho = 0.2$. In (d), $\lambda_c = 10$, $\lambda_b = 100$ and $\lambda_a = 200$,
$\delta_c = 3$, $\delta_b = 5$, $\gamma_b = 0.1$ and $\gamma_a = 1$ with $\rho = 0.3$.

3 Solving through integrability

Integrability is an important means for solving systems, since it means that
we can construct the spectrum and the eigenstates of the underlying Markov
operator. The equation governing the evolution of the probability distribution
$P(\mathcal{C}, t)$ with time is

$$\frac{d}{dt}P(\mathcal{C}, t) = \sum_{\mathcal{C}'} P(\mathcal{C}', t)M(\mathcal{C}', \mathcal{C}) - \sum_{\mathcal{C}'} P(\mathcal{C}, t)M(\mathcal{C}, \mathcal{C}')$$

where $M(\mathcal{C}, \mathcal{C}')$ is the transition rate between configurations $\mathcal{C}$ and $\mathcal{C}'$. To get
a model which can be analyzed, and possibly solved, we impose cancellations
conditions for the nonlinear terms [9] in order to get a so-called free "fermionic

point". Such restrictions between the rates renders the model solvable for some specific choice:

$$\lambda_a = \gamma_{ab} + \gamma_{ba}, \quad \lambda_b = \delta_{ab} + \gamma_{ba} = \delta_{aa}^2 + \gamma_{bb}^2, \quad \lambda_{ab} = \lambda_a - \delta_{aa}^1 - \gamma_{bb}^1.$$

The interaction term has then the form $-\lambda_a \sum_i n_i^a - \lambda_b \sum_i n_i^b = hN$ of a chemical potential with h playing the role of an average hopping rate operator, the operators $n_i^{a,b}$ are local operators counting particles of each sort.

Another limiting case occurs when we consider only the coagulation/decoagulation part of the model. This case can be dealt with help of the empty interval method [1] and describes a densely packed road with cars of two types. Then we can write a system of equations for the queues of cars:

$$P_t^{a,b}(i, i+1, \ldots, i+m-1) = \mathbb{E}^t(n_i^{a,b} n_{i+1}^{a,b} \cdots n_{i+m-1}^{a,b}).$$

Taking into account the Markovian evolution, the equations of the corresponding process can be written as a system of linear equations when $\gamma_{ab} = \gamma_{ba} = \gamma_{bb}^2 = 0$ and $\lambda_{ab} = \gamma_{bb}^1$:

$$\frac{d}{dt}P_t^a(x,y) = \delta_{ba} P_t^a(x-1,y) - \left(2\lambda_{ab} + (y-x)(\delta_{aa}^1 + \delta_{aa}^2) + \delta_{ab} + \delta_{ba}\right) P_t^a(x,y)$$

$$+ (\lambda_{ab} - \delta_{aa}^1 + \delta_{ab}) P_t^a(x, y+1) + \lambda_{ab} P_t^a(x+1, y).$$

Such equations can be solved in terms of Bessel functions. A more general structure of the cluster functions is possible as well, to describe intermediate cases between the two ones described above (see [9] for details).

4 Product form of jams at steady-state

Taking advantage of the mapping of the process to a generalized tandem queue process, we study in this section the conditions under which the stationary state has a product form. The queuing processes which are obtained [9] have dynamical service rates, meaning that each single queue $i \in \mathcal{N}$ is represented by a vector $z_i(t) = (n_i(t), \mu_i(t)) \in E_i \subset \mathbb{Z}^+ \times \mathbb{R}^+$, where $n_i(t)$ is the number of clients and $\mu_i(t)$ is a service rate. It represents the global transition rate from z_i to $z_i' = (n_i - 1, \mu_i') \in V_i^-(z_i)$, the set of points in E_i having one client less than z. Two sets of transition probability matrices $p_i^\pm(z, z')$ and one set of transition rates $q_i^0(z, z')$ are introduced to be complete. When a client get served in queue i, the state of the departure queue z_i is modified according to the set $p_i^-(z, z')$ with $z' \in V^-(z)$, and the state z_{i+1} of the destination queue is modified according the set $p_{i+1}^+(z, z')$, $z' \in V^+(z)$. We have the normalizations,

$$\sum_{z' \in z} p_i^\pm(z, z') = 1, \qquad \forall z' \in V^\pm(z). \tag{1}$$

Additional internal transitions are allowed, where the service rate μ_i of queue i changes independently of any arrival or departure. The intensities of these transitions are given by the set $q_i^0(z, z')$, $z' \in V_i^0(z)$ of transition rates, with $V_i^0(z)$ the set of points in E_i having the same number of clients as z. For this model we can prove the following [9].

Theorem 1. *Let π_i^λ denote the steady state probability corresponding to queue i taken in isolation and fed with a Poisson process with rate λ. If the following partial balance equations are satisfied,*

$$\sum_{z \in V^+(z_i)} \mu(z) p_i^-(z, z_i) \pi_i^\lambda(z) = \lambda \pi_i^\lambda(z_i), \tag{2}$$

$$\mu(z_i) \pi_i^\lambda(z_i) + \sum_{z \in V_i^0(z_i)} q_i^0(z_i, z) \pi_i^\lambda(z_i) =$$

$$\sum_{z \in V^-(z_i)} \lambda p^+(z, z_i) \pi_i^\lambda(z) + \sum_{z \in V_i^0(z_i)} q_i^0(z, z_i) \pi_i^\lambda(z), \tag{3}$$

then the following product form holds at steady state:

$$P(S = \{z_i, i \in \mathcal{N}\}) = \frac{\prod_{i \in \mathcal{N}} \pi_i^\lambda(z_i)}{P(\sum_i n_i = N)} \tag{4}$$

Note that reversible processes are special cases of processes satisfying (2,3) and, in this respect, our result is an adaptation of Kelly's general result concerning product forms in queueing networks [5]. Some non-reversible examples of this partial balance property can actually be found [9].

References

1. ben Avraham, D., Havlin, S.: Diffusion and Reactions in Fractals and Disordered Systems. Cambridge University Press (2000)
2. Cantini, L.: Algebraic bethe ansatz for the two species asep with different hopping rates. J. Phys. A: Math. Theor. **41**, 095001 (2008)
3. Furtlehner, C., Lasgouttes, J.: A queueing theory approach for a multi-speed exclusion process. In: Traffic and Granular Flow ' 07. pp. 129–138 (2007)
4. Karimipour, V.: A multi-species asep and its relation to traffic flow. Phys. Rev. **E59**, 205 (1999)
5. Kelly, F.P.: Reversibility and stochastic networks. John Wiley & Sons Ltd. (1979)
6. Kerner, B.: The Physics of Traffic. Springer Verlag (2005)
7. Liggett, T.M.: Interacting Particle Systems. Springer, Berlin (2005)
8. Nagel, K., Schreckenberg, M.: A cellular automaton model for freeway traffic. J. Phys. I,2 pp. 2221–2229 (1992)
9. Samsonov, M., Furtlehner, C., Lasgouttes, J.: Exactly solvable stochastic processes for traffic modelling. Tech. Rep. 7278, Inria (2010)
10. Schönhof, M., Helbing, D.: Criticism of three-phase traffic theory. Transportation Research 43, 784–797 (2009)
11. Spitzer, F.: Interaction of markov processes. Adv. Math. **5**, 246 (1970)
12. Sugiyama, Y., et al.: Traffic jams without bottlenecks: experimental evidence for the physical mechanism of the formation of a jam. New Journal of Physics 10, 1–7 (2008)

Actor Petri net Model: toward Suitable and Flexible Level Representation of Scientific Workflows

Nanshan Du[1,2], Qing Li[1], Yiwen Liang[2], Farong Zhong[3]

[1] Department of Computer Science, City University of Hong Kong, Kowloon, Hong Kong, China dunanshan@163.com, itqli@cityu.edu.hk
[2] School of Computer, Wuhan University, Wuhan, Hubei, China 430072 dunanshan@163.com, ywliang@whu.edu.cn
[3] Department of Computer Science, Zhejiang Normal University, Jinhua, Zhejiang, China 321004 zfr@zjnu.cn

Abstract. Applications of scientific workflows are going to be more widespread and important to our living and lives. The intrinsic characteristics of scientific workflows are data- and computing-intensive, heterogeneous data representation and distributed execution environments. Scientists use different equipment to retrieve source data by monitoring objects and then store or process on many different workstations. Actor Petri net Model (APnM) helps develop scientific workflows effectively and efficiently within collaboration and cooperation work mode. Scientific workflow environments based on APnM can help scientists pay close attention to functional components development, and choose flexible mechanisms on error management, transaction and exception management, and priority processing. Scientific workflows represented based on APnM can be operated both on design and run time to support trial and error development. From the perspective of software engineering, it is a suitable level of indirection to resolve the development, testing, and simulation complexity of scientific workflows.

1 Introduction

Computing is going to be a more and more important part of science and engineering. An advertisement "A Computer Wanted" appeared in 1892 in the New York Times [1] when computer had not been created. It means that computing has been an indispensable part of experiment and engineering since the 19th century. Many applications of scientific workflows are going to be more widespread and important to our living and lives, such as Mesoscale Meteorology, Seismic Hazard Analysis, and Ecological Niche Modeling [15, 6].

Many characteristics and challenges make scientific workflows different from traditional workflows [9, 3]. From the user perspective, scientists are the main users to design their scientific workflows, rather than professional software developers. With regard to processes, workflows are the objects to be operated in trial-and-error cycles of the research procedure: proposing hypotheses, designing experiments, running or simulating workflows, observing results online, making changes on the fly, and verifying proposed hypotheses. In terms of the work mode, scientists cooperate and coordinate with each other through making their results self describing or self-reflective on how to

E. Gelenbe et al. (eds.), *Computer and Information Sciences*, Lecture Notes in Electrical Engineering 62, DOI 10.1007/978-90-481-9794-1_16,
© Springer Science+Business Media B.V. 2010

be used easily. With regard to the functions that a software environment should provide for workflows, they need to deal with complex and heterogeneous data, flexible and dynamic skeletons, and distributed computing environments that can integrate many different computing devices to solve data- and computing-intensive applications.

Dynamic Data Driven Applications Systems (DDDAS) [5] are classical scientific worklows. They are generally composed of four main functional components: measuring data from real environments, simulating and forecasting the possible results in a period of time, assimilating data from both previous parts, and visualizing data. Actor Petri net Model (APnM) can be a suitable computing model of DDDAS on how to process data. On the other hand, DDDAS are suitable cases to test and evaluate the suitability and flexibility of APnM.

In this paper, we advocate APnM to meet the challenges of scientific workflows. In particular, the scientific workflow environment based on APnM provides a dynamic type system, flexible operations on workflows at design time or run time, and advanced features of computing. We stipulate on what the workflow environment need to support/provide in order for APnM-based scientific workflows to work simply and intuitively based on our experience of prototyping such a scientific workflow system.

2 Related Work

There are many representation methods of workflows from various perspectives by different research teams. The relationship with APnM can be found in our previous work [7]. There are also some works on workflow evolution or dynamic workflow. Workflow management systems supply a set of primitives to support runtime changes upon corresponding workflow specifications [4, 12]. Frequently used operations includes *AddTask, RemoveTask, ForkTask, JoinTask, AltRoute* and so on. For each operation, the runtime workflow should satisfy some structure and data constraints. Besides, some meta-models are proposed to specify workflows [8, 13]. As in the meta-model ML-DEWS, main objects are *Process, Activity, Event, Rule, FlowNet, FlowComp*. Changes can be achieved according to different modalities by supplying operations. Data constraints should be held to make sure the changed workflow valid [17]. However, all the workflows are operated with a global view, and workflow engines need to embrace all kinds of evolution according to primitives. As a result, when workflows are running in distributed environments, it will be formidable to ask all platform to supply consistent behaviors on dynamic operations.

There are many pioneering projects in supporting scientific workflows, such as Taverna [14], Kepler [11], Virtual Data Toolkit [16], and so on. Taverna is a workbench for workflow composition and enactment developed as part of the ^{my}Grid project, the focus of which is bioinformatic applications. Kepler provides a graphical user interface for composing workflows. A workflow in Kepler is composed of independent actors communicating through well-defined interfaces. The execution order and the communication mechanisms of the actors in the workflow are defined in a director object. VDT is a system for deriving data rather than generating them explicitly from a workflow. Each project has a specific workflow representation language. Until now, they have concentrated on supporting domain functional applications, and they do not take distributed dynamic tasks and heterogenous data compatibility into account.

3   Actor Petri net Model

As earlier work presented [7], APnM is derived from many other workflow representation models with modifications to deal with characteristics and challenges in scientific workflows. It is a simple and basic model for applications with characteristics of heterogeneous data and distributed computing. Unlike traditional representation models, APnM can also be used as a runtime model. As to scientific workflows, scientists can monitor and change their applications at any time to speed up the application development.

Definition 1. *(Actor Petri net Model.) An Actor Petri net Model is a 5-tuple:*
$\langle Set_A\ Set_R\ Set_P\ R\ D_T \rangle$ *where: Set_A is a finite set of Actors, Set_R is a finite set of Routers, Set_P is a finite set of Pools, R is a set of relationships specified by a finite set of links so that each one is between a Pool and a port of an Actor or a Router, D_T is a distribution of Tokens (to be defined next).*

   An actor is a functional component to satisfy a simple and single function requirement. It takes tokens from pools linked with its input ports, and produce tokens to pools linked with its output ports. A router is a special actor concentrating on data operations, such as *split, join,* and operations in Nested Relational Calculus (NRC) [10]. Routers in a workflow offer sufficient information on dataflows. They are important to deal with heterogeneous data. A pool is a place to store and retrieve data. Data in pools can be subject to complex management functionalities. The set of relationships indicates where actors or routers retrieve tokens from and store to. In a distribution, tokens can be placed in pools, actors, or even routers as needed.
   A skeleton is an APnM without Tokens.

Definition 2. *(Token.) A token is a pair: $\langle V\ S_T \rangle$ where V is a value of a particular type in a data type system, S_T is a stack of Traces (to be defined next) identifying and specifying the position of the value in its corresponding value with a collection type.*

   A token has two parts: the value part is of simple data to be processed in applications, and the trace part offers routers information on how to handle data value. To cooperate with NRC, the type system should provide at least a collection data type for representing the nested data. To deal with complex and heterogeneous data, the type system should be dynamic so that it can be expanded easily to represent complex data, and flexible enough to do transformation between different types.

Definition 3. *(Trace.) A trace is a pair: $\langle ID\ A\ L \rangle$ where ID is the identifier of the corresponding nested data, A is the rank of that data, and L is a list of positions specifying data sources referring to that data.*

4 Workflow Execution

If actors and routers are substituted by transitions, relations on their ports are reattached to corresponding transitions, and pools are substituted by places, then the structure of APnM is identical to Petri nets. Nevertheless, most of the results obtained from verification studies on Petri nets are not applicable to APnM, because actors and routers can be more complicated components.

Firing Mechanism For an actor or a router e, the state firing rule F is

$$F : \pi_{\bullet e}(D_T) \quad S_e \rightarrow S_e \quad \pi_{e\bullet}(D_T) \tag{1}$$

where π is a projection operation which projects a distribution of tokens to some pools, $\bullet e$ is the set of input pools of e, S_e is the state set of e, $e\bullet$ is the set of output pools of e.

Rule 1 means that e consumes some tokens from its input pools and produce some tokens to its output pools. In fact, the execution of workflows is not exactly equal to a sequence of firing. Because when a token is consumed or produced, it will influence firing of linked components. Workflow execution is communications of actors and routers through tokens in pools. Whether the workflow execution succeeds or not depends on coordination and cooperation of all the components. This different state management and execution strategies result in very complex semantics but simple and intuitive application development methodologies. Each component can be developed independently under few constraints: pulling tokens from input pools and pushing tokens to output pools, continuously sensing environments through tokens and publishing its running states if necessary.

Error Management For distributed and parallel systems, it is very difficult to advance adaptive software development process because of various data sequences and network or application errors. Data sequences can be accumulated to an empirical data set. To advance application development, the general method is to accumulate components one by one and combine error information from assembling components to get clues on whether application runs according to their want. Based on APnM, scientists can combine errors of components flexibly and easily. They just need to redirect published state pools of those components.

Transaction and Exception Management Transaction is almost the most fundamental feature in parallel systems to hold ACID properties of data. Exception is used in languages to reverse the running application to a previously legal control point after some rescue, which is very useful in interactive systems. For workflows based on the APnM, these two features need to be attached to tokens so that components can be aware. Due to control-flow is weakened to be data driven, only D_T needs to be considered. To support transaction and exception management on APnM will be difficult and different from their original essence. Weaker transaction and exception model are needed to support fault tolerance. For example, some data processing errors do not influence the subsequential data processing.

Priority Processing Sometimes urgent and critical data need to be processed before others even though they are produced later. When a special data item of priority among tokens is in one pool, it is relatively simple that we just need to extend the pool to support the specific priority. When the priority is among tokens in different pools, we should extend routers to support it as a supplement, by transforming this scenario to the single pool scenario.

To cope with scientific workflows like DDDAS, more flexible skeletons are needed to support appliations running fluently along with dynamic computing resources. Hereby, intelligent workflow engines, which can perceive the computing environment changes, are needed to distribute and direct the actors and tokens of applications.

Components Distribution Inputs: workflow dimention containing workflow, input tokens frequency and size, components computing complexity and features (viz. law of distribution, law of association and law of commutation), output tokens frequency and size; computing resources dimension containing workstations network, workstations' idle computing power. Targets: higher perfomance, less communication traffic, fault tolerance (e.g., only the failed partial work needs to be redone.)

The workflow engine for APnM-based scientific workflow environment needs to at least cope with the static scenarios, and preferably be able to accommodate the dynamic scenarios as much as possible.

5 Conclusions and Future Work

We have advocated APnM as a basic model of scientific workflows after articulating scientific workflow characteristics. APnM is a simple and intuitive model to represent workflows no matter in running state or not. From the perspective of software engineering, it is a suitable level of indirection to resolve the development, testing, and simulation complexity of scientific workflows. Based on APnM, we have developed a graphic workflow editor on Qt Development Platform [2]. Our views and considerations on supporting scientific workflow development and workflow engine design are particularly stipulated in this paper. Currently, we are engaged in developing the workflow engine as our ongoing work.

Acknowledgement: This work has been supported by the Natural Science Foundation of China with the project 60873234.

References

1. A Computer Wanted. http://query.nytimes.com/gst/abstract.html?res=9F07E0D81438E233A25751C0A9639C94639ED7CF, 1892.
2. Actor Petri net Model. http://sites.google.com/site/dunanshan.
3. R. Barga and D. Gannon. Scientific versus business workflows. In I. J. Taylor, E. Deelman, D. Gannon, and M. S. Shields, editors, *Workflows for e-Science: Scientific Workflows for Grids*, pages 9–16. Springer-Verlag, NJ, USA, 2007.
4. F. Casati, S. Ceri, B. Pernici, and G. Pozzi. Workflow evolution. *Data & Knowledge Engineering*, 24(3):211–238, 1998.

5. F. Darema. New software technologies for the development and runtime support of complex applications. *International Journal of High Performance Computing Applications*, 13(3):180–190, 1999.
6. E. Deelman. Grids and Clouds: Making Workflow Applications Work in Heterogeneous Distributed Environments. *International Journal of High Performance Computing Applications*, 2009.
7. N. Du, Q. Li, and Y. Liang. Actor petri net model for scientific workflows: Model, design and system. In *Proceedings of the 4nd international conference on Ubiquitous information management and communication*, Suwon, Korea, 2010. ACM.
8. C. Ellis and K. Keddara. ML-DEWS: Modeling language to support dynamic evolution within workflow systems. *Computer Supported Cooperative Work (CSCW)*, 9(3):293–333, 2000. 10.1023/A:1008799125984.
9. J. Hendler. Communication: Enhanced: Science and the semantic web. *Science*, 299(5606):520–521, 2003.
10. J. Hidders, N. Kwasnikowska, J. Sroka, J. Tyszkiewicz, and J. Van den Bussche. DFL: A dataflow language based on petri nets and nested relational calculus. *Information Systems*, 33(3):261–284, 2008.
11. Kepler. http://www.kepler-project.org/.
12. M. Reichert and P. Dadam. ADEPT_flex—supporting dynamic changes of workflows without losing control. *Journal of Intelligent Information Systems*, 10(2):93–129, 1998. 10.1023/A:1008604709862.
13. R.-Z. Sun and M.-L. Shi. A meta-model supporting dynamic changing workflow. *Acta Electronica Sinica*, 30(1):2052–2056, 2002.
14. Taverna. http://taverna.sourceforge.net/.
15. I. J. Taylor, E. Deelman, D. Gannon, and M. S. Shields, editors. *Workflows for e-Science: Scientific Workflows for Grids*. Springer-Verlag, NJ, USA, 2007.
16. Virtual Data Toolkit. http://vdt.cs.wisc.edu/.
17. L. Wang, Z. Huang, and M. Luo. Supporting dynamic workflow adaptation in a dataflow-constrained workflow net. In *NISS '09: Proceedings of the 2009 International Conference on New Trends in Information and Service Science*, pages 1000–1005, Washington, DC, USA, 2009. IEEE Computer Society.

3 Bioinformatics & Bioengineering

Developing a Scoring Function for NMR Structure-based Assignments using Machine Learning

Mehmet Çağrı Çalpur[1], Hakan Erdoğan[1], Bülent Çatay[1], Bruce R. Donald[2] and Mehmet Serkan Apaydın[1]

[1] Sabanci University
Faculty of Engineering and Natural Sciences
Tuzla Istanbul, 34956, TURKEY
[2] Duke University, Department of Computer Science
Duke University Medical Center, Department of Biochemistry
Durham NC 27708, USA

Abstract. Determining the assignment of signals received from the experiments (peaks) to specific nuclei of the target molecule in Nuclear Magnetic Resonance (NMR[1]) spectroscopy is an important challenge. Nuclear Vector Replacement (NVR) ([2, 3]) is a framework for structure-based assignments which combines multiple types of NMR data such as chemical shifts, residual dipolar couplings, and NOEs. NVR-BIP [1] is a tool which utilizes a scoring function with a binary integer programming (BIP) model to perform the assignments. In this paper, support vector machines (SVM) and boosting are employed to combine the terms in NVR-BIP's scoring function by viewing the assignment as a classification problem. The assignment accuracies obtained using this approach show that boosting improves the assignment accuracy of NVR-BIP on our data set when RDCs are not available and outperforms SVMs. With RDCs, boosting and SVMs offer mixed results.

1 Introduction

The gold standard in determining the protein structure is wet-lab experiment, the primary ones being X-ray crystallography (XRC) and NMR spectroscopy. In order to understand a protein's function and do rational drug design, it is necessary to determine the protein structure.

Structure-based assignment (SBA) aims to determine the assignments using a template structure. This template is homologous to the target. Previous techniques for NMR SBA include NVR-EM [3], NVR-BIP [1], MARS [4], NOE-net [5], Hus et al. [6].

---

[1] Abbreviations used: NMR, Nuclear Magnetic Resonance; NVR, nuclear vector replacement; NOE, Nuclear Overhauser Effect; BIP, binary integer programming; SVM, Support Vector Machine; RDC, Residual Dipolar Coupling; XRC, X-ray Crystallography; PDB, Protein Data Bank; SBA, Structure-based Assignment; EM, Expectation Maximization.

E. Gelenbe et al. (eds.), *Computer and Information Sciences*, Lecture Notes in Electrical Engineering 62, DOI 10.1007/978-90-481-9794-1_17,
© Springer Science+Business Media B.V. 2010

NVR-BIP works comparably well on the proteins on which NVR-EM was tested. Furthermore it provides significantly better accuracies on four novel proteins. However the scoring function of NVR involves simple addition of the contribution of 7 different terms although these terms are not independent. The goal of this work is to explore machine learning techniques to learn optimal ways of combining these terms.

To the best of our knowledge, this is the first approach that uses classification techniques to develop a scoring function for NMR SBA. Our contributions in this paper are:

- the combination of the components of NVR-BIP's scoring function using SVMs and boosting
- incorporation of the novel scoring function into NVR-BIP and
- testing the novel scoring function on NVR-BIP's data set and comparison with the results reported in [1].

The rest of the paper is as follows: Section 2 describes the proposed algorithm, followed by the implementation in Section 3. Section 4 presents the experimental study and discusses the results. Finally, concluding remarks are given in the last section.

2   Methods

The data set is divided into two components: A training set and a test set. The training set consists of data corresponding to those proteins that are homologous to the target, except the template with which the SBA will be performed and which forms the test set.

The goal is to learn a classifier that distinguishes the correct peak-residue pair from incorrect ones. SVMs and boosting return scores corresponding to how confidently the corresponding classification is made. The output of the learning algorithm is used as the scoring function of the BIP model, which solves the SBA problem. After the initial assignments are made, an alignment tensor is computed and then the components of the scoring function corresponding to RDCs are included.

3   Implementation

The training data set belongs to two classes, +1 and -1. Positive label represents the correct peak-residue assignment pair and negative label represents incorrect assignments. Roughly there are 2000 positively labeled instances and 100,000 negatively labeled instances. SVMs require weighting adjustment to the data, in order not to classify all instances as -1. The +1 instances are multiplied by the weight factor (-1/+1 instance ratio). We solve the BIP problem using ILOG OPL Studio CPLEX solver.

The execution times for the BIP solution change according to the number of available peak-residue assignments. Without RDCs, using the boosting scores, the CPLEX solver runs for an average of 5 minutes to solve the system for ubiquitin. Adding RDC information to the process greatly reduces the number of available assignments, therefore reducing the problem size, and the average execution time for boosting scores becomes 45 seconds on an Intel Celeron 560 computer with 2.13 Ghz processor with 2GB memory.

4   Results

The experimental results are reported in Table 1. Both the results without and with RDCs are provided. In addition, the results obtained by the addition of scoring function components, which are used in NVR-BIP [1] are given as a reference and is labeled the addition method. It can be seen that, without RDCs, for most of the proteins SVM accuracies are about the same as the accuracies obtained using the addition method. Boosting accuracies are 7-16% higher than addition method. On the other hand, with RDCs, boosting and addition method's accuracies are similar. The SVM results given in the following table are obtained with RBF Kernel. The boosting results given in Table 1 are the results achieved by Gentle AdaBoost algorithm. Results on more proteins are available in our technical report.

Table 1. Results on Ubiquitin without and with RDCs.

PDB ID	without RDCs			with RDCs		
	addition	SVM	boosting	addition	SVM	boosting
1UBI	87%	84%	97%	$97\%^a$ $100\%^b$	$97\%^a$ $97\%^b$	$97\%^a$ $100\%^b$
1UBQ	87%	87%	100%	$97\%^a$ $100\%^b$	$97\%^a$ $100\%^b$	$100\%^a$ $100\%^b$
1G6J	87%	87%	100%	$97\%^a$ $93\%^b$	$94\%^a$ $93\%^b$	$100\%^a$ $90\%^b$
1UD7	81%	81%	97%	$97\%^a$ $97\%^b$	$89\%^a$ $89\%^b$	$97\%^a$ $100\%^b$
1AAR	79%	83%	86%	$97\%^a$ $100\%^b$	$93\%^a$ $93\%^b$	$93\%^a$ $93\%^b$

[a] with NH RDCs in two media
[b] with NH and CH RDCs.

5   Conclusion

In this study, we combine the SVM and boosting techniques with BIP within NVR's framework to perform SBA. The tests without RDCs show that boosting has better assignment accuracy than the addition method. With RDCs, our accuracies are comparable to the addition method for both SVM and boosting. This may be explained by the fact that with RDCs, the RDCs dominate the feature vectors and they don't allow separating the positive examples from negative ones. Boosting method is therefore especially suitable for use when RDCs are not available. When RDCs are available, our method could be used to accelerate converging to the best assignment by providing a better assignment from which a better alignment tensor estimate could be obtained.

Our results also indicate that, the training set for a protein from the homologous protein data provides good assignment accuracies. However this limits our approach to those proteins for which homologous proteins and their corresponding assignments are known. As future work we are interested in developing a Bayesian scoring function for SBA that does not have this requirement.

Acknowledgments

We thank Dr. Nanjiang Shu for discussions. We thank Dr. Pei Zhou for providing us with the NMR data. We acknowledge funding from the Scientific and Technical Research Council of Turkey (TUBITAK)[program code 1001; 109E027] to M.S.A. and from the NIH [GM-65982] to B.R.D.

References

1. Apaydın, M. S., Çatay, B., Patrick N. and Donald, B. R.: NVR-BIP: Nuclear Vector Replacement using Binary Integer Programming for NMR Structure-Based Assignments. The Computer Journal, Advance Access published on January 6, 2010; doi: doi:10.1093/comjnl/bxp120.
2. Langmead, C., Yan, A., Lilien, R., Wang, L., and Donald, B.: A Polynomial-Time Nuclear Vector Replacement Algorithm for Automated NMR Resonance Assignments (2003) In Proc. The Seventh Annual International Conference on Research in Computational Molecular Biology (RECOMB) Berlin, Germany, April 1013: ACM Press. appears in: J. Comp. Bio. (2004), 11 (2-3), pp. 277-98 pp. 176-187.
3. Langmead, C. and Donald, B.: An expectation/maximization nuclear vector replacement algorithm for automated NMR resonance assignments (2004), Journal of Biomolecular NMR. 29(2), 111-138.
4. Jung, Y. and Zweckstetter, M.: Mars – robust automatic backbone assignment of proteins (2004), Journal of Biomolecular NMR 30(1), 11-23.
5. Stratmann, D., van Heijenoort, C. and Guittet, E.: NOEnet-Use of NOE networks for NMR resonance assignment of proteins with known 3D structure, Bioinformatics (2009), 25(4):474–481
6. Hus, J., Prompers, J., and Bruschweiler, R.: Automated NMR assignment and protein structure determination using sparse dipolar coupling constraints (2002), J. Mag. Res. 157(1), 119-125.

Data and Model Driven Hybrid Approach to Activity Scoring of Cyclic Pathways

Zerrin Işik[1], Volkan Atalay[1], Cevdet Aykanat[2], and Rengül Çetin-Atalay[3]

[1] Department of Computer Engineering, Middle East Technical University
[2] Department of Computer Engineering, Bilkent University
[3] Department of Molecular Biology and Genetics, Bilkent University, Ankara, TURKEY

Abstract. Analysis of large scale -omics data based on a single tool remains inefficient to reveal molecular basis of cellular events. Therefore, data integration from multiple heterogeneous sources is highly desirable and required. In this study, we developed a data- and model-driven hybrid approach to evaluate biological activity of cellular processes. Biological pathway models were taken as graphs and gene scores were transferred through neighbouring nodes of these graphs. An activity score describes the behaviour of a specific biological process was computed by flowing of converged gene scores until reaching a target process. Biological pathway model based approach that we describe in this study is a novel approach in which converged scores are calculated for the cellular processes of a cyclic pathway. The convergence of the activity scores for cyclic graphs were demonstrated on the KEGG pathways.

1 Introduction

Microarray experiments produce transcriptome data which reflects the biological behaviour of several genes under particular conditions. A microarray data analysis method initially generates lists of significant genes hopefully related with the particular condition of the experiment. Researchers focus on integrating biological pathways and gene lists to associate genes to a specific cellular process. Biological pathways represent several experimental interactions in the form of graphs. The vertices and edges of these graphs represent genes/molecules and relations between genes/molecules, respectively. Several tools have been developed to visualize microarray data by considering existing biological pathways [1–3]. Generally, these pathway analysis tools identify significant genes or pathways based on traditional statistical tests. However, the analysis capacity of such tools depends on the initially identified differentially expressed gene set. Moreover, existing tools do not integrate individual gene information with pathway models to provide more biologically significant results.

In our previous study, we integrated transcriptome data to evaluate acyclic signaling cascades under the control of specific biological process [4]. In this study, we describe a hybrid approach integrating large scale data (microarray

---

E. Gelenbe et al. (eds.), *Computer and Information Sciences*, Lecture Notes in Electrical Engineering 62, DOI 10.1007/978-90-481-9794-1_18,
© Springer Science+Business Media B.V. 2010

gene expression and ChIP-seq) to quantitatively assess paths in a cyclic pathway under the control of a biological process. We use the integrated data as the attribute of a node and we transfer this attribute to en route of the cyclic pathway as scores which explain the current activity of analyzed pathway. Our main contribution in this study is to assess biological activity of cyclic pathways by developing a linear-time graph cascading algorithm combined with a rank product gene scoring method.

2   Material and Methods

The proposed approach is made up of two main stages: *data integration* and *pathway scoring* (Figure 1). In the *data integration* stage, we perform the integration of large scale heterogeneous transcriptome data. For this purpose, ChIP-seq and microarray gene expression data both performed on HeLa cells under control and oxidative stress conditions were selected from public databases [5, 6]. After performing raw data analysis, we assign a rank measure for the genes both from ChIP-seq and microarray data. For this purpose, we ordered these genes by sorting their read counts and fold-change measurements in the ascending order. These individual ranking scores of genes were integrated by taking their rank products [7]. These scores are used as *integrated gene scores* in the rest of the analysis.

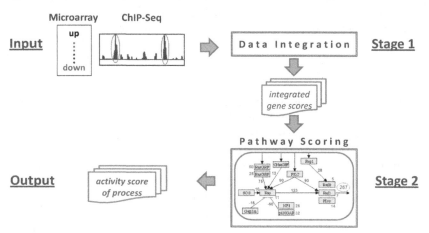

Fig. 1. Process diagram of the developed system.

In the *pathway scoring* stage, several signaling cascades from KEGG PATHWAY database are used as the models of our method. An activity score for a biological process in a pathway is computed by using flow mechanism of integrated gene scores. For this purpose, a KEGG pathway is converted into a directed graph $\mathcal{G} = (\mathcal{V}, \mathcal{E})$ by using KGML files. A node in the graph represents gene product, or target process linking current signal to another pathway. The edges represent the relations (i.e., activation or inhibition) between the nodes. In $\mathcal{G}$, let $outAdj(x)$ denote the out-adjacency list of node x, that is

$outAdj(x) = \{y : (x, y) \in \mathcal{E}\}$ and similarly $inAdj(x)$ denotes the in-adjacency list of node x. The directed graph $\mathcal{G}$ is converted into a cascade form by applying Breadth-First Search (BFS)-like algorithm which effectively propagates visiting levels starting from nodes of zero indegree. Let $\mathcal{V}_0, \mathcal{V}_1, \mathcal{V}_2, \ldots, \mathcal{V}_{L-1}$ denote the node levels of this cascade form of $\mathcal{G}$, where $\mathcal{V}_0$ denotes the set of nodes with zero indegree. This cascade form enables us to solve the score convergence problems of some cyclic graphs. Algorithm 1 describes the biological activity score computation for each pathway. The for-loop in initialization part computes the sum of the self-scores of the nodes in out-adjacency of each node which is necessary in out-score computations. The score computation part works in iterative manner which updates the score of the nodes in a level-wise fashion. The statement in the third for-loop computes the out-score of node x by dividing among the nodes in $outAdj(x)$ according to the self-scores of those nodes. Therefore, the nodes with small self-scores will get small share of $outScore(x)$ compared to the nodes having large self-scores. The reason of the iterative approach is the existence of cyclic cascades in KEGG PATHWAY database, because the out-scores of the nodes in a cycle need to be computed many times. For this purpose, we execute the while loop until obtaining converged out-scores for all nodes in the graph. The error threshold for convergence criteria and set to 10^{-6}. After convergence, the out-score (*activity score*) of each gene and process are returned as the output of the algorithm.

The BFS-like levelization algorithm run in linear-time ($\mathcal{O}(\mathcal{V} + \mathcal{E})$) in the size of the pathway graph $\mathcal{G}$. The initialization for-loop also makes a single scan over all vertices and edges of $\mathcal{G}$. The while-loop of Algorithm 1 processes each vertex once. Therefore, Algorithm 1 can be considered as a linear-time algorithm if constant number of iterations suffices for convergence.

Algorithm 1 : Computing Activity Score of Biological Pathway

Input:
Directed graph $\mathcal{G}$ stored in-adjacency and out-adjacency list format
Score: indicates self-score of each node given by our method
outScore: contains out-score of each node
sign : keeps edge types: activation (1) or inhibition (-1)
Levelization info $\mathcal{V}_0, \mathcal{V}_1, \mathcal{V}_2, \ldots, \mathcal{V}_{L-1}$ obtained by running BFS-like algorithm.
Initialization:
for each vertex $x \in \mathcal{V}$ **do**
  $outScore(x) = Score(x)$
  $totOutSelfScore(x) = 0$
  for each vertex $y \in outAdj(x)$ **do**
    $totOutSelfScore(x) = totOutSelfScore(x) + Score(y)$
Score Computation:
while not converged **do**
  for each level $\ell = 0, 1, 2, \ldots, L - 1$ **do**
    for each vertex $x \in \mathcal{V}_\ell$ **do**
      for each vertex $y \in outAdj(x)$ **do**
        $outScore(y) = outScore(y) + sign(x, y) * Score(x) * \frac{Score(y)}{totOutSelfScore(x)}$
  return $\{outScore\}$

---

3   Results and Discussion

In our approach, identification of an activated process under experimental conditions is easily provided by mapping gene scores and flowing them over the pathways. We applied our approach to several KEGG pathways: Pathways in cancer, Cell cycle, P53 signaling, Insulin signaling, Regulation of actin cytoskeleton, Jak-STAT, Apoptosis, TGF-β, and MAPK signaling pathways. These pathways have 3 - 7 target cellular processes and include several cycles. We compute score of the nodes in a cycle and transfer this score to the neighbouring nodes, then iterate over the entire graph until obtaining convergence of node scores. Therefore, the Algorithm 1 may run 10-50 times over entire the cyclic graph until the convergence.

The significant biological process are specific to biological function of a given pathway and this fact is more in correlation with the cellular machinery. The behaviour of *Apoptosis* target process is discriminative one, since it produced higher activity scores with oxidative stress data in most of the pathways. This results was an expected one, since the response of a cell to a condition either normal or stressed is expected to be differential; therefore as a result of our analysis some of the target processes are activated whereas others are down-regulated.

References

1. Dahlquist,K.D., Salomonis,N., Vranizan,K., Lawlor,S.C. and Conklin, B.R. (2002) GenMAPP, a new tool for viewing and analyzing microarray data on biological pathways. *Nat. Genet.*, **31**, 19–20
2. Mlecnik,B., Scheideler,M., Hackl,H., Hartler,J., Sanchez-Cabo,F. and Trajanoski,Z. (2005) PathwayExplorer: web service for visualizing high-throughput expression data on biological pathways. *Nucleic Acids Res.*, **33**, W633–W637.
3. Goffard N. and Weiller G. (2007) PathExpress: a web-based tool to identify relevant pathways in gene expression data. *Nucleic Acids Res.*, **35**, W176–W181.
4. Isik Z., Atalay V., and Cetin-Atalay R. (2010) Evaluation of Signaling Cascades Based on the Weights from Microarray and ChIP-seq Data. *Journal of Machine Learning Research, Workshop and Conference Proceedings*, **8**, 44–54.
5. Kang J., Gemberling M., Nakamura M., Whitby F.G., Handa H., Fairbrother W.G., Tantin D. (2009) A general mechanism for transcription regulation by Oct1 and Oct4 in response to genotoxic and oxidative stress. *Genes Dev.*, **23(2)**, 208–222.
6. Murray J.I., Whitfield M.L., Trinklein N.D., Myers R.M., Brown P.O., Botstein D. (2004) Diverse and specific gene expression responses to stresses in cultured human cells. *Mol Biol Cel*, **15(5)**, 2361–2374.
7. Breitling R., Armengaud P., Amtmann A., Herzyk P. (2004) Rank products: a simple, yet powerful, new method to detect differentially regulated genes in replicated microarray experiments. *FEBS Letters*, **573**, 83-92.

A Novel Hybrid Electrocardiogram Signal Compression Algorithm with Low Bit-Rate

Hakan Gürkan[1], Umit Guz[1], B.Siddik Yarman[2]

[1]Isık University, Engineering Faculty, Electronics Eng. Dept., Istanbul, Turkey
[2]Istanbul University, College of Engineering, Elect.-Electronics Eng. Dept., Istanbul, Turkey
hakan@isikun.edu.tr, guz@isikun.edu.tr, yarman@istanbul.edu.tr

Abstract. In this paper, a novel hybrid Electrocardiogram (ECG) signal compression algorithm based on the generation process of the Variable-Length Classified Signature and Envelope Vector Sets (VL-CSEVS) is proposed. Assessment results reveal that the proposed algorithm achieves high compression ratios with low level reconstruction error while preserving diagnostic information in the reconstructed ECG signal. The proposed algorithm also slightly outperforms others for the same test dataset.

Keywords: Electrocardiogram, data compression, classified and envelope vector sets, energy based ECG segmentation.

1 Introduction

An ECG signal is an essential biological signal for the monitoring and diagnosis of heart diseases. ECG signals are most widely used in applications such as monitoring or long-term recording. The amount of ECG data grows depending upon sampling rate, sampling precision, number of lead and recording time. Evidently, huge amount of ECG data needs high storage capacity. Therefore, an effective ECG compression algorithm which removes redundant information from the ECG signal is required, while retaining all clinically significant features [1]. In the literature, several powerful ECG compression algorithms were reported in [2-4]. In our previous research work, ECG signals were modeled by using predefined signature and envelope vector sets [5].

2 Proposed Compression Algorithm

In the proposed algorithm, each ECG signal is first normalized to 500 Hz using cubic spline interpolation technique for the purpose of standardization and then, is normalized between the values 0 and +1. After that, the energy based segmentation method that splits ECG signal into two different lengths according to the energy variation of the signal is utilized to improve the compression performance of the proposed algorithm is carried out. This segmentation method divides the ECG frames with high energy into the short segments whose length is 16 samples while the ECG

E. Gelenbe et al. (eds.), *Computer and Information Sciences*, Lecture Notes
in Electrical Engineering 62, DOI 10.1007/978-90-481-9794-1_19,
© Springer Science+Business Media B.V. 2010

frames with low energy are divided into the long segments whose each contains 64 samples. After the preprocessing stage, the signature and the envelope vectors are generated by using the procedure given [5]. There were a lot of signature vectors which are similar to each other. This type of repetitive similarity properties have also observed among the envelope vectors. The vectors in the signature and envelope set were clustered by using an effective k-means clustering algorithm [1] and the centroid vectors of each cluster were determined for these two vector types which are called as classified signature vectors (CSV) and classified envelope vectors (CEV). The CSVs are collected under either the Classified Signature Set-16 (CSS$_{16}$) or the Classified Signature Set-64 (CSS$_{64}$) according to their segment length. The CSVs are represented by Ψ_{NS}. In the same way, the CEVs are collected under either the Classified Envelope Set-16 (CES$_{16}$) or the Classified Envelope Set-64 (CES$_{64}$) according to their segment length. The CEVs are represented by Φ_{NS}. Afterwards, CSS$_{16}$, CES$_{16}$, CSS$_{64}$, and CES$_{64}$ are collected in the VL-CSEVS.

Step 1: The original ECG signal first is normalized and segmented in the preprocessing stage. If the segment length is 16 the switch-codebook bit b_{SWCB} is assigned as 1. Otherwise, b_{SWCB} is equal to 0.

Step 2a: An appropriate CSV from either CSS$_{16}$ or CSS$_{64}$ according to the value of b_{SWCB} is pulled such as the error which is given below is minimized for all $\tilde{R} = 1,2,\dots,R,\dots,N_S$

$$\delta_R = min\{\|V_{i1} - \Psi_R\|^2\} = \|V_{i1} - \Psi_R\|^2$$

Step 2b: The index number R that refers to CSV is stored.

Step 3a: An appropriate CEV from either CES$_{16}$ or CES$_{64}$ according to the value of b_{SWCB} is pulled such as the error shown below is minimized for all $\tilde{K} = 1,2,\dots,K,\dots,N_E$.

Step 3b: The index number K that refers to CEV is stored.

$$\delta_K = min\{\|X_i - C_R\Phi_R\Psi_R\|^2\} = \|X_i - C_R\Phi_K\Psi_R\|^2$$

Step 4: A new gain coefficient factor C_i is replaced with C_R by computing as follows,

$$C_i = \frac{(\Phi_K\Psi_R)^T X_i}{(\Phi_K\Psi_R)^T(\Phi_K\Psi_R)}$$

so that the global error which is given below is minimized.

$$\delta_{GLOBAL} = \|X_i - C_R\Phi_K\Psi_R\|^2$$

Step 5: At this step, the segment X_{Ai} is approximated by

$$X_{Ai} = C_i\Phi_K\Psi_R$$

Step 6: The above steps is repeated to determine the model parameters R, K, and C_i for each segment of ECG signal and $\hat{X}_{rec}$ is reconstructed.

$$\hat{X}_{rec} = [X_{A1} \quad X_{A2} \quad X_{A3} \quad \dots \quad X_{AN_F}]$$

Step 7: Residual error is figured out by subtracting $\hat{X}_{rec}$ from the original ECG signal.

$$err = X - \hat{X}_{rec}$$

Step 8: The residual error is down-sampled by two using cubic spline interpolation technique and three-level discrete wavelet transform using Biorthogonal wavelet (Bior 4.4) is applied to the down-sampled residual signal.

Step 9: The modified two-role encoder [4] is employed for coding the obtained wavelet coefficient, and thus, the encoded residual bit stream is obtained.

Step 10: The encoded bit stream of the index number of R and K is obtained by using Huffman coding.

Step 12: The new gain coefficients C_i are coded by using 6 bits.

Algorithm 1. The Encoder part of the proposed algorithm

Step 1: The encoded bit stream of the index number of R and K are decoded by using Huffman decoder.

Step 2: For each segment, the index number of R and K are used to pull the appropriate CSV and CEV from the VL-CSEVS according to the switch-codebook bit b_{SWCB}.

Step 3: The each segment X_{Ai} is approximated by the following mathematical model.

$$X_{Ai} = C_i \Phi_K \Psi_R$$

Step 4: The reconstructed ECG signal $\hat{X}_{rec}$ is produced by

$$\hat{X}_{rec} = [X_{A1} \quad X_{A2} \quad X_{A3} \quad \cdots \quad X_{AN_F}]$$

Step 5: The encoded bit stream of the residual signal is decoded by using the modified two-role decoder [4].

Step 6: The reconstructed residual signal err_{rec} is produced by applying the inverse wavelet transformation and up-sampling process by a factor of two, respectively.

Step 7: In the final step, the reconstruction process of the ECG signal was accomplished by adding the reconstructed residual signal to the reconstructed ECG signal as follows.

$$X_{rec} = \hat{X}_{rec} + err_{rec}$$

Algorithm 2. The Decoder part of the proposed algorithm

3   Simulation Results

Arrhythmia MIT-BIH Database [6] was used in this paper. In this experiment, VL-CSEVS which was constructed contains two different segment length, 16 and 64 as shown in Table 1. In order to carry out fair comparison, the same test dataset used in [2-4] were chosen. This test dataset taken from MIT-BIH arrhythmia database contains first of 6.4-sec length of data extracted from records 100, 101, 102, 103, 107, 109, 111, 115, 117, 118 and 119. Since acceptable values of PRD[1] were reported as less than 9% in the literature, it can be emphasized that the results obtained in the proposed compression algorithm provides high compression ratio with very good PRD levels. The newly proposed algorithm was compared to three powerful ECG compression methods SPITH [2], Blanco-Valesco [3], and Benzid [4] in terms of average PRD and average CR as shown in Figure 1.

4   Conclusion

In this research work, both the size of VL-CSEVS and the computational complexity of the searching and matching process are reduced drastically in comparison with our previous work [5]. As a result of that, the CR of the proposed algorithm is significantly improved in comparison with the results of our previous method [5]. Besides, the low PRD is ensured by applying the residual error coding. Moreover, the average encoding and decoding time are 0.78 and 0.347 second, respectively. In this sense, it can be emphasized that it is suitable for real-time implementation. The

---

[1] Each signal in the MIT-BIH Arrhythmia Database included a baseline of 1024 added for storage purpose. Consequently, the PRD is computed by subtracting 1024 from each sample.

performance of the proposed algorithm is evaluated and compared to the three powerful ECG compression methods mentioned in [2-4]. The results of the performance evaluations show that the proposed algorithm provides slightly better results than the other methods in terms of average CR and PRD.

Table 1. The number of CSV, CEV, and the required total bit in the VL-CSEVS

L_F	N_S	N_E	$b_{total}=b_{SWCB}+b_C+b_R+b_K$
16	8	64	1+6+3+6=16
64	8	128	1+6+3+7=17

Fig. 1. Comparison results of the proposed algorithm

Acknowledgements. The present work was supported by Scientific Research Fund of ISIK University, Project Number 06B302.

References

1. Rangayyan, R.M.: Biomedical Signal Analysis: A Case Study Approach, Wiley (2002)
2. Lu, Z., Kim, D.Y., Pearlman, W.A.: Wavelet Compression of ECG Signals by the Set Partitioning in Hierarchical Trees (SPIHT) Algorithm. IEEE Transactions on Biomedical Engineering, Vol. 47, No. 7, 849--856 (2000)
3. Blanco-Valesco, M., Cruz-Roldan, F., Godino-Llorente, J.I., Barner, K.E.: ECG compression with retrieved quality guaranteed. Electron Letters, Vol. 40, No. 23, 1466--1467 (2004)
4. Benzid, R., Marir, F., Bouguechal, N.E.: Electrocardiagram Compression Method based on the Adaptive Wavelet Coefficients Quantization Combined to a Modified Two-Role Encoder. IEEE Signal Processing Letters, Vol. 14, No. 6, 373--376 (2007)
5. Gurkan, H., Guz, U., Yarman, B.S.: Modeling of Electrocardiogram Signals Using Predefined Signature and Envelope Vector Sets. EURASIP Journal on Applied Signal Processing Special issue on Advances in Electrocardiogram Signal Processing and Analysis. Vol. 2007, Article ID. 12071, Doi. 10.1155/2007/12071, 1--12 (2007)
6. Moody, G.B.: The MIT-BIH Arrhythmia Database CD-ROM. Second Ed., Harvard-MIT Division of Health Sciences and Technology (1992)

4 Data Engineering

A Roadmap for Semantifying Recommender Systems Using Preference Management

Dilek Tapucu[1], Fatih Tekbacak[1], Murat Osman Ünalır[2], Seda Kasap[1]

[1] Izmir Institute of Technology, 35430 Urla, Izmir, Turkey,
[2] Ege University[2],35100 Bornova, Izmir, Turkey.

[1] {dilektapucu, fatihtekbacak,sedakasap}@iyte.edu.tr
[2] murat.osman.unalir@ege.edu.tr

Abstract. The work developed in this paper presents an innovative solution in the field of recommender systems. Our aim is to create integration architecture for improving recommendation effectiveness that obtains user preferences found implicitly in domain knowledge. This approach is divided into four steps. The first step is based on semantifying domain knowledge. In this step, domain ontology will be analyzed. The second step is to define an innovative hybrid recommendation algorithm based upon collaborative filtering and content filtering. The third step is based on preference modeling approach. And in the fourth step preference model and recommendation algorithm will be integrated. Finally, this work will be realized on Netflix movie data source.

Keywords: Recommender System, User Preference, Ontology.

1 Introduction

Preference management has a key role in order to provide effective personalization [1]. Our model proposes associating any preference model to any ontology resource model. It allows to manipulate the ontology model through its meta-model [4]. In this model, the ontology's instances are taken into account by referring to their corresponding ontology's entities.

Recommender systems represent user preferences for the purpose of suggesting items [2]. Effective recommendation includes filtering methods to predict if a suggesting item will please a user or not.

In this paper, an innovative solution in the field of recommender systems is examined. Our contribution is to propose architecture for using our preference model to represent user preferences. Furthermore, proposed architecture has been integrated with recommendation algorithm(s) in the literature. The main goal of our work consists of improving recommendation effectiveness. The remainder of this paper is organized as follows. In Section 2, we give the domain ontology analysis. In Section 3, we summarize existing work related with Recommender Systems. In Section 4, main feature of the Preference Modeling approach is given. In Section 5, we explain proposed architecture. Then conclusion and future work is determined.

E. Gelenbe et al. (eds.), *Computer and Information Sciences*, Lecture Notes in Electrical Engineering 62, DOI 10.1007/978-90-481-9794-1_20,
© Springer Science+Business Media B.V. 2010

2 Domain Ontology Analysis

To obtain properties of ontology related individuals of domain classes, domain ontology should be analyzed. Users that log in the system can choose their preference attributes and fill them appropriately. Meanwhile, reusable design strategy has to be thought for an adaptive recommendation approach. So that changing domain ontology can't affect the whole system while searching the ontology in granular way. Then different domain ontologies can be loaded and analyzed by the system using stored preferences of users.

3 Recommender Systems

This section presents a general review of recommender system literature. These systems act as personalized decision guides, aiding users in decisions on matters related to personal taste [5]. The key concept to develop an efficient recommender system is better understanding of both users and items. However, traditional recommender systems consider limited data (ratings, keywords) to compute predictions and do not take into account different factors necessary to understand reasons behind a user's judgment. Actual Recommender Systems can be divided in three categories as Content Based (CB), Collaborative (CF) and Hybrid recommender Systems [2], [5], [6].

4 Preference Meta-Model

In this section we present an ontology-based preference modeling approach. This approach includes three model elements: **Ontology Model Resource**: In order to attach preferences to instances of a given ontology, we need to model semantic resource definitions. In this approach [4], the `Property_Or_Class` resource is used to represent data elements of the ontology model, and `Property_Or_Class_Instance` is defined as an instance of that resource definition. Notice that this resource can be defined in all existing ontology model. `Preference` and `Property_Or_Class` resources are composed to `Pref_link` for combining each other. **Preference Model:** The definition of our preference model compiles the different types of preferences (*boolean, interval, numeric etc.*) found in the literature [4]. **Preference Link**: The last part of model consists of a link establishing an association between the preference of the preference model and the class or property definition of the ontology model.

5 Integration Architecture

In this section, we propose why we need semantifying recommendation system to obtain user preferences. In our application, user's preferences are found implicitly in domain knowledge. The corresponding system architecture is a multi-tier application with a *front-end* and a *back-end* level. The *front-end* level includes all those modules that implement the communication between the user and system, while the *back-end* level refers to all those modules that implement the recommendation mechanism. This architecture is clarified in two steps that is explained below:

Analysis and Design: Increasing number of Recommender System approaches are based on text-based documents or database entries. By the need of accessing personal data around the Internet, each user wants to have an identifier document that includes his/her preferred knowledge. With the analysis of this problem, FOAF documents[1] have been determined as an appropriate solution. Recommender Systems use generally predefined algorithms in the literature and the hybrid solutions using them as told in Section 3. To measure performance of these algorithms, a flexible, fast collaborative filtering engine named as Apache Mahout Taste have been used in this project[2]. This project helps us to predict rating values for the user interests. To test our system, we firstly divided our Netflix[3] dataset in two pieces. After doing this process, usage of a semantic web enabled inference engine and a programming environment named Jena[4] has been decided.

Implementation Layer: In Figure 1, our implementation architecture is described with a *front-end* and a *back-end* level in a detailed manner:

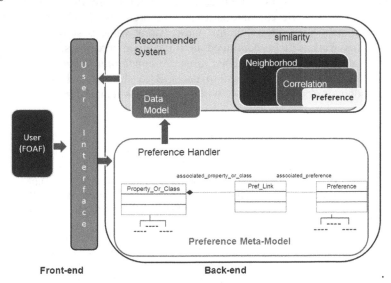

Fig. 1. System Architecture.

[1] http://www.foaf-projects.org/
[2] http://lucene.apache.org/mahout/taste.html
[3] http://www.netflix.com/Default
[4] http://jena.sourceforge.net/

Front-end level consists of;

- *The User Interface Module*: It is responsible for communicating between the users and system. This interface is used for users' login and new user registration. It obtains rating from the users and provides recommendation to the active user. It has two areas: 1. *Test interface:* Developer is able to see the performance of the algorithm on the previously collected "test" dataset. 2. *Real Time Recommendations*: A new user is able to create a FOAF document and rate a small set of M movies.

Back-end level includes;

- *The Preference Handler Module*: It is composed of preferences identified in the literature that is attached to domain ontology [3, 4]. In this paper `Numeric_Preference` type definition which is interpreted by *numeric value* is used. This type of preference is specified with two attributes; `number_value` is a defined type based on integer values, `pref_attributes` associates a `Numeric_Preference` with a list of `Preference_URI` identifier.
- *Recommender System Module:* This module uses the required preference type as an input. The final output of a recommender module is a set of recommended item for a user. The dataset for our study is a subset of the Netflix[4] collection.

6   Conclusion

In this paper, we proposed integration architecture for improving recommendation effectiveness. While movie characteristics are ignored, user preferences are used implicitly in domain knowledge. For this view, rating value is stored as a numeric preference. This work will be continued in three main directions: a), we plan to extend our example (*After Jack watched fantastic movie that is called AVATAR, he recommends it to John*), b) we want to use CB to show social net and CF for semantifying domain knowledge, c) we will try to discuss social search approach.

References

1. Toninelli, A., Corradi, A., Montanari R..: Semantic-based discovery to support mobile context-aware service Access. Computer Communications archive, **31(5)**, 935--949, (2008)
2. Resnick, P. and Varian, H. R.: Recommender Systems, Communications of the ACM, **40** (3), 56-58 (1997)
3. Tapucu, D., Can, Ö., Bursa O., Ünalir, M. O.: Metamodeling Approach to Preference Management in the Semantic Web", IAAA, M-PREF2008 USA, 116--123, (2008)
4. Tapucu, D., Jean S., Aït-Ameur Y., and Ünalir M. O., An Extention of Ontology Based Databases to Handle Preferences, ICEIS 2009, Milan, Italy, 208--214, (2009)
5. Lampropoulou P.S., Lampropoulos A.S., and Tsihrintzis G.A., A Mobile Music Recommender System based on a Two-level Genre-Rating SVM Classifier enhanced by Collaborative Filtering, Interactive Multimedia Sys., SCI 226, 361--368, (2009)
6. Terveen, L. and Hill, W: 2001, Human-Computer Collaboration in Recommender Systems. In: J. Carroll (ed.): Human Computer Interaction in the New Millenium, (2001)

Summarization of Documentaries

Kezban Demirtas[1]   Ilyas Cicekli[2]   Nihan Kesim Cicekli[1]

[1] Department of Computer Engineering, Middle East Technical University, Ankara, Turkey
[2] Department of Computer Engineering, Bilkent University, Ankara, Turkey
kezbandemirtas@gmail.com, ilyas@cs.bilkent.edu.tr, nihan@ceng.metu.edu.tr

Abstract. Video summarization algorithms present condensed versions of a full length video by identifying the most significant parts of the video. In this paper, we propose an automatic video summarization method using the subtitles of videos and text summarization techniques. We identify significant sentences in the subtitles of a video by using text summarization techniques and then we compose a video summary by finding the video parts corresponding to these summary sentences.

Keywords: Video Summarization, Text Summarization.

1 Introduction

Video content is being used in a wide number of domains ranging from commerce, security, education and entertainment. People want to search and find the video content according to its semantics. Creating searchable video archives becomes an important requirement for different domains as a result of the increase in the amount of multimedia contents. Video summarization helps people to decide whether they really want to watch a video or not. Video summarization algorithms present a condensed version of a full length video by identifying the most significant parts of the video.

In this paper, we propose an automatic video summarization system in order to present summaries to the users so that they can decide easily whether the selected video is of any interest to them. We aim to use text information only to determine how only the text data associated with the video is helpful in searching the semantic content of videos. The subtitles provide the speech content with the time information which is used to retrieve the relevant video pieces. For this purpose, we have chosen documentary videos as the application domain. In documentary videos, the speech usually consists of a monolog and it mentions the things seen on the screen.

For automatic summarization, we make use of two text summarization algorithms [1,3] and combine the results of these two algorithms to constitute a summary. Text summarization techniques identify the significant parts of a text to constitute a summary. We extract a summary of video subtitles with these summarization algorithms and then we find the video parts corresponding to these summary parts. By combining the video parts, we create a moving-image summary of the original video. In our summarization approach, we take the advantage of the documentary video characteristics. For example, in a documentary about "animals", when an animal is seen on the screen, the speaker usually mentions that animal. So, when we find the video parts corresponding to the summary sentences of a video, those video parts are

E. Gelenbe et al. (eds.), *Computer and Information Sciences*, Lecture Notes in Electrical Engineering 62, DOI 10.1007/978-90-481-9794-1_21,
© Springer Science+Business Media B.V. 2010

closely related with the summary sentences. Hence we obtain a semantic video summary giving the important parts of a video.

Text features associated with a video can be viewable text placed on the screen or transcript of the dialog which can be provided in the form of closed captions, open captions or subtitles. Text features plays an important role in video summarization as it contains detailed information about the video content. Pickering et al. [4] make summarization of television news by using the accompanying subtitles. They extract news stories from the video and provide a summary for each story by using lexical chain analysis. Tsoneva et al. [5] creates automatic summaries for narrative videos using textual cues available in subtitles and scripts. They extract features like keywords, main characters' names and presence, and according to these features they identify the most relevant moments of video for preserving the story line. In our video summarization system, we extract moving-image summaries of documentaries using video subtitles and text summarization methods.

The rest of the paper is organized as follows. Section 2 describes our video summarization approaches and we present evaluations of these approaches in Section 3. Finally in Section 4, conclusions and possible future work are discussed.

2 Video Summarization

We find the summary sentences of the subtitle file by using the text summarization techniques [1,3]. Then we find the video segments corresponding to these summary sentences. By combining the video segments of summary sentences, we create a video summary. Subtitle files contain the text of the speech, the number and time of speech. In the text preprocessing step, the text in the subtitle file is extracted by striping the number and time of the speech, and it is given to the "Text Summarization" module. "Text Summarization" module finds the summary sentences of the given text. We use three algorithms for finding the summary sentences; TextRank algorithm [3], Lexical Chain algorithm [1] and a combination of these two algorithms. After the summary sentences are found by one of these approaches, the output can be given to the "Text Smoothing" module. This module applies some techniques to make summary sentences more understandable and smoother. "Video Summarization" module creates the video summary by using the summary sentences. This module finds the start and end times of sentences from the video subtitle file. Then the video segments corresponding to start and end times are extracted. By combining the extracted video segments, a video summary is generated.

The TextRank algorithm [3] extracts sentences for automatic summarization by identifying sentences that are more representative for the given text. To apply TextRank, we first build a graph and a vertex is added to the graph for each sentence in the text. To determine the connection between vertices, we define a "similarity" relation between them, where "similarity" is measured as a function of their content overlap. The content overlap of two sentences is computed by the number of common tokens between them. To avoid promoting long sentences, the content overlap is divided by the length of each sentence.

In [1] automated text summarization is done by identifying the significant sentences of text. The lexical cohesion structure of the text is exploited to determine the importance of sentences. Lexical chains can be used to analyze the lexical cohesion structure in the text. In the proposed algorithm, first, the lexical chains in the text are constructed. Then topics are roughly detected from lexical chains and the text is segmented with respect to the topics. It is assumed that the first sentence of a segment is a general description of the topic, so the first sentence of the segment is selected as the summary sentence.

We also propose a new summarization approach by combining the two summarization algorithms, TextRank algorithm [3] and Lexical Chain algorithm [1]. In this approach, we find the summary sentences of a text by using both the TextRank algorithm and the Lexical Chain algorithm. Afterwards, we determine the common sentences of two summaries and select these sentences to be included in the summary. Both algorithms determine the summary sentences of a text in a sorted manner, that is, the summary sentences are sorted with respect to their importance scores. After selecting the common sentences, we select the most important sentences of the two algorithms up to the length of the desired summary.

In order to improve the understandability and completeness of the summary, some smoothing operations are done after text summarization. It is observed that some of the selected sentences start with a pronoun and if we do not have the previous sentences in the summary, these pronouns may be confusing. In order to handle this problem, if a sentence starts with a pronoun, the preceding sentence is also included in the summary. If the preceding sentence also starts with a pronoun, its preceding sentence is also added to the summary sentence list. The backward processing of the sentences goes at most two steps. We observed that if a sentence starts with a pronoun, including just the preceding sentence solves the problem in most cases and the summary becomes more understandable.

3 Experiments and Evaluation

The evaluation of video summaries is a hard job because summaries are subjective. Different people will compose different summaries for the same video. The evaluation of video summaries could be conducted by requesting people watch the summary and asking them several questions about the video. However, in our summarization system, since we use text summarization algorithms, we prefer to evaluate the text summarization algorithms only. We believe that the success of the text summarization directly determines the success of video summarization in our system. For the evaluation of text summarization, we use ROUGE (Recall-Oriented Understudy for Gisting Evaluation) algorithm [2] which makes evaluation by comparing the system generated output summaries to model summaries written by humans.

In our video summarization system, we tried six algorithms (three text summarization algorithms with or without smoothing the result) by using the documentaries from BBC. We asked students to compose summaries of the selected documentaries by selecting the most important twenty sentences from the subtitles. The same documentaries were also summarized by our video summarization system which generated summaries composed of twenty sentences by using our algorithms. In order to compare the system outputs with human summaries, the ROUGE scores are calculated, and given in Table 1. From Table 1, we can observe that smoothing improves the performance of all the algorithms. Our best method is the combination of two algorithms using smoothing, and our best scores are comparable with the scores of the state of the art systems in the literature.

Table 1. ROUGE Scores of Algorithms in Video Summarization System

Summarization Algorithm	ROUGE-1	ROUGE-L	ROUGE-W
TextRank	0,33877	0,33608	0,13512
TextRank_Smooth	0,34453	0,34184	0,13686
LexicalChain	0,24835	0,24600	0,10413
LexicalChain_Smooth	0,25211	0,24976	0,10529
Mix	0,34375	0,34140	0,13934
Mix_Smooth	0,34950	0,34716	0,14108

4 Conclusions

This paper presents a system which performs automatic summarization of documentary videos with subtitles. We perform video summarization by using video subtitles and employing text summarization methods. In this work, we take the advantage of the characteristics of the documentary videos. In documentary videos, the speech and the display of the video have a strong correlation in the way that mostly both of them give information about the same entities.

In the evaluation of video summaries, we evaluate the text summaries of videos. We compare the program summaries with human generated summaries and find the ROUGE score of program summaries. As a future work, we want to perform the detailed user evaluation of video summaries. Video summaries could be watched by viewers and the viewers could evaluate the results.

Acknowledgments

This work is partially supported by The Scientific and Technical Council of Turkey Grant ''TUBITAK EEEAG-107E234, and The Scientific and Technical Council of Turkey Grant "TUBITAK EEEAG-107E151".

References

1. G. Ercan, and I. Cicekli. Lexical cohesion based topic modeling for summarization. In Proceedings of the CICLing 2008, pp. 582–592.
2. C.Y. Lin, and E.H. Hovy. Automatic evaluation of summaries using n-gram co-occurrence statistics. In Proceedings of HLT-NAACL-2003, Edmenton, Canada, 2003.
3. R. Mihalcea, and P. Tarau. TextRank - bringing order into texts. In Proceedings of the Conference on Empirical Methods in Natural Language Processing (EMNLP 2004), Barcelona, Spain.
4. M. Pickering, L. Wong, and S. Ruger. ANSES: Summarization of News Video. In Proceedings of CIVR-2003, University of Illinois, IL, USA, July 24-25, 2003.
5. T. Tsoneva , M. Barbieri, and H. Weda. Automated summarization of narrative video on a semantic level, In Proceedings of the International Conference on Semantic Computing, pp.169-176, September 17-19, 2007.

A Content Boosted Collaborative Filtering Approach for Movie Recommendation Based on Local & Global Similarity and Missing Data Prediction

Gözde Özbal, Hilal Karaman, Ferda Nur Alpaslan

Department of Computer Engineering, Middle East Technical University
06531 Ankara, Turkey
gozbalde@gmail.com, hilal_karaman@yahoo.com, alpaslan@ceng.metu.edu.tr

Abstract. Many recommender systems lack in accuracy when the data used throughout the recommendation process is sparse. Our study addresses this limitation by means of a content boosted collaborative filtering approach applied to the task of movie recommendation. We combine two different approaches previously proved to be successful individually and improve over them by processing the content information of movies, as confirmed by our empirical evaluation results.

Keywords: Recommender Systems, Collaborative Filtering, Pearson Correlation Coefficient, Floyd Warshall Algorithm

1 Introduction

An important shortcoming of Collaborative Filtering (CF) is that when users in the system have rated just a few items in the collection, the user-item rating matrix becomes very sparse. This leads to a reduced probability of finding a set of similar users. Our study addresses this problem with a content boosted CF approach applied to the task of movie recommendation. Our main motivation is to investigate whether further success can be obtained by combining 'Local & Global User Similarity' [1] and 'Effective Missing Data Prediction' [2] approaches.

With sparse data, Global User Similarity (GUS) improves the performance of the algorithm introduced by [2], which uses only Local User Similarity. But the approach of [1] is only an improvement of user-based algorithm. Therefore, [1] asserts that approaches using both user and item-based algorithms can employ its approach to replace the traditional user-based approach to obtain a higher performance. Based on this assertion, we use a combination of EMDP and GUS concepts in our prediction technique. In addition, we process the content information of each movie to enhance these approaches.

2 System Description

We extract all necessary movie metadata from IMDb [4] by using a Python package called IMDbPY [5]. We represent each movie by a set of features including type, country, cast, genre, language, company, writer and keyword. We use two different methods for the distance measure calculation. The first one, applied to strings, checks whether two strings are equal. The second, which is used for lists, measures the cardinality of the intersection of the two lists divided by the length of the first list.

For user and item similarity calculations, we use the Pearson Correlation Coefficient (PCC) method and adopt the solution of [2], which proposes a correlation significance weighting factor in order to devalue the similarity weights based on a small number of co-rated items.

Traditional CF approaches do not take the content information into account while calculating the similarity of two items with PCC algorithm. This algorithm can work without problem for a dense user-item matrix, while there might be crucial problems with sparse data. As a solution, we process the content information of the items while calculating their similarity. We adopt the definition of [3] for the similarity between items. We use the distance measures previously mentioned and the weight values introduced by [3]. The formula that we use for the overall item similarity calculation is:

$$\text{OverallItemSim}(i,j) = (1-\beta) \times \text{CollabSim}(i,j) + \beta \times \text{ContentSim}(i,j) \qquad (1)$$

where β determines the extent to which item similarity relies on CF methods or content similarity.

To prevent the possibility of generating dissimilar users with the Top-N algorithm, we use the thresholds introduced in [2] with an update: if the similarity between the neighbor and user is bigger than η, the former is added to the potential neighbor list sorted in terms of similarity values. The real neighbors are determined as the minimum of N and the size of the list. Item similarity calculations are done similarly.

In order to find more neighbors of users with few or no immediate neighbors, we adopt the approach of [1] so that first a user graph is constructed considering the users as nodes and the local similarity values as the weight of edges. Pairwise user maximin distance is calculated as their GUS, using Floyd-Warshall algorithm [7].

EMDP addresses data sparsity by using available information to predict the rating for a movie unrated by a user. Each prediction is assessed independently of other predictions.

3 Evaluation

3.1 Data Set, Metrics and Comparison

We conducted our experiments using the MovieLens [6] dataset containing 100,000 ratings on a scale of 1 to 5 for 1682 movies by 943 users, where each user has rated at least 20 movies. We created the same 9 configurations as [1] and [2], and used Mean Absolute Error (MAE) metrics to make the results comparable.

Table 1 - MAE comparison with state-of-the-art algorithms on MovieLens

Training Users	Methods	Given5	Given10	Given20
	CBCFReM	0.7889	0.7653	0.7541
100	CFReM	0.7893	0.7665	0.7553
	LU&GU	0.791	0.7681	0.7565
	EMDP	0.7896	0.7668	0.7806
	CBCFReM	0.7816	0.7628	0.7533
200	CFReM	0.7884	0.7637	0.7588
	LU&GU	0.7937	0.7733	0.7719
	EMDP	0.7997	0.7953	0.7908
	CBCFReM	0.7637	0.7562	0.7384
300	CFReM	0.7653	0.7616	0.7394
	LU&GU	0.7718	0.7704	0.7444
	EMDP	0.7925	0.7951	0.7552

The parameters and thresholds used for the prediction process were set to $\lambda = 0.6$, $\gamma = 30$, $\delta = 25$, $\eta = \theta = 0.6$, numberOfNeighbors $= 35$, and $\alpha = 0.5$ like the experimental setup of [1]. β was set to 0.5 for evaluating our CBCF approach. In Table 1, MAE comparison of our two separate prediction techniques including the one using a pure CF approach without content information (CFReM), and the other one exploiting content information (CBCFReM), with Effective Missing Data Prediction (EMDP) [2], and Local & Global User Similarity (LU&GU) [1] are summarized. It can be observed that either by using content information or not, our approach improves the recommendation quality and outperforms these algorithms in various configurations. And just like [1] asserted, when EMDP employed LU&GU to replace traditional user-based approaches, a better performance is achieved. As another conclusion, using content information in item similarity calculations improves the recommendation accuracy for all configurations.

3.2 Impact of β

To determine the sensitivity of β, we conducted several experiments on all configurations in which β varied from 0 to 1. The results of these experiments on movieLens100 are shown in Figure 1. Similar trends have been observed also for movieLens200 and movieLens300. During the item based prediction of a rating for a specific item, the ratings of other users in the system for that item are not processed directly. These ratings only have a contribution to the calculation of the average rating of the item. As a design issue, while making user based prediction, the users who have not rated that item are not considered as similar to the user, whereas while making item based prediction, the items who have not been rated by the user are not considered as similar to the item. Due to the second statement, in order to be able to use the content information of the items similar to the item for which rating will be predicted, the user should have rated these items. Thus, the number of ratings given by a user has importance for our overall prediction mechanism.

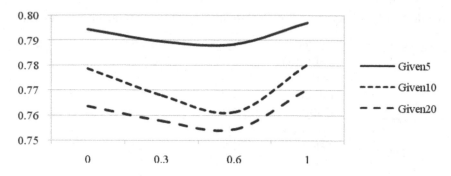

Figure 1 - Impact of β (*x* axis) on MAE (*y* axis) on movieLens100

For these reasons, a decrease in the MAE was observed for all configurations, when the number of user ratings increased. Experimental results also show that more accurate predictions are obtained for $\beta \approx 0.5$. In this way, the prediction can exploit both CF and content based similarity in similar amounts, which shows that both approaches have an important and indispensable role for rating prediction.

4   Conclusion

In this paper, we presented a movie recommender system which uses a CBCF approach combining the local/global user similarity and EMDP techniques and exploits content information of the movies to handle the sparsity problem.

Empirical analysis shows that when LU&GU is employed by EMDP to replace traditional user-based approaches, a better performance is achieved. Moreover, using content information during item similarity calculations improves the recommendation quality of CF approach.

References

1. Heng Luo, Changyong Niu, Ruimin Shen, Carsten Ullrich, "A collaborative filtering framework based on both local user similarity and global user similarity," in *Proc.* of *ECML/PKDD* 2008.
2. Ma, H., King, I., and Lyu, M. R., "Effective missing data prediction for collaborative filtering," in *Proc. of SIGIR* 2007.
3. Souvik Debnath, Niloy Ganguly, Pabitra Mitra, "Feature weighting in content based recommendation system using social network analysis," *WWW*, 2008
4. The Internet Movie Database (IMDb), http://www.imdb.com
5. IMDbPY, http://imdbpy.sourceforge.net/
6. MovieLens, www.movielens.umn.edu
7. Floyd, Robert W. (June 1962). "Algorithm 97: Shortest Path". *Communications of the ACM* **5** (6): 345.

A Hybrid Named Entity Recognizer for Turkish with Applications to Different Text Genres

Dilek Küçük[1] and Adnan Yazıcı[2]

[1] Power Electronics Group
TÜBİTAK UZAY
06531 Ankara, Turkey
[2] Department of Computer Engineering
Middle East Technical University
06531 Ankara, Turkey

Abstract. In this study, we present a hybrid named entity recognizer for Turkish, which is based on a previously proposed rule based recognizer. Since rule based systems for specific domains require their knowledge sources to be manually revised when ported to other domains, we turn the rule based recognizer into a hybrid one so that it learns from annotated data and improves its knowledge sources accordingly. Both the hybrid recognizer and its predecessor are evaluated on the same corpora and the hybrid recognizer achieves comparably better results. The current study is significant since it presents the first hybrid –manually engineered and learning– named entity recognizer for Turkish texts.

Key words: named entity recognition, information extraction, Turkish

1 Introduction

Named entity recognition is defined as the extraction of identifiers of people, locations, and organizations as well as some temporal and numeric expressions [1]. The task is known to be given rare attention on Turkish texts. Related studies on Turkish include [2] where a language-independent named entity recognizer is proposed and evaluated on Turkish texts along with texts in some other languages; [3] which presents a statistical information extraction system carrying out various tasks including named entity recognition; [4] which proposes a person name extractor for financial news texts based on the determination of local patterns; [5] where a person mention extractor for news texts using a set lexical resources is presented together with a string matching based coreference resolver; [6] which proposes a rule based named entity recognizer for news texts, and finally [7] where an information extraction architecture for processing business documents in Turkish is described.

In this paper, we present a hybrid named entity recognizer for Turkish texts which is built upon the rule based recognizer proposed in [6] for news texts. We extend and turn this recognizer into a hybrid one so that it can learn from annotated data and thereby support new text genres as well. The rest of the

E. Gelenbe et al. (eds.), *Computer and Information Sciences*, Lecture Notes
in Electrical Engineering 62, DOI 10.1007/978-90-481-9794-1_23,
© Springer Science+Business Media B.V. 2010

paper is organized as follows: In Section 2, the details of the hybrid named entity recognizer are provided. Section 3 presents the evaluation results of the hybrid recognizer and its rule based predecessor, and finally Section 4 concludes the paper.

2   The Hybrid Named Entity Recognizer

The rule based named entity recognizer for Turkish news texts [6] employs a set of lexical resources and pattern bases. The lexical resources include a list of person names and lists of well-known people, locations, and organizations. As for the set of pattern bases employed, they contain rules for the extraction of location/organization names, and temporal/numeric expressions. We arrive at these resources after examining several sample news articles and try to make their coverage as high as possible[3]. A morphological analyzer for only noun inflections is utilized by the recognizer to validate the candidate entities. Interested readers are referred to [6] for the details of the recognizer.

The hybrid named entity recognizer, based on this rule based recognizer, has the ability to enrich its lexical resources with those that it learns from annotated texts through rote learning. Rote learning is one of the learning approaches experimented to improve information extraction in [8] where it turns out to yield high precision rates. A rote learner for information extraction as described in [8] basically extracts and groups annotated entities with two statistical features: n denoting the number of occurrences of the entity and p denoting the number of occurrences which happen to be annotated. Hence p/n for each annotated entity can be used as a confidence value for that entity. The rule based recognizer is turned into a hybrid recognizer by equipping it with a rote learner component and with the ability to enrich its information sources with those entities which have a confidence value above 0.5. The resulting recognizer can be executed by providing the genre of the input or not. If the genre of the input is specified by the user, the recognizer first uses the learned lexical resources for that genre and then uses the initial lexical resources and pattern bases. If the input text genre is not specified, the recognizer first executes exactly the same as the rule based recognizer. Then, it employs all learned resources to annotate the resulting text.

3   Evaluation and Discussion

Information on the evaluation data sets belonging to the genres of news texts (from METU Turkish corpus [9]), financial news texts (from Anadolu Agency where only person and organization names are tagged), child stories, and historical texts is provided in Table 1.

---

[3] The final forms of the resources employed by the recognizer are available at http://www.ceng.metu.edu.tr/~e120329/ResourcesForNERinTurkish.V.1.1.zip under the Lesser General Public License for Language Resources (LGPL-LR), http://www-igm.univ-mlv.fr/~unitex/lgpllr.html.

Table 1. Summary Information on the Evaluation Data Sets of Different Text Genres.

Data Set	Word Count	Named Entity Count
News Text Data Set	101700	11206
Financial News Text Data Set	84300	5635
Child Stories Data Set	19000	1084
Historical Text Data Set	20100	1173

The evaluation results of the initial rule based recognizer on these data sets are provided in Table 2 in terms of the metrics of precision, recall, and f-measure as utilized in [10]. These metrics are calculated as follows:

$$Precision = (Correct + 0.5 * Partial)/(Correct + Spurious + 0.5 * Partial)$$
$$Recall = (Correct + 0.5 * Partial)/(Correct + Missing + 0.5 * Partial)$$
$$F-Measure = (2 * Precision * Recall)/(Precision + Recall)$$

Table 2. Evaluation Results of the Rule Based Named Entity Recognizer.

Data Set	Precision	Recall	F-Measure
News Text Data Set	84.66%	82.97%	83.81%
Financial News Text Data Set	71.47%	50.31%	59.05%
Child Stories Data Set	71.82%	76.25%	73.97%
Historical Text Data Set	53.64%	70.59%	60.96%

Though the data sets are not comparable in size or in terms of the number of named entities that they contain, the recognizer achieves the best results on the news text data set as expected, since news texts constitute its target genre. For the other texts, the recognizer achieves considerably lower rates.

Table 3. 10–Fold Cross Validation Results of the Hybrid Named Entity Recognizer.

Data Set	Precision	Recall	F-Measure
News Text Data Set	84.84%	87.13%	85.95%
Financial News Text Data Set	77.73%	71.99%	74.23%
Child Stories Data Set	76.59%	95.82%	85.06%
Historical Text Data Set	58.26%	79.71%	66.96%

Table 3 presents 10–fold cross validation results of the hybrid named entity recognizer on the same data sets. The results in Table 3 and Table 2 reveal that the hybrid approach leads to comparably better results than its predecessor. For all of the genres, even for the news text data set which belongs to the initial target genre of the recognizer with a modest improvement of 2.14% in f-measure, the hybrid approach results in considerable improvements in the success rates over the sole rule based approach.

4   Conclusion

In this paper, a hybrid named entity recognizer for Turkish texts is proposed. The hybrid recognizer is based on a rule based recognizer and also has the ability to extend its information sources through learning from annotated data. Both the hybrid recognizer and its core rule based predecessor are evaluated on data sets of four different genres: news texts, financial news texts, child stories, and historical texts. Performance evaluations show that the hybrid recognizer achieves considerably better success rates compared to its predecessor, on all of the date sets. To the best of our knowledge, this is the first hybrid named entity recognizer proposed for Turkish texts. As future work, the hybrid recognizer can be used to extract named entities to be used as index terms for information retrieval systems for Turkish. It can also be used on multimedia texts to automatically annotate the corresponding multimedia data with the extracted entities.

Acknowledgments. This work is supported in part by a research grant from TÜBİTAK EEEAG with grant number 109E014.

References

1. Nadeau, D., Sekine, S.: A survey of named entity recognition and classification. Lingvistica Investigationes **30**, 1 (2007) 3–26
2. Cucerzan, S., Yarowsky, D.: Language independent named entity recognition combining morphological and contextual evidence. In: Proceedings of the Joint SIGDAT Conference on Empirical Methods in Natural Language Processing and Very Large Corpora. (1999)
3. Tür, G., Hakkani-Tür, D., Oflazer, K.: A statistical information extraction system for Turkish. Natural Language Engineering **9**, 2 (2003) 181–210
4. Bayraktar, Ö., Taşkaya-Temizel, T.: Person name extraction from Turkish financial news text using local grammar based approach. In: Proceedings of the International Symposium on Computer and Information Sciences (ISCIS). (2008)
5. Küçük, D., Yazıcı, A.: Identification of coreferential chains in video texts for semantic annotation of news videos. In: Proceedings of the International Symposium on Computer and Information Sciences (ISCIS). (2008)
6. Küçük, D., Yazıcı, A.: Named entity recognition experiments on Turkish texts. In: Proceedings of the International Conference on Flexible Query Answering Systems (FQAS). (2009)
7. Adalı, S., Sönmez, A.C., Göktürk, M.: An integrated architecture for processing business documents in Turkish. In: Proceedings of the Conference on Text Processing and Computational Linguistics (CICLing). (2009)
8. Freitag, D.: Machine Learning for Information Extraction in Informal Domains. PhD thesis, Computer Science Department, Carnegie Mellon University (1998)
9. Say, B., Zeyrek, D., Oflazer, K., Özge, U.: Development of a corpus and a treebank for present-day written Turkish. In: Proceedings of the 11th International Conference of Turkish Linguistics (ICTL). (2002)
10. Maynard, D., Tablan, V., Ursu, C., Cunningham, H., Wilks, Y.: Named entity recognition from diverse text types. In: Proceedings of the Conference on Recent Advances in Natural Language Processing. (2001)

Translation Relationship Quantification: A Cluster-Based Approach and its Application to Shakespeare's Sonnets

Fazlı Can, Ethem F. Can, Ceyhun Karbeyaz

Bilkent University
Department of Computer Engineering
Ankara 06800, Turkey
{canf, efcan, karbeyaz}@cs.bilkent.edu.tr

Abstract. We introduce a method for quantifying translation relationship between source and target texts. In this method, we partition source and target texts into corresponding blocks and cluster them separately using word phrases extracted by a suffix tree approach. We quantify the translation relationship by examining the similarity between source and target clustering structures. In this comparison we aim to observe that their similarity is meaningful, i.e., it is significantly different from random. The method is based on the hypothesis that similarities and dissimilarities among the source blocks will not be lost in translation and reappear among target blocks. For testing we use Shakespeare's sonnets and its translation in Turkish. The results show that our method successfully quantifies translation relationships.

1 Introduction

During translation a text in a particular source language is comprehended and expressed in another target language by retaining the same meaning. Different translations of a given source text can communicate the same message without losing the original meaning. Researchers define objective and quantitative metrics to evaluate the accuracy and quality of translations. In some fields, like automotive service information, there are some metrics for measuring translation quality. Such metrics usually focus on lexical, semantic, and syntactic errors.

In this work, we introduce a method that aims to quantify translation relationship with no information other than the texts themselves. The method is simple and intuitive. In order to quantify translation relationship, we divide source text and its translation into corresponding blocks and cluster source and target blocks separately by defining each text block by a document description vector as is done in information retrieval. After clustering, similar blocks become the member of joint clusters and dissimilar blocks appear in different clusters. Intuitively we expect to have significant similarity between source and target clustering structures, since source and target texts are supposed to have the same meaning and hence similarities/dissimilarities among source blocks reappear among target blocks. For meaningful translations we aim to quantify the similarity between source and target texts and show that their similarity is significant, i.e., not by chance and significantly different from random. In the experiments we use all 154 sonnets of Shakespeare [1] and their Turkish translations by Halman [2]. The experiments show that our findings match with the observations of [3, pp. 352-353].

The main contribution of this study is a statistical, language-independent translation relationship quantification method. The method works without requiring any knowledge about the languages involved. We perform an in depth analysis of Shakespeare's sonnets with Turkish translations. This paper provides some sample results from our findings.

Previous work on the problem of phrasal translation comparison is done by Munteanu and Marcu [4]. They use suffix trees for both source and target languages and benefit from a bilingual lexicon to provide correspondence between them. They successfully create alignments for the source and target languages that have the same word order (e.g. English and French). Unlike their approach of comparing the languages having a common word order, in this study we analyze English and Turkish literary works which have different grammar forms and we use sonnet numbers instead of words as our cluster members.

2   The Method

For translation relationship quantification we first divide the source text into blocks. In some cases blocking may be available in a natural way (for example in our experiments each sonnet of Shakespeare is treated as a block). Word phrases are identified before indexing operation performed. Phrases and words used for indexing are referred to as terms. We make use of a generalized suffix tree approach to identify the word phrases. Rather than simply using single words we aim to identify frequently used phrases, since we intuitively expect that word phrases will be a better reflection of translations. Next, we cluster the source documents and target documents using the k-means clustering algorithm for $k = \{3, 5, 7, ..., 51\}$. After obtaining the clusters we compare source and target clustering structures to measure the similarity between them.

We hypothesize that if target text is a (meaningful) translation of source text, then the clustering structures C_s (source) and C_t (target) should have a meaningful similarity, i.e., a similarity which is significantly different from random, and hence, this implies a meaningful translation relationship.

We use a modified form of the formula developed by Yao [5] for measuring the similarity between source and target clustering structures. Originally, Yao's formula determines the number of disk pages to be accessed to retrieve the related records of a query under the assumption that database records are randomly distributed among the same size pages. Later Can and Ozkarahan [6] adapted the formula for environments for pages (clusters) with different sizes. For using Yao's formula in our problem we treat the individual clusters of C_s as queries and determine how their members (like the related documents of a query) are distributed in the clustering structure C_t.

We use the Monte Carlo approach [7] and generate a large number of random clustering structures for C_t (during randomization the number of clusters and the size of the individual clusters of C_t are kept the same as given to and determined by the k-means clustering algorithm). We obtain the baseline distribution for n_{tr} values (average number of target cluster in random clustering), which is the similarity between C_s and these randomized C_t clustering structures. We decide that n_t value (actual number of target clusters in C_t) is significantly different from the n_{tr} value if it is smaller than most of the random observations. In the experiments we generate 1000 random cases. We refer to the entity n_t as the Translation Relationship Index (TRI) and check the merit of the index by comparing it with the value of n_{tr}. The existence of n_{tr}, which can be directly computed by the modified Yao's formula [6], gives TRI the attribute of a measurement criterion, since n_{tr} provides a benchmark or a reference point. If the observed TRI value indicates that the relationship is different from random (i.e., if n_t is smaller than n_{tr}), we obtain the baseline distribution for n_{tr} using the Monte Carlo approach to decide if the difference is significant.

3   Experimental Results

Before performing indexing operation, we remove the punctuation marks in the blocks and all letters are converted to lower case. During indexing we use three stemming approaches. One is no stemming, in this approach words are used as they are. The others are a pseudo stemmer, which uses the first five characters of words (we prefer a pseudo stemming approach because of its simplicity) for Turkish translation, and Porter Stemming Algorithm [8] for the original documents.

Table 1. Similarity between original sonnets of Shakespeare and their Turkish translations by Halman: n_t vs. n_{tr} values ($k = 33$, μ: mean value, σ: standard deviation).

Stemming	n_t	n_{tr}: μ (σ)
No Stem.	3.76	4.16 (0.094)
With Stem.	3.63	4.24 (0.089)

Considering the different values of k during the clustering process, $k = 33$ provides the most significant difference, i.e., the lowest p-values which are computed using z-scores. The results for Shakespeare's sonnets and their Turkish translations by Halman can be seen in Table 1. The n_{tr} mean values are exactly the same as the ones obtained by the modified Yao's formula.

As provided in Table 1, TRI values (n_t) are smaller than those of the Monte Carlo n_{tr} values. This means that the cluster formations for the translator show a similarity to the clustering structure of the original sonnets, which is different from random. In most of the cases considering the different values of k, the results of two-tailed z-tests indicate that, for both stemmed and unstemmed versions, those cases are statistically significantly different from random.

4   Conclusion and Future Work

In this study, we propose a cluster-based approach for quantifying translation relationship between source and target texts. Our method can only indicate that a translation retains the meaning of source text and does not say anything about the style. It can be used with any pair of languages without requiring any knowledge about them. In the experiments we successfully quantify relationship between Shakespeare's sonnets and its Turkish translations.

Our method can complement and be used in connection with other more conventional translation quality measurement methods which are based on lexical, semantic, and syntactic type information. As future work, further experiments with additional data can be interesting, e.g., doing a similar investigation using translations of the sonnets in other languages. It would be interesting to investigate the effects of block size granularity on performance. Furthermore, the method can be used for plagiarism detection both in intra- and inter-language platforms.

Acknowledgments. This research is supported by the Scientific and Technical Research Council of Turkey (TÜBİTAK) under the grant number 109E006. We would like to thank Pınar Duygulu, Jon M. Patton, and literary scholars Talât Sait Halman and Bülent Bozkurt for their helpful pointers and constructive comments.

References

1. Ledger, G.:   Shakespeare's   sonnets.   http://www.shakespeares-sonnets.com/sonn01.htm (2010)
2. Halman, T.S.: William Shakespeare Soneler, 8th ed. Dünya Kitapları, İstanbul (2004)
3. Enginün, İ.: Türkçede Shakespeare. Dergah Yayınları, İstanbul (2008)
4. Munteanu, D.S., Marcu, D.: Processing comparable corpora with bilingual suffix trees. In: EMNLP '02: Proceedings of the ACL-02 conference on Empirical methods in natural language processing, Morristown, NJ, USA (2002) 289–295
5. Yao, S.B.: Approximating block accesses in database organizations. Commun. ACM **20**(4) (1977) 260–261
6. Can, F., Ozkarahan, E.A.: Concepts and effectiveness of the cover-coefficient-based clustering methodology for text databases. ACM Trans. Database Syst. **15**(4) (1990) 483–517
7. Jain, A.K., Dubes, R.C.: Algorithms for Clustering Data. Prentice Hall (1988)
8. Porter, M.F. In: An algorithm for suffix stripping. Morgan Kaufmann Publishers Inc., San Francisco, CA, USA (1997) 313–316

Conceptual Hierarchical Clustering of Documents using Wikipedia knowledge

Gerasimos Spanakis, Georgios Siolas and Andreas Stafylopatis

Intelligent Systems Laboratory
School of Electrical and Computer Engineering
National Technical University of Athens
15780, Zografou, Athens, Greece

Abstract. In this paper, we propose a novel method for conceptual hierarchical clustering of documents using knowledge extracted from Wikipedia. A robust and compact document representation is built in real-time using the Wikipedia API. The clustering process is hierarchical and creates cluster labels which are descriptive and important for the examined corpus. Experiments show that the proposed technique greatly improves over the baseline approach.

1 Introduction

Nowadays, Wikipedia has become one of the largest knowledge repositories with many advantages (size, dense link structure between articles, brief anchor texts e.t.c). This paper introduces an efficient Conceptual Hierarchical Clustering (CHC) technique of documents, using a document representation based on Wikipedia knowledge and exploiting Wikipedia article features (ingoing/outgoing links etc.) Clusters produced have labels, informative of the content of the documents assigned to each specific cluster.

2 Related work

There has been a growing amount of research in ways of enhancing text categorization and clustering by introducing Wikipedia external knowledge [3], [1]. Gabrilovich and Markovitch [3], propose a method to improve text classification performance by enriching document representation with Wikipedia concepts. Banerjee et al. [1] extend the method applied in [3] by using query strings created from document texts to retrieve relevant Wikipedia articles. Both methods only augment document representation with Wikipedia concepts content without considering the hierarchical structure of Wikipedia or any other features of the ontology. All of the papers mentioned above, rely on existing clustering techniques (mostly k-Nearest Neighbors and Hierarchical Agglomerative Clustering) whereas in this paper we extend the idea of [5] and introduce a novel clustering technique, Conceptual Hierarchical Clustering (CHC).

E. Gelenbe et al. (eds.), *Computer and Information Sciences*, Lecture Notes in Electrical Engineering 62, DOI 10.1007/978-90-481-9794-1_25,
© Springer Science+Business Media B.V. 2010

3   Document Representation Model using Wikipedia

Our goal is to extract Wikipedia concepts which are described by one or more consecutive words of the document. In our approach, we overcome the bottle-neck of extracting all possible N-grams, by choosing to annotate each document's text with Part-of-Speech information using the TreeTagger tool provided by [8]. Wikipedia articles have descriptive titles, so it is not necessary to perform stemming or remove stop words during document preprocessing. After this procedure, we keep those consecutive words which are nouns and proper nouns (singular or mass or plural) along with prepositions, subordinating or coordinating conjunctions and the word *to* (POS tags in the Penn Treebank Tagset [6]). By grouping consecutive words with the previous POS tags we perform full *Noun Phrase* extraction, forming our candidate concepts.

For each candidate concept, we automatically check "on-the-fly" whether it exists or not as a Wikipedia article using the Wikipedia API. If the concept has multiple senses (so there are multiple Wikipedia articles referring to the same Noun Phrase), we use the disambiguation technique proposed by [2] in order to choose the most appropriate sense. Once we obtain a unique mapping between the candidate concept and Wikipedia, the concept is selected as a component of the document vector which is about to be formed. At the same time, using the Wikipedia API, for every selected concept i, we extract the features presented below :

- $Content_i$: the corresponding Wikipedia article text
- $Links_i$: links from the corresponding article to other articles
- $BackLinks_i$: articles which have a link to the examined article
- $PageHits_i$: the articles in which the examined article (Noun Phrase) is simply present, either as link or not (plain text)

After the extraction of the features mentioned above for every concept i in a document j, we combine them with the original document features, as described in the equations below, in order to form a richer document representation.

- Weighted Frequency ($Wfreq$) is defined by :

$$WFreq_{j,i} = size_i * frequency_{j,i} \qquad (1)$$

where : $size_i$ is the number of words that form concept i and $frequency_{j,i}$ stands for how many times concept i occurs in document j.

- $LinkRank$ is a measure of how many links a concept has in common with the total of those contained in a document, thus it is a measure of the importance of the concept to the document and is formally defined as :

$$LinkRank_{j,i} = \frac{|Links_i \cap Links_{Doc_j}|}{|Links_{Doc_j}|} \qquad (2)$$

where : $Links_i$ is the set of Links of concept i and $Links_{Doc_j}$ is the set of Links of document j, defined as all the links of all concepts that represent document j.

- *ConceptSim* is the similarity between the document and the article text of a concept contained in the document, computed in the classic term frequency - inverse document frequency $(tf - idf)$ vector space, which is given by the following equation :

$$ConceptSim_{j,i} = \cos(\mathbf{v}_j, \mathbf{v}_i) \tag{3}$$

where : $\mathbf{v}_j$ is the $tf - idf$ vector of document j, $\mathbf{v}_i$ is the $tf - idf$ vector of the Wikipedia article text corresponding to concept i and cos is the cosine function which computes the similarity between the two vectors.

- *OrderRank* is a measure which takes larger values for concepts that appear at the beginning of the document, based on the observation that important words often occur at the beginning of a document. Formally it is defined as:

$$OrderRank_{j,i} = 1 - \frac{arraypos_i}{|j|} \tag{4}$$

where : $arraypos$ is an array containing all words of the document in the order that they occur in the document, $arraypos_i$ represents the position of the first occurrence of concept i in the array (if a concept consists of more than one word, then we take into consideration the position of occurrence of the first word of the concept) and $|j|$ is the size of document j, i.e. how many words form the document.

- *Keyphraseness* is a global measure adapted from [7], which has a specific value for each different concept, regardless of the document we refer to, and is an indication of how much descriptive and specific to a topic a concept is. It is defined as:

$$Keyphraseness(i) = \frac{BackLinks_i}{PageHits_i} \tag{5}$$

A concept with high *Keyphraseness* value has more descriptive power than a concept with low *Keyphraseness* value, even if the latter may occur more times in Wikipedia, but less times as a link. *Keyphraseness* is normalized in the interval $[0, 1]$, after the extraction of all concepts from all documents in the corpus, so that the highest *Keyphraseness* value is set to 1 and the lowest to 0.

After completing the disambiguation process, we linearly combine features (1) to (4) in order to construct a vector representation for each document. The final weight of concept i in document j is given by the following equation:

$$\begin{aligned} Weight(j,i) = \alpha * WFreq_{j,i} + \beta * LinkRank_{j,i} + \gamma * OrderRank_{j,i} + \\ +(1 - \alpha - \beta - \gamma) * ConceptSim_{j,i} \end{aligned} \tag{6}$$

The coefficients α, β and γ are determined by experiments and their value range is the interval $[0, 1]$.

4   Conceptual Hierarchical Clustering

Our clustering method extends the idea of frequent itemsets [5], aiming to provide a cluster description based on the Wikipedia concepts extracted from the
corpus examined. Let us introduce some definitions: (a) A *global important concept* is a concept that: has a *Keyphraseness* value greater than a specific threshold, defined as *minimum keyphraseness threshold* and appears in more than a
minimum fraction of the whole document set, defined as *minimum global frequency threshold*. A *global important k-concept-set* is a set of k global important
concepts that appear together in a fraction of the whole document set greater
than the minimum global frequency threshold, (b) A global important concept
is *cluster frequent* in a cluster C_m, if the concept is contained in some minimum fraction of documents assigned to C_m, defined as *minimum cluster support*
and (c) The *cluster support* of a concept in a cluster C_m is the percentage of
documents in C_m that contain this specific concept.

The method consists of two steps. At the first step, initial clusters are constructed (based on the *Keyphraseness* of concepts and on the frequency of
concepts and concept-sets using definitions (a) through (c)) where the *cluster
label* of each cluster is defined by the global important concept-set that is contained in all documents assigned to the cluster. At the second step, clusters get
disjoint according to a *Score* function which shows how "good" a cluster C_m is
for a document Doc_j :

$$Score(C_m \leftarrow Doc_j) = [\sum_x Weight(j,x) \cdot cluster\_support(x)]$$
$$-[\sum_{x'} Weight(j,x') \cdot Keyphraseness(x')] \tag{7}$$

where : x represents a global important concept in Doc_j, which is cluster-frequent
in C_m, x' represents a global important concept in Doc_j, which is not cluster-
frequent in C_m, $Weight(j,x)$ is the weight of concept x in Doc_j as defined by
Equation (6), $Weight(j,x')$ similarly as the previous one, $cluster\_support(x)$ is
given by definition (c), $Keyphraseness(x')$ is given by Equation (5).

A cluster tree can be broad and deep, depending on the minimum global
threshold and the *Keyphraseness* values we define, therefore, it is likely that
documents are assigned to a large number of small clusters, which leads to poor
accuracy. By treating one cluster as a document (by combining all the documents in the cluster) and measure its score using the *Score* function defined by
Equation (7), we are in position to define the similarity of a cluster C_b to C_a :

$$Sim(C_a \leftarrow C_b) = \frac{Score(C_a \leftarrow Doc(C_b))}{\sum_x Weight(Doc(C_b),x) + \sum_{x'} Weight(Doc(C_b),x')} + 1 \tag{8}$$

where : $Doc(C_b)$ stands for combining all the documents in the subtree of C_b into
a single document, x represents a global important concept in $Doc(C_b)$ which is
also cluster frequent in C_a, x' represents a global important concept in $Doc(C_b)$
which is not cluster frequent in C_a, $Weight(Doc(C_b),x)$, $Weight(Doc(C_b),x)$

are the weights of concepts x and x' respectively in document $Doc(C_b)$. To explain the normalization by the denominator in (8), notice that, in the *Score* function, the *Cluster_Support* and *Keyphraseness* take values in the interval $[0, 1]$, thus the maximum value of *Score* function would be $\sum_x Weight(j, x)$ and the minimum value $-\sum_{x'} Weight(j, x')$. So, after the proposed normalization, the value of *Sim* would be in the interval $[-1, 1]$. To avoid negative values for similarity, we add the term $+1$ and we end up with the above equation. Please notice that the range of the *Sim* function is $[0, 2]$.

The cluster similarity between C_a and C_b is computed as the geometric mean of the two normalized scores provided by Equation (8) :

$$Similarity(C_a \longleftrightarrow C_b) = \sqrt{Sim(C_a \leftarrow C_b) \times Sim(C_b \leftarrow C_a)} \qquad (9)$$

In our method, *Similarity* value 1 is considered the threshold for considering two clusters similar. The pruning criterion computes the *Similarity* function between a child and its parent and is activated when the value of *Similarity* is larger than 1, i.e. the child is similar to its parent. Sibling merging is a process applied to similar clusters at level 1 (recall that child pruning is not applied at this level). Each time, the *Similarity* value is calculated for each pair of clusters at level 1 and the cluster pair with the highest value is merged.

5   Experiments

We evaluated our method by comparing its effectiveness with two of the most standard and accurate document clustering techniques: Hierarchical Agglomerative Clustering (HAC) (the UPGMA variant) and k-Nearest Neibghbor (k-NN) (the bisecting k-NN variant). Two well-known datasets were used for the evaluation, 10.000 documents from the 20-newsgroup collection of USENET news group articles and 6.000 documents of the Reuters 21578 dataset. For the evaluation of clustering quality we adopt a quality measure widely used in text clustering techniques, the *F-measure* [?].

We experimented with various values for the α, β and γ parameters of Equation (6) in order to define the effect of *WFreq*, *LinkRank*, *OrderRank* and *ConceptSim* on document representation. *LinkRank* and *ConceptSim* have the biggest effect on document representation with weights 0.4 and 0.3 respectively, whereas *Wfreq*'s weight is 0.2 and *OrderRank*'s is 0.1.

We also experimented on the *minimum keyphraseness threshold* (MinKeyph) and the *minimum global frequency* threshold (MinFreq) by choosing values which create clusters with descriptive labels. Numerous experiments showed that, if a dataset contains less than 5.000 documents, MinFreq should be set between 0.03 and 0.05, otherwise MinFreq should be set between 0.01 and 0.04. Experiments show that a value for MinKeyph around 0.5 always yields good results in different datasets, provided that there are at least a few hundreds of documents available.

The clustering results in comparison to those of HAC and k-NN, for the 20-NG and Reuters datasets are shown in Table 1.

Table 1. Experimental Results

	Dataset F-measure		Improvement	
Clustering method	20-NG	Reuters	20-NG	Reuters
HAC	0.452	0.521	**80.09%**	**58.92%**
k-NN	0.671	0.737	**21.31%**	**12.35%**
Proposed	0.814	0.828		

6   Conclusions - Future Work

In this paper, we proposed a novel method for Conceptual Hierarchical Clustering of documents using knowledge extracted from Wikipedia. The proposed method exploits Wikipedia textual content and link structure in order to create a rich and compact document representation which is built real-time using the Wikipedia API, whereas the clustering approach is hierarchical. We are currently investigating ways to improve the proposed clustering technique. These include the introduction of a novel disambiguation method, the improvement of clustering accuracy by introducing new strategies and the application of the concept based representation model to text classification tasks.

References

1. Banerjee, S., Ramanathan, K. and Gupta, A.: Clustering short texts using Wikipedia. In Proceedings of the 30th Annual International ACM SIGIR Conference on Research and Development in Information Retrieval (2007) 787–788
2. Wang, P. and Domeniconi, C.: Building Semantic Kernels for text classification using Wikipedia. In Proceedings of the 14th ACM SIGKDD International Conference on Knowledge Discovery and Data Mining (2008) 713–721
3. Gabrilovich, E. and Markovitch, S.: Overcoming the brittleness bottleneck using Wikipedia: Enhancing text categorization with encyclopedic knowledge. In Proceedings of the 21st National Conference on Artificial Intelligence (2006) 1301–1306
4. Hu, J., Fang, L., Cao, Y., Zeng, H., Li, H., Yang, Q., and Chen, Z.: Enhancing text clustering by leveraging Wikipedia semantics. In Proceedings of the 31st Annual international ACM SIGIR Conference on Research and Development in information Retrieval (2008) 179–186
5. Fung B., Wang K., Ester M.: Hierarchical Document Clustering Using Frequent Itemsets. In Proceedings of the SIAM International Conference on Data Mining (2003)
6. Marcus, M., Santorini, B., and Marcinkiewicz, M.A.: Building a large annotated corpus of English: The Penn Treebank. In Computational Linguistics (1993) Volume 19, Number 2, 313–330
7. Mihalcea, R. and Csomai, A.: Wikify!: linking documents to encyclopedic knowledge. In Proceedings of the Sixteenth ACM Conference on information and Knowledge Management (2007) 233–242
8. Schmid, H.: Probabilistic Part-of-Speech Tagging Using Decision Trees. In Proceedings of the International Conference on New Methods in Language Processing (2004)

Data Engineering in Graph Databases

Byron Choi, Haibo Hu, Jianliang Xu,
William K.W. Cheung, Chun-Hung Li, and Jiming Liu

Department of Computer Science, Hong Kong Baptist University
{choi, haibo, xujl, william, chli, jiming}@comp.hkbu.edu.hk

Abstract. Graph-structured databases have a wide range of emerging applications, *e.g.*, the Semantic Web, eXtensible Markup Language (XML), biological databases and network topologies. To-date, there has already been voluminous real-world (possibly cyclic and schemaless) graph-structured data. Therefore, data engineering in graph-structured databases has recently received a lot of attention, where there are limitations as well as scope for significant developments. In these databases, there exist many different indexes and different query languages, *e.g.*, XQuery, regular expressions, Web Ontology Langauge and subgraph isomorphism, while there are few graphical user interfaces for effectively querying subgraphs. In this paper, we examine and evaluate the current state-of-the-art in graph-structured databases with respect to (i) query languages, (ii) dynamic aspects, (iii) data mining, (iv) graphical user interfaces, and (v) modern computer architecture on graph-structured data. In addition, the incremental maintenance of graph indexes/views will be addressed.

Keywords: Graph databases, data engineering, query formalisms, updates, data mining, GUI, computer architecture, assessment, survey

1 Introduction

Graph-structured data (or simply graph data) has been ubiquitous nowadays. Examples of graph data include social networks, biological and chemical databases, web ontologies [46], the Semantic Web [44], eXtensible Markup language (XML) and semistructured data [1, 2]. Some examples of graphs that are popular in recent database research are presented in [30]. The recent emergence of graph data offers an expanding array of challenges and opportunities to database research. *In this paper, we provide a critical assessment of some key developments of graph databases, which will have a direct bearing on their future evolution.* For ease of exposition, we summarize selected recent research, that may be contributed by other researchers, which forms a collection of references of graph databases.

2 Assessment

Assessment 1: Query Formalisms. Graph data model (*a.k.a* network model) has been flexible and versatile to support a wide range of recent applications. It is fair to say that

E. Gelenbe et al. (eds.), *Computer and Information Sciences*, Lecture Notes
in Electrical Engineering 62, DOI 10.1007/978-90-481-9794-1_26,
© Springer Science+Business Media B.V. 2010

the graph data may be retrieved differently in different applications. *Our first assessment recognizes the co-existence of a diverse query formalism for graph databases.* Unlike relational and XML (hierarchical) counterparts, where there have been standard query languages, namely SQL, XQuery and XSLT, there are various popular query formalisms for graph databases. The current popular query formalisms can be arguably categorized into navigation, pattern matching and transformation.

1. *Navigation.* Navigation on a graph can be specified through paths or twig queries. For example, regular path expressions and XPath have been a mechanism for describing a navigation on a graph and XML, respectively. Indexes have been studied extensively for regular path expressions, *e.g.,* [16, 31] and XPath, *e.g.,* [20, 56]. Another navigation-like query addresses checking reachability between nodes in a graph. These formalisms *select* the nodes that are reachable via the navigation.
2. *Pattern matching.* Subgraph isomorphism has been another popular tool for specifying the patterns users wanted to retrieve from a graph database. It is well-known that determining subgraph isomorphism has been a NP-complete problem. Ullman [45] proposed a classical worst-case exponential-time algorithm for this problem. Indexing techniques, *e.g.,* [9,11,18,40,43,48,50–52,59], have been extensively studied for determining subgraph isomorphism. Supergraph isomorphism has been proposed to retrieve subgraphs of a given query graph, *e.g.,* [9,57].
3. *Transformation.* There have been proposals for a "full-fledged" query language for semi-structured data, *e.g.,* Lorel [2] and UnQL [7]. UnQL proposes to use structural recursions as a basis to retrieve and transform a graph. This work influences the design of XML-QL [14], a language that supports transformations of XML data (hierarchical data). Quilt [8] is an XML query langauge for heterogeneous data sources. W3C XML Query Working Group recommends XQuery which draws ideas from XML-QL and Quilt, among others. While there have been proposals for query languages for graph data (*e.g.,* SPARSQL [47]), the design of languages is still in its infancy. The languages mentioned above provide syntax for *transforming and constructing* result graphs, not simply selecting nodes or subgraphs.

While a general query language may subsume navigation and pattern matching, the latter two have more efficient implementations. Up-to-date, there does not seem to be a standard graph query language and there does not seem to be a trend to converge.

Assessment 2: Dynamic Aspects. Nowadays, various query formalisms for querying graphs are being used in practice, as discussed in Assessment 1. A natural consequence is that there are various implementations for querying graphs. Consider indexing as an example. There has been a variety of proposals on indexes for reachability tests, *e.g.,* [12, 13, 36, 37, 49], path queries, *e.g.,* [10, 16, 20, 31], and subgraph isomorphism, *e.g.,* [9, 17, 23, 24, 53, 58].

Update has been an inseparable part of a database system. However, updates have not received as much research attention as retrieval of graphs. *Our second assessment acknowledges the demand for update supports of graph databases, which also appear to have a wide range of implementations.* It is straightforward that different implementations for the same problem may offer very different update performance. For example, our experience in supporting updates in XML publishing [4] tells us that the underlying implementation of an XML view has clear impacts on update performance.

To illustrate updates in graph databases can be technically involved, we summarize our experience [5,6] on updating a reachability index, namely *2-hop* labeling, for large graphs. Minimal *2-hop* labels are constructed in an iterative heuristic algorithm, which minimizes the size of *2-hop* labeling. For example, two heuristics for *2-hop* construction are derived from the SET COVER heuristics [12,13]. To support efficient updates, our heuristics consider not only the size of *2-hop* cover but also the *node-separation property* [5]. When *2-hop* labeling exhibits the node-separation property, the deletion of *2-hop* labeling becomes simple. (In any case, insertions are simple.) We derive *2-hop* construction heuristics based on cut vertices, minimum bisections and node deletions, to guarantee the node-separation property. We show, through extensive experiments, that it is possible to spare some *2-hop* labeling size for simpler updates.

Assessment 3: Mining Dynamic Networks. In addition to query processing, graph data mining is needed to gain more in-depth insights on the data in graph databases, *e.g.*, social networks and the Semantic Web. Among others, community mining is one of the important graph mining tasks where a community refers to a tightly connected set of nodes based on certain relationships or similarities. Many methods have been proposed for community mining on unsigned weighted static graphs, including (i) graph theoretic and spectral methods [33, 34, 41]; (ii) hierarchical and divisive methods derived based on structural similarity and betweenness metrics [35, 38]; and (iii) methods proposed for detecting Web communities [15,22]. Real-world social networks (*e.g.*, blogosphere) evolve over time and pose challenges on conventional analysis techniques, which presume static networks and ignore edge polarity.

Our third assessment recognizes the importance of mining non-conventional networks. Some of our recent contributions to the field include developing community mining algorithms for graph data which represent (i) networks with signed edges using a random-walk approach [54], (ii) networks with time-stamped edges using a probabilistic framework [27], and (iii) distributed and dynamically evolving networks using an autonomy-oriented computing approach [55].

Assessment 4: Graphical User Interfaces. The syntax of graph query languages is often complex. Formulating a graph query demands considerable cognitive effort and programming skills from users. In many real-life domains, it is far from reasonable to assume users are proficient in deriving an accurate syntactically correct query. For example, in biological databases, biologists may require to be familiar with PQL (Pathway Query Language) [26] to query biology networks. Complex query syntax may hinder biologists from using a great deal of database technology. In recent self-assessment of database research [42], researchers recognize the importance of a simple and intuitive graphical user interface to spread database technology to a wider community.

Our fourth assessment identifies that graphical query interfaces are vital to graph databases. This can be justified by the fact that the visual representation of graph data and queries are more succinct and intuitive than the textual representation.

Recently, Bhowmick *et al.* [19] proposes GBlender – a graphical user interface for subgraph isomorphism on graph databases. A usability test shows that novice users can formulate given queries faster with a graphical interface than a textual interface. GBlender shows that graphical user interface offers a new optimization opportunity. Specifically, classical querying paradigm involves two steps: (i) query formulation and then (ii) query evaluation. With a graphical interface, GBlender evaluates partial queries as the user is formulating (drawing) them. That is, graphical interface realzes a unique query processing paradigm by *interleaving* query evaluation with query formulation.

Assessment 5: Modern Computer Architectures. While graph data model is flexible and versatile, it is the relational model the most popular data model. A vast amount of revenue is still being generated from relational database applications nowadays. A reason could be that graph data model has been too flexible such that many important data-engineering problems, *e.g.*, query optimization, become intractable. However, with the advance of hardwares, many intractable problems are solved in reasonable time.

With our fifth assessment we recognize the advance in computer hardwares makes more data engineering problems of graph databases feasible. On the one hand, Moore's law prediction – the CPU speed and memory capacity double in approximately two years – remains practically accurate. On the other hand, new hardwares are introduced in a rapid pace, which offers a new array of engineering opportunities.

For instance, the emergency of Solid-State Drives (SSDs), *a.k.a* flash, as an alternative secondary storage, sparks a host of research on flash-based database management. Kawaguchi *et al.* [21] proposes to simulate traditional hard disks on SSDs. Lee and Moon [25] investigate an in-page logging of flash-based DBMS. Join algorithms have been revisited by Shah *et al.* [39] and Li *et al.* [29]. Indexes (B+ trees) are revisited recently, *e.g.*, [3, 28, 32]. These studies focus on relational databases, whereas it is still open how SSDs, among others, affect data engineering in graph databases.

3   Conclusion

In this paper, we make our critical assessment on selected state-of-the-art of graph databases and identify some research opportunities: (i) There co-exist multiple query formalisms for graphs. (ii) With an unprecedented diverse implementation for graph databases, a diverse update implementation may be needed. (iii) Evolving graphs, *e.g.*, social networks, pose new opportunities for analysis. (iv) Graphs and their queries can be readily visualized and GUIs are preferable. (v) Modern hardwares may make some data-engineering problems in graph databases practically solvable.

Acknowledgements. This work is supported by GRF HKBU210409 & FRG/07-08/I-59.

References

1. S. Abiteboul, P. Buneman, and D. Suciu. *Data on the web : from relations to semistructured data and XML.* Morgan Kaufmann, San Francisco, 2000.
2. S. Abiteboul, D. Quass, J. Mchugh, J. Widom, and J. Wiener. The Lorel query language for semistructured data. *International Journal on Digital Libraries*, 1:68–88, 1997.
3. D. Agrawal, D. Ganesan, R. K. Sitaraman, Y. Diao, and S. Singh. Lazy-adaptive tree: An optimized index structure for flash devices. *PVLDB*, 2(1):361–372, 2009.
4. R. Bramandia, J. Cheng, B. Choi, and J. X. Yu. Optimizing updates of recursive XML views of relations. *The VLDB Journal*, 18(6):1313–1333, 2009.
5. R. Bramandia, B. Choi, and W. K. Ng. On incremental maintenance of 2-hop labeling of graphs. In *WWW*, pages 845–854, 2008.

6. R. Bramandia, B. Choi, and W. K. Ng. Incremental maintenance of 2-hop labeling of large graphs. *TKDE*, 22:682–698, 2010.

7. P. Buneman, M. Fernandez, and D. Suciu. UnQL: a query language and algebra for semistructured data based on structural recursion. *The VLDB Journal*, 9(1):76–110, 2000.

8. D. Chamberlin, J. Robie, and D. Florescu. Quilt: An XML query language for heterogeneous data sources. In *LNCS; Vol. 1997*, pages 1–25. Springer-Verlag, 2000.

9. C. Chen, X. Yan, P. S. Yu, J. Han, D.-Q. Zhang, and X. Gu. Towards graph containment search and indexing. In *VLDB*, pages 926–937, 2007.

10. Q. Chen, A. Lim, and K. W. Ong. D(k)-index: an adaptive structural summary for graph-structured data. In *SIGMOD*, pages 134–144, 2003.

11. J. Cheng, Y. Ke, W. Ng, and A. Lu. FG-index: towards verification-free query processing on graph databases. In *SIGMOD*, pages 857–872, 2007.

12. J. Cheng, J. X. Yu, X. Lin, H. Wang, and P. S. Yu. Fast computation of reachability labeling for large graphs. In *EDBT*, pages 961–979, 2006.

13. E. Cohen, E. Halperin, H. Kaplan, and U. Zwick. Reachability and distance queries via 2-hop labels. *Journal of Computing*, 32(5):1338–1355, 2003.

14. A. Deutsch, M. Fernandez, D. Florescu, A. Levy, and D. Suciu. XML-QL: A query language for XML. http://www.w3.org/TR/NOTE-xml-ql/, 1998.

15. G. W. Flake, S. Lawrence, C. L. Giles, and F. M. Coetzee. Self-organization and identification of web communities. *Computer*, 35(3):66–71, 2002.

16. R. Goldman and J. Widom. Dataguides: Enabling query formulation and optimization in semistructured databases. In *VLDB*, pages 436–445, 1997.

17. G. Jeh and J. Widom. Mining the space of graph properties. In *SIGKDD*, pages 187–196, 2004.

18. H. Jiang, H. Wang, P. S. Yu, and S. Zhou. Gstring: A novel approach for efficient search in graph databases. In *ICDE*, pages 566–575, 2007.

19. C. Jin, S. S. Bhowmick, X. Xiao, J. Cheng, and B. Choi. Gblender: Towards blending visual query formulation and query processing in graph databases. In *SIGMOD*, 2010.

20. R. Kaushik, P. Shenoy, P. Bohannon, and E. Gudes. Exploiting local similarity for indexing paths in graph-structured data. In *ICDE*, page 129, 2002.

21. A. Kawaguchi, S. Nishioka, and H. Motoda. A flash-memory based file system. In *TCON '95*, pages 13–13, Berkeley, CA, USA, 1995. USENIX Association.

22. J. M. Kleinberg. Authoritative sources in a hyperlinked environment. *J. ACM*, 46(5):604–632, 1999.

23. M. Kuramochi and G. Karypis. Frequent subgraph discovery. In *ICDM*, pages 313–320, 2001.

24. M. Kuramochi and G. Karypis. An efficient algorithm for discovering frequent subgraphs. *TKDE*, 16(9):1038–1051, 2004.

25. S.-W. Lee and B. Moon. Design of flash-based DBMS: an in-page logging approach. In *SIGMOD*, pages 55–66, 2007.

26. U. Leser. A query language for biological networks. *Bioinformatics*, 21(1):33–39, 2005.

27. J. Li, W. K. Cheung, J. Liu, and C. H. Li. On discovering community trends in social networks. *WIIAT*, pages 230–237, 2009.

28. Y. Li, B. He, Q. Luo, and K. Yi. Tree indexing on flash disks. In *ICDE*, pages 1303–1306, 2009.

29. Y. Li, S. T. On, J. Xu, B. Choi, and H. Hu. Digestjoin: Exploiting fast random reads for flash-based joins. In *MDM*, pages 152–161, 2009.

30. Z. Lin, B. He, and B. Choi. A quantitative summary of XML structures. In *ER*, pages 228–240, 2006.

31. T. Milo and D. Suciu. Index structures for path expressions. In *ICDT*, 1999.

32. S. T. On, H. Hu, Y. Li, and J. Xu. Lazy-update B+-tree for flash devices. In *MDM*, pages 323–328, 2009.
33. G. Palla, I. Derenyi, I. Farkas, and T. Vicsek. Uncovering the overlapping community structure of complex networks in nature and society. *Nature*, 435(7043):814–818, 2005.
34. P. Pons and M. Latapy. Computing communities in large networks using random walks. In *ISCIS*, pages 284–293, 2005.
35. F. Radicchi, C. Castellano, F. Cecconi, V. Loreto, and D. Parisi. Defining and identifying communities in networks. *PNAS*, 101(9):2658–2663, 2004.
36. R. Schenkel, A. Theobald, and G. Weikum. Hopi: An efficient connection index for complex XML document collections. In *EDBT*, pages 237–255, 2004.
37. R. Schenkel, A. Theobald, and G. Weikum. Efficient creation and incremental maintenance of the hopi index for complex XML document collections. In *ICDE*, pages 360–371, 2005.
38. J. Scott. *Social Network Analysis: A Handbook*. Sage Publications, second. edition, 2000.
39. M. A. Shah, S. Harizopoulos, J. L. Wiener, and G. Graefe. Fast scans and joins using flash drives. In *DaMoN*, pages 17–24, 2008.
40. H. Shang, Y. Zhang, X. Lin, and J. X. Yu. Taming verification hardness: an efficient algorithm for testing subgraph isomorphism. *PVLDB*, 1(1):364–375, 2008.
41. J. Shi and J. Malik. Normalized cuts and image segmentation. In *CVPR*, page 731, 1997.
42. M. Stonebraker *et al*. The Lowell database research self-assessment. *Comm. of the ACM*, 48(5):111–118, 2005.
43. S. Triβl and U. Leser. Fast and practical indexing and querying of very large graphs. In *SIGMOD*, pages 845–856, 2007.
44. O. Udrea, A. Pugliese, and V. S. Subrahmanian. GRIN: a graph based RDF index. In *ICAI*, pages 1465–1470, 2007.
45. J. R. Ullmann. An algorithm for subgraph isomorphism. *JACM*, 23(1):31–42, 1976.
46. W3C. OWL web ontology language overview. http://www.w3.org/TR/owl-features, 2004.
47. W3C. SPARQL query language for RDF. http://www.w3.org/TR/rdf-sparql-query, 2008.
48. H. Wang, H. He, J. Yang, P. S. Yu, and J. X. Yu. Dual labeling: Answering graph reachability queries in constant time. In *ICDE*, page 75, 2006.
49. X. Wu, M. L. Lee, and W. Hsu. A prime number labeling scheme for dynamic ordered XML trees. In *ICDE*, page 66, 2004.
50. X. Yan and J. Han. gSpan: Graph-based substructure pattern mining. In *ICDM*, page 721, 2002.
51. X. Yan, P. S. Yu, and J. Han. Graph indexing: a frequent structure-based approach. In *SIGMOD*, pages 335–346, 2004.
52. X. Yan, P. S. Yu, and J. Han. Graph indexing based on discriminative frequent structure analysis. *TODS*, 30(4):960–993, 2005.
53. X. Yan, P. S. Yu, and J. Han. Substructure similarity search in graph databases. In *SIGMOD*, pages 766–777, 2005.
54. B. Yang, W. Cheung, and J. Liu. Community mining from signed social networks. *TKDE*, 19(10):1333–1348, 2007.
55. B. Yang, J. Liu, and D. Liu. An autonomy-oriented computing approach to community mining in distributed and dynamic networks. *AAMAS*, 20(2):123–157, 2010.
56. C. Zhang, J. F. Naughton, D. J. DeWitt, Q. Luo, and G. Lohman. On supporting containment queries in relational database management systems. In *SIGMOD*, pages 425–436, 2001.
57. S. Zhang, J. Li, H. Gao, and Z. Zou. A novel approach for efficient supergraph query processing on graph databases. In *EDBT*, pages 204–215, 2009.
58. P. Zhao, J. X. Yu, and P. S. Yu. Graph indexing: tree + delta <= graph. In *VLDB*, pages 938–949, 2007.
59. L. Zou, L. Chen, J. X. Yu, and Y. Lu. A novel spectral coding in a large graph database. In *EDBT*, pages 181–192, 2008.

Distributed Database Design with Genetic Algorithm and Relation Clustering Heuristic

Ender Sevinç, Ahmet Coşar

Middle East Technical University, 06531 Ankara/Turkey
Computer Engineering Department

Abstract. We describe a genetic algorithm based heuristic for distributed database (DDB) design, Relation Clustering (RC). Relations in a database are allocated to nodes of a distributed database such that the total cost of executing a set of queries (each with a given frequency) over a time period is minimized. The experimental results are compared with another earlier GA based algorithm which shows about 15% improvement.

Keywords: Genetic Algorithm, Distributed Database Design, Relation Clustering

1 Introduction

Earlier work on distributed database query optimization have used several techniques which are sub-optimal greedy heuristics [8], genetic algorithm based solutions [1, 7, 11], dynamic programming [2, 5, 10] and other randomized techniques [3].

The goal of this paper is to find an optimal allocation of database relations to a set of distributed database nodes. A set of distributed database queries are assumed to be repeatedly executed and the execution cost of a query will be minimized if all relations accessed by a query are allocated on the same node. The parameters are;
  Q: a set of frequently issued queries
  N: query issuing nodes and frequencies of those queries in Q
  R: a set of relations which are used to answer queries in Q
  G: graph showing connectivity of nodes and bandwidths (LAN/WAN)
The chromosome structure used for optimization of a single DDB query is explained in [11]. The objective function of DDB algorithm is to decide the DDB schema while minimizing the combination of both the communication time and the CPU execution time for a given query set.

2 Design of Distributed Database Schema Using GA

The DDB GA chromosome consists of two genes, *"FragmentID"* and *"NodeNumber"*, which keep the node number for each relation fragment. The cost of a chromosome is the total cost of given query set where the best plan for each query in this set is determined by another GA based DDB query optimization heuristic[11].

E. Gelenbe et al. (eds.), *Computer and Information Sciences*, Lecture Notes in Electrical Engineering 62, DOI 10.1007/978-90-481-9794-1_27,
© Springer Science+Business Media B.V. 2010

2.1 Crossover and Mutation Operators

Crossover operator for a DDB chromosome works as follows. First, two parent chromosomes, P1 and P2, are chosen and truncate with 2-point crossover technique is used. Secondly, the genes of P1 that will not be crossed are carried to the offspring in their existing order. Finally, the genes that are crossed are substituted with the genes of the other parent, P2.

Mutation operator doesn't allow the same *FragmentID* to appear twice (i.e. assigned to two or more different nodes) in a DDB chromosome, it simply changes the node number of a randomly selected gene. This makes the chromosome size fixed and no replication of fragments is possible.

Optimization of queries is done by running our New GA (**NGA**) [11] algorithm separately for each query and a fitness value is calculated for DDB schema as the weighted (by query frequencies) sum for input query set. For solving the distributed database design problem we employ a nested genetic algorithm as defined in [4, 6, 9]. In the experiments, we compare quality of solutions generated by our DDB Design Algorithm (**DGA**) against the optimal solutions given by Exhaustive Search Algorithm (**ESA**) and an earlier nested GA (**RGA**) described in [6].

2.2 DDB Design Using Relation Clustering

We define a new method, CGA, based on *Relation Clustering* (RC) that gathers related relations into the same or nearest nodes in order to increase the performance of DGA. We generate the initial pool of promising DDB designs using RC heuristic, rather than creating it randomly. This causes a remarkable performance increase as the problem size gets bigger. The algorithm is given below.

```
Input   : QL[], array of N queries
Output  : RN[], assigned node for each relation
begin
  for i:= 1 to N do
    COST[i]:= CALCULATE_COST(Q_i);                      (1)
  for i:= 1 to M do
    RN[i]:= -1;
    QL := SORT_DESCENDING(QL);                          (2)
    {sort the queries using their costs}
  for k:= 1 to M do                                     (3)
    for i:= 1 to N do                                   (3.1)
      if RN[k]<0 then RN[k]:=NODE(Q_i);                 (3.2)
      else if Rand()<P(Q_i,R_k) then
              RN[k]:= NODE(Q_i);                         (3.3)
end.
Hint: {P(Q_i,R_k):={Cost(Q_i)/TotalCost(all queries using R_k}
```

3 Experimental Results

Our experiments have shown that DGA always performs better than RGA and finds solutions in shorter time. We further improve DGA by employing relation clustering in CGA. In Figure 1(a), the query execution times found by ESA, RGA and CGA are shown. In Figure 1(b), relative comparison of DGA and CGA is presented. CGA continues to give better performance while problem size grows with increasing number of queries. Each point on the graph is average of 20 runs. In all cases our CGA gave better results and took shorter time to find a solution.

(a)

(b)

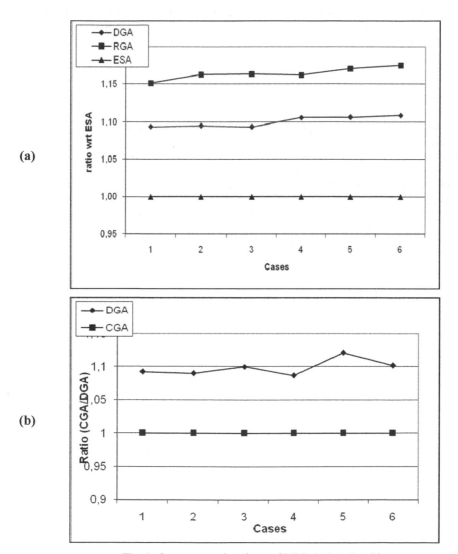

Fig. 1. Query execution times of DDB design algorithms.

4   Future Work and Conclusions

In this work, we have compared a relation clustering based GA with a previously defined GA. We have also implemented exhaustive and random algorithms so that we will be able to compare with upper and lower bounds for the solution costs determined by GA. Our experimental results show that our proposed DDB design algorithm generates DDB schemas which are about 10% to 15% worse than the best achievable solution. Compared to a previous GA based design algorithm our CGA design algorithm is about 10% faster.

We are also currently working on extending this work by including replicated fragments. Update transactions can also be included in order to better model real world DDB environments.

References

1. Goldberg, D.E., Genetic Algorithms in Search, Optimization, and Machine Learning, Addison- Wesley, (1989)
2. Hellerstein, J.M., *"Optimization Techniques for Queries with Expensive Methods,"* ACM Transactions on Database Systems, Vol. 23, No. 2, pp. 113–157 (1998)
3. Ionnidis, Y.E. and Kang, Y.C., *"Randomized Algorithms for optimizing large join queries,"* In Proc. ACM SIGMOD, pp. 312-321 (1990)
4. Johansson, J.M., March, S.T. and Naumann, J.D., *"Modeling Network Latency and Parallel Processing in DDB design,"* Decision Sciences, vol. 34 no. 4, pp. 677-706 (2003)
5. Kossmann, D., Stocker, K., *Iterative dynamic programming: a new class of query optimization algorithms.* ACM Transactions on Database Systems, vol. 25/1, pp. 43 – 82 (2000)
6. March, S.T. and Rho, S., *"Allocating data and operations to nodes in a distributed database design,"* IEEE Transactions on Knowledge and Data Engineering, vol. 7, no. 2, pp. 305-317 (1995)
7. Nahar, S., Sahni, S. and Shragowitz, E., *Simulated Annealing and Combinatorial Optimization,* Proc. of the 23rd Design Automation Conference, pp 293-299 (1986)
8. Ozsu, M.T. and Valduriez, P., **Principles of Distributed Database Systems**, Prentice Hall, 2nd ed. (1999)
9. Rho, S., March, S.T., *"Optimizing distributed join queries: A genetic algorithm approach,"* Annals of Operations Research, pp.199 – 228 (1997)
10. Selinger, P., Astrahan, M., Chamberlin, D., Lorie, R. and Price, T., *Access Path Selection in a Relational Database Management System.* In Proc. of the ACM SIGMOD Conf. on Management of Data, pp. 23–34, Boston, USA (1979)
11. Sevinç, E., Coşar, A., "An Evolutionary Genetic Algorithm for Optimization of Distributed Database", The Computer Journal, Advance Access Jan. 15 (2010)

5 Learning and Clustering Methods

Density Sensitive Based Spectral Clustering

Qingsheng Zhu, Peng Yang[1,]

[1] School of Computer Science, Chongqing University,
400030, Chongqing, China
llylab@21cn.com

Abstract. The clustering effect by using spectral method depends heavily on the description of similarity between instances of the datasets. In this paper, we introduce a density sensitive distance measure which squeezes the distances in high density regions while widening them in low density regions. Experimental results show that compared with conventional spectral clustering algorithms, our proposed algorithm with density sensitive similarity measure can obtain desirable clusters with high performance.

Keywords: spectral clustering; density sensitive; similarity function

1 Introduction

In recent years, spectral clustering has become quite popular for data analysis because it can be solved efficiently by standard linear algebra tools and do not suffer from the problem of local optima [1][2][3][4]. The key problem of spectral clustering is the selection of distance measure which will be smooth with respect to the intrinsic structure of data points. Objects in the same group should have high similarity and follow space consistency. While dealing with complex dataset, however, the similarity simply based on Euclidean distance may not reflect the data distributing, which will result in the poor performance of spectral clustering. In this paper, we propose a density sensitive similarity measure, which can squeeze the distances in high density regions while widening those in low density regions. Finally, a density sensitive spectral clustering algorithm with cluster number automatically determined is present and it can achieve better performance while grouping on most real life datasets.

2 The Proposed Clustering Algorithm with Density Sensitive

Generally, clustering is one of the unsupervised methods in machine learning. However, utilizing some prior knowledge in dataset can improve clustering performance. An important information about given dataset is the prior assumption of consistency, which means nearby data points are likely to have higher similarity, and

E. Gelenbe et al. (eds.), *Computer and Information Sciences*, Lecture Notes
in Electrical Engineering 62, DOI 10.1007/978-90-481-9794-1_28,
© Springer Science+Business Media B.V. 2010

data points on the same structure (typically referred to as a cluster or a manifold) are likely to have higher similarity. This argument is often called the cluster assumption.

Let $G = (V, E)$ be the graph derived from the dataset such that the nodes represent the data points, $V=\{x_1,x_2,\ldots,x_n\}$. The edges $(i, j) \in E$ are weighted by a given distance based function. Since the graph is used to derive pair-wise similarity between data points, we consider to squeeze the distances in high density regions while widen them in low density regions. Thus, we suggest that a pair of data points in the graph will be highly similar if there exists a series of links in the dense regions between them. Otherwise, they will be assigned lower similarity. Let $P=\{p_1,p_2,\ldots,p_l\}\in V$ denote the path from p_1 to p_l with length $l=|P|$, where $(p_k,p_{k+1})\in E$, $1\leq k<l$. Let P_{ij} denote the set of paths connecting with v_i and v_j, $1\leq i,j\leq n$. To find the shortest distance between the two points in graph with different manifolds, a density sensitive distance metric can be defined as follow:

$$D_{ij} = \min_{P\in P_{ij}} \sum_{k=1}^{l-1} (e^{\rho dist(p_k,p_{k+1})} - 1)^{1/\rho} \tag{1}$$

Dijkstra algorithm can be used to calculate the shortest path between two nodes. We construct the k nearest neighbor graph rather than the fully connected graph to model the local neighborhood relationships since the time complexity of the algorithm will be $O(n^3)$ in the latter graph. In such graph, it is to connect vertex v_i with vertex v_j if v_j is among the k nearest neighbors of v_i. To void a directed graph, it needs to ignore the directions of the edges, i.e., we connect v_i and v_j with an undirected edge if v_i is among the k nearest neighbors of v_j and vice versa. The resulting graph is the k nearest neighbor graph. After connecting the appropriate vertices we weight the edges by adjustable line segment length.

The similarity of two instances is dependent on the distance between them. Using the density sensitive distance metric, a new similarity function w.r.t v_i and v_j in graph can be defined as

$$S_{ij} = \frac{1}{D_{ij} +1} \tag{2}$$

Note that the denominator plus 1 is to guarantee its nonzero. Comparing with traditional similarity measure such as Gaussian kernel function which is not adapted to the multi-scale clustering problem, the clustering results by using the new similarity function are little sensitive to parameter ρ than σ[5].

Note that the cluster number is a key parameter needed to be estimated in advance. One conventional approach estimates such number by examining the largest eigenvalues of the affinity matrix P. If the datasets consist of clearly separated, convex and not too elongated clusters, there should be a significant drop between dominant and non-dominant eigenvalues derived from the corresponding affinity matrix.

Let $\{ \lambda_n, v_n\}$ and $\{ \lambda_n^M, v_n \}$ be the eigensystem of P and P^M respectively. For an idempotent orthogonal basis $\{T_n\}_{n=1}^N$, if λ_n is very close to 1, such that λ_n^M is also close to 1, then T_n survives the random walk and is related to stable groups in the data, otherwise is related to unstable groups. The higher is the value of λ_n^M, the larger is the scale of the structure revealed by v_n. The cluster number can be inferred from the location of the maximal eigengap, as defined by:

$$\Delta(M) = \max_k(\lambda_k^M - \lambda_{k+1}^M) \tag{3}$$

It means that the optimal cluster number is k, which let $\Delta(M)$ achieve the maximum.

Given dataset $X=\{x_1,x_2,...,x_n\}$, the proposed spectral algorithm can partition it to $C_j(1 \leq j \leq k)$ Clusters, which involves the following steps:

Step 1. Form the similarity matrix $S \in R^{n \times n}$ by using Eq. (2) if $i \neq j$, and $S_{ii}=0$;

Step 2. Let E be the diagonal matrix whose (i, i)-element is the sum of S's i-th row;

Step 3. Compute P and obtain its eigensystems $\{\lambda_i, u_i\}_{i=1}^n$;

Step 4. Compute $\Delta(M)$ according to Eq. (3) and select the corresponding value k of the maximal $\Delta(M)$ as the number of clusters;

Step 5. Find u_1, u_2,... u_k, the k largest eigenvectors of the generalized eigensystem $Sx=\lambda Dx$ and form the matrix $Y=[y_2,... y_k] \in R^{n \times n}$ by stacking the eigenvectors in columns;

Step 6. Treating each row of Y as a point in R^k, cluster them into k clusters via k-means algorithm;

Step 7. Assign the original point x_i to cluster C_j if and only if row i of the matrix Y is assigned to cluster C_j.

3   Experimental Results

In this section, we conduct extensive experiments to evaluate the effects of our spectral clustering algorithm on different datasets. For comparison, we implement other two spectral clustering algorithms with the reciprocal of the Euclidean distance and Gaussian kernel function as their similarity functions respectively. The results show that our algorithm may perform reasonably well on most datasets. All experiments are performed on a 1.6 GHz Pentium PC with 1G of main memory running on Windows XP. We can use the Rand Index (RI) and Variation of Information (VI) to evaluate the performance of clustering algorithm [6].

The results are summarized in table 1. As can be seen from the table, D-SC algorithm nearly achieves the highest performance. Bold entries in the table indicate which algorithm has the highest performance. On eight among the ten datasets, D-SC algorithm outperforms against the other algorithms. It indicates that density sensitive similarity function used in the D-SC algorithm can appropriately represent the similarity between instances. It squeezes the distances in high density regions while widening them in low density regions, which can effectively meet the multi-scale clustering problems in complex datasets.

While clustering on dataset Soybean-L and Sponges with unevenly distributed structure, the performance of all the three algorithms was relatively poor, because some small clusters tend to be merged with other larger cluster. Moreover, since 5% noise is added to monk-3, it had great effect on clustering result for all the three algorithms on Monk dataset. However, D-SC can acquire 40% superiority than E-SC, and 38% superiority than G-SC. In summary, D-SC is able to deal with unevenly distributed datasets and more robust to perturbed noise.

Table 1. RI and VI for Different Clustering Algorithms

Dataset	E-SC	G-SC	D-SC
Annealing	0.951/0.390	**0.953/0.307**	0.950/0.354
Hepatitis	0.793/0.518	**0.794/0.515**	0.785/0.520
Iris	0.900/0.450	**0.980/0.350**	**0.980/0.350**
Soybean-L	0.401/0.910	0.510/0.812	**0.785/0.605**
Teaching	0.823/0.900	0.867/0.756	**0.965/0.300**
Zoo	0.810/0.450	0.823/0.414	**0.962/0.212**
Flags	0.872/0.518	0.883/0.412	**0.971/0.304**
Heart	0.501/0.634	0.612/0.550	**0.795/0.312**
Monk	0.517/0.875	0.523/0.788	**0.724/0.574**
sponges	0.530/0.814	0.586/0.800	**0.789/0.672**

4   Conclusions

In this paper, a spectral algorithm based on random walk is proposed for clustering. We define a density sensitive similarity measure to effectively reflect the original distribution and structure of the dataset. It squeezes the distances in high density regions while widening them in low density regions. Furthermore, the optimal cluster number can be inferred from the location of the maximal eigengap by calculating the eigensystem of the affinity matrix. Experimental results show that the new algorithm outperforms those with traditional similarity functions on most real life datasets.

Acknowledgment

This work is supported by the National Science & Technology Pillar Program (No. 2007BAH08B04) and the Chongqing University Postgraduates' Science and Innovation Fund (No. 200811A1B0080297).

References

1. D. Verma and M. Meil,a, "A Comparison of Spectral Clustering Algorithms", UW CSE. Technical report 03-05-01, (2003)
2. M. Meila, J. Shi, "A random walks view of spectral segmentation," Proceedings of the 8th International Workshop on Artificial Intelligence and Statistics, (2001)
3. M. Meila, J. Shi, "Learning Segmentation by Random Walks," Neural Information Processing Systems 13, (2001)
4. A. Y. Ng, M. Jardan, Y. Weiss, "On spectral clustering: analysis and an algorithm," Neural Information Process- ing Systems 14, (2002)
5. WANG Ling, BO Liefeng, JIAO Licheng, "Density Sensitive Spectral Clustering," ACTA ELECTRONICA SINICA, Vol. 35, No. 8, pp. 1577-1581, (2007)
6. M. Meila, "Comparing Clusterings - An Axiomatic View," Proceedings of the 22nd International Conference on Machine Learning, (2005)

Dependence Analysis for Regression Test Suite Selection and Augmentation

Hasan Ural[1], Hüsnü Yenigün[2]

[1]SITE, University of Ottawa
800 King Edward Avenue, Ottawa, Ontario, K1N 6N5, Canada
ural@site.uottawa.ca

[2]FENS, Sabancı University
Orhanlı Tuzla 34956 İstanbul, Turkey
yenigun@sabanciuniv.edu

Abstract. Using dependence analysis for model-based regression test suite (RTS) selection and augmentation from Extended Finite State Machine (EFSM) representations of system requirements is proposed. Given an EFSM representing the requirements of a system under test (SUT) and a set of modifications (i.e., adding, deleting, and changing transitions) on the EFSM, dependencies between transitions in the EFSM are identified. These dependencies capture the effects of the model on the modifications, the effects of the modifications on the model, and the side-effects of the modifications. The proposed method selects and augments a subset of a given test suite to form an RTS by examining dependencies covered by test cases in the given test suite.

Keywords: Regression testing, Extended finite state machine, Control dependence, Data dependence, Regression test suite selection

1 Introduction

Software maintenance is an integral part of developing evolving systems where both the specification and implementation of the software are subject to modifications. Regression testing is an essential process to ensure that the unchanged parts of the modified software (i.e. system under test (**SUT**)) have not been adversely affected by the modifications [9].

Research on regression testing techniques spans a wide variety of topics [see for example, 6, 9]. While code-based techniques have paid considerable attention to the topic of regression test suite (RTS) selection [see for example, 5, 7, 10], there is very limited research on requirement-based regression testing and the focus is on regression test suite reduction [8, 11, 2, 3, 4].

Korel et al. presented a requirement-based regression test suite reduction approach in [8] that used dependence analysis of a given EFSM model to reduce the size of a given RTS. For each modification (i.e., addition or deletion of a transition) in the given set of modifications, *data and control dependencies* are used to capture potential interactions between EFSM transitions. During the traversal of each test case in the given RTS, these interactions are computed, and only those test cases that at least one of their interactions is not produced for any other test case in the given RTS

E. Gelenbe et al. (eds.), *Computer and Information Sciences*, Lecture Notes
in Electrical Engineering 62, DOI 10.1007/978-90-481-9794-1_29,
© Springer Science+Business Media B.V. 2010

are included in the reduced RTS. Xie formalized the work of Korel et al. in her thesis [11] and provided an implementation for this approach.

Chen et al's work [2, 3, 4] differed from the work of Korel et al. and Xie in terms of its coverage: it considered change of a transition as another modification type, identified additional dependencies, proposed approaches to reduce a given RTS [2, 4] or generated a reduced RTS [3].

In practice, a modified SUT is tested to ensure that the changed parts of the SUT behave as intended. Thus, a regression test suite needs to be formed by selecting test cases from the test suite that is used for testing the previous version of the SUT and possibly an additional test suite designed for testing the modifications. This paper proposes the use of dependence analysis for selecting and augmenting a subset of these given test suites according to a given set of modifications on an EFSM model of the requirements of a SUT. Specifically, we consider the following problem: Given

-an EFSM model M representing the requirements before the modifications

-a set of modifications on M to construct M' representing the modified requirements where each modification is an added, deleted or changed transition (note that the changed transition's beginning and ending states are not changed)

-test suite $T1$ used for testing implementation I before it is modified

-test suite $T2$ used for testing implementation I' to ensure that the modified parts of I behave as intended with respect to the added, deleted and changed transitions,

consider M and M' and select (and augment if necessary) a subset R of $T1 \cup T2$ for regression testing of I' to ensure that the unchanged parts from I have not been adversely affected by the modifications.

This selection (and augmentation) is based on dependence analysis to identify the side effects of each modification on the unchanged parts from I. All side effects need to be tested since they indicate the indirect interactions within the unchanged parts from I. If test cases selected from $T1 \cup T2$ do not cover all identified side effects, additional test cases must be constructed to augment R to cover remaining side effects.

This paper also proposes that for dependence analysis to be used beyond regression testing of I' to increase our confidence to the modified parts of I behave as intended, one needs to examine the test cases in $T1 \cup T2$ for the coverage of direct interactions between the model and modifications. That is, one needs to identify the effects of the model on each modification and the effects of each modification on the model by using dependence analysis. Each of these dependencies should have been covered by test cases in $T2$. However, if this is not the case, then one needs to examine test cases in $T1$ to see whether it is possible to select test cases from $T1$ to cover the remaining ones (in an effort to avoid incurring the cost of constructing test harness for new test cases). When this is not possible, new test cases have to be constructed to cover the remaining direct interactions between the model and modifications.

The rest of the paper is organized as follows. Section 2 reviews the basic terminology used throughout this paper. Section 3 discusses the RTS selection using dependencies reflecting indirect effects of the modifications within the unchanged part of the SUT.

Section 4 presents the approach for ascertaining the coverage of dependencies reflecting direct effects introduced by modifications on the changed part of the SUT. Section 5 gives our conclusions.

2 Preliminaries

Dependence analysis focuses on identifying data and control dependencies between transitions in an EFSM. Each (state) transition in an EFSM is associated with an input event, an optional enabling predicate, an optional sequence of actions, and an optional output event. Before defining data and control dependencies, we first adopt the following terminology [2]. In an EFSM, a *definition* (*def*) of a variable v is an occurrence of v in a transition by which v takes a value. That is, an occurrence of v on the left hand side of an action or in the parameter list of an input event. A *use* of a variable v is an occurrence of v in a transition by which the value of v is referenced. That is, an occurrence of v on the right hand side of an action, in an enabling predicate, or in the parameter list of an output event [2].

A sequence of consecutive transitions $(t_1\ t_2\ ...\ t_{m-1}\ t_m)$ of an EFSM is called a *def-clear path from t_1 to t_m with respect to (w.r.t.)* a variable v if v is not defined at $t_2\ ...\ t_{m-1}$. Def of v at t_1 and use of v in t_m is a *du-pair* w.r.t. v if def of v at t_1 is the last def of v at t_1, use of v at t_m is a use of v in t_m (before v is possibly redefined at t_m), and there is a def-clear path from t_1 to t_m w.r.t. v [4]. Given that t and t' are transitions, and v is a variable in an EFSM, there is a *data dependence from t to t'* w.r.t. v, denoted (t, t', v), iff there is a du-pair (def of v in t, use of v in t') w.r.t. v. There is a *control dependence from t to t'*, denoted (t, t'), if there exists another transition t'' that if executed instead of t prevents t' to be executed, and t' cannot be executed without execution of t, and in every path in which t is executed t' is also executed.

A test case is a sequence of consecutive (not necessarily distinct) transitions corresponding to a path from the start state to the exit state in an EFSM [2]. A modification on a SUT requires a certain part of the SUT to be tested in a specific way. Such testing requirements will be denoted using the notation given below.

Case 1) $[+t+t']$: Such a test obligation denotes the requirement that the transitions t and t' must be executed, in this order but not necessarily consecutively. A test case $\tau = (t_1\ t_2\ ...\ t_m)$ *satisfies a test obligation* $[+t+t']$ if there exist two indices $1 \leq j < k \leq m$ such that $t = t_j$ and $t' = t_k$.

Case 2) $[+t+t'+t'']$: Similar to Case 1, the transitions $t, t',$ and t'' need to be executed in this order. Formally a test case $\tau = (t_1\ t_2\ ...\ t_m)$ *satisfies a test obligation* $[+t+t'+t'']$ if there exist three indices $1 \leq j < k < l \leq m$ such that $t = t_j$, $t' = t_k$, and $t'' = t_l$.

Case 3) $[+t+t']^v$: This case is the same as Case 1 except that there is an additional requirement for a def-clear path. A test case $\tau = (t_1\ t_2\ ...\ t_m)$ *satisfies a test obligation* $[+t+t']^v$ if there exist two indices $1 \leq j < k \leq m$ such that $t = t_j$, $t' = t_k$, and the subpath $(t_j\ t_{j+1}\ ...\ t_k)$ of τ is a def-clear path w.r.t. v.

Case 4) $[+t+t'+t'']^v$: This case is the same as Case 2 except that there is an additional requirement for a def-clear path. A test case $\tau = (t_1\ t_2\ ...\ t_m)$ *satisfies a test obligation* $[+t+t'+t'']^v$ if there exist three indices $1 \leq j < k < l \leq m$ such that $t = t_j$, $t' = t_k$, and $t'' = t_l$ and the subpath $(t_j\ t_{j+1}\ ...\ t_l)$ of τ is a def-clear path w.r.t. v.

Case 5) [+*t*-*t'*-*t''*]: This test obligation denotes the requirement that the transition *t* must be executed at some point in the test case after which the transitions *t'* and *t''* do not occur. Formally a test case $\tau = (t_1 \ t_2 \ \ldots \ t_m)$ *satisfies a test obligation* [+*t*-*t'*-*t''*] if there exists an index $1 \leq j \leq m$ such that $t = t_j$ and for all $j < k \leq m$, $t' \neq t_k$, and $t'' \neq t_k$.

Case 6) [+*t*-*t'*+*t''*-*t'''*]: Such a test obligation denotes the requirement that the transitions *t* and *t''* must be executed, in this order but not necessarily consecutively. Furthermore, the transition *t'* (respectively, *t'''*) must not be executed between the executions of *t* and *t''* (respectively, after the execution of *t''*). Given a test case $\tau = (t_1 \ t_2 \ \ldots \ t_m)$, τ is said to *satisfy a test obligation* [+*t*-*t'*+*t''*-*t'''*] if there exist two indices $1 \leq j < k \leq m$ such that $t = t_j$, $t' = t_k$, and for all $j < l < k < n$, $t' \neq t_l$, and $t''' \neq t_n$.

3   RTS Selection

A modification on an existing implementation has three kinds of effects. First, the modification may affect what already is implemented in the SUT. Second, what is already implemented in the SUT may affect the modification. Finally, the modification may result in some interaction between two different unmodified parts of the SUT in a way they did not interact before. Model based regression testing approaches follow this classification and perform three types of tests [8]: **Type 1)** tests for checking the effects of the model on the modification; **Type 2)** tests for checking the effects of the modification on the model; **Type 3)** tests for checking the side-effects of the modification on the unmodified parts of the model.

The first two types of tests are related to the correct implementation of the modifications in the SUT. The third type of tests is for checking any unintentional effect of the modification on the unmodified parts of the SUT. Let us call the collection of all test cases used to test the system before the current version *T*1. After the current version is obtained an additional test suite will be built for checking the correct implementation of the modifications. Let's call this test suite *T*2. Obviously, *T*2 would include elements for Type 1 and Type 2 tests given above, since *T*2 is mainly introduced for checking the correct implementation of the modifications. However, tests of Type 3 for checking any adverse affects of the modifications on the unmodified parts of the SUT may not take place intentionally in *T*2.

The reason for a modification to have a side effect on the unmodified parts is due to an interaction (respectively, an absence of an interaction) between two unmodified parts that did not exist (respectively, existed) before the modification. Previous work in the literature [8, 11, 2, 3, 4] identifies possible side effects of a modification as one of the following four dependence types.

Activation Data Dependence. An activation data dependence is a data dependence that does not exist in *M* but exists in *M'*. For a modified transition *t* (an addition or a change), the test suite *T*2 is expected to have test cases for checking dependencies in which *t* actively participates. In other words, if for a transition *t'''*, there is a control dependence of the form (*t'''*, *t*) or (*t*, *t'''*), or for a transition *t'''* and a variable *v*, there is a data dependence of the form (*t'''*, *t*, *v*) or (*t*, *t'''*, *v*) in the modified model *M'*, the test suite *T*2 is expected to have test cases exercising these kind of dependencies. However, if there is an activation data dependence from *t* to a data dependence (*t'*, *t''*, *v*), since *t'* and *t''* may not even be modified transitions, *T*2 may not have a test case checking such a dependence. An activation data dependence from t to a data dependence (t', t'', v) requires a test obligation $[+t'+\underline{t}+t'']^v$. Intuitively, the test case satisfying this test obligation must go through a path that caused this new dependence to exist, and that is only possible by using a def-clear path w.r.t. v on which t itself occurs.

Activation Control Dependence. An activation control dependence is a control dependence that does not exist in M but exists in M'. For a modified transition t there may be three types of test obligations, which are $[+t'+t'']$, $[+t-t'-t'']$, and $[+t'+t+t'']$. depending on the way the activation control dependence is formed.

Activation Ghost Data Dependence. If there is an activation ghost data dependence from a deleted or a changed transition t to the data dependence (t', t'', v) in M', then we know that the last def-clear path causing the existing data dependence is removed. Testing such a removal means testing non—existence of a path and that means there is no test obligation.

Activation Ghost Control Dependence. If there exists an Activation Ghost Control Dependence from an added or a deleted transition t to the control dependence (t', t'') in M' then there are cases to consider: (1) When t is an added transition, the test obligation $[+t'-t''+t'-t'']$ arises (2) When t is a deleted transition, we know that a path required to form the control dependence (t', t'') is disappearing. Hence we cannot test non—existence of a path, no test obligation arises.

While testing SUT I', it is sufficient to use a subset T of $T1 \cup T2$ such that T satisfies the same set of test obligations as the tests in $T1 \cup T2$.

4 RTS Augmentation

Note that there may be some test obligations raised by the modifications that cannot be satisfied by test cases in $T1 \cup T2$. Such unsatisfied test obligations can be brought to the attention of test designers. This might be valuable for the test designers to augment RTS with more test cases as it makes it explicit what needs to be tested, but not being tested.

A similar helpful analysis can also be performed for $T2$ to see if it includes sufficient test cases for checking the correct modification of the implementation. In fact, just like $T1$ is used in Section 3 to complement $T2$ for satisfying the test obligations raised by the side effects of the modifications, $T1$ can again be used to satisfy some of the test obligations of testing the effects of the modifications on the model and that of the model on the modifications. We again utilize the definitions of dependencies introduced by earlier work [8, 11, 2, 3, 4] and present test obligations of each related dependence below.

Affecting Data Dependence. In order to require a test case to exercise an affecting data dependence from a transition t' to an added or changed transition t w.r.t. v in M', a test obligation in the form $[+t'+t]^v$ is needed.

Affecting Control Dependence. An affecting control dependence from a transition t' to an added transition t will require a test obligation $[+t'+t]$.

Affected Data Dependence. An affected data dependence from an added or changed transition t to t' w.r.t. v in M' will require a test obligation $[+t+t']^v$.

Affected Control Dependence. An affected control dependence from an added transition t to a transition t' in M' will require the test obligation $[+t+t']$.

There are four other dependence types in the taxonomy, namely Affecting Ghost Data Dependence, Affecting Ghost Control Dependence, Affected Ghost Data Dependence, and Affected Ghost Control Dependence. All of these dependencies are based on non-existence of a path with certain properties and therefore they require no test obligation.

5 Conclusions

We have presented a regression test suite (RTS) selection method for a given set of modifications (i.e., additions, deletions, and changes of transitions) on an EFSM model based on dependence analysis. We characterized test obligations to be fulfilled for covering the effects of the model on the modifications, the effects of the modifications on the model, and the side-effects caused by the modifications. Then, considering a given set of modifications on an EFSM model of a system under test (SUT), we presented a method to select test cases for regression testing of the SUT from a given test suite that will cover the indirect effects of the modifications on the unchanged parts of the SUT. In order to increase our confidence on the changed parts of the SUT, we proposed an approach for augmenting the selected test cases with those that satisfy the unfulfilled test obligations for complete testing of the direct effects of the modifications on the changed parts of the SUT.

Acknowledgments

This work was supported in part by the Natural Sciences and Engineering Research Council of Canada, and the Ontario Centres of Excellence, and by Sabanci University.

References

1. Belina, F., and Hogrefe, D.: The CCITT-Specification and Description Language SDL. Computer Networks and ISDN Systems. 16, pp. 311--341 (1989)
2. Chen, Y., Probert, R. L., Ural, H.: Model-based Regression Test Suite Generation Using Dependence Analysis. In: ISSTA (AMOST)'07, pp. 54--63. London (2007)
3. Chen, Y., Probert, R. L., Ural, H.: Regression Rest Suite Reduction Using Extended Dependence Analysis. In: ESEC/FSE (SOQUA)'07, pp. 62--69. Dubrovnik (2007)
4. Chen, Y-P., Probert, R., Ural, H.: Regression Test Suite Reduction Based on SDL Models of System Requirements. Journal of Software Maintenance and Evolution. 21(6), pp. 379—405 (2009)
5. Gupta, R., Harrold, M.J., Soffa, M.L.: An Approach to Regression Testing Using Slicing. In: ICSM'92, pp. 299--308. Washington DC (1992)
6. Harrold, M.J., Gupta, R., Soffa, M.L.: A Methodology for Controlling the Size of a Test Suite. ACM Trans. Soft. Eng. Methodology (TOSEM), pp. 270--285. (1993)
7. Harrold, M.J., Jones, J.A., Li, T., Liang, D.: Regression Test Selection for Java Software. In: OOPSLA'01, pp. 312--326. Tampa Bay, USA (October 2001)
8. Korel, B., Tahat, L.H., Vaysburg, B.: Model-based Regression Test Reduction Using Dependence Analysis. In: ICSM'02, pp. 214--223. Montréal, Canada (2002)
9. Rothermel, G., Harrold, M.J.: Analyzing Regression Test Selection Techniques. IEEE Trans. Soft. Eng. 22, pp. 529--551 (Aug. 1996)
10. Rothermel, G., Harrold, M.J., Dedhia, J.: Regression Test Selection for C++ Software. Journal of Soft. Test, Verification and Reliability. 10(2), pp. 77—109 (2000)
11. Xie, B.: Requirement-Based Regression Test Suite Reduction Using Dependence Analysis. Master's Thesis, University of Ottawa, Ottawa, Canada (2005)

FLIP-ECOC: A Greedy Optimization of the ECOC Matrix

Cemre Zor[1] [2], Berrin Yanikoglu[1], Terry Windeatt[2], Ethem Alpaydin[3]

[1]Sabanci University, Tuzla, Istanbul, Turkey, 34956
(cemre, berrin)@sabanciuniv.edu
[2]Center for Vision, Speech and Signal Processing, University of Surrey, UK, GU2 7XH
t.windeatt@surrey.ac.uk
[3]Bogazici University, Bebek, Istanbul, Turkey, 34342
alpaydin@boun.edu.tr

Abstract. Error Correcting Output Coding (ECOC) is a multiclass classification technique, in which multiple base classifiers (dichotomizers) are trained using subsets of the training data, determined by a preset code matrix. While it is one of the best solutions to multiclass problems, ECOC is suboptimal, as the code matrix and the base classifiers are not learned simultaneously. In this paper, we show an iterative update algorithm that reduces this decoupling. We compare the algorithm with the standard ECOC approach, using Neural Networks (NNs) as the base classifiers, and show that it improves the accuracy for some well-known data sets under different settings.

1 Introduction

In multiclass classification, ensembles of suboptimal classifiers are preferred over single classifiers due to the advantages they offer in terms of accuracy, complexity and flexibility. The Error Correcting Output Coding (ECOC) is one such technique [3] , where multiple base classifiers are trained according to a preset *code matrix*. Consider an ECOC matrix C, where a particular element $C_{ij}\epsilon(+1,-1)$ indicates the desired label for class i, to be used in training the base classifier j. The base classifiers are the dichotomizers which carry out the two-class classification tasks per each column of the ECOC matrix, according to the input labelling. Each row, called a *codeword*, indicates the desired output for the whole set of base classifiers for the class it is indicating.

During decoding, a given test sample is classified by computing the similarity between the output (hard or soft decisions) of each base classifier and the codeword for each class by using a distance metric, such as the Hamming (L1 Norm) or the Euclidean (L2 norm) distance. The class with the minimum distance is then chosen as the estimated class label. The method can handle incorrect base classification results up to a certain degree. Specifically, if the minimum Hamming distance (HD) between any pair of codewords is d, then up to $\lfloor (d-1)/2 \rfloor$ single bit errors can be corrected. A good practice in code matrix design is to ensure large HD between codewords of different classes in order to have large error correction capacity and large HD between pairs of *columns,* in order to end up with uncorrelated outputs of deterministic classifiers [3].

Although the tasks of the base classifiers are significantly simplified compared to the overall classification problem, the sub-problems are still non-trivial generally. While the individual base errors may be corrected by using the ECOC approach, the encoding and the decoding of ECOC matrix are open problems. Our aim in this paper is to optimize the original matrix so as to better match the trained base classifiers. This is done by considering the performances of base classifiers over the individual classes, and changing the ECOC matrix whenever it is deemed beneficial, while taking the HD information into account.

2   Previous Work

ECOC is a powerful ensemble method for multiclass classification. For encoding the ECOC matrix, there are some commonly used data-independent techniques such as one-versus-all, one-versus-one, dense random and sparse random [4] in addition to the computationally expensive exhaustive codes, which do not guarantee the best performance. By using data dependent ECOC designs to create subproblems which can better fit the decision boundaries of the main problem, the aim is to increase the overall accuracy and overcome expensive parameter optimizations [2]. Although problem dependent coding approaches are successful, it has been theoretically and experimentally proven that the randomly generated long or deterministic equidistant code matrices are also close to optimum performance when used with strong base classifiers [9,10].

As for the decoding of the ECOC matrix, apart from the usual $L1$ decoding with the HD, weighted decoding approaches, "Centroid of Classes", "Least Squares" and "Inverse Hamming Distance" methods[11] can be used. Many static and dynamic pruning methods are also applied to the ECOC so as to increase the efficiency and accuracy.

Other than the research on encoding, there has been little work to update the ECOC matrix, or to analyze the performance of the base classifiers. In [8] Alpaydin et al train a multilayer perceptron to learn the new ECOC code matrix, allowing small modifications from the original. In [7], the update of the one-versus-one coding matrix has been carried out in a problem-dependent way and the generalization capability of the system is shown to increase.

Our approach is applicable to any ECOC matrix design. The experiments are carried out on random ECOC matrices of varying column sizes for systems having NNs as base classifiers. When the number of nodes and epochs used in NNs is small, increases up to 16% in the overall classification accuracy are obtained through 10-fold cross validation (CV). Since long random matrices used with strong base classifiers are proven to perform close to ideal, there is no remarkable change under this setting.

3   Proposed Method

Consider the ECOC matrix C, C_{ij} as the entry of the matrix on row i and column j, and A_{ij} as the accuracy of the base classifier j, with regard to class i. A_{ij}, measured on a validation set, is the proportion of the samples in class c_i that are correctly classified by j according to the target value specified by C_{ij}.

We propose to flip C_{ij} entries that have corresponding A_{ij} values lower than 0.5 so as to better match what is learned by the base classifiers; i.e. if the decision of the base classifier does not match the target, we consider changing the target. However, to keep the decisions of the individual base classifiers as uncorrelated from each other as possible and avoid deterioration of the row-wise and column-wise HDs, we have a certain criterion on the flipping process. Without any stopping criterion, flipping can yield a decrease in the HD between classes; which can adversely affect the small accuracy gain obtained on a single class by flipping the decision of a single base classifier.

In our method, we first list the C_{ij} entries in ascending order according to their corresponding A_{ij} values until 0.5. By using a hill climbing method, which results in a suboptimal solution due to the greedy decisions it takes in each iteration, the C_{ij} entries are sequentially proposed for flipping. In each iteration, a flip and therefore an ECOC update is accepted if the validation set accuracy does not decrease when the updated ECOC matrix is used in the decoding process instead of the current one. By considering the validation accuracy in this stage, we expect the method to take care of the row and column-wise HD information together with the error correction capacity, and therefore carry out updates without causing any degradation. In Algorithm 1, pseudo-code for the method can be found.

Algorithm 1 FLIP-ECOC

1: calculate A and C matrices
2: list C_{ij} s.t $A_{ij} < 0.5$ is in ascending order
3: noElements←number of elements in the list
4: current state←original ECOC matrix, C
5: **for** $t = 1 :$ noElements **do**   ▷ start hill climbing
6:     nextState←flip t^{th} element of C
7:     $\Delta gain$ ←valAccuracy[nextState]−valAccuracy[currentState]
8:     **if** $\Delta gain \geq 0$ **then**
9:         currentState←nextState   ▷ currentECOC←updatedECOC
10:     **end if**
11: **end for**

We have also studied a ternary ECOC [4] extension of the proposed method, in which the elements C_{ij} are flipped if their corresponding A_{ij} values are below a threshold (e.g. 0.4) as in the Flip-ECOC method, whereas the elements between that lower and a proposed upper threshold (e.g. 0.6) are set to zero. The use of a third label, namely zero, allows us to handle the cases where the classifier

Table 1. Summary of the 5 UCI MLR datasets

	# Training Samples	# Test Samples	# Attributes	# Classes
Glass Identification	214	-	10	6
Dermatology	358	-	33	6
Segmentation	4435	2000	36	6
Landsat Satellite Image	210	2100	19	7
Yeast	1484	-	8	10

decisions are not strong enough to justify a labelling to either class. However, our results with the extension have not shown remarkable improvement over Flip-ECOC and we only present Flip-ECOC outcomes in the experiments session. We believe that this is due to the problematic decoding of ternary ECOC matrices [6] and aim to address this problem as a future work. Finally, we also applied simulated annealing as a greedy search technique. As the results are not significantly different than those of the hill climbing, hill-climbing has been selected as the search procedure for the sake of decreased test complexity.

4   Experimental Results

Experiments have been carried out on 5 UCI MLR [5] datasets. NNs (using the Levenberg-Marquart algorithm) are used as the base classifiers, random coding as the coding strategy and the HD as the metric in the decoding stage (i.e. the standard approach). In the experiments, the number of columns of the ECOC matrix varies between 10 and 150 (namely 10,15,25,75 and 150), that of NN nodes between 2 and 16, and the level of training between 2 and 15 epochs.

Table 2 shows the summary of the 5 datasets. For the datasets having separate test sets, the input training samples have been randomly split into a training and a validation set. The average results are recorded for 10 independent runs. For the rest, 10-fold CV has been applied together with a random split of the training samples into two as above. The size of the validation set has been selected to be equal to that of the training, as it plays an important role both as a flipping and a stopping criterion in the Flip-ECOC algorithm.

In Figure 1, the relative accuracy gain of Flip-ECOC against the standard approach is presented. The trend in the graphs show that the power of the method increases when simpler ensembles with fewer number of nodes and/or epochs and/or columns are used. Figure 2 presents the actual and the updated accuracies for some datasets. When the ECOC setup is close to optimum (i.e. when large number of columns are used with strong base classifiers under random coding scheme), the method starts to lose its capacity to increase the overall accuracy as expected; however there is no significant decrease either.

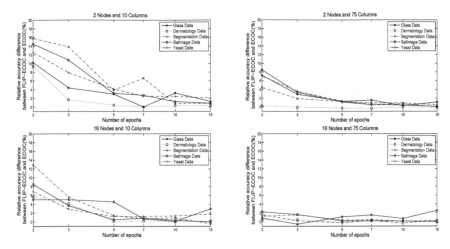

Fig. 1. Relative accucary difference between the Flip-ECOC and standard ECOC approaches vs. number of epochs. First Row: for 2 Nodes and 10 (left), 75(right) Columns Second Row: for 16 Nodes and 10 (left), 75 (right) Columns

5   Discussion

The proposed method improves the default ECOC accuracy in almost all problems and settings. The extent of the improvement varies up to 16% in certain cases. Significant improvements are observed when the base classifiers and the corresponding decision boundaries are simpler; either when fewer number of nodes are used, resulting in a less complex classifier, or when the networks are trained using fewer epochs, resulting in a less tuned decision boundary.

The improvements are larger when the number of columns is small (e.g. < 75). When the number of columns is large, more flips are necessary to change the overall accuracy, due to the large HD already helping with the decoding. However, when there are too many flips the HD between certain class pairs may decrease and counter-balance the improvements to be gained from updated individual base classifier accuracies. Therefore, we may end up with smaller accuracy gains compared to the ones obtained by using fewer columns.

Finally, the proposed method is less applicable when highly accurate base classifiers and long random ECOC matrices are employed, where it is already proven to yield results close to optimal. While theoretically interesting, the use of ECOC approach with large number of accurate base classifiers is not practical, due to prohibitive training time. Therefore, we believe that the reliable improvements gained with very small effort in simpler ECOC ensembles are significant.

Techniques on updating the matrix can be further examined by concentrating on the settings in which improvements were small. Future work is also aimed at using ECOC matrices other than random ones together with different types of base classifiers and different decoding techniques.

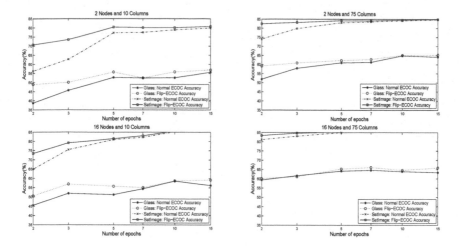

Fig. 2. Accuracies of the Flip-ECOC and standard ECOC approaches vs. number of epochs. First Row: for 2 Nodes and 10 (left), 75(right) Columns Second Row: for 16 Nodes and 10 (left), 75(right) Columns

References

1. Tumer K., Ghosh, J.: Error Correlation and Error Reduction in Ensemble Classifiers. Connection Science, Special Issue on Combining Artificial Neural Networks: Ensemble Approaches, 8(3) 385–404 (1996)
2. Escalera, S., Tax, D. M. J., Pujol, O., Radeva, P., Duin, R. P. W.: Subclass Problem-Dependent Design for Error-Correcting Output Codes. In: IEEE Trans. Pattern Analysis and Machine Intelligence, vol. 30, no. 6, pp. 1041-1054 (2008)
3. Dietterich, T.G., Bakiri, G.: Solving Multi-class Learning Problems via Error-Correcting Output Codes. J. Artificial Intelligence Research 2. 263–286 (1995)
4. Allwein, E., Schapire, R., Singer, Y.: Reducing Multiclass to Binary: A Unifying Approach for Margin Classifiers. JMLR 1. 113–141 (2002)
5. Asuncion, A., Newman, D.J.: UCI Machine Learning Repository, http://www.ics.uci.edu/~mlearn/MLRepository.html. School of Information and Computer Science, University of California, Irvine, CA (2007)
6. Escalera, S., Pujol, O., Radeva, P.: On the Decoding Process in Ternary Error-Correcting Output Codes. In: CIARP, vol. 4225, pp. 753–763 (2006)
7. Escalera, S., Pujol, O., Radeva, P.: Recoding Error-Correcting Output Codes. Proceedings of the 8th International Workshop on MCS, vol. 5519, pp. 11–21 (2009)
8. Alpaydin, E., Mayoraz, E.: Learning error-correcting output codes from data. In: Proc. Int. Conf. Neural Networks (ICANN) (1999)
9. James, G. M.: Majority Vote Classifiers: Theory and Applications. PhD Thesis, Department of Statistics, University of Standford (1998)
10. James, G. M., Hastie, T.: The Error Coding Method and PICT's, Computational and Graphical Statistics, vol. 7, no. 3, pp. 377-387 (1998)
11. Windeatt, T., Ghaderi R.: Coding and Decoding Strategies for Multi-class Learning Problems. Information Fusion, 4(1), pp. 11-21 (2003)

Learning in the feed-forward Random Neural Network:
A Critical Review

Michael Georgiopoulos[1], Cong Li [1] and Taskin Kocak[2]

[1] School of EECS, University of Central Florida, United States,
[2] Department of Computer Engineering, Bahcesehir University, Turkey

michaelg@mail.ucf.edu, licong@knights.ucf.edu, taskin.kocak@bahcesehir.edu.tr

Abstract. The Random Neural Network (RNN) has received, since its inception in 1989, considerable attention and has been successfully used in a number of applications. In this critical review paper we focus on the feed-forward RNN model and its ability to solve classification problems. In particular, we paid special attention to the RNN literature related with learning algorithms that discover the RNN interconnection weights, suggested other potential algorithms that can be used to find the RNN interconnection weights, and compared the RNN model with other neural-network based and non-neural-network based classifier models. In review, the extensive literature review and experimentation with the RNN feed-forward model provided us with the necessary guidance to introduce six critical review comments that identify some gaps in the RNN related literature and suggest directions for future research.

1 Introduction

The random neural network (RNN) introduced by Gelenbe ([1]) has motivated a number of theoretical papers and application papers (see [2] and [3]). What is unique about the RNN compared to other neural network models in the literature (e.g., multi-layer perceptron (MLP) in [4]), where the activity of a neuron is either a binary variable or a continuous variable, is that in RNN each neuron is represented by a non-negative integer potential, resulting in a more granular representation of its state. Furthermore, signals in the RNN are transmitted from one neuron to another in the form of spikes of a certain rate, which represents more closely how signals are transmitted in a biophysical neural network.

In 1993 (see [5]), Gelenbe introduced a learning algorithm for the recurrent RNN, which is a gradient descent learning procedure applied on an appropriately defined error function. The majority of the RNN papers that have appeared in the literature use gradient descent as the learning algorithm with a few exceptions (e.g., see [6], and [7]). It is a well known fact that the gradient descent (GD) procedure suffers from the slow convergence rate to a solution. Gradient descent learning within the context of an MLP neural network has been substituted by more efficient algorithms, examples of which are Delta-Bar-Delta [8], RPROP [9], and many others. Optimization problems where the objective function to be optimized is differentiable have also been solved by techniques that are referred to as evolutionary techniques. These techniques avoid the problem of getting stuck in local minima that plagues the derivative-based approaches, and the problem of calculating derivatives, which at times can be a computationally complex task. An example of an evolutionary approach that has received considerable attention in the literature is the particle swarm optimization technique (PSO), introduced in [10].

In this paper, we focus on the class of feed-forward RNN models and on mapping problems that are classification problems, so the focus is much narrower than what is available in the RNN literature (see [2] and [3]). Nevertheless, a thorough review of the RNN literature identified a good number of RNN papers dealing with the feed-forward RNN model (e.g., [6] and [7], RNN application papers dealing with image and video compression, assessing video quality in packet networks, recognizing land-mines, recognizing the onset of malicious attacks in computer networks, and others). It is worth noting that a significant portion of the recent RNN literature deals with reinforcement learning of the RNN weights in the context of computer networks, referred to as Cognitive Packet Networks [11], and Self-Aware Networks [12]; this literature is out of the scope of this paper. The purpose of this paper is to provide appropriate critical review comments regarding potential avenues of research related to feed-forward RNNs used for solving classification problems. Some of these research recommendations are applicable to recurrent RNNs, as well. To provide justification for these critical review comments, experiments with the feed-forward RNN were conducted (e.g. applying evolutionary learning techniques to learn the RNN weights) and the literature was reviewed, but only a small sample of this literature is reported here, due to lack of space. It is expected that the critical review comments will spur additional RNN research by academics and practitioners in the field.

2   The RNN Model

The random neural network model has been extensively described in the literature in a variety of papers such as [1], and [5], among others, and we assume that the reader is familiar with this model. Fig. 1 shows a feed-forward RNN model with I, H, O input, hidden and output nodes, its representative interconnection weights, and equations to calculate its outputs (i.e., the steady probabilities q_v's). The type of problems that we focus on this paper is classification problems. In particular, we assume that a training collection of input/output pairs, $\{\Lambda(p), \lambda(p); d(p)\}, 1 \leq p \leq PT$ are available to us, and the objective is to map the input vector $(\Lambda(p), \lambda(p))$ to its corresponding desired output vector $d(p)$, for all $p: 1 \leq p \leq PT$. The parameter PT corresponds to the number of input/output pairs in the training set. The P-th input output pair from the training collection that is presented to the RNN is designated by $(\Lambda^{(p)}(p), \lambda^{(p)}(p))$. We assume that $\Lambda^{(p)}(p), \lambda^{(p)}(p)$ are vectors of dimensionality I, and their i-th component is designated as $\Lambda_i^{(p)}(p), \lambda_i^{(p)}(p)$. We also assume that $d^{(p)}(p)$ is an O-dimensional vector, and its corresponding o-th component is designated by $d_o^{(p)}(p)$. We define an error function (for all input/output pairs), as follows:

$$E = \sum_{p=1}^{PT} E(p) = \frac{1}{2} \sum_{p=1}^{PT} \sum_{o=1}^{O} [q \qquad (1)$$

In [5], a learning algorithm (gradient descent procedure) has been developed to minimize this error function by updating (learning) the network's weights.

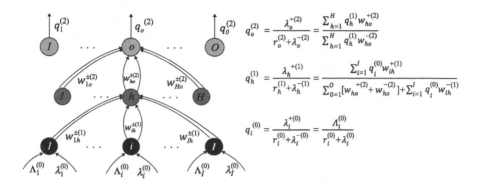

$$q_o^{(2)} = \frac{\lambda_o^{+(2)}}{r_o^{(2)}+\lambda_o^{-(2)}} = \frac{\sum_{h=1}^{H} q_h^{(1)} w_{ho}^{+(2)}}{\sum_{h=1}^{H} q_h^{(1)} w_{ho}^{-(2)}}$$

$$q_h^{(1)} = \frac{\lambda_h^{+(1)}}{r_h^{(1)}+\lambda_h^{-(1)}} = \frac{\sum_{i=1}^{I} q_i^{(0)} w_{ih}^{+(1)}}{\sum_{0=1}^{O}[w_{ho}^{+(2)}+ w_{ho}^{-(2)}]+\sum_{i=1}^{I} q_i^{(0)} w_{ih}^{-(1)}}$$

$$q_i^{(0)} = \frac{\lambda_i^{+(0)}}{r_i^{(0)}+\lambda_i^{-(0)}} = \frac{\Lambda_i^{(0)}}{r_i^{(0)}+\lambda_i^{(0)}}$$

Fig. 1. A feed-forward RNN architecture, with I input nodes, H hidden nodes and O output nodes. All the inputs, outputs and representative interconnection weights are depicted in the figure. The equations to compute the RNN outputs are also provided.

3 Critical Review Comments

Critical Review Comment 1: Our examination of the relevant RNN literature showed that there is not an exhaustive investigation of the different derivative-based approaches to solve the associated sum of the squared error problem. Some papers related to this topic have appeared in the literature (e.g., [6], [7]) but all of them compare their learning algorithms with the gradient descent approach on a limited set of problems. On the other hand, the multi-layer perceptron (MLP) neural network and its associated back-propagation learning algorithm (gradient descent applied on the sum of the squared errors function defined for the MLP model) has received significant attention in the literature by a variety of researchers who have suggested improvements to its speed of convergence (e.g., [8], [9], and many others). There is a need for a more thorough investigation of which of the many derivative-based methods is most efficient with the RNN model and this investigation should be applied to a good number of benchmark problems.

  Critical Review Comment 2: Our examination of the relevant RNN literature showed that there has not been a thorough examination of the feed-forward RNN's performance on classification problems, an important class of problems for a variety of application domains. On the other hand, for a wide variety of other classifier models (e.g., see [13], [14]) results pertaining to their comparative performance on a good number of benchmark classification problems have been provided. Therefore, a thorough investigation of RNN's classification performance, size, and complexity needs to be conducted and contrasted against other popular classifier models, such as

MLP, ART (Adaptive Resonance Theory), SVMs (Support Vector Machines), decision trees (such as CART), and others.

Critical Review Comment 3: Our examination of the relevant RNN literature showed that in finding the interconnection weights of the RNN, primarily first and second order derivative methods have been considered. Our limited experimentation (see Section 4 of the paper) has illustrated that there might be an advantage in using existing evolutionary approaches, such as PSO [10], as well as other evolutionary methods, to optimize the weights of an RNN in an effort to avoid getting trapped in local minima, which has been one of the problems of first and second order derivative based learning methods (e.g., see [15]).

Critical Review Comment 4: Our examination of the relevant RNN literature showed that the majority, if not all, of the RNN papers (e.g., [5], [6], and [7]) consider the minimization of the frequently used sum of the squared errors function to find the RNN interconnection weights. Although this function is appropriate for regression problems, it might not be the most appropriate one for classification problems. As the literature is suggesting (e.g., [16], [17], and many others papers), as well as our limited experimentation (see Section 4 of the paper) with the RNN and the cross-entropy error function [18], there might be advantages considering alternative error functions to find the weights in a neural network. Therefore, the RNN learning algorithm procedures (derivative based or not) should be examined with other error functions in addition to the frequently used squared error function, especially if RNN addresses classification problems.

Critical Review Comment 5: Our examination of the relevant RNN literature showed that there has been no attempt to co-jointly optimize the weights and the structure of the RNN network using a multi-objective optimization approach. Considering the extensive literature on the topic of multi-objective optimization of classifiers and the good results obtained therein (e.g., [14], many others), it is worth considering a multi-objective optimization of the structure and the interconnection weights of an RNN model.

Critical Review Comment 6: A review of the RNN literature revealed that a careful analysis of the functionality of the feed-forward RNN model has not been conducted, while such an analysis has been carried through for other classifier models, such as the MLP (e.g., see [19], many others) This research avenue will facilitate the future work, suggested by all critical comments 1-5, which are primarily of experimental nature, but whose successful implementation relies on a good understanding of the feed-forward RNN model, its capabilities and its limitations.

4. Experiments with the RNN

To justify some of the critical review comments that we provided in the previous section we conducted some experiments. In particular, we used 12 datasets: G05, G15, G25, G40, C00, C15, C25, IRIS (IR), Bupa (BU), Pima (PI) and Magic (MA). The first eight datasets are artificial, while the last 4 datasets are real datasets obtained from the UCI Machine Learning repository. The G datasets are 2-dimensional, 2-class Gaussian data with different amounts of overlap (5% for G05, 15% for G15, 25% for

G25 and 40% for G40). The C datasets are off-springs of the famous circle in the square dataset with different amounts of noises in the data (0% noise for C00, 15% noise for C15, 25% noise for C25, and 40% noise for C40). In our experiments we trained an RNN feed-forward model with a training set until a criterion of convergence was met (maximum number of epochs reached, or error did not change appreciably over a number of epochs). Then, we evaluated the performance of the trained RNN model on a different set of data, the test set. The results are shown in Table 1 and they provide justification for critical review comments 3 and 4.

In [14] we performed an exhaustive comparison of MO-GART (an ART variant), SVM, and CART classifiers on a number of datasets, some of which are the datasets that we experimented with the RNN (see Table 1 below). In all the experiments with the G datasets the attained classification performance of MO-GART, SVM and CART was optimal, using the smallest possible size of a classifier (2). For the C00 dataset the results were: 99.80 (2) [MO-GART], 99.67 (88) [SVM], 97.56% (28) [CART]. For the IRIS dataset the results were: 95.24% (2) [MO-GART], 95.06% (64) [SVM], 94.02% (2) [CART]. For the PIMA dataset the results were: 82.67% (2) [MO-GART], 73.71% (2) [SVM], and 73.70% (4) [CART]; the numbers in parentheses are sizes of the classifier models. Obviously, a more thorough experimentation with a variety of classifier models and RNN on a more extensive list of benchmark datasets is needed, as critical review comment 2 suggests.

Table 1: Percentage of Correct Classification (rows 1, 3, 5), and Number of Epochs Needed for Training (rows 2, 4, 6) for RNN-RPROP, RNN-PSO, and RNN-PSO (e). RNN-PSO (e) minimizes the entropic error function instead of the more typical mean squared error function of equation (1). RNN has five hidden nodes. Results are averages over 20 experiments.

Algorithm	G05	G15	G25	G40	C00	C05	C15	C25	IR	BU	PI	MA
RNN-RPROP	91.4	82.7	73.8	61.2	72.7	66.8	64.9	62.5	89.7	61.1	75.8	73.0
RNN-RPROP	537	1053	631	500	1274	1486	1724	1843	264	500	1908	2335
RNN-PSO	92.1	82.8	74.5	61.4	78.5	75.0	69.7	65.7	90.2	63.2	76.0	75.4
RNN-PSO	100	168	100	100	250	100	200	370	132	199	100	385
RNN-PSO (e)	95.2	84.8	74.9	61.1	88.4	84.5	77.2	66.1	94.2	66.1	75.6	73.4
RNN-PSO (e)	262	179	100	95	500	500	478	400	200	200	194	430

5. Summary

In this paper we focused on the feed-forward RNN model and its associated learning algorithms. Furthermore, we emphasized classification problems. This focus was intentional, so that we can narrow the breath of the RNN knowledge to a manageable level. We provided six critical review comments that suggested future research with the feed-forward RNN model within the context of solving classification problems. These comments were substantiated through references to the available literature and sometimes through limited but appropriate experimentation.

Acknowledgments. Georgiopoulos and Li were supported by NSF grants: 0341601, 0647018, 0717674, 0717680, 0647120, 0525429, 0806931, 0837332, and 0963146.

References

1.   Gelenbe, E.: Random Neural Networks with Negative and Positive Signals and Product Form Solution. Neural Computation 1, 502-510 (1989)
2.   Bakircioglu, H. Kocak, T.: Survey of random neural network applications. European Journal of Operational Research 126 319-330 (2000)
3.   Timotheou, S.: The Random Neural Network: A Survey. Computer Journal 53 (3) 251-267, (2010)
4.   Rumelhart, D. E., Hinton, G. E., Williams, R. J.: Learning Internal Representations by Error Propagation. In: Rumelhart, D. E., McClelland, J. L., PDP Research Group (eds.) Parallel Distributed Processing; Explorations in the Microstructure of Cognition. MIT Press, Cambridge, MA (1986)
5.   Gelenbe, E.: Learning in the Recurrent Neural Network. Neural Computation 5, 154-164 (1993)
6.   Likas, A., Stafylopatis, A.: Training the Random Neural Network using Quasi-Newton Methods. European Journal of Operational Research 126, 331-339 (2000)
7.   Basterrech, S., Mohammed, S., Rubino, G., Soliman, M.: Levenberg-Marquardt Training Algorithms for Random Neural Networks. The Computer Journal (2009).
8.   Jacobs, R. A.: Increased Rates of Convergence through Learning Rate Adaptation. Neural Networks 1, 151-160 (1988)
9.   Riedmiller, M., Braun, H.: A Direct Adaptive Method for Faster Back-Propagation Learning: The RPROP Algorithm. In: Proceedings of the International Conference on Neural Networks, pp. 586-591 (1993)
10. Kennedy, J., Eberhart, R.: Particle Swarm Optimization. In: Proceedings of the IEEE International Conference on Neural Networks, vol. 4, pp. 1942-1947. Perth, Australia (1995)
11. Gelenbe, E., Gellman, M., Lent, R., Liu, P., Su, P.: Autonomous Smart Routing for Network QoS. In: Proceedings of the First International Conference on Autonomic Computing, 232–239. New York, NY, May 2004
12. Gelenbe, E.: Steps toward self-aware networks. Communications ACM, 52(7) 66-75 (2009)
13. Lim, T., Loh, W., Shih, Y.: A Comparison of Prediction Accuracy, Complexity, and Training Time of Thirty-Three Old and New Classification Algorithms. Machine Learning 40, 203–229 (2000)
14. Kaylani, A., Georgiopoulos, M., Mollaghasemi, M., Anagnostopoulos, G. C., Sentelle, C., Zhong, M.: An Adaptive Multi-Objective Approach to Evolving ART Architectures. IEEE Transactions on Neural Networks 21, 529-550 (2010).
15. Jordanov, I., Georgieva, A.: Neural Network Learning with Global Heuristic Search. IEEE Transactions on Neural Networks 18, 937-942 (2007)
16. van Ooyen, A., Nienhuis, B.: Improving the Convergence of the Back-Propagation Algorithm. Neural Networks 5, 465-471 (1992)
17. Nedeljkovic, V.: A Novel Multi-Layer Neural Networks Training Algorithm minimizes the Probability of Classification Error. IEEE Transactions on Neural Networks 4, 13-16 (1993)
18. Bishop, C. M.: Neural Networks for Pattern Recognition. Oxford University Press (2008)
19. Gibson, G. J., Cowan, C. F. N.: On the Decision Regions of Multi-Layer Perceptrons. Proceedings of the IEEE 78, 1590-1594 (1990).

6 Computer and Wireless Networks

An Energy Efficient Location Service for Mobile Ad Hoc Networks

Zijian Wang[1], Eyuphan Bulut[1] and Boleslaw K. Szymanski[1],

[1] Department of Computer Science, Rensselaer Polytechnic Institute,
Troy, NY 12180 USA
{wangz, bulute, szymansk}@cs.rpi.edu

Abstract. Location based routing protocols are heavily dependent on location services which provide the position information of the desired destination node. Seldom location service schemes include energy efficiency metrics when evaluating their performance in forwarding location update and query packets. We propose a novel location service that aims at decreasing the distance traveled by the location update and query packets and, thus, at reducing the overall energy cost. Simulation results are presented to demonstrate that the new scheme achieves energy efficiency while maintaining all the other performance metrics comparable to the previously published algorithms.

Keywords: Location service, mobile ad hoc networks, routing

1   Introduction

A critical issue for location based routing protocols is to design efficient location services that can track the locations of mobile nodes. The earliest of location service protocols were based on flooding-based approaches. Then, to restrict the resulting location update and query flooding, quorum-based protocols were proposed. Recently, hashing-based protocols have been proposed, which can further be divided into flat or hierarchical ones. In the first category [1-2], each node's identifier is mapped to a home region consisting of one or more nodes within a fixed location. However, a large overhead is introduced during the location update procedure and frequent location queries and replies cause early death of the nodes within such home region. In the second category [3-5], the network area is recursively divided into a hierarchy of squares. For each node, one or more nodes in each square at each level of the hierarchy are chosen as its location servers. Thus, the location update cost is significantly reduced and location servers are scattered all over the network.

However, the main goal of the hierarchical hashing-based protocols is just to find the location of the destination nodes. They seldom take energy efficiency issue into consideration during design of forwarding location update and query packets. We propose a novel location service scheme which attempts to decrease the distance

E. Gelenbe et al. (eds.), *Computer and Information Sciences*, Lecture Notes
in Electrical Engineering 62, DOI 10.1007/978-90-481-9794-1_32,
© Springer Science+Business Media B.V. 2010

traveled by the location update and query packets and, thus, to reduce the overall energy cost.

2   Energy Efficient Location Service

2.1   Network Partition and Coordinate System

Each node knows its own position and the positions of its neighbors. The whole square network area is recursively divided into a hierarchy of squares which are known to each node in the network. At the top level, the entire area is called a level-N square. Each of level-i ($1 < i \le N$) squares is further divided into four level-(i-1) quadrants, until the entire region is divided into $4^{(N-1)}$ level-1 squares. Given L as the side length of the whole network area, the side length of a level-i square is $L_i = L/2^{N-i}$. Fig. 1(left) illustrates an example of a 4-level hierarchy network.

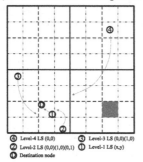 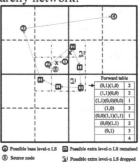

④ Level-4 LS (0,0)   ③ Level-3 LS (0,0)(1,0)
② Level-2 LS (0,0)(1,0)(0,1) ① Level-1 LS (x,y)
⑩ Destination node

⑩ Possible base level-n LS   ⑪ Possible extra level-n LS remained
⑤ Source node   ⑪ Possible extra level-n LS dropped

Fig. 1. An example for a 4-level hierarchy network (left) and location query procedure and forward table (right)

Using the lower left point as the origin, we define the address of level-i square as a sequence of coordinate pairs $(a_x^{N-1}, a_y^{N-1})...(a_x^i, a_y^i)$ ($a_{x|y}^i$ in short) computed as:

$$a_{x|y}^i = (s_{x|y}^i - \sum_{k=1}^{N-i-1} L_{N-k} \bullet a_{x|y}^{N-k})/L_i,$$ where (s_x^i, s_y^i) ($s_{x|y}^i$ in short) is the lower left

coordinate of the level-i square. For example, the address sequence for the marked level-1 square in Fig. 1(left) is (1,0)(1,0)(0,1). Inversely, the lower left coordinate of

the level-i square can be computed as follows: $s_{x|y}^i = \sum_{k=1}^{N-i} L_{N-k} \bullet a_{x|y}^{N-k}$. Given a node's

coordinate (n_x, n_y), the address sequence $(na_x^{N-1}, na_y^{N-1})...(na_x^i, na_y^i)$ ($na_{x|y}^i$ in short) of the level-i square to which this node belongs is calculated as:

$$na_{x|y}^i = floor((n_{x|y} - \sum_{k=1}^{N-i-1} L_{N-k} \bullet na_{x|y}^{N-k})/L_i).$$

2.2   Location Update

Each node selects one level-i location server in each level-i square in which it resides. The position of the level-i location server (ls_x^i, ls_y^i) (referred to as location server point) for each node in level-i square is determined as: $(ls_x^i, ls_y^i) = (s_x^i, s_y^i) + hash(ID, L_i)$, where ID is the unique identifier of the node. Hash is a global function known to each node that maps a node's ID to a relative position in a level-i square.

In our method, each location server maintains a list of nodes whose location information it stores. Each element of the list stores the following information: node ID (32 bits), location server level (log_2N bits), location information (introduced in the following), and expiration time (32 bits). Please note that the destination node's exact location information is only stored at level-1 location servers. At all other levels, the location servers only store the address sequence of the square in which the level-(i-1) location server resides, as shown in Fig. 1(left). Thus, 1) the memory usage is reduced; 2) the size of the location update packet is also reduced; 3) the location information at level-i location server needs to be updated only when the destination node moves out of the corresponding level-(i-1) square, which significantly reduces the frequency of location updates, thereby saving a lot of energy.

In previous methods, all the location update packets are sent to location servers individually. In our method, if one node needs to send a location update to more than one location server, it first calculates the distances traveled by the update messages both for sending them to each desired location server individually (referred as d-indiv) and sending them in one packet which traverse all the desired location servers (referred as d-one). If d-indiv is smaller than d-one, the location update messages are sent to each desired location server individually. Otherwise, all the update messages are integrated into one packet that is forwarded according to a forward table which indicates the sequence of location servers to be visited. Traversing multiple points in a plane is a kind of Hamiltonian path problem. We use a simple greedy solution in which the next visited node is always the nearest one to the currently visited node. Any intermediate node greedily forwards location update packet to the neighbor nearest to the position of the next location server in the forward table. Once the location update packet reaches a location server at certain level, the corresponding location information will be stored at this server and the next entry in the forward table pops up. All the outdated table entries are deleted.

2.3   Location Query

When the source node resides within a level-s (predefined parameter, we set it to 1) square that is beside the boundary of any level-h (predefined parameter, we set it to N-1) square, the search proceeds as follows. The source node calculates all candidate location server points (from level-N to level-1) that fall into the adjacent level-s squares (we refer to them as candidate adjacent squares) located on the opposite side of the boundary of a level-h square. If any level-k candidate location server point is found in each adjacent level-s square, there is no need to find level-i (i<k) candidate

location server points in the same level-s square. Hence, only the highest candidate location servers in every adjacent square searched need to be found (we refer to them as *extra location servers*). Then, the source node follows HIGH-GRADE method [5] (abbreviated HGM) and calculates, from the lowest level to the highest, all candidate level-i location server points of squares in which source node resides until such level is reached that its square contains also the destination node (we refer to them as *base location servers*). Both of these two kinds of location points (if the extra location servers exist) are sorted into a list that can be traversed by a path starting from the source node, using the same greedy Hamiltonian path method as used in sending location update packets. If any high level base location server is in front of low level base location server, the lower one is deleted from the list because if the location query packet checks the high level base location server points first, then there is no need to check the low level base location server points. But for extra location servers, we need to check all of them in each adjacent level-s square, so we keep all of them.

An example in which the source node resides in the level-1 square which is beside the boundary of level-3 square is shown in Fig. 1(right). The source node calculates all candidate location server points in the adjacent squares (there are at most five of them, as shown in Fig. 1(right)). There are two candidate location server points in adjacent level-1 square $(1,0)(0,1)(0,1)$ (one is level-1, the other is level-3). Only the level-3 one will be kept. Then, all candidate location servers are sorted in the order shown in Fig. 1(right), as defined by the path traversing from the source node. Since the level-2 base location server is in front of level-1 base location server on this sorted list, the level-1 base location server will be removed from the list.

4   Simulations

We used NS-2.33 to evaluate our scheme and compared it with the HIGH-GRADE method [5]. The whole network is deployed over a 1000 m by 1000 m area partitioned into 4-level squares. The following metrics are evaluated: (1) the total distance (measured in meters and hops) traveled by all location update packets for all nodes; (2) the average distance traveled by location query packets; (3) the average distance traveled by location query packet for specific destination node (for this kind of location query, we select the source node that resides within a level-1 square that is beside the boundary of level-3 square; moreover, there is at least one location server for the destination node residing in the adjacent level-1 square which is also beside the boundary of level-3 square on the opposite side); (4) the average energy usage; and (5) the location query success rate.

In static network scenario, we keep the average number of neighbor nodes constant and vary the number of nodes from 200 to 600. For each randomly generated topology, nodes send location update packets at first, then, 20 randomly location queries start. In the mobile network scenario, nodes move according to the random way-point model with no pause time. We keep the number of nodes at 400 but vary the maximum nodal speed V_{max} from 2.5 m/s to 7.5 m/s.

Table 1 gives the average results for metric (1) to (3). Clearly, the location update cost for our method is much lower than for HGM. This is mainly because the location update messages in our method could be sent in one packet. It is also clear that the cost of a specific location query in our method is much lower than for HGM. This advantage is the result of its properties: quick search within the adjacent low level squares and visiting higher level candidate location server first. However, for randomly selected location queries, the costs of the two compared methods are almost the same. The reason is that the quick search within adjacent low level squares does not always find the desired location servers. In such cases, the distance traveled by the quick search just increases the cost without any benefit. However, our method still benefits from visiting higher level candidate location servers first, preventing unnecessary travel by a location query packet.

Table 1. Simulation results for the first three metrics

Static network scenario for metric (1)			
Node Number	200	400	600
Our method: distance (hops)	154129.1(1259.6)	302726.2(3285.0)	452976.9(5845.0)
Compared method: distance (hops)	227285.2(1736.0)	435527.5(4495.4)	649542.7(8037.4)
Mobile network scenario for metric (1)			
V_{max} (m/s)	2.5	5	7.5
Our: distance (hops)	324755.9(3581.9)	352415.3(3903.1)	388754.6(4528.7)
Compared: distance (hops)	475739.1(4946.3)	529158(5736.5)	575242.9(6327.1)
Static network scenario for metric (2)			
Node Number	200	400	600
Our method: distance (hops)	1288.6(9.9)	1315.5(13.9)	1317.1(16.6)
Compared method: distance (hops)	1299.3(10.0)	1303.4(13.7)	1365.5(17.2)
Mobile network scenario for metric (2)			
V_{max} (m/s)	2.5	5	7.5
Our method: distance (hops)	1021.6(10.7)	1017.5(11.0)	967.3(10.4)
Compared method: distance (hops)	959.2(10.1)	1055.1(11.3)	1080.8(11.7)
Static network scenario for metric (3)			
Node Number	200	400	600
Our method: distance (hops)	878.6(7.2)	966.8(10.3)	1098.3(14.4)
Compared method: distance (hops)	1443.9(11.2)	1424.8(14.5)	1497.1(18.7)

Static network scenario   Mobile network scenario

Fig. 2. Simulation results for metric (4), the energy usage

The energy usage for both methods is shown in Fig. 2. The energy usage for our method is lower, in the range of 74% to 88% of the HGM energy use. Table 2 shows the location query success rate results. This rate is a little higher for our method.

Table 2.   Simulation results for metric (5), the location query success rate

Node Number	200	400	600	V_{max} (m/s)	2.5	5	7.5
Our method:	99%	96%	96%	Our method:	80%	72%	59%
Compared method:	91%	94%	93%	Compared method:	74%	69%	56%

5   Conclusion

In this paper, we introduced a novel location service that aims at reducing the overall energy cost by decreasing the distance traveled by the location update and query packets. Extensive simulations are performed to demonstrate that the new scheme achieves energy efficiency while maintaining all the other performance metrics.

Acknowledgement

Research was sponsored by US Army Research Laboratory and the UK Ministry of Defence and was accomplished under Agreement Number W911NF-06-3-0001. The views and conclusions contained in this document are those of the authors and should not be interpreted as representing the official policies, either expressed or implied, of the US Army Research Laboratory, the U.S. Government, the UK Ministry of Defence, or the UK Government. The US and UK Governments are authorized to reproduce and distribute reprints for Government purposes notwithstanding any copyright notation hereon.

References

1. Woo, S. C., Singh, S.: Scalable Routing Protocol for Ad Hoc Networks. ACM Wireless Networks, vol. 7(5), pp. 513--529 (2001)
2. Das, S. M., Pucha, H., Hu, Y. C.: Performance Comparison of Scalable Location Services for Geographic Ad Hoc Routing. In: 24th Annual Joint Conference of the IEEE Computer and Communications Societies (INFOCOM), pp. 1228--1239. IEEE Press, New York (2005)
3. Yan, Y., Zhang, B. X., Mouftah, H.T., Ma, J.: Hierarchical Location Service for Large Scale Wireless Sensor Networks with Mobile Sinks. In: IEEE Global Telecommunications Conference (GLOBECOM), pp. 1222--1226. IEEE Press, New York (2007)
4. Ahmed, S., Karmakar, G. C., Kamruzzaman, J.: Hierarchical Adaptive Location Service Protocol for Mobile Ad Hoc Network. In: IEEE Wireless Communications and Networking Conference (WCNC), pp. 1--6. IEEE Press, New York (2009)
5. Yu, Y. Z., Lu, G.-H., Zhang, Z.-L.: Enhancing Location Service Scalability with HIGH-GRADE. In: IEEE International Conference on Mobile Ad-hoc and Sensor Systems (MASS), pp. 164--173. IEEE Press, New York (2004)

A Low-latency and Self-adapting Application Layer Multicast

Ricardo Lent, Omer H. Abdelrahman, and Gokce Gorbil

Electrical and Electronic Engineering Department
Imperial College London, UK
{r.lent, o.abd06, g.gorbil}@imperial.ac.uk

Abstract. The paper evaluates a simple, yet effective, application-layer multicast algorithm (AMUCAST) targeted to medium-scale applications with low-latency requirements. A distributed tree construction and maintenance mechanism combines metric measurement and link selection to produce consistent and self-adaptable trees. The paper presents results from an extensive simulation study that quantify the performance of the approach and experimental data collected on a network testbed.

1 Introduction

Many interactive group communication applications need efficient data delivery service that can adapt to changing workload and network conditions in order to satisfy their stringent delay requirements. Network layer (IP) multicast provides a low cost bandwidth efficient mechanism for delivering data to a group of recipients. However, ubiquitous deployment of IP multicast in the Internet has been hindered by several practical challenges [1] which have shifted the interest toward Application Layer Multicast (ALM). With ALM, multicast functionalities such as packet replication, routing and group membership management are implemented at the application layer on the end hosts rather than in the network routers.

One approach to ALM is for group members to self-organize into an overlay network and to take on the responsibility of forwarding data between themselves using only unicast connections. This approach conforms to the smart-host dumb-network paradigm that has driven the internet, allowing for immediate deployment at the cost of less efficient utilization of network resources in comparison to IP multicast due to duplicate packet transmissions over same physical links.

Designing efficient ALM protocols consists mainly in constructing high quality and self-adapting overlays with minimal complexity and overhead. Building such overlays requires knowledge of the underlying physical network and its performance metrics which are usually estimated using measurement techniques such as round-trip time (RTT). However, gathering measurements for all pairs of nodes introduces a large overhead which grows with the group size. As a result, an ALM protocol needs to achieve good trade-off between topology estimation and measurement cost.

E. Gelenbe et al. (eds.), *Computer and Information Sciences*, Lecture Notes in Electrical Engineering 62, DOI 10.1007/978-90-481-9794-1_33,
© Springer Science+Business Media B.V. 2010

2   AMUCAST Algorithm

AMUCAST delivery tree T is source-specific and it is composed of three types of nodes: a sender s (tree root), a set of receivers M and a set of deputies D, which may be an empty set, i.e. $T = \{s \cup M \cup D\}$. Each node $n \in T$ maintains two information sets: (i) the set of children C_n, which consists of n's current children in the distribution tree, and (ii) the set of possible successors N_n, which contains nodes that can potentially be selected as the children of n in the next tree construction cycle. Note that $C_l = \emptyset$ for all leaf nodes $l \in T$ and members of C_n may potentially change over time $\forall n \in T$ as the tree adapts itself to changing conditions. The set N is used to reduce the search space (i.e. the distributed broadcast space during tree (re-)construction) when the number of receivers ($|M|$) is large. Therefore, $N \subseteq M$.

The tree construction proceeds as follows. Sender s creates a candidate set Z_s, which consists of possible children of s in the to-be-constructed multicast tree, and sets $C_s = \emptyset$. The possible children are selected from N_s based on their fitness as observed from previous tree constructions. Note that $N_s = \{M \cup D - s\}$ when there are no previous observations (i.e. during the first tree construction). Sender s unicasts L copies of the Tree Build Message (TBM) to each node in Z_s. Each TBM carries a unique tree identifier assigned by s along with the sender's identifier and predecessor. Each node remembers the last tree identifier, so stale (delayed) TBMs can be easily discarded.

A node that receives a TBM will immediately repeat the process described above with its own candidate set after appending its node identifier to the Tabu List B in the TBM. The Tabu List B in the TBM helps units to construct more efficient candidate sets and loop-free trees by excluding previously used units in the tree construction process (i.e. $Z = N \cup D - s - B$). A node receiving the first L TBMs from the same predecessor will send a Child Attach Message (CAM) to the predecessor. A copy of each CAM is sent to the root to inform it of the new attachment. A node receiving a CAM will add the sending node to its child set C. Once s receives attachment notifications from all nodes in M, it will start using the new tree. Data transmission proceeds by each node retransmitting data arrivals to nodes in its C set. The tree performance is constantly monitored and new constructions may be triggered either after detecting a node failure or performance degradation [2].

3   Simulation Study

The study consisted in observing the performance of AMUCAST when running over a simulated network that reflected the Autonomous System-level Internet topology [3] as of 01 January 2009. Each AS was represented as a single node (excluding stubs) making a total of 1679 nodes and 110620 full-duplex links. Each link had a 500-packet output buffer and transmission rates exponentially distributed in the range 32 Kbps to 1 Mbps with a fixed propagation latency of 1 ms.

A root unit and 20 receivers were instantiated with each run for a 1 Kbps (64-byte messages) UDP flow for a duration of 90 simulated seconds. Extra unicast flows (10 Kbps with 512-byte packets) were also established from the root to K random receivers to create obstruction to the AMUCAST traffic for added realism. It was assumed a zero-threshold configuration for tree construction, which implies that multicast trees are always constructed even under low traffic conditions.

AMUCAST's candidate set was constructed either by including all receivers (producing results labeled with the postfix $F = 1$) or by fitness selection ($F = 0$). Fitness was determined by historic performance. Figure 1 depicts the results along with their 95% confidence intervals: average message latency (1a) and leaf message latency (1b). While the interfering flows can rapidly impact the multicast traffic flows and increase the average delay, AMUCAST was able to substantially produce lower latency than unicasting . A similar observation can be drawn from the delivery ratio depicted in Figure 1c.

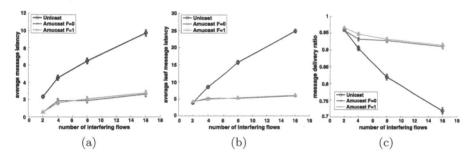

$$\text{(a)} \qquad\qquad\qquad \text{(b)} \qquad\qquad\qquad \text{(c)}$$

Fig. 1: AMUCAST under obstructing traffic: (a) average message delay, (b) message delay to leaf nodes and (c) message delivery ratio.

4   Implementation and Experimentation

An AMUCAST implementation was developed and integrated into the communication services layer (CL) of the DIESIS middleware [4], which is a software developed to create the basis for a European modeling and simulation e-Infrastructure. The current AMUCAST implementation can support different transport protocols in the substrate network. It can also expose the state of a node as a web service, which allows convenient remote inspection and monitoring of the protocol operation for testing and verification purposes.

A testbed consisting of 6 computers running UNIX-based OS was deployed at various points of the department's network as shown in Figure 2a, with the purpose of illustrating the utility of AMUCAST for very small scale applications with critical delay requirements such as *federated simulations*. The computers are connected to the network via Ethernet and each computer runs a number of AMUCAST units. We used TCP so that the measured delay would be affected by both TCP flow and congestion windows as well as losses and delays of the substrate network. Node `fed0` runs the sender (root), which transmits a test traffic flow of 2600-byte messages on average at approximately 1 message per second. Figures 2b and 2c depict the leaf round-trip delay over time and the long-term average delay for a single experiment run under AMUCAST and unicast, respectively. It can be appreciated that unicast produced roughly twice as high delay for the same flow of messages and network setting.

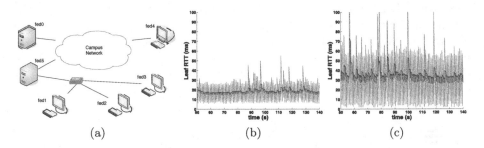

| (a) | (b) | (c) |

Fig. 2: (a) The network testbed. Measured message round trip delay to leaf units with (b) AMUCAST and (c) multiple unicasts.

5   Conclusions

This paper has evaluated AMUCAST, an application-layer multicast protocol, that is suitable for applications with low-delay requirements. A key property of AMUCAST is self-adaptation, which is achieved by allowing changes in the multicast tree in response to network conditions. To detect network changes, AMUCAST implements a continuous but non-obtrusive monitoring of the round-trip delay to leaf nodes. The results have shown that AMUCAST can significantly boost the performance of multicast applications as compared to multicasting by repeating unicasts. Finally, we have shown the utility of AMUCAST on a network testbed.

References

1. Diot, C., Levine, B., Lyles, B., Kassem, H., Balensiefen, D.: Deployment issues for the IP multicast service and architecture. IEEE Network **14**(1) (Jan./Feb. 2000) 78–88
2. Lent, R., Abdelrahman, O.H., Gorbil, G., Gelenbe, E.: Fast message dissemination for emergency communications. In: Proc. 1st Annual Workshop on Pervasive Networks for Emergency Management, Mannheim, Germany (Apr. 2010)
3. Internet Topology Collection. http://irl.cs.ucla.edu/topology/
4. DIESIS project web page. http://www.diesis-project.eu/

A Data-Centric Framework for Network Enabled C4ISR Software Systems

Hüseyin N. Karaca[1], H.Mehmet Yüksel[1], Eray Tüzün[1], İsmail Kılınç[1], Buyurman Baykal[1],

[1] Havelsan A. Ş., Peace Eagle Program, Research and Development Team, ODTU Teknokent, 06531, Ankara
{hkaraca,myuksel,etuzun,ikilinc, bbaykal}@havelsan.com.tr

Abstract. In this paper a data centric, platform and hardware communication protocol independent, standard compliant and net enabled C4ISR Software Framework which is envisioned to be used for all types of mission critic processing and display applications in distributed command and control projects is presented.

Keywords: C4ISR framework, Network enabled capability, data distribution service, software reuse.

1 Introduction

C4ISR stands for Command, Control, Communications, Computers, Intelligence, Surveillance and Reconnaissance. Those elements work together according to the principle which is called Boyd's Observe Orient Decide and Act (OODA) Loop [1].

In this paper, a Command and Control Software Framework (CCSF) for C4ISR domain is presented. Various architectural views are built using the Views and Beyond (V&B) approach [2] and several standards such as Data Distribution Services (DDS) for Real Time Systems 1.2 Specification [3] approved by Object Management Group (OMG), GO-1 Application Objects standard [4] by Open Geospatial Consortium (OGC), the tactical display military standards MIL-STD-2525B/C, App6A/B and Electronic Chart Display and Information System (ECDIS) standards are applied to CCSF. CCSF consists of two decoupled sub-frameworks; Tactical Display Framework (TDF) for presentation layer and Mission Processing Framework (MPF) for the business logic of the C4ISR systems.

2 Background Information

It is a common problem in C4ISR software companies to effectively utilize common knowledge and build reusable software components. A commonality/variability analysis on a set of primary functionalities that are critical for the command and control domain has been performed based on C4ISR projects of HAVELSAN. It is

E. Gelenbe et al. (eds.), *Computer and Information Sciences*, Lecture Notes in Electrical Engineering 62, DOI 10.1007/978-90-481-9794-1_34,
© Springer Science+Business Media B.V. 2010

observed that a framework for different C4ISR applications is highly needed to support systematic reuse and reduce the system development cost. CCSF must be able to deal with consuming and providing lots of sensor data in a real or near real time manner for both in-platform and inter-platform (net-enabled) usage. Packing the business functions into independent services and defining loosely coupled providers and consumers for these services were also crucial design goals of CCSF. According to these requirements, DDS with publish/subscribe messaging mechanism is chosen as the middleware of the CCSF. It is the one that covers the entire spectrum from non-real time to extreme real time [5]. In [6], there is a real time performance analysis of DDS versus to other messaging schemes.

Network Centric Warfare (NCW) is based on adopting a new way of thinking - network centric thinking - and applying it to military operations with information superiority approach. NCW is not narrowly about only technology, but broadly about an emerging military response to the Information Age [7]. More details about the NCW theory can be found in [8].

CCSF has requirements to support whole military operational spectrum from tactical to strategic command and control domains. Because of interoperability issues and as well as to be able to easily design, develop and deploy of services in a loosely coupled manner, Service Oriented Architecture (SOA) is accepted as the architectural concept of CCSF.

In this study, CCSF is compared with the similar products in the market: Gizmo SDK [9], SAF [10], [11] and Tacticos [12]. CCSF is the only one provides pub/sub mechanism, platform independency, application domain independency (air, naval and ground) , tactical display support and net centric support at the same time.

3 System Architecture

CCSF consists of two basic layers. Platform Layer includes all the libraries and third party products which provide Operating System (OS) independency, network communications abstraction, graphics abstraction and DDS middleware imple-mentations. Framework Layer provides reusable components and services for the domain applications, abstraction of DDS and hardware communication protocols. It also contains the MPF and TDF sub-frameworks.

Fig.1 shows the deployment view of CCSF defining the allocation of the components over hardware nodes. An application uses the functions provided by the components of the CCSF and communicates with another application through the DDS middleware where the functions of DDS are encapsulated within Data Distribution and Monitoring (DDM).

DDM consists of Tactical DDM (T-DDM) and Strategic DDM (S-DDM). T-DDM provides services for tactical level where real time requirements are necessary and S-DDM provides services for the strategic level where being real-time is not necessary. Currently S-DDM supports web services [13]. However, if the Request For Proposal (RFP) in [14] is added to the OMG DDS specification, S-DDM will use Web-Enabled DDS. All the services are defined in xml based configuration files and the contract/interface of the services are created automatically.

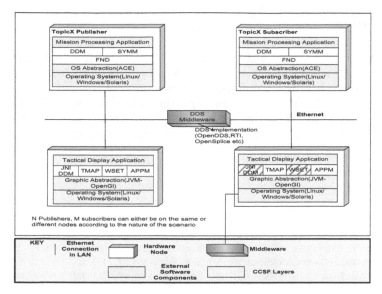

Fig. 1. The deployment view of CCSF.

In the MPF; Foundation Infrastructure (FND) provides memory management, concurrency, exception handling and logging etc. System Management and Monitoring (SYMM) manages lifecycles of the software components. Hardware Abstraction Layer (HAL) abstracts the applications from the underlying hardware communication protocols like MIL-STD-1553, ARINC-429, EIA-485, EIA-422-B and MIL-STD-1397c [15]. Checkpoint & Recovery (CPR) holds the minimum healthy data to recover a component from a failover. Recording & Playback (REC) is responsible for recording the mission data in order to play it for post mission analysis. Utilities (UTIL) provides utility libraries including geodesy functions (loading DTED maps or line of side analysis-los-), math and state machine implementation. Mission Time (MTIME) provides synchronized mission time. In the TDF; Tactical map (TMAP) is used for visualization of geographic data on a display area. Widget set (WSET) is the building blocks for GUI window components. Application manager (APPM) combines tactical map, application windows and DDS abstraction.

Since reliability is one of the important concerns, an automated testing framework is applied. The details of this automated test framework and continous integration platform is given in in [16].

4 Application Domain Experiences

CCSF is tested with platform, simulation and network enabled application domains. A naval and an air command and control software system are developed with CCSF for platform applications. A small scaled tactical environment simulator is developed with CCSF for simulation domain and a network enabled capability scenario is developed for network enabled applications. Requirements of all these domain specific applications are implemented and tested successfully.

5 Conclusion

CCSF supports both tactical and strategic levels. Easy and fast application design, development and testing are achieved by CCSF. It also provides loose coupling and ease of integration because of abstraction of both hardware communication protocols and DDS vendors. For network centric capability, CCSF provides a framework for designing, creating and deploying services. In short term, CCSF will be used as a reference architecture for the software product line engineering transition [17].

References

1. Boyd, R.J.: An organic design for Command and Control. In: Department of the Navy, Marine Corps Doctrinal Publication 6, Command and Control, ch 2. pp. 63--64. (1996)
2. Clements, P., Bachmann, F., Bass, L., Garlan, D., Ivers, J., Little R., Nord, R., Stafford, J.: Documenting Software Architectures. Addison-Wesley, (2002)
3. Data Distribution Service (DDS) Specification v1.2, http://www.omg.org/cgi-bin/doc?formal/07-01-01
4. OpenGIS Geographic Objects Implementation Specification, http://www.opengeospatial.org/standards/go
5. A collaborative activity of the USN PEO for C4I and Space, the USAF Electronic Systems Center, and the Defense Information Systems Agency: Net-Centric Enterprise Solutions for Interoperability (NESI), v3.0.0, pp. 70 -- 85. (2009)
6. Oh, S., Kim, J, H., Fox, G.: Real-Time Performance Analysis for Publish/Subscribe Systems. Future Generation Computer Systems, vol. 26, no. 3, pp. 318—323. (2010)
7. Alberts, S.A., Garstka, J.J., Stein F.P.: Network Centric Warfare Developing and Leveraging Information Superiority. 2nd Ed, (2000)
8. Croser, C.: Commanding the Future: Command and Control in a Networked Environment. Defense & Security Analysis, vol. 22, no. 2, pp. 197—202. (2006)
9. Gizmo Sdk, http://www.gizmosdk.com
10. Sioutis C., Foster K., Temple P., Dominish D.: Achieving Information Interoperability Using Data Distribution Middleware. MilCIS, Australia (2008)
11. Foster K., Iannos A., Lawrie G., Temple P., Tobin B: Exploring a Net Centric Architecture using the Net Warrior Airborne Early Warning and Control Node. Air Operations Division DSTO Defence Science and Technology Organisation. (2007)
12. Tacticos, http://www.thalesgroup.com/Portfolio/Defence/TACTICOS/?pid=1568
13. Saiedian, H., Mulkey, S.: Performance evaluation of eventing web services in real-time applications. In: IEEE Commun. Mag. 46(3), pp. 106--111. (2008)
14. Web-Enabled DDS RFP, http://www.omg.org/cgi-bin/doc?mars/2009-09-19
15. Yilmaz E., Karaca H., N.: A Data Centric Hardware Abstraction Layer for C4ISR Software Systems (in Turkish), a submitted paper to SAVTEK Turkey (2010)
16. Yüksel, M., E., Tüzün, E., Gelirli, E., Bıyıklı, E, Baykal, B.: Using Continuous Integration and Automated Test Techniques for a Robust C4ISR System. ISCIS, pp 743--748, (2009)
17. Tekinerdogan B., Tüzün E., Şaykol, E.: Exploring the Business Case for Transitioning from a Framework-based Approach to a Software Product Line Engineering Approach, in submitted conference paper to Software Product Line Conference (2010)

A Decentralised, Measurement-based Admission Control Mechanism for Self-Aware Networks

Georgia Sakellari

Imperial College London
Intelligent Systems and Networks Group
Electrical & Electronic Engineering Dept.
SW7 2BT London, UK
Email: g.sakellari@imperial.ac.uk

Abstract. This paper presents a decentralised Admission Control (AC) algorithm, based on the centralised proposed in [1–4]. Our algorithm is a multiple criteria AC algorithm, where each user can specify the QoS metrics that interest him/her, and decides whether a new call should be allowed to enter the network based on measurements of the QoS metrics on each link of the network before and after the transmission of probe packets. Our algorithm will be briefly described and we will present experimental results, conducted in a large laboratory test-bed, under highly congested circumstances.

1 Introduction

High demand and network congestion can prevent multimedia applications and users from obtaining the network service they require for a successful operation. Admission control (AC) is the process that determines whether an incoming request should be accepted or rejected. This usually requires estimation of the level of QoS that a new user session will need and investigation of whether there are enough resources available to service that session without affecting the QoS of the existing users of the network. So, when a flow requests real-time service, the network needs to be able to characterise the requirements of the new flow and make an admission decision based on an estimation of its current and projected state. Here we describe a decentralised AC algorithm which is based on the centralised, multiple-criteria, measurement-based AC algorithm presented in [1–4]. Our algorithm is targeted for self-aware networks (SAN) [5] and more specifically for the Cognitive Packet Network (CPN) [6] used by the SANs for two reasons. Firstly because the CPN protocol is directly related to the QoS desired by the end user and each user can specify different QoS goals based on which the routing decisions are being made. Secondly, CPN constantly collects real-time QoS data, so their is no need for special monitoring mechanisms which would work on top of the network layer, capturing packets and creating log files at specific time intervals.

E. Gelenbe et al. (eds.), *Computer and Information Sciences*, Lecture Notes
in Electrical Engineering 62, DOI 10.1007/978-90-481-9794-1_35,
© Springer Science+Business Media B.V. 2010

2 Our proposed algorithm

Our AC algorithm consists of three stages. In the identification stage the network identifies the quality criteria of a new user request and translates them into QoS metrics. In the probing stage each input node estimates the impact that its new flow will have to the network, based on personal link QoS information acquired by sending probe packets to the desired destination and by receiving information from the rest of the nodes about their finding from similar probings. Finally, in the decision stage each node searches for a feasible path that can accommodate the new call by considering the impact of its new flow on the network. All of the stages are similar to those of the centralised AC described in [1, 4], the only difference is that now, instead of collecting QoS information about all links to a central data centre where the decision is being made, each input node collects its personal information, about specific links, and decides independently.

2.1 Configuration of the experiments

In order to evaluate our mechanisms we conducted experiments in a real, 46-node testbed located at Imperial College London (same as in [4]. All links have the same capacity $(10\,Mbits/s)$. All users have the same QoS requirements: $delay \leq 150\,ms$, $jitter \leq 1\,ms$, and $packetloss \leq 5\,\%$. There are 7 Source-Destination (S-D) pairs that correspond to 7 users. After making a request, the user will wait for a random time W and then make a request again. We set the random waiting time W among requests in order to have different rate for the arrivals. W is chosen to be uniformly distributed in the range of values $[0, 15]$ seconds. We set the probing rate at 40% of the user's rate and the probing duration at $2s$. When a call is accepted, the source generates UDP traffic of $1Mbps$ constant bit rate that lasts for $600s$. Thus, the load on the system is constantly increasing at least until the $600th$ second. Since the capacity of each link is $10Mbps$, this means that the network becomes highly congested very quickly. Each experiment, lasts for $15min$ $(900s)$ and was conducted 5 times. The results presented here are the average values of those runs.

Our experiments covered three cases: (i) The Admission Control is disabled (NoAC), (ii) i) the centralised AC, proposed in [1], is enabled (CAC) and (iii) the decentralised AC is enabled (DAC).

In figures 1, 2 and 3 we compare the average packet loss, delay and jitter of a user in the network in all three cases. We observe that in both cases where the AC algorithm is enabled, the satisfaction of the user is much higher than when there is no AC. By satisfaction we mean the percentage of time throughout the experiment duration that all three QoS criteria, that user $D1$ has specified, are met. In the case of the centralised AC user $D1$ is satisfied 81.09% of the time, contrary to the decentralised AC mechanism where the user is satisfied 18.92% of the time. When the AC is disabled, this percentage drops even further to 8.11%. It needs to be noted that even if the percentage of the decentralised AC is low the user's QoS values are much closer to the requested ones than when we don't have AC.

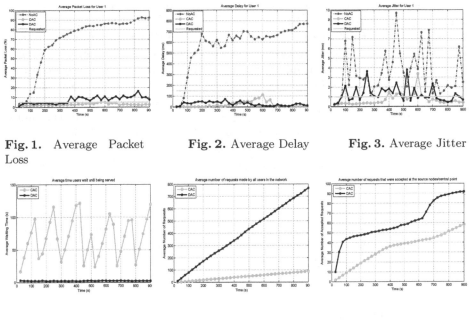

Fig. 1. Average Packet Loss

Fig. 2. Average Delay

Fig. 3. Average Jitter

Fig. 4. Average time a user waits in the "request queue" before being served

Fig. 5. Average Number of Requests

Fig. 6. Average Number of Accepted Requests

Figure 4 shows the average time a user has to wait until it is accepted into the network, when the AC is enabled. In the case of the centralised AC the users queue at the central point while in the decentralised version there are individual "request queues" at each input node. Here we present the average waiting time over all these queues. When the AC is disabled, users do not wait in a queue but are served as quickly as possible. In our experiments, a user has to wait on average $68.11s$ when the AC procedure is centralised and only $2.49s$ when the AC decision is taken independently at each input node.

Figures 5, 6 report the number of requests made in the whole network and the number of accepted requests respectively, when the AC schemes are enabled. We observe that with the decentralised algorithm the number of requests served and accepted into the network is much higher. This is due to the fact that the users's do not need to wait in a single queue at the central point and are therefore served much faster.

3   Node coordination

In order to further improve the performance of our decentralised AC, we tried two simple coordination mechanisms between the input nodes. The admission decision of our decentralised algorithm is based on the limited personal QoS information that each input node has from the links that are affected by the probe traffic and from the existing flows initiated by that node. In the experiments presented at the previous section we observed that the satisfaction of the accepted users in the decentralised version is worse than in the centralised one. This is mainly because each input node has limited information and does not know the QoS values of all the links like in the centralised version. Also, multiple probes are in the network and the estimation of the algorithm is not accurate.

Here we test two simple coordinating mechanisms in order for all the input nodes to have more "global" information about the links of the network. First we exchanging messages between all the input nodes. Every time a node measures link information it sends those values along with the time it measured them to all of the other input nodes. When a node wants to make a decision it bases it on the most recent link values taken from all the nodes.

Having nodes to exchange messages every time they measure a different link QoS value introduces additional overhead in the network. Therefore we also implemented a lighter coordination mechanism. In this mechanism, every time an input node has new QoS measurements instead of sending them to every source node in the network it randomly chooses one and only sends it to it.

3.1   Experimental results

The experiments have the same configuration as in section 2.1 and cover three cases: (i) the decentralised AC with no coordination between the input nodes (DAC), (ii) the decentralised AC with full coordination between the input nodes (DAC-Full) and (iii) the decentralised AC with random coordination between the input nodes (DAC-Rand).

From figures 7, 8 and 9 we observe that the satisfaction of the user improves when coordination is used. Same as before, in the case of the decentralised AC user $D1$ is satisfied 18.92% of the time. When we apply full coordination the user satisfaction increases to 27.03% and when we have random coordination the satisfaction surprisingly increases further to 40.54%. Additionally, the percentage of the satisfaction is still low mainly because of the jitter restriction. This is maybe because we use CPN with only delay as QoS goal and therefore CPN chooses the smallest delay paths while our AC algorithm looks at delay jitter and loss. We believe that if you use a combinatory QoS goal the results will improve.

Figure 10 shows that when we have coordination, the waiting time is slightly longer due to the message exchanges. More specifically, for DAC the average waiting time is 2.49s, while for the fully coordinated DAC it is 2.69s and for the randomly coordinated is 2.56s.

Figure 11 shows that almost the same number of requests are being made in all three cases while figure 12 shows that by having coordination more users are accepted into the network. So, when coordination is used not only the satisfaction is improved but also the number of users accepted into the network increases. This is because with the coordination the input nodes have more information about the network status. Additionally, with the random coordination even more users are accepted since fewer messages are exchanged between the input nodes.

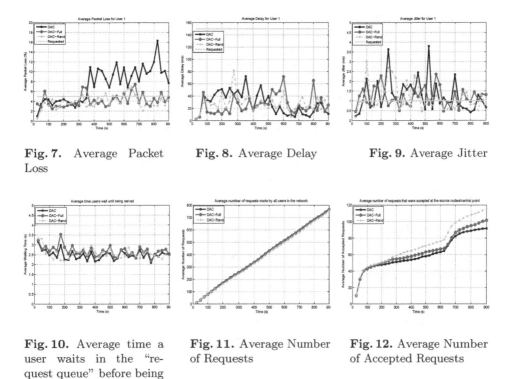

Fig. 7. Average Packet Loss

Fig. 8. Average Delay

Fig. 9. Average Jitter

Fig. 10. Average time a user waits in the "request queue" before being served

Fig. 11. Average Number of Requests

Fig. 12. Average Number of Accepted Requests

Regardless of the fact that the QoS values experienced by the users are very close to the requested ones, the satisfaction of the users is still quite low. This is because the sources probe the network at the same time making the estimations inaccurate. A way to overcome this could be by making the algorithm stricter, for example by decreasing the requested QoS values or by putting a restriction on the feasible path's size. Of course making the algorithm too strict could lead to poor use of the network resources and low utilisation. Another way would be to use a token passing mechanism for the probing stage, but this would increase the waiting times. Another idea is to use the distributed algorithm when the demand is small and then serialise the admission process by an auction process when the demand gets high. We are currently investigating the latter.

4   Conclusions

It is obvious that having a centralised AC mechanism raises security issues, since there is a single point and if this fails the system collapses. Also in the centralised version users have to wait for a relatively long time in order to be served. On the other hand, in the decentralised version each input node bases its decisions on restricted information. Also, each source node probes the network independently causing false estimations and additional traffic to the network. The experimental results showed that by decentralising our AC algorithm the network does not get over-congested and the QoS values are kept close to the required ones, but, as far as the satisfaction of the users is concerned, it is less likely that the user-specified QoS requirements will be met. A direction towards improving the decentralised AC could be to look into other coordination mechanisms between the decision (input) nodes. An idea would be to use an auctioning mechanism to supervise the decision stage.

Acknowledgment

The author would like to thank the ALADDIN (Autonomous Learning Agents for Decentralised Data and Information Networks) project which is jointly funded by a BAE (British Aerospace) Systems and EPSRC (Engineering and Physical Sciences Research Council) strategic partnership (EP/C548051/1) and the SATURN (Self-organizing Adaptive Technology underlying Resilient Networks) project which is sponsored by the UK Technology Strategy Board as part of the Saturn Consortium.

References

1. Gelenbe, E., Sakellari, G., D' Arienzo, M.: Admission of QoS Aware Users in a Smart Network. ACM Transactions on Autonomous and Adaptive Systems **3**(1) (Mar. 2008) 4:1–4:28
2. Sakellari, G., D' Arienzo, M., Gelenbe, E.: Admission Control in Self Aware Networks. In: Proceedings of the 49th annual IEEE Global Telecommunications Conference (GLOBECOM 2006), San Francisco, CA, USA (Nov./Dec. 2006) 1–5
3. Gelenbe, E., Sakellari, G., D' Arienzo, M.: Controlling Access to Preserve QoS in a Self-Aware Network. In: Proceedings of the First IEEE International Conference on Self-Adaptive and Self-Orginizing Systems (SASO 2007), Boston, MA, USA (Jul. 2007) 205–213
4. Sakellari, G., Gelenbe, E.: A Multiple Criteria, Measurement-Based Admission Control for Self-Aware Networks. In: Proceedings of the third International Conference on Communications and Networking in China (CHINACOM'08), Hangzhou, China (Aug. 2008)
5. Gelenbe, E., Lent, R., Nunez, A.: Self-Aware Networks and QoS. Proceedings of the IEEE **92**(9) (Sep. 2004) 1478–1489
6. Gelenbe, E., Xu, Z., Seref, E.: Cognitive Packet Networks. In: Proceedings of the 11th International Conference on Tools with Artificial Intelligence (ICTAI '99), Chicago, IL, USA, IEEE Computer Society Press (Nov. 1999) 47–54

A heuristic for fast convergence in interference-free channel assignment using D1EC coloring

Fabio Campoccia[1], Vincenzo Mancuso[2]

[1]Università degli studi di Palermo, Italy, [2]INRIA Sophia Antipolis, France

Abstract. This work proposes an efficient method for solving the Distance-1 Edge Coloring problem (D1EC) for the assignment of orthogonal channels in wireless networks with changing topology. The coloring algorithm is performed by means of the *simulated annealing* method, a generalization of Monte Carlo methods for solving combinatorial problems. We show that the simulated annealing-based coloring converges fast to a suboptimal coloring scheme. Furthermore, a stateful implementation of the D1EC scheme is proposed, in which network coloring is executed upon topology changes. The stateful D1EC reduces the algorithm's convergence time by one order of magnitude in comparison to stateless algorithms.

Keywords: Channel assignment, Edge coloring, Simulated annealing.

1 Introduction

Tremendous growth of 802.11 wireless networks in the last years allows adopting protocols that optimize the usage of the narrow available radio spectrum. In particular, the main problem that degrades network performance is the interference between concurrent transmissions, i.e., packet collisions. To avoid collisions, it is necessary to coordinate the transmitters within the network to access the wireless media through a multiple access scheme based on time, code or frequency. The availability of orthogonal channels (e.g., in CDMA or OFDMA systems) allows to assign dedicated channels to node pairs that would otherwise interfere with each other, so that multiple simultaneous transmissions can successfully occur. However, the number of available orthogonal channels is limited. Thereby, it is not always possible to assign a different channel to each different node pair.

Channel assignment can be seen as a graph coloring problem [1], by using, e.g., the "distance-1 edge coloring" (D1EC) described in [2]. We propose a heuristic for D1EC which uses a centralized algorithm and exploits a global knowledge of the network topology and the node activity. Our channel assignment algorithm uses a combinatorial method called *simulated annealing* [3]. In particular, we propose a stateful approach to further improve the coloring algorithm performance by running the coloring scheme from an initial channel assignment whose cost is near to the minimum. We developed a Java simulator to validate our proposal.

1.1 Definitions

Here we recall the basic definitions about graph coloring and simulation annealing.
Graph coloring. It consists in assigning a color to each edge of a graph, so that no two adjacent edges share the same color. A k-coloring is an assignment of edges to k colors. We say that a graph G is *k-colorable* if there exists a k-coloring for G. Given a k-colorable graph G, finding a k-coloring is solvable in polynomial time for $k = 2$, but

E. Gelenbe et al. (eds.), *Computer and Information Sciences*, Lecture Notes in Electrical Engineering 62, DOI 10.1007/978-90-481-9794-1_36,
© Springer Science+Business Media B.V. 2010

NP-hard for $k \geq 3$ [4]. Since graph coloring is NP-complete, the channel assignment problem is also NP-complete, and therefore an optimal assignment cannot be found in polynomial time. Several approaches have been developed to define a channel assignment problem as a graph coloring problem, e.g., in cellular radio networks [5-6], and in IEEE 802.11-based mesh networks [7-8].

Link distance. Given a graph G, and two nodes u and v contained in G, a link l_{uv} is defined as the edge contained in G that connects node u to node v. Let the distance $d(u_1, u_2)$ between two nodes u_1 and u_2 in a graph G be the minimum number of hops in G from u_1 to u_2. Then the distance between two links l_{u1u2} and l_{v1v2} is the minimum of distances between one node in $\{u_1, u_2\}$ and one node in $\{v_1, v_2\}$.

Hence, zero-distance between two links means that the two links share a common node; distance one means that at least one edge connects one node of the first link to one node in the second link, hence simultaneous transmissions interfere. Distances greater than one are achieved if no edges connect a node in the first link to a node in the second link. So, channels can be reused over links whose distance is two or more.

D1EC channel assignment. Given a graph G and a sub-graph $A \subseteq G$, "the Distance-1 Edge Coloring (D1EC) problem seeks a mapping of colors to links in A such that any two links in A that are at distance one with respect to G are assigned different colors" [2]. The authors of [2] do not discuss the time needed for the coloring to be computed and show the network throughput for a colored static topology, i.e., a static channel assignment is calculated before starting the experiments.

Simulated annealing. It was originally proposed by Kirkpatrick *et al.* [3] and Cerny [9]: a system has a set S of possible *conformations* s, each having a cost $K(s)$ and a set of neighbors $N(s)$ representing the possible state transitions from s. A transition from s to $s' \in N(s)$ occurs according to the Metropolis criterion [10], i.e.: if the cost difference $\Delta K = K(s') - K(s)$ is negative then the s' becomes the new conformation; else, a random number R between 0 and 1 is generated according to a uniform distribution, and the resulting conformation is accepted if $e^{-\Delta K/C} > R$. The parameter C is a constant called control parameter. It regulates the percentage of new configurations that are accepted in case ΔK is positive. A *cooling process*, in simulated annealing applications, is emulated by decreasing C progressively from C_0 to C_f through a function $f(C) = uC$. Note that C_0 is critical in order to engage the simulating annealing process, while C_f allows to define a final condition for the algorithm.

2 Dynamic channel assignment through simulated annealing

An active network topology is a subnet that only contains nodes that are sending and receiving packets, and edges that connect these nodes. If the active network changes, also the interference map changes. Furthermore, static coloring of the entire network results in using an unnecessary high number of colors to assign channels to edges that will not really contend most of the time. In practice, with a dynamic coloring scheme, channel assignment could be performed for the sub-graph comprising the *active nodes only*, and *online*, e.g., when the set of active nodes changes or on a fixed schedule. To speed-up the online coloring update procedure, we further exploit the fact that, upon topology changes, the current coloring is likely to be close to the optimal coloring for the new active topology. Hence we run D1EC via simulated annealing as soon as the traffic matrix changes. The contention degree, i.e., the number of interfering links, represents the cost in the Metropolis criterion. We developed a Java simulator to evaluate the coloring scheme, as well as to design and test the simulated annealing parameters. The details about the simulator and the Java code are omitted due to space constraints. Our simulations show that applying D1EC to the set of active nodes is efficient, and initializing D1EC with the colors in use in the previous subinterval converges faster than starting from a non-colored graph (*stateful initial condition*).

2.1 Design of a D1EC-suitable simulated annealing

Different *perturbation methods* are used for promoting state transitions in simulated annealing and obtain a fast convergence to a coloring conformation which is close to the optimal one. Since the algorithm tuning depends on the network topology, we considered different topologies for which we found similar results. Hence we only show results for the network of Fig. 1, which is an extraction from the Chaska's 802.11 network, and contains 45 vertex and 75 edges. As baseline, we considered an algorithm that does not use the Metropolis criterion, and hence accept state transitions only if $\Delta K > 0$. We call this algorithm

Fig. 1 - Graph, extracted from the Chaska network.

NOT-SA, and we compared its performance to the one of a legacy perturbation method (SA) in which we (*i*) select all edge pairs that have the same color and whose distance is one, (*ii*) assign a random color to those edge, and (iii) use the Metropolis criterion. Following [3] we found that the optimal values for C_0 is 4, and $u = 0.95$. C_f was set such that SA effectively converges. Results-not shown here due to lack of space-show that SA outperforms NON-SA. In particular, SA reaches a significant cost reduction within little iteration, while NON-SA converges more slowly.

3 Evaluation

All tests reported here were repeated 10 times, and results are shown in terms of average statistics. We first consider a stateless version of our algorithm, and then we show that the stateful algorithm is ten times faster than the stateless one. In order to show the advantage of using the *stateful initial condition*, we simulate D1EC with simulation annealing in a network in which one node pair is activated after the other, following a random order. When a node pair is activated, the shortest path between the two nodes is computed, and all nodes and links on the path are added to the active network topology. This way, we simulate the impact of multihop wireless traffic.

In Fig. 2, we report the performance of the D1EC when all computations are initialized with a monochromatic assignment, and 3 to 19 colors are available for D1EC. In the figure, the cost decreases dramatically with respect to the initial cost, and fifty iterations are enough to reduce the cost to less than 10% of the initial cost when using at least seven colors. With three colors, the network under test cannot be colored with zero cost. Anyway, also in that case, the minimum possible cost is approached in as few as fifty iterations. Further iterations do not really reduce the cost remarkably. The convergence time is shown in Fig. 3, which reports the number of iterations required to converge after a node pair is added to the active topology: the x-

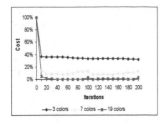 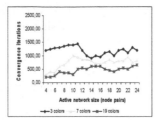 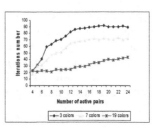

Fig. 2 – Cost convergence (all nodes).

Fig. 3 - Convergence time (stateless).

Fig. 4 - Convergence time (stateful).

axis represents the number of node pairs already in the network when the topology changes, and the y-axis shows the iterations to convergence after the topology change. A few hundreds of iterations are needed in order to converge at each step. In the results of Fig. 4, D1EC uses the last active coloring scheme as initial coloring for the updated network graph, and newly added edges are initialized with a same random color. Noticeably, whatever the number of available colors, the stateful algorithm converges in few tens of iterations, ten times faster than the stateless algorithm.

4 Conclusions

We proposed a simulated annealing-based dynamic channel assignment algorithm, and demonstrated that it can quickly compute a good suboptimal coloring. In particular, we introduced a state in the algorithm, which makes the coloring ten times faster by using an initial channel assignment whose cost is near to the minimum.

References

1. W. K. Hale, "Frequency assignment: Theory and applications." In Proc. IEEE, vol. 68, pp. 1497–1514, Dec. 1980.
2. E. Aryafar, O. Gurewitz, E.W. Knightly, "Distance-1 Constrained Channel Assignment in Single Radio Wireless Mesh Networks." In Proc. of IEEE INFOCOM 2008.
3. S. Kirkpatrick, C.D. Gelatt Jr., M.P. Vecchi, "Optimization by simulated annealing," Science, vol. 220, no. 4598, pp. 671-680, May 13, 1983.
4. Chun-Chen Hsu, Pangfeng Liu, Da-wei Wang, Jan-Jan Wu, "Generalized Edge Coloring for Channel Assignment in Wireless Networks." In Proc. of ICPP 2006, pp. 82 – 92.
5. R. Battiti, A. Bertossi, D. Cavallaio, "A Randomized Saturation Degree Heuristic for Channel Assignment in Cellular Radio Networks." IEEE Trans. on Vehicular Technology, Vol. 50, issue 2, pp. 364-374, 2001.
6. M.I. Islam, A.B.M. Siddique Hossain, "Channel Allocation of Mobile Cellular Network Based on Graph Theory." In Proc. of IEEE TENCON 2004, 21-24 November 2004.
7. J. Riihijarvi, M. Petrova, P. Mahonen, "Frequency Allocation for WLANs Using Graph Colouring Techniques." In Proc. of the WONS 2005, pp. 216-222, January 19-21, 2005
8. C.L. Barrett, V.S.A. Kumar, M.V. Marathe, S. Thite, G. Istrate, "Strong Edge Coloring for Channel Assignment in Wireless Radio Networks." In Proc. of PERCOMW 2006, p. 106.
9. V. Cerny, "Thermodynamical approach to the travelling salesman problem: an efficient simulation algorithm." Journal on Opt. Theory Appl., vol. 45, pp. 41-51, 1985.
10. N. Metropolis, A. Rosenbluth, M. Rosenbluth, A. Teller, E. Teller, "Equation of state calculations by fast computing machines." Jour. of Ch. Phys., vol. 21, pp. 1087-1092, 1953.

Combining Monitoring and Privacy-Protection Perspectives in a Semantic Model for IP Traffic Measurements

Georgios V. Lioudakis[1], Giuseppe Tropea[2], Iakovos St. Venieris[1], Dimitra I. Kaklamani[1],
Nicola Blefari-Melazzi[2]

[1] School of Electrical and Computer Engineering, National Technical University of Athens
Athens, Greece
gelioud@icbnet.ntua.gr, venieris@cs.ntua.gr, dkaklam@mail.ntua.gr
[2] CNIT- Consorzio Nazionale Interuniversitario per le Telecomunicazioni,
Rome, Italy
giuseppe.tropea@cnit.it, blefari@uniroma2.it

Abstract. Several research efforts have focused on the topic of unified data models for IP traffic measurements. However, this domain is so rich in semantics and comprises so many challenges that a standard for sharing and handling datasets is difficult to achieve consensus on. This work is backed by the know-how coming from two projects dealing with unified, privacy-aware access to network data and aims to achieve an integrated model, combining the various concepts involved.

Keywords: Network monitoring, privacy, ontology, semantic model, access control.

1   Introduction

Activities related to network monitoring hold an outstanding position among the ICT technologies threatening personal privacy. While useful and important for purposes such as network operation, management, planning and maintenance, security protection, law enforcement and scientific research based on real traffic traces, network monitoring not only may lead to privacy violations but it is also surrounded by legal implications.

The FP7 projects PRISM [1] and MOMENT [2] have dealt with unified, privacy-aware access to network data, proposing two different, albeit complementary, approaches. Both projects acknowledge the manifold advantages of using ontologies in the design of traffic monitoring infrastructures. This work conducts a survey of the similarities and differences between the two approaches, drawing from different backgrounds and originating from different scientific communities, in order to achieve possible added value in a unified view of the IP traffic measurement domain. This work is motivated by and contributes to the activities of the "Monitoring Ontology for IP traffic" (MOI) [3] ETSI ISG.

E. Gelenbe et al. (eds.), *Computer and Information Sciences*, Lecture Notes
in Electrical Engineering 62, DOI 10.1007/978-90-481-9794-1_37,
© Springer Science+Business Media B.V. 2010

2   Two Perspectives on the IP Traffic Measurement Domain

The MOMENT project has developed an approach comprising all aspects of the IP measurement domain. It includes four ontologies: Data, Metadata, Upper and Anonymization [4]. The latter (Fig. 1) serves for the definition of possible anonymization strategies to be applied to the data, prior to their release. The *PolicyObject* is the cornerstone class; it associates a number of *UserRole*s and *UsagePurpose*s, applied to a number of *PrivacyScope*s. The *PolicyObject* specifies a well-defined *AnonymizationStrategy* and an associated *AcceptableUsePolicy*. The former consists of a group of *AnonymizationTarget*s and an *AnonymizationBackend* to support and implement that strategy. The latter represents an informative structured document, about what the provider expects from the user regarding the use of data that the provider is willing to release. An innovative idea is reflected by the *DataAge* class, capturing the concept that the age of a measurement makes it less sensitive and a looser scheme could be enforced.

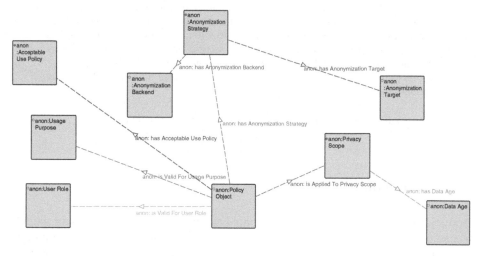

Fig. 1. MOMENT Anonymization ontology.

On the other hand, the PRISM ontology [5] (Fig. 2) has been developed in order to become the semantic implementation of a privacy-aware access control and authorization model, specifically devised for the protection of network monitoring data [6]. It defines access control *Rules* as associations of *PersonalData*, *Purposes* and *Roles*. The rules are also associated with contextual *Conditions*, as well as meta-rules, reflecting concepts such as inheritance and privacy obligations. The data types may become members of *ExclusiveCombinations*, preventing their combinatorial disclosure, while a set of software *Components* enables the definition of *DataTransformations*, e.g., for adjusting precision.

3   Towards a Combined Approach

Table 1 summarizes the main points of the two approaches. Each approach's rationale differentiates the overall design; while MOMENT mostly targets interoperability, PRISM focuses on policies and reasoning. As interoperability is the bottom-line requirement for standardization, the MOMENT approach is the basis of unification, incorporating certain PRISM features; their integration point is the MOMENT Anonymization Ontology.

Concerning the representation of data, monitoring purposes and roles, the MOMENT model already defines such entities; for becoming PRISM-enabled, the corresponding classes are replaced by the PRISM equivalents. For relieving the latter from their interoperability restrictions, they are extended by the flexible string matching approach of MOMENT [4]; this way, the unified approach takes advantage of both the detailed PRISM hierarchies and the interoperability and flexibility features of MOMENT.

With respect to rules definition, PRISM lacks pre-defined anonymization patterns, while MOMENT does not support real-time strategies specification. The solution adopted is to extend MOMENT strategies with privacy obligations and to make them integral to the PRISM real-time decision making procedures. An interesting aspect is the so-called "privacy context" that should affect final decisions, where the two projects have followed quite different approaches. PRISM's *Conditions* class is extended with MOMENT's data age concept. This class becomes related with both the rules themselves, as well as the anonymization strategies, for their conditional application, while it is also supported by the MOMENT fuzzy matching mechanism PRISM's *ExclusiveCombinations* is also adopted.

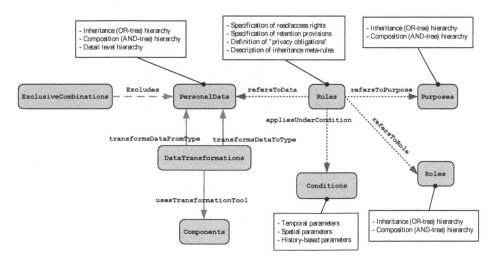

Fig. 2. PRISM ontology.

Table 1. Summary of the MOMENT and PRISM approaches.

Aspect	MOMENT Perspective	PRISM Perspective
General structure	4 discrete ontologies, classes-based	Integrated ontology, instances-based
Data types representation	Sub-classes of the *AnonymizationTarget* class	Instances of the *PersonalData* class, with three different hierarchies
Purposes representation	Sub-classes of the *UsagePurpose* class	Instances of the *Purposes* class, with two hierarchies (AND-, OR-tree)
Roles representation	Sub-classes of the *UserRole* class	Instances of the *Roles* class, with two hierarchies (AND- and OR-tree)
Rules definition	Rules serve for the association of anonymization strategies to roles, purposes and anonymization targets	Access control rules, with additional provisions regarding conditions, obligations
Anonymization strategy definition	Static; the Anonymization Ontology defines some pre-specified anonymization strategies	Dynamic; the strategies are specified in real-time by means of ontological reasoning
Anonymization implementation	The Anonymization module calls external anonymization back-ends, with Java AAPI wrapper included	The ontology contains "semantic pointers" to PRISM software components (including AAPI wrapper)
Obligations	N/A	Per rule definition, using properties
Exclusive data disclosure	N/A	Implemented by means of the *ExclusiveCombinations* class
Additional "privacy context"	Data age	Temporal, spatial and history context, exclusive data combinations
Management of measurements	Measurements are represented as instances of the *Measurement* class	Measurements are managed outside the ontology

References

1. FP7 ICT project PRISM, http://fp7-prism.eu/.
2. FP7 ICT project MOMENT, http://fp7-moment.eu/.
3. ETSI ISG "Measurement Ontology for IP Traffic" (MOI), http://portal.etsi.org/MOI/.
4. A. Salvador, J. E. López de Vergara, G. Tropea, N. Blefari-Melazzi, Á. Ferreiro, Á. Katsu, "A Semantically Distributed Approach to Map IP Traffic Measurements to a Standardized Ontology", *International Journal of Computer Networks & Communications*, Vol. 2, No. 1, January 2010.
5. G. V. Lioudakis, F. Gogoulos, A. Antonakopoulou, D. I. Kaklamani, I. S. Venieris, "Privacy Protection in Passive Network Monitoring: an Access Control Approach", in *Proceedings of the 23rd IEEE International Conference on Advanced Information Networking and Applications (AINA-09)*, Bradford, UK, May 26 – 29, 2009.
6. F. Gogoulos, A. Antonakopoulou, G. V. Lioudakis, A. Mousas, D. I. Kaklamani, I. S. Venieris, "Privacy-Aware Access Control and Authorization in Passive Network Monitoring Infrastructures", in *Proceedings of the 3rd IEEE International Symposium on Trust, Security and Privacy for Emerging Applications (TSP-10)*, Bradford, UK, June 29 – July 1, 2010.

Priority Encoding of Image Data in Wireless Multimedia Sensor Networks for Border Surveillance

Kerem Irgan[1], Cem Unsalan[2] and Şebnem Baydere[1]

[1] Department of Computer Engineering,
[2] Department of Electrical and Electronics Engineering,
Yeditepe University, 34755 Istanbul Turkey

Abstract. In this study, we propose dynamic prioritization of image macro-blocks for Wireless Multimedia Sensor Networks (WMSN). An encoding scheme is employed at the source node by labeling the blocks as "important" or "not-important" based on the information they contain. We introduce a set of novel priority measures to weigh importance of macro-blocks using their intrinsic properties. Experimental results reveal that the priority encoding scheme gracefully adapts itself to the application's quality requirements while reducing the required bandwidth fairly.

1 Introduction

A wide range of emerging wireless sensor network applications may benefit from multimedia capabilities [1]. Border surveillance is such an application, where sensor nodes equipped with low-power cameras can be utilized in an intrusion detection scenario. Resource utilization is one of the main issues in WMSN. Transmitting the informative parts of images instead of the whole scene helps to utilize resources effectively. Although there are some work in the literature devoted to data extraction from images, compression and transmission over WMSN, these are still in their early stages [2]. Complex encoding techniques those require processing of the full image data prior to its transmission may not be suitable for sensor nodes due to memory and processing resource constraints.

Packet prioritization has been extensively studied in the literature for differentiated services networks. One of the pioneering work is by Albanese *et al.* [3]. However, in WMSN the problem becomes more specific due to resource constraints and the dynamic nature of the environment. Therefore, static resource allocation methods are not convenient for WMSN. Soro *et al.* [1] indicate that multimedia packet prioritization remains an open challenge. Lecuire *et al.* [2] performed packet prioritization of wavelet sub-bands. Their main aim is the energy efficiency of image transmission. On the other hand, the present study focuses on packet prioritization at the network layer which adapts itself to the application layer requirements and environmental changes using a simple encoding mechanism.

E. Gelenbe et al. (eds.), *Computer and Information Sciences*, Lecture Notes in Electrical Engineering 62, DOI 10.1007/978-90-481-9794-1_38,
© Springer Science+Business Media B.V. 2010

In this study, we propose a priority encoding scheme that is applicable to image partitions rather than the full image. N M 8-bit grayscale images are partitioned into m m pixel macro-blocks. These macro-blocks are serially passed to the network layer for encoding. The network layer employs a cost effective image measure to the macro-blocks and labels them as "important" or "not-important" based on the information they contain. Then, only the packets labeled as "important" are transmitted through fully reliable paths. In this method, *priority threshold value* is the critical network parameter that has to be set carefully for successful labeling. Determining the threshold value should be adaptive based on the setup of the sensor nodes and the images to be transmitted. In the border surveillance application, the image parts containing humans are valuable. Therefore, their successful transmission to the sink node is more important than transmitting the background image. To this end, different priority measures are considered: *entropy, edge* and *reproducibility*. To quantitatively measure their performances, we propose a new metric called as *Object-Transmission-Rate* (OTR). It reflects the object quality in the transmitted images. We compare the performance of the priority encoding when different image measures are used. Transmissions over lossy links without any encoding case is used as the baseline for the comparisons. The implementation costs of the proposed measures are also examined on real sensor nodes.

2   Packet Prioritization for Images

Generally, the image to be transferred in a WMSN is not homogeneous. Some of its parts contain more information compared to others. In this section, we provide several measures to weigh the importance of a given macro-block. Our motivation is border surveillance with WMSN. Therefore, the measures should emphasize objects in the image and label the ones containing objects as "important". The proposed measures are *entropy, edge* and *reproducibility*.

Entropy measure can be taken as the probabilistic information measure of a given macro-block [4]. For each image macro-block, entropy is calculated by its normalized grayscale intensity histogram. This is actually the sample probability mass function of the macro-block.

Edge measure is based on the edge amount in the image. If there is an object in the image, it should have edges. Therefore, if a measure can be developed based on the edge information, then it can also be used for packet prioritization. In this study, the simplest edge detection method based on Haar filter (with coefficients $\{+1 \ -1\}$) is used without direction selectivity. The absolute values of these edge filter responses in the image macro-block are summed and taken as the edge measure.

Reproducibility measure is based on the well-known technique in image processing called as image inpainting [5]. In this measure, each macro-block is represented by the mean value of its grayscale pixel values. If the mean value of a macro-block is close to the mean values of its neighboring macro-blocks, in general terms it resembles its neighbors. Hence, it is possible to reproduce it. If the mean values are different, then the macro-block differs from its neighbors and it may not be easy to reproduce it, so it is "important". The weight for the macro-block p is calculated as $R_p = \sum_{n=1}^{8} |\mu(p) - \mu(p_n)|$ where $\mu(p)$ is the mean value of p. p_n for $n = 1 \ldots 8$ are the eight neighbors of p.

3   Experiments

In the experiments, we assume that sensor nodes do not fail during image transmission and a reliable communication path between the source and the sink is established prior to image transmission. Each macro-block is labeled as "important" or "not-important" in accordance with the selected priority measure and corresponding priority threshold value. Then, the "important" macro-blocks are transmitted in seperate data packets through the reliable channel with a transmission probability $p = 1$. The "not-important" macro-blocks are dropped from the network buffer. Therefore, the number of prioritized macro-blocks are equal to the transmitted packets.

In this study, we selected test images in accordance with their suitability to surveillance applications. For this purpose, we picked 26 images from [6]. We first implemented the *entropy*, *edge*, and *reproducibility* measures under Matlab. Applying each measure to test images, we obtain *macro-block weight matrices* for each measure-image pair.

Along with the weights, a *threshold value* is determined to label macro-blocks of an image for each priority measure. We determine the threshold values for each measure by taking the medians of the macro-block measure weights of all 26 images together. By applying the thresholds to the macro-block weights, we obtained different *Prioritized-Packet-Rates* (PPRs) for each measure-image pair.

We evaluate the efficiency of the proposed encoding scheme and the priority measures by the rate of the transmitted objects which are subjects of the application, in the image. We call this metric as *Object-Transmission-Rate* (OTR).

3.1   Results and Implementation Costs

We conducted a set of Monte Carlo simulations under Matlab to compare the results of the proposed measures. As a performance criterion, we consider the number of tests in which OTR is greater than the corresponding OTR_{sim}. In this way, we attain 85% success rate for *entropy* and *edge* measures, and 100% success rate for *reproducibility* measure.

Another consideration is on the relation between OTR and PPR. To assess this relation, we generate the *Object Transmission Index* (OTI) which is calculated as $OTI = OTR/PPR$. This index gives us the best measure in which maximum amount of objects are transmitted with minimum amount of packets. OTI's of the measures are given in Table 1. As can be seen in this table, *reproducibility* measure is the most successful one in terms of OTI.

We implemented each measure on Telos [7] compatible *Tmote Sky* sensor nodes as summarized in Table 2. The edge based measure needs lowest memory and fairly low CPU cycles.

Table 1. Object transmission index values.

Measures	$\mu(OTR)$	$\mu(PPR)$	$\mu(OTI)$
Entropy	0.8164	0.5176	1.58
Edge	0.8186	0.4832	1.69
Reproducibility	0.8782	0.4845	1.81

Table 2. Implementation costs of the measures.

Measures	CPU Cycles	Program Memory (bytes)	Data Memory (bytes)	Network Buffer (bytes)
Entropy	8270	206	454	64
Edge	2800	126	72	64
Reproducibility	1820	514	154	4480

4   Conclusions

In this study, we first introduced a set of novel packet priority measures for the network layer. Each measure achieves high OTRs and has different advantages. While the *reproducibility* measure needs the lowest processing time, *edge* measure has the minimum memory requirement. Hybrid usage of these measures should be examined as a future work. Second, the proposed encoding scheme enables packets to be labeled as "important" or "not-important" without referencing the full image. Experimental results indicate that the labeling can successfully be done using adaptive group based thresholding. By using priority encoding in this scenario approximately half of the bandwidth is saved.

References

1. Soro, S., Heinzelman, W.: A Survey of Visual Sensor Networks. Advances in Multimedia **2009** (2009) 1–22
2. Lecuire, V., Duran-Faundez, C., Krommenacker, N.: Energy-efficient image transmission in sensor networks. International Journal of Sensor Networks **4** (2008) 3747
3. Albanese, A., Blomer, J., Edmonds, J., Luby, M., Sudan, M.: Priority encoding transmission. IEEE Transactions on Information Theory **42** (1996) 1737–1744
4. Lathi, B.P., Ding, Z.: Modern Digital and Analog Communication Systems. 4. edn. Oxford University Press (2009)
5. Ballester, C., Bertalmio, M., Caselles, V., Sapiro, G., Verdera, J.: Filling-in by joint interpolation of vector fields and gray levels. IEEE Transactions on Image Processing (2001) 1200–1211
6. Olivia, A., Torralba, A.: Modeling the shape of the scene: a holistic representation of the spatial envelope. Int. Journal of Computer Vision **42** (2001) 145–175 http://people.csail.mit.edu/torralba/code/spatialenvelope/.
7. Polastre, J., Szewczyk, R., Culler, D.: Telos: enabling ultra-low power wireless research. In: Information Processing in Sensor Networks, 2005. IPSN 2005. Fourth International Symposium on. (2005) 364–369

Energy-aware Routing with Two-group Allocation in Ad Hoc Networks

Jihai Zhou, Mustafa Gurcan, and Anursorn Chungtragarn

Department of Electrical and Electronic Engineering
Imperial College London, UK
{jihai.zhou06,m.gurcan,a.chungtragarn09}@imperial.ac.uk

Abstract. A new energy-aware disjoint routing discovery scheme for wireless ad-hoc networks is developed. With a novel energy per bit measurement technique incorporated with a two-group allocation method, the information bits can be allocated to each path such that the overall amount of energy consumed is minimized.

Key words: energy-aware routing, two-group allocation, ad hoc network

1 Background

The constrained energy problem in wireless ad-hoc networks renders the need for energy-efficient routing protocols, especially when multi-path routing [1] is considered. Instead of identifying routing paths with the smallest hop counts and transmitting fixed-sized packets, routing paths with the smallest energy per bit requirement can be selected using a two-group allocation scheme and a novel energy consumption per bit measurement technique to adjust the packet sizes on each path, hence satisfying the minimum energy requirement.

There are two main strategies of multi-path routing in literature; the best route selection scheme and the load balancing method. The former measures parameters such as the hop count [1] and the probability of successful transmission [5] to find the best path and the latter considers multiple routing paths [3, 4] to minimize energy utilization, improve fault tolerance and network lifetime, alleviate traffic congestion and maximize the data rate.

In this paper a novel routing path discovery algorithm is proposed to identify multiple routing paths by minimizing energy consumption while maximizing data rates. To achieve this objective, the paper is organized as follows. Section 2 formulates and defines this research problem. The account of the proposed routing path discovery scheme is given in Section 3. Section 4 presents the results and Section 5 concludes this paper.

2 Problem Formulation

Consider a total of M bits to be transmitted over T seconds through Z paths linking a source to a destination node in a wireless ad hoc network with N randomly distributed immobile nodes, where disjoint multi-path routing is assumed.

Each hop between two adjacent nodes, i and j, in path z allows L_z bit packet size to be transmitted over a service time of $\overline{T}_{i,j}$ for $i, j \in J_z$ where J_z represents a set of numbers denoting all nodes in path z for $z = 1, \ldots, Z$. If a total of m_z bits are transmitted over T seconds using path z where $M = \sum_{z=1}^{Z} m_z$, the amount of energy consumed in path z over T seconds can be written as

$$E_z = P_{MAC,z} T = m_z P_T N_{PG} T_c \sum_{i \in J_z} \frac{1}{r_{i,l}} \tag{1}$$

where $P_{MAC,z} = \frac{m_z P_T N_{PG} T_c}{T} \sum_{i,l \in J_z} \frac{1}{r_{i,l}}$ is the required MAC power for path z, P_T is the transmission power, N_{PG} is the processing gain, T_c is the chip period and $r_{i,l}$ is the data rate required for transmission between node i and l, where $i, l \in J_z$. From (1), the consumed energy per bit for path z can be expressed as

$$E_{b,z} = \frac{E_z}{m_z} = P_T N_{PG} T_c \sum_{i,l \in J_z} \frac{1}{r_{i,l}} \tag{2}$$

Hence, the main aim of this paper is to minimize the total energy $E_T = \sum_{z=1}^{Z} m_z E_{b,z}$ such that the total data rate in bits per second is achieved as

$$\frac{M}{T} = \sum_{z=1}^{Z} \frac{m_z}{T} = \sum_{z=1}^{Z} \frac{L_z}{\max_{i,l \in J_z}(\overline{T}_{i,l})} \tag{3}$$

considering the maximum permissible MAC rate over each path z, $R_{MAC,z,MAX} = \frac{L_z}{\max_{i,l \in J_z}(\overline{T}_{i,l})}$. To minimize E_T, all routing paths $z = 1, \ldots, Z$ with the least consumed amounts of energy per bit, $E_{b,z}$ are identified using (2), which requires optimization of the data rate, $r_{i,l}$ that can be realized by the two-group resource allocation scheme [2]. Once $E_{b,z}$ is discovered, the number of bits that should be allocated to path z can be determined as

$$m_z = \frac{M}{E_{b,z} \sum_{z=1}^{Z} \frac{1}{E_{b,z}}}, \tag{4}$$

where the energy consumed per path, E_z is equal for all paths. Having m_z, the packet size, L_z for path z is calculated from equation (3) as follows

$$L_z \geq \frac{m_z}{T} \max_{i,l \in J_z}(\overline{T}_{i,l}), \tag{5}$$

where the minimum energy utilization requirement is met with equality and the maximum service time, $\max_{i,l \in J_z}(\overline{T}_{i,l})$ is calculated using the approach presented in [2]. In the next section, modified disjoint multi-path routing algorithms to address this energy minimization problem are proposed.

3   Modified Disjoint Multi-path Routing Discovery

Two techniques are developed to discover the least cost disjointed routing paths, in which none of the nodes between the source and the destination nodes are shared, where the cost is the energy per bit calculated using (2).

3.1   The Trellis-hop Diagram Approach

Given an N-node network topology, all possible routing paths can be identified using a trellis-hop diagram. The N nodes are arranged in each column of an N-column trellis diagram. All routing paths can be discovered by drawing the links from the source node on the top-left corner of the diagram to the connected neighbouring nodes, which are denoted in the next column until the drawn routing paths reach the destination node on the last row of the diagram. The least cost disjointed routing path is then identified using (2). Once this path is known, all other nodes connected to it are disconnected to reconstruct a new network topology from which the next least cost routing path is discovered. This process is repeated until all least cost routing paths are identified. However as N grows larger, the required computational load increases significantly. To address this problem, a modified Viterbi algorithm is proposed next.

3.2   The Modified Viterbi Algorithm

There are two main parts of this algorithm. The first part discovers all low cost routing paths of the current network topology by grouping the routing paths in different levels, R_k based on the hop count, k, where $k = 1, 2, \ldots, N - 1$. From the lowest level, R_1, the link cost is calculated using equation (2) for all uncompleted routing paths until the highest level is reached. At each level, the routing paths which arrive at the destination node are considered complete, hence recorded in the completed routing path table before being removed from the uncompleted routing path table. If more than one uncompleted routing paths pass through the same link, the routing path with the lowest sum of the link costs is selected before being removed from the uncompleted routing path table.

Once all low cost routing paths are found, the next part of the algorithm is to identify the lowest cost path from these paths. After knowing this path, all nodes along it are removed and a new network topology is formed from the rest of the nodes to find the remaining disjointed routing paths using the first part of this algorithm. In the next section, some simulation results are presented to demonstrate the advantage of applying the proposed scheme.

4   Simulation Results

To measure performance of the proposed schemes, networks with 50 randomly distributed nodes are produced and tested. Using the modified Viterbi algorithm, four least cost routing paths are discovered from four different topologies constructed from a 50-node network, as shown in Figure 1a.

Figure 1b shows the energy consumed per bit when the proposed energy-aware disjoint single-path routing (EADSR) and the ad hoc on demand distance vector (AODV) schemes are tested with five different network topologies, given source-to-destination pairs under different scenarios. The lowest cost routing paths are chosen for both cases while the two-group algorithm is compared with

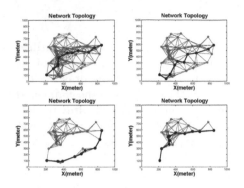

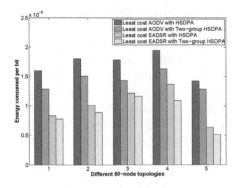

(a) Disjoint multiple routing path discovery   (b) Energy consumption comparison

Fig. 1: Discovered routing paths with energy consumption measurement

the standard high speed downlink packet access (HSDPA) equal rate allocation scheme. It clearly shows that the EADSR, which can be further enhanced by the two-group allocation scheme, consumes the least amount of energy.

5   Conclusion

In this paper, an energy-aware disjoint routing scheme is proposed for wireless ad hoc networks. With a novel energy per bit measurement technique equipped with the two-group algorithm, energy consumption is minimized while maximizing the transmission rate over the routing paths chosen.

References

1. M. K. Marina and S. R. Das, "On-demand Multi-path Distance Vector Routing in Ad Hoc Networks", *IEEE Ninth International Conference on Network Protocols*, Nov. 2001, pp: 14-23
2. J. Zhou and M. K. Gurcan, "An Improved Multicode CDMA Transmission Method for Ad Hoc Networks", *IEEE Wireless Communications and Networking Conference (WCNC)*, Budapest, Hungary, April 2009.
3. A Tsirigos and Z. J. Haas, "Analysis of Multi-path Routing - Part I: The effect on The Packet Delivery Ratio". *IEEE Trans. Wireless Communication*, 3(1) (2004), pp/ 138-146.
4. S Zhang, G Xu, "Rate Allocation Strategies for Energy-efficient Multi-path Routing in Ad Hoc Networks towards B3G," *The Journal of China Universities of Posts andTelecommunications*, Vol. 14, Issue 2, June 2007, pp. 84-88.
5. Bacelli, F., B. Blaszczyszyn, and P. Muhlethaler, "Time-space Opportunistic Routing in Wireless Ad Hoc Networks: Algorithms and Performance Optimization by Stochastic Geometry," *The Computer Journal*, June 2009.

ProFID: Practical Frequent Item Set Discovery in Peer-to-Peer Networks

Emrah Çem[1] and Öznur Özkasap[1*]

Koç University, Istanbul, Turkey

Abstract. This study addresses the problem of discovering frequent items in unstructured P2P networks. We propose a fully distributed Protocol for Frequent Item set Discovery (ProFID) where the result is produced at every peer. We also propose a practical rule for convergence of the algorithm. Finally, we evaluate the efficiency of our approach through an extensive simulation study on PeerSim.

1 Introduction

Peer-to-Peer (P2P) systems are very dynamic and scalable, hence centralized approaches are not as functional, reliable, and robust as decentralized approaches. Peers may need a system-wide information such as network size, query/event counts, or mostly contacted peers for specific files in order to perform various tasks such as load-balancing or topology optimization [1]. Database applications [2], wireless sensor networks [3], and security applications can also make use of frequent item discovery protocol, as well as P2P applications [1,4]. Hence, efficient discovery of frequent items would be a valuable service for distributed systems.

We propose a fully distributed gossip-based approach named ProFID using pairwise averaging function and convergence rule which is novel in frequent item discovery problem. Our approach for data aggregation in ProFID is inspired by [3] and the main differences are that it works for multiple items and utilizes aggregation for frequent item set discovery. The work of [3] presents a distributed way of calculating aggregates such as averages, sums, and extremal values. They use topology information while determining the termination time, which is not practical since it may not be available at all peers. Another related study [5] proposes a push-synopses protocol using uniform gossip for aggregate computation and analyzes the scalability, reliability and efficiency of their approach. Algorithm converges to true average only if all peers have a knowledge about all items in the system, which might be an inconvenient requirement for large networks without centralized agents. In [4], gossip protocol is used for the first time in frequent item discovery problem. In order to identify frequent elements, a threshold mechanism is used, and by using sampling, the communication load is decreased. However, a uniform gossip is performed, which is not a realistic assumption for large networks.

* Research supported by TUBITAK (The Scientific and Technical Research Council of Turkey) under CAREER Award Grant 104E064.

E. Gelenbe et al. (eds.), *Computer and Information Sciences*, Lecture Notes in Electrical Engineering 62, DOI 10.1007/978-90-481-9794-1_40,
© Springer Science+Business Media B.V. 2010

2   ProFID: Protocol for Frequent Item Set Discovery

We consider a network consisting of N peers denoted as $P=\{P_1, P_2, \ldots, P_N\}$ and M item types denoted as $D=\{D_1, D_2, \ldots, D_j, \ldots, D_M\}$, where D_j has a global frequency g_{D_j}. Parameters N, M, and g are system-wide information, hence they are unknown to all peers a priori. Each peer (P_i) has a local set of items $S_i \subseteq D$ and each local item (D_j) has a local frequency f_{i,D_j} such that

$$g_{D_j} = \sum_{i=1}^{N} f_{i,D_j}, \quad D_j \notin S_i \Longrightarrow f_{i,D_j} = 0$$

Peers form an unstructured network and communicate in rounds with a fixed duration. A peer may leave or join the network at any time. Furthermore, peers' local clocks do not need to be synchronized because peers use clocks just to perform periodic operations.

We provide a gossip-based fully distributed approach with pairwise averaging function in ProFID, utilizing pairwise averaging function with gossip-based aggregation and a practical convergence rule (Fig. 1). Our pairwise averaging function uses push-pull scheme meaning that a peer sends its state (in a push message) to a target peer and the target peer performs averaging operation using its own state and incoming state, then replies the average of incoming items (in a pull message) back to the sender. Then, sender updates its state. By this way, a single push-pull based pairwise averaging operation is completed. In order to prevent misleading calculations, this operation must be performed atomically. For this purpose, we used buffering and timeout mechanisms. Since we aim to find frequent items, knowing averages of items is not enough, we also need to calculate the system size N at each peer. In order to calculate system size, an initiator peer adds a unique item named ui in its local item set. The local frequency of this item is set to 1. Since only one peer has that unique item, average frequency of that item would converge to $\frac{1}{N}$ from which N can be extracted by each peer. Using both estimated average frequency of items and the network size, each peer can calculate the frequencies of items. Due to page limitation, we refer interested reader to [6] for details of our study.

3   Simulation Results

We used PeerSim [7] simulator to build the model for ProFID. We evaluated the behavior and performance of ProFID through extensive large-scale distributed scenarios. Random graphs with average degree 10 is used in the experiments and items are distributed randomly to all peers. Moreover, all the simulation data points are the average of 50 experiments. We evaluate the effects of convergence parameters (ε and $convLimit$) on the accuracy and efficiency of ProFID, as well as the performance of pairwise averaging function.

Fig. 2a depicts the scalability of ProFID in terms of time complexity. Our results (for number of rounds to converge) agree with the $O(logN)$ time complexity of epidemic dissemination [8]. Fig. 2b illustrates that even though the

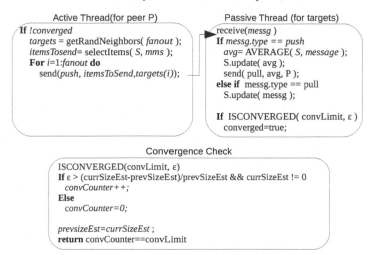

Fig. 1: ProFID Algorithms: Active thread, passive thread, and convergence check

link drop probability is around 5%, convergence error of the pairwise averaging is almost negligible. In this simulation, the message loss probability of each link is independent and identically distributed. As depicted in Fig. 2c, algorithm converges faster for larger values of fanout since a peer exchanges its state with more neighbors and its state is disseminated faster to the network.

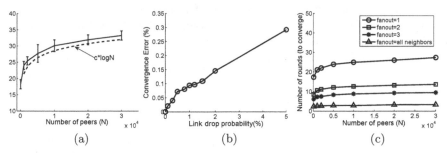

Fig. 2: (a) Number of gossip rounds needed for all peers to converge. (b)The effect of link drop probability on the accuracy of pairwise averaging. (c) The effect of fanout on convergence time

Fig. 3a shows that increasing ε, decreases both average number of messages sent per peer and number of rounds to converge because convergence rule increments *convCounter* value with more probability, which results in faster convergence. Since algorithm converges faster, peers communicate less and average number of messages sent per peer decreases. In contrast to ε parameter, increasing *convLimit* increases both the average number of messages sent per peer and number of rounds to converge because *convCounter* needs to be incremented more to reach *convLimit*. Fig. 3c illustrates the effects of convergence param-

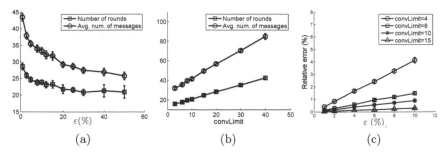

(a)   (b)   (c)

Fig. 3: The effects of ε (a) and *convLimit* (b) on convergence time and average number of messages sent per peer. (c) The effects of convergence parameters on relative error.

eters on converge time. The fastest convergence occurs whenever ε parameter takes its largest value and *convLimit* takes its smallest value, which agrees with the convergence rule. However, there is a tradeoff between convergence time and accuracy as depicted in Fig. 3c.

In conclusion, our results confirm the practical nature, ease of deployment and efficiency ProFID. As future directions, we aim to evaluate ProFID in peer churn scenarios, and investigate the effect of limited gossip message sizes. For comparison, we are developing the well-known push-synopses protocol [5] by adapting it to the problem of frequent item discovery and practical P2P network settings. Furthermore, we aim to conduct network tests of ProFID on the PlanetLab.

References

1. Li, M., Lee, W.C.: Identifying Frequent Items in P2P Systems. ICDCS. (2008) 36–44
2. Manjhi, A., Shkapenyuk, V., Dhamdhere, K., Olston, C.: Finding (Recently) Frequent Items in Distributed Data Streams. ICDE. (2005) 767–778
3. Jelasity, M., Montresor, A., Babaoglu, O.: Gossip-Based Aggregation in Large Dynamic Network. ACM Ttrans. Comput. Syst. **23** (2005) 219–252
4. Lahiri, B., Tirthapura, S.: Computing Frequent Elements Using Gossip. SIROCCO. (2008) 119–130
5. Kempe, D., Dobra, A., Johannes., G.: Gossip-Based Computation of Aggregate Information. FOCS. (2003) 482–491
6. Çem, E., Özkasap, Ö.: ProFID: Practical Frequent Item Set Discovery in Peer-to-Peer Networks. Technical Report, Koç University, March 2010.
7. The Peersim simulator. http://peersim.sf.net.
8. Özkasap, Ö., Çaglar, M., Yazici, E. S., Küçükçifçi, S.: An analytical framework for self-organizing peer-to-peer anti-entropy algorithms. Perform. Eval. **67** (2010) 141–159

7 Computer Vision and Image Processing

Face Signatures Derived from the Trace Transform

Marsyita Hanafi and Maria Petrou

Imperial College, South Kensington Campus, London SW7 2AZ

Abstract. Face signatures computed from the Trace transform offer alternative face representations. They may be used in tasks like face authentication and face recognition. We demonstrate the usefulness of the constructed features with experiments on the BANCA and FERET databases.

1 Introduction

Problems concerned with human faces are of two types: face authentication (verification) and face recognition (identification) [1]. In the authentication task, one of the most successful methods is based on the Trace transform [1]. However, this method is very computationally intensive. Inspired by this method, our goal here is to explore some other options of the Trace transform and construct signatures from it. The produced face signatures are used in authentication tasks.

2 Methodology

The Trace transform is produced by calculating a functional, T, over parameter t along tracing lines. Each of the tracing lines is characterized by two parameters, which are its distance from the centre of the axes, p, and its orientation, φ. In our implementation, instead of considering lines at various orientations, we follow [4] and rotate the image instead, while keeping the tracing lines at fixed orientation $\varphi = 90°$. The tracing lines are two pixels apart, i.e., $\triangle p = 2$ and each line is sampled with points two pixels apart, i.e., $\triangle t = 2$. Different Trace functionals produce different Trace transforms [3]. In our work, we used the following 7 Trace functionals [2]:

$$T_1 : \left| \sum_{j=1}^{n} e^{i5lnr_{1_j}} r_{1_j} f(r_{1_j}) \triangle t \right| \qquad T_3 : \left| \sum_{j=1}^{n} e^{i4lnr_{1_j}} (r_{1_j})^{0.5} f(r_{1_j}) \triangle t \right|$$

$$T_2 : \left| \sum_{j=1}^{n} e^{i3lnr_{1_j}} r_{1_j} f(r_{1_j}) \triangle t \right| \qquad T_6 : \left| \sum_{j=1}^{n} r_j^2 f(r_j) \triangle t \right| \qquad T_7 : \left| \sum_{j=1}^{n} r_j f(r_j) \triangle t \right|$$

$$T_4 : \text{median}\left(\{|(t_k - c_1)f(t_k - c_1)|\}_{t_k > 0}, \{|f(t_k - c_1)|^{1/2}\}_{t_k > 0} \right)$$

$$T_5 : \text{median}\left(\{|f(t_k - c_1)|\}_{t_k > 0}, \{|f(t_k - c_1)|^{1/2}\}_{t_k > 0} \right)$$

$$(1)$$

E. Gelenbe et al. (eds.), *Computer and Information Sciences*, Lecture Notes in Electrical Engineering 62, DOI 10.1007/978-90-481-9794-1_41, © Springer Science+Business Media B.V. 2010

The so called circus function is produced by applying a diametric functional to the columns of the Trace transform, to produce a function that depends only on φ. In this work, 6 diametric functionals were used:

$$P_1 : \sum_{k=1}^{N} |g(p_{k+1}) - g(p_k)| \qquad P_2 : \text{median}\left(\{g(p_k)\}_k, \{|g(p_k)|\}_k\right)$$

$$P_3 : \sum_{k=1}^{N} |FourierTrans(g(p_k))\omega_k|^4 \triangle p$$

$$P_4 : \left|\sum_{k=1}^{N} e^{i4lnr_{1_k}} (r_{1_k})^{0.5} f(r_{1_k}) \triangle p\right| \qquad P_6 : \left|\sum_{k=1}^{N} r_k^2 f(r_k) \triangle p\right|$$

$$P_5 : \text{median}\left(\{|(p_k - c_1)g(p_k - c_1)|\}_{p_k > 0}, \{|g(p_k - c_1)|^{1/2}\}_{p_k > 0}\right)$$

$$(2)$$

The combination of the 7 Trace functionals and 6 diametric functionals produced a total of 42 circus functions, denoted as $h(\varphi)$. Then, following [2] we produced the associated circus functions using $h_a(\varphi) \equiv \text{sign}(h(\varphi))|h(\varphi)|^{-\frac{1}{v}}$ where v is a number characterizing the pair of functionals used [5]. The produced associated circus functions are normalised so that they differ from each other only by rotation and a positive scaling [5]. So, each face in the database is represented by 42 signatures. In an authentication task, the same signatures are computed for the query face. Then, the system should verify whether the query face is identical with the reference face (client) or not (impostor). To perform this task, we compare the corresponding signatures, one from a reference face and one from the query face, by computing their normalised correlation coefficient (NCC), for the shift that maximises it.

3 Experiments

We demonstrate our work using the BANCA and FERET databases. The BANCA database [6] consists of 312 faces of 56 subjects (6 faces per subject captured in three different sessions). These faces are divided into three sets: training set, evaluation set and testing set. The subjects are randomly divided into 25 clients, 12 evaluation impostors and 15 test impostors. The training set is used to build the client models and the evaluation set is used to select the combinations of trace and circus functionals that best discriminate between clients and impostors and to define the threshold for the score of similarity. The faces in the testing set are used to simulate the authentication test. The FERET database [7] consists of 450 faces of 150 subjects (3 faces per subject). The subjects from this database are randomly divided into 50 clients, 50 training impostors and 50 testing impostors. The performance is observed using False Acceptance (FA) and False Rejection (FR). FA and FR are measured by $FA = (EI/I) \times 100\%$

and $FR = (EC/C) \times 100\%$. EI is the number of impostor acceptances, I is the number of impostor claims, EC is the number of clients rejected and C is the number of client claims. Three thresholds are chosen so that they make the two error rates, when computed for the evaluation set, to be $FA_e = FR_e$, $FR_e = 0$ and $FA_e = 0$: $T_{\mathrm{FA}_e=\mathrm{FR}_e}$, $T_{\mathrm{FR}_e=0}$ and $T_{\mathrm{FA}_e=0}$, respectively, where letter e indicates that these error rates refer to the evaluation dataset.

During training, we computed the normalised correlation coefficients, between face signatures of the same client, for all clients, and between signatures that correspond to all combinations of clients and impostors. The normalised histograms of these values were constructed in order to help us identify which face signatures are good discriminators. For the BANCA database, the selected circuses are those produced by the following pairs of functionals: (T_1, P_1), (T_2, P_1), (T_4, P_1), (T_6, P_1), (T_7, P_1), (T_6, P_4), (T_7, P_4), (T_6, P_5) and (T_7, P_5), while for the FERET database, the selected circuses are those produced by: (T_1, P_1), (T_2, P_1), (T_4, P_2), (T_5, P_2), (T_4, P_4), (T_5, P_4), (T_1, P_5), (T_2, P_5), (T_3, P_5) and (T_5, P_5). The scores obtained from these circuses for the evaluation sets are represented by the normalised histogram shown in Fig. 1 and 2, for the two databases, respectively. From these graphs, the three thresholds, $T_{\mathrm{FA}_e=\mathrm{FR}_e}$, $T_{\mathrm{FR}_e=0}$ and $T_{\mathrm{FA}_e=0}$ were obtained.

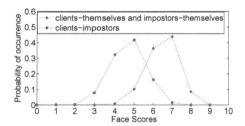

Fig. 1. The normalised histogram of the face scores of the BANCA database.

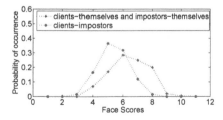

Fig. 2. The normalised histogram of the face scores of the FERET database.

In the testing, the scores of similarity between the impostors in the testing set and the clients in the training set, and the scores between clients in the testing set and the training set were calculated. Using the BANCA database, the total number of scores for the clients-impostors is 4500 (25 clients × 2 shots × 15 impostors × 6 shots) and for the clients-themselves is 100 (25 clients × 4 shots), while for the FERET database, the total number of scores for the clients-impostors is 7500 (50 clients × 1 shots × 50 impostors × 3 shots) and for the clients-themselves is 50 (50 clients × 1 shot). The calculated error rates from the BANCA and FERET databases are shown in Table 1.

Table 1. Error rates from (a) BANCA and (b) FERET

	(a)			(b)		
	$T_{FA_e=0}$	$T_{FR_e=0}$	$T_{FA_e=FR_e}$	$T_{FA_e=0}$	$T_{FR_e=0}$	$T_{FA_e=FR_e}$
FA	0%	44.8%	3.9%	0.1%	90.9%	4.9%
FR	47.0%	0%	7.0%	98.0%	0%	8.0%
TER	47.0	44.8	10.9	98.1	90.0	12.9

4   Conclusions

The results presented in Table 1 show a total error rate of $10 - 13\%$. This is too high for an authentication system to be used in practice. However, it shows that the face signatures we constructed can be used as features, in combination with other features for a practical authentication system.

References

1. Srisuk, S., Petrou, M., Kurutach, W., Kadyrov, A.: Face Authentication using the Trace Transform. In: IEEE Computer Society Conference on Computer Vision and Pattern Recognition, pp. I-305– I-312 (2003)
2. Kadyrov, A., Petrou, M.: Object signatures invariant to affine distortions derived from the trace transform. J. Image and Vision Computing, pp. 1135–1143 (2003)
3. Kadyrov, A., Petrou, M.: The Trace Transform and Its Application. IEEE Transactions on Pattern Analysis and Machine Intelligence, 811–828 (2001)
4. Fahmy, S.A., Bouganis, C-S., Cheung, P.Y.K., Luk, W.: Real-time hardware acceleration of the trace transform. J. Real-Time Image Processing, pp. 235–248 (2007)
5. Petrou, M., Kadyrov, A.: Affine Invariant Features from the Trace Transform. IEEE Transactions on Pattern Analysis and Machine Intelligence, pp. 30–44 (2004)
6. Biometric Access Control for Networked and E-Commerce Applications, http://www.ee.surrey.ac.uk/CVSSP/banca
7. Phillips, P. J., Wechsler, H., Huang, J., Rauss, P.: The FERET database and evaluation procedure for face recognition algorithms. J. Image and Vision Computing, vol. 16, pp. 295–306 (1998)

This article was processed using the LaTeX macro package with LLNCS style

Automatic and Self-adaptive Facial Expression Tracking

Jing chi [1]

[1] Department of Computer Science and Technology, Shandong Economic University, Ji'nan, China

Abstract. We present a novel automatic and self-adaptive technique for facial expression tracking. The face point clouds are acquired at video rate with 3D scanner or reconstructed from 2D images. A single time-varying deformable mesh model is computed with our new metric to track these point clouds. A normal constraint is presented and introduced in the new metric to measure the direction consistency of vertex normal and vertex motion in the tracking process. Combined with other constraints in the new metric, it can automatically ensure the vertices move to optimal position. The normal constraint also works effectively where the model is very different from the point clouds in geometry. Experiment results show that the new technique can well track facial expression without manual aid.

1 Introduction

In recent years, 3D facial expression tracking with dynamic face point clouds has become an important and challenging problem in computer graphics. These point clouds are captured at video rate with 3D scanner or recovered from 2D video flow, which records the facial time-varying expression. Each point cloud can be reconstructed as a mesh to reflect the expression at a certain time. But these meshes have different geometry and topology, which makes it difficult to accurately reflect the facial expression variation and reanimate the captured expressions. So, we need to build a sequence of meshes with the same topology and integrally represent the mesh sequence as a single deformable mesh model. The mesh sequence will reflect the time-varying expression and the single model can support further processing such as expression editing, surface deformation analysis, and so on.

Because the facial physical structure is complex, and humans are sensitive to the unnatural expression variation, it is necessary to track all the subtleties of expression. In addition, to improve the tracking efficiency, the manual aid should be decreased in the tracking process. Moreover, the tracking process should get suggested results no matter how different the facial shapes are. To address those problems, we present a novel more automatic and self-adaptive technique for 3D facial expression tracking in this paper. We use a single deformable mesh model to fit each captured mesh under our new metric in order to track the facial expression. The new metric extends iterative closest point (ICP) idea to non-rigid deformation while retaining the convergence properties of ICP, and introduces the normal constraint to enforce the directional consistency of the vertex normal and the vertex intra-frame motion, which can avoid the manual aid in tracking process and improve the adaptability to different facial shapes.

E. Gelenbe et al. (eds.), *Computer and Information Sciences*, Lecture Notes in Electrical Engineering 62, DOI 10.1007/978-90-481-9794-1_42,
© Springer Science+Business Media B.V. 2010

2 Prior Work

[1,2] focus on accurately tracking facial features from 2D video sequences. [3,4] use a deformable 3D face model to track a image sequence. The model has not enough degrees of freedom to capture all the subtle expressions. [5-7] focus on capturing the subtle expressions. All these methods in [1-7] can not track facial expression automatically.

[8-11] introduce non-rigid deformation to create a single deformable mesh model. [9] uses a multi-resolution deformable face model to fit the captured mesh sequence. Global rigid deformations are performed on the coarse level of the model, and local non-rigid deformations on the fine level. The non-rigid deformation integrates an implicit shape representation and the B-spline based Free Form Deformation (FFD). The implicit representation increases computations and FFD decrease intuitive control on deformation. [10] extends the ICP framework to non-rigid deformation by incorporating additional constraints in the closest point search. The framework can accurately recovers the facial expression, but work poorly when the model and the captured mesh have very different facial shapes. The methods in [8-11] all take feature correspondences as an important factor to constraint the deformation of the model. It requires users to select facial feature points for each captured mesh. The selection spends tremendous amount of skill and time. In our method, the normal constraint will be used to avoid manual aid in tracking process.

[12] uses a multi-scale face model to track the facial wrinkles motion. The method does not need manual aid, but the wrinkles on actor's face should be marked with different diffuse colors in order to automatically form the feature correspondences. This data acquisition is time-consuming and make actor uncomfortable. [13-15] use optical flow to constraint the deformation of the facial model, so as to automatically fit the model to the captured mesh sequence. Though almost all the correspondence information can be derived from images by computing optical flow, image sequence is not always acquired. In many cases, estimation of optical flow is not robust, which will result in unwanted deformation. In our method, the normal is used to guide the automatic tracking of the mesh sequence, which can overcome the limitation of optical flow.

3 New Method

We use a high-resolution deformable mesh model to track the facial expression in this paper. The expression data acquired from 3D scanner or reconstructed from 2D images exists in the form of a mesh sequence. A new metric is presented for computing optimal deformations of the model to fit each mesh. The model can be a user defined mesh or the first frame of the mesh sequence. If the model is a user defined mesh which may be very different from the captured meshes, we first fit the model to the first mesh of the sequence, initialized with a small amount of user guidance, and then automatically fit the initial deformed model to the rest meshes under our new metric. If the model comes from the first mesh of the sequence, we directly fit the model to the mesh sequence under our new metric automatically.

Let $S = (V, E)$ be an n-vertex deformable triangle mesh, with vertex set $V = \{v_i\}$ and edge set $E = \{(i_1, i_2)\}$. We call S source mesh. Let $\Upsilon = \{T_m \mid m = 1, 2, ..., M\}$, be a captured mesh sequence with M frames. Each frame in the sequence can be represented as $T_m = (V_m, E_m)$, where V_m is vertex set and E_m is edge set. We call T_m target mesh. To fit the target mesh, we assign a displacement d for each vertex of S, and then use a new metric to solve for these unknown displacements so that the deformed mesh S' with vertex set $\{v_i + d_i\}$, optimally approximate the target mesh. The new metric consists of a closest-point term, a normal term, and a smoothness term. Automatic and self-adaptive tracking can be achieved with the new metric.

3.1 Closest-point constraint

The closest-point term measures the distance between the deformed source mesh and the target mesh. Naturally the distance should be small. This term is expressed as

$$E_a(\{d_i\}) = \sum_{v_i \in V} w_i \|(v_i + d_i) - q_i\|^2 \tag{1}$$

where, $v_i + d_i$ is the new location of v_i after being displaced, i.e., the vertex on the deformed mesh S', and its closest compatible point on target mesh T is denoted by q_i. $\|(v_i + d_i) - q_i\|$ is the Euclidean distance between $v_i + d_i$ and q_i. w_i is a weight factor which is set to zero when no compatible point could be found. In our method, a point v on S' and a point q on T is considered to be compatible if the difference in orientation of normals at v and q is less than 90° and the distance between v and q is within a threshold. In closest compatible point search, normal compatibility is judged beforehand to remove large numbers of unnecessary distance computations, which accelerates the closest point computation.

3.2 Normal constraint

The computed deformation of the source mesh only with closest-point constraint is generally unwanted. For example, as shown in Fig.1, when the source mesh S with vertices $\{v_i\}$ does not completely cover the target mesh T, S may be deformed to S' with vertices $\{v_i'\}$ only with closest-point constraint. Here, the vertices of S' bunch together in some regions of T while still approximate T closely. In fact, it is more reasonable in this case to move the vertices of S along their normal directions (denoted by red dashed arrow, e.g., N_{v_1} is the vertex normal on v_1), which could guide S to deform to cover the whole target mesh T after several iterations. So, we introduce a normal constraint in the metric to measure the directional consistency of the vertex normal and the displacement vector on the vertex. Specifically

$$E_{b1}(\{d_i\}) = \sum_{v_i \in V} angle^2(N_{v_i}, d_i) \tag{2}$$

where N_{v_i} is the vertex normal on v_i, $angle(N_{v_i}, d_i)$ is the angle between N_{v_i} and d_i. Eq.(2) performs usefully when there is large difference between the source mesh and the target mesh.

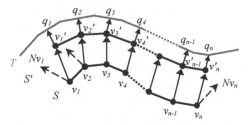
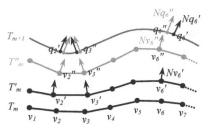

Fig. 1. The computed optimal deformation with closest-point constraint deforms source mesh S to S' whose vertices $\{v_i'\}$ bunch together in some regions of target mesh T. Here, q_i is the closest point for v_i'.

Fig. 2. Illustration of the normal constraint in automatic fitting.

The normal also plays an import role in automatic mesh fitting. In our method, the mesh sequence is captured at video rate, so adjacent frames of the sequence are very close, and the deformation between adjacent frames is small. As shown in Fig.2, the m-th frame T_m is very close to the $(m+1)$-th frame T_{m+1}. Here, T_m can be regarded as source mesh and T_{m+1} as target mesh. We aims to deform the source mesh to optimally fit the target mesh. In ideal case, each source vertex after being displaced could map onto a point on the target mesh, and has the same normal direction with the target point. This means that the distance between the deformed source mesh and the target mesh should be small, and the directional difference between normals on the displaced source vertex and its corresponding target point should also be small. As shown in Fig.2, only with the closest-point constraint, T_m may be deformed to T'_m. The vertex v_6 is displaced to v_6' whose closest point on T_{m+1} is q_6'. However, the vertex normal $N_{v_6'}$ on v_6' is very different from the surface normal $N_{q_6'}$ on q_6'. The cases of v_2 and v_3 are similar with v_6. It means that the computed displacements are not optimal in this case. It may be more reasonable to deform T_m to T''_m. Here, v_6 is displaced to v_6'' on which the direction of vertex normal $N_{v_6''}$ is consistent with the surface normal $N_{q_6''}$ on q_6'' - the closest point to v_6''. So, it is necessary to adjust the deformation considering normal consistency as well as distance minimization. The normal consistency constraint will ensure the directional consistency of vertex normal on the displaced source vertex and surface normal on the corresponding target point. Specifically,

$$E_{b2}(\{d_i\}) = \sum_{v_i \in V} \varphi_i angle^2(N_{v_i+d_i}, N_{q_i}) \tag{3}$$

where q_i is defined as Eq.(1), $N_{v_i+d_i}$ is the vertex normal on the vertex $v_i + d_i$, N_{q_i} is the surface normal on q_i, and $angle(N_{v_i+d_i}, N_{q_i})$ is the angle between $N_{v_i+d_i}$ and N_{q_i}. φ_i is a weight factor which is set to zero where no corresponding point could be found.

If the source mesh is a user defined mesh which may be very different from the captured mesh sequence, we will use Eq.(2) as normal constraint to compute optimal deformation. Assuming the source mesh has been deformed to optimally fit the first frame of the mesh sequence and been denoted as S_1 (or the first frame can be directly used as S_1), then starting from S_1, we recursively get S_{m+1} that optimally fit the $(m+1)$-th frame by deforming S_m that has fitted the m-th frame. In the recursive fitting process, Eq.(3) is used as normal constraint. Combination of Eq.(1) and Eq.(3)

will ensure that the deformed mesh matches the target mesh as well as the vertex motion matches the normal consistency. As discussed above, the optimal deformation can be ensured without manual aid since the adjacent frames of the sequence are very close.

3.3 Smoothness constraint

Generally, the computed deformation with the closest-point and the normal constraints would still not result in a very attractive mesh, because the neighboring vertices on the source mesh may displace to disparate parts of the target mesh. For example, when the target mesh does not completely cover the source mesh, the source mesh may deform without penalty where there is no data. So, a smoothness term is introduced to enforce neighboring source vertices to undergo similar displacements. Specifically,

$$E_c(\{d_i\}) = \sum_{(i_1, i_2) \in E} \left\| d_{i_1} - d_{i_2} \right\|^2 \tag{4}$$

3.4 New metric and tracking steps

The new metric in our method is a weighted sum of Eqs. (1)-(4), specifically

$$E(\{d_i\}) = \alpha E_a + \beta_1 E_{b1} + \beta_2 E_{b2} + \gamma E_c \tag{5}$$

where the weights α, β_1, β_2 and γ are tuned to guide the optimization. By minimizing Eq. (5), we can get the displacements that optimally fit the source mesh to the target mesh. We solve the minimization using L-BFGS-B algorithm [16], and implement our new method in two steps.

Step 1. The source mesh is deformed to fit the first frame of the captured sequence. If the source mesh is automatically obtained from the first frame, this step can be skipped. In this step, E_{b1} in Eq.(2) is used as normal constraint in minimizing Eq.(5) , i.e., $\beta_2 = 0$. To initialize the optimization, we first select some corresponding feature points on both the source and target mesh, and use them to solve for an over-constrained global affine transformations to get the initial deformation of the source mesh, then, based on the deformed source mesh, we use the displacements obtained in initial deformation as initial values of unknowns to minimize Eq.(5). In iterative optimization, α will be increased to finally dominate the optimization. After this step, the feature correspondences are no longer used for the following fitting.

Step 2. Let S_1 be the deformed source mesh obtained in step1, we would use it to automatically fit the rest meshes of the sequence. E_{b2} in Eq.(3) is used as normal constraint in minimizing Eq.(5) to ensure the consistency of vertex normal and vertex intra-frame motion. So, let $\beta_1 = 0$ in this step. Starting from S_1, we recursively get S_{m+1} given S_m, which has fitted the m-th frame, by optimizing Eq. (5).

Our new method could automatically fill in missing data. The weights in Eqs.(1) and (3) are set to zero for source vertices whose closest point is located on a boundary edge of the target mesh, then the displacements on these vertices are only affected by the smoothness term. So, the hole on the target mesh will be filled in by seamlessly transformed parts of the source mesh. See Fig.3, the details not available in the captured meshes can be filled effectively from the source mesh.

4 Experimental Results

Fig.3 shows the results of tracking a captured mesh sequence. Fig.3 (a) is the source mesh obtained from a user defined model. Fig.3 (b) and (d) are two meshes in the captured sequence. The captured meshes do not scan well, so some details are lost. For example, the scanned face in Fig.3 (b) has a hole around the right brow, and the one in Fig.3 (d) has holes around the left eye and left brow. Our new method not only tracks the captured sequence automatically, but also fills in the holes automatically. Fig.3(c) is the source mesh after being deformed to fit the scanned face in (b), note that the hole has been filled in. Fig.3 (e) shows the result to fit the scanned face in (d). Likewise, the holes have been filled in.

To measure the fit quality in the tracking process, we use two measures for objective estimation of the fit results. In the first measure, we average over the squared Euclidean distance of corresponding points of the source mesh after being deformed and the target mesh. In the second measure, we average over the angle between the normals of corresponding points on the source mesh after being deformed and the target mesh. Intuitively, if the source mesh has been deformed to optimally fit the target mesh, the normals of corresponding points should have approximately the same direction, that is, the average angle should be small. The average squared Euclidean distance and the average angle obtained from the two deformations in Fig.3(c) and (e) are shown in Fig.3 (f).

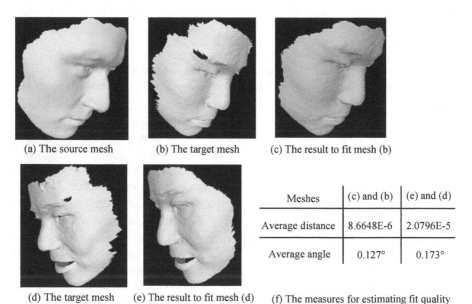

(a) The source mesh   (b) The target mesh   (c) The result to fit mesh (b)

Meshes	(c) and (b)	(e) and (d)
Average distance	8.6648E-6	2.0796E-5
Average angle	0.127°	0.173°

(d) The target mesh   (e) The result to fit mesh (d)   (f) The measures for estimating fit quality

Fig. 3. The results of tracking a mesh sequence having lost details.

Fig.4 shows the tracking results with a user defined source mesh. Fig.4 (a) is the user defined source mesh and (c) is the first frame of the captured mesh sequence. Fig.4 (b) and (d) are respectively the close-up view of the geometry and topology around the nose of (a) and (c), which are marked by red circles. It can be seen that, the source mesh (a) is very different from the target mesh (c) in facial shape as well as geometry and topology. The optimal deformation of mesh (a) is computed as discussed as step 1 of section 3.4, and (a) is deformed to (e) which optimally fit (c). In the flowing tracking process, as discussed as step 2 of section 3.4, optimal deformation is computed without manual aid in fitting each captured mesh. Fig.4 (f)-(h) are some selected meshes after tracking the source mesh through the whole sequence.

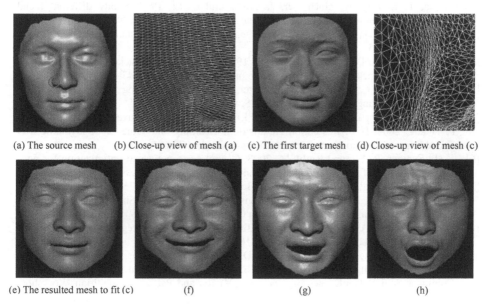

(a) The source mesh   (b) Close-up view of mesh (a)   (c) The first target mesh   (d) Close-up view of mesh (c)

(e) The resulted mesh to fit (c)   (f)   (g)   (h)

Fig. 4. The automatic tracking results obtained by the new method.

5 Discussion

In this paper, we have developed a new automatic and self-adaptive method for 3D facial expression tracking. The expression data are acquired at video rate with 3D scanner or recovered from 2D video flow. The normal constraint E_{b1} in our new metric can ensure more reasonable deformation of the source mesh where the shape of source mesh is very different from the target mesh. The constraint E_{b2} can enforce the consistency of the vertex normal and the vertex intra-frame motion, so as to automatically track through the captured sequence. Additionally, our method can automatically fill in missing data of the captured sequence.

The presented normal constraint works effectively on automatic fitting between adjacent frames which are close enough, but may generate unwanted results where the time-space interval of two frames is large. Improving the generality of the method is our future work.

Acknowledgements

We are grateful to Prof. Li Zhang at the University of Washington, for the help of 3D face data acquisition. This research has been supported by the Science and Technology Planning Project of Shandong Provincial Education Department grant J08LJ72.

Reference

[1] J. Lien, T. Kanade, A. Zlochower, J. Cohn, and C. Li. 1998. Subtly different facial expression recognition and expression intensity estimation. In CVPR'98, 853-859.
[2] Y. Yacoob and L. Davis. 1994. Computing spatio-temporal representations of human faces. In CVPR'94, 70-75.
[3] Pighin, F., Salesin, D. H., and Szeliski, R. 1999. Resynthesizing facial animation through 3D model-based tracking. In Proc. Int. Conf. on Computer Vision, 143-150.
[4] Blanz, V., Basso, C., Poggio, T., and Vetter, T. 2003. Reanimating faces in images and video. In Proceedings of EUROGRAPHICS, vol. 22, 641-650.
[5] Y. Wang, X. Huang, C-S. Lee, S. Zhang, Z. Li, D. Samaras, D. Metaxas, A. Elgammal, and P. Huang. 2004. High Resolution Acquisition, Learning and Transfer of Dynamic 3-D Facial Expressions. Computer Graphics Forum, 23(3), 677-686.
[6] Li, H., Sumner, R. W., and Pauly, M. 2008. Global correspondence optimization for non-rigid registration of depth scans. In Symposium on Geometry Processing, 27(5).
[7] M. Wand, B. Adams, M. Ovsjanikov, A. Berner, M. Bokeloh, P. Jenke, L. Guibas, H.-P. Seidel, A. Schilling. 2009. Efficient Reconstruction of Nonrigid Shape and Motion from Real-Time 3D Data. ACM Transactions on Graphics 28(2), #15.
[8] J. Feldmar and N. Ayache. 1996. Rigid, affine and locally affine registration of free-form surfaces. Int. Journal of Computer Vision, 18(2), 99–119.
[9] Xiaolei Huang, Song Zhang, Yang Wang, D. Metaxas, D., Samaras. 2004. A Hierarchical Framework For High Resolution Facial Expression Tracking. In proceedings of IEEE Computer Society Conference on Computer Vision and Pattern Recognition Workshop, 22-29.
[10] B. Amberg, S. Romdhani, T.Vetter. 2007. Optimal Step Nonrigid ICP Algorithms for Surface Registration. IEEE Conference on Computer Vision and Pattern Recognition, 1-8.
[11] Yang Wang, Mohit Gupta, Song Zhang, Sen Wang, Xianfeng Gu. 2007. dimistris Samaras and Peisen Huang. High Resolution Tracking of Non-Rigid Motion of Densely Sampled 3D Data Using Harmonic Maps, international journal of computer vision, 76(3), 283-300.
[12] B. Bickel, M. Botsch, R. Angst, W. Matusik, M. Otaduy, H., Pfister, M. Gross. 2007. Multi-Scale Capture of Facial Geometry and Motion. ACM Tansactions on Graphics (TOG), 26(3), #33.
[13] Decarlo, D., and Metaxas, D. 2002. Adjusting shape parameters using model based optical flow residuals. IEEE Trans. on Pattern Analysis and Machine Intelligence 24(6), 814-823.
[14] D. DeCarlo and D. Metaxas. 2000. Optical flow constraints on deformable models with applications to face tracking. International Journal of Computer Vision, 38(2), 99–127.
[15] Li Zhang, Noah Snavely, Brain Curless, Steven M. Seitz. 2004. Spacetime Faces: High Resolution Capture for Modeling and Animation. ACM Transaction on Graphics, 23(3), 548-558.
[16] Zhu, C., Byrd, R. H., Lu, P., and Nocedal, J. 1997. Algorithm 778. L-BFGS-B: Fortran subroutines for Large-Scale bound constrained optimization. ACM Transactions on Mathematical Software 23, 4 (Dec.), 550-560.

Eye contact with a virtual character using a vision-based head tracker

M.L.Yuan, G.G Chua, F. Farbiz and S. Rahardja

Institute for Infocomm Research, A*STAR

1 Fusionopolis Way, #21-01, Singapore, 138632

Abstract. Eye contact with virtual character can provide a realistic illusion to a user in an immersive virtual reality (VR) environment. This allows more believable eye communication between a user and a computer-generated virtual character. In this paper, an effective eye contact mechanism by innovatively combining a vision-based head tracker and an eye animation method is shown. Together, a robust color classification method to track the user's face is developed which includes extracting the 3D information of the tracked face available from a stereo camera without the need for any handheld devices or special sensors attached on the user. Through the use of the vision-based head tracker, the virtual character will be aware of the user's movements and can react to the user in a believable and pleasing manner by moving the head and the eyes to gaze at the user when the user is looking at the virtual character, or turning away when the user is not looking, or be in idle mode when the user is not around. The proposed eye contact method has been successfully applied in a virtual reality interactive game.

Keywords: Virtual reality, eye contact, color classification, stereo vision and tracking

1 Introduction

Modern virtual reality (VR) is a compelling visualization tool that provides a user a feeling of being truly immersed in a virtual environment. With advancement of human action interaction (HCI) techniques, researchers have paid much attention to the next generation of computer tools for visualization and interaction [1-4]. The effectiveness of such interaction between the virtual characters and real humans will depend on many aspects such as tracking, action recognition and the intelligence level of the virtual characters etc. Among many elements to achieve those mentioned above, eye contact is one of the essential steps in achieving interaction with a virtual character in a virtual environment [3, 7]. This can let the virtual character to be aware of the user and react in a believable and pleasing manner by moving the head and eyes of the virtual character to communicate with the user.

Some impressive progresses have been reported in this field [3-6]. State [3] proposed a simple yet effective method for achieving accurate, believable eye contact between humans and virtual characters. In [4], Masuko and Hoshino proposed a new head-eye animation method, which allowed the head-eye movements of the computer graphics characters to be synchronized with the conversation. Chai et al. used a vision-based approach to track facial details in order to control the facial animation of a virtual character [5]. However, the method did not utilize any head tracking methods for eye contact.

In literature, few works have been reported on using vision-based head tracking methods for eye-contact between a virtual character and a real human. The main advantage of the vision-based eye contact method is that no handheld device or special sensors are needed for the user. Head tracking is commonly used to move the user's point of view in the virtual world. This can greatly enhance the experience of interacting with a virtual character. In this paper, a solution is proposed to solve the eye contact problem using a computer vision-based approach. A color-based face tracking method is first used to track the face in 2D. This is then coupled with the depth information obtained from a stereo camera to estimate the 3D position of the center of the tracked face, i.e., the approximate position of the eye. This assumption is reasonable, as the distance between the virtual character and the real human is normally much farther compared to the distance between the center of the two eyes of the human and the center of the tracked faces. Through the use of the vision-based head tracker, a virtual character is aware of the user and react to the user in a believable and pleasing manner by moving the head and eyes to gaze at the user when the user is looking at her, or turning away when the user is not looking, and be in idle mode when the user is not around.

It should be noted that similar color classification methods have been proposed in [11, 12]. However, these works are mainly used to track pen-like objects in 2D. We have expanded on that by adding depth information to enable robust 3D tracking of the face. In combination with an eye animation method, our solution provides a novel eye contact mechanism which can enhance the communication between the virtual character and the user, and give the user a more engaging experience in a VR environment.

The remaining sections of this paper are organized as follows: Section 2 describes the system overview of the proposed method. Section 3 describes the details of the eye animation from the viewpoint of computer graphics. In Section 4, a robust color-based head tracker is presented. Section 5 describes the implementation details and some examples are given to demonstrate the performance of the proposed method. Conclusions and future work are given in the last section.

2   System Overview

Fig. 1 shows the structure of the eye contact system proposed in this paper. The system includes two major modules: the vision-based head tracking module and virtual character animation module. In the vision-based head tracking module, a robust color classification technique is used to track the user's face in real-time. Based on the tracked face, the depth information available from a stereo camera is applied to estimate the 3D position of center of the tracked face, which is approximated as the center of the user's two eyes for the eye animation of the virtual character. In the virtual animation module, we define a series of rules to model the eye animation. The 3D position of the head obtained from the vision module is transmitted to the eye animation module to drive the eye animation.

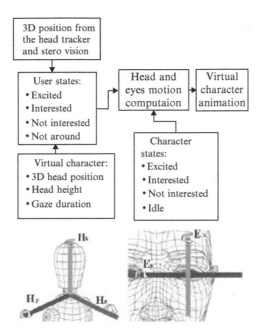

Fig. 1. System diagram of the proposed method   **Fig. 2.** Angles of head-eye movement [4].

3   Eye Animation

In the eye animation module, the following information is used to estimate the user's states:

- 3D Position of user's head
- 3D Position of the virtual character
- 3D Position and orientation of the character's head
- View radius of the virtual character's body (i.e., half the virtual character's height)
- View radius of the virtual character's head (i.e., half the height of the virtual character's head)
- Gaze duration period (set to 1 second)

In order to determine the user's states, a set of rules is defined to model the eye animation:

- If the user maintains a gaze around the view radius from the virtual character's head for a fixed Gaze duration period, then the user's state is considered as EXCITED.
- If the user maintains a gaze around the view radius from the virtual character's body for a fixed Gaze duration period, then the user's state is considered as INTERESTED.
- If the user does not maintain the gaze around the view radius of the virtual character's body for a fixed gaze duration period, then the user's state is considered as NOT INTERESTED.
- If the head tracker outputs invalid data, then the user's state is NOT AROUND.

To calculate the necessary rotational angles for the virtual character's head and eyes, we adopted the rotational coordinate system in [4], as shown in Fig 2.

If the user's head center is at position $[X_u, Y_u, Z_u]$ and the virtual character's eyes center (the middle point of the two eyes) is at position $[X_c, Y_c, Z_c]$, then the viewing angles of V_x and V_y when the virtual character looks at the user's head are calculated as follows:

$$V_x = \tan^{-1}\left(\frac{X_u - X_c}{Z_u - Z_c}\right),$$

$$V_y = \tan^{-1}\left(\frac{Y_u - Y_c}{Z_u - Z_c}\right).$$

(1)

Through a combination of the head and the eye rotations (H and E in Equation 2), the virtual character will be able to satisfy the following viewing angles:

$$V_x = H_x + E_x$$
$$V_y = H_y + E_y$$

(2)

In this paper, an equation to depict the rotation priorities for the head and eyes is proposed. The first 30 degrees of the viewing angle for the virtual character are supplied by the eye rotation and the rest will be satisfied through the head rotation:

$$E_x = sign(V_x)\min(30°, |V_x|),$$
$$E_y = sign(V_y)\min(30°, |V_y|),$$
$$H_x = V_x - E_x,$$
$$H_y = V_y - E_y.$$

(3)

The ratio of the head and eye rotations is changed based on the following rules:

- If the user's state is EXCITED or INTERESTED and the virtual character's state is EXCITED or INTERESTED, then the virtual character will turn to face the user directly using Equation (3) for head and eye rotations.
- If the user's state is NOT INTERESTED and the virtual character's state is EXCITED or INTERESTED, then the character will turn only its eyes to look at the user, subject to physical constraints.
- If the virtual character's state is NOT INTERESTED, then the character's eyes will follow the user, subject to physical constraints.

- If character's state is NOT AROUND, then the head-eye animation is turned off and the character goes to the IDLE mode.

Based on these pre-defined rules and the 3D position of the head obtained from the head tracker, the virtual character will be aware of the user and react to the user in a believable and pleasing way by moving its head and eyes to gaze at the user.

4 Color-based Head Tracker

Face has a certain skin color distribution [8] which can be classified into a number of color clusters using related classification techniques. In a tracking procedure, the classified color clusters can be used to recognize the face in each incoming frame in real time. In this paper, a randomized list structure [10] with adaptive influence field thresholds to classify the color clusters is used.

The randomized list classifier is applicable to dealing with pattern recognition problems in which data classes are represented by disjoint class distributions, linearly and non-linearly separable class distributions, as well as non-separable classes whose class distributions overlap. It is an efficient classifier since the classification is very fast and the data structure can be well maintained. Furthermore, using a randomized list classifier, the number of the clusters can be automatically determined. Each color cluster is characterized by five parameters: class C, weight vector ω, color cluster threshold λ, pattern count t and smoothing factor σ. ω represents the set of weighted connections between the color clusters and each of the input signals, i.e., training data. λ describes a hyper-spherical region of influence around the color clusters in the color space. t indicates the number of times that a color cluster has responded to the input color signals submitted to the randomized list structure. σ represents a radial decaying coefficient of the hyper-spherical influence field.

At the beginning, the user is required to specify one or more regions on a face to obtain the training data to generate a color classifier. The classifier is stored into a randomized data structure. When the training procedure is completed, the training results will be saved automatically. Later, when the user initiates the face tracking algorithm, the system will automatically load the training results and execute the tracking procedure. This provides the advantage of automatic initialization and save processing time. This is necessary for natural and intuitive interaction to initialize the system automatically. The training data is represented in the L*a*b* color space [8]. In response to an input signal, i.e., an input vector of each pixel, the Euclidean distance, i.e., $d_i = \sqrt{\sum_{j=1}^{3}(\omega_{ij} - x_j)^2}$, between the input vector and its corresponding weight in each color cluster is computed. For the first input signal presented to the training procedure, a new color cluster C_1 is created first and this input signal is loaded as a weight vector of this new color cluster. The pattern count in this color cluster is set to 1. The color cluster is assigned a threshold λ. This assignment creates an influence field around the color cluster. In the case of the first color cluster to be created, the cluster is assigned λ, which is a use-specified parameter that defines the largest size of the influence fields of any color clusters. Later, new color clusters will have their own threshold sets either at λ or at some values less than λ based on their positions with respect to the other clusters in the list structure. During training, an input signal is included in the cluster C_i if its distance to the cluster center is less than a pre-defined threshold. Subsequently, the pattern counter is incremented by 1. Otherwise, a new color cluster will be created and the current input vector is loaded as the weight vector of this cluster .

In response to an input color signal X, related probability response model are commonly used, in which each cluster will output a probability value to determine which cluster will be activated for the incoming input signal. A fast response mode is used, in which the classifier computes the distance between the input signal and the weights in the color clusters, and then directly compares whether this distance is less than the predefined threshold, that is

$$p_i = \begin{cases} 1 & if\ d_i < \lambda_i \\ 0 & if\ d_i \geq \lambda_i \end{cases} \tag{4}$$

If d_i is less than or equal to a pre-defined threshold of a color cluster, the cluster will become active to trigger its associated color class C. Otherwise, the cluster will not respond this input signal.

The output pattern with the maximum conditional probability indicates an optimal identification of the input signal with that color class. Figs. 4 shows some head tracking results. In this example, the center of the face is marked with the symbol "○" and the values of the X, Y, Z coordinates of the center are annotated. The details on how to estimate the values of the X, Y, Z coordinates is given in the following sections. It is worth noting that in the last two examples in Fig 3, the user wears a pair of stereo glasses and the proposed method can still robustly track the face. This is why the proposed color classification technique is used to track the user's face instead of using the OpenCV's face detection method [9]. As when the user wears a pair of stereo glasses, the OpenCV's face detection method will fail to track the face while the proposed tracking method can still do so. Another advantage is that the proposed tracking method can still track the face under poor lighting condition, as shown in Fig. 5.

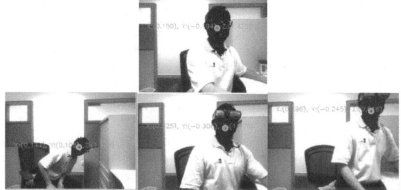

Fig. 3. Some face tracking results where the user wears a pair of stereo glasses. In some cases, the surrounding box of the detected face may include some areas from the background which might have similar color distribution as the face, as shown in

Fig. 4(a). Thus, the tracking results should be refined. Since the depth information is available from a stereo camera and assuming the depth for background pixels is larger than the foreground pixels, the tracking results can be easily refined using the depth information.

A simple but intuitive method is used in this paper. Given that the user is facing an interactive system, it is assumed that the closer an object is to the camera, the more likely the object is the user's body, including the face. Next, the trained classified is used to segment the face. The initial average depth D_f is first obtained with the depth standard deviation S_{Df}, of the pixels belong to the user's face by judging whether the depth of the pixel of the tracked area belongs to $\left[Z_{init\_\min}, Z_{init\_\max}\right]$. In the system, $Z_{init\_\min}$ and $Z_{init\_\max}$ are set to 0.5 and 2.1, respectively. Then these two variables are updated in consecutive frames by calculating the average and standard deviation of face pixels in every frame.   Hence, based on the depth information d_i of each pixel, the equation below is used to determine whether a pixel belongs to the face:

$$p_i = \begin{cases} 1 & if \ d_i \in \left[D_f - 2S_{Df}, D_f + 2S_{Df}\right] \\ 0 & otherwise \end{cases} \tag{5}$$

As can be seen in Fig. 4(b), we can effectively remove the background pixels using Equation (5).

(a)   (b)

Fig. 4. Examples of the depth-based refinement: (a) an initial tracking result; (b) the final tracking result.

5 Implementation

The proposed eye contact method is implemented using Visual Studio 2005 under Windows XP on a 3.0GHz Xeon 2.66GHz CPU with 3GB RAM. The hardware items include a Barco Galaxy 12 HB++ projector, a BumbleBee stereo camera and a pair of CrystalEyes shutter glasses.

In the vision tracking module, it is assumed that the user is always facing to the 3D display system and the stereo camera is located at the top of the display. Combining with the depth information, the face detection algorithm can output the 3D position of each pixel on the tracked face in 3D Cartesian coordinate system attached to the right camera of the stereo camera system. In the system, the average values of the face points in three dimensions are used as the face center point for interaction purposes.

Due to the noises of the tracked face, a low-pass filter is further applied to attenuate the current 3D position of the face center point using the previous one in order to reduce the jitters, thus making the interaction more stable and robust. The low-pass filter is defined as follows:

$$P_i = \alpha * P_i + (1-\alpha)P_{i-1} \tag{6}$$

where α ($0 < \alpha < 1$)) is the smoothing factor to determine the output samples in terms of the input samples. Fig. 5(a) shows an example indicating the 3D position of the face center point based on Equation (6) in which α is set to 0.75.

Normally, the users move their heads at a normal speed. However, when the users move their heads very fast, the face tracking results may be lost. Thus, the previous face center point is preserved and the users can move their faces near the position of the previous point to easily re-track their faces without any manual re-initialization. Otherwise, the new face center point will be directly considered as the current position (without applying the low-pass filter) after few seconds.

Maintaining eye contact between the virtual character and the user is performed by sending the 3D position of the head obtained from the head tracker to the eye animation module in real-time. The user is required to wear a pair of CrystalEyes glasses to see the immersive stereo effect. Fig. 5 shows some examples of eye contact between the virtual character and the user, in which the virtual character will be aware of the user's movements and can react to the user in a believable and pleasing manner.

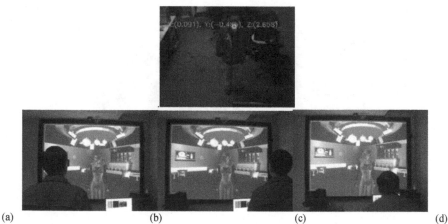

(a)   (b)   (c)   (d)

Fig. 5. Examples of eye contact between a virtual character and a user. For reader's visual clarity, the display in these figures is shown in 2D format.

6   Conclusions

In this paper, an effective eye contact method between a virtual character and a user based on a robust vision-based head tracker is presented. The method enhances the communication between the virtual character and the user. It also provides the user a realistic illusion in an immersive virtual reality environment. The proposed method is simple and easy to use without any handheld devices or any special sensors attached on the user. It can be potentially applied in wide range of applications where a real human interacts with a virtual character such as computer games and virtual world simulations. It can also be applied in education and industry training.

References

1. Taylor, R., Torres, D., Boulanger, P., Torres D., and Boulanger P., 2005, Using music to interact with a virtual character, Conference on New Interfaces for Musical Expression, Vancouver, 220-223.
2. Cayazza M., Charles F. and Steven J.M., 2002, Interacting with Virtual Characters in Interactive Storytelling, the first international joint conference on Autonomous agents and multiagent systems: part 1, Bologna, Italy, 318-325.
3. State A., 2007, Extract eye contact with virtual humans, Lecture Notes in Computer Science, Vol. 4796, 138-145.
4. Masuko S. and Hoshino J., 2007, Head-eye Animation Corresponding to a Conversation for CG Characters, Eurographics, 26(3).
5. Chai J.X., Xiao J. and Jodgins J., 2003, Vision-based Control of 3D Facial Animation, Eurographics, 193-206.
6. Kim K.N. and Ramakrishna R.S., 1999, Vision-Based Eye-Gaze Tracking for Human Computer Interface, IEEE International Conference on Systems, Man, and Cybernetics, 324-329.
7. Yuzer T.V., 2007, Generating Virtual Eye Contacts through Online Synchronous Communications in Virtual Classroom Applications, Turkish Online Journal of Distance Education, 8(1).
8. Yin, X.M. and Xie, M., 2001, Hand image Segmentation using Color and RCE Neural Network, Journal of Robotics and Autonomous Systems, 34(4), pp. 235-250.
9. Viola P. and Jones J.J, 2001, Rapid Object Detection using a Boosted Cascade of Simple Features, IEEE Conference on Computer Vision and Pattern Recognition, Hawaii, USA.
10. Williams B., Klein G. and Reid I., 2007, Real-time SLAM Relocalisation, IEEE Conference on Computer Vision.
11. Yuan, M. L., Ong, S. K. and Nee, A. Y. C., 2006, Augmented reality for assembly guidance using a virtual interactive tool, International Journal of Production Research, 46(7), 1745–1767.
12. Yuan, M. L., Ong, S. K. and Nee, A. Y. C., 2004, The virtual interaction panel: an easy control tool in augmented reality system, Computer Animation and Virtual Worlds, 15, 425-432.

Gender and Age Groups Classifications for Semantic Annotation of Videos

Gökhan Yaprakkaya [1], Nihan Kesim Cicekli [1], İlkay Ulusoy [2]

[1] Department of Computer Engineering, METU, Ankara, Turkey
[2] Department of Electrical and Electronics Engineering, METU, Ankara, Turkey
e134811@metu.edu.tr , nihan@ceng.metu.edu.tr, ilkay@metu.edu.tr

Abstract. This paper presents a combination of methods for gender identification and age group classification for semantic annotation of videos. The system has two different running modes as 'Training Mode' and 'Classification Mode'. The gender classifier achieves over 96% accuracy and the age group classifier achieves over 87% accuracy in age group classification

Keywords: Age Group Classification, Gender Classification, LBP features, DCT Mod2 Features, Adaboost, Random Forest, Face Tracking

1 Introduction

As the vast majority of the videos contain humans, the extraction of faces from videos has become a necessity. Human faces provide lots of information about the gender and age of that human such as facial landmarks, wrinkles, eyebrows, hair, lips. The prediction of gender and age group of a person requires the detection of frontal faces, the extraction of facial features and training classifiers with these features, and use of the trained classifiers for prediction. In this study we aim to decribe a robust method to identify genders from human face, and determine the age group under uncontrolled illumination or non-uniform background. The suggested algorithms are highly competitive with the best currently available classification methods in terms of both accuracy and computational cost. DCT Mod2 and LBP feature extraction methods are extensively used in face identification and verification.

2 Face and Facial Landmark Detection and Normalization

The system mainly consists of two running modes. The first mode is the 'Training Mode' and the second mode is the 'Classification Mode'. The descriptions of the two modes are summarized in Fig. 1 and Fig.2. In order to detect faces in videos, a robust face detector is used. The main assumption of the face detection method of the system is that, whatever the ethnic group, the skin color is localized in a precise subset of the chrominance space [3,4]. Therefore, a skin-color probability model is constructed in the form of a bi-dimensional Gaussian function. The function's parameters are determined on FERET color face image database. A threshold has to be set on the probability values in order to reach a binary skin/non-skin decision for each pixel. A LUT-type boosted cascade classifier based on the concept of Viola and Jones [2] is used as face detector and skin color identifier helps to eliminate false positives. The detected frontal faces are tracked by the condensation tracking algorithm. By this way every detected face is tracked as a human and we collect four different face images of

E. Gelenbe et al. (eds.), *Computer and Information Sciences*, Lecture Notes
in Electrical Engineering 62, DOI 10.1007/978-90-481-9794-1_44,
© Springer Science+Business Media B.V. 2010

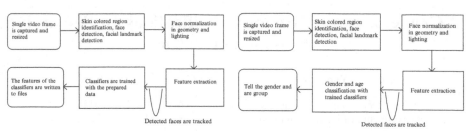

Fig. 1. Training Mode   **Fig. 2.** Classification Mode

that human. Eyes, mouth and nose are searched on the resized face images. Cheeks and forehead positions are approximated with the available positions of eyes, mouth and nose. Eyes, mouth and nose detectors are boosted cascade classifier similar with the face detector. We used the available classifiers for eyes [8], for nose and mouth [9]. The detected eye coordinates are used to rotate the face to equalize both eyes' y-coordinates. Then histogram equalization method is executed on the face images to equalize the brightness distribution of the image. Finally, the required rigid transforms are computed on images (mapping facial landmarks to defined positions; like left eye at 25% of image width, and right eye at 75% of image width).

3   Gender Classification

First, 256 bins LBP feature vectors for all images are calculated. The calculated feature vector is processed using Random Forest [5]. In random trees there is no need for any accuracy estimation procedures, such as cross-validation or bootstrap, or a separate test set to get an estimate of the training error, and there are fewer parameters than SVM to be set. In some situations, random forest outperforms SVM. When the training set for the current tree is drawn by sampling with replacement, some vectors are left out (out-of-bag data). The classification error is estimated by using this out-of-bag data.

Our second classifier is an adaboost classifier which is trained with the data extracted from comparisons of LBP values of pixels on 20x20 pixels face image. We used ten types of pixel comparison operators: (Let L_1 is LBP value of $pixel_1$ and L_2 is LBP value of $pixel_2$) $L_1 > L_2$, $L_1 < 5 * L_2$, $L_1 < 10 * L_2$, $L_1 < 25 * L_2$, $L_1 < 50 * L_2$, $L_2 > L_1$, $L_2 < 5 * L_1$, $L_2 < 10 * L_1$, $L_2 < 25 * L_1$, $L_2 < 50 * L_1$. This algorithm is same as the algorithm in [1] except the comparison operators. Each comparison yields a binary feature. We use these binary features as weak classifiers which are only required to have accuracy slightly better than random chance. The output of the classifier is the value of the binary feature. If the value of any binary feature is 1, the output is male, otherwise female. In this method, we used 20x20 pixels face image and this yields to 10x400x399 = 1596000 distinct weak classifiers. Adaboost algorithm is used to combine these weak classifiers together. Its primary goal is to form a single strong classifier with better accuracy. The computation of the accuracy in each iteration is a time consuming process but it only effects the training time, not the classification time. Randomly selecting weak classifiers in all iterations can reduce the training time. We select the best 1000 weak classifiers to construct a strong classifier. We sorted weak classifiers by their accuracy on the training images. If a training image is a male face image and the weak classifier gives the correct output for that image, the weak classifier's point is incremented by one. All the randomly selected weak classifiers are graded in this way and finally they are sorted by their total point. We select the best 1000 of the weak classifiers and write their pixel coordinates and their operators to a file which will be used to load to build strong classifier.

Gender classification module takes two face image sets which are prepared by the "face, facial landmark detection and face normalization module". In "Classification Mode", if the classifier prediction on face images for a human contains more "male" result, the "male" outputted for random tree classifier. The second classifier, namely "Adaboost Classifier" takes the 20x20 pixels image set as input and, calculates the 1000 selected (weak classifiers) binary operation results, and calculates the genders of the faces. Finally, if the results of these two classifications are same, the gender of the face is determined as the result of any classifier.

4 Age Classification

We divide human ages into four classes, 0–20, 20–40, 40–60 and 60–100. In order to classify the age group of faces, we use two distinct age classifiers. The first classifier is based on DCT Mod2 features and Random Forest. In this method, the set of face images are 40x40 pixel size, are given to DCT Mod2 feature extraction method. In this method the given face image is analyzed on a block by block basis [6,7]. In our implementation, the block size is 8x8 pixels size. Therefore, the feature vector of a face image has a size 1458. "Random Forest" classifier is trained with these features. Our second classifier is based on LBP features of selected face regions and "Random Forest". In this classification, LBP features of some selected regions of the face are computed first. Wrinkle structures around the eyes, cheeks and forehead have different characteristics which can differentiate by the age.

The calculation of LBP features yields to a 256 bin histogram. "Random Forest" classifier is trained with these features. In "Classification Mode" the DCT Mod2 Features Random Forest Classifier takes the 40x40 pixels image set as input and it extracts its DCT Mod2 feature vectors, then it predicts the age group of the face images separately with the trained classifier. The output of this classifier is the average of the results of all predictions on the given face image set of a person. The Region's LBP Features Random Forest Classifier takes the 80x80 pixels image set as input and it extracts its LBP feature vectors, then it predicts the age group of the face images separately with trained classifier. The output of this classifier is the average of the results of all predictions on a given face image set of a person. Finally, the final output is determined by averaging the results and taking floor of the average value.

5 Experiments and Results

We divided our experiments into two parts: *Gender Classification* and *Age Classification*. The captured face images from videos are grouped as males and females in the first experiment. Both groups contained 2500 images. The detected faces are stored with eyes, nose and mouth coordinates. Then face normalization methods are executed. Feature extraction methods are applied and feature vectors are stored in related files. Classifier methods are trained with stored values and classifier data are stored in xml files (for random forest), text file (for adaboost). In *Age Classification*, there were 750 images in all groups. Classifier methods are trained with extracted features and classifier data are stored in xml files. Then, we tested the classifiers with 600 detected faces in testing videos. The results were satisfactory (see Tables 1 and 2). The running time of our method changes between 2 and 4 ms on Intel(R) Core(TM) 2 Duo CPU T5850 @ 2.16GHz, 2.99 GB RAM notebook.

Table 1. Real-time Gender Classification in Videos

Classifier	# of training images	Success Rate (%)
LBP and RF	5000	91.5
Pixel comp.& Adaboost	5000	92.0
Combination	5000	96.5

Table 2. Real-time Age Group Classification in Videos

Classifier	# of training images	Success Rate (%)
DCT Mod2 & RF	3000	80.75
Selected Region LBP and RF	3000	83.25
Combination	3000	87.25

6 Conclusions and Future Work

The accuracy of gender classification is found as 96.5% in our experiments. This ratio is higher than our expectations and most of the accuracy rates reported in the literature. This result shows the impressiveness of the proposed method on gender classification. "Age Group Classification" module contains two distinct age group classifiers as gender classification module. The combination of two classifiers has 87.25% accuracy rates on 600 detected faces of test videos. 87.25% is a high success rate for a process of classification of age groups on videos. The main contribution of this work is adopting LBP and DCT Mod2 used mainly on face verification and recognition to gender and age classification from faces. Future work can be done in adding these methods to an ontological semantic video annotation framework. Our methods can be used as a personal information extractor for a semantic video annotation framework.

Acknowledgments

This work is partially supported by The Scientific and Technical Council of Turkey Grant "TUBITAK EEEAG-107E234.

References

1. Baluja, S., Rowley, H., Boosting Sex Identification Performance, Intl Journal of Computer Vision, v.71 n.1, p.111-119, 2007.
2. Viola, P., Jones, M., Rapid Object Detection using a Boosted Cascade of Simple Features, CVPR 2001.
3. Yang, M.-H., et al. Detecting faces in images: a survey, IEEE Trans. Pattern Analysis and Machine Intelligence, 24(1), 2002, pp. 34-58.
4. Hjelmås, E., Low, B. K., Face detection, a survey, Computer Vision and Image Understanding, 83(3), 2001, pp. 236-274.
5. http://stat-www.berkeley.edu/users/breiman/wald2002-2.pdf
6. Sanderson, C., Paliwal,, K. K., Fast feature extraction method for robust face verification, Electronics Letters, vol. 38, no. 25, pp. 1648-1650.
7. Eickler, S., Muller, S., and Rigoll, G., Recognition of JPEG compressed face images based on statistical methods, Image Vis. Comput., 2000, 18, (4), pp. 279–287.
8. http://www-personal.umich.edu/~shameem/haarcascade_eye.xml
9. http://mozart.dis.ulpgc.es/Gias/modesto.html

Analysis of Face Recognition Algorithms for Online and Automatic Annotation of Personal Videos

Mehmet C. Yilmaztürk,[1] Ilkay Ulusoy,[1] Nihan Kesim Cicekli[2]

[1] Department of Electrical and Electronics Engineering, Middle East Technical University, Ankara, Turkey

[2] Department of Computer Engineering, Middle East Technical University, Ankara, Turkey

e134623@metu.edu.tr, ilkay@metu.edu.tr, nihan@ceng.metu.edu.tr

Abstract. Different from previous automatic but offline annotation systems, this paper studies automatic and online face annotation for personal videos/episodes of TV series considering Nearest Neighbourhood, LDA and SVM classification with Local Binary Patterns, Discrete Cosine Transform and Histogram of Oriented Gradients feature extraction methods in terms of their recognition accuracies and execution times. The best performing feature extraction method and the classifier pair is found out to be SVM classification with Discrete Cosine Transform features

Keywords: Facial Feature Extraction, Classification, Support Vector Machines with Multiple Kernels.

1 Introduction

In order to be able to query the semantic content of multimedia data, it must be annotated with some metadata. An efficient approach is content-based indexing and retrieval which provides some degree of automation by automatically extracting features the data. In order to speed up the labeling process, face recognition methods are employed. The literature [5, 6] considers face recognition methods for mostly offline annotation applications.

For video based recognition, methods have been tested on the videos of movies, news and TV series which include many characters and scenes. In this way, the proposed methods were used for automatic naming of characters [8, 10]. The recognition of faces in videos is challenging because of the dynamic nature of the videos involving bizarre conditions which distort the faces. Some works combined facial features with others such as information extracted from clothing or hair [8, 10] but we restrict ourselves to facial features alone because clothing or hair may show more variations than the appearance of the face.

This work focuses on the evaluation of face recognition methods that can be used for an online and semi automatic face annotation system for personal videos. All combinations of the considered state-of-the-art facial-feature extraction methods and classification methods are evaluated and compared in terms of recognition accuracies and execution times. We have evaluated Nearest Neighborhood, Linear Discriminant Analysis and Support Vector Machines with single and multiple kernels as face recognition methods where various features such as DCT, LBP and HOG are used.

E. Gelenbe et al. (eds.), *Computer and Information Sciences*, Lecture Notes in Electrical Engineering 62, DOI 10.1007/978-90-481-9794-1_45,
© Springer Science+Business Media B.V. 2010

We have made our tests on datasets which are composed of face images extracted from an episode of "How I Met Your Mother" TV series. We have observed that SVM with DCT features performs the best.

2   Considered Algorithms for Face Recognition

Three facial feature extraction algorithms, namely DCT, LBP and HOG features are used to extract information from face images. These features have been selected as they are robust state-of-the-art features and can be computed fast enough to use in an online learning system. For the classification Nearest Neighborhood, LDA, SVM and multiple kernel SVM are selected since these are also among the most popular algorithms and can be extended for online learning by using their sequential variants.

2.1   Feature Extraction

Since direct pixel values are sensitive to noise and localization errors, three alternative feature extraction methods have been implemented to represent data. These include DCT Features [3], LBP Features [2] and HOG features [9]. For the DCT Features 48 blocks are used which produces feature vectors of 480 dimensions. Basic LBP features with 8 neighbours are of 256 dimensions and HOG features with 35 blocks have 1260 dimensions.

2.2   Classification

Nearest Neighbor (NN). NN method is widely used in annotation applications especially as a baseline method. We take the dot product of the two vectors and normalize the result with their magnitudes to calculate their similarity measure.

Linear Discriminant Analysis (LDA). We have implemented LDA to reduce the dimension of input data. We retain 95% of the total energy. During classification, the nearest class center, which is the mean value of the projected samples for a given class, is used to find the nearest neighbor for the test samples.

Support Vector Machines with Single and Multiple Kernels. "One vs. the Rest" method has been considered for multi-class classification. Gaussian RBF Kernel function is used for the single kernel SVM and also for the Multiple Kernel SVM as base kernels.

 For the multiple kernel SVM, instead of using a single kernel, linear combinations of base kernels are used. Each base kernel corresponds to a different block of the feature vector. For the DCT and HOG features, these base kernels are applied for each of the data blocks created during the feature extraction stage. Hence the number of base kernels is 35 for HOG features and 48 for DCT features. are the base kernels and are the weights corresponding to each base kernel.

3   Experiments and Results

Recognition accuracies are plotted. The execution times are also plotted for both training and testing phases as the number of training and testing samples changes. All tests are made for two distinct face datasets. The first dataset is a collection of hand-labeled face detection outputs. Viola-Jones face detector [1] has been run for every single frame throughout an episode of "How I Met Your Mother" TV series and the detected faces of target people are manually clustered. The second dataset is created by using a face tracker algorithm on the same episode. OpenCV implementation of Camshift Color Based face tracker [4] is used to track faces throughout the video. The resulting face tracks are also manually labeled and clustered. Samples from both datasets are fed to an illumination compensation algorithm before recognition is performed. In all tests, 5-fold cross validation technique is used.

3.1 Illumination Compensation

Sample face images are converted to gray-scale and resized to have a standard size of 64 (height) x 48 (width) pixels. Next, a basic and fast algorithm of illumination compensation is performed (1).

$$I_{comp}(x, y) = a + b \, log \left(I_{raw}(x, y) * H_{hp}(x, y) \right), \tag{1}$$

H is a high-pass filter. In our application a = 10 and b = 2 and H is a binomial high-pass filter of size 5 x 5 pixels.

3.2 Execution Times

All of the tests are performed on an Intel Core 2 Duo 2.20 GHz PC with 1 GB RAM. DCT and HOG feature extraction methods has been implemented in MATLAB. For LBP feature extraction, a MATLAB implementation available in [29] has been used. Nearest Neighborhood and LDA algorithms are implemented in MATLAB environment. For Single Kernel and Multiple Kernel SVM, a MATLAB interface for LIBSVM implementation [14] is used. For the calculation of the execution times, the number of classes is selected as 6.

Nearest Neighborhood. For NN, there is no training. The execution times are shown for different numbers of gallery samples (Figure 1). For each method, three different graphs are plotted with different numbers of testing samples used.

LDA. A major change in terms of execution times is observed for different features (Figure 1). This is expected since most of the computation is due to the construction of the scatter matrices and calculation of the eigenvectors where the number of feature vector dimensions determines the size of the scatter matrices. 3000 samples are used to construct an eigenspace model.

SVM. SVM training times are shown on Figure 1 for 6 SVM models (6 classes) with a total of 3000 training samples used. Most of the computation is due to the kernel construction. In the testing phase, most of the computation is due to the construction of kernels as well; hence the number of returned support vectors is indicated for each method. Having returned a smaller number of support vectors, Multiple Kernel SVM models have smaller testing times compared to the SVM with DCT features.

3.3 Recognition Precisions

The general trend of decreasing recognition precision in Figure 2 is due to the fact that while the number of samples per person increases, the diversity of the model also becomes more complex with different looking samples of the face.

In all tests, LDA classification is observed to degrade and perform poorly with the insufficient number of training samples. SVM performs as the best classification method, but SVM training is a heavy process compared to NN and LDA. Single Kernel SVM with DCT features works best. But the testing time is higher than other SVM methods. This is due to the high number of returned support vectors.

4 Conclusions

Several state-of-the-art feature extraction and classification methods have been implemented and compared in terms of precision and execution times. Our focus is on determining a fast and robust face recognition method which can be used in an online learning application where face recognition for personal videos is to be performed. We have observed that single kernel SVM trained with DCT features gives the highest recognition accuracy. On the other hand in this method, the number of Support Vectors found is great and this yields relatively long testing times. SVM with Multiple Kernels, on the other hand, have comparable recognition accuracy to single kernel SVM, though training times are longer due to a more complex process of kernel construction. But tests show that in multiple Kernel SVM methods, fewer number of support vectors is sufficient to define the separating hyperplane which led to shorter testing times.

There is a tradeoff between testing times and training times when we consider the usage of SVM with single and Multiple Kernels. If long testing times are acceptable, Single Kernel SVM with DCT coefficients has the highest recognition accuracy. For the online automatic face annotation system where encountered face tacks are to be classified, the number of testing samples per query is not large, residing between typical ranges of 10-100 samples. And training times can be considered more important for an online learning system as the newly encountered samples are sequentially learnt in data chunks, repetitive sessions of long trainings may discourage the user from working with the system.

As a conclusion, we have decided to use a SVM with DCT features for our online automatic annotation purposes.

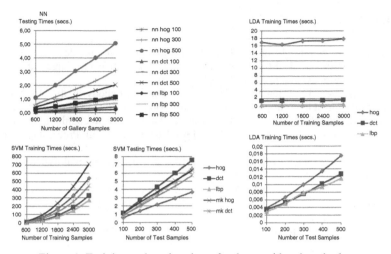

Figure 1. Training and testing times for the considered methods.

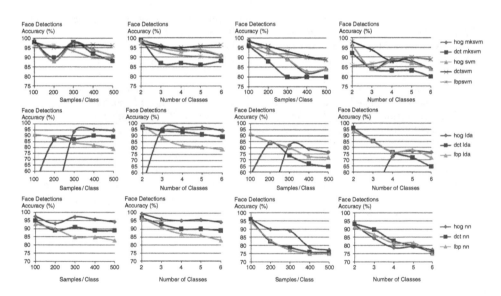

Figure 2. Recognition accuracies for different numbers of training samples and classes.

Acknowledgments. This work is partially supported by The Scientific and Technical Council of Turkey Grant ''TUBITAK EEEAG-107E234''.

References

1. Viola, P., Jones, M.: Rapid object detection using a boosted cascade of simple features. Proceedings of the 2001 IEEE Computer Society Conference on Computer Vision and Pattern Recognition, vol. 1, pp. 511--518 (2001)
2. Wolf, L., Hassner, T., Taigman, Y.: Descriptor Based Methods in the Wild. Real Life Images Workshop at the European Conference on Computer Vision (ECCV) (2008)
3. Ekenel, H.K., Stiefelhagen, R.: Local Appearance Based Face Recognition Using Discrete Cosine Transform. in Proceedings of the 13th European Signal Processing Conference (2005)
4. Bradski, G.R.: Computer Vision Face Tracking for Use in a perceptual user interface. Intel Technology Journal, 2nd Quarter (1998)
5. Jiang, R. M., Sadka, A.H., Zhou, H.: Automatic human face detection for content based image annotation. International Workshop on Content-Based Multimedia Indexing, CBMI 2008, pp. 66--69 (2008)
6. Poh, N., Chan, C.H., Kittler, J.: Face video Competition at ICB2009. Int'l Conf. on Biometrics (ICB) (2009)
7. Satoh, S.: Comparative Evaluation of Face Sequence Matching for Content-based Video Access. Fourth IEEE International Conference on Automatic Face and Gesture Recognition, pp. 163--168 (2000)
8. Ramanan, D., Baker, S., Kakade, S.: Leveraging archival video for building face datasets. IEEE 11th International Conference on ICCV 2007, pp. 1--8 (2007)
9. Dalal, N., Triggs, B.: Histogram of Oriented Gradients for human detection. IEEE Computer Society Conference on Computer Vision and Pattern Recognition, vol. 1, pp. 886--893 (2005)
10. Everingham, M., Sivic, J., Zisserman, A.: Taking the bite out of automated naming of characters in TV video. Image and Vision Computing, vol. 27, issue 5, pp. 545--559 (2009)
11. Sivic, J., Everingham, M., Zisserman, A.: "Who are you?" – Learning person specific classifiers from video. IEEE Conference on Computer Vision and Pattern Recognition, pp. 1145--1152 (2009)
12. Bach, F., Lanckriet, G., Jordan, M.: Multiple kernel learning, conic duality and the SMO algorithm. In International Conference on Machine Learning (2004)
13. University of Oulu, Machine Vision Group, http://www.ee.oulu.fi/mvg/page/lbp_matlab
14. Chang, C.C., Lin, C.J.: LIBSVM : a library for support vector machines. 2001. Software available at http://www.csie.ntu.edu.tw/~cjlin/libsvm

Classification of Multispectral Satellite Land Cover Data by 3D Local Discriminant Bases Algorithm

Habil Kalkan[1,2], Çagrı Tekinay[1,3], Yasemin Yardımcı[1]

[1]Middle East Technical University, Ankara, Turkey
[2]Suleyman Demirel University, Isparta, Turkey
[3] Delft University of Technology, Delft, Netherlands

habil@mmf.sdu.edu.tr, C.Tekinay@tudelft.nl, yardimy@ii.metu.edu.tr

Abstract. In this study, a 3D Local Discriminant Bases based algorithm is developed to extract the discriminative features from multispectral satellite/airborne data. The developed algorithm, first localizes the information in hyperspectral data by the trees generated both along the spectral and spatial-frequency axis. These trees are then automatically pruned to obtain the location of the discriminative features in data space. The extracted features are ranked by feature selection algorithms to eliminate the irrelevant ones for classification. This combination of feature extraction and selection algorithms also identifies the specification of the relevant spectral bands including center frequency and bandwidth in imaging. The algorithm is implemented on a multispectral airborne data set from Tippecanoe County, Indiana for classifying five vegetative species and an average classification error of 8.85% is achieved with three extracted features.

Keywords: Remote Sensing, Multispectral Imaging, Classification

1 Introduction

Hyperspectral imaging is the process of imaging the objects with various spectral bands providing high amount of information with rich spectral content. However, increasing the data dimension not only increases the computational complexity but also decreases the classification accuracy when a limited number of training data is available [1, 2]. The number of training samples should be increased exponentially in order to retain the accuracy of classifier [1] or the hyperspectral data dimension should be reduced by feature extraction and selection methods. Pal [3] used margin-based feature selection methods for the classification of 8 vegetation classes in DAIS data of 65 spectral bands and 9 vegetation classes of AVIRIS data of 185 spectral bands, separately. He reduced the data dimension and classification accuracy from 65 to 24 and 185 to 65 by reaching 92.6% and 82.4%, respectively. A similar study was performed on Flightline C1 (FLC1) 12 band multispectral data [4] by using two different extraction methods, Binary Tree Edge Sensing Demosaicking (BTES) and Binary Tree Bilinear Interpolation (BTBI), and achieved the classification accuracies of 21.57% and 22.21% with three features.

E. Gelenbe et al. (eds.), *Computer and Information Sciences*, Lecture Notes
in Electrical Engineering 62, DOI 10.1007/978-90-481-9794-1_46,
© Springer Science+Business Media B.V. 2010

In this study, we propose a method which adaptively searches the data space along both the spectral and spatial- frequency axs to extract the relevant features in multispectral data. The feature extraction is followed by a filter based feature selection algorithm in order to optimize the feature vector dimension. The developed algorithm not only extracts the most discriminative features but also identifies the relevant optical filters of the multispectral imaging system with their properties such as center frequency and bandwidth. The developed method was validated on Flightline C1 (FLC1) 12 band multispectral data which were also used in [4].

2 Materials and Methods

Flightline C1 (FLC1) multispectral data [5] covering the southern part of Tippecanoe County, Indiana in 12-band multispectral form with the wavelength from 400 to 1000 nm was used to in the study. Based on the ground truth data of FLC1, the data set was divided into five classes (corn, soybeans, wheat, oat and red clover).

A method based on Local Discriminant Bases (LDB) algorithm is developed for feature extraction. The LDB algorithm is extensively used in signal classification problems for finding the discriminative features by decomposing the time axis into local cosine packets or frequency axis into wavelet packets. To adapt the algorithms to hyperspectral imaging the spectral axis is regarded as the time axis. Both the spectral and frequency information are employed in this study by extending the original LDB algorithm to 3D space of which the 1D is spectral and 2D for spatial-frequency axis.

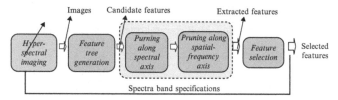

Fig. 1. Block diagram of the proposed discriminative feature extraction algorithm

The developed algorithm (Fig. 1) starts with generating features trees along the spectral and spatial-frequency axes to localize the features in data space. These trees are then pruned sequentially to extract the most discriminative ones for classification. The extracted features are then selected by feature selection algorithm to obtain the highest classification accuracy with fewer numbers of features. Two energy based feature trees along spectral and spatial-frequency axis are generated to localize the information in multispectral data. In the first tree, the reflectance energies of spectral images are placed on the (lowest) level of the tree from left to right. The energy value of the mother nodes at the higher levels is assumed to be the sum of the energies of their child nodes. The second feature tree is generated by decomposing the spectral images into wavelet frequency subbands to locate and process the local patterns in images. Therefore, the spectral images separated into m level full wavelet subbands of

LL, LH, HL and *HH* in a quad tree formation to generate the spatial-frequency feature tree where the first character shows the filtering (Low or High) along the row and second shows the filtering through the image columns.

The feature extraction step (Fig. 1) starts with pruning along the spectral (color) axis and the pruned spectral band tree is further pruned by performing a pruning in the second spatial frequency tree (wavelet tree). The pruning operation is basically performed by comparing the mother nodes with their children. In pruning, A mother node is kept if its discrimination potential is higher that any of its children. Otherwise, the children survive and the most discriminant one is assigned as mother for further pruning. The pruning operations provide a feature map along both spectral and spatial-frequency axes but the features in that map need to be ranked for further dimension reduction. Therefore, the extracted features are then sorted by feature selection algorithms.

A Linear Discriminant Analysis (LDA) classifier was used for classification purposes. The LDA is selected because of its linear behavior and simplicity which supports our focus on feature extraction rather than classification. More enhanced classifier could give better classification accuracies. The *C*-class problem was transform into *h* two class problems. The proposed algorithm provides class-specific feature maps for each pair of classes to obtain better classification accuracies. Therefore, independent hyperplanes are constructed for these *h* class pairs by using these feature maps. At the testing phase, *h* number of feature vectors whose size and features are defined by the feature maps were obtained for each test samples and tested in each classifier. The classification results were then combined to get a final decision by using majority voting principle. In the case of equality, the distances to hyperplanes are considered for that decision.

3. Experimental Results

All vegetation fields in the image were divided into subfields and these subfields are randomly distributed to the train and test set ensuring that at least one sub-label from each label is included in the training set. The 12 spectral bands constituted 4 level binary tree. The second tree was constructed by two levels wavelet decomposition. That gives us a total of 252 spatial-frequency candidate patterns. The pruning fused some of the patterns and feature selection algorithm ranked these patterns which constructed the feature map. The following feature map (Fig.2) was obtained for oat-red clover class pair. The darkness and also the numbers on the maps show this ranking. The algorithm reduced the data dimension to 33 subbands from the possible 252 sub-bands. The fusing in both spectral and spatial-frequency axis can be observed in Fig.2 (left). The minimum classification accuracy of 8.85% is achieved with the first three most discriminative features which were extracted from three spectral bands. When the classification error was considered in pixel scale, it is observed that 1578 pixels out of 66534 pixels are misclassified. The misclassified regions in fields were marked in black color in Fig.2 (right).

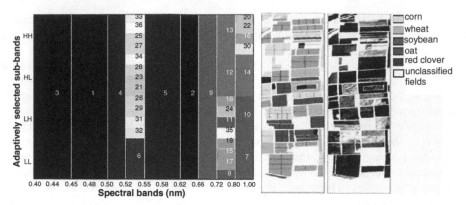

Fig. 2. The feature map of oat-red clover features (left) and the overall classification results of FLC1 data (right)

The developed algorithm was also applied in food safety area for two-class (binary) classification of fungal contaminated hazelnut kernels from the uncontaminated ones[6] and a classification accuracy of 97.4% was achieved.

4. Conclusions

In this study, the LDB algorithm is modified to 3D search structure to develop a new feature extraction algorithm for hyperspectral and multispectral data. The algorithm is specifically implemented on multispectral airborne FLC1 data set to classify the corn, soybeans, red clover, wheat, and oat vegetation classes. This five class classification problem is transformed into 10-class pairs for pairwise solution to get a final decision of a test pattern.   The mean error rate of 8.85% was obtained with three most discriminative features which is superior to the methods in study [4] that obtained an error of 22.26% with the same number of features.

5. References

1. Hsu, P.H.: Feature Extraction of HyperSpectral Images Using Matching Pursuit. Proc. of the XXth ISPRS Congress, Istanbul, (2004)
2. Landgrebe, D.A.: Signal The. Met. in Multi. Remote Sensing. John Wiley & Sons (2003)
3. Pal, M.,: Margin-based Feature Selection for Hyperspectral Data. Int. Jour. of App. Earth Obser. and Geoinformation 11(3) (2009) 212-220
4. Miao, L., Qi, H., Ramanath, R.,Snyder, W.E.: Binary tree-based generic demosaicking algorithm for multispectral filter arrays. IEEE Tr. on Image Proc.: 15(11) (2006) 3550-3558
5. Ghassemian H. and Landgrebe D.A.: On-Line Object Feature Extraction for Multi spectral Scene Representation, TR-EE 88-34. Purdue Univ., West Lafayatte. (1988)
6. Kalkan, H.:Feature Extraction from Acoustic and Hyperspectral Data by 2D-LDB Search, PhD Thesis, METU, Ankara, Turkey. (2008)

Binary and Ternary Coded Structured Light 3D Scanner for Shiny Objects

Rıfat Benveniste and Cem Ünsalan

Computer Vision Research Laboratory
Department of Electrical and Electronics Engineering
Yeditepe University
İstanbul, 34755 TURKEY
{*rifatb,unsalan*}*@yeditepe.edu.tr*

Abstract. Three dimensional range data provides useful information for computer vision, computer graphics, and object recognition applications. For these, extracting the range data reliably is utmost important. Therefore, various range scanners based on different operating principles are proposed in the literature. Although these scanners can be used in diverse applications, most of them cannot be used to scan shiny objects under ambient light. This is a severe restriction. We propose color invariant based binary and ternary coded structured light range scanners to solve this problem. We hypothesize that, by using color invariants we can eliminate the effects of highlights and ambient light in the scanning process. Therefore, we can extract the range data of shiny and matte objects in a robust manner. We implemented three different range scanners to test our hypothesis. We performed tests on various objects and provided their range data.

1 Introduction

Various computer vision, computer graphics, and object recognition applications benefit from 3D information. These require reliable range data acquisition. For this purpose, various types of range scanners are proposed in the literature [1]. Although these scanners can be used in most applications, they cannot be used to scan shiny objects under ambient light. This is a severe restriction, since applications such as outdoor scanning cannot avoid this type of problem. The mentioned problem can be clearly seen in binary coded structured light scanners. In a previous study, we focused on the same problem in line stripe based range scanners [2]. In this study we propose new systems based on binary and ternary coded structured light systems to solve this problem. Our method depends on using color information instead of black and white stripes in binary coding. In the literature, there are several structured light methods based on color information [3–5]. Our method differs from these studies, since we use a set of color invariants (different from our previous study) to extract the stripe information in extracting codewords from the camera image. To test our method, we developed prototype range scanners using a commercial projection machine and an industrial color

E. Gelenbe et al. (eds.), *Computer and Information Sciences*, Lecture Notes
in Electrical Engineering 62, DOI 10.1007/978-90-481-9794-1_47,
© Springer Science+Business Media B.V. 2010

camera. In the next section, we provide the specifications of these scanners. Then, we focus on our color invariant based stripe extraction method. Finally, we provide range scan results of several test objects with our scanners.

2   The Developed Structured Light based Range Scanners

To scan shiny surfaces reliably, we developed both binary and ternary coded structured light scanners in this study. In implementation, the only difference between the binary and ternary coded structured light scanners is in the pattern codification step. In other saying, the same hardware can be used for both scanners with a change in the pattern projection step. The hardware of our system is as follows. We project structured light patterns onto the test object by a Hitachi CP-RS57 Multimedia 3 LCD projection machine. The images of the patterns projected onto the object surface is grabbed by a Sony DXC-390P 3 CCD color camera. We calibrate the camera projection machine setup by using Bouguet's [6] calibration toolbox. We use Matlab as our coding platform. For the binary coded structured light scanner, we project eight patterns (having different widths) with either red-green or blue-green color pairs. For the ternary coded structured light scanner, we project five patterns with red, green, and blue colors. For both scanner systems, we use Gray coding in projecting the patterns.

3   Stripe Segmentation using Color Invariants

Color invariants are used to overcome the effects of imaging conditions on color extraction such as, the illumination of the environment, surface properties of the object, and the angle of view. To scan shiny object surfaces, we benefit from the set of color invariants (c_1, c_2, c_3) introduced by Gevers and Smeulders [7]. In this section, we benefit from these to extract binary and ternary patterns projected onto the test object.

3.1   Segmenting Binary Patterns

We implement the binary coded structured light scanner in two different ways using c_1 and c_3 separately. To use the first color invariant, c_1, we project red and green colored patterns onto the object. For c_3, we use blue and green colored patterns. To extract these projected patterns from the grabbed camera images, we apply thresholding after obtaining the color invariant image. We explain this method in detail in our previous study [8]. In this study, we also benefit from matched filtering to obtain a more reliable segmentation, hence the pattern.

3.2   Segmenting Ternary Patterns

For the ternary coded pattern, we use red, green, and blue colors. Unlike binary coding, on ternary coding the thinnest lines are not so thin. Hence, there is no dominant sensor cross-talk problem. Therefore, we did not use matched filtering for ternary coding. On the other hand, the not so thin stripes cause lower resolution compared to the binary coding. We will see the effect of this in the experiments section. We can define a new value for stripe segmentation as $s = c_1 - c_3$. Then, for the red colored stripes, $s > 0$; for the green colored stripes $s \approx 0$; for the blue colored stripes $s < 0$. Therefore, we can use s to segment the red, green, and blue stripes from the ternary image. In implementation, we divided the range of the s value to three and applied segmentation based on these.

4   Experiments

To test our scanners, we used five different objects having different colors on them. These objects are: Polyester Atatürk with shiny acrylic paint, porcelain teapot, porcelain dove, soft green frog, and porcelain green cat. We provide the range data obtained by binary (using c_1), and ternary pattern based range scanners in Fig. 1.

Fig. 1. Point clouds of test objects. Column wise: Atatürk, teapot, dove, soft green frog, green cat. Row wise: Test objects, binary scanner results, ternary scanner results.

As can be seen in Fig. 1, the binary range scanner based on c_1 extracted all of the range data from five objects reliably. If we check the range data results of the ternary scanner, we observe that only the frog object has some missing parts. All other objects have fairly good range data. However, the resolution of the range data is not as good as the binary coded scanner. Please remember that, the ternary range scanner needs five projection patterns. On the other hand, the binary range scanners need eight projection patterns. As a benchmark we also implemented a black and white range scanner. Unfortunately it gives poor results on shiny objects. It can only extract the range data of matte objects reliably.

The range data for some test objects are not complete. There are some minor missing parts. We should remember that, these scan results are obtained only from one viewing direction. When the objects are scanned from more than one direction, then these missing parts can be filled. On the other hand, if the scanner produces extra or wrongly coded parts (as in the black and white range scanner), they cannot be deleted easily.

5 Final Comments

In this study, we proposed a framework to solve the problem of scanning shiny objects using color pattern projection and color invariants. We developed three range scanners based on two binary and one ternary color patterns. The binary range scanners need eight patterns for coding. The ternary range scanner needs five projection patterns. In all systems, we project colored patterns onto the object. As a benchmark, we also implemented the black and white range scanner. We tested all range scanners on several test objects having different properties. Although the black and white binary structured light scanner could not extract the range data of the shiny objects, our color invariant based range scanners were able to extract the range data in a reliable manner.

6 Acknowledgements

This work is supported by TUBITAK under project no 108E196.

References

1. Salvi, J., Pages, J., Batlle, J.: Pattern codification strategies in structured light systems. Pattern Recognition **37** (2004) 827 – 849
2. Benveniste, R., Ünsalan, C.: A color invariant for line stripe based range scanners. The Computer Journal (In press)
3. Caspi, D., Kiryati, N., Shamir, J.: Range imaging with adaptive color structured light. IEEE Transactions on Pattern Analysis and Machine Intelligence **20** (1998) 470–480
4. Chen, C.S., Hung, Y.P., Chiang, C.C., Wu, J.L.: Range data acquisition using color structured lighting and stereo vision. Image and Vision Computing **15** (1997) 445–456
5. Rocchini, C., Cignoni, P., Montani, C., Pingi, P., Scopigno, R.: A low cost 3d scanner based on structured light. In: Proceedings of Eurographics. (2001) 299–308
6. Bouguet, J.Y.: Complete camera calibration toolbox for Matlab (2008) *http : //www.vision.caltech.edu/bouguetj/calib_doc/*.
7. Gevers, T., Smeulders, A.W.M.: Color based object recognition. Pattern Recognition **32** (2000) 453–464
8. Benveniste, R., Unsalan, C.: A color invariant based binary coded structured light range scanner for shiny objects. In: Proceedings of ICPR. (2010) In Press

Gender Classification via Gradientfaces

K. Berker Loğoğlu[1,2], Ahmet Saracoğlu[1,3], Ersin Esen[1,3] and A. Aydın Alatan[3]

[1]TUBITAK Space Technologies Research Institute,
[2]Graduate School of Informatics, Middle East Technical University
[3]Electrical and Electronics Engineering, Middle East Technical University
{berker.logoglu, ahmet.saracoglu, ersin.esen}@uzay.tubitak.gov.tr, alatan@eee.metu.edu.tr

Abstract. In this paper illumination invariant, pose and facial expression tolerant gender classification method is proposed. A recently introduced feature extraction method, namely *Gradientfaces,* is utilized together with Support Vector Machine (SVM) as a classifier. Image regions obtained from cascaded Adaboost based face detector is used at the feature extraction step and faster classification is achieved by using only 20-by-20 pixel region during feature extraction. For performance evaluation, two well-known face databases, FERET and Yale B are tested and the algorithm is compared against a pixel-based algorithm on these datasets. The results indicate that *Gradientfaces* significantly outperform the pixel-based methods under severe illumination, pose and facial expression variances.

Keywords: Gender Classification, Gradientface, Support Vector Machine

1 Introduction

Although face detection and consequently face recognition have been intensely researched in the past years, gender classification has drawn less attention. However, successful gender classification methods can be extremely important for various application areas. In surveillance systems, gender classification can improve the analytic capacity of the whole system, for instance by collecting information regarding the number of women entering a store or mall area. Furthermore, user experience of the human-computer interaction can be enhanced by incorporating gender of the user. Moreover, for visually-impaired, gender of a person can be a vital information.

Gender classification methods can be categorized according to input of the system as *gait*-based [6], *speech*-based [12] and *face*-based [1] methods. In gait-based methods, particular walking manner of males and females are tried to be captured and classified whereas in speech-based methods gender models are obtained from audio signals. Face-based methods on the other hand identify gender from face images. Even though for a versatile and complete gender classification system all of the previously mentioned information sources should be utilized, in this paper a face-based approach is proposed.

Lately, many successful algorithms utilizing face images are reported in the literature. These methods can be classified into three categories corresponding to the

E. Gelenbe et al. (eds.), *Computer and Information Sciences,* Lecture Notes
in Electrical Engineering 62, DOI 10.1007/978-90-481-9794-1_48,
© Springer Science+Business Media B.V. 2010

type of data, classification is performed on i.e.: pixel-based, global feature-based and local feature based. Moghaddam [1] uses Support Vector Machine (SVM) directly on the face images to identify gender. Classification is carried out on relatively low resolution face images which are 21x12 and achieved error rates as low as %3.4 furthermore; Moghaddam reports only 1% improvement by using a larger face image size. In a different approach, Makinen [5] evaluates different gender classification methods and concludes that SVM performs best with high classification rates and input face image size has little effect on the performance.

As one of the global feature-based methods, Lu [7] proposes a fusion based method in which multiple facial sub-regions are integrated into classification in order to make the gender identification facial expression tolerant. On the other hand, Hadid [9] employs a dynamic texture analysis approach in which facial expression movements together with the local binary patterns (LBP) is used. Additionally, Jain [8] proposes to use independent component analysis on face images along with a classifier of SVM and this method achieved recall rates up to 95.67%.

As an alternative, Toews and Arbel recently utilized scale-invariant local features for gender classification [4]. In their work, Toews adopts object class invariant models in order to handle arbitrary viewpoint cases.

It should be noted that face-based methods are influenced from many factors including lighting conditions, pose of the head, facial expression and possible occlusions. Thus, a gender classification method robust to these effects is crucial. In this paper, pose, illumination and facial expression invariant gender classification method is proposed. In this approach, a recently proposed feature extraction method dedicated to face recognition is utilized [2] and furthermore the performance of the method is compared against some pixel-based approach. In the following section, the approach is described in detail. In Section 3, experimental setup and corresponding results are provided. Finally, in the last section concluding remarks are given.

2 Proposed Algorithm

Basic building blocks of the proposed approach are presented in Fig 1. As the first step, face detection via the cascaded detector of Viola & Jones is employed [3]. In this face detection method, integral images are utilized and thus a very fast feature extraction is possible. Additionally, method employs a cascaded AdaBoost as a feature classifier. Due to these advantages, this method has been selected as face detector in our approach.

The second stage of our approach involves the extraction of a feature vector from the detected face region. It should be noted that after face detection, the face region is further shrunk in order to decrease the cluttering effects of ears, hairs and background. Zhang et al. in [2] employed *Gradientfaces* for illumination invariant face recognition and showed that this method is robust for uncontrolled and natural lighting conditions. Furthermore, it has been reported that Gradientfaces is superior to pixel-based approaches [2].

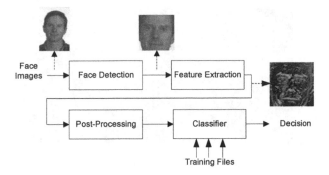

Fig 1. Block Diagram of the Gender Classification System

2.1 Gradientfaces

Gradientfaces approach is derived from the fact that the ratio of the y-gradient of image $I(x, y)$ to the x-gradient of image is an illumination invariant measure, as shown in [2]. This said, in our approach gender classification is made on this measure computed as the following equation;

$$g = \arctan\left(\frac{I_y}{I_x}\right), g \in [0, 2\pi)$$ (1)

in which I_x and I_y represent x- and y-gradients of the image, respectively.

However, since computation of image derivatives/gradients is ill-posed due to noise and quantization, to compute stable image gradients and more importantly to extract an illumination invariant measure that is robust to noise, image is firstly smoothed by a Gaussian kernel function given below.

$$G(x, y, \sigma) = \frac{1}{2\pi\sigma^2} e^{-\frac{x^2 + y^2}{2\sigma^2}}$$ (2)

where σ is the variance of the kernel.

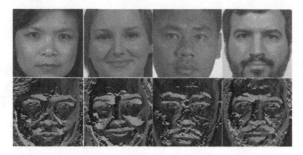

Fig 2 Example Gradientfaces obtained from FERET face dataset images

In Fig 2, Gradientfaces computed from male and female face images are depicted. At the post-processing stage images are further cropped and down sampled to 20-by-20. Down sampling size is chosen empirically in order to both achieve fast training / detection and high accuracy rate.

2.2 Gender Classification

At the last step of the proposed method, extracted features are classified by a Support Vector Machine (SVM). Several kernel functions satisfying the Mercer's theorem has been presented in the literature however, in this work Radial Basis Functions (RBF) have been employed.

$$K(x, y) = e^{-\gamma(x-y)^2} \qquad\qquad (3)$$

where γ is the spread of the kernel.

3 Experiments

Experiments are conducted on two different face datasets; the colored FERET database [11] and Yale Face Database-B [12]. Performance results obtained on different image subsets are reported. Furthermore, in order to compare our approach, a pixel-based gender classification system is also incorporated in the experiments. In the pixel-based approach after face detection face region is downscaled and directly classified by an SVM without any feature extraction step. From the FERET dataset only frontal images that consists 874 female and 1594 male images are used throughout the experiments. The Yale dataset is included in the experiment because of the fact that it contains face images in varying lighting conditions as well as varying pose and expression contents. 286 female, 3466 male images are used from the Yale dataset. Although both datasets can be used for training, only the FERET dataset is incorporated for the training of SVM classifier, since FERET dataset is more structured compared to Yale dataset.

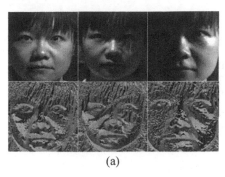
(a)

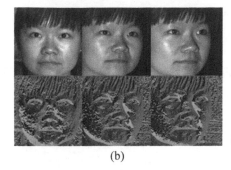
(b)

Fig 3. Example face images and corresponding Gradientfaces from (a) illumination subsets (b) pose subsets of Yale dataset

In the first phase of the experiments, 250 female and 250 male images are randomly selected from FERET dataset as test images and the rest of the face images from FERET are used for training the classifier. Gaussian smoothing kernel size and standard deviation in Gradientfaces approach are empirically chosen as 7-by-7 and 0.75, respectively, after preliminary experiments. Moreover, it should be noted that, in pixel-based method, a histogram equalization step is incorporated before the classification with SVM in order to decrease the effect of illumination. Recall rates obtained in this test are given in Table 2. The performances of both algorithms are almost same in this setup.

Table 1. Performance obtained on FERET dataset.

	FERET	**Yale Face B**
	Overall / Male / Female	**Overall / Male / Female**
Pixel-based	92.20 / 91.20 / 93.20	71.51 / 71.84 / 67.48
Gradientfaces	92.40 / 90.00 / 94.80	90.94 / 91.92 / 79.02

For tests on Yale dataset, all the chosen frontal images from FERET dataset (874 female and 1594 male) are used in the training. The obtained recall rates are given in Table 2. Since Yale dataset consists of images with varying pose, expression and illumination; further experiments are conducted for each category. Poses in the Yale dataset vary between $0°$ and $24°$ whereas the illumination varies up to $130°$ in azimuth and $90°$ in elevation with respect to camera optical axis. According to the illumination direction, dataset can be categorized into 5 subsets and plus one more subset with no illumination (ambient illumination). The illumination direction is varied from $0°$ to $12°$ in Subset 1, from $13°$ to $25°$ in Subset 2, from $26°$ to $50°$ in Subset 3, from $51°$ to $77°$ in Subset 4 and from $78°$ to $130°$ in subset 5. The overall accuracy obtained for the varying illumination direction is given in Table 3. Furthermore, accuracy on different pose angles is shown in Table 4.

Table 3. Overall Accuracy Performance Obtained from Illumination Subsets of Yale Face Database-B.

	Subset 1	**Subset 2**	**Subset 3**	**Subset 4**	**Subset 5**
Pixel based	77.28	77.38	67.65	60.98	75.85
Gradientfaces	90.29	90.82	91.15	90.98	91.3

Table 4. Overall Accuracy Performance Obtained from Different Pose Angles of Yale Face Database-B.

	0°		1°-12°		13°-24°	
	Male	Female	Male	Female	Male	Female
Pixel based	65.43	91.43	67.25	62.13	81.60	68.29
Gradientfaces	97.22	85.71	93.91	74.56	86.76	85.37

4 Conclusion

A recently proposed illumination insensitive feature extraction method for face recognition, namely Gradientfaces, is used for gender classification. In this work, discriminative power of the approach is shown to be highly applicable for gender classification. The proposed algorithm is compared to a pixel based method [1] in two well known datasets with highly varying illumination, pose and facial. It could be concluded that by using Gradientfaces, much higher correct classification rates (90.94% overall) than the pixel based method (71.51% overall) are achieved especially in extreme lighting conditions; thus, making this method more appropriate for real life applications, where illumination varies highly.

Acknowledgements: This work is funded by TÜBİTAK (The Scientific and Technological Research Council of Turkey) KAMAG TARAL 1007 (Support Programme for Research Projects of Public Institutions 1007) Research Programme, Project no. 107G229.

References

1. Moghaddam, B.; Ming-Hsuan Yang: Learning gender with support faces. IEEE Trans. on Pattern Analysis and Machine Intelligence, vol.24, no.5, 707-711, (2002)
2. Taiping Zhang; Yuan Yan Tang; Bin Fang; Zhaowei Shang; Xiaoyu Liu: Face Recognition Under Varying Illumination Using Gradientfaces. IEEE Transactions on Image Processing vol.18, no.11, pp.2599-2606, (2009)
3. Viola, P. and Jones, M. J.: Robust Real-Time Face Detection. *Int. J. Comput. Vision* 57, 2 137-154 (2004)
4. Toews, M.; Arbel, T.: Detection, Localization, and Sex Classification of Faces from Arbitrary Viewpoints and under Occlusion. IEEE Transactions on Pattern Analysis and Machine Intelligence, vol.31, no.9, pp.1567-1581, (2009)
5. Makinen, E.; Raisamo, R.: Evaluation of Gender Classification Methods with Automatically Detected and Aligned Faces. IEEE Transactions on Pattern Analysis and Machine Intelligence. vol.30, no.3, pp.541-547, (2008)
6. Shiqi Yu; Tieniu Tan; Kaiqi Huang; Kui Jia; Xinyu Wu: A Study on Gait- Based Gender Classification IEEE Transactions on Image Processing, vol.18, no.8, pp.1905-1910, (2009)
7. Li Lu; Pengfei Shi: A novel fusion-based method for expression-invariant gender classification. IEEE International Conference on Acoustics, Speech and Signal Processing, pp.1065-1068, (2009)

8. Jain, A.; Huang, J.: Integrating independent components and support vector machines for gender classification. 17th IEEE International Conference on Pattern Recognition. pp. 558- 561 Vol.3, 23-26 (2004)
9. Hadid, A. and Pietikinen, M.: Combining appearance and motion for face and gender recognition from videos. Pattern Recogn. 42, 11, 2818-2827. (2009)
10. A. S. Georghiades, P. N. Belhumeur, and D. J. Kriegman: From few to many: Illumination cone models for face recognition under variable lighting and pose. IEEE Trans. Pattern Analysis and Machine Intelligence, vol. 23, no. 6, pp. 643--660, (2001)
11. P.J. Phillips, H. Moon, S.A. Rizvi, P.J. Rauss: The FERET Evaluation Methodology for Face Recognition Algorithms. IEEE Trans. Pattern Analysis and Machine Intelligence, Vol. 22, pp. 1090-1104, (2000)
12. H. Harb and L. Chen: Gender identification using a general audio classifier. Int. Conf. Multimedia and Expo, pp. 733–736, (2003)

Adult Image Content Classification Using Global Features and Skin Region Detection

Hakan Sevimli[1,2], Ersin Esen[1,3], Tuğrul K. Ateş[1,3], Ezgi C. Ozan[1,3],
Mashar Tekin[1,2], K. Berker Loğoğlu[1,4], Ayça Müge Sevinç[1,4], Ahmet Saracoğlu[1,3],
Adnan Yazıcı[2] and A. Aydın Alatan[3]

[1] TÜBİTAK Space Technologies Research Institute
[2] Department of Computer Engineering, M.E.T.U.
[3] Department of Electrical and Electronics Engineering, M.E.T.U.
[4] Graduate School of Informatics, M.E.T.U.

{hakan.sevimli, ersin.esen, tugrul.ates, ezgican.ozan, mashar.tekin, berker.logoglu,
muge.sevinc, ahmet.saracoglu}@uzay.tubitak.gov.tr
yazici@ceng.metu.edu.tr, alatan@eee.metu.edu.tr

Abstract. A method for adult content classification and nudity detection is presented. Objective of this method is to classify images into different classes, varying on the degree of adult content. We utilize MPEG-7 descriptors to represent visual information. Skin regions are detected to model adult content more precisely, as well as to eliminate false-positives. Proposed method is tested with conventional image sets. Experimental results indicate that the algorithm has an acceptable detection performance.

Keywords: adult image classification, nudity detection, MPEG-7 visual descriptors, close-up face detection, skin color detection

1 Introduction

The amount of visual content available on the internet is well beyond manual analysis. Adult classification of images is one of the major tasks for semantic analysis of visual content. Modern approach to this problem is introducing rating mechanisms to prevent unsolicited access to this type of content. This prevention is especially critical for children [1]. It is an obvious fact that such a rating mechanism should make use of automatic analysis. One desired property of such a system is the opportunity to dynamically adjust the content severity level. For instance, different clients may require different restriction levels at different times [2].

In the literature, different adult image filtering methods are presented. The detection of skin areas is investigated in [3] where skin color is used in combination with other features such as texture and color histograms. Most of these systems build on neural networks or Support Vector Machines [4] as classifiers. One of the pioneering works is done by Forsyth *et al.* [5] where they combine tightly tuned skin filter with smooth texture analysis. After skin detection, geometric analysis is applied to detect of bare parts in human body figures. Another work is conducted by Duan *et al.*

E. Gelenbe et al. (eds.), *Computer and Information Sciences*, Lecture Notes
in Electrical Engineering 62, DOI 10.1007/978-90-481-9794-1_49,
© Springer Science+Business Media B.V. 2010

[6]. Their study is based purely on skin color detection and SVM. The images are first filtered by skin model and outputs are classified. Rowley *et al.* [7] propose a system that includes both skin color and face detection where they utilize a face detector to eliminate the effects of skin regions that belong to face area on the skin map. Yoo [8] suggests retrieving labeled images from a database where an image is labeled as adult content if most of the similar images are labeled that way.

Previous studies on this topic show that images which contain close-up face(s) mislead adult content classification systems [9], since these images have the same characteristics with ordinary nude images regarding skin color features. These studies suggest the use of face detection systems to overcome this problem.

Our aim is to rate any image as being in one of the classes defined in [10]: *normal*, *swimming suit*, *topless*, *nude* and *sexual content*. We present a system with four components. First component is skin color detection. Second component is close-up face detection. Third component is feature extraction from images by using shape, color and texture descriptors. The fourth component is to classification.

2   Proposed Algorithm

The proposed algorithm has four fundamental components: close-up face detection, skin color detection, feature extraction and classification. The general system structure is shown in Fig. 1.

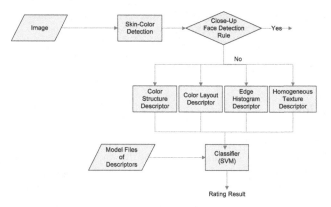

Fig. 1. Overall flow of adult rating classification algorithm.

2.1   Skin Region Detection

For the skin region detection step of this study, the method proposed by Jones and Rehg [3] is utilized. This method is based on inferring pixels on statistical skin and non-skin models, which are represented and trained with GMM. Jones and Rehg utilize millions of skin pixels for training. Mean and covariance results of this study are directly used in our method. Skin masks are obtained from skin detection and connected component labeling algorithms as shown in Fig. 2-a and 2-b. The skin mask is used to determine the regions that contain human bodies or body parts in the original image. These regions define the bounding box, which encapsulates all the parts that shows the skin color characteristics. Also skin detection is used for face elimination phase which will be described in the next section.

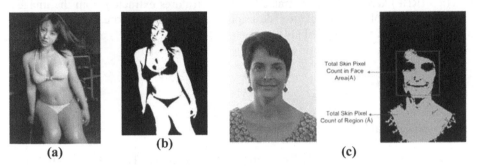

Fig. 2. (a) Input image, (b) its skin mask and (c) An example for close-up face elimination. Rectangular box indicates the face box given by the face detector.

2.2 Face Detection and Close-up Face Rule

Images containing many faces or a close-up face can be classified as nude images [9] causing false alarms. To solve this problem, we should be able to detect and eliminate close-up faces. For face detection, the method of Viola and Jones [13] is utilized.

By combining the face areas with skin masks, the ratio of total skin pixels that lie on the face area over the total skin pixel count of skin region can be calculated. If this ratio is large enough, it indicates that body parts other than the face may be found in the image. This means corresponding input images may contain nudity. Otherwise the image should be labeled as non-nude. The ratio can also be interpreted as a measure to determine the scale of human bodies in the image. Fig. 2-c shows an example of a query image, where total area of skin regions are large compared to image proportions. The test rule is $T = \tilde{A} - A / \tilde{A}$. If T is below a certain threshold, then the image is labeled as non-nude.

2.3 Feature Extraction

In feature extraction step, visual descriptors are extracted by using four different methods. These four low-level feature extraction methods are chosen from MPEG-7 descriptors [11, 12]. These are *Color Structure Descriptor* (CSD), *Color Layout Descriptor* (CLD), *Edge Histogram Descriptor* (EHD) and *Homogeneous Texture Descriptor* (HTD). These four different descriptors capture the visual information from different perspectives and provide compact representations.

2.4 Classification

We employ pattern classification on extracted features with SVM's due to their well reported potential in the literature [4]. We use multi-category SVM with a radial basis function (RBF) kernel. SVM are trained with the features extracted from the images by using the color and texture descriptors mentioned before. The OpenCV implementation of SVM is used [14].

3 Experiments

3.1 Experimental Setup

The system extracts four MPEG-7 descriptors for each image. The data set [10] that is used in the experiments has five different classes, which are *normal* images (class 1), *swimming suit* images (class 2), *topless* images (class 3), *nude* images (class 4) and *sexual activity* images (class 5).

The experimental image set consists of 1702 images for each class [10]. For each of the five classes, 1000 images are used for training and 500 images are used for testing. The image dataset, which is used to measure the success rates of close-up face elimination rule, consists of 799 frontal female faces of the FERET dataset [15]. If face elimination labels as non-nude, the classification is accomplished successfully.

3.2 Results

The classification results of the proposed system are shown in Table 1. It should be emphasized that whole image area is utilized for inactive skin detection case during training and test phases. These results indicate that color descriptors are more suitable than texture descriptors to adult image classification.

Comparing the results in Table 1 according to the use of skin color detection reveals that skin color detection slightly increases the performance. Compared to a very similar study [10], success rates of the proposed system are relatively higher, since Kim *et al.* [10] have not utilized any skin detection mechanism. Besides rating adult images with respect to their content, the results give an idea about nudity detection. It is obvious that rating images is a much more complex task than nudity detection. The results of nudity detection, where the classes 2, 3, 4 and 5 are combined into a single nude class, are represented in Table 2. In the second stage of the experiments, the effectiveness of the close-up face elimination rule is observed. Exact counts of eliminated images with respect to adult classes and the female set are shown in the Table 3. False eliminations on classes 1 to 5 are rare.

The close-up face check eliminates the images that are not likely to contain nudity. Thus they are classified as class 1 (normal images). Remaining images are classified with four feature descriptors and obtained results given in Table 4. Texture descriptors do not contribute much to the close-up face elimination process but color descriptors are more successful.

Table 1. Classification confusion matrices of experiments (with/without skin detection).

Descriptor	Query Class	Predicted Class				
		None	Swimsuit	Topless	Nude	Sexual
Color	None	**92.4/92.8**	2.8/3.8	2.6/2	1.6/1	0.6/0.4
Structure	Swimsuit	6.8/8	**51.8/51.8**	7.6/7.2	27.6/27.2	6.2/5.8
	Topless	7.4/10	18/20.6	**55.4/50.2**	17.8/17.8	1.4/1.4
	Nude	13.615.4	22.2/29	6.4/3.8	**56.8/50.8**	1/1
	Sexual	1/1	39/34	3/2.6	11.4/14.8	**45.6/47.6**
Color	None	**80.2/75.4**	5.4/9.4	7.6/9	1.2/0	5.6/6.2
Layout	Swimsuit	8/8.2	**22.6/27.4**	15.6/22.6	12.2/2.8	41.6/39
	Topless	5.2/6.4	20.4/23	**42/44.8**	4.6/2.4	27.8/23.4
	Nude	14/10.6	17.2/25	18.8/23.2	**12.6/10**	37.4/31.2
	Sexual	3/3.6	20/16.4	19.6/30.8	5.6/2.2	**51.8/47**
Edge	None	**82.2/80.8**	4.8/5.6	5.5/4.6	2.2/2.6	5.6/6.4
Histogram	Swimsuit	7.8/8	**41.4/34**	19.8/24.4	18.2/16.8	16/16.8
	Topless	15/15.4	25.4/30.8	**25.4/23.4**	18.2/13.4	16/17
	Nude	12.8/14.4	20/15.4	8.4/15.2	**47.4/43.8**	11.4/11.2
	Sexual	4.2/4.4	13/14.2	9/7.6	8.6/7.4	**65.2/66.4**
Homogeneous	None	**74.4/74.2**	3.4/3.8	12.8/13	4.6/4.8	4.8/4.2
Texture	Swimsuit	10.8/11	**28.8/25.2**	16.2/17.8	25/28.6	19.2/17.4
	Topless	7.4/7.2	16.6/15.4	**54.8/54.2**	8.2/8.4	13/14.8
	Nude	4.8/4.8	19/14.4	15/15	**31.6/36.8**	29.6/29
	Sexual	2.4/2.6	18/16.2	7.6/7.8	22/22.4	**50/51**

Table 2. Success rates of nudity detection when classes 2, 3, 4 and 5 are combined

Desc	w. Skin Detection	wo. Skin Detection
CSD	92.80	91.40
CLD	92.45	92.80
EHD	90.05	89.45
HTD	93.65	93.60

Table 3. Number of images that are labeled non-nude by face elimination rule

Image Set	Eliminated	Percentages
None	1	0.06(incorrect)
Swimsuit	28	1.64(incorrect)
Topless	33	1.94(incorrect)
Nude	7	0.41(incorrect)
Sexual	25	1.47(incorrect)
FERET Female	576	72.1(correct)

Table 4. Confusion values for FERET frontal female image set.

Descriptor	Resulting Class				
	None	Swimsuit	Topless	Nude	Sexual
Color Structure	**91.61**	2.13	0.13	6.13	0.0
Color Layout	**83.60**	5.89	1.00	3.13	6.38
Edge Histogram	**74.34**	7.13	5.63	2.38	10.51
Homogeneous Texture	**72.47**	7.88	5.51	4.38	9.76

4 Conclusion

In this study, a method that makes use of visual descriptors with skin detection is proposed for adult image classification. Additionally, we incorporate a close-up face elimination mechanism to get rid of false alarms. Experiments indicate that the proposed system can distinguish nude and non-nude cases. An important observation is that descriptors and decision of using skin detection or not is very crucial.

Acknowledgements. This work is funded by TÜBİTAK (The Scientific and Technological Research Council of Turkey) KAMAG TARAL 1007 (Support Programme for Research Projects of Public Institutions 1007) Research Programme, Project no. 107G229.

References

1. Zheng Q.F., Zeng W., Wen G., Wang W.Q., Shape-Based Adult Image Detection. In 3rd International Conference on Image and Graphics, pp. 150—153 (2004).
2. Deselaers T., Pimenidis L., Ney H., Bag-of-Visual-Words Models for Adult Image Classification and Filtering. In 19th International Conference on Pattern Recognition, pp. 1--4 (2008)
3. Jones M.J., Rehg J.M., Statistical Color Models with Application to Skin Detection. In International Journal of Computer Vision, Vol 46, No. 1, pp. 81--96 (2002).
4. Duda R.O., Hart P.E., Stork D.G., Pattern Classification. John Wiley & Sons, USA (2001)
5. Fleck, M., Forsyth, D.A., Bregler, C., Finding Naked People. In 4th European Conference on Computer Vision, pp. 593--602. Springer (1996).
6. Duan L., Cui G., Gao W., and Zhang H., Adult Image Detection Method Base-on Skin Color Model and Support Vector Machine. In 5th Asian Conference on Computer Vision. pp. 780--797 (2002).
7. Rowley H. A., Jing Y., Baluja S., Large Scale Image-Based Adult-Content Filtering. In 1st International Conference on Computer Vision Theory. pp. 290--296 (2006).
8. Yoo S.J., Intelligent Multimedia Information Retrieval for Identifying and Rating Adult Images. In 8th International Conference on Knowledge-Based Intelligent Information & Engineering Systems. vol. 1of Lecture Notes in Artificial Intelligence 3213, pp. 164--170 (2004).
9. Jeong C.Y., Kim J.S., Hong K.S., Appearance-Based Nude Image Detection. In 17th International Conference on Pattern Recognition, pp. 467--470 (2004).
10. Kim W., Yoo S.J., Kim J.S., Nam T.Y., Yoon K., Detecting Adult Images Using Seven MPEG-7 Visual Descriptors. In Human. Society@ Internet, pp. 336-339 (2005).
11. Manjunath B.S., Introduction to MPEG-7: Multimedia Content Description Interface. John Wiley & Sons (2002).
12. Manjunath B.S., Ohm J.S., Vasudevan V.V., Yamada A., Color and Texture Descriptors. In IEEE Transactions on Circuits and Systems for Video Technology. pp. 703--715 (2001).
13. Viola P., Jones M., Rapid Object Detection using a Boosted Cascade of Simple Features. In IEEE Computer Society Conference on Computer Vision and Pattern Recognition. vol. 1, pp. 511 (2001).
14. Open Computer Vision Library, http://sourceforge.net/projects/opencvlibrary
15. Phillips P.J., Moon H., Rizvi S.A., Rauss P.J., The FERET Evaluation Methodology for Face Recognition Algorithms. IEEE Transactions on Pattern Analysis and Machine Intelligence. vol. 22, pp. 1090--1104 (2000).

Texture Classification and Retrieval Based on Complex Wavelet Subbands

Turgay Celik and Tardi Tjahjadi

School of Engineering, University of Warwick, Coventry CV4 7AL, U.K.
{t.celik,t.tjahjadi}@warwick.ac.uk

Abstract. This paper proposes a multiscale texture classifier which uses features extracted from both magnitude and phase responses of subbands at different resolutions of the dual-tree complex wavelet transform decomposition of a texture image. The mean and entropy in the transform domain are used to form a feature vector. The superior performance and robustness of the proposed classifier is shown for classifying and retrieving texture images from image databases.

Key words: Texture retrieval, texture classification, multiscale analysis, discrete wavelet transform, dual-tree complex wavelet transform.

1 Introduction

A typical content-based image retrieval (CBIR) system involves extracting features such as shape, texture and colour, which constitute the image signature of the content of an image, and using image signatures and an appropriate distance metric to measure the similarity of a query image to the images in database. The ability to classify texture, where texture is used to represent the content of an image, is a fundamental requirement of a CBIR system. Gabor filters, wavelet transforms, finite impulse response filters have been widely used for this task. The Gabor filter is appealing due to its simplicity and support from neurophysiological experiments [1, 2]. The DWT based methods [3, 4] employ multiscale decomposition to extract high-frequency components from wavelet subbands for texture representation. However, DWT is not shift invariant and lacks direction selectivity [5] for robust feature representation. Gabor wavelets have been designed to be directionally selective. They are robust to shift since they are non-decimated, but they are therefore overcomplete and hence computationally expensive. The dual-tree complex wavelet transform (DT-CWT) has been shown to be approximately shift invariant and has limited redundancy [5].

The afore-mentioned advantages of DT-CWT and its multiscale structure make it appealing for texture classification and retrieval. Our previous multiscale texture classifier [6] uses the mean and standard deviation of the magnitude of DT-CWT subbands in different scales. In this paper, we improve the performance of our previous work by using both magnitude and phase of the complex subbands of DT-CWT. The additional information provided by the phase combined with the magnitude of the complex subbands results in more discriminative feature vectors. We also modified the texture feature vector structure to increase its discriminability. The new classifier is applied to both supervised texture classification and texture retrieval problems.

E. Gelenbe et al. (eds.), *Computer and Information Sciences*, Lecture Notes
in Electrical Engineering 62, DOI 10.1007/978-90-481-9794-1_50,
© Springer Science+Business Media B.V. 2010

2   Proposed method

The DT-CWT decomposition of an $W \times H$ image I results in a decimated dyadic decomposition into $s = 1, 2, \ldots, S$ scales, where each scale is of size $W/2^s \times H/2^s$. Each decimated scale has a set of six subbands of complex coefficients, $C_s = \{\alpha_1^{(s)} e^{i\theta_1^{(s)}}, \ldots, \alpha_6^{(s)} e^{i\theta_6^{(s)}}\}$, that respectively correspond to responses of the six subbands orientated at $-15°$, $-45°$, $-75°$, $15°$, $45°$, and $75°$. Each subband at scale s has magnitude $(\alpha_i^{(s)})$ and phase $(\theta_i^{(s)})$ responses, $i = 1, \ldots, 6$, that are normalized as

$$\alpha_i^{(s)} = \frac{\alpha_i^{(s)}}{E(\alpha_i^{(s)})}, \quad \theta_i^{(s)} = \frac{\theta_i^{(s)}}{E(\theta_i^{(s)})} \tag{1}$$

where $E(\alpha_i^{(s)}) = \sum_{y=1}^{H/2^s} \sum_{x=1}^{W/2^s} \alpha_i^{(s)}(x,y)^2$, $E(\theta_i^{(s)}) = \sum_{y=1}^{H/2^s} \sum_{x=1}^{W/2^s} \theta_i^{(s)}(x,y)^2$.

Texture features are extracted using image statistics. Unlike in [6] where the variance and entropy are defined in terms of magnitude of the subbands, in this paper we define a variance $M_1(r)$ and an entropy $M_2(r)$ that incorporate both magnitude and phase responses as the features for $r, r \in \{\alpha_i^{(s)}, \theta_i^{(s)}\}$, i.e.,

$$M_1(r) = \frac{2^{2s}}{HW} \sum_{y=1}^{H/2^s} \sum_{x=1}^{W/2^s} (r(x,y) - \mu(r))^2,$$

$$M_2(r) = \frac{-2^{2s}}{HW} \sum_{y=1}^{H/2^s} \sum_{x=1}^{W/2^s} r(x,y)^2 \log(r(x,y)^2) \tag{2}$$

where $\mu(r) = \frac{2^{2s}}{HW} \sum_{y=1}^{H/2^s} \sum_{x=1}^{W/2^s} r(x,y)$. Using $M_k(r)$, $k \in \{1, 2\}$, the following feature vectors are defined for scale s using the set C_s:

$$\mathbf{F}_{M_k, \alpha, s} = \frac{[M_k(\alpha_1^{(s)}) \ldots M_k(\alpha_6^{(s)})]}{\|[M_k(\alpha_1^{(s)}) \ldots M_k(\alpha_6^{(s)})]\|}, \mathbf{F}_{M_k, \theta, s} = \frac{[M_k(\theta_1^{(s)}) \ldots M_k(\theta_6^{(s)})]}{\|[M_k(\theta_1^{(s)}) \ldots M_k(\theta_6^{(s)})]\|},$$

$$\mathbf{F}_{\alpha, s} = [\mathbf{F}_{M_1, \alpha, s} \mathbf{F}_{M_2, \alpha, s}], \mathbf{F}_{\theta, s} = [\mathbf{F}_{M_1, \theta, s} \mathbf{F}_{M_2, \theta, s}], \mathbf{F}_s = \left[\frac{\mathbf{F}_{\alpha, s}}{\|\mathbf{F}_{\alpha, s}\|} \frac{\mathbf{F}_{\theta, s}}{\|\mathbf{F}_{\theta, s}\|}\right], \tag{3}$$

where $\|.\|$ is the second norm (i.e., the signal energy).

Given an image I, the multiscale feature vector is extracted by combining different realizations of Eq. 3 for different values of scales s, i.e.;

$$\mathbf{F}_S^I = \frac{[\mathbf{F}_1 \mathbf{F}_2 \cdots \mathbf{F}_S]}{\|[\mathbf{F}_1 \mathbf{F}_2 \cdots \mathbf{F}_S]\|} = [f_{S,1}^I \; f_{S,2}^I \; f_{S,3}^I \; \cdots \; f_{S,24S-2}^I \; f_{S,24S-1}^I \; f_{S,24S}^I] \tag{4}$$

where $\mathbf{F}_S^I$ is a vector of $24S$ elements.

Assume that each training set for texture class t consists of K texture samples. To perform a supervised texture classification, we use the following learning stage for the texture classifier based on that in [6] but modified to include phase information and the newly defined feature vectors for each class:

(i) Decompose k^{th} training texture image $I_t^{(k)}$ and generate feature vector $\mathbf{F}_S^{I_t^{(k)}}$ for decomposed texture image according to Eq. 4.

(ii) Repeat step (i) for all sample images in the same texture class and generate texture feature set $\mathbf{F}_{t,S} = \{\mathbf{F}_S^{I_t^{(k)}}\}$, and store them in the database.

After the features have been learned for each texture class, the following classification stage is performed to classify an unknown image I_u:

(i) Decompose an unknown texture image I_u using S levels of DT-CWT and extract its feature vector $\mathbf{F}_S^{I_u}$ using Eq. 4.

(ii) Calculate the distance between $\mathbf{F}_S^{I_u}$ and texture feature set $\mathbf{F}_{t,S}$ of each class t as $D_t = d(\mathbf{F}_S^{I_u}, \mathbf{F}_{t,S})$, where $d(\ )$ is similarity function, and then assign the unknown texture to texture class i if $D_i < D_j$ for all $i \neq j$.

In [6], the similarity function between the query texture and texture class t is simply the normalized Euclidian distance between the feature vectors of the query texture and the mean feature vector of the texture class t. In this paper, the average of the distances between a query feature vector and feature vectors of each sample in each texture class is used, i.e.,

$$d(\mathbf{F}_S^{I_u}, \mathbf{F}_{t,S}) = \frac{1}{K} \sum_{k=1}^{K} \sqrt{\frac{1}{24S} \sum_{i=1}^{24S} \left(\frac{f_{S,i}^{I_u} - f_{S,i}^{I_t^{(k)}}}{\sigma_{t,i}} \right)^2},$$

where for texture class t, $\sigma_{t,i} = \sqrt{\frac{1}{(K-1)} \sum_{k=1}^{K} (f_{S,i}^{I_t^{(k)}} - \mu)^2}$ and $\mu = \frac{1}{K} \sum_{k=1}^{K} f_{S,i}^{I_t^{(k)}}$.

Texture retrieval is viewed as a search for the best N, i.e., most similar, images to a given query image I_q from a database of a total M images, $I_m, m = 1, 2, \cdots, M$. For this purpose, each image is represented by a feature vector as in Eq. 4. The similarity between two images is measured by the distance between the corresponding feature vectors. The goal is to select among the M possible distances images with the N smallest distances, in a ranked order, that are most similar to I_q.

Given two images I_q and I_m, and let $\mathbf{F}_S^{I_q}$ and $\mathbf{F}_S^{I_m}$ represent the corresponding feature vectors extracted according to Eq. 4. We define two distance measures between two feature vectors $\mathbf{F}_S^{I_q}$ and $\mathbf{F}_S^{I_m}$ as

$$d_1(\mathbf{F}_S^{I_q}, \mathbf{F}_S^{I_m}) = \sum_{i=1}^{24S} |f_{S,i}^{I_q} - f_{S,i}^{I_m}|, \text{ and } d_2(\mathbf{F}_S^{I_q}, \mathbf{F}_S^{I_m}) = \sum_{i=1}^{24S} \frac{|f_{S,i}^{I_q} - f_{S,i}^{I_m}|}{\sigma_i}, \quad (5)$$

where $\sigma_i = \sqrt{\frac{1}{(M-1)} \sum_{m=1}^{M} (f_{S,i}^{I_m} - \mu_i)^2}$ and $\mu_i = \frac{1}{M} \sum_{m=1}^{M} f_{S,i}^{I_m}$.

3 Experimental results

3.1 Data

We evaluate the performance of our overall texture classification/retrieval system on the same database as that used in [6]. For this purpose we used 40

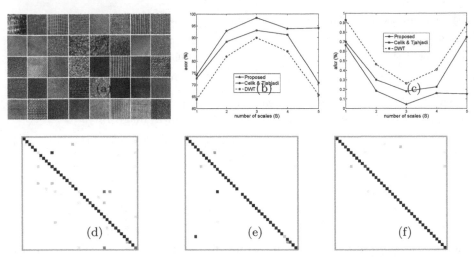

Fig. 1. Performance comparisons of different schemes: (a) Texture samples from MIT VisTex database [7] and Brodatz album [8] that are used in experiments; (b) *accr* versus S; (c) *afcr* versus S and confusion matrices for different schemes when $S = 3$: (d) DWT-based scheme; (e) the scheme in [6]; and (f) the proposed method.

texture samples from MIT VisTex database [7] and Brodatz album [8] as shown in Figure 1(a). Each texture image has a size of 512×512, with 256 grey levels. Each image is divided into two non-overlapping parts of size 256×512, one for training and one for testing. Sets of overlapped random patches of size $W \times H$ are generated from the training texture images. Each set consists of K samples, where $K = 10$ samples are used for each texture class. After training, randomly selected patches of size $W \times H$ from the testing samples are used to evaluate the performance of the texture classifier. In this study $W = H = 128$. From each testing texture image, 100 overlapping patches are selected.

Each of the 512×512 images was divided into sixteen 128×128 non-overlapping subimages, thus creating a test database of 640 texture images for experiments on texture retrieval.

3.2   Performance evaluation metrics

The performance of a texture classifier is measured using a confusion matrix **CM** [9]. **CM** is a $L \times L$ matrix for L different texture classes and $\mathbf{CM}(i, j)$ refers to the classification rate when samples from class i are identified as class j. Two figure of merits are used in conjunction with **CM**: average correct classification rate ($accr = \sum_{\forall(i,j),i=j} \mathbf{CM}(i,j)/L$) and average false classification rate ($afcr = \sum_{\forall(i,j),i\neq j} \mathbf{CM}(i,j)/(L \times (L-1))$).

In the experiments for texture retrieval, a query image is any one of the 640 images in our database. The relevant images for each query are defined as

Table 1. Average retrieval rate $R_{T_i}^{(d_i)}$ of the proposed texture retrieval algorithm using different distance measure d_i according to the number of best matches (T_i) considered for different number of scales S.

T_i	$S = 1$		$S = 2$		$S = 3$		$S = 4$		$S = 5$	
	$R_{T_i}^{(d_1)}$	$R_{T_i}^{(d_2)}$	$R_{T_i}^{(d_1)}$	$R_{T_i}^{(d_2)}$	$R_{T_i}^{(d_1)}$	$R_{T_i}^{(d_2)}$	$R_{T_i}^{(d_1)}$	$R_{T_i}^{(d_2)}$	$R_{T_i}^{(d_1)}$	$R_{T_i}^{(d_2)}$
15	68.77	68.93	83.40	83.74	88.98	89.46	89.35	90.42	88.95	90.72
20	75.84	75.85	87.52	87.83	92.11	92.34	92.50	93.28	92.75	94.10
40	87.25	87.29	93.32	93.29	96.24	96.35	96.75	97.16	97.02	97.49
60	91.27	91.30	95.51	95.70	97.79	97.82	97.91	98.32	98.28	98.51
80	93.73	93.79	96.92	97.07	98.39	98.63	98.63	98.90	98.91	99.06
100	95.21	95.30	97.77	97.96	98.86	99.04	99.00	99.18	99.18	99.26
Δ	0.00%		0.13%		0.19%		0.4255%		0.4258%	

the other 15 subimages from the same image in the database. We evaluated the performance of the proposed system in terms of the average rate of retrieving relevant images as a function of the number of best retrieved images given a distance measure d used for comparing feature vectors, i.e., $R_{T_i}^{(d)} = \frac{1}{640} \sum_{k=1}^{640} \frac{P_{T_i}^{(k)}}{15}$, where $R_{T_i}^{(d)}$ is the average retrieval rate of the database when the best T_i images are retrieved from the database, and $P_{T_i}^{(k)}$ is the number of correctly retrieved images among the T_i retrieved images when k^{th} image is the query image.

3.3   Evaluation of texture classification capability

The first experiment compares the proposed texture classifier with our previous classifier [6] and the DWT implementation of the structure of the proposed classifier. The results in Figure 1(b)-(c) clearly show that the proposed classifier outperforms the other two classifiers for different values of S. The best performance is achieved when $S = 3$ where $accr$ is 98.32% and $afcr$ is 0.04%. The performance of the proposed classifier, like the other classifiers, becomes worse when $S > 3$. This is mainly due to insufficient number of data points when $S > 3$ to extract discriminative features for the feature vector. The corresponding confusion matrices for $S = 3$ are shown as images in Figure 1(d)-(f), where white and black squares respectively correspond to 0 and 1, and values between 0 and 1 are denoted by squares of varying grey shades. Thus, more black squares along the diagonal of an image indicates a better performance, i.e., the proposed method achieves the best performance.

3.4   Evaluation of texture retrieval capability

Since the performance of the proposed texture classifier is better than our previous classifier [6], we only evaluate the texture retrieval capability of the proposed classifier. Table 1 shows its performance in terms of $R_{T_i}^{(d_i)}$, the average rate of retrieving relevant images as a function of the number of best retrieved images for different number of scales S when different similarity measures are used. It shows that the proposed algorithm achieves best performance when $S = 5$ at the expense of an increase in computational complexity for both distance measures (i.e., d_1 (Eq. (5)) and d_2 (Eq. (5)). It achieves almost the same performance for both distance measures when $S < 3$ but the performance differs when S increases, i.e., $S >= 3$. As a result, the mean difference of the performances when the two distance measures are used, i.e., $\Delta = \frac{1}{18}\sum_{i=1}^{18}(R_{T_i}^{(d_2)} - R_{T_i}^{(d_1)})$ are computed and shown in the last row of Table 1. It is clear that the performance is better when d_2 is used, but at an extra normalization by σ_i (see Eq. (5)).

The performance of the proposed algorithm is compared with the algorithms in [3, 4] by comparing with the results tabulated in [4]. For this purpose we used the same set of 40 texture images as used in [3, 4]. The average retrieval rate is calculated for the best 15 ($T_i = 15$) images retrieved from the database for each query texture image from the database. In the experiments, $S = 5$ is used. The average retrieval rates for DWT, [3], [4] and the proposed method are 75.62%, 80.78%, 76.57%, and 87.60%, respectively. The best performance is achieved by the proposed algorithm. This is mainly due to the structure of the texture classifier and the directional data representation of the DT-CWT.

4   Conclusion

In this paper, we proposed a new texture classifier structure which uses both the magnitude and phase of DT-CWT subbands. It is shown that for texture classification the proposed classifier outperforms our previous multiscale texture classifier [6] both in high $accr$ and low $afcr$. The capability of the proposed classifier in retrieving texture images is empirically shown to achieve high performance. The average retrieval rate of the proposed texture retrieval algorithm increases when the number of the scales S increases. However, the increased in performance is achieved at the expense of an increase in computational load.

References

[1] Faugeras, O.: Texture analysis and classification using a human visual model. In: Proc. IEEE Int. Conf. Pattern Recognit. (1978) 549–552
[2] Arivazhagan, S., Ganesan, L., Priyal, S.: Texture classification using gabor wavelets based rotation invariant features. Pattern Recognit. Letts. **27**(16) (Dec 2006) 1976–1982
[3] Do, M., Vetterli, M.: Wavelet-based texture retrieval using generalized gaussian density and kullback-leibler distance. IEEE Trans. Image Proc. **11**(2) (Feb 2002) 146–158
[4] Kokare, M., Biswas, P., Chatterji, B.: Texture image retrieval using rotated wavelet filters. Pattern Recognit. Letts. **28** (2007) 1240–1249
[5] Kingsbury, N.: Complex wavelets for shift invariant analysis and filtering of signals. Applied and Computational Harmonic Analysis **10**(3) (2001) 234–253
[6] Celik, T., Tjahjadi, T.: Multiscale texture classification using dual-tree complex wavelet transform. Pattern Recognit. Letts. **30** (2009) 331–339
[7] MITVisTex: Vision texture database. http://www.media.mit.edu/vismod/ (1998)
[8] Brodatz, P.: Textures: A Photographic Album for Artists and Designers. Dover, New York, USA (1966)
[9] Kohavi, R., Provost, F.: Glossary of Terms. Volume 30. Kluwer Academic Publishers, Hingham, MA, USA (1998)

A COMPRESSION METHOD BASED on COMPRESSIVE SENSING for 3-D LASER RANGE SCANS of INDOOR ENVIRONMENTS

Oguzcan Dobrucali and Billur Barshan

Department of Electrical and Electronics Engineering, Bilkent University
06800, Bilkent, Ankara, Turkey
{dobrucali, billur}@ee.bilkent.edu.tr

Abstract. When 3-D models of environments need to be transmitted or stored, they should be compressed efficiently to increase the capacity of the communication channel or the storage medium. We propose a novel compression technique based on compressive sensing, applied to sparse representations of 3-D range measurements. We develop a novel algorithm to generate sparse innovations between consecutive range measurements along the axis of the sensor's motion, since the range measurements do not have highly sparse representations in common domains. Compared with the performances of widely used compression techniques, the proposed method offers the smallest compression ratio and provides a reasonable balance between reconstruction error and processing time.

1 Introduction

Many techniques have been developed for extracting 3-D models of environments, which allow describing objects with undefined or arbitrary shapes or patterns [1]. One approach to constructing 3-D models is to use laser range finders that measure the distance between the sensor and the objects within the field of view. The model is acquired by using either a conventional 3-D laser scanner, which is an expensive device, or a number of translating and/or rotating 2-D laser scanners [2].

In this study, we consider an indoor environment scanned in 3-D with a single 2-D laser range finder, rotating around a horizontal axis above ground level. The device used in this study is SICK LMS200 with its maximum range 80 m, field of view 180°, range resolution 1 mm, and angular resolution 0.5° [3]. Since the 3-D model is composed of a considerable number of 2-D scans that are themselves comprised of a large number of range measurements, the measurements need to be compressed when they are transmitted or stored.

The *compression ratio* (CR), which is the ratio of the size of the compressed output to the size of the original data, and the *speed of compression* are two important criteria for measuring compression performance. The CR is between zero and one (or zero and 100%), such that the closer the CR is to zero, the

E. Gelenbe et al. (eds.), *Computer and Information Sciences*, Lecture Notes
in Electrical Engineering 62, DOI 10.1007/978-90-481-9794-1_51,
© Springer Science+Business Media B.V. 2010

greater the amount of compression. In terms of the CR, a compression method can be considered efficient when the size of the original data is reduced by more than one half, so that the capacity of the communication channel or data storage medium is at least doubled [4].

2   Review of Compressive Sensing

Compressive sensing is a technique that samples a signal in $\Re^N$, where N is very large, at a rate lower than the signal's Nyquist rate, using a linear sampling model with an optimization procedure for reconstructing the sampled signal [5].

The sampling model is composed of the *sparsifying basis* and the *measurement model* that satisfy *sparsity* and *incoherence* properties, respectively. Sparsity requires the signals to have sparse projections onto the sparsifying basis in which only a small number of the coefficients (K) will have large values, whereas the majority $(N - K)$ will be close to zero. The sparsifying basis is an orthonormal basis denoted by $\Psi = [\psi_1, .., \psi_N]$ which is spanned by $\{\psi_i\}_{i=1}^N$. Thus, the sampled signal can be represented as $\mathbf{x} = \sum_{i=1}^N s_i \psi_i = \Psi \mathbf{s}$, where $\mathbf{s} = [s_1, ..., s_N]^T$ in which $s_i = <\mathbf{x}, \psi_i>$. Notice that, $\mathbf{x}$ and $\mathbf{s}$ are different representations of the same signal in time and Ψ domains, respectively. The measurement model determines M measurements, where $M \ll N$, using a linear operator $\Phi = [\phi_1^T, ..., \phi_M^T]^T$ composed of $\{\phi_i\}_{i=1}^M$, each of which is in $\Re^N$. The measurement model should be chosen so that $\{\phi_i\}_{i=1}^M$ cannot sparsely represent $\{\psi_i\}_{i=1}^N$, which is a requirement of the incoherence property. Baraniuk suggests in [6] that the measurement model, in which each entry is chosen from a Gaussian distribution with zero mean and $\frac{1}{N}$ variance, is incoherent with any sparsifying basis with high probability. Given N and K, the lower bound on M is determined by:

$$M \geq cK \ln \left(\frac{N}{K} \right) \tag{1}$$

where c is a small positive constant [6]. Eventually, the measurement vector denoted by $\mathbf{y} = [y_1, ..., y_M]^T$, where $y_i = <\mathbf{x}, \phi_i>$, is obtained such that $\mathbf{y} = \Phi \mathbf{x} = \Phi \Psi \mathbf{s} = \Theta \mathbf{s}$. The signal is then reconstructed by determining $\mathbf{s}$, given $\mathbf{y}$ and Θ. Since Θ is an $M \times N$ matrix with $M \ll N$, there is no unique solution to $\mathbf{y} = \Theta \mathbf{s}$. Therefore, the optimal solution is found by [7]:

$$\hat{\mathbf{s}} = \arg\min \|\mathbf{s}\|_1 \text{ such that } \mathbf{y} = \Theta \mathbf{s}. \tag{2}$$

Finally, the original signal is approximated from $\hat{\mathbf{x}} = \Psi \hat{\mathbf{s}}$ with little distortion.

3   The Proposed Method

In compressive sensing, although determining the measurement model is straightforward, determining the sparsifying basis is not so simple. One of the main objectives of this study is to obtain sufficiently sparse representations of the 2-D scans that form the 3-D model.

The experimental data set [8] used in this study is composed of 29 3-D scans from different indoor environments, each of which is acquired by taking 2-D scans as the sensor is rotated in 471 steps around a horizontal axis above ground level. As a consequence, every 3-D scan in the data set constitutes 471 2-D scans, sequentially acquired as vectors in $\Re^{361}$ (i.e., $N = 361$).

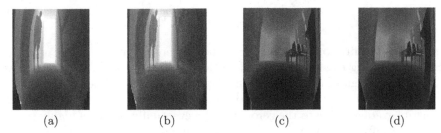

(a)   (b)   (c)   (d)

Fig. 1: (a) and (c): sample 3-D scans, (b) and (d): their reconstructions.

To apply the sampling model described in Sect. 2, we first consider the projections of a 3-D scan from the data set, illustrated in Fig. 1(a), onto some of the well-known sparsifying bases. The 2-D scans forming the 3-D scan are projected one at a time onto $N \times N$ sparsifying bases formed by using Fourier [9], Gabor [9], and Haar [10] dictionaries. After lowering the small values to zero, the average number of non-zero coefficients in these projections are around 270, 220, and 320, respectively. The projections are not sufficiently sparse, so both the CR and the distortion on the reconstruction would be high, if compressive sensing were used with one of these sparsifying bases and the measurement model mentioned in Sect. 2 [7]. Therefore, we propose a novel technique to generate more sparse innovations with approximately 40 non-zero coefficients on the average, for the same scan data.

The proposed method involves sparsifying, measurement, and reconstruction stages: The sparsifying model generates sparse innovations for each scan, and then the measurement model samples the innovations with the minimum number of samples. Finally, the reconstruction model rebuilds each scan from the samples encoded by the measurement model. In the following subsections, these three stages are described in more detail.

3.1 The Sparsifying Model

In the sparsifying model, we generate innovations between the currently acquired scan $\mathbf{x}$, and the previous scan $\tilde{\mathbf{x}}$. First, $\tilde{\mathbf{x}}$ is generated at the encoder by employing the reconstruction procedure that the decoder follows, to adapt the sparsifying parameters according to the reconstructions at the decoder. Then, $\tilde{\mathbf{x}}$ is approximated to $\mathbf{x}$ by shifting $\tilde{\mathbf{x}}$ along the vertical and horizontal axes by amplitude (ϵ) and phase (δ) shifts, respectively.

We define an error function $\mathcal{E}^2 = \sum_{k=1}^{N} [x[k] - (\tilde{x}[k + \delta] + \epsilon)]^2$, where k is the discrete-time index, and set its partial derivatives with respect to ϵ and δ to zero, to find the optimal ϵ and δ. Ignoring the δ term in $\frac{\partial \mathcal{E}^2}{\partial \epsilon}$, we determine ϵ as:

$$\epsilon = \frac{1}{N} \sum_{k=1}^{N} (x[k] - \tilde{x}[k]) \tag{3}$$

which corresponds to the average amplitude difference between $\mathbf{x}$ and $\tilde{\mathbf{x}}$. Since δ is assumed to be very small compared to N, $\tilde{x}[k+\delta]$ is expressed using the first two terms of its *Taylor series* expansion around k. Then, we find δ as:

$$\delta = \frac{\sum_{k=1}^{N} \tilde{x}'[k]\,(x[k] - \tilde{x}[k] - \epsilon)}{\sum_{k=1}^{N} \tilde{x}'[k]^2} \tag{4}$$

where $\tilde{x}'[k]$ is the first-order difference of the sequence $\tilde{\mathbf{x}}$ at k.

Shifting $\tilde{\mathbf{x}}$ along the horizontal and vertical axes by ϵ and δ, respectively, we obtain an approximation $\hat{\mathbf{x}}$ to $\mathbf{x}$. Then, the innovation is defined as $\mathbf{v} = \mathbf{x} - \hat{\mathbf{x}}$ and is vertically shifted in either positive or negative direction by the offset Δ, to bring its average value to the zero level. We eventually obtain a highly sparse innovation $\hat{\mathbf{v}}$ after nulling very small variations around zero. Consequently, $\mathbf{x}$ is represented with ϵ, δ, Δ, and $\hat{\mathbf{v}}$, respectively. When the *mean square error* (MSE) between $\mathbf{x}$ and $\hat{\mathbf{x}}$ is very low, $\hat{\mathbf{v}}$ becomes very small, so $\mathbf{x}$ is represented without $\hat{\mathbf{v}}$. When the MSE is greater than a preset threshold, $\hat{\mathbf{v}}$ becomes not as sparse as we would like, so $\mathbf{x}$ is not encoded.

3.2 The Measurement Model

The measurement model gets the minimum number of samples from $\hat{\mathbf{v}}$ by using either simple coding (SC) or compressive sensing (CS). Simple coding encodes $\hat{\mathbf{v}}$ using the location and amplitude of the non-zero components. The measurement size M is $2K$, and the reconstruction error is zero. Compressive sensing measures arbitrary linear combinations of the components in $\hat{\mathbf{v}}$. In this case, M is determined using (1), and the reconstruction error increases with K.

When M required by SC is lower than M required by CS, using SC is advantageous over using CS, in terms of the zero reconstruction error and lower M. Therefore, we obtain the measurements $\mathbf{m}$ applying either SC when $K \leq K^*$, or CS, otherwise. Here, K^* is the value of K that makes M for SC equal to M for CS. We include a special character (i.e., π) at the beginning of $\mathbf{m}$ when SC is applied to inform the decoder that we are using SC instead of CS. When $K > \frac{N}{2}$, $\hat{\mathbf{v}}$ cannot be considered sparse, since the reconstruction error would be very high if $\hat{\mathbf{v}}$ were sampled using CS. In that case, $\mathbf{x}$ is not encoded.

At the output of the measurement model, $\mathbf{x}$ is represented with $\{\epsilon,\ \delta,\ \Delta,\ \mathbf{m}\}$ if it is encoded. Otherwise, $\mathbf{x}$ is left as is.

3.3 The Reconstruction Model

The reconstruction model rebuilds $\mathbf{x}$ from the output generated by the encoder. When $\mathbf{x}$ is encoded, the output is $\{\epsilon, \delta, \Delta, \mathbf{m}\}$ with length $(M+3)$ less than N. Otherwise, the output is $\mathbf{x}$ with length N. Therefore, the output is stored directly as the reconstruction of $\mathbf{x}$ if its length is N. Otherwise, the reconstruction model is applied to the output.

The reconstruction model first decomposes the output into ϵ, δ, Δ, and $\mathbf{m}$. After this step, to obtain $\hat{\mathbf{x}}$, $\tilde{\mathbf{x}}$ is shifted along the vertical and horizontal axes by ϵ and δ, respectively. Afterwards, $\mathbf{v}$ is rebuilt from $\mathbf{m}$ and Δ. In this step, if the first value of $\mathbf{m}$ is π, then $\hat{\mathbf{v}}$ is rebuilt, decoding the rest of $\mathbf{m}$ with respect to the SC scheme, which involves filling an empty signal in $\Re^N$ with the values of location and amplitude pairs given in the measurements. Otherwise, $\hat{\mathbf{v}}$ is rebuilt, decoding $\mathbf{m}$ with respect to the CS scheme, which involves solving (2), where $\Theta = \Phi$, by following the procedure in [7]. Then, $\mathbf{v}$ is acquired by shifting the amplitude of $\hat{\mathbf{v}}$ by Δ. Eventually, $\mathbf{x}$ is reconstructed by adding $\mathbf{v}$ to $\hat{\mathbf{x}}$.

The reconstruction model is used at the decoder, as well as at the encoder, to estimate the reconstructions generated by the decoder.

4   Comparing the Proposed Method with Some Well-Known Compression Techniques

In this section, we compare the compression performance of the proposed method with some well-known and widely used lossless and lossy compression techniques that are applied to every 2-D scan independently in all of the 3-D scans in the data set. Thus, for each technique in the comparison, we compare the CR, the average of the *root mean square error* between the 2-D scans and their reconstructions (E), and the time required for encoding (t_{enc}) and decoding (t_{dec}). These values are found by averaging over the values obtained for the whole data set, including $4,930,899$ ($= 29$ 3-D sets $\times$ 471 2-D scans $\times$ 361 measurements) range measurements in total.

We first compress the scan data using four of the lossless techniques: *Huffman* [11], *arithmetic* [11], *ZLIB* [12], and *GZIP* [13]. Besides, we also apply two of the lossy compression methods to the data set: *JPEG* [11] and 3-level *wavelet transform* using the *Haar dictionary* [14]. The results are given in Table 1.

	method	CR (%)	E (cm)	t_{enc} (s)	t_{dec} (s)
lossless	Huffman coding	41.7	0	165.6	610.6
	arithmetic coding	11.1	0	37.6	48.9
	ZLIB	65.3	0	0.4	0.2
	GZIP	76.7	0	0.5	0.3
lossy	JPEG	25.4	184.2	0.8	0.2
	wavelet transform	12.7	37.3	0.1	0.1
	proposed	**10.9**	**12.9**	**15.3**	**14.5**

Table 1: Table of CR, E, t_{enc}, and t_{dec} for compression using different methods.

Finally, the data set is encoded using the proposed method. In this method, since the measurement model in CS is determined arbitrarily in each trial, small fluctuations in the compression performance are observed ($\pm 2\%$ in CR). Therefore, CR, E, t_{enc}, and t_{dec} are obtained as in Table 1, after the whole data set is encoded 10 times, and the results are averaged. On the average, the data set is compressed by 89% with about 13 cm distortion in the reconstructions. In this case, 57% of the 2-D scans are encoded with ϵ, δ, and Δ; 24% are encoded with ϵ, δ, Δ, and $\mathbf{m}$ obtained using SC; 16% are encoded with ϵ, δ, Δ, and $\mathbf{m}$ obtained using CS. Only 3% are not encoded. When the 3-D scans illustrated in Fig. 1(a) and (c) are compressed by 89% and 85%, the resulting average distortions are 12 and 16 cm, respectively. The reconstructed scans are shown in Fig. 1(b) and (d) to allow comparison with their originals.

The proposed method compresses the experimental data more than all the lossy and lossless techniques we have considered. In terms of speed, the proposed method is much faster than Huffman and arithmetic coding, but much slower than ZLIB, GZIP, JPEG, and the wavelet transform. However, the proposed method compresses more than the latter four. Moreover, the proposed method provides much less reconstruction error than the latter two.

5   Conclusion

In this study, we consider 3-D modelling of indoor environments employing the SICK LMS200 laser range finder. The 2-D range scans forming the 3-D model are compressed so that they can be stored or transmitted efficiently. From this perspective, we propose a novel compression technique based on compressive sensing for sequentially acquired 2-D scans.

According to the criteria described in Sect. 1, the proposed method is fast and efficient in terms of CR, and provides a reasonably good balance between reconstruction accuracy and speed [11]. It is recommended for applications where both CR and speed are crucial. However, a lossless compression technique can be used in applications where the accuracy of the range measurements is more important. Our future work involves improving the compression performance of the proposed method, and extending its application to 3-D range measurements of outdoor environments.

References

1. C. Brenneke, O. Wulf, B. Wagner: Using 3-D laser range data for SLAM in outdoor environments. Proc. IEEE/RSJ Int. Conf. Intelligent Robots Syst. (2003) 188–193
2. D. Borrman, J. Elseberg, K. Lingemann, A. Nüchter, J. Hertzberg: Globally consistent 3-D mapping with scan matching. Robot. Auton. Syst. **56** (2007) 130–142
3. SICK AG: Quick Manual for LMS Communication Setup (March 2002) Ver. 1.1.
4. D. Salamon: A Guide to Data Compression Methods. Springer, New York, U.S.A. (2002)
5. E. J. Candes and M. B. Wakin: An introduction to compressive sampling. IEEE Signal Proc. Mag. **25** (2008) 21–30
6. R. G. Baraniuk: Compressive sensing. IEEE Signal Proc. Mag. **24** (2007) 118
7. E. Candes, J. Romberg: Signal recovery from random projections. Proc. SPIE. Vol. 5674. (2005)
8. Nüchter, A.:   Osnabruck University and Jacobs University Knowledge-based Systems Research Group Repository (2009) http://kos.informatik.uni-osnabrueck.de/3Dscans/
9. S. S. Chen: Basis Pursuit. PhD thesis, Stanford University, Department of Statistics, California, U.S.A. (1995)
10. I. Daubechies: Ten Lectures on Wavelets. Society for Industrial and Applied Mathematics, Philadelphia, Pennsylvania (1992)
11. K. Sayood: Introduction to Data Compression. Academic Press, San Diego, U.S.A. (2000)
12. G. Roelofs, M. Adler: The ZLIB Homepage (August 2009) http://www.zlib.net/
13. J. Gailly, M. Adler: The GZIP Homepage (July 2003) http://www.gzip.org/
14. G. Strang and T. Nguyen: Wavelets and Filterbanks. Wellesley-Cambridge Press, Wellesley MA, U.S.A. (1997)

Two-Dimensional Mellin and Mel-Cepstrum for Image Feature Extraction

Serdar ÇAKIR and A. Enis ÇETİN*

Department of Electrical and Electronics Engineering
Bilkent University, 06800, Ankara, Turkey
{cakir,cetin}@bilkent.edu.tr

Abstract. An image feature extraction method based on two-dimensional (2D) Mellin cepstrum is introduced. The concept of one-dimensional (1D) mel-cepstrum which is widely used in speech recognition is extended to two-dimensions both using the ordinary 2D Fourier Transform and the Mellin transform in this article. The resultant feature matrices are applied to two different classifiers (Common Matrix Approach and Support Vector Machine) to test the performance of the mel-cepstrum and Mellin-cepstrum based features. Experimental studies indicate that recognition rates obtained by the 2D mel-cepstrum based method are superior to the recognition rates obtained using 2D PCA and ordinary image matrix based face recognition in both classifiers.

1 Introduction

Mel-cepstral analysis is one of the most popular feature extraction technique in speech processing applications including speech and sound recognition and speaker identification. Two-dimensional (2D) cepstrum is also used in image registration and filtering applications [1, 2]. To the best of our knowledge 2-D mel-cepstrum which is a variant of 2D cepstrum is not used in image feature extraction, classification and recognition problems. The goal of this paper is to define the 2-D mel-cepstrum and 2-D Mellin-cepstrum and show that they are viable image representation tools.

Fourier-Mellin transform (FMT) is a mathematical feature extraction tool which is used in some pattern recognition applications [3]. The FMT is generally implemented by performing a log-polar mapping followed by the Fourier transform (FT) [3]. The main idea behind this approach is to represent rotation and scaling as translations along some axes and to take advantage of the translation invariance property of the Fourier Transform.

Ordinary 2D cepstrum of a 2D signal is defined as the inverse Fourier Transform of the logarithmic spectrum of the signal and it is computed using 2D FFT. As a result it is independent of pixel amplitude variations or gray-scale changes, which leads to robustness against illumination variations. Since it is a FT based

---

* This work is supported by European Commission Seventh Framework Program with EU Grant: 244088(FIRESENSE)

method it is also independent of translational shifts [3]. 2D mel-cepstrum which is based on logarithmic decomposition of frequency domain grid also has the same shift and amplitude invariance properties as the 2D cepstrum. In addition, 2D Mellin-cepstrum has rotation and amplitude invariance properties. The proposed feature extraction technique is applied to the face recognition problem that is still an active and popular area of research. It should be pointed out that our aim is not the development of a complete face recognition system but to illustrate the advantages of the 2-D cepstral domain features.

In 2D mel-cepstrum and Mellin-cepstrum, the logarithmic division of the 2D DFT grid provides the dimensionality reduction. This is also an intuitively valid representation as most natural images are low-pass in nature. Unlike the ordinary Fourier or DCT domain features high-frequency DFT and DCT coefficients are not discarded in an ad-hoc manner. They are combined in bins of frequency values in a logarithmic manner during the 2D mel-cepstrum computation.

The rest of the paper is organized as follows. In Section 2, proposed 2D cepstral domain feature extraction methods are described. In Section 3, the well-known classification method SVM and a subspace based pattern recognition method called Common Matrix Approach are briefly explained. In Section 4, experimental results are presented.

2   The 2D Mel- and Mellin-Cepstrum

In the literature, the 2D cepstrum was used for shadow detection, echo removal, automatic intensity control, enhancement of repetitive features and cepstral filtering [1, 2]. In this article, 2D mel-cepstrum and Mellin-cepstrum are used for representing images or image regions.

We first introduce the 2-D mel-cepstrum using the definition of 2D cepstrum which is defined as follows. 2D cepstrum $\hat{y}(p, q)$ of a 2D image $y(n_1, n_2)$ is given by

$$\hat{y}(p, q) = F_2^{-1}(log(|Y(u, v)|^2)) \tag{1}$$

where (p, q) denotes 2D cepstral quefrency coordinates, F_2^{-1} denotes 2D Inverse Discrete-Time Fourier Transform (IDTFT) and $Y(u, v)$ is the 2D Discrete-Time Fourier Transform (DTFT) of the image $y(n_1, n_2)$. In practice, Fast Fourier Transform (FFT) algorithm is used to compute DTFT.

In 2D mel-cepstrum the DTFT domain data is divided into non-uniform bins in a logarithmic manner and the energy $|G(m, n)|^2$ of each bin is computed as follows

$$|G(m, n)|^2 = \sum_{k, l \in B(m, n)} |Y(k, l)|^2 \tag{2}$$

where $Y(k, l)$ is the Discrete Fourier Transform (DFT) of $y(n_1, n_2)$, and $B(m, n)$ is the $(m, n) - th$ cell of the logarithmic grid. Cell or bin sizes are smaller at low frequencies compared to high-frequencies. This approach is similar to the mel-cepstrum computation in speech processing. Similar to speech signals most natural images including face images are low-pass in nature. Therefore, there is more signal energy at low-frequencies compared to high frequencies. Logarithmic division of the DFT grid emphasizes high frequencies. After this step 2D mel-frequency cepstral coefficients $\hat{y}_m(p,q)$ are computed using either inverse DFT or DCT as follows

$$\hat{y}_m(p,q) = F_2^{-1}(log(|G(m,n)|^2)) \qquad (3)$$

The size of the Inverse DFT (IDFT) is smaller than the size of the forward DFT used to compute $Y(k,l)$ because of the logarithmic grid. It is also possible to apply different weights to different bins to emphasize certain bands as in speech processing. Since several DFT values are grouped together in each cell, the resulting 2D mel-cepstrum sequence computed using the IDFT has smaller dimensions than the original image. Steps of the 2D mel-cepstrum based feature extraction scheme is summarized below.

- N by N 2D DFT of input images are calculated. The DFT size N should be larger than the image size. It is better to select $N = 2^r > dimension(y(n_1, n_2))$ to take advantage of the FFT algorithm during DFT computation.
- The non-uniform DTFT grid is applied to the resultant DFT matrix and the energy $|G(m,n)|^2$ of each cell is computed. Each cell of the grid can be also weighted with a coefficient. The new data size is M by M where $M \leq N$. In most images, edges and important facial features generally contribute to high frequencies. In order to extract better representative features, high frequency component cells of the 2D DFT grid is multiplied with higher weights compared to low frequency component bins in the grid. As a result, high frequency components are further emphasized.
- Logarithm of cell energies $|G(m,n)|^2$ are computed.
- 2D IDFT or 2D IDCT of the M by M data is computed to get the M by M mel-cepstrum sequence.

It is possible to achieve illumination invariance in cepstral domain because of the logarithm operation during cepstrum computation.

Fourier-Mellin features are rotation, scale and translation invariant [3]. The 2D Mellin cepstrum feature extraction technique is a modified version of the 2D mel-cepstrum algorithm. It takes advantage of the Mellin transform and provides rotation, scale and illumination invariant features. Steps of 2D-Mellin cepstrum computation is summarized below:

- N by N 2D DFT of input images are calculated. The DFT size N should be larger than the image size. It is better to select $N = 2^r > dimension(y(n_1, n_2))$ to take advantage of the FFT algorithm during DFT computation.
- Logarithm of magnitudes of the DFT coefficients are computed.
- Non-uniform DFT grid is applied to the resultant matrix and the mean of each cell is computed. Each cell of the grid is represented with this mean and the cell is weighted with a coefficient. The new data size is M by M where $M \leq N$.
- Cartesian to Log-polar conversion is performed using bilinear interpolation. This is the key step of the Fourier-Mellin transform providing rotation and scale invariance.

- 2D IDFT of the M by M log-polar data is computed.
- Absolute value or the magnitude of the IDFT coefficients are calculated to get the M by M Mellin-cepstrum sequence.

Invariance of cepstrum to the pixel amplitude changes is an important feature. In this way, it is possible to achieve robustness to illumination invariance. Let $Y(u, v)$ denote the 2D DTFT of a given image matrix $y(n_1, n_2)$ and $cy(n_1, n_2)$ has a DTFT $cY(u, V)$ for any real constant c. The log spectrum of $cY(u, V)$ is given as follows

$$log(|cY(u, v)|) = log(|c|) + log(|Y(u, v)|) \tag{4}$$

and the corresponding cepstrum is given as follows

$$\psi(p, q) = \hat{a}\delta(p, q) + \hat{y}(p, q) \tag{5}$$

where $\delta(p, q) = 1$ for $p = q = 0$ and $\delta(p, q) = 0$ otherwise. Therefore, the cepstrum values except at $(0, 0)$ location (DC Term) do not vary with the amplitude changes. Since the Fourier Transform magnitudes of $y(n_1, n_2)$ and $y(n_1 - k_1, n_2 - k_2)$ are the same, the 2D cepstrum and mel-cepstrum are shift invariant features.

Another important characteristic of 2D cepstrum is symmetry with respect to $\hat{y}[n_1, n_2] = \hat{y}[-n_1, -n_2]$. As a result only a half of the 2-D cepstrum or MxM 2-D mel-cepstrum coefficients are enough when IDFT is used.

3   Feature Classification

In this article, Common Matrix Approach (CMA) and multi-class SVM are used in feature classification. The CMA directly uses feature matrices as input. The Common Matrix Approach (CMA) is a 2D extension of Common Vector Approach (CVA), which is a subspace based pattern recognition method [4]. In this article, the CMA method is implemented as given in the reference [5] and used as a classification engine. On the other hand SVM needs a matrix to vector conversion process to convert the 2D cepstral domain feature matrices to vectors. SVM is a supervised machine learning method based on the statistical learning theory. The method constructs a hyperplane or a set of hyperplanes in a high dimensional space that can be used in classification tasks. In this work, SVM with a multi class classification support [6] with RBF kernel is used. The multi-class classification method uses "one-against-one" strategy [6].

4   Experimental Results

In this paper, AR Face Image Database [7], ORL Face Database [8] and Yale Face Database [9] are used to demonstrate the effectiveness of the proposed features. AR face database created by Aleix Martinez and Robert Benavente contains 4000 facial images of 126 subjects. In this work, 14 non-occluded poses of 50 subjects are used. The second database used in this work is ORL face database. The ORL database contains 40 subject and each subject has 10 poses. In this article 9 poses of each subject are used. The last database used in this work is the Yale Face Database. The database contains 165 facial images belonging to 15 subjects.

In order to compare performances of various features, the proposed 2D cepstral domain features, 2D Fourier Mellin Transform (FMT) based features, actual image pixel matrices, and 2D PCA based features are applied to CMA and multi-class SVM as inputs. In order to achieve robustness in recognition results, "leave-one-out" procedure is used.

In the calculation of 2D cepstral domain features, different non-uniform grids are used. Due to these different non-uniform grids, new M by M 2D cepstrum based features are generated.($M = 49, 39, 35, 29$). The 2D cepstrum based features giving the best performance are used in the comparison with the FMT based features, 2D PCA features and actual image matrices. The size of the cepstral features given in Table 1 and Table 2 differ for that purpose.

Actual image pixel matrices, 2D PCA based feature matrices, 2D FMT and 2D cepstrum based feature matrices are applied to the CMA. These features are also applied to SVM by converting these feature matrices to feature vectors. For each face database, average recognition rates of both classifiers are obtained and displayed in the Table 1 and Table 2.

Table 1. Recognition Rates (RR) of CMA classifier with different feature sets.

Features	Face Databases					
	AR		ORL		YALE	
	RR	Feature Size	RR	Feature Size	RR	Feature Size
Original Images	97.42%	100 × 85	98.33%	112 × 92	71.52%	152 × 126
2D PCA	97.71%	100 × 12	98.33%	112 × 15	71.52%	152 × 9
2D FMT	98.28%	60 × 60	98.61%	60 × 60	73.33%	60 × 60
Proposed 2D Mel-Cepstrum	99%	20 × 39	99.44%	18 × 35	77.57%	20 × 39
Proposed 2D Mellin Cepstrum	99.28%	25 × 49	100%	15 × 29	77.57%	20 × 39

Based on the above experiments, the 2D PCA and 2D FMT based features do not provide better results than the proposed cepstrum based features. The Yale Face database contains face images having large illumination variations. Since CMA can not cope with large illumination changes, the recognition rates become significantly lower than the rates obtained by using SVM.

The computational complexity of 2D PCA and 2D FMT based features are higher than 2D mel-cepstrum based features which are computed using FFT. The cost of computing a 2D mel-cepstrum sequence for an N by N image is $O(N^2 log(N)) + M^2 log(M)$ and an additional $M^2/2$ logarithm computations which can be implemented using a look-up table. 2D Mellin-cepstrum requires an additional log-polar conversion step in the Fourier domain.

Table 2. Recognition Rates (RR) of SVM based classifier with different feature sets.

Features	Face Databases					
	AR		ORL		YALE	
	RR	Feature Size	RR	Feature Size	RR	Feature size
Original Images	96.85%	8500	98.05%	10304	88.00%	19152
2D PCA	96.85%	1200	98.33%	1680	87.87%	1368
2D FMT	97.85%	3600	98.61%	3600	90.90%	3600
Proposed 2D mel-cepstrum	98.71%	630	98.61%	630	94.54%	780
Proposed 2D Mellin-cepstrum	98.85%	630	99.44%	435	96.96%	780

5   Conclusion

In this article, a 2D mel-cepstrum and Mellin-cepstrum based feature extraction techniques are proposed for image representation. Illumination invariance and invariance to translational shifts are important properties of 2D mel-cepstrum and 2D cepstrum. In addition, 2D Mellin-cepstrum provides robustness against rotation and scale invariance. 2D Cepstral domain features extraction techniques provide not only better recognition rates but also dimensionality reduction in feature matrix sizes in the face recognition problem. Our experimental studies indicate that 2D cepstral methods are superior to classical feature extraction baseline methods in facial image representation with lower computational complexity.

References

1. Toreyin, B.U., Cetin, A.E.: Shadow detection using 2D cepstrum. Acquisition, Tracking, Pointing, and Laser Systems Technologies XXIII **7338** (2009) 733809
2. Lee, J.K., Kabrisky, M., Oxley, M.E., Rogers, S.K., Ruck, D.W.: The complex cepstrum applied to two-dimensional images. Pattern Recogn. **26** (1993) 1579 – 1592
3. Gueham, M., Bouridane, A., Crookes, D., Nibouche, O.: Automatic recognition of shoeprints using fourier-mellin transform. In: Adapt. Hardw. and Sys., 2008. AHS '08. NASA/ESA Conf. (2008) 487 –491
4. Gulmezoglu, M., Dzhafarov, V., Barkana, A.: The common vector approach and its relation to principal component analysis. IEEE T Speech Audi. P. **9** (2001) 655–662
5. Turhal, U.C., Gulmezoglu, M.B., Barkana, A.: Face recognition using common matrix approach. In: European Signal Processing Conference. (2005)
6. Chang, C.C., Lin, C.J.: LIBSVM: a library for support vector machines. (2001)
7. Martinez, A., Benavente, R.: The AR face database. CVC Tech. Report # 24 (1998)
8. Samaria, F.S., Harter, A.C.: Parameterisation of a stochastic model for human face identification. In: App. Comput. Vision, 1994., Proc. Second IEEE Workshop. (2002) 138–142
9. Yale: Yale Face Database. http://cvc.yale.edu/projects/yalefaces/yalefaces.html (1997)

Similarity-Transformation Invariant Reversible Watermarking for 3D Models

Xifeng Gao[1], Caiming Zhang[1,2], Yan Huang[1], Xia Hu[1] and Anping Zhu[1]

[1] Shandong University, School of Computer Science and Technology, China
[2] Shandong Economic University, School of Computer Science and Technology, China

Abstract. In this paper, we present a reversible watermarking method for 3D models with arbitrary topology based on histogram shifting. We use similarity-transformation invariants to generate histogram such that the proposed method is invariant to similarity transformations including translation, rotation and uniform scaling. By adjusting the range of a histogram adaptively, our proposed method provides a tunable capacity and invisibility for watermarking. The computational complexity of our proposed method is also very low. Experimental results demonstrate the high effectiveness of our proposed algorithm.

1 Introduction

Watermarking has been proposed as part of the solution to authentication of 2D still images, audio, video clips, and 3D models. Inevitably, embedded information changes the digital content, even though the introduced distortion is imperceptible to the human visual system. However, no distortion is tolerable for digital contents with a high-precision requirement. Example applications are medical diagnosis, law enforcement, and artwork preservation, where a marked digital content must be restored to its original state. Reversible watermarking techniques which can losslessly invert a watermarked media back to its orginal state are explored to solve this problem.

Recent research of reversible data hiding techniques mostly works on 2D still images, audio, and videos through lossless compression [1], difference expansion [2], and histogram shifting [3]. However, due to the topological complexity and irregularity of 3D models, there are few existing watermarking methods for 3D models which can restore watermarked models to their original ones correctly, efficiently, and effectively. Based on a public verifiable digital signature protocol, Dittmann and Benedens [4] proposed the first reversible authentication method for 3D mesh models. Using Predictive Vector Quantization (PVQ), Lu and Li in [5] proposed a reversible watermarking algorithm where obtained recovered models are slightly different from the original ones. In [6], Wu and Dugelay proposed a large capacity but low invisibility reversible watermarking method by extending Difference Expansion (DE) as described in [2].

In this paper, we propose an adaptive reversible watermarking method for 3D models based on histogram shifting. For each vertex in an input model, we first calculate its associated similarity-transformation invariant ratios. Then, we map these ratios into an integer range to generate the histogram. After shifting the histogram appropriately, we embed a payload into the 3D model, and simultaneously adjust the coordinates of vertices where watermark information is embedded. By controlling the range of the integers used for length ratio mapping, we adjust the capacity and invisibility of the proposed watermarking method flexibly. Our proposed watermarking method can exactly recover an original model with a very low computation cost, and the extracted watermark can be used for authentication.

In section 2, we introduce the proposed similarity-transformation invariants and describe its construction procedure for 3D models. Section 3 presents the embedding and extraction process of our proposed method. Section 4 presents the experimental results and conclusions of our work are presented in section 5.

2   Similarity-Transformation Invariants

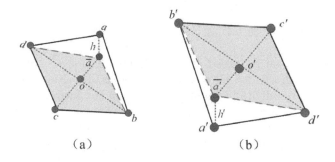

Fig. 1. Projected length ratios are preserved under any similarity transformations.

Our definition of similarity-transformation invariants can be illustrated in Fig. 1. Let $a, b, c, d, \bar{a}$ be five points in three-dimension and $\bar{a}$ is the projected point from a to plane $\triangle bcd$(Fig. 1a). Let r_1 be the ratio of $\bar{a}o$ and $\bar{a}c$ and r_2 be bo/bd. Then r_1 and r_2 are preserved under any similarity transformations. Let a', b', c', d' and $\bar{a}'$ be the corresponding five points after any similarity transformations of $a, b, c, d, \bar{a}$, let $r'_1 = \bar{a}'o'/\bar{a}'c'$ and $r'_2 = b'o'/b'd'$. Then $\bar{a}'$ is the projection point from a' to plane $\triangle b'c'd'$ (as seen in Fig. 1b) and $r_1 = r'_1$ and $r_2 = r'_2$.

Considering a 3D model with V vertices and E edges. Let v_i denote the ith vertex. We define the $1-ring$ neighbors of v_i as $N(v_i) = \{v_j | \exists (v_i, v_j) \in E \cup v_i\}$. In our watermarking method, we employ the similarity-transformation invariants described above to embed watermarks for 3D models. Given $N(v_i)$ consisting of vertex indices in the input model, we define n_i as the number of vertices in $N(v_i)$. The total number of all four-point sets in $N(v_i)$ is then calculated as $C_{n_i}^4$. For a four-point set $\{a, b, c, d\}$ in $N(v_i)$, there are four projection cases:

$\{\bar{a}, b, c, d\}$, $\{a, \bar{b}, c, d\}$, $\{a, b, \bar{c}, d\}$, and $\{a, b, c, \bar{d}\}$, where $\bar{a}, \bar{b}, \bar{c}, \bar{d}$ are the projection points from a, b, c, d to planes Δbcd, Δacd, Δabd, and Δabc respectively. In the proposed method, for each vertex, we generate all these projected quadrilaterals one by one, and choose the first convex quadrilateral as the candidate for the similarity-transformation invariant construction.

3   Watermarking Process

3.1   Embedding Process

- **Ratio Set Construction.** Given a convex coplanar quadrilateral $\{\bar{a}, b, c, d\}$ as defined in Fig. 1(a), in order to unambiguously identify r_1 and r_2 for both embedding and extracting, we select r_1 and r_2 which can satisfy the following relationship:

$$0.5 \leq r_1, r_2 < 1. \tag{1}$$

  For each vertex v_i in a 3D model, we construct its r_1 and r_2 from a projected coplanar quadrilateral as illustrated in section 2, and add them to the ratio set Ω. Note that, for vertices in $N(v_i)$ that have been used in former length ratio calculations, we discard them during the quadrilateral construction of v_i in order to ensure that ratios are calculated independently.

- **Ratio Mapping.** Given Ω of floating numbers, we map its values to an integer range of $(1, G]$, where G is a tunable parameter related with the embedding capacity and invisibility of our proposed method. The mapping function is given as follows:

$$g = \left\lfloor \frac{(\omega - 0.5) \times G}{0.5} \right\rfloor + 1, \tag{2}$$

  where $\omega \in \Omega$, and $g \in (1, G]$.

- **Watermark Insertion Based on Histogram Shifting.**
    - We collect the distribution of each g with a histogram H. Given H, we find the maximum point $h(a)$ and the minimum point $h(b)$. If $h(b) > 0$, we record the indices of those vertices whose length ratios are mapped on b. Then, we set $h(b) = 0$.
    - Without loss of generality, let's assume $a < b$. We shift the part of the histogram within $[a+1, b-1]$ to the right by one unit, while their corresponding similarity-transformation invariant ratios are also added by a histogram bin width of $0.5/G$. Details of invariant ratios' modification is illustrated in section 3.2.
    - For length ratios mapped to "a", we scan them one after another. Meanwhile we check the watermark bit by bit. Assuming the ith bit of the watermark is "1", we modify the mapping result of the ith length ratio from "a" to "a+1", and the corresponding length ratio is added by $0.5/G$. If the ith bit is "0", no modification is performed.

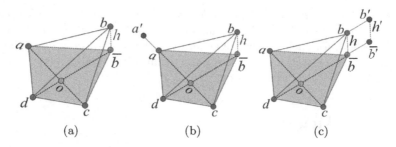

Fig. 2. Modification of invariant ratios. (a) $\bar{a}\bar{b}cd$ is the projected quadrilateral of four–points set a, b, c, d. (b) When $r_1 = ao/ac$ and r_1 is added by $0.5/G$, we move a outward along ac. (c) When $r_2 = \bar{b}o/\bar{b}d$ and r_2 is added by $0.5/G$, we move $\bar{b}$ and b outward along the direction of $\bar{b}d$.

3.2   Invariant Ratio Modification

For a selected four-point set$\{a, b, c, d\}$ of v_i, let's assume the corresponding convex quadrilateral is $a, \bar{b}, c, d$ as shown in Fig. 2a. If the vertex to be changed is not a projection point (i.e. $a, c,$ or d), we change its coordination as the following:

$$a' = \frac{a(1 - r_1) + c(r_1 - r_1')}{1 - r_1'}, \tag{3}$$

where a moves to a' (Fig. 2b), and r_1' is the subtraction or addition result of r_1. If the vertex to be changed is a projected point, for example $\bar{b}$, the new position b' of b is shown in Fig. 2c and the calculation can be given by (4).

$$b' = b + \frac{(r_2 - r_2')}{1 - r_2'}\bar{b}d, \tag{4}$$

where r_2' is the result from subtraction or addition of r_2.

As described above, the coordinate of o keeps constant when we change r_1, or r_2, or both. Therefore, the changes of r_1 and r_2 are mutually independent.

3.3   Extracting Process

In the extracting process, a watermarked 3D model undergoes three steps and the first two steps are the same as those described in the embedding process. The third step called watermark extraction procedure is the reverse of watermark insertion procedure carried out in the embedding process. Note that, if overhead information is detected in the extracted data, we retrieve the vertex indices of those length ratios mapped to b. Due to the facts that we change length ratios with a constant value of $0.5/G$ and both the embedding and extracting processes follow the same rule for histogram shifting, an original model can be completely recovered without any distortion.

3.4   Computational Complexity

Considering a model with V vertices, the most computationally expensive operations of the proposed method are local neighborhood construction $(O(3V))$, four-point set selection$(O(KV))$, and watermark embedding and extracting $(O(PV))$, where K and P are both constants. Therefore, the proposed method has a computational complexity of $O(3V) + O(KV) + O(PV) = O(V)$ altogether.

4   Experiments

We conduct a series of experiments to test the embedding capacity and invisibility of our proposed watermarking algorithm using two manifold models Fandisk (6475 vertices, 12946 faces) and Bunny (35947 vertices, 69451 faces), and one non-manifold model, Maple-tree (45499 vertices, 43530 faces).

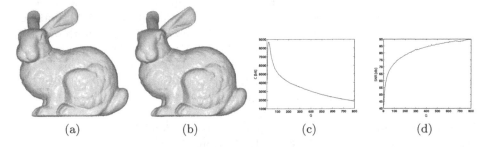

(a)   (b)   (c)   (d)

Fig. 3. (a) The original bunny model. (b) The watermarked models. (c) Curves of the relation between C and G. (d) Curves of the relation between SNR and G.

The actual data embedding capacity C can be calculated by (5).

$$C = h(a) - h(b) \times \log(V), \tag{5}$$

where $log(V)$ is the number of bits used for the representation of vertex indices in a 3D model. We show the relation between C and G for the bunny model in Fig. 3c. In the figure, we can see that when G gets smaller, C increases accordingly. However, as G gets small enough, there is a sharp decrease in C. This is because the increase of $h(a)$ incurred by G modification is much slower than that of $h(b) \times \log(V)$ according to (5). Table 1 lists the values of $h(a)$, $h(b)$, and the capacity for three models, given different G.

We employ the commonly used signal-to-noise ratio (SNR) as the means of measuring the geometrical difference between the watermarked and the original models. The invisibility of our proposed method is tunable by adjusting the value of G as illustrated in Fig. 3d. Fig. 3d shows that as G increases, the SNR increases accordingly. It also shows that the values of SNR have a bit fluctuation with the increase of G. This can be explained by the fact that the geometrical

Table 1. Embedding capacity and invisibility of the three models given different G.

Models	Vertices	G	$h(a)$	$h(b)$	C[bit]	SNR[db]
Fandisk	6475	40	1473	1	1460	57.83
Bunny	35947	20	10062	86	8686	58.44
Maple-tree	45499	70	3520	0	3520	56.92

distortion of watermarked models are decided not only by the number of length ratios mapped to a, but also the distance between the maximum point a and the minimum point b as the distance determines the amount of bits moved in histogram shifting. Table 1 lists the SNR of the three watermarked models, and the corresponding visual effects of bunny are shown in Fig. 3b.

5   Conclusions

In this paper, we propose a novel reversible watermarking method which embeds/extracts watermarks through extended histogram shifting for 3D models with arbitrary topology. Advantages of the proposed method include the invariance to similarity transformations, tuneable capacity and invisibility, and low computational complexity ($O(V)$). These superior advantages enable us to apply it in a wide range of applications where authentication of 3D models and the lossless recovering of 3D models are required.

Acknowledgment This work is supported by National 863 High-Tech programme of China (2009AA01Z304), the National Natural Science Foundation of China (60933008), Shandong Province National Nature Science Foundation (No.Z2006G05), National Research Foundation for the Doctoral Program of Higher Education of China (20070422098).

References

1. Fridrich, J., Goljan, M., Du, R.: Invertible authentication. In: Proc. SPIE Security Watermarking Multimedia Contents III, **4314**, 197–208 (2001)
2. Tian, J.: Reversible data embedding using a difference expansion. In: IEEE Trans. Circuits Syst. Video Technol., **13(8)**, 890–896 (2003)
3. Ni, Z., Shi, Y. Q., Ansari, N., Su, and W.: Reversible data hiding. In: IEEE Transactions on Circuits and Systems for Video Technology, **16(3)**, 354–362 (2006)
4. Dittmann, J., Benedens, O.: Invertible authentication for 3D meshes. In: Proceedings of SPIE, Security and Watermarking of Multi-media Contents V, **5020**, 653–664 (2003)
5. Lu, Z. M., Li, Z.: High capacity reversible data hiding for 3D meshes in the PVQ domain. In: Proceedings of the 6th International Workshop on Digital Watermarking, 593–596 (2007)
6. Wu, H. T., Dugelay, J. L.: Reversible watermarking of 3D mesh models by prediction-error expansion. In: 10th IEEE Workshop on Multimedia Signal Processing, 797–802 (2008)

A Novel Image Compression Method Based on Classified Energy and Pattern Blocks: Initial Results

Umit Guz[1] , Hakan Gurkan[1], and B. Siddik Yarman[2]

[1] Isik University, Engineering Faculty, Department of Electronics Engineering,
Sile, Istanbul, Turkey
[2] Istanbul University, Engineering Faculty, Department of Electrical-Electronics
Engineering, Istanbul, Turkey

guz@isikun.edu.tr , hakan@isikun.edu.tr , yarman@istanbul.edu.tr

Abstract. In this work, a new method for the compression of the images based on the generation of the so called classified energy and pattern blocks is introduced and the initial results are presented. The initials results proved that the new method provides considerable image compression ratios and image quality even at low bit rates.

Keywords: Image compression, image representation, image coding.

1 Introduction

More recently, especially in image compression area a variety of powerful and sophisticated WT based coding schemes have been developed and established [1]. The compression performance of DCT based coders (JPEG) generally degrades the image especially at low bit rates mainly because of underlying block based DCT scheme [2]. PCA has a computational complexity based on the computation of the covariance matrix of the training data [3]. Although able to achieve much faster compression than PCA, DCT leads to relatively great degradation of compression quality at the same compression ratio compared to PCA [4].

In this work, a new image compression scheme is proposed based on the generation of the block sets so called Classified Energy Blocks (CEB) and Classified Pattern Blocks (CPB). The initial results of the newly proposed method promises high compression ratios and acceptable image quality even at low bit rates.

2 Method

The new method consists of two major parts; Construction of the Classified Energy and Pattern Blocks (CEPB) Sets and Reconstruction Algorithm [5].

E. Gelenbe et al. (eds.), *Computer and Information Sciences*, Lecture Notes
in Electrical Engineering 62, DOI 10.1007/978-90-481-9794-1_54,
© Springer Science+Business Media B.V. 2010

2.1 Construction of the CEPB

Let the image data Im(m,n) is an $M \times N$ (in our cases, $M=N=512$) matrix with integer entries in the range of 0 to 255 (or the real values in the range of 0 to 1) where m and n are row and column pixel indices of the whole image, respectively. The input image is first divided into non-overlapping image blocks, $B_{r,c}$ of size $i \times j$, where the image block size is $i=j=8,16$ etc.. All the image blocks $B_{r,c}$ from left to the right direction are reshaped as column vectors and constructed a new matrix denoted as B_{Im}.

In the construction of the two block sets (CEPB), a certain number of image files are determined as a training set from the whole image database. Each image file in the training set are divided into the 8×8 ($i=j=8$) or 16×16 ($i=j=16$) image blocks and then each image block is reshaped as a column vector called image block vector (vector representation of the image block) which has $i \times j$ pixels.

All the image files have the same number of pixels ($512 \times 512 = 262.144$) and equal number of image blocks N_B. After the blocking process the image matrix will be given as below,

$$\text{Im} = \begin{bmatrix} B_{1,1} & B_{1,2} & \cdots & B_{1,(N/j)-1} & B_{1,(N/j)} \\ B_{2,1} & B_{2,2} & \cdots & B_{2,(N/j)-1} & B_{2,(N/j)} \\ \cdots & \cdots & \cdots & \cdots & \cdots \\ B_{(M/i)-1,1} & B_{(M/i)-1,2} & \cdots & B_{(M/i)-1,(N/j)-1} & B_{(M/i)-1,(N/j)} \\ B_{(M/i),1} & B_{(M/i),2} & \cdots & B_{(M/i),(N/j)-1} & B_{(M/i),(N/j)} \end{bmatrix} \tag{1}$$

Let construct a new matrix which its column vectors are the image blocks of the matrix, Im.

$$B_{Im} = \begin{bmatrix} B_{1,1} & \cdots & B_{1,(N/j)} & B_{2,1} & \cdots & \cdots & B_{(M/i),(N/j)} \end{bmatrix} \tag{2}$$

The columns of the matrix B_{Im} is called as image block vector (*IBV*) and the length of the *IBV* is represented by $L_{IBV}= i \times j$ ($8 \times 8=64$ or $16 \times 16=256$ etc.).

As it is explained above, in the method that we proposed the *IBV*s of an image can be represented by a mathematical model which consists of the multiplication of the three quantities; scaling factor, classified energy and pattern blocks.

In our method it is proposed that any ith *IBV* of length L_{IBV} can be approximated as $IBV_i=G_i P_{IP} E_{IE}$ ($i=1,...,N_B$), where the scaling coefficient, G_i of the *IBV* is a real constant, $IP \in \{1,2,...,N_{IP}\}$, $IE \in \{1,2,...,N_{IE}\}$ are the index number of the CPB and index number of the CEB where N_{IP} and N_{IE} are the total number of the CPB and CEB indices, respectively. *IP*, *IE*, N_{IP} and N_{IE} are all integers.

The CEB in the vector form is represented as $E_{IE}^{T} = \begin{bmatrix} e_{IE1} & e_{IE2} & \cdots & e_{IEL_{IBV}} \end{bmatrix}$ and it is generated utilizing the luminance information of the images and it contains basically the energy characteristics of IBV_i under consideration in broad sense. Furthermore, it will be shown that the quantity $G_i E_{IE}$ carries almost maximum energy of IBV_i in the least mean square (LMS) sense. In this expression the contribution of the G_i is to scale the luminance level of the IBV_i. P_{IP} is a diagonal matrix such that,

$$P_{IP} = diag \begin{bmatrix} p_{IP1} & p_{IP2} & p_{IP3} & \cdots & p_{IPL_{IBV}} \end{bmatrix} \tag{3}$$

P_{IP} acts as a pattern term on the quantity, $G_i E_{IE}$ which also reflects the distinctive properties of the image block data under consideration.

It is well known that, each *IBV* can be spanned in a vector space formed by the orthonormal vectors $\{\phi_{ik}\}$. Let the real orthonormal vectors be the columns of a transposed transformation matrix (Φ_i^T) [6].

$$\Phi_i^T = \begin{bmatrix} \phi_{i1} & \phi_{i2} & \cdots & \phi_{iL_{IBV}} \end{bmatrix} \tag{4}$$

$$IBV_i = \Phi_i^T \times G_i \tag{5}$$

$$G_i^T = \begin{bmatrix} g_1 & g_2 & \cdots & g_{L_{IBV}} \end{bmatrix} \tag{6}$$

From the property of $\Phi_i^T = \Phi_i^{-1}$, the equations $\Phi_i IBV_i = \Phi_i \Phi_i^{-1} G_i$ and $G_i = \Phi_i IBV_i$ can be obtained respectively.

Thus, *IBV$_i$* can be written as a weighted sum of these orthonormal vectors.

$$IBV_i = \sum_{k=1}^{L_{IBV}} g_k \phi_{ik}, \quad k = 1,2,3,...,L_{IBV} \tag{7}$$

From the equation above, the coefficients of the *IBV*s can be obtained as

$$g_k = \phi_{ik}^T IBV_i, \quad k = 1,2,3,...,L_{IBV} \tag{8}$$

Let $IBV_{it} = \sum_{k=1}^{t} g_k \phi_{ik}$ be the truncated version of *IBV$_i$* such that $1 \le t \le L_{IBV}$. It is noted that, if $t=L_{IBV}$ then *IBV$_i$* will be equal to *IBV$_{it}$*. The approximation error (ε_t) is

$$\varepsilon_t = IBV_i - IBV_{it} = \sum_{k=t+1}^{L_{IBV}} g_k \phi_{ik} \tag{9}$$

ϕ_{ik} are determined by minimizing the E[ε_t] with respect to ϕ_{ik} in the LMS sense. The above mentioned LMS process results in the following eigenvalue problem.

$$R_i \phi_{ik} = \lambda_{ik} \phi_{ik} \tag{10}$$

R_i is correlation matrix. It is real, symmetric with respect to its diagonal elements, positive-semi definite, and toeplitz. λ_{ik} and ϕ_{ik} are the eigenvalues and eigenvectors of the R_i. λ_{ik} are also real, distinct, and non-negative. Moreover, ϕ_{ik} are all orthonormal. Let λ_{ik} be sorted in descending order such that $\left(\lambda_{i1} \ge \lambda_{i2} \ge \lambda_{i3} \ge ... \ge \lambda_{iL_{IBV}} \right)$ with corresponding ϕ_{ik}. The simplest form of (7) can be obtained taking ϕ_{i1}. The eigenvector ϕ_{ik} is called energy vector. That is to say, the energy vector, which has the highest energy in the LMS sense, may approximate each image block belonging to the *IBV$_i$*. Thus,

$$IBV_i \cong g_1 \phi_{i1} \tag{11}$$

In this case, one can vary the L_{IBV} as a parameter in such way that almost all the energy is captured within the first term and the rest becomes negligible. That is why ϕ_{i1} is called the energy vector since it contains most of the useful information of the original *IBV* under consideration. Once (11) is obtained, it can be converted to an equality by means of a pattern term P_i which is a diagonal matrix for each *IBV*. Thus, *IBV$_i$* is computed as

$$IBV_i = G_i P_i \phi_{i1} \tag{12}$$

In (12), diagonal entries p_{ir} of the matrix P_i are determined in terms of the entries of ϕ_{i1r} of the energy vector ϕ_{i1} and the entries (pixels) IBV_{ir} of the IBV_i by simple division. Hence,

$$p_{ir} = \frac{IBV_{ir}}{G_i \phi_{i1r}}, \quad (r = 1,2,...,L_{IBV})$$ (13)

In this research, several tens of thousands of IBVs were investigated and several thousands of energy and pattern blocks were generated. It was observed that the energy and the pattern blocks exhibit repetitive similarities. In this case, one can eliminate the similar energy and pattern blocks and thus, constitute the so called classified energy and classified pattern block sets with one of a kind, or unique blocks. For the elimination process Pearson correlation coefficient is utilized. Hence, similar energy and pattern blocks are eliminated accordingly. Thus, the energy blocks which have unique shapes are combined under the set called classified energy block CEB=$\{ E_{n_{ie}} ; n_{ie}=1,2,3,..., N_{IE} \}$ set. The integer N_{IE} designates the total number of elements in this set. Similarly, reduced pattern blocks are combined under the set called classified pattern block CPB=$\{ P_{n_{ip}} ; n_{ip}=1,2,3,..., N_{IP} \}$ set. The N_{IP} designates the total number of unique pattern sequences in CPB set.

2.2   Reconstruction Algorithm

Inputs:
1) Image file $\{Im(m,n), M \times N=512 \times 512\}$ to be modeled.
2) Size of the IBV of the Im(m,n) $\{L_{IBV}=i \times j=8 \times 8$ or $L_{IBV}=i \times j=16 \times 16\}$.
3) The CEB=$\{E_{IE} ; IE=1,2,...,N_{IE}\}$, The CPB=$\{P_{IP} ; IP=1,2,...,N_{IP}\}$.
Computational Steps:
Step1: Divide Im(m,n) into the image blocks and then B_{Im} of column length L_{IBV}.
Step 2a: For each IBV_i pull an appropriate E_{IE} from CEB such that the distance or the total error $\delta_{I\tilde{E}} = \|IBV_i - G_{I\tilde{E}} E_{I\tilde{E}}\|^2$ is minimum for all $I\tilde{E} = 1,2,3,..., IE,..., N_{IE}$. This step yields the index IE of the E_{IE}. In this case, $\delta_{IE} = \min\{\|IBV_i - G_{I\tilde{E}} E_{I\tilde{E}}\|^2\} = \|IBV_i - G_{IE} E_{IE}\|^2$.

Step2b: Store the index number IE that refers to E_{IE}, in this case, $IBV_i \approx G_{IE} E_{IE}$.
Step3a: Pull an appropriate P_{IP} from CPB such that the error is further minimized for all $I\tilde{P} = 1,2,3,..., IP,..., N_{IP}$. This step yields the index IP of P_{IP}.

$$\delta_{IP} = \min\{\|IBV_i - G_{IE} P_{I\tilde{P}} E_{IE}\|^2\} = \|IBV_i - G_{IE} P_{IP} E_{IE}\|^2.$$

Step 3b: Store the index number IP that refers to P_{IP}. At the end of this step, the best E_{IE} and the best P_{IP} are found by appropriate selections. Hence, the IBV_i is best described in terms of the patterns of P_{IP} and E_{IE}. i.e. $IBV_i \cong G_{IE} P_{IP} E_{IE}$.
Step 4: Having fixed P_{IP} and E_{IE}, one can replace G_{IE} by computing a new block scaling coefficient $G_i = (P_{IP} E_{IE})^T IBV_i / (P_{IP} E_{IE})^T (P_{IP} E_{IE})$ to further minimize the distance between the vectors IBV_i and $G_{IE} P_{IP} E_{IE}$ in the LMS sense. In this case, the global minimum of the error is obtained and it is given by $\delta_{Global} = \|IBV_i - G_i P_{IP} E_{IE}\|^2$. At this step, $IBV_{Ai} = G_i P_{IP} E_{IE}$.

Step 5: Repeat the above steps for each *IBV* to reconstruct approximated version
($\hat{B}_{Im}$) of the B_{Im} . $\hat{B}_{Im} = \begin{bmatrix} \hat{B}_{1,1} & \cdots & \hat{B}_{1,(N/j)} & \hat{B}_{2,1} & \cdots & \cdots & \hat{B}_{(M/i),(N/j)} \end{bmatrix}$

Step 6: Reshape $\hat{B}_{Im}$ to obtain the reconstructed version of the original image data.

3   Experiments and Initial Results

In our data set 67 gray-scale, 8 bit, JPEG images of size 512x512, were used. The
experiments are implemented in two groups which correspond different sizes of
image blocks ($L_{IBV} = i \times j = 8 \times 8$ and $L_{IBV} = i \times j = 16 \times 16$). In the 1st group of experiments,
randomly selected 7 files and 9 files are chosen as training and test set, respectively.
In the 2nd group of experiments, we enlarged the training set to 58 files and remained
the test data set as used in the 1st group of experiments. In the 1st group of
experiments the total number of bits required to represent the 8x8 blocks for each file
is (8x8)x8bits=512bits. The size of the CEB is $31 < 2^5$ and the size of the CPB is
$15.607 < 2^{14}$. N_{IE} and N_{IP} are represented with 5 bits and 14 bits, respectively. For the
representation of the block scaling coefficient 5 bits are good enough. In this case in
order to represent the 8x8 blocks we need 24 bits in total. In the 2nd group of
experiments the total number of bits required to represent the 16x16 blocks for each
file is (16x16)x8bits=2.048bits. The total number of CEB is $179 < 2^8$ and the size of
the CPB is $52.229 < 2^{16}$. N_{IE} and N_{IP} are represented with 8 bits and 16 bits,
respectively. 5 bits are required to represent the coefficient. In this case, in order to
represent the 16x16 blocks, 29 bits are required in total. In order to obtain lower bit
rates the size of the CEB and CPB is also reduced to 64 and 16.384, respectively. In
this case the number of bits required to represent the image block is reduced to 25bits.
In order to reach lower bit rates we also established the same experiments using an
efficient clustering algorithm. In this case the size of the CEB and CPB is reduced to
31and 4096, respectively. Therefore, the number of bits required is reduced to 22bits.

Table 1. The average results of the first group of experiments

Group of experiment	Clustering	Block size	Bit per pixel (bpp)	Compression Ratio (CR)	MSE	PSNR (dB)
1st	no	8×8	0.3750	21.33	0.001055	30.10
1st	yes	8×8	0.3438	23.27	0.001235	29.41
2nd	no	16×16	0.1133	70.62	0.002274	26.76
2nd	yes	16×16	0.0977	81.92	0.002435	26.47

4   Conclusion

In this work, a new image compression algorithm based on the classified energy and
pattern block (CEPB) sets are proposed. In the method first the CEB and CPB sets are
constructed and an image data can be reconstructed block by block using a scaling
coefficient and the index numbers of the classified energy and pattern blocks placed

in the CEB and CPB. The CEB and CPB sets are constructed for different size of image blocks such as 8×8 or 16×16 with respect to different compression ratios desired. The initial results proved that the proposed method provides high compression ratios while preserving the image quality at acceptable level. In our future works we will be focused on better designed CEB and CPB in order to increase the level of the PSNR while reducing the number of bits required representing the image blocks. Currently, we are also working on improving the quality of the images that we reconstructed using an efficient post processing algorithms.

Fig 1. Original (left side) and reconstructed images; Lenna:0.375bbp, CR=21.33, PSNR=28.89dB, Lenna: 0.1133bbp, CR=70.62, PSNR=25.27dB.

References

1. Vetterli, M., Kovacevic, J.: Wavelets and Subband Coding, Englewood Cliffs, NJ, Prentice Hall, (1995).
2. Rao, K. Yip, P.: Discrete Cosine Transforms-Algorithms, Advantages, Applications, Academic Press, (1990).
3. Jolliffe, I. T.: Principal Component Analysis, Springer Series in Statistics, Springer, (1993).
4. Zhang, D., Chen, S.: Neurocomputing, 68, pp. 258-266, (2005).
5. Guz, U., Gurkan, H., Yarman, B. S.: A New Method to Represent Speech Signals via Predefined Signature and Envelope Sequences, EURASIP Journal on Applied Signal Processing, Hindawi, Vol. 2007, Article ID. 56382, pp. 1-17, (2007).
6. Akansu, A.N., Haddad, R.A.: Multiresolution Signal Decomposition, Academic Press, (1992).

An SVD based Common Matrix Method for Face Recognition: Single Image per Person

Meltem Apaydın[1], Ü. Çiğdem Turhal[1], Alpaslan Duysak[2]

[1] Electric and Electronics Engineering Department, Bilecik University, Turkey , [2] Computer Engineering Department, Dumlupınar University, Turkey
meltem.apaydin@bilecik.edu.tr , ucigdem.turhal@bilecik.edu.tr ,
aduysak@dumlupinar.edu.tr

Abstract. Common Matrix (CM) fails to work when there is only one image available in the training set. In this paper, an approach to solve this problem is proposed. By using singular value decomposition (SVD) null space of the image matrices are obtained. By projecting the image matrix onto the null space, common matrices are obtained for each class. After obtaining the common matrices, optimal projection vectors will be those that maximize the total scatter of the common matrices.

Keywords: Face recognition, Common vector (CV) approach, Common Matrix (CM), Single training image per person, Singular value decomposition (SVD).

1 Introduction

Recognition performances of the most common recognition techniques rely on the size of the training set. They will suffer serious performance drop or even recognition failure if there are not enough samples presented. This problem is called "one sample per person problem".

One of the methods which will fail to work in the case of one sample per person problem is Fisher linear discriminant analysis (FLDA) [1]. Feature extraction using FLDA depends on the estimation of the scatter matrices of training samples. In case of when there is only one training sample is available the within-class scatter matrix is zero and the FLDA-based algorithms fail. Gao et al. [2] presented a method to solve this problem by evaluating the within-class scatter matrix from the available single training sample. Common Vector (CV) [3] and its extension into 2 dimensional case that is called Common Matrix (CM) [4] approaches are also other face recognition methods which will fail to work in case of one sample per person problem. In each of these two methods, within-class scatter matrix is used for feature extraction. So, for each person both of these two methods require at least two different images.

E. Gelenbe et al. (eds.), *Computer and Information Sciences*, Lecture Notes
in Electrical Engineering 62, DOI 10.1007/978-90-481-9794-1_55,
© Springer Science+Business Media B.V. 2010

In this paper, an SVD based common matrix (CM) method to solve the single image per person problem is proposed. This method does not requires the computation of a within class scatter matrix explicitly. Instead, null space of the single training sample is used as the within-class scatter matrix.

2. SVD-based Common Matrix Method

In this section we propose an extension of an SVD-based FLDA solution which is proposed as a solution to one sample per person problem given in [2] to CM approach.

The vectors that span the null space of the training sample are used as the optimal projection vectors. Projection of the training sample onto its null space is performed. With this projection, common matrices are obtained for each class. Then a new set of optimal projection vectors, that maximize the total scatter of the common matrices in all classes are obtained and used for classification.

2.1 Obtaining Common Matrix by Using the Null Space of Image Matrix

Given a face image $X \in R^{mxn}$ and $m \geq n$, we have the following expression according to SVD [5].

$$X = \sum_{i=1}^{n} \sigma_i u_i v_i^T \tag{1}$$

where u_i and v_i are the *ith* column of $U \in R^{mxm}$ and $V \in R^{nxn}$ which are called the left and the right singular matrices respectively. σ_i is the singular values of image matrix and given in decreasing order ($\sigma_1 \geq \sigma_2 \geq .... \geq \sigma_n$).

The rank is given as $r = rank(X)$. Thus, the null space of X (right null space) is spanned by the $(n-r)$ columns of V and the null space of X^T (left null space) is spanned by the last $(m-r)$ columns of U.

The projections onto the null space of the image matrix do not make any contributions of the general appearance of the image as corresponding singular values are zero. That is why the null space can be considered of the within class scatter matrix, which reflects the common properties of the class. It is the point in the proposed method that the vectors which span the null space of an image matrix can be used as the optimal projection vectors, which minimizes the within-class scatter matrix.

The proposed method now can be summarized as follows:

Step 1: Using SVD find the left null space of the single training sample in each class.

Step 2: Take the projection of the image matrix X^i onto the null space and use this matrix as the common matrix X^i_{com} of the i_{th} class.

$$X^i_{com} = X^i - X^i QQ^T = \overline{Q}\,\overline{Q}^T X^i \qquad (2)$$

where $\overline{Q}$ is a matrix whose columns are the left singular vectors which corresponds to the zero singular values that span the left null space of the image matrix and Q is a matrix whose columns are the left singular vectors which corresponds to the non-zero singular values that span the range space of image matrix.

Step 3: After obtaining the common matrices X^i_{com}, optimal projection vectors will be those that maximize the total scatter of the common matrices S_{com}.

$$S_{com} = \sum_{i=1}^{C} (X^i_{com} - \Psi_{com})(X^i_{com} - \Psi_{com})^T \qquad (3)$$

where $\Psi_{com} = \dfrac{1}{C}\sum_{i=1}^{C} X^i_{com}$, the mean of all common matrices.

Then common matrices are projected onto the optimal projection vectors that maximize the total scatter of the common matrices in all classes. Discriminative feature matrices are obtained for each class and are used for classification.

Step 4: To recognize a test image, a remaining matrix is obtained for each class using Eq.2 and then remaining image is projected onto the optimal projection vectors which maximize the total scatter matrix given in Eq.3. A discriminative feature matrix for the test image is obtained and then compared with the discriminative feature matrices which belong to the classes. The discriminative feature matrix of a class which found to be the closest to the discriminative feature matrix of the test image used to identify the test image.

3. Experimental Studies and Conclusions

In the experimental study, performance of the proposed method is evaluated using Ar-Face [6] database. This database includes frontal view of nonoccluded face images with changes in illumination conditions and facial expressions. 37 people are used from Ar-Face database. 20 of them are males and 17 of them are females. Each person has 27 different images. The images are cropped with size of 50x40 without any other preprocessing step.

Three different experiments are performed in the experimental study.

In the first experiment 27 images including illumination condition and facial expression changes which belong to 37 people are used. One randomly selected image matrix supposed to be the training image. Remaining 26 images are used as the test set. This experiment is repeated 10 times and the average of the 10 experiments is given in Table 1.

In the second and in the third experiments new databases are constructed from the Ar-Face database. These images have the same facial expression including only lightning condition changes among each other. 9 images are used for 37 people and leave-one-out strategy is used in order to find the recognition rates. In the second experiment face images with normal facial expression and in the third experiment face images with smiling facial expression are used.   Recognition results for both experiments are given in Table 1.

Table 1. Recognition rates for AR-Face face database.

	Recognition Rate (%)
First Experiment	77.28
Second Experiment	99.68
Third Experiment	99.39

Table 1 reveals that the proposed method yields satisfactory recognition results. As the next step, the developed algorithm will be applied to other data bases and will be compared to other well known algorithms.

References

1. P.N.Belhumeur, J.P.Hespanha, and D.J.Kriegman, "Eigenfaces vs. Fisherfaces: Recognition Using Class Specific Linear Projection," IEEE Trans. on Pattern Analysis and Machine Intelligence, Vol.19, No.7, pp.711-720 (1997)
2. Q. Gao, L. Zhang, D. Zhang, "Face Recognition using FLDA with Single Training Image per Person", *Applied Mathematics and Computation,* vol. 205, issue 2, November 2008, pp. 726-734.
3. M. B. Gulmezoglu, V. Dzhafarov, M. Keskin and A. Barkana, "A Novel Approach to Isolated Word Recognition", *IEEE Transactions on Speech and Audio Processing*, vol. 7, no. 6, November 1999, pp. 620-628.
4. Ü. Ç. Turhal, M. B. Gülmezoğlu, and A. Barkana, " Face Recognition Using Common Matrix Approach" 13 Th. European Signal Processing Conference, Eusipco05, September 4-8, 2005, Antalya
5. G. Golub, C. Loan, "*Matrix Computations*", The Johns Hopkins University Press, Baltimore, MD, 1983
6. Martinez A. M. and Benavante R., The Ar Face Database, CVC Tech. Report *J* 24 (1998)

Shape and Texture based Face Recognition on Overlapping 3D Sub-regions

Göksel Günlü[1] and Hasan S. Bilge[2],

[1] Electrical-Electronics Engineering, Gazi University, Ankara, Turkey
[2] Computer Engineering, Gazi University, Ankara, Turkey
{goksel, bilge}@gazi.edu.tr

Abstract. In this study, we present a new method for handling facial expression variations by dividing face into overlapping 3D sub-regions and extracting independent features by using 3D DCT from each sub-region. By the proposed method, 99.66% rank-one recognition rate is achieved using FRGC ver2.0 database.

Keywords: Face recognition, 3D DCT, shape and texture information, region based feature extraction.

1 Introduction

3D face data includes shape data which has higher descriptive information especially in high security scenarios in comparison to 2D data which includes only texture information.

One of the challenges in face recognition is expression variation. To overcome this problem, it is suggested to use the least affected regions such as nose and eye [1]. Another method is the multi region selection approach. In this method, Chang et.al [1] proposed to use multiple overlapping nose regions in order to increase performance. ICP is used to match these regions.

Another approach is to discard the effect of expression and to divide the face into separate parts extracting features from each part studied in 2D. In previous studies, (Cook et.al [2]) 3D data was represented as range image and was divided into 2D sub-images. In addition, a constant number of features from each region were used for matching. Unlike the previous studies, we divided 3D faces into smaller sub-voxel structures and applied 3D transformation to extract features from these voxels.

The first contribution, which is the main subject, is the use of shape and texture information together with only one feature extraction method, 3D DCT. 3D DCT is applied to voxel representation of the 3D face, including both shape and texture. Information fusion can be applied at various levels; e.g. at feature level and at decision level [3].In this paper, we proposed the data level fusion method and tested it with the FRGC database. That is the second 4D face recognition method which fuse shape and texture information at data level other than Papatheodorou's [4] 4D face recognition. Second contribution of this paper is the division of the voxel structure

E. Gelenbe et al. (eds.), *Computer and Information Sciences*, Lecture Notes
in Electrical Engineering 62, DOI 10.1007/978-90-481-9794-1_56,
© Springer Science+Business Media B.V. 2010

into overlapping sub-voxel structures. Sub-voxel structure increases recognition rate when using the whole face. Lastly the third contribution is that it has shown that recognition rate using only nose region is higher than the recognition rate using he whole face.

This paper is an extension of our study in [5] and is organized as follows. In the second section the details of the method are given; alignment, registration, overlapping sub-voxel structure based feature extraction. Section 3 explains experimental results on FRGC database. Finally in Section 4 and 5, we conclude our investigations.

2   3D Face Recognition

In this study, we are investigating 3D face recognition by using shape and texture information. Face Recognition Grand Challenge (FRGC) ver2.0 [6] is the largest and most popular dataset for 3D face recognition [7]. This database contains a large number of recordings that comprise a challenge for most algorithms.

2.1   Preprocessing

Preprocessing is performed in 3 steps: alignment, cropping and registration.For the alignment of the 3D face data, nose tip is used because it is the most significant points of the 3D face. The nose tip becomes the origin of the 3D coordinate system, and all faces are aligned according to this point. After the nose tip is determined and set as the origin, several ellipsoid regions are cropped from each face. These regions of interest may be used as a whole. However we also investigate the case when they are partitioned into 3D sub-regions and observe the recognition performance in this case. The center and radius values of the ellipsoid regions are given in Table 1. These regions are also shown in Fig. 1.

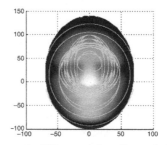

Fig. 1. Cropping the region of interest; different regions from whole face to nose region.

After alignment and cropping of faces, each cropped region is registered to average face.

2.2 Feature Extraction

In this paper, we modified the previous 3D DCT based feature extraction method [5]. In that method, 3D DCT coefficients from all 3D face data are used as features. But here, 3D DCT is applied to 3D sub-regions in order to improve the performance. The cropped face region (region of interest) will be divided into several 3D face sub-regions, independent features will be extracted from different face sub-regions. The sub-regions are shown in Fig. 1. The partitioning of region of interest in face recognition is previously studied in only 2D, but here we investigate the partitioning in 3D voxel structure.

Overlapping sub-region approach. Since there is scaling differences in the FRGC database, each sub-region may correspond to another area of the face for different subjects. Therefore in this study, the use of overlapping in sub-regions is also investigated. For this purpose, the 3D face is divided into overlapping sub-regions as seen in Fig. 2.

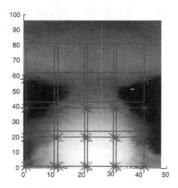

Fig. 2. Partitioning of the nose region into 16 sub-regions with 80% overlapping. The cross signs indicate the left-bottom corner of each sub-region.

Shape and texture information. In this study, we also proposed a new method in terms of information fusion. In our previous study, 3D DCT is directly applied to voxel structure which encodes only the shape information. Here, texture information is also added to the voxel structure. Instead of setting the value of "1" to voxels corresponding to face surface, voxels have values of gray levels. These gray levels come from pixels in 2D face texture data. Therefore, shape and texture information are fused at data level and 3D DCT coefficients convey both information. That method resembles Papatheodorou's 4D ICP based algorithm. In that study, Papatheodorou developed a 4D (x, y, z and texture) registration which includes textural information in ICP method. 4D distances between points in the source and probe faces give similar scores. Our method and Papatheodorou's method are very similar, but distinct from each other in terms of information fusion.

After the feature extraction, most discriminating 3D DCT coefficients are selected using PoV [8,9].Selected features are used for Euclidian distance based nearest neighbor classifier.

3 Experimental Results

In the experiments the FRGC ver2.0 face database was used.
We perform five experiments for 24 different ROIs. Experiments differ in only the feature extraction stage.

Table 1. Recognition rates.

#reg.	Ellipsoid centers			ROI Dimension			2D DCT	Shape only			Shape + Texture
	x	y	z	r_x	r_y	r_z	whole	whole	4 over. sub-reg.	16 over. sub-reg.	16 over. sub-reg.
1	0	15	0	72	108	52	83.96	91.23	96.60	97.42	98.79
2	0	15	0	64	90	52	88.58	94.38	97.83	98.63	99.05
3	0	35	0	24	48	68	93.76	96.49	98.56	99.28	99.30
4	0	35	0	24	56	68	92.6	96.70	98.94	99.36	99.38
5	0	35	0	24	64	68	89.92	95.95	98.27	98.97	99.18
6	0	35	0	30	48	68	94.12	96.62	98.56	99.18	99.33
7	0	35	0	30	56	68	92.5	96.49	98.76	99.30	99.43
8	0	35	0	30	64	68	90.9	95.95	98.63	98.94	99.28
9	0	35	0	36	48	68	94.23	96.31	98.50	99.20	99.33
10	0	35	0	36	56	68	93.14	96.57	98.74	99.30	99.38
11	0	35	0	36	64	68	90.44	95.69	98.14	98.99	99.23
13	0	10	0	48	72	52	92.68	96.42	95.95	99.12	99.20
14	0	35	0	36	48	60	94.77	96.91	98.71	99.38	99.33
15	0	30	0	36	48	60	95.44	97.60	98.48	99.41	99.41
16	0	25	0	36	48	60	96.26	98.32	98.66	99.30	99.54
17	0	35	0	40	48	60	94.33	97.11	98.92	99.46	99.48
18	0	30	0	40	48	60	95.02	97.71	98.79	99.48	99.48
19	0	25	0	40	48	60	96.52	98.45	98.61	99.66	99.61
20	0	25	0	44	48	60	96.34	98.48	98.74	99.51	99.56
21	0	25	0	44	48	56	95.85	98.45	98.71	99.61	99.64
22	0	25	0	44	52	52	94.79	98.12	98.27	99.25	99.43
23	0	25	0	48	52	52	95.2	97.73	98.22	99.41	99.46
24	0	25	0	48	56	52	94.74	97.11	97.76	99.30	99.54
						Mean :	93.27	96.72	98.26	99.20	99.36
						Std. :	2.89	1.55	0.77	0.44	0.19

In the first experiment, 2D DCT is directly applied to the range image of the whole ROI.

In the second experiment, 3D DCT is directly applied to the binary voxel data of the whole ROI including shape information.

In the third experiment, 3D DCT is applied to 4 different 50% overlapping sub-regions for each ROI including shape information.

In the fourth experiment, 3D DCT is applied to 16 different 50% overlapping sub-regions for each ROI including shape information.

In the fifth experiment, 3D DCT is applied to 16 different 50% overlapping sub-regions for each ROI including shape and texture information.

Rank-one recognition results are given in Table 1 for each experiment.

4 Discussion

From Table 1, we see that dividing the face into overlapping sub-regions increases the recognition rate. There is no significant performance increase in fusing shape and texture information for the nose region. However, shape and texture information fusion increase performance when the whole face is used for recognition

An important debate is in the dimension that is used for face recognition; namely the 2D and 3D modalities. When features are extracted by using DCT coefficients as in our case, 3D DCT gives better results than 2D DCT (Fig. 3).

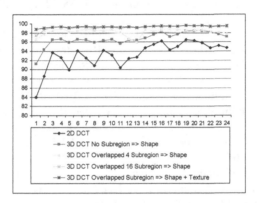

Fig. 3. Recognition rates of 5 experiments with the change of the sub-region number in Table I

Another aspect is finding out which face region gives better results. Facial expression affects each point at different rates. Faltemier et.al [10] report that the mouth region does not increase the recognition rate. Our results support that as well, In **Table 1** ,using only the nose region and eye region (reg.15-21) information gives better results than when the whole face (reg.1,2) is used.

5 Results

In this study, we present a new approach to increase performance against facial expression variations. We divide the face into 3D sub-regions and apply 3D DCT for each sub-region. Unlike previous methods, dividing is made in 3D, not in 2D, and each sub-region consists of voxels. It is seen that most of the discriminating features are extracted from the nose and eye regions. Another novelty is the application of 3D DCT into voxel structure including both shape and texture information. Therefore, features convey both shape and texture information. The proposed method is evaluated by using the FRGC ver2.0 face database. We achieved a 99.66% rank-one recognition. Sub-region structure increases recognition rate when using the whole face.

References

[1]   Chang, K.I., Bowyer, K.W., Flynn, P.J.: Multiple Nose Region Matching For 3D Face Recognition Under Varying Facial Expression. IEEE Transactions on Pattern Analysis and Machine Intelligence. vol. 28:10, pp. 1695--1700 (2006)

[2]   Cook, J., Chandran, V., Fookes, C.: 3D Face Recognition Using Log-Gabor Templates. In: The 17th British Machine Vision Conference (BMVC) (2006)

[3]   Jain, A., Nandakumar, K., Ross, A.: Score Normalization in Multimodal Biometric Systems. Pattern Recognition. vol. 38:12, pp. 2270-2285, Elsevier (2005)

[4]   Papatheodorou, T., Rueckert, D.: Evaluation of Automatic 4D Face Recognition using Surface and Texture Registration. In: Sixth International Conference on Automated Face and Gesture Recognition, pp. 321--326 (2004)

[5]   Gunlu, G., Bilge, H.S.: Face Recognition with Discriminating 3D DCT Coefficients, The Computer Journal, 2010, DOI 10.1093/comjnl/bxq031

[6]   Phillips, P. J., Flynn, P. J., Scruggs, T., Bowyer, K. W., Chang, J., Hoffman, K., Marques, J., Min, J., Worek, W.: Overview of the Face Recognition Grand Challenge. In: IEEE Conference on Computer Vision and Pattern Recognition, pp. 947--954 (2005)

[7]   Mian, A.S., Bennamoun, M., Owens, R.: An Efficient Multimodal 2D-3D Hybrid Approach to Automatic Face Recognition. IEEE Trans. Pattern Anal. Mach. Intell. vol. 29:11, 1927--1943 (2007)

[8]   Bartlett, M.S., Movellan, J.R., Sejnowski, T.J.: Face recognition by independent component analysis. IEEE Transactions on Neural Networks, vol. 13:6, pp. 1450--1464 (2002)

[9]   Yuen, P.C., Lai, J.H.: Face Representation using Independent Component Analysis. Pattern Recognition. vol. 35:6, pp. 1247--1257 (2002)

[10]   Faltemier, T. C., Bowyer, K. W., Flynn, P. J.: A Region Ensemble for 3-D Face Recognition. IEEE Transactions on Information Forensics And Security. vol. 3:1 (2008)

Cepstrum Based Method for Moving Shadow Detection in Video

Fuat Cogun and A. Enis Cetin *

Bilkent University, Bilkent 06800, Ankara, Turkey
fuatc@ee.bilkent.edu.tr, cetin@bilkent.edu.tr

Abstract. Moving shadows constitute problems in various applications such as image segmentation and object tracking. Main cause of these problems is the misclassification of the shadow pixels as target pixels. Therefore, the use of an accurate and reliable shadow detection method is essential to realize intelligent video processing applications. In this paper, the cepstrum based method for moving shadow detection is presented. The proposed method is tested on outdoor and indoor video sequences using well-known benchmark test sets. To show the improvements over previous approaches, quantitative metrics are introduced and comparisons based on these metrics are made.

1 Introduction

In many computer vision applications, moving shadows may lead to inaccurate moving object detection results. All moving points of both objects and shadows are detected at the same time in most common video foreground object detection methods requiring inter-frame differentiation or background subtraction. In addition, moving shadow pixels are normally adjacent to moving object pixels. Hence, moving shadow pixels and object pixels merge in a single blob causing distortions of the object shape and model. Thus, object shape is falsified and the geometrical properties of the object are adversely affected by shadows. As a result of this, some applications such as classification and assessment of moving object position (normally given by the shape centroid) give erroneous results. For example, shadow detection is utmost important in forest fire detection applications [1] because shadows are confused with smoke regions as shown in Fig. 1. Another problem arises when shadows of two or more close objects create false adjacency between different moving objects resulting in detection of a single combined moving blob. Shadow regions retain underlying texture, surface pattern, color and edges in images. In [2] it is pointed out that Hue-Saturation-Value (HSV) color space analysis as a shadow cast on a background does not change significantly its hue. There have been some further studies on HSV color space analysis for shadow detection such as [3] and [4]. In the study of Jiang and Ward [5, 6], classification is done on the basis of an approach that shadows

---

* This work is supported by European Commission Seventh Framework Program with EU Grant: 244088(FIRESENSE)

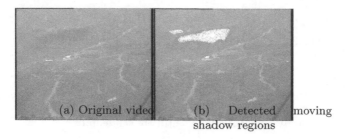

(a) Original video   (b)   Detected   moving
shadow regions

Fig. 1.: The source of the shadow regions are the moving clouds

are composed of two parts: self-shadow and cast shadow. The shadow detection approaches are classified as statistical and deterministic type and comparisons of these approaches are made in [9], [10] and [11]. In this paper, a deterministic two-dimensional cepstrum analysis based shadow detection method is proposed. The method is composed of two steps. In the first step, hybrid background subtraction based moving object detection is implemented to determine the candidate regions for further analysis. The second step involves the use of a non-linear method based on cepstrum analysis of the candidate regions for detecting the shadow points inside those regions.

The next section presents the proposed cepstrum based shadow detection method. Results of the proposed method and comparisons with previous approaches are presented in Section 3.

2   Cepstrum Analysis for Moving Shadow Detection

The proposed method for moving shadow detection consists of two parts. In the first part, a method based on hybrid background subtraction [12] is used to determine the moving regions. After determining moving regions, cepstrum analysis is carried out on detected moving regions for yielding the regions with shadows.

The proposed cepstrum analysis method for shadow detection is composed of two parts. The first part includes the separation of the moving regions into 8x8 blocks and the application of the 2D cepstrum to the blocks of interest and their corresponding background blocks to decide whether the texture and color properties are preserved for that moving block or not. If it is decided that the properties are preserved for the block, the algorithm proceeds with the second part. If not, the detection algorithm marks the block as moving object block. In the second part, a more detailed pixel-based approach is considered. 1D cepstrum is applied to each pixel belonging to the block to decide if the pixel is a moving shadow pixel or object pixel. The following subsections present the parts of the proposed cepstrum analysis method.

Part I. Cepstral Analysis of Blocks: The cepstrum $\hat{x}[n]$ of a signal x is defined as the inverse Fourier transform of the log-magnitude Fourier spectrum of x. Let $x[n]$ be a discrete signal, its cepstrum $\hat{x}[n]$ is defined as follows:

$$\hat{x}[n] = F^{-1}\{\ln(|F\{x[n]\}|)\}$$

where $F\{.\}$ represents the discrete-time Fourier Transform, $|.|$ is the magnitude, $\ln(.)$ is the natural logarithm and $F^{-1}\{.\}$ represents the inverse discrete-time Fourier Transform operator. In our approach, we use both one-dimensional (1D) and two-dimensional (2D) cepstrums for shadow detection.

Moving regions in video are divided into 8x8 moving blocks as a subset of the whole moving region. Let the i-th moving 8x8 block be defined as $\mathbf{R}_i$. Then, 2D cepstrum of $\mathbf{R}_i$, $\hat{\mathbf{R}}_i$ is defined as follows:

$$\hat{\mathbf{R}}_i = F_{2D}^{-1}\{\ln(|F_{2D}\{\mathbf{R}_i\}|)\}$$

where $F_{2D}\{.\}$ is the 2D discrete-time Fourier Transform and $F_{2D}^{-1}\{.\}$ is the inverse discrete-time Fourier Transform operator.

Similarly, let the i-th corresponding background block for the current image frame be defined as $\mathbf{B}_i$ and its 2D cepstrum as $\hat{\mathbf{B}}_i$. A difference matrix $\mathbf{D}_i$ for the i-th block can be defined as: $\mathbf{D}_i = |\hat{\mathbf{R}}_i - \hat{\mathbf{B}}_i|$. Theoretically if the block of interest is part of a shadow it should have the following property:

$$\mathbf{R}_i = \alpha\, \mathbf{B}_i$$

where α is a positive real number less than 1. The effect of this on the difference matrix in the 2D cepstral domain is: $\mathbf{D}_i$ having only the (1,1)-indexed value different than zero because of the scaling by constant α. Other entries of $\mathbf{D}_i$ should be equal to zero. So the distance metric is defined as:

$$m_i = \sum_{(a,b)\neq(1,1)} \mathbf{D}_i(a,b)$$

Notice that this operation is done for R, G and B values of the block separately. Therefore, the distance metric M_i is used as follows:

$$M_i = \sqrt{m_{i,r}^2 + m_{i,g}^2 + m_{i,b}^2}$$

where $m_{i,r}$, $m_{i,g}$ and $m_{i,b}$ is the R, G and B component distance metric, respectively. Therefore, the decision algorithm for the first part is:

$$R_i : \begin{cases} \text{moving shadow block,} & \text{if } M_i < \kappa \\ \text{moving object block,} & \text{otherwise} \end{cases}$$

where κ is a determined threshold. After detecting possible candidate 8 by 8 shadow regions, we examine each pixel of such regions one by one to determine the exact boundary of shadow pixels as follows.

Part II. Cepstrum Analysis of Pixels: Red, Green and Blue values and the estimated background values of the pixel positioned at $\mathbf{x} = (x_1, x_2)$ in the nth frame are defined as:

$$\mathbf{v}_{\mathbf{x},n} = (r_{\mathbf{x},n} \ g_{\mathbf{x},n} \ b_{\mathbf{x},n}) \quad \mathbf{b}_{\mathbf{x},n} = (br_{\mathbf{x},n} \ bg_{\mathbf{x},n} \ bb_{\mathbf{x},n})$$

Theoretically, a shadow pixel positioned at $\mathbf{x}$ in n^{th} frame should have the property: $\mathbf{v}_{\mathbf{x},n} = \alpha \mathbf{b}_{\mathbf{x},n}$, where α is a positive real number less than 1. Thus, the shadow pixel frame value is an α scaled version of the same positioned background pixel value in the RGB-space. As a result of this, we obtain the following cepstral relation:

$$\hat{\mathbf{v}}_{\mathbf{x},n}[1] \neq \hat{\mathbf{b}}_{\mathbf{x},n}[1] \tag{1}$$

$$\hat{\mathbf{v}}_{\mathbf{x},n}[i] = \hat{\mathbf{b}}_{\mathbf{x},n}[i], \ i = 2, 3, \ldots \tag{2}$$

We use a DFT of size 4 in our implementation and check the second, third and fourth cepstral coefficients, $\hat{\mathbf{v}}_{\mathbf{x},n}[2], \hat{\mathbf{v}}_{\mathbf{x},n}[3], \hat{\mathbf{v}}_{\mathbf{x},n}[4]$ and their counterpart cepstral coefficients of background location, $\hat{\mathbf{b}}_{\mathbf{x},n}[2], \hat{\mathbf{b}}_{\mathbf{x},n}[3], \hat{\mathbf{b}}_{\mathbf{x},n}[4]$. They should be equal if the pixel of interest is a shadow pixel. First cepstral coefficients, $\hat{\mathbf{v}}_{\mathbf{x},n}[1]$ and $\hat{\mathbf{b}}_{\mathbf{x},n}[1]$ should be different due to the effect of the natural logarithm of coefficient α. Using this fact, we define a difference vector: $\mathbf{d}_{\mathbf{x},n} = |\hat{\mathbf{v}}_{\hat{\mathbf{x}},n} - \hat{\mathbf{b}}_{\hat{\mathbf{x}},n}|$. Shadow detection method for moving pixels inside the block is given as follows:

$$\mathbf{x} : \begin{cases} \text{moving shadow pixel,} & \text{if } \mathbf{d}_{\mathbf{x},n}[2] \ \& \ \mathbf{d}_{\mathbf{x},n}[3] \ \& \ \mathbf{d}_{\mathbf{x},n}[4] < \tau \\ \text{moving object pixel,} & \text{otherwise} \end{cases} \tag{3}$$

where τ is an adaptive threshold changing its value as a function of the background pixel value for the current image frame.

3   Experimental Results and Conclusions

In this section, the outcomes of the proposed algorithm are presented and comparisons with some of the previous approaches are made. The benchmark test set available in [14] is used in this paper as it is widely referenced by most of the researchers working in the field. Each video sequence in the benchmark test set has different sequence type, shadow strength, shadow size, object class, object size, object speed and noise level.

The video sequences of campus raw (Fig. 2a) have very low shadow strength as well as high noise level. In Fig. 2b, it is clearly seen that two moving objects are detected perfectly and most of the moving shadow points on the ground are marked with success. In order to compare the performance of the proposed method with the others, quantitative measures are used. In this study, shadow detection accuracy η and shadow discrimination accuracy ξ metrics introduced in [10] are used as the quantitative measures for comparison purposes. The reason for selecting [10] for comparison is due to the existence of detailed classification schemes and utilization of different approaches available in the literature

(a) Original video frame (b) ject and shadow regions

Fig. 2.: "Campus" video sequence

for shadow detection in its content. Table 2 and Table 3 summarizes the performance of the proposed method and the other methods using the same benchmark test set. In the tables, the abbreviations SNP, SP, DNM1, DNM2 and CB stands for the statistical non-parametric approach, statistical parametric approach, deterministic non-model based approach using color exploitation, deterministic non-model based approach using spatial redundancy exploitation and the proposed cepstrum based approach, respectively. The ξ and η values in percentage for the proposed approach are commonly better than the SNP, SP, DNM1 and DNM2 approaches used by the other researchers in the literature.

Table 1.: Shadow detection accuracy (η) values in percentage

	Campus	Highway I	Highway II	Intelligent Room	Laboratory
SNP	80.58	81.59	51.20	78.63	84.03
SP	72.43	59.59	46.93	78.50	64.85
DNM1	82.87	69.72	54.07	76.52	76.26
DNM2	69.10	75.49	60.24	71.68	60.34
CB	**84.21**	**77.38**	**62.73**	**80.67**	**83.26**

Table 2.: Shadow discrimination accuracy (ξ) values in percentage

	Campus	Highway I	Highway II	Intelligent Room	Laboratory
SNP	69.37	63.76	78.92	89.92	92.35
SP	74.08	84.70	91.49	91.99	95.39
DNM1	86.65	76.93	78.93	92.32	89.87
DNM2	62.96	62.38	72.50	86.02	81.57
CB	**81.35**	**85.34**	**86.88**	**93.56**	**94.90**

The proposed cepstral domain method can determine shadow regions retaining the underlying color and texture of the background region. In benchmark data test sets, it is observed that proposed method gives successful results. The shadow pixels and object pixels are segmented accurately in all video sequences. Finally, quantitative measures are defined for comparison with previous approaches. The detection and discrimination rate comparisons show that the proposed method gives better results than other approaches available in the literature.

References

1. Toreyin, B. U., Cetin, A. E.: Shadow Detection Using 2D Cepstrum. In: Proceedings of SPIE, the International Society for Optical Engineering, vol. 7338, pp 733809-733809-7 (2009)
2. Cucchiara, R., Grana, C., Piccardi, M., Prati, A.: Detecting Objects, Shadows and Ghosts in Video Streams by Exploiting Color and Motion Information. In: Proceedings of the 11th International Conference on Image Analysis and Processing, pp. 360-365 (2001).
3. Cucchiara, R., Grana, C., Piccardi, M., Prati, A., Sirotti, S.: Improving Shadow Suppression in Moving Object Detection with HSV Color Information. In: Proceedings of IEEE International Conference on Intelligent Transportation Systems, pp. 334-339 (2001)
4. Chen, B.: Indoor and Outdoor People Detection and Shadow Suppression by Exploiting HSV Color Information. In: Proceedings of the The Fourth International Conference on Computer and Information Technology, pp. 137-142 (2004)
5. Jiang, C., Ward, M. O.: Shadow Identification. In: Proceedings of IEEE International Conference on Computer Vision and Pattern Recognition, pp. 606-612 (1992)
6. Stauder, J., Mech, R., Ostermann, J.: Detection of Moving Cast Shadows for Object Segmentation. In: IEEE Transactions on Multimedia, vol. 1, no. 1, pp. 65-76 (1999)
7. Onoguchi, K.: Shadow Elimination Method for Moving Object Detection. In: Proceedings of Fourteenth International Conference on Pattern Recognition. vol. 1. pp. 583-587 (1998)
8. Sonoda, Y., Ogata, T.: Seperation of Moving Objects and Their Shadows, and Their Application to Tracking on the Loci in the Monitoring Images. Proceedings of Fourth International Conference on Signal Processing, vol. 2, pp. 1261-1264 (1998)
9. Prati, A., Mikic, I., Grana, C., Trivedi M. M.: Shadow Detection Algorithms for Traffic Flow Analysis: A Comparative Study. In: Proceedings of IEEE International Conference on Intelligent Transportation Systems, pp. 340-345 (2001)
10. Prati, A., Mikic, C., Trivedi, M. M., Cucchiara, R.: Detecting Moving Shadows: Algorithms and Evaluation. In: IEEE Transactions on Pattern Analysis and Machine Intelligence, vol. 25, no. 7, pp. 918-923 (2003)
11. Prati, A., Cucchiara, R., Mikic, C., Trivedi, M. M.: Analysis and Detection of Shadows in Video Streams: a Comparitive Evaluation. In: Proceedings of IEEE International Conference on Computer Vision and Pattern Recognition, vol. 2, pp. 571-576 (2001)
12. Colins, R., Lipton, A., Kanade, T.: A System for Video Surveillance and Monitoring. 8-th Int Topical Meeting on robotics and remote systems, American Nuclear Society, (1999)
13. Joshi, A., Atev, S., Masoud, O., Papanikopoulos, N.: Moving Shadow Detection with Low- and Mid-Level Reasoning. In: Proceedings of IEEE International Conference on Robotics and Automation, (2007)
14. Video Surveillance Online Repository, http://www.openvisor.org

This article was processed using the LaTeX macro package with LLNCS style

Joint Utilization of Appearance and Geometry for Scene Logo Retrieval

Medeni Soysal[1,2] and A. Aydın Alatan[2]

[1]Video and Audio Processing Group, TÜBİTAK UZAY, Ankara, Turkey
[2]Electrical and Electronics Engineering Department, Middle East Technical University, Ankara, Turkey
medeni.soysal@uzay.tubitak.gov.tr, alatan@eee.metu.edu.tr

Abstract. A novel approach, involving the comparison of appearance and geometrical similarity of local patterns simultaneously via a combined description is presented. The proposed algorithm proved itself in scene logo retrieval domain, where significant appearance changes, especially due to affine transformations take place.

Keywords: Scene logo detection, local descriptors, geometrical descriptors.

1 Introduction

Detecting instances of a specific logo in images and video is of great importance for various applications. Logos can serve as an important cue for the presence of many semantic concepts, such as political parties, companies and even illegal organizations.

In the literature, many methods have been proposed for logo detection [1-5]. However, the research has been mostly on the detection side within some constrained environments[1-3]. In contrast to logo detection in constrained environments, there are only a few algorithms proposed for the natural scene logo detection domain. An important research [4], which aims at detecting scene logos in frames of sport videos, utilizes edges, shapes and color composition. More recent work by Joly *et al.* [5] addresses the problem by using local interest point features. In this work, SIFT [6] descriptors extracted from template and test images are matched using L_2 distance and then matches are filtered by a geometric consistency checking step.

In this paper, a novel approach involving the evaluation of appearance and geometry via a combined description is presented. This description utilizes quantized appearance descriptors of SIFT points to avoid comparing a test descriptor to all template descriptors in contrast with [5] and [6]. Geometrical descriptions are based on multiple small groups of points, namely *quads*, instead of a single large group. These advantages render the proposed algorithm robust to significant appearance changes, while being robust to random false matches through simultaneous utilization of geometrical description. The experimental results showing the robustness of the method by comparing it against a baseline algorithm is given in Section 3 before conclusions.

E. Gelenbe et al. (eds.), *Computer and Information Sciences*, Lecture Notes in Electrical Engineering 62, DOI 10.1007/978-90-481-9794-1_58,
© Springer Science+Business Media B.V. 2010

2 Utilization of Appearance and Geometry for Scene Logo Retrieval

In the proposed approach, appearance is represented by a codebook generated via clustering of SIFT descriptions. Geometric constraints, on the other hand, are enforced on interest points by means of barycentric coordinates [7], scale and orientation. The process of systematically combining appearance and barycentric coordinates is illustrated in Fig 1a-d. Combined definitions of template images in terms of codewords, barycentric coordinates and interest point spatial properties (i.e. scale, orientation) are together denoted as *Combined Visual Knowledge Base (CVKB)* for clarity in further references.

The developed system searches patterns that are automatically extracted from the template images and converted into a database, i.e. *CVKB*. Each of these patterns are represented in the form $q_i : (cw_i, \sigma_i, \Theta_i, b_i)$. Let *CVKB* consist of N quads q_i, i ∈ {1,...,N}. Each quad has four elements, i.e. interest points q_{ij}, with corresponding codewords cw_{ij}, scales σ_{ij}, and dominant orientations Θ_{ij} for j ∈ {1,...,4}. Barycentric Coordinates of each quad q_i are represented by b_{ik}, where i ∈ {1,...,N} and k ∈ {1,...,3}. Let a test image quad be defined as q_t: ($cw_t, \sigma_t, \Theta_t, b_t$). Compatibility of q_t with a CVKB quad q_i is assessed as follows:

1. If ∀j ∈ {1,...,4}, $cw_{ij} = cw_{tj}$, then continue; else quads are incompatible.
2. Compute $\Delta\sigma = (\Delta\sigma_1, \Delta\sigma_2, \Delta\sigma_3, \Delta\sigma_4)$ and $\Delta\Theta = (\Delta\Theta_1, \Delta\Theta_2, \Delta\Theta_3, \Delta\Theta_4)$, where,

$$\Delta\sigma_j = \left\lfloor \log_2 \frac{\sigma_{tj}}{\sigma_{ij}} \right\rfloor \tag{1}$$

$$\Delta\Theta_j = \left\lfloor \frac{\left((\Theta_{tj} - \Theta_{ij}) \bmod 2\pi\right) \bullet 12}{2\pi} \right\rfloor \tag{2}$$

3. Compute barycentric coordinate distance d_b as in [7].
4. q_i is compatible with q_t, if and only if
    a. $d_b < thr_b$
    b. $\max(\Delta\sigma_j) - \min(\Delta\sigma_j) < thr_\sigma$
    c. $\max(\Delta\Theta_j) - \min(\Delta\Theta_j) < thr_\Theta$

$\Delta\sigma$ is the quantized $\log_2$ scale ratio vector between two quads. Similarly $\Delta\Theta$ is the quantized orientation difference vector, with a bin size of $\pi/6$ radians. Three parameters that control the geometrical consistency are: (a) thr_b for overall geometrical consistency of two quads, (b) thr_σ for heterogeneity in scale change due to the affine transformation, (c) thr_Θ for heterogeneity in local orientation change of patches that construct a quad. In addition to the previously explained parameters, an extension, which is denoted as *Artificial Template Extension (ATE)* throughout the text, that consists of artificially applying viewpoint(6) and scale(4) changes on template images is applied. The performance of the proposed algorithm is also compared with a baseline algorithm (Fig. 2c), which is the recommended matching method for SIFT [6]. Sample retrieval results are given in Fig. 2d.

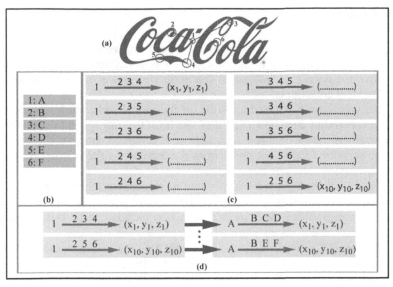

Fig. 1. (a) Neighbors of interest point 1 are 2,3,4,5,6. One of the combinations (2,3,4) is also illustrated, (b) Example codeword assignment, (c) barycentric coordinates of combinations, (d) quad representations of first and last combinations in (c).

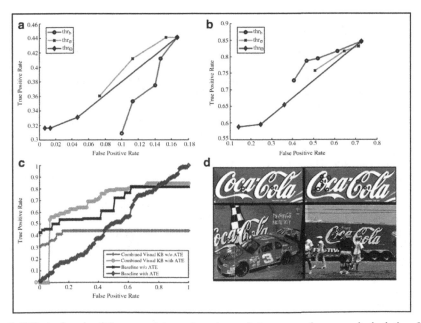

Fig. 2. Effect of each of the parameters, thr_b, thr_σ and thr_Θ on performance in isolation for (a) single template case, (b) ATE case. (c) Comparison of the proposed algorithm with baseline for single template and ATE cases. (d) Two representative results of the proposed algorithm. Template interest points are shown in the upper row, test interest points and images are given below them.

3 Conclusions

In the proposed template-based matching approach, robustness of appearance representation is enhanced by using clustered local descriptors, while compensating the side effect of decreased individual discriminative power by the help of group-based geometrical constraints.

The experiments are conducted to assess the individual and combined power of the geometrical constraints and shown that they can limit the upsurge in false positive rate while true positive rate is boosted with additional template data. On the other hand, the baseline algorithm could not profit from the increase in the number of templates due to the upsurge in false positive rate.

The proposed method provides a robust way to achieve template matching with large template sets and using marginally discriminative yet repeatable local features. After appropriate modifications, the approach can be adapted to classification and other high-level problems as an intermediate layer.

Acknowledgements. This works is funded by TÜBİTAK (The Scientific and Technological Research Council of Turkey) KAMAG TARAL 1007 (Support Programme for Research Projects of Public Institutions 1007) Research Programme, Project no. 107G229.

References

1. Seiden, S., Dillencourt, M., Irani, S., Borrey, R., and Murphy, T.: Logo detection in document images. In: Proc. CISST (1997)
2. Albiol, A., Ch, M. J., Albiol, F. A., Torres, L.: Detection of TV Commercials. In: ICASSP 2004, IEEE (2004)
3. Esen, E., Soysal, M., Ates, T.K., Saracoglu, A. and Alatan, A.A.: A Fast Method For Animated TV Logo Detection. In: Sixth International Workshop on Content-Based Multimedia Indexing (2008)
4. Kovar, B. and Hanjalic, A.: Logo detection and classification in a sport Video: video indexing for sponsorship revenue control. In: Proc. SPIE Storage and Retrieval for Media Db.s, pp. 183--193 (2002)
5. Joly, A., Buisson, O.: Logo retrieval with a contrario visual query expansion. In: Proceedings of the seventeen ACM international conference on Multimedia , pp. 581--584. ACM, New York (2009).
6. Lowe, D.: Distinctive image features from scale-invariant keypoints. Int. J. Computer Vision, pp. 91--110. Springer, Netherlands (2004)
7. Soysal, M., Alatan, A.A., Karadeniz, T.: Joint Utilization of Appearance and Geometry for Determining Correspondences. In: 24th of the International Symposium on Computer and Information Sciences (ISCIS), pp. 60--65. IEEE (2009)

Author Queries

AQ1: We renumber the list 4 to 3 please check it is appropriate.

Spatial Sampling for Image Segmentation

Mariano Rivera[1], Oscar Dalmau[1] and Washington Mio[2]

[1] Centro de Investigacion en Matematicas A.C, Guanajuato GTO 36000, Mexico
[2] Florida State University, Tallahassee FL 32306, USA

Abstract. We present a framework for image segmentation based on the ML estimator. A common hypothesis for explaining the differences among image regions is that they are generated by sampling different Likelihood Functions. We adopt last hypothesis and, additionally, we assume that such samples are *i.i.d.* Thus, the probability of a model generates the observed pixel value is estimated by computing the likelihood of the sample composed with the surrounding pixels.

1 Introduction

Image segmentation consists in partitioning an image in regions with similar characteristics: color, texture, local orientation, *etc.* Although there are many strategies for segmenting images, we can classify such algorithms in *hard* and *soft* segmentation approaches. Hard segmentation methods try to directly estimate the label map, meanwhile soft approaches compute a membership map. Given that, in a Bayesian framework, the uncertainties can be represented by probabilities, then soft segmentation procedures are commonly named Probabilistic Segmentation (PS) approaches.

We use the following notation: we assume that the observed image $g : \Omega \to \mathbb{R}^n$ ($n = 1$ for gray scale images and $n = 3$ for color images) is generated by sampling unknown probability density functions named models $\mathcal{M} = \{M_k\}_{k=1}^K$ with parameters $\theta_1, \theta_2, \ldots, \theta_K$; Ω denotes the set of all the pixels in a regular lattice and $\mathcal{K} = \{1, 2, \ldots, K\}$ the label set such that the label field $c : \Omega \to \mathcal{K}$ indicates the source for each pixel. Then the task is to solve the inverse problem: to segment the image g (to estimate c) into K classes. This task may require one of estimating possible unknown parameters θ. We denote by

$$v_k(r) = P(g(r)|\theta_k, c(r) = k). \tag{1}$$

the likelihood of observing $g(r)$ given the model k. This can be seen as the preference of the data, $g(r)$, for the model k. Thus the Maximum Likelihood (ML) estimator (classification) is given by $c^{ML}(r) = \text{argmax}_k v_k(r)$. This Winner Takes All (WTA) assignment is used as estimate of the true label, $c(r)$. A disadvantage of the ML estimator if its sensibility to noisy data that results in noisy segmentations. For improving those segmentations of a noisy image one has two choices:

1. To increase the number of samples per pixel, *i.e.*, to acquire a set of independent observations $\{g_i(r)\}_{i=1}^I$. The samples' noise contributions are averaged and therefore improving the ML estimator; where the likelihood is given by

$$v_k(r) = \prod_i P(g_i(r)|\theta_k, c(r) = k). \tag{2}$$

E. Gelenbe et al. (eds.), *Computer and Information Sciences*, Lecture Notes
in Electrical Engineering 62, DOI 10.1007/978-90-481-9794-1_59,
© Springer Science+Business Media B.V. 2010

2. To use prior knowledge that promotes smooth solutions. If this prior is coded as the probability $P(c)$, then, by using the Bayes' rule, the MAP estimator can be computed from the posterior probability:

$$c^{MAP} = \underset{c}{\operatorname{argmax}} \prod_r \prod_k v_k(r) P(c). \tag{3}$$

Both strategies allows one to estimate simultaneously the segmentation and the model parameter. This joint estimation can be implemented by an EM strategy [2]. Futhermore, note that both strategies are not mutual exclusive: the likelihood in (3) can be improved by the use of multiple samples. However from last two options, Bayesian regularization is the preferred strategy given that, in general, we are limited to a single image [3,7]. In such a case, one can find a vast literature for solving the optimization problem stated in (3). Such techniques can be classified as combinatorial optimization approaches (the ones that try to directly estimate the c^{MAP}) [3,1,5,9,6] and probabilistic approaches (the ones for estimating a hidden real variable that represents the probability that $c(r)$ takes a particular label, a PS) [8,11,4].

2   Spatial Sampling

We present a method for improving the likelihood in the lack of multiple observations. Our improved likelihoods can be used for directly compute the segmentation by means of the ML estimator or used as prime matter for a Bayesian segmentation method that solve (3). The general idea is simple, we assume that all the pixels are *i.i.d.* samples of generative models and the source is determined by the label map c. Since the image regions are relative large (this assumption is frequently codified as a prior in Bayesian regularization), then the pixels in a small neighborhood are very likely samples of a unique model. Thus the small pixel neighborhood can be assumed as multiple observations of the central pixel. This simple idea is actually the underlaying idea of all spatial filtering techniques in image processing. Inspired on that, we porpose a novel and efficient framework for image probabilistic segmentation. Our approach, differently from those frameworks that regularize (smooths) the pixel values, regularizes the likelihood density functions.

Let $\mathcal{N}_r$ be a neighborhood of pixels centered at r and $\mathcal{G}_r = \{g(s) : s \in \mathcal{N}_r\}$ their corresponding pixels values. For the moment, we assume the simple neighbothood $\mathcal{N}_r = \{s : \|r - s\|^2 \le \rho\}$, —in section 3 we discuss the neighborhood selection. We can note that $\mathcal{G}_r$ is a sample with mixed likelihood:

$$P(\mathcal{G}_r | \theta, c, \pi) = \sum_k \pi_k(r) \left[\prod_{s \in \mathcal{N}_r} P(g(s) | \theta_k, c(s) = k) \right] = \left(\pi^T \tilde{v} \right)(r); \tag{4}$$

where we define the spatial likelihood

$$\tilde{v}_k(r) \overset{def}{=} \prod_{s \in \mathcal{N}_r} v_k(s) \tag{5}$$

and $\pi(r) \in \mathbb{S}^K$ is a vector whose components are unknown mixture coefficient. Where we denote by $\mathbb{S}^K$ the simplex with all the positive vector that sum one: $z \in \mathbb{S}^K \Longleftrightarrow$

$z \geq 0, \sum_k z_k = 1$ for $k = 1, 2, \ldots, K$. Thus $\pi_k(r)$ is the fraction of the sample $\mathcal{G}_r$ generated with the kth model.

Then, the image segmentation can be estimated from an estimator of π if an appropriated $\mathcal{N}_r$ is selected, subsection 3. Next we investigate two estimators of π:

1. A hard segmentation can be computed by the maximization of (4), a Linear Programming problem. It is easy to prove that this ML estimator is the indicator vector: $p^{(1)}(r) = e_{k^*}$, where e_k is the kth basis vector and $k^* = \text{argmax}_k \tilde{v}_k(r) = \text{argmax}_k \hat{v}_k(r)$; where the normalized spatial likelihood is given by

$$\hat{v}_k(r) = \tilde{v}_k(r) / \sum_i \tilde{v}_i(r). \qquad (6)$$

2. A soft estimation of π can be computed by the maximization: $p^{(2)}(r) = \text{argmax}_\pi (\pi^T \hat{v})(r) / \|\pi(r)\| \|\hat{v}(r)\|$; that results in $p^{(2)}(r) = \hat{v}(r)$.

Therefore, in any of the last two cases, the estimation of π is reduced to the computation of $\hat{v}_k(r)$: spatial products of individual likelihoods, or sums of log-likelihoods:

$$\hat{v}_k(r) \propto \prod_{s \in \mathcal{N}_r} v_k(s) = \exp \left(\sum_{s \in \mathcal{N}_r} \log v_k(s) \right). \qquad (7)$$

Now we extend the above introduced probabilistic segmentation to the case of multiple sources, *i.e.*, to combine independent segmentation from different clues. After that, we will be in the capability of presenting the neighborhood choices and their algorithmic implications. First, we note that (7) can be written as

$$\hat{v}_k(r) \propto v_k(r) \bar{v}_k(r) \quad \text{with} \quad \bar{v}_k(r) = \prod_{s \in \mathcal{N}_r \setminus \{r\}} v_k(s). \qquad (8)$$

Eq. (8) can be understood as the combination of two independent sources: the likelihood estimated from the observed value, $v_k(r)$, and the likelihood, $\bar{v}_k(r)$, estimated with the neighbor pixels except r. We can give a further step by generalizing (8) to J independent sources and introducing their confidence factor. Then α_j is our grade of confidence in the jth–source (the $v^{(j)}$ likelihood) and it holds $\alpha \in \mathbb{S}^J$. So that $\alpha_j = 1$ means that the jth–source has the largest possible confidence and it becomes irrelevant as $\alpha_j \to 0$. Thus:

$$\hat{v}_k(r) \propto \prod_{j=1}^J \left[v_k^{(j)}(r) \right]^{\alpha_j} = \exp \left(\sum_{s=1}^J \alpha_j \log v_k^{(j)}(s) \right); \qquad (9)$$

this, Eq. (9), is a simple form of combining a set of likelihoods (probabilistic segmentations). The different PS (sources) can result from the use of different clues as, for instance, color and local statistical descriptors for texture.

3   On the Neighborhood Selection

An accurate segmentation depends on selecting a pixel neighborhood such that its majority belongs to the correct class. Note that the right side of (9) defines a spatial filtering in the log-space of the likelihoods. Our derivation for distinct filters, both linear and

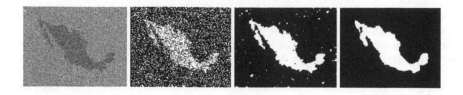

Fig. 1. ML segmentation with a squared neighborhood ($\mathcal{N}_r = \{s : \|r - s\|_\infty \leq \rho\}$) for different values of ρ. The data corresponds to a binary map (left) corrupted with Gaussian noise [$N(m = 0, \sigma = 0.7)$] and the segmentations to $\rho = 0, 2$ and 4.

nonlinear, constructs on the assumption that each neighbor pixel $s \in \mathcal{N}_r$ is an independent source for estimating the likelihood at the pixel of interest, r.

Homogeneous Windows (HW). The simplest neighborhood is a regular window centered at the pixel r: $\mathcal{N}_r = \{s : \|r - s\|_m \leq \rho\}$, where the parameter ρ controls the sample size and $\|\cdot\|_m$ is a given metric. For instance, the L_∞ norm leads to a square–shaped neighborhood((7) is reduced to a box–filter in the logarithmic space). The segmentations based on the ML estimator for different values of ρ. are shown in Fig. 1. Large ρ–values reduce the granularity but at the same time over–smoothed small details .

General Homogeneous Windows (GHW). The use of the previous HW is equivalent to apply a box-shape linear filter in the log-domain. This result can be generalized to any arbitrary linear filter if each neighbor pixel is considered an independent source [10,12,7]. . Then, similar to (9), the sources (neighbor pixels) are combined with a confidence factor that depends on its spatial distance to the central pixel r:

$$\hat{v}_k(r) \propto \prod_{s \in \mathcal{N}_r} [v_k(s)]^{\alpha(s)} = \exp\left(\sum_{s \in \mathcal{N}_r} \alpha(s) \log v_k(s)\right). \tag{10}$$

The Gaussian filtering results of choosing $\alpha(s) \propto \exp\left(-(r - s)^T \Sigma^{-1} (r - s)\right)$, where Σ is a covariance matrix and the simple homogeneous membrane is implemented as [8]:

$$d^* = \underset{d:\Omega \to \mathbb{R}^K}{\operatorname{argmin}} \sum_{r:C(r)=0} \left\{ \|d(r) - \log v(r)\|^2 + \frac{\lambda}{2} \sum_{s \in \mathcal{N}_r} \|d(r) - d(s)\|^2 \right\}. \tag{11}$$

Spatially Adapting Windows (SAW). The shape neighborhood can be adapted by depending on the local properties of the image.

4   Experiments

We developed an interactive procedure for multiclass image segmentation based on ML segmentation. The models are empirically initialized from user marked data (scribbles) on the image. The purpose is to demonstrate that the final segmentation is improved by combining multiples sources (likelihood vectors) and the source combination is naturally implemented in our proposal.

In interactive image segmentation the user's scribbles define the multimap $C : \Omega \to \{0\} \cup \mathcal{K}$ such that $C(r) \in \mathcal{K}$ indicates that the pixel r is labelled as member of class

Fig. 2. Original image (first column). Segmentation using: just color distribution (second column) and with multiple clues (last column).

k and $C(r) = 0$ if such a pixel is unlabeled and hence its label needs be estimated. The segmentation procedure is as follows. Let $g = \{g_i\}_{i=1}^3$ be the original image (in RGB space), then we computed for each pixel and color layer the local structure tensor $\Sigma_g = \{\Sigma_1, \Sigma_2, \Sigma_3\}$; where

$$\Sigma_i(r) = \begin{bmatrix} g_{i11}(r) & g_{i12}(r) \\ g_{i12}(r) & g_{i22}(r) \end{bmatrix} \quad \text{for } i = 1, 2, 3. \tag{12}$$

is a symmetric semi–positive definite matrix: Then we group the original data and tensor's coefficients in four feature sets that will be consider four independent segmentation sources: $g = \{g_i\}$, $g_{11} = \{g_{i11}\}$, $g_{12} = \{g_{i12}\}$, and $g_{22} = \{g_{i22}\}$; for $i = 1, 2, 3$. The additional feature sets [g_{11}, g_{12} and g_{22}] codify the local texture information. Afterward, we compute four Spatial Likelihoods $\{v^{(j)}\}_{j=1}^4$. The Likelihood Functions are estimated by histograms with $64 \times 64 \times 64$ bins and the dynamic range of each feature image is linearly mapped into the interval $[1, 64]$.

The confidence factor of a Likelihood Function set (says the jth set) is its capability for predict the correct pixel class. In our interactive scheme, such a confidence α_j is large if the likelihoods of the hand-labeled pixels are large for their respective models (and small for the other ones). In particular the confidence of the jth source for of the kth class is $\alpha_{jk} = \sum_r v_k^{(j)}(r)\delta(k - C(r))/\sum_r \delta(k - C(r))$. Figure 2 shows images segmented with the proposed procedure. The confidence scores are shown in Table 1. This Table shows in bold font the more confident source for each image. Note that if the color source is the one with largest confidence, then the color based segmentation is qualitatively as good as the one with four sources, these are the case of the *Elephant* image. However, the accuracy of the single source (color) segmentation is reduced as the confidence on such a source is reduced. Indeed, in all our experiments the best segmentation was computed with the proposed integration of all the sources. The filter used was the simple homogeneous membrane (11) with $\lambda = 20$.

5   Conclusions

The presented probabilistic segmentation strategy computes the uncertainty (probability) associated to each particular label. We start our development by noting that the

Table 1. Confidence factor to combine the probabilistic segmentations, see Fig. 2

Image	g	g_{11}	g_{12}	g_{22}
Cheetah	0.2284	**0.2714**	0.2411	0.2592
Elefant	**0.3280**	0.2270	0.2156	0.2294

spatial sampling is an alternative to the lack of multiple pixels' observations. Differently from multiple observations, the pixel neighborhood is a mixed sample and the estimated mixture coefficients can be used as the probability for the labels. We have noted that the neighborhood selection is an important issue to obtain a good segmentation. Our strategy allows us to combine multiple sources (probabilistic segmentations) in a natural way and is general enough to be applied in the development of algorithms for different computer vision applications.

Acknowledgement. This work was partially supported by Conacyt, Mexico: grant 61367, sabbatical stance for M. Rivera and scholarship for O. Dalmau.

References

1. Boykov, Y., Veksler, O., Zabih, R.: Fast approximate energy minimization via graph cuts. IEEE Trans. Pattern Anal. Machine Intell. 23(11), 1222–1239 (2001) 2
2. Dempster, A., Laird, N., Rubin, D.: Maximum likelihood from incomplete data via the EM algorithm. J. Roy. Statist. Soc. B 39, 1–38 (1977) 2
3. Geman, S., Geman, D.: Stochastic relaxation, Gibbs distribution and the Bayesian restoration of images. IEEE PAMI 6(6), 721–741 (1984) 2
4. Kohli, P., Torr, P.H.S.: Dynamic graph cuts for efficient inference in Markov random fields. IEEE Trans. Pattern Anal. Mach. Intell. 29(12), 2079–2088 (2007) 2
5. Kolmogorov, V., Zabih, R.: What energy functions can be minimized via graph cuts. IEEE Trans. Pattern Anal. Mach. Intell. 26(2), 147–159 (2004) 2
6. Komodakis, N., Tziritas, G., Paragios, N.: Performance vs computational efficiency for optimizing single and dynamic MRFs: Setting the state of the art with primal–dual strategies. Computer Vision and Image Understanding 112, 14–29 (2008) 2
7. Li, S.Z.: Markov Random Field Modeling in Image Analysis. Springer-Verlag, Tokyo (2001) 2, 4
8. Marroquin, J.L., Velazco, F., Rivera, M., Nakamura, M.: Probabilistic solution of ill–posed problems in computational vision. IEEE Trans. Pattern Anal. Machine Intell. 23, 337–348 (2001) 2, 4
9. Olsson, C., Eriksson, A.P., Kahl, F.: Improved spectral relaxation methods for binary quadratic optimization problems. Computer Vision and Image Understanding 112, 30–38 (2008) 2
10. Perona, P., Malik, J.: Scale-space and edge-detection using anisotropic diffusion. IEEE Trans. Pattern Anal. Mach. Intell. 12(7), 629–639 (1990) 4
11. Rivera, M., Ocegueda, O., Marroquin, J.L.: Entropy-controlled quadratic Markov measure field models for efficient image segmentation. IEEE Trans. Image Processing 8(12), 3047–3057 (Dec 2007) 2
12. Terzopoulos, D.: Regularization of inverse visual problems involving discontinuities. IEEE Trans. Pattern Anal. Mach. Intell. 8(4), 413–424 (1986) 4

Kernel and Spectral Methods for Learning the Semantics of Images

Horace H.S. Ip

Image Computing Group, Department of Computer Science
Centre for Innovative Applications of Internet and Multimedia Technologies
City University of Hong Kong, Kowloon, Hong Kong
cship@cityu.edu.hk

Abstract. In order to bridge the semantic gap, learning the semantics of images automatically using visual features alone has been an area of active research. Recently, visual keywords extracted from images have been shown to provide a useful intermediate representation for image characterization and retrieval. A challenging problem is to find effectively ways of extracting, representing and using the context of visual keyword for learning image semantic. In this paper, we will present a number of kernel and spectral methods which our research group has developed for learning the semantics of images, which can be applied to a variety of image annotation, categorization and retrieval tasks. To capture the context of visual keywords, we propose two contextual kernels, called spatial Markov kernel and spatial mismatch kernel, respectively. The first kernel is defined based on Markov models, while the second kernel is motivated from the concept of string kernel and derived without the use of any generative models. The experimental results show that the context captured by our kernels is very effective for learning the semantics of images. Moreover, to learn a semantically compact (or high level) vocabulary, we further propose a spectral embedding method to capture the local intrinsic geometric (i.e. manifold) structure of the original abundant visual keywords. This spectral method can also be applied to manifold learning on textual keywords for image annotation refinement. The experimental results show that our spectral methods lead to significant improvement in performance by capturing the manifold structure of visual or textual keywords.

Keywords: semantic gap, contextual kernel, spectral embedding, image annotation, annotation refinement.

1 Introduction

To search the rapidly growing image archives more effectively, many content-based image annotation and retrieval systems have been developed. Because of the semantic gap between the low-level visual features and the high-level semantics of images, these techniques are still far from satisfactory for practical use. To reduce this semantic gap, methods [1, 2] have been proposed to learn the semantics of images directly. In this paper, we present our recent development of methods that aim to

E. Gelenbe et al. (eds.), *Computer and Information Sciences*, Lecture Notes
in Electrical Engineering 62, DOI 10.1007/978-90-481-9794-1_60,
© Springer Science+Business Media B.V. 2010

reduce the semantic gap through: (i) capturing the context within images using kernel methods, and (ii) learning the visual and semantic manifolds across the entire dataset using spectral methods. The main advantage of our kernel and spectral methods is that they can be readily combined and used with other machine learning techniques such as Relevance Model [3] and Multi-label propagation [4] for learning the semantics of images for the purpose of annotation and categorization.

It is generally accepted that context provides useful cues for learning the semantics of images, e.g. through helping to reduce the ambiguity of visual keywords. Recently, methods [5-7] have been proposed to capture the context of visual keywords. Since kernels play the role of a similarity measure in many machine leaning techniques (e.g. manifold learning), we capture the context within images through defining two contextual kernels, called spatial Markov kernel [8] and spatial string kernel [9], respectively.

In the literature, typically thousands of visual keywords are used to obtain better performance on a relatively large image dataset and this visual vocabulary may contain a large amount of information redundancy. To learn a semantically compact visual vocabulary, we propose a spectral embedding method which learns the local intrinsic geometric (i.e. manifold) structure of the original abundant visual keywords. It should be noted that the manifold structure of visual keywords has not been previously investigated. Similarly, our spectral method for learning the visual manifolds can be extended to learn the semantic manifold structure of textual keywords, which can be further used for image annotation refinement [10].

The proposed kernel and spectral methods can be unified in a single framework for learning the semantics of images. Within such a framework [Fig. 1], visual manifolds are first learnt from the original visual vocabulary using our spectral method and spectral clustering is then performed in the embedding space to generate a new and compact visual vocabulary. Furthermore, both contextual kernels and textual keywords are combined for keyword propagation such that the resulting annotations (i.e. the output of keyword propagation) can be further refined based on the learnt semantic manifolds.

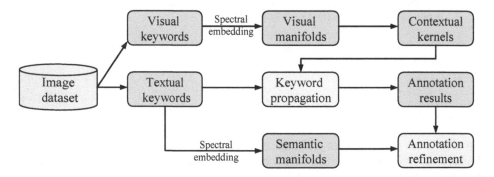

Fig. 1. A unified framework for semantic learning that integrates our kernel and spectral methods

2 Kernel Methods for Capturing the Context within Images

To capture the context within images, we have proposed two contextual kernels based on the image representation using visual keywords. The first kernel is defined based on 2D Markov models, while the second kernel is actually derived from string kernel without using any generative models [9]. Due to the shortage of space, in this paper, we focus on our spatial string kernel (particularly spatial mismatch kernel). Detail of the spatial Markov kernel and its applications can be found in [6-8].

Given an image, to learn the associated set of visual keywords, we first divided the image into blocks on a regular grid, and a feature vector that describes the color and texture characteristics of the block is extracted for each of the blocks. Based on the block feature vectors, a vocabulary of M visual keywords, $V = \{w_i: i = 1,...,M \}$, that capture the content (visual) similarities among the blocks is generated through k-means clustering. Block feature extraction and visual keywords generation have been extensively covered elsewhere, e.g. [6, 11] and will not be repeated here. With this learnt universal vocabulary V, each block of the image is automatically assigned a visual keyword that best describes the visual characteristic of the block and the entire image can subsequently be represented compactly as a 2D sequence Q of visual keywords on the regular grid. The sequence of visual keywords provides a succinct intermediate representation of the image.

The 2D sequence Q can be further decomposed into two parallel 1D sequences, i.e. a row-wise Q^r and column-wise Q^c. The 1D sequence Q^r (or Q^c) can be obtained by a row-wise (or column-wise) raster scan on the regular grid. In the following, we will give the details on the feature mapping for the row-wise sequences. The column-wise sequences can be mapped to a feature space similarly.

For each k-length subsequence α in a row-wise sequence Q^r (i.e. $\alpha \square Q^r$), the (k,m)-neighborhood $N_{(k,m)}(\alpha)$ generated by α is the set of all k-length sequences β from the vocabulary V (i.e. $\beta \in V^k$) that differ from α by at most m mismatches. We then define the following $\Phi_{(k,m)}$ that maps α to a M^k-dimensional feature space:

$$\Phi_{(k,m)}(\alpha) = (\delta_\beta(\alpha))_{\beta \in V^k}, \qquad (1)$$

where $\delta_\beta(\alpha)=1$ if $\beta \in N_{(k,m)}(\alpha)$, and $\delta_\beta(\alpha)=0$ otherwise. That is, a k-length subsequence contributes weight to all the coordinates in its mismatch neighborhood. For a row-wise sequence Q^r, we extend the above feature mapping additively by summing the feature vectors for all the k-length subsequences α in Q^r:

$$\Phi(Q^r) = \sum_{\alpha \in V^k, \alpha \subset Q^r} \Phi_{(k,m)}(\alpha). \qquad (2)$$

When $k=1$ and $m=0$, the above feature vector is equivalent to the histogram of visual keywords (i.e. the conventional bag-of-words representation). Similar feature mapping can be obtained for the column-wise sequence Q^c.

Given Q and $\tilde{Q}$, we can define our spatial mismatch kernel that compares the contextual similarity between the two images using the following inner-product:

$$K(Q,\tilde{Q}) = < \Phi(Q^r), \Phi(\tilde{Q}^r) > + < \Phi(Q^c), \Phi(\tilde{Q}^c) >, \qquad (3)$$

Since the feature vectors given for our kernel definition are extremely sparse, it can be computed efficiently.

To the best of our knowledge, this is the first application of string kernel for matching 2D sequence of visual keywords. Here, it is worth noting that string kernels were originally developed for protein classification [12] where the number of amino acids (similar to visual keywords used here) used for kernel definition was very small. In the present work, string kernels are used to capture and compare the context of a large number of (e.g. thousands of) visual keywords within an image, so that the associated problem of (2D) sequence matching is significantly more challenging.

The advantage of our spatial string kernel over the spatial Markov kernel approach is that the former does not make use of any generative models which typically require some prior assumptions of the data property.

3 Spectral Methods for Learning Visual and Semantic Manifolds

To learn a semantically compact vocabulary, we propose a spectral embedding method to capture the local intrinsic geometric (i.e. manifold) structure of the original abundant visual keywords. This spectral method can be extended to manifold learning on textual keywords.

3.1 Learning Visual Manifolds

To learn the manifolds hidden among visual keywords, we first extract and measure the correlation of visual keywords using the Pearson product moment (PPM) correlation measure [13]. Given a set of N training images and the visual vocabulary $V = \{w_i: i = 1,...,M \}$, we collect the histogram of visual keywords as $\{c_n(w_i): n = 1, ...,N\}$ $(i = 1, ...,M)$, where $c_n(w_i)$ is the count of times that visual keyword w_i occurs in image n. The PPM correlation between two visual keywords w_i and w_j can be defined by:

$$a_{ij} = \frac{\sum_{n=1}^{N}(c_n(w_i) - \mu(w_i))(c_n(w_j) - \mu(w_j))}{(N-1)\sigma(w_i)\sigma(w_j)}, \qquad (4)$$

where $\mu(w_i)$ and $\sigma(w_i)$ are the mean and standard deviation of $\{c_n(w_i): n = 1, ...,N\}$, respectively. Similarly, we can also collect the correlation information of textual keywords, which is vital for subsequently learning the semantic manifolds hidden among them by spectral methods.

Using the set of visual keywords as the vertex set, we construct an undirected weighted graph for manifold learning. We construct the affinity matrix $A = \{a_{ij}\}_{M \times M}$ based on PPM to measure the similarity between keywords. Here, it is worth noting that the PPM correlation value a_{ij} will be negative if w_i and w_j are not positively correlated. In this case, we set $a_{ij} = 0$ to ensure that the affinity matrix A is nonnegative. As PPM is a parameter-less measure, the distinct advantage of using PPM to compute the elements of the affinity matrix A is that, unlike other similarity measures that are based on parameterized functions such as the Gaussian function, we have eliminated the need of parameter tuning for graph construction. Parameter tuning can significantly affect the performance and has been noted as an inherent weakness of graph-based methods.

The goal of manifold learning is to represent each vertex in the graph as a lower dimensional vector that preserves similarities between the vertex pairs. Such goals can be achieved by spectral embedding through finding the leading eigenvectors of the normalized graph Laplacian $L = I - D^{-1}A$, where D is a diagonal matrix with its (i, i)-element equal to the sum of the i-th row of the affinity matrix A. Without loss of generality, we consider one type of normalized graph Laplacian that was proposed in [14]. Let $\{(\lambda_i, \mathbf{v}_i) : i = 1, ..., M\}$ be the set of eigenvalues and the associated eigenvectors of the normalized Laplacian L, where $0 \le \lambda_1 \le ... \le \lambda_M$ and $\mathbf{v}_i^T \mathbf{v}_i = 1$. The spectral embedding of the graph can be represented by

$$E = (\mathbf{v}_1, ..., \mathbf{v}_s),$$
(5)

with the j-th row $E_{j\cdot}$ being the new representation for vertex w_j. Since we usually set $s < M$, the visual keywords have been represented as lower dimensional vectors.

Based on this new low-dimensional representation, we can learn a semantically more compact visual vocabulary of size s by spectral clustering using k-means from the original set of visual keywords which has a much higher cardinality. The learnt compact visual vocabulary can be used to represent the semantic content of an image in the form of bag-of-words so that we can similarly define a histogram intersection kernel or our contextual kernels (see Fig. 1).

3.2 Learning Semantic Manifolds

The above spectral method for learning visual manifolds can be extended to manifold learning on textual keywords. More concretely, we first compute the affinity matrix A using the PPM measure between textual keywords, and then learn the semantic manifolds hidden among textual keywords by spectral embedding using the computed affinity matrix. An example of exploiting the learnt semantic manifolds for annotation refinement can be found in our recent work [10]. Here, it should be noted that the semantic manifolds hidden among textual keywords help to reduce the semantic ambiguity in semantic learning.

4 Conclusions

The experimental results reported in [8, 10] demonstrate that the proposed kernel and spectral methods for learning the semantics of images lead to improved performance and even outperform the state-of-the-art methods. For example, our spatial string kernel can achieve 13% gain over spatial pyramid matching (SPM) [11] on the Corel-5K annotation dataset, and our spectral method for learning visual manifolds can increase the performance of SPM by an average of 5% on the Scene-8 image dataset. In the future work, as general machine learning techniques, our kernel and spectral methods will be tested in other challenging applications such as video content analysis and retrieval.

Acknowledgments. The author would like to thank the contributions and dedications of his past and present students, Feiyang Yu, Wendy Wang, and Zhiwu Lu, to the work presented in this paper. The work presented in this paper was supported by a City University of Hong Kong Strategic Research Grant 7008040 and a Hong Kong SAR Research Grants Council grant No. 114007.

References

1. Feng, S., Manmatha, R, Lavrenko, V.: Multiple Bernoulli Relevance Models for Image and Video Annotation. In: IEEE Computer Society Conference on Computer Vision and Pattern Recognition (CVPR), pp. 1002--1009. IEEE Press (2004)
2. Lu, Z., Peng, Y., Ip, H.: Image Categorization via Robust pLSA. Pattern Recognition Letters, 31 (1), 36--43 (2010)
3. Lu, Z., Ip, H.: Generalized Relevance Models for Automatic Image Annotation. In: Pacific-Rim Conference on Multimedia (PCM), pp. 245--255. Springer Press (2009)
4. Lu, Z., Ip, H., He, Q.: Context-Based Multi-Label Image Annotation. In: ACM International Conference on Image and Video Retrieval (CIVR). ACM Press (2009)
5. Li, J., Wang, J.: Automatic Linguistic Indexing of Pictures by a Statistical Modeling Approach. IEEE Trans. on Pattern Analysis and Machine Intelligence, 25 (9), 1075--1088 (2003)
6. Yu, F., Ip H.: Automatic Semantic Annotation of Images Using Spatial Hidden Markov Model. In: International Conference on Multimedia and Expo (ICME), pp. 305--308. IEEE Press (2006)
7. Wang, L., Lu, Z., Ip, H.: Image Categorization Based on a Hierarchical Spatial Markov Model. In: International Conference on Computer Analysis of Images and Patterns (CAIP), pp. 766--773. Springer Press (2009)
8. Lu, Z., Ip, H.: Combining Context, Consistency, and Diversity Cues for Interactive Image Categorization. IEEE Trans. on Multimedia, 12(3), 194--203 (2010)
9. Lu, Z., Ip, H.: Image Categorization with Spatial Mismatch Kernels. In: IEEE Computer Society Conference on Computer Vision and Pattern Recognition (CVPR), pp. 397--404. IEEE Press (2009)
10. Lu, Z., Ip, H.: Learning the Semantics of Images Using Visual and Semantic Context. IEEE Trans. on Multimedia. (Under second round review)
11. Lazebnik, S., Schmid, C., Ponce, J.: Beyond Bags of Features: Spatial Pyramid Matching for Recognizing Natural Scene Categories. In: IEEE Computer Society Conference on Computer Vision and Pattern Recognition (CVPR), pp. 2169--2178. IEEE Press (2006)
12. Leslie, C., Eskin, E., Noble, W.: The Spectrum Kernel: A String Kernel for SVM Protein Classification. In: Pacific Symposium on Biocomputing, pp. 566--575. (2002)
13. Rodgers, J., Nicewander, W: Thirteen Ways to Look at the Correlation Coefficient. The American Statistician, 42 (1), 59--66 (1988)
14. Liu, J., Yang, Y., Shah, M.: Learning Semantic Visual Vocabularies Using Diffusion Distance. In: IEEE Computer Society Conference on Computer Vision and Pattern Recognition (CVPR), pp. 461--468. IEEE Press (2009).

8 Web Systems

A Context-Sensitive Approach for Ontology Mapping Using Concepts Substitution Semantics

Islam Elgedawy

Computer Engineering Department
Middle East Technical University
Northern Cyprus Campus,
Guzelyurt, Mersin 10, Turkey
(elgedawy@metu.edu.tr)

Abstract. Existing approaches for ontology mapping are known of having limited accuracy, as they are basically based on generic schematic relations (such as Isa and Part-of), and ignore the usage context as well as the logic of the involved operation. To overcome this limitation, this paper proposes a novel approach for ontology mapping that uses concepts substitution semantics to resolve concepts incompatibilities in a context-sensitive manner. Experiments results show that the proposed approach is more accurate than existing generic ontology mapping approaches.

Keywords: Ontology Mapping, Substitution Semantics, Context-Sensitive

1 Introduction

Business systems use application domain ontologies in their modeling and design in order to standardize their models and to facilitate systems interaction, integration, evolution and development. This is because application domain ontologies provide a common shared understanding of application domains that can be communicated across people, applications, and systems. An ontology can range from a simple taxonomy, to a thesaurus (words and synonyms), to a conceptual model (where more complex relations are defined), to a logical theory (formal axioms, rules, theorems, and theories are defined). Ontologies incompatibilities result due to many reasons. For example, two different concepts could be used to describe the same entity. An entity could appear as an attribute in a given ontology and appear as a concept in other ontology. Two different operations could be used to describe the same transaction, etc. Hence, when two systems adopt different ontologies and need to interact with each other, ontology mapping becomes mandatory to perform such interactions. However, ontology mapping is a very complex process as it requires identification of semantically related entities, and then resolving their appearing differences according to application domain semantics and the usage contexts.

E. Gelenbe et al. (eds.), *Computer and Information Sciences*, Lecture Notes
in Electrical Engineering 62, DOI 10.1007/978-90-481-9794-1_61,
© Springer Science+Business Media B.V. 2010

There are many research efforts have been proposed to provide systematic straightforward approaches for ontology mapping such as [1] [2] [3] [4] [5]. For example, work in [1] determines the mapping between different models without translating the models into a common language. Such mapping defined as a set of relationships between expressions over the given model, where syntactical inferences are used to find matching elements. Work in [2] proposed a metric for determining objects similarity using hierarchical domain structure (i.e. Isa relations) in order to produce more intuitive similarity scores. Work in [3] provides an ontology mapping approach based on tree structure grammar. They try to combine between internal concept structure information and rules provided by similarity languages. Work in [4] developed a translation system for symbolic knowledge. It provides a language to represent complex syntactic transformations and uses syntactic rewriting (via pattern-directed rewrite rules) and semantic rewriting (via partial semantic models and some supported logical inferences) to translate different statements. Its inferences are based on generic taxonomic relationships. Work in [5] proposed a language for specifying correspondence rules between data elements adopting a general structure consisting of general ordered labeled trees. A good survey about existing ontology mapping approaches could be found in [6].

As we can see, existing ontology mapping approaches try to provide a general translation model that can fit in all contexts using generic schematic relations (such as Isa and Part-of relations), which definitely cannot guarantee to achieve high accuracy mapping results in all contexts [7] [8]. We argue that in order to guarantee having the correct mapping results, ontology mappings should be determined in a customized manner according to the usage context as well as the logic of the involved application domain operation (i.e. the transaction needs to be accomplished by interacting systems or users). Therefore, in this paper, we propose an approach for ontology mapping that is able to resolve appearing entities incompatibilities in a context-sensitive manner. The proposed approach uses conditional aggregate substitution semantics of application domain concepts to resolve appearing incompatibilities between application domain entities. Such semantics are captured by the proposed Concepts Substitutability Enhanced Graph (CSEG) in a context-sensitive manner and with respect to every application domain operation. The proposed approach adopts a meta-ontology approach for modeling application domain ontologies to ensure having CSEG semantics captured in different application domain ontologies. Experiments results show that the proposed approach is more accurate than generic ontology mapping approaches.

The rest of the paper is organized as follows. In section 2, we discuss the proposed meta-ontology for capturing concepts substitution semantics in a machine-understandable format, and show how concepts incompatibilities are resolved in a context sensitive-manner. In section 3, we provide some comparative simulation experiments for the proposed approach and comment on the obtained results, and finally we conclude the paper.

2 A meta-ontology for application domains

Adopting a meta-ontology approach for application domain conceptualization provides users with the flexibility to use different ontologies provided that these ontologies follow a common structure indicating the entities and the types of semantics to be captured. A meta-ontology should consist of two layers: a schematic layer and a semantic layer. The schematic layer defines which application domain entities need to be captured in the ontology, which will be used to define the systems models and their interaction messages. The semantic layer defines which entities semantics need to be captured in the ontology such that they can be used to resolve appearing entities incompatibilities. In the meta-ontology schematic layer, we propose to capture the application domain concepts and operations. An application domain concept is represented as a set of features defined in an attribute-value format. An application domain operation is represented as a set of features defined in an attribute-value format. In addition it has a set of input concepts, a set of output concepts, a set of pre-conditions and a set of post-conditions. We also represent the usage context as a set of conditions formulated based on the attributes of application domain concepts and operations. In the meta-ontology semantic layer, we propose to use a graph data structure, known as the Concepts Substitutability Enhanced Graph (CSEG). This graph extends the concept substitutability graph previously proposed in [7] [8] to capture the aggregate concept substitution semantics in a context-sensitive manner with respect to every application domain operation, as the old version was only capturing bilateral substitution semantics between application domain concepts.

CSEG consists of a collection of segments, where each segment is corresponding to one of the application domain operations. Each segment consists of a collection of substitution patterns corresponding to the operation input and output concepts. Each substitution pattern consists of a scope, a set of substitution conditions, and a conversion function. A substitution pattern scope is a set of concept that contains at least one application domain concept. A substitution condition is a condition that must be satisfied by the usage context in order to consider such substitution as valid. A conversion function indicates the logic needed to convert the scope into the corresponding operation concepts or vice versa. A substitution pattern for an input concept represents the collection of concepts that can substitute the input concept, while a substitution pattern for an output concept represent the collection of concepts that can be substituted by the output concept. A substitution pattern could correspond to a subset of concepts. For example, a substitution pattern for a subset of input concepts represents the set of concepts (i.e. the pattern scope) that can substitute such subset of input concepts, while a substitution pattern for a subset of output concepts represents the set of concepts that can be substituted by such subset of output concepts. Figure 1 provides a graphical representation for a CSG segment. The figure indicates the substitution patterns corresponding to a given operation input and output concepts. For example, the input concept $C1$ has three substitution patterns. The first pattern indicates that the concepts $C5$, $C6$, and $C7$ can substitute the concept. Table 1 indicates an example of an input and an output substitution patterns for *Payonline* operation. The input pattern indicates that a *CreditCard, Amount,* and *Currency* concepts can be replaced by the *Payment* concept only if credit card details and the currency are not null, and the amount is greater than zero. The output pattern indicates we can substitute the concept *Confirmation* by the concept *Receipt* only when conformation is not null. As we can see, substitution patterns are valid only in the contexts satisfying their substitution conditions. CSG systemizes the ontology mapping process, as all what need to be done is to add the suitable substitution patterns between the ontologies concepts with respect to every domain operation.

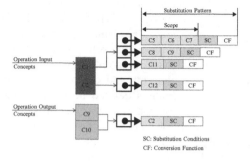

Figure 1: CSEG Segment

Table 1: An example for an input and an output substitution patterns

Operation	Concepts	Scope	Conversion Function	Substitution Condition
PayOnline	Input: CreditCard Input: Amount Input: Currency	Payment	Payment.Method= Credit Payment.Details = CreditCard.Details Payment.Currency = Currency Payment.CreditAmt = Amount	CreditCard.Details ≠ NULL Amount >0 Currency ≠ NULL
	Output: Receipt	Confirmation	Receipt= Confirmation	Confirmation ≠ NULL

Concepts mapping is determined by checking if there exists a sequence of transformations (i.e. substitution patterns) that can carried out to transform a given concept or a group of concepts into another concept or group of concepts. This is done by checking if there exists a path between the different concepts in the CSG segment corresponding to the involved application domain operation. Having no path indicates there is no mapping between such concepts according to the logic of the involved operation. We identify the concepts as reachable if such path is found. However, in order to consider reachable concepts as substitutable, we have to make sure that the usage context is not violated by such transformations. This is done by checking if the conditions of the usage context satisfy the substitution conditions defined along the identified path between the concepts. More details about this concept mapping approach as well as the adopted condition satisfiability approach could be found in [8].

3. Experiments

To verify the proposed approach, we use a simulation approach to compare between the proposed approach and the generic mapping approach that adopts only

Isa relations to match concepts. The used comparison metric is the F-measure metric. F-measure metric combines between the retrieval precision and recall metrics and is used as an indicator for accuracy, that approaches with higher values means that they are more accurate. F-measure is computed as $(2 \times \text{Precision} \times \text{Recall}) / (\text{Recall} + \text{Precision})$.

The experiment starts by generating two random sets of independent concepts (representing two different ontologies). One set will be used as the original dataset, and the second one will be used as a query set. For each concept in the query set, we randomly generate an Isa relation to a corresponding concept in the original dataset (i.e. mapping using Isa relation). For each pair of concepts having an Isa relation, we generate a corresponding substitution pattern in the CSEG. For simplicity, the substitution pattern is generated as follows. The scope is equal to the original dataset concept. The substitution condition is generated as greater than condition with a randomly generated integer number (e.g. $C1 >10$). The conversion function is just an equality function (e.g. $C1=C2$). For each concept in the query set, we generate a corresponding context. For simplicity, the context will consist of one equality condition with a randomly generated integer number (e.g. $C1=20$). Hence, not all the substitution pattern defined in the CSEG will be valid according to the generated contexts. We submit the query set to the two approaches, to find matches in the original dataset, and based on the retrieved concepts the F-measure is computed. Figure 2, depicts the results. As we can see, the generic approach ignores the contexts and retrieves the whole original dataset as answers, which results in low F-measure values, while the proposed approach succeed to reach 100%.

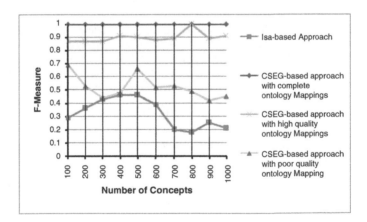

Figure 2: Experiments Results

However, this result could be misleading, as the experiment is done with complete CSEG patterns. In practice, an ontology designer may skip some substitution patterns when defining CSEG patterns. Therefore, the proposed approach will not be able to resolve the cases with missing patterns. In other words, the accuracy of the proposed approach mainly depends on the quality of the defined ontology mappings. To show such effect, we repeated the experiment except that we store only a portion of the generated substitution patterns. A high-quality ontology mappings means up to 25%

of the generated patterns are missing. A low-quality ontology mappings means from 50% to 80% of the generated patterns are missing. Then we compute the F-measure values for each case. Results are depicted in Figure 2. As we can see, when low-quality mappings are used, the proposed approach accuracy does not differ much from the generic approach, however when high-quality mappings are used the proposed approach provides a much higher accuracy values.

4. Conclusion

In this paper we proposed a context-sensitive approach for ontology mapping. The approach resolves concepts incompatibilities based on the conditional substitutability semantics of application domain concepts. Such semantics are captured in the proposed concepts substitutability graph using a meta-ontology approach. The graph consists of as a set of concepts substitution patterns, which are defined for each application domain operation. Identified concept substitution patterns are considered valid only when the usage context satisfies the required substitution conditions. Finally, we presented some simulation experiments for comparing our approach against generic ontology mapping approaches. Experiments results have shown that our approach succeeds to provide more accurate results when complete or nearly complete substitution patterns are provided.

References

1. Madhavan, J., Bernstein, P.A., Domingos, P., and Halevy A.: Representing and reasoning about mappings between domain models. In Proceedings of the 18th National Conference on Arti¯cial Intelligence (AAAI'02), Canada, 2002.
2. Ganesan, H., Molina, G. and Widom, J.: Exploiting hierarchical domain structure to compute similarity. ACM Transactions on Information Systems, 21(1):64–93, 2003.
3. Sheng L., Heping H., Xian H.,: An Ontology Mapping Method Based on Tree Structure, Semantics, Knowledge and Grid, International Conference on, p. 87, Second International Conference on Semantics, Knowledge, and Grid (SKG'06), 2006.
4. Chalupksy, H.: OntoMorph: A Translation System for Symbolic Knowledge. In Proceedings of the 17th International Conference on Knowledge Representation and Reasoning (KR-2000), Colorado, USA, April 2000.
5. Abiteboul, S., Cluet, S., and Milo, T.: Correspondence and translation for heterogeneous data. Theoretical Computer Science, (275):179{213, March 2002.
6. Kalfoglou, Y. and Schorlemmer, M.: Ontology mapping: the state of the art. The Knowledge Engineering Review, 18 (1). pp. 1-31, 2003.
7. Elgedawy, I., Tari, Z., and Thom, J. A.: A High-Level Functional Matching for Semantic Web Services, in Proc. of the third International Conference on Service Oriented Computing (ICSOC), pages 115-129, Amsterdam, Netherlands, 2005.
8. Elgedawy, I., Tari, Z., and Thom, J. A.: Correctness-Aware High-Level Functional Matching Approaches For Semantic Web Services, ACM Transactions on the Web, Special Issue on SOC, vol. 2, no. 2, April, 2008.

Providing Scalability for an Automated Web Service Composition Framework

Ertay Kaya[1], Mehmet Kuzu[2], Nihan Kesim Cicekli[1]

[1] Department of Computer Engineering, Middle East Technical University
06531 Ankara TURKEY
[2] Department of Computer Science, University of Texas at Dallas
Richardson, TX 75080 U.S.A.

e1356948@ceng.metu.edu.tr, mxk093120@utdallas.edu, nihan@ceng.metu.edu.tr

Abstract. This paper describes an automatic web service composition and execution system which provides a practical significance with its scalability, i.e. the ability to operate on large service sets in reasonable time. In addition, the service storage mechanism utilized in this system presents an effective method to maintain large service sets. Our system implements some pre-processing to extract information from service descriptions. This information is then used to filter potentially useful services for a composition problem. Only filtered services are used during the AI planning phase which actually generates the composition and execution of web services.

Keywords: Semantic web services, automated service composition and execution, scalability, service filtering.

1 Introduction

Since the emergence of semantic web services and service desription standards like OWL-S [5] and WSDL [6], automated web service composition problem has attracted high attention. In [1], an interleaved web service composition and invocation framework is described, which uses semantic service descriptions annotated with OWL-S and utilizes a novel AI planner called Simplanner [2]. The resiliency of Simplanner to dynamic environments makes replanning possible in case a service fails to execute. The framework also employs some recovery mechanisms to compansate the world altering effects of failed services before initiating replanning. However, this framework fails to be scalable and it is time inefficient in case of data sets containing thousands of services. A promising solution to find the composition is applying some filtering to the available web service domain before running the planner. With the help of filtering, the planner runs on a smaller set of candidate services and returns the plan fastly. Since filtering algorithms deal with large service sets, it becomes mandatory to do some pre-processing which is independent of the given problem.

In this paper, we describe a system which enhances the framework in [1] with scalability and service domain maintenance. Scalability is provided by adapting the pre-processing and filtering steps in [5] to PDDL domain and providing some improvements to these steps. In order to provide domain maintenance, our system uses an in-memory relational database to store the information about available services, which provides a significant improvement to the overall system performance. Our system consists of two modules. The *pre-processing module* takes a set of OWL-S service descriptions with their WSDL representations and converts them to PDDL [12]. These PDDL and WSDL descriptions are stored in a domain database to be used by the *User Request Handling module*.

2   Pre-processing of available services

The main purpose of this module is to decrease the time required for the filtering process by exploiting and storing the service information that can be used by this process. Furthermore, this module enables maintaining large service sets with the help of an in-memory relational domain database. Figure 1 presents the general architecture of the Pre-processing module.

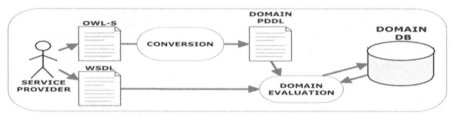

Fig. 1. Pre-processing module and the data flow between its two components

The service conversion component converts the service domain represented in OWL-S to PDDL. The domain evaluation component evaluates some properties of the actions defined in PDDL domain and stores this information in the domain database. The stored information includes PDDL types and predicates with their ontological relationships, PDDL actions and possible chains between actions. Supertypes and subtypes are used to create super-predicates and sub-predicates of PDDL predicates and these are stored in the domain database with the corresponding types and predicates. Possible chains (i.e. whether an action effect can be matched with a precondition predicate so that it can be used by the actions having that precondition) are created by considering the ontological relationships of actions' precondition and effect predicates. Furthermore, user data dependencies of actions are stored. This is done by adapting the term "user data-dependent service" in [5] to PDDL domain: An action with a precondition predicate p, is called an *initial state dependent action* if there is no action in the domain, one of whose effects can be chained with p. In this case, the action can be invoked only if the initial state of the problem provided by the user contains p or one of its sub-predicates. Furthermore, we define an action as *dependent action* if an initial state dependent action is the only action that provides one of the preconditions of this action. This dependent action is also recorded as the initial state dependent action and this process continues in a recursive manner. We also extend the definition in [5] to cover the actions being dependent on the user goal in a similar manner. In addition to PDDL information, WSDL descriptions of the services corresponding to the PDDL actions are also stored in domain database to be used for real service execution. Initial state dependent actions and the goal state dependent actions are together named *user data dependent actions*. These actions are checked during filtering to determine whether they can be used to solve the composition problem.

3 Handling the User Request

In this module, the OWL problem specification provided by user is converted to a PDDL problem and passed to the Filtering component for action selection. After this step, the Composition-Execution component uses the selected actions to find a composition and execute it. Figure 2 shows the overall architecture of this module.

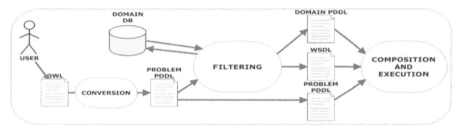

Fig. 2. User Request Handling module and the data flow between its two components: Filtering and Composition-Execution

3.1 Filtering web services

This component is used to filter the services stored in the domain database and eliminate the ones that cannot be used in the composition. The filtering is done based on the user problem in PDDL format. In this component, three different processes run in parallel: 1. Finding unusable actions from the initial state, 2. Finding unusable actions from the goal state, 3. Forward chaining. The first two processes check the initial state and goal state dependent actions which are determined and recorded during pre-processing. Initially all actions in the domain are assumed to be usable. If the initial state does not provide the predicates required by an initial state dependent action, that action is marked as unusable in the domain database. Similarly, the goal state of the problem description is checked for goal state dependent actions. A forward chaining algorithm is used to determine the actions that will be passed to the Composition-Execution module. Firstly, this algorithm retrieves the predicates provided in the problem initial state and finds the actions that can be invoked with the given initial state. Then, the effects of these actions are added to the available predicates and the new actions that can be invoked with the new available predicate set are retrieved from domain database. Ontological hierarchies of predicates are considered in this process. The available predicates are updated again and the algorithm continues to retrieve new usable actions and update the available predicates until the predicates required by the problem goal are satisfied or no more actions can be chained. The algorithm considers the usability of actions while retrieving the actions from the domain database which is determined by the previous two processes concurrently. Filtering module creates a new PDDL domain including the filtered actions only. In addition, WSDL descriptions corresponding to these actions are retrieved from domain database. These two descriptions are passed to the Composition-Execution module with problem PDDL description.

3.2 Composition and Execution

This component retrieves the problem PDDL, filtered domain PDDL and WSDL descriptions of the services from the Filtering module and uses this data to find and execute the composition. The composition and execution processes are executed in an interleaved manner with the help of Simplanner and some service invocation mechanisms. The details of Composition-Execution module are explained in [1].

4 Conclusion

We have described a system that provides two important practical aspects to the web service composition and execution framework described in [1] which are scalability and the ability to maintain large service sets. In the future, we plan to enable parallel execution of Filtering and Composition-Execution components to execute faster composition. This will be achieved by making changes in Simplanner so that it runs with dynamic action domains. With the help of this, Composition-Execution component will run in parallel with Filtering module and the possible actions selected by Filtering module in each level will be added to the dynamic domain of Composition-Execution component.

References

1. Kuzu, M., Automatic Web Service Composition with AI Planning M.Sc. Thesis in Computer Engineering, Department of Middle East Technical University (2009).
2. Sapena, O., Onaindia, E.: Planning in Highly Dynamic Environments: An Anytime Approach for Planning Under Time Constraints. In: Journal of Applied Intelligence, Volume 29, Number 1, pages 90-109 (2007)
3. Polleres A.: AI Planning For Web Service Composition. Presentation, Ilog, Paris, France (2004)
4. Agrawal V., Chafle G., Mittal S., Srivastava B.: Understanding Approaches for Web Service Composition and Execution, IBM Research Report (2007)
5. Bartalos P., Bielikova M.: Semantic Web Service Composition Framework Based on Parallel Processing, 2009 IEEE Conference on Commerce and Enterprise Computing, pp. 495-498 (2009)

Suggest Me a Movie: A Multi-Client Movie Recommendation Application on Facebook

Seda Cakiroglu and Aysenur Birturk[1]

Middle East Technical University, Ankara, Turkey

Abstract. In this study, an online movie recommendation engine that serves on Facebook is developed in order to evaluate social circle effects on user preferences in a trust-based environment. Instead of using single-user profiles, virtual group profiles that present common tastes of the social environments are used.

1 Introduction

Recommender systems aim serving more personalized way of information filtering considering the preferences of people. As a recommendation methodology, Collaborative Filtering emphasizes the importance of user profiles' similarities on the recommendation generations [1]. In this study, the virtual representations of users' social circles are tried to be analyzed based on their linked friend information on social network Facebook.

The strategy of seeing a group of people as a single person and building a single memory structure on these groups has been already studied in the organizational area [3]. Since it has been identified that the recommendations of friends are always preferable to the recommendations of the recommender engines [2], in this study the suggestions are generated considering users' social circles.

1.1 Motivation and Problem Description

Through this paper, the social circle effects on the user preferences are tried to be identified in the recommendation area on a trustful social network platform, Facebook. The aim is generating more innovative suggestions in a more trustable way.

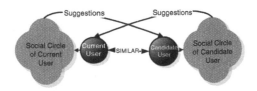

Fig. 1. Similar Users Algorithm

E. Gelenbe et al. (eds.), *Computer and Information Sciences*, Lecture Notes in Electrical Engineering 62, DOI 10.1007/978-90-481-9794-1_63,
© Springer Science+Business Media B.V. 2010

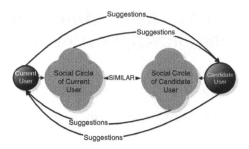

Fig. 2. Similar Social Circles Algorithm

As the first algorithm, the success of the recommendations that are generated based on the common preferences of the social circles of similar users is tried to be indicated (Figure 1). As the second algorithm, the similarity between social circles are considered regardless from personal similarity and the recommendations are generated based on the similar social circles (Figure 2).

In the social circle identification phase, with the aim of increasing virtual social profile trust, instead of the usage of the entire Facebook friend list, inclusion of close related friends is performed by the users themselves by referring the owner of their memorized movie critics. Moreover, the studies showed that what the users really want is understanding the reason of the suggested recommendations [4]. Regarding to this, the generation methodology of the recommendations are shared with the users.

The movie recommendation application, 'Suggest me a Movie' (http://apps. facebook.com/suggestmeamovie) is published on Facebook platform with the intention of gathering data from the users. It is asked to users to comment on movie related questions based on personal experiences and their memorized critics. In the application, personal specific comments include 'I liked it', 'I didn't like it', 'I like to watch' and 'I don't like to watch'. Whereas social environment specific comments include 'My friend, XXX suggested it', 'My friend, YYY says it is bad' with or without personal referring and 'I have never heard it before'.

2   Solution Approach

2.1   Recommendation Generation Based on Social Circles of Similar Users

In Social Circles of Similar Users algorithm, the idea is generating suggestions based on the social circle information of the most similar users.

Here is a representation of idea behind the Social Circles of Similar Users Algorithm (Figure 3). In the diagram the current user bobble symbolizes the user for who suggestions are generated whereas the bobble Candidate User symbolizes any random user that share the same movie taste with the current user. For the current user, suggestions are generated based on the data of social circle of candidate user instead of the data of the candidate user directly.

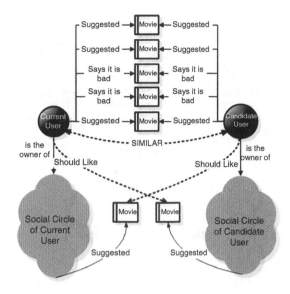

Fig. 3. Usage of User Similarity

The steps of the algorithm are as follows;

1. Retrieve user profile vector of current user. Calculate PCC value between current user profile vector and all user profile vectors in the application.
2. Order the PCC values, select the highest 15 PCC values and add the owner users of corresponding vector to the similar users array.
3. Add all the users that are referred in the application to the similar users array. Find the social circle vectors of the users in the similar user array.
4. Predict a rate for the included items in the selected social circle vectors. Predict for the ones that are not rated by the current user.
5. Order the items based on predicted rates. Start suggesting from the highest rated item to the lowest one.

In the suggestions phase, the virtual social circle profiles of the selected similar users are evaluated irrelevantly from their personal profiles. The movies with higher predicted ratings that are not rated by the current user are selected and suggested to the user [5].

2.2   Recommendation Generation Based on Similar Social Circles

In Similar Social Circles algorithm, the idea is generating suggestions based on the similar social circle information of the users.

In the figure 4, the idea behind the algorithm is stated. The current user bobble indicates the user for who recommendations are generated whereas the candidate user bobble is a random user whose social circle shares the similar

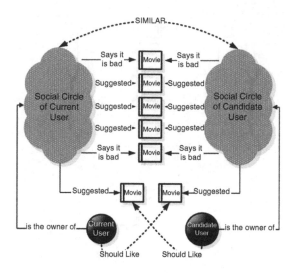

Fig. 4. Usage of Social Circle Similarity

common movie preferences with the social circle of the current user. The suggestions are generated based on the information of social circle of candidate user and candidate user itself to the current user.

The steps of the algorithm are as follows;

1. Retrieve social circle profile vector of current user. Calculate PCC value between current social circle profile vector and all other social circle profile vectors in the application.
2. Order the PCC values and select the highest 15 PCC values and add these groups to the similar group array. Add the owner user profile vectors of the selected groups in the similar group array.
3. Predict a rate for the included items in the selected social circle and user vectors in the similar group array. Predict for the ones that are not rated by the current user.
4. Order the items based on their predicted rates. Start suggesting from the highest rated item to the lowest one.

2.3   Similarity Rank and Predicted Ratings Evaluation

Pearson Correlation Coefficient factor is calculated with the aim of evaluating the similarity rank between two selected vectors [6].

$$PCC_{xy} = \frac{\sum_{h=1}^{n'}(r_{u_x,i_h} - \overline{r_{u_x}}) - (r_{u_y,i_h} - \overline{r_{u_y}})}{\sqrt{\sum_{h=1}^{n'}(r_{u_x,i_h} - \overline{r_{u_x}})^2}\sqrt{\sum_{h=1}^{n'}(r_{u_y,i_h} - \overline{r_{u_y}})^2}} \tag{1}$$

Where, u_x and u_y are the vectors of x user/group and y user/group. n' is the total number of the items that are rated in u_x and/or u_y. r_{u_x,i_h} is the rating that x gives to item i_h. $\overline{r_{u_x}}$ is the average rating of x for all the rated items.

The predicted ratings for the items that are included in the recommendation data profile vectors are evaluated linearly with the given equation [5].

$$\hat{u}_{ij} = \overline{U_i} + \frac{\sum_{j=1}^{k} PCC_{mi}(u_{mj} - \overline{U_m})}{\sum_{j=1}^{k} |PCC_{mi}|} \tag{2}$$

Where, $\hat{u}_{ij}$ is the predicted rating that user i gives to the item j. u_{mj} is the rating that is included in any vector m. $\overline{U_i}$ is the average of user i's ratings.

3   Evaluation

User specific recommended item sets are shared with the users in order to retrieve their real ideas about the suggested movies. The user similarity based recommendations and the social circle similarity based recommendations are served to the users separately indicating their generation algorithms.

Statistical accuracy metrics, mean absolute error (MAE) and root mean squared error (RMSE) are used for the determination of accuracy of the recommendation algorithms [7]. MAE is defined as the average absolute difference between the predicted ratings and the actual user ratings. On the other hand, RMSE is a quadratic equation in which sample set ratings are squared and averaged.

3.1   Evaluation Results

At the end of the cold start phase, the number of the users that commented more than 40 movies is 52. The average number of movies that are commented by these 52 users is 44. However, only 44 of the 52 users have evaluated the recommended data until now. The estimations are performed on those 44 users.

For the 'Recommendation Generation Based on Social Circles of the Similar Users' algorithm, MAE value is estimated as 3.73 and RMSE value is calculated as 0.36. On the other hand, for the algorithm 'Recommendation Generation Based on Similar Social Circle', MAE value is estimated as 2.84 where RMSE value is calculated as 0.26. Considering these results, it is concluded that similar social circle algorithm generates more successful suggestions compared to the social circles of similar users algorithm. Also regarding to the small RMSE values, it is accurate to say that the predictions are very close to the real ranks that are supplied by the users.

Based on the user comments, it is identified that the recommendations that are generated through 'Social Circles of Similar Users' algorithm generates more correct suggestions comparing to the 'Similar Social Circles'algorithm. 38 of 44 users says correct for the recommendations of social circle of similar user algorithm where 35 users says correct for the recommendations of the similar social circle algorithm.

On the other hand, it is identified that users find 'Similar Social Circles' algorithm more innovative comparing to the 'Social Circles of Similar Users' algorithm. All of the users state similar social circle algorithm recommendations as innovative where 41 of 44 users says that the recommendations of social circles of similar users algorithm recommendations are innovative.

Although, the methodology is not exactly the same, for comparison the study of Jung can be declared [8]. Jung applied Friend of Friend methodology on MovieLens data set. The experimental studies show that MAE value range is 2.5-1.75. Although it was better from the current study results, it is necessary to remark that the huge data set of Jung's study is an advantage for generating more accurate suggestions.

4   Conclusions and Future Work

In this paper, a new recommendation algorithm that considers users with their social circles is analyzed through a Facebook application. Two different recommendation algorithms, which are 'Social circles of similar users' and 'Similar social circles', are implemented. The evaluation shows that social circles of similar users algorithm generates more accurate suggestions whereas similar social circles algorithm generates more innovative ones. As future work, grouping of the friends based on different parameters can be applied in order to compare the impact of social groups.

References

1. Sarwar, B. M., Karypis, G., Konstan, J. A., Reidl, J.: Item-based collaborative filtering recommendation algorithms. World Wide Web (2001) 285–295
2. Sinha, R., Swearingen, K.: Comparing recommendations made by online systems and friends. Proceedings of the DELOS-NSF Workshop on Personalization and Recommender Systems in Digital Libraries (2001)
3. Ackerman, M. S.: Augmenting organizational memory: a field study of answer garden. ACM Trans. Inf. Syst. 16 (1998) 203–224
4. Herlocker J., Konstan J. and Riedl J.: Explaining Collaborative Filtering Recommendations. Conference on Computer Supported Cooperative Work (2000) 241–250
5. Papagelis M, and Plexousakis D.: Recommendation Based Discovery of Dynamic Virtual Communities. CAiSE'03, 15th Conference on Advanced Information Systems Engineering (2003)
6. Papagelis M, and Plexousakis D.: Qualitative analysis of user-based and item-based prediction algorithms for recommendation agents. CIA'04, 9th International Workshop on Cooperative Information Agents (2004)
7. Mingrui W.: Collaborative Filtering via Ensembles of Matrix Factorizations. KDD Cup and Workshop (2007)
8. Jung J.: Visualizing Recommendation Flow on Social Network. J-Jugs (2005) 1780–1791

This article was processed using the LaTeX macro package with LLNCS style

Optimal Design of Web Information Contents
for E-Commerce Applications

Alfredo Milani[1], Valentino Santucci[1], Clement Leung[2]

[1]University of Perugia, via Vanvitelli, 1 – Perugia, Italy
{milani@unipg.it, valentino.santucci@dipmat.unipg.it}

[2]Hong Kong Baptist University, Hong Kong
{clement@comp.hkbu.edu.hk}

Abstract. Optimization of web content presentation poses a key challenge for e-commerce applications. Whether considering web pages, advertising banners or any other content presentation media on the web, the choice of the appropriate structure and appearance with respect to the given audience can obtain a more effective and successful impact on users, such as gathering more readers to web sites or customers to online shops. Here, the collective optimization of web content presentation based on the online discrete Particle Swarm Optimization (PSO) model is presented. The idea behind online PSO is to evaluate the collective user feedback as the PSO objective function which drives particles' velocities in the hybrid continuous-discrete space of web content features. The PSO coordinates the process of sampling collective user behaviour in order to optimize a given user-based metric. Experiments in the online banner optimization scenario show that the method converges faster than other methods and avoid some common drawbacks such as local optima and hybrid discrete/continuous features management. The proposed online optimization method is sufficiently general and may be applied to other web marketing or business intelligence contexts.

Keywords: Web marketing optimization, collective behaviour mining, collaborative intelligence.

1 Introduction and Related Work

In Web-based information systems adopting an appropriate structure and appearance with respect to the given user community can raise its impact and effectiveness [11][12]. This is particularly true for e-commerce applications and social networking sites whose aims are to attract more customers or increase the rate of participation. Online advertising is a key enabler of e-commerce and in an advertising banner scenarios, a designer has to compose a web banner by considering a variety of options such as different background colours, available pictures of the product, presentation phrases, font types, and sizes. Typically, the banner designer employs his own skills and his model of the target customer in order to design what he consider the best eye catching or attention catching advertising. The only way for the designer to know if the banner is effective is to submit it to the web and consider users reactions. Managing

E. Gelenbe et al. (eds.), *Computer and Information Sciences*, Lecture Notes
in Electrical Engineering 62, DOI 10.1007/978-90-481-9794-1_64,
© Springer Science+Business Media B.V. 2010

this interactive process for a large number of users is nearly impossible for a banner designer, on the other hand an automatic optimization [13] of the content presentation can exploit the feedback of a large number of online users. Some applications [1][13] has been proposed which try to select the optimal presentation using a voting mechanism (i.e. user feedback, such as number of clicks) among a fixed set of candidate ones, e.g. a set of candidate banners, or by tuning some features parameters by randomly generating candidates to vote [2]. The limit in the first case is that the optimal solution could not be in the fixed set of candidates, while a purely random strategy can hardly find an optimal solution because of combinatorial explosion, especially in presence of features with nearly continuous values, such as colours or image sizes. Particle swarm optimization (PSO) [3][4] technique has recently emerged as an effective strategy for a variety of multidimensional optimization problems. PSO uses the algorithmic metaphor of the dynamic of swarm behaviour in order to coordinate a set of particles, i.e. computational units, which move through a given features domain space. Evolutionary approaches to adaptive web content selection has been previously used in the field of web newspapers and multimedia information retrieval in [5][6] [7].

In this paper, we formulate a strategy based on PSO for generating candidate presentation instances, which eventually converge to the optimal content presentation. A single particle has a current position in the features space, i.e. it represents a content presentation instance. Each particle in the swarm sends a candidate presentation to a set of online users which provide a feedback. Particle positions are updated according to PSO strategy based on the user feedback. Experiments show that the PSO strategy for web content presentation is effective and converges very fast, minimizing the number of sampled candidate presentations, i.e. minimizing the number of non-optimal presentations delivered.

2   PSO for Web Marketing

The principle underlying PSO has been introduced in [3]. The metaphor receives its inspiration from particles models of objects and simulation of collective behaviour of flocks of birds. In PSO, a swarm is composed of a set of particles $P=\{p_1, p_2, ..., p_k\}$. The position of a particle in the n-dimensional space $\mathfrak{R}^n$ corresponds to a candidate solution of a given optimization problem represented by an objective function f: $\Theta \rightarrow \mathfrak{R}$, with $\Theta \subseteq \mathfrak{R}^n$, to be maximized (or minimized).

At any step t, each particle p_i has associated a position $x_{i,t}$, a velocity $v_{i,t}$, where position and velocity are n-dimensional vectors, and $b_{i,t}$ the particle personal best, i.e. the best position of p_i has ever visited until time step t. Moreover, particles are interconnected in a network and can communicate only with their neighbors l_i; in this way each particle can maintains the best position ever found among his l_i's neighbors denoted by $l_{i,t}$.

Each particle in the swarm moves according to its velocity. Position is updated by the vector expression $x_{i,t+1} = x_{i,t} + v_{i,t+1}$, while velocity is updated by $v_{i,t+1} = \omega v_{i,t} + \varphi_1 \beta_{1,t}(b_{i,t} - x_{i,t}) + \varphi_2 \beta_{2,t}(l_{i,t} - x_{i,t})$, where the weights respectively represent the inertia ω, the acceleration factors φ_1, φ_2 and the random factors $\beta_{1,t}, \beta_{2,t}$ which are distributed in

[0,1]. The contribution $(b_{i,t} - x_{i,t})$, the distance from the personal best, has been interpreted as a cognitive component, while $(l_{i,t} - x_{i,t})$ is a social component.

A number of variations to PSO has been proposed for velocity updating or other aspects. A very common one assumes that particles are connected by a complete network and in this case $l_{i,t}$ are substituted by a global l which can be maintained more efficiently. This simple variation is the one used in our approach.

As pointed out in [10] and [3] PSO seems to benefit from the local monotony of objective function f in continuous search spaces, but the same property does not hold in the discrete feature spaces generated by combinatorial problems. Solutions have been proposed for discrete PSO since [8] and more recently [9], while a distinction should be made between *ordered discrete* features, for which a discrete approximation of local monotony hold, and *pure combinatorial* feature for which it does not. Let consider the *discrete* feature *temperature T*, whose domain D_T, is the finite set of ordered values $D_T=\{veryCold, cold, cool, mild, warm, veryWarm, hot, veryHot\}$, if the best value so far for f has been found in position $T=veryWarm$ then is likely that f does not differ much for values close to *veryWarm*. On the other hand a *pure combinatorial* feature domain has a finite number of values which cannot be ordered according to some notion of distance for which an approximation of continuity properties of objective function f hold. For instance the feature *product name* $D_{PN}=\{WeatherPlus, allWeatherInfo, EveryWeather, FastForecasting, Sun\&Rain\}$, containing candidate names for a weather forecasting web site, is *pure combinatorial* since it contains values which have no significant ordering relationship inducing local monotony in objective function f. Moreover the distinction among continuous, discrete ordered and pure combinatorial domains is not so sharp: discrete ordered domains of very large size can be easily managed by continuous approximation, while discrete ordered domain of small cardinality are better regarded as pure combinatorial.

3   An Online PSO Model for Web Marketing Content Presentation

The search space here consists of admissible content presentations. The content presentation search space is described by a feature vector $C=[c_1,...,c_n]$ with $c_i \in D_i$, where D_i are possible alternatives provided by the content presentation designer. In content presentation problems, the domains D_i are, in general, a mix of continuous, discrete and pure combinatorial domains. The particle swarm algorithm proposed here uses a fully connected particle swarm. At each iteration each particle generates a new candidate presentation configuration by moving to a new position $x_{i,t}$ in the search space D. The evaluation of the objective function $f(x_{i,t})$ is realized by submitting the candidate presentation to web users and measuring their feedback.

The users feedback is used in order to determine the personal best, absolute best and in order to perform velocity update. The algorithm aims at maximizing the feedback function. A scheme of the online algorithm is shown in Fig. 1. The set P of particles is initially distributed in a random way in the search space. If the content designer has his own preferred or best candidate it is directly assigned to one particle. Personal best and global best are initially assigned to zero for all particles (i.e. no feedback observed). Velocity updating has an important role in the proposed algorithm. Since it is supposed to have a hybrid continuous/discrete features space, different update functions are used for different classes of dimensional domains. The purpose is to exploit the local continuity for continuous and discrete domains and emphasize the exploration for pure combinatorial domains. In the following is described the update phase of velocity and position which varies, as mentioned above, depending on the domain to which the feature belongs.

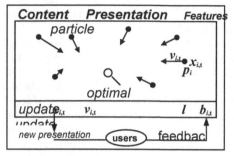

Features(#×size)	C_{eucl}	P_{schw}	C_{schw}	P_{ack}	C_{ack}
Mix (6×2⁶)	860	1.00	980	0.62	1360
Mix (6×2⁶)	1000	0.76	1680	1.00	5800
Cont.(8×2⁷)	800	0.76	1820	0.40	2480
Discrete 1(6×2⁷)	220	1.00	320	1.00	9640
Discrete 2(8×2⁷)	360	1.00	51820	0.80	18580
Discrete 3(10×2⁷)	520	0.00	---	0.00	---
Pure Comb.1(3×2⁶)	2600	1.00	220	1.00	14060
Pure Comb.2(4×2⁶)	44800	1.00	18000	0.57	108920
Pure Comb.3(5×2⁶)	---	0.85	122560	0.00	---

Fig. 1. (a) Online PSO scheme for content presentation and (b) Experimental results

Continuous Features

Position and velocity of continuous features are updated according to the updating functions given above. Features with many discrete values, like *pictureSize*, are considered discrete approximation of continuous position and velocity. Out of bound exceptions are managed by randomly restarting the particle dimension.
$$x_{i,t}$$

Pure Combinatorial Features
The domain of a *pure combinatorial* feature consists of a discrete set of values for which an ordering is not defined. In this case a random extraction which combines both domain exploration and the behaviour of classical PSO approach is used.
For each particle p and for each pure combinatorial feature domain D_c, an appropriate *probability distribution* $P_{Dc,p}$ over the values of D_c is built. Let d_b, d_p, d_l the values of feature D_c respectively for the *global best* position, the *current* particle position and the particle *local best* position, then the distribution is defined as

$$P_{Dc,p}(d_p)=(1+\omega)/n \cdot 1/N_{Dc} \qquad P_{Dc,p}(d_b)=(1+\varphi_1)/n \cdot 1/N_{Dc}$$
$$P_{Dc,p}(d_l)=(1+\varphi_2)/n \cdot 1/N_{Dc} \qquad P_{Dc,p}(d)=1/n \cdot 1/N_{Dc} \quad \forall\ d\in D_c\ d\notin\{ d_b, d_p, d_l \}$$

where $n=|D_c|$ and $N_{Dc,p}$ is a normalization factor: $N_{Dc} = 1+(\omega+\varphi_1+\varphi_2)/n$. The probability distribution used to extract the next particle value can be interpreted as considering all the values equiprobable, except d_b, d_p, d_l, whereas the amplification factors ω, φ_1 and φ_2 gives a greater probability to d_b, d_p and d_l. In other words the amplification factors respectively express, the tendency to remain in the current position (inertial factor ω), and the tendency to move toward the global best (social factor φ_1) or the local best positions (cognitive factor φ_2).

Discrete Ordered Features
Discrete ordered features are content features for which a total order exists. Let $D_d=\{d_1,\dots, d_n\}$ the values of a discrete ordered domain D_j then a probability distribution $P_{Dd,p}$ is built similarly to the case of pure combinatorial features, but reflecting the additional property that "close feature values have close probabilities". The probability distribution is obtained by smoothing the probabilities in the contour of the "centers" d_p d_b and d_l. Initially a quantity $1/n$ is assigned to each value d_i and then

the values in the centers and in the points to their left and to their right are incrementally amplified. Let $\alpha \in \{1+\omega, \ 1+\varphi_1, \ 1+\varphi_2\}$ the amplification factor for a center d_k and let $\beta = \alpha/(\lambda+1)$ where is 2λ is the amount of values centered in d_k whose probability will be amplified with *smoothness* β. All the λ values d_{k-j} (d_{k+j}) at the left (right) of index k will be amplified with parameter $\alpha_j = \beta^* |\lambda +1-j|$, process is iterated for every center d_p, d_b and d_l and the final quantities are then normalized to obtain the probability distribution $P_{Dd,p}$. The parameter λ determines the interval of features values where the $(1+\alpha_j)$ amplification is applied, it is easy to see that values near the *global optimum*, *local optimum*, and *current* particle values tend to be preferred, while the initial distribution $1/n$ ensures that each domain value has a non null probability of being selected.

4 Experiments and Discussion

Experiments have been carried out using the hidden values technique developed in [1] where the PSO algorithm make external call to different online user feedback functions. Three different *user feedback functions* has been experimented: (1) the *Euclidean feedback* f_{eucl}, which returns the Euclidean distance from the optimal solution, (2) f_{schw} a relaxed version of the *Schwefel*'s double sum function [2] and (3) the *Ackley* function f_{ack} [2].

$$f_{eucl}(x) = \sqrt{\sum_{i=1}^{D} x_i^2} \tag{1}$$

$$f_{schw}(x) = \sum_{i=1}^{D} \sum_{j=1}^{i} x_j^2 \tag{2}$$

$$f_{ack}(x) = -20 \exp\left(-0.2\sqrt{\frac{1}{D}\sum_{i=1}^{D} x_i^2}\right) - \exp\left(\frac{1}{D}\sum_{i=1}^{D}\cos\left(2\pi x_i^2\right)\right) + 20 + e \tag{3}$$

[1]. Feedback function f_{eucl} and f_{schw} are unimodal functions, while f_{ack} is a multimodal function, in order to investigate the behaviour of online PSO approach both with single optimal value and multiple local optima. For each of the three benchmark *user feedback* functions, nine different types of domain combinations with homogeneous and hybrid features have been tested: the hybrid features mix (*Mixed Banner Real*), an hybrid artificial case (*Mixed Banner Artificial)* and six cases of homogeneous features of different type and size which has been used for performance comparison (*Continuous, Discrete1-3, Purely Combinatorial 1-3*).

The results shows that the performance of convergence probability drops with purely combinatorial domains, or with an increasing number of discrete ordered features (f_{schw} and f_{ack} do not converge with 10 discrete ordered features of size 128) with respect to continuous domains. On the other hand the algorithm always determines the optimal content design in all hybrid cases, *Mixed Banner Real* and *Mixed Banner Artificial*, it also converge (62%) with "difficult" user models like the *Ackley* function f_{ack} where multiple local minima are present.

The convergence speed for the hybrid cases is also quite encouraging: the $\underline{C_{best}}$ value of NFE in all the user feedback models lies within a range of one to six thousands fitness evaluations, i.e. user contacts, which appears to be a realistic size for many online applications.

5 Conclusions

A method based on online PSO has been introduced and experimented in order to model the process of optimizing the design of content presentations by evaluating the collective feedback of online users, which is regarded as PSO fitness.

The PSO particles moves in the features space of the presentation objects, each new position correspond to a new content presentation, the PSO dynamics guided by user feedback guarantees convergence toward the optimal content presentation.

A novel method to manage *purely combinatorial* and *discrete ordered* feature domains has been introduces. The method is based on building probabilities distributions biased toward the global optimal, the local optimal and the current particle feature values. The biased probabilities reflect the typical PSO inertial, local and global search strategies. Experiments shows that the online PSO method converges for a realistic hybrid feature mix after a realistic number of user feedback evaluation.

References

[1] M. Bolin, M. Webber, P. Rha, T. Wilson, R.C. Miller. "Automation and customization of rendered web pages". In Proc. 18th ACM Symp. on User interface Software and Technology, ACM Press, New York, USA 2005, pp. 163-172.

[2] K. Marriott, B. Meyer, L. Tardif. "Fast and efficient client-side adaptivity for SVG". In Proc.11th Int.Conf.onWorld Wide Web, Hawaii, USA, May 07, 2002.

[3] J. Kennedy, R. Eberhart. "Particle swarm optimization". In Proc. of IEEE Conf. on Neural Networks, IEEE Press, 1995, pp. 1942-1948.

[4] R. Poli, J. Kennedy, T. Blackwell. "Particle swarm optimization. An overview.". Swarm Intelligence, 1(1): 33-57, 2007.

[5] A. Milani. "Online genetic algorithms", in International Journal of Information Theories and Applications, n.1 Vol.11, pp.20-28, (2004), ISSN 1310-0513.

[6] J.H. Lin, C.K. Wang, C.H. Lee (Taiwan). "Particle swarm optimization for web newspaper layout problem" in J.T. Yao (Ed) Web Technologies, Applications, and Services – 2006 pp. 524-026 ISBN0-88986-575-2.

[7] C. Leung, A. Chan. "Community adaptive search engines" in Int.J.of Advanced Intelligence Paradigms(IJAIP), Special Issue on Intelligent Techniques for Personalization and Recommendation, Inderscience, 2008, ISSN 1755-0386.

[8] J. Kennedy, R. Eberhart. "A discrete binary version of the particle swarm algorithm". In Proc. of the IEEE Conf. on Systems, Man, Cybernetics, IEEE Press, 1997, pp. 4104-4108.

[9] X.H. Zhi, X.L. Xing, Q.X. Wang, Zhang. "A discrete PSO method for generalized TSP problem", 2004. Proceedings of 2004 Int. Conference on Machine Learning and Cybernetics Vol. 4, 26-29 Aug. 2004, pp. 2378-2383.

[10] R. Poli. "Analysis of the publications on the applications of particle swarm optimisation", J. of Artificial Evolution and Applications, Article ID 685175, 10 pages, 2008. ISSN 1755-0386.

[11] W.S. Chan, A. Milani, C.H.C. Leung, J. Liu. "An architectural paradigm for collaborative semantic indexing of multimedia data objects", LNCS in Springer Verlag.

[12] A. Bunt, G. Carenini, C . Conati. "Adaptive co/ntent presentation for the web", in P. Brusilovsky, A. Kobsa, & W. Nejdl (Eds.), The Adaptive Web. Berlin: Springer, (2007), pp. 409-432.

[13] A. Jameson. "Adaptive interfaces and agents", in Jacko, J., Sears, A. (eds.): Human-Computer Interaction Handbook, Erlbaum, Mahwah, NJ (2003), pp. 305-330.

Semantic Music Information Retrieval Using Collaborative Indexing and Filtering

C. H. C. Leung and W. S. Chan

Hong Kong Baptist University, Hong Kong
{clement@comp.hkbu.edu.hk}

Abstract. With the rapid development of multimedia technology, digital music has become increasingly available and it constitutes a significant component of multimedia contents on the Internet. Since digital music can be represented in various forms, formats, and dimensions, searching such information is far more challenging than text-based search. While some basic forms of music retrieval is available on the Internet, these tend to be inflexible and have significant limitations. Currently, most of these music retrieval systems only rely on shallow music information (e.g., metadata, album title, lyrics, etc). Here, we present an approach for deep content-based music information retrieval, which focuses on high-level human perception, incorporating subtle nuances and emotional impression on the music (e.g., music styles, tempo, genre, mood, instrumental combinations etc.). We also provide a critical evaluation of the most common current Music Information Retrieval (MIR) approaches and propose an innovative adaptive method for music information search that overcomes the current limitations. The main focus of our approach is concerned with music discovery and recovery by collaborative semantic indexing and user relevance feedback analysis. Through successive usage of our indexing model, novel music content indexing can be built from deep user knowledge incrementally and collectively by accumulating users' judgment and intelligence.

Keywords: Collaborative filtering, multimedia indexing, music information retrieval.

1 Introduction and Related Work

Digital music has become increasingly prevalent and it constitutes a significant component of multimedia contents on the Internet. Since digital music can be represented in various forms, formats, and dimensions, searching such information is far more challenging than text-based search. While some basic forms of music retrieval is available on the Internet, these tend to be inflexible and have significant limitations. Currently, most of these music retrieval systems only rely on shallow music information (e.g., metadata, album title, lyrics, etc). Here, we present an approach for deep content-based music information retrieval, which focuses on high-level human perception, incorporating subtle nuances and emotional impression on the music (e.g., music styles, tempo, genre, mood, instrumental combinations etc.).

E. Gelenbe et al. (eds.), *Computer and Information Sciences*, Lecture Notes
in Electrical Engineering 62, DOI 10.1007/978-90-481-9794-1_65,
© Springer Science+Business Media B.V. 2010

The chief objective of effective music information retrieval is the accurate transfer of musical information from a database to a user [1], [4], [6], [11], [12]. Since music can have different characteristics and its content can be represented in various ways and formats, effectively retrieving music from a large music database can be very challenging. In an effective "concept-based" music retrieval system, efficient and meaningful indexing is necessary [7], [8]. Due to current technological limitations, it is impossible to extract the semantic content of music data objects automatically [13], [14].

Present music information retrieval approaches are mainly focused on shallow music content, such as melody search from users entering via a piano keyboard interface [10], query by humming QBH [3], contour-based parsons code search [10], rhythm-based tapping search [10], and collaborative social tagging [2]. However, these approaches only support limited music elements in the search domain and do not provide high-level semantic concept search (e.g. human perceptions of the music). In [9], a music search engine based on the automatic derived descriptions by making use of methods from Web Retrieval and Music Information Retrieval (MIR) is proposed. Their method makes use of the information found in the ID3 tags, such as the values of the fields "artist", "album" and "title", of the music files. However, this approach only focuses on the metadata (e.g., title, album, track number, etc.) of the music files. While this kind of information is easily extracted, semantic music information extraction is far more difficult (e.g., music style, musical arrangements, chord progressions, etc.). In [15], a creative MIR approach based on personal emotion is suggested, which is closer to our proposed method. However, our proposed method is not just exclusively concerned with the human personal subjective perception, but also the general human perception of the community since we collect their perceptions through analyzing their search history and behviour. Here, we base our innovative concept-based approach on music search by adaptive collaborative indexing.

2 System Structure

Our system consists of different levels for supporting music search. It includes the user level, the interface level, and the database level. The database level contains two sublevels, query level and index level.

2.1 The User and System Interface Levels

The users are the ones who interact with the search system via the system interface. They can search music objects by submitting query with keywords. After the system has processed a query, they can receive search results from the system interface and proceed to provide feedback through the system interface. The system interface acts as a bridge between users and ultimately the system database. It captures user query input with search criteria, search result feedback and selection from the user, and employ the information to update the index.

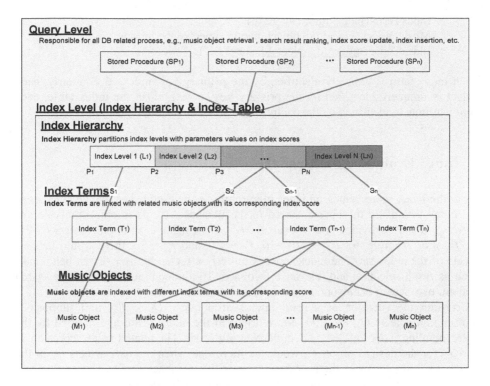

Fig. 1. The System Database Level

2.2   The System Database Level

The system database level is the core part of the system. It consists of a query level and an index level (Fig. 1). The query level consists of stored procedures that are responsible for all database related processes, such as index insertion, index score updating, object ranking and retrieval for the entire system. The index level is an index table organized as a hierarchy, which links music objects and index terms with the corresponding index score. The index score indicates the importance of the index term that is related to the music object. The following sections will focus on discussing the system database level.

We consider a set of music objects $\{O_j\}$, where the characteristics or semantic contents of each object O_j cannot be extracted automatically. Typically, a music object would be a song, represented in digital formats such as mp3, midi, or wave. More generally, it may be a computer-generated music score or manually produced manuscript. For every O_j, it links with an index set I_j that consists of a number of elements: $I_j = \{e_{j1}, e_{j2}, ..., e_{jMj}\}$. Each index element e is a triple, such that $e_{jk} = (t_{jk}, s_{jk}, o_j)$, where t_{jk} is an index term ID, s_{jk} is the score associated with t_{jk}, and O_j is the object ID. The higher the score s_{jk}, the more important is the index term t_{jk} to the object O_j. The relationship of t_{jk}, s_{jk}, and O_j can be represented as:

IndexTerm (<u>index_id</u>, index_term)
MusicObject (<u>object_id</u>, object_name, object_description, …)
IndexTable (<u>index_id</u>, <u>object_id</u>, score, …)

Each index term is uniquely identified by the primary key, index_id. Similarly, each object is uniquely identified by the primary key, object_id. In the index table, each item is uniquely identified by the composite key, index_id and object_id.

3 Index Evolution and Growth

From the index score values, an index hierarchy may be established, which consists of the index sets of all the objects stored in the database. By partitioning the value of score s_{jk}, it can be divided into N levels $L_1, L_2, …, L_N$ using a set of parameters $P_1, P_2, …, P_N$. For example, for $P_1 = 0$, $P_2 = 10$, $P_3 = 20$, and $P_4 = 30$, there would be four levels of the index set. The index score is directly affected by user search behaviour, such as result selection and relevance feedback. By the continuous use of the search system, user search behaviour can be collected and analyzed.

Consider the situation of a user input search query $Q(T_1, T_2)$, and suppose N multimedia objects $O_1, O_2,…,O_n$ are returned in the query result and ordered by the corresponding score $S_1, S_2, …., S_n$ in descending order. The related index scores on T_1 and T_2 for the desired object O_x would be increased when the user selects O_x in the query result list, or when the user provides positive feedback on O_x. These two cases would increase the related index scores on T_1 and T_2 for the desired object O_x by a predefined value. In contrast, the related index scores on T_1 and T_2 for the desired object O_x would be decreased when the user provides negative feedback on O_x. Furthermore, the related index scores on T_1 and T_2 for all objects $O_1, O_2,…,O_n$ in the query result would be decreased when the user does not select any object on the query result list. These two cases would decrease the related index scores by a predefined value.

In the index growth approach, consider an object K that is indexed with a term T_1. K can be searched by a user query which contains T_1 and many objects may be returned in the query result since many objects are indexed with T_1. Among these returned objects, a user can distinguish objects by adding another index term T_2 to K. Thus, the user can search the desired object by entering both index terms in the search query. Consider the searching of the song "Clair de Lune", composed by Debussy, and we assume that the music object is indexed with the term "Debussy" initially. Users can search this song by the term "Debussy", but sometimes, some user query would be more specific, with both search terms "Debussy" and "Clair de Lune" used. The same objects would be returned in the result when searching by the term "Debussy", since the term "Clair de Lune" is not indexed yet. Eventually, the user would select the object "Clair de Lune" and this suggests that a new index term, "Clair de Lune", may be useful for indexing this data object. Thus, the new index term would be included in the lowest level of the index hierarchy for this object. For every query that specifies both terms, "Debussy" and "Clair de Lune", the user on selecting this music object will cause an increase in the score of the index terms for that object. Thus, the score of the index would be gradually increased and the new index term would be properly installed. Through progressive usage, the indexing of music objects would be enriched, and such attributes as "Slow Bossa", "Oistrakh", "Tremelo Strings" "Arpeggios" or "Stradivarius" may be indexed for a music object.

To ensure that newly added music objects have a reasonable chance of being discovered and processed, our system incorporates a degree of variation in the return of search results. After considerable usage, the high scored multimedia objects always rank near the top of the search results. Generally, users tend to be interested in the highly ranked objects. Consequently, the high scored objects always have greater chance of increasing the score while the chance for the newly added objects appearing in the result list would be reduced. Thus, the newly added objects would be ranked very low and nearly "hidden". In order to optimize the search results, our search system would introduce small degrees of perturbations so as to allow constructive variations in the result. When considering a large number of objects returned by a query result, the users may not reach their desired object since the target object always rank very low and nearly hidden. By exploiting the random variations introduced through Genetic Algorithms, those "hidden" objects would have a chance of being promoted to a higher ranking position and discovered eventually.

4 Conclusions

Digital music has been increasing at an accelerated pace, and a mismatch of creation and indexing rates necessitates a radically new approach to solve the music object retrieval problem. Individual indexing of music objects is labour intensive and has a number of disadvantages. In the context of ROC analysis [5], these are (i) false positives – i.e. wrongly adding an index term through personal subjectivity which is not shared by the wider community, and (ii) false negatives – i.e. the omission of relevant properties due to the inability to cover and capture all the nuances and deep semantics of the music.

Our system is able to overcome (i) by having a resilient, community validated structure which allows personal subjectivity to be filtered off through a robust scoring system, and (ii) by exploiting collective assessment and perception of music objects through continuous usage by the community. By capturing, analyzing and interpreting user response and query behaviour, the patterns of searching and finding music objects may be established. Within the present paradigm, the semantic index may be dynamically constructed, validated, and built-up, and the performance of the system will tend to increase as time progresses. Our system also incorporates a high degree of robustness and fault-tolerance whereby inappropriate index terms will be gradually eliminated from the index, while appropriate ones will be reinforced. By incorporating genetic variations into the design, our system will allow music objects which may otherwise be hidden to be discovered.

Acknowledgements. This research is supported by HK Research Grants Council GRF 210709.

References

1. Crawford, T.: "Music Information Retrieval and the Future of Musicology", Technical Report for the Online Chopin variorum Edition project, (2005).
2. Bischoff, K., Firan, C. S., Nejdl, W., and Paiu, R.: "Can All Tags be Used for Search?" In CIKM '08: Proceedings of the 17th ACM Conference on Information and Knowledge Management, pages 193-202, New York, NY, USA, ACM, (2008).
3. Dannenberg, R. B., Birmingham, W. P., Pardo, B., Hu, N., Meek, C., and Tzanetakis, G.: "A Comparative Evaluation of Search Techniques for Query-By-Humming using the Musart Testbed", Journal of the *American* Society for Information *Science* and *Technology*, 58(5): 687-701 (2007).
4. Downie, J. S.: "Music Information Retrieval", Annual Review of Information Science and Technology, 37:295– 340, (2003).
5. Fawcett, T.: "An Introduction to ROC Analysis", Pattern Recognition Letters, 27:861–874, (2006).
6. Fingerhut, M.: "Music Information Retrieval, or How to Search for (and maybe find) Music and Do Away with Incipits", In Proceedings of the IAML-IASA Congress, (2004).
7. Go'mez, J. and Vicedo, J. L.: "Next-generation Multimedia Database Retrieval", IEEE Multimedia, 14(3):106 – 107, (2007).
8. Goth, G.: "Multimedia Search: Ready or Not?", Distributed Systems Online, IEEE, 5(7). (2004).
9. Knees, P. et al.: "A Music Search Engine Built Upon Audio-based and Web-based Similarity Measures," In Proceedings of the ACM SIGIR 2007, Amsterdam (2007).
10. Musicpedia: The Open Music Encyclopedia. http://www.musicpedia.org
11. Lesaffre, M.: "Music Information Retrieval: Conceptual Framework, Annotation and User Behaviour", PhD thesis, Faculty of Arts and Philosophy, Department of Art, Music and Theatre Sciences, Ghent University, (2006).
12. Orio, N.: "Music Retrieval: A Tutorial and Review", Foundations and Trends in Information Retrieval, 1(1):1-90. Now Publishers Inc. (2006).
13. Snoek, C. G. M., Worring, M., Gemert, J. C. van, Beusebroek, J. M., and Smeulders, A. W. M.: "The Challenge Problem for Automated Detection of 101 Semantic Concepts in Multimedia", In Multimedia '06: Proceedings of the 14th annual ACM international conference on Multimedia, pages 421-430, New York, NY, USA, ACM, (2006).
14. Yang, B. and Hurson A. R.: "Ad Hoc Image Retrieval using Hierarchical Semantic-based Index", In AINA '05: Proceedings of the 19th international conference on advanced information networking and applications, pages 629-634, Washington, DC, USA, IEEE Computer Society, (2005).
15. Yang, Y.H. et al.: "Personalized Music Emotion Recognition," In Proceedings of the SIGIR 2009, Boston, Massachusetts (2009).

9 Discovery Science

Efficient Algorithms for Discovering Frequent and Maximal Substructures from Large Semistructured Data

Hiroki Arimura

Division of Computer Science, Hokkaido University
N14, W9, Sapporo 060-0814, Japan
Tel: +81-11-706-7678, Fax: +81-11-706-7680
E-mail: arim@ist.hokudai.ac.jp

Abstract. In this paper, we review recent advances in efficient algorithms for *semi-structured data mining*, that is, discovery of rules and patterns from structured data such as sets, sequences, trees, and graphs. After introducing basic definitions and problems, We present efficent algorithms for frequent and maximal pattern mining for classes of sets, sequences, and trees. In particular, we explain general techniques, called the *rightmost expansion* and *PPC-extension*, which are powerful tools for designing efficient algorithms. We also give examples of applications of semi-structured data mining to real world data.

1 Introduction

Data mining. By rapid progress of high-speed networks and large-scale storage technologies in 1990s, a huge amount of electronic data has been available on computers and databases distributed over the Internet. *Knowledge Discovery in Databases* or *Data Mining* [2] is a formal study on efficient methods for discovering interesting rules or patterns in these massive electronic data. The study of data mining started since the early 1990s, quickly expanded in thoery and practice in the late 1990s, and became one of the major branches of computer science and data engineering. Although data mining has its roots in machine learning, statistics, the current data mining technologies focus on efficiency and scalability of mining algorithms as well as identificaition of unknown rules and patterns.

Semi-structured data. Massive electronic data of new types, called *semi-structured data*, have been emerged in the late 1990s [1]. The largest example of semi-structured data is the World Wide Web (WWW), which is the collection of Web pages and XML documents on the Internet, which is sometimes reffered to as the largest collection of knowledge that the human being ever had. Hence, there exist demands for efficient algorithms to extract useful knowledge from these semi-structured data.

Traditionally, data mining mainly deals with well-structured data, e.g., transaction databases or relational databases, which have table-like structures. On the

E. Gelenbe et al. (eds.), *Computer and Information Sciences*, Lecture Notes
in Electrical Engineering 62, DOI 10.1007/978-90-481-9794-1_66,
© Springer Science+Business Media B.V. 2010

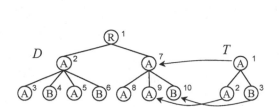

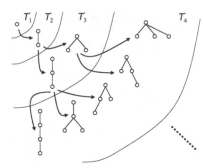

Fig. 1. A data tree D and a pattern tree T on the set $\mathcal{L} = \{A, B\}$ of labels

Fig. 2. A search graph for (unlabeled) ordered trees

other hand, these semi-structured data are (i) *huge*, (ii) *heterogeneous* collections of (iii) *weakly-structured* data that do not have rigid structures. Thus, we cannot directly apply these traditional data mining technologies to semi-structured data. For this reason, semi-structured data mining has been extensively studied since 2000.

In this paper, we present efficient semisturucured data mining algorithms for discovering rules and patterns from structured data such as sequence, trees, and graphs. Especially, we describe basic techniques, called *rightmost expansion* and *PPC-extension*, for designing efficient algorithms for frequent and maximal pattern discovery from such semi-structured data.

2   Efficient Frequent Pattern Mining Algorithms

2.1   Frequent Ordered Tree Mining

Tree mining is to find all subtrees appearing more than a specified number of times in a given tree-structured data. We presented an efficient algorithm FREQT [3] that finds all frequent ordered tree paterns in a given tree database. The key is efficient enumeration of labeled ordered trees [3, 25].

In tree mining, data and patterns are modeled by *labeled ordered trees* as shown in Fig. 1. An *ordered tree* over a label alphabet $\Sigma = \{A\ B\ ...\}$ is a rooted tree T where each node x is labeled with a symbol $lab_T(x)$ from Σ, and the order of siblings matters. We denote by V_T and $root_T$ the node set and the root of T, respectively. We denote by $\mathcal{OT}$ and $\mathcal{UT}$ the classes of labeled ordered trees and unordered trees. For ordered trees P and T, we say P matches Q ($P \sqsubseteq Q$) if there exists a *matching function* $\phi : V_P \to V_T$ from P to T that satisfies the following conditions (i) – (iv): (i) ϕ is one-to-one; (ii) ϕ preserves the parent-child relation; (iii) ϕ preserves the sibling relation; (iv) ϕ preserves the node label. Intuitively, P matches T if P is a substructure of T. Then, the node $y = \phi(root_P)$ is called an *occurrence* of P in T. We denote by $\Phi(P\ T)$ the set of all matching functions from P to T.

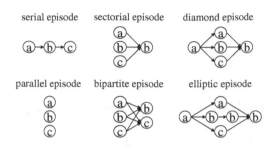

Fig. 3. Examples of subclasses of episodes

Problem. (frequent tree mining) Given an input collection $\mathcal{T} = \{T_1 \ldots T_m\} \subseteq \mathcal{OT}$ of ordered trees and a nonnegative integers $0 \leq \sigma \leq |T|$ called a *minimum frequency threshold*, find all *frequent* ordered trees $P \in \mathcal{OT}$ appearing in $\mathcal{T}$ with frequency $freq(P\ \mathcal{T}) = |\{\ \phi(root_P) : \phi \in \Phi(P\ T)\ \}| \geq \sigma$.

A basic idea of the algorithm is to build a spanning tree on the search space of frequent ordered tree patterns, called an *enumeration tree* $\mathcal{E}$ (Fig. 2). By using $\mathcal{E}$, we can systematically enumerate all the distinct ordered tree patterns without duplicates by starting from the empty tree $\perp$ of size 0 and by expanding (or *growing*) an already generated tree of size $k-1$ (a *parent tree*) by attaching a new node to yield a larger tree of size k (a *child tree*) for every $k \geq 1$.

However, a straightforward implementation of this idea leads exponential number of the duplication for one tree. To avoid duplicates, we developed a technique called the *rightmost expansion* ([3, 25]), where attachment of a new node is restricted to only the rightward positions on the rightmost branch of the parent tree. We extended FREQT for frequent unordered tree mining by canonical tree technique [4].

2.2   Frequent Sequence Episode Mining

It is one of the important tasks in data mining to discover frequent patterns from time-related data. Mannila et al. [21] introduced the episode mining to discover frequent episodes in an event sequence. An *episode* is an acyclic labeled digraphs (DAGs) as shown in Fig. 3, where labels correspond to events and arcs represent a temporal precedent-subsequent relation in an event sequence. Classes of episodes are rich representation of temporal relationship in time-series data. Furthermore, we can use additional constraints formulated by a sliding window of a fixed time width.

Mannila et al. [21] presented efficient algorithms for mining classes of *parallel and serial episodes*, which are sets and linear chains of events, respectively. They also considered a mining of general episodes that have DAG structures. Unfortunately, its complexity is rather high due to the inherent computational hardness of subgraph matching. To overcome this difficulty, we presented efficent episode mining algorithms for subclasses of episodes such as *sectoria, diamond, elliptic*, and *bipartite episodes* [19,18]. (Fig. 3). All of these algorithms have polynomial delay and space complexities, and thus they find all frequent episodes in polynomial time per episode with small memory footprint.

3   Efficient Maximal Pattern Mining Algorithms

Maximal Pattern Discovery. Maximal pattern discovery (or *closed* pattern discovery) is one of the most important topics in recent studies of data mining. Assuming a class of patterns and associated partial ordering over patterns indicating a generalization or subsumption order, a *maximal pattern* is such a pattern that is maximal with respect to the subsumption ordering (or the generalization relation) among an equivalence class of patterns having the same set of occurrences in a database.

For some known classes of patterns, such as itemsets and sequence motifs [2], maximal patterns enjoy a nice property that maximal patterns are uniquely determined in each equivalence class of patterns w.r.t. a given database. Also, it is known that the number of frequent maximal patterns is much smaller than that of frequent patterns on most realworld datasets, while the frequent maximal patterns still contain the complete information of the frequency of all frequent patterns. Thus, the complete set of maximal patterns give a compact representation for all frequent patterns. Maximal pattern discovery is useful to increase the performance and the comprehensivity of data mining.

Depth-first Maximal Pattern Discovery algorithms. For maximal pattern discovery, we have developed the following efficient algorithms for finding all maximal patterns from a given collection of data.

- LCM (*Linear-time Closed Itemset Miner*) for maximal sets [24]. (Fig. 4)
- MAXMOTIF (*Maximal Motif Miner*) for mining maximal sequences [5].
- CLOATT (*Closed Atribute Tree Miner*) for mining maximal trees [6].
- MAXGEO (*Maximal Geometric Subgraph Miner*) for mining maximal geometric graphs [9].
- MAXPICTURE for mining maximal 2-dimensional subpictures [7].

All algorithms adopt depth-first search strategy unlike the previous maximal pattern algorithms, and are light-weight high-speed mining algorithms that operate in polynomial time per pattern and in polynomial space with respect to the input size only and in dependent of the number of output maximal patterns. For the purpose, we developed as a basic technique for maximal pattern discovery, the PPC-extension (prefix-preserving extension) technique. Fig 4 shows the search structure of PPC-extension in LCM algorithm. For details, see [24].

Recently, we succeeded to give a uniform algorithmic framework [11] for constructing polynomial delay polynomial space algorithms for maximal pattern mining by generalizing the above results including mining closed sequences, graphs, and pictures.

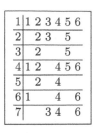

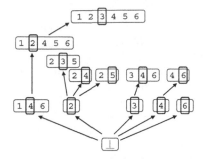

Fig. 4. A transaction database $\mathcal{T}$ on items $\Sigma = \{1,2,3,4,5,6\}$ (left), where each row represents a record. All maximal (closed) item sets generated (right), where each arrow indicates a generation of a child from a parent by the PPC extension.

4   Conclusion

In this talk, we reviewed efficient mining algorithms for large semi-structured data. Finally, we mention applications of semi-structured data mining. Frequent tree miners and optimized tree miners, such as FREQT and OPTT are used to apply standard statistical machine learning techniques, such as *support vector machines* (SVM) and *statistical modeling* to tree and graph structured data [23, 22]. They are also used for the *tree/graph boosting* by extending Boosting algorithms, such as ADABOOST [15], to tree data. We also applied a set of sequential episode mining algorithms to bio-medical data mining, e.g. [19, 20], to extract a collection of episodes representing interaction patterns among a set of antibiotics and bacteria, such as *replacements of bacteria*, in bacterial culture data obtained in the real clinical record data. Further applications will be an interesting future problem.

Acknowledgment. The results presented in this talk are obtained in the joint works with Takeaki Uno, Shin-ichi Nakano, Shin-ich Minato, Tatsuya Asai, Takashi Katoh, and Kouichi Hirata. The author would like to express sincere thanks to them.

References

1. S. Abiteboul, P. Buneman, D. Suciu, *Data on the Web*, Morgan Kaufmann, 2000.
2. R. Agrawal, H. Mannila, R. Srikant, H. Toivonen, A. I. Verkamo, Fast discovery of association rules, *Advances in Knowledge Discovery and Data Mining, Chapter 12*, AAAI Press / The MIT Press, 1996.
3. T. Asai, K. Abe, S. Kawasoe, H. Arimura, H. Sakamoto, S. Arikawa, Efficient Substructure Discovery from Large Semi-structured Data, *Proc. SDM'02*, 2002.
4. T. Asai, H. Arimura, T. Uno, S. Nakano, Discovering frequent substructures in large unordered trees, Discovery Science 2003, LNCS 2843, 47–61, 2003.
5. H. Arimura, T. Uno, An efficient polynomial space and polynomial delay algorithm for enumeration of maximal motifs in a sequence, *Journal of Combinatorial Optimization*, 13, 243–262, 2006.

6. H. Arimura, T. Uno, An output-polynomial time algorithm for mining frequent closed attribute trees, *Proc. ILP'05*, LNAI 3625, 1–19, August 2005.
7. H. Arimura and T. Uno, A polynomial space and polynomial delay algorithm for enumerating maximal two-dimensional patterns with wildcards, *Technical Report*, TCS-TR-A-06-19, DCS, Hokkaido Univ., 18 July 2006.
8. H. Arimura, Efficient algorithms for mining frequent and closed patterns from semi-structured data (invited talk), *Proc. PAKDD'08, LNAI 5012*, 2–13, 2008.
9. H. Arimura, T. Uno and S. Shimozono, Time and space efficient discovery of maximal geometric graphs, *Proc. Discovery Science 2007*, LNAI 4755, 42–55, 2007.
10. Hiroki Arimura and Takeaki Uno, Mining Maximal Flexible Patterns in a Sequence, *Proc. LLLL'07*, LNAI 4914, 2008.
11. H. Arimura and Takeaki Uno, Polynomial-delay and polynomial-space algorithms for mining closed sequences, graphs, and pictures in accessible set systems, *Proc. the 9th SIAM Int'l Conf. on Data Mining (SDM2009)*, 1087-1098, 2009.
12. T. Asai, H. Arimura, K. Abe, S. Kawasoe, S. Arikawa, Online algorithms for mining semi-structured data stream, *Proc. ICDM'02*, IEEE, 27–34, 2002.
13. T. Asai, H. Arimura, T. Uno, S. Nakano, Discovering frequent substructures in large unordered trees, *Proc. Discovery Science 2003*, LNAI, Springer, 2003.
14. D. Avis, K. Fukuda, Reverse search for enumeration, *Discrete Applied Mathematics*, 65(1–3), 21–46, 1996.
15. Y. Freund, R. E. Schapire, A decision-theoretic generalization of on-line learning and an application to boosting, J. Comput. Syst. Sci., 55(1): 119-139, 1997.
16. D. Gunopulos, H. Mannila, R. Khardon, and H. Toivonen, Data mining, hypergraph transversals, and machine learning, *Proc. PODS'97*, ACM, 209–216, 1997.
17. A. Inokuchi, T. Washio, H. Motoda, Complete mining of frequent patterns from graphs: mining graph data, *Machine Learning*, 50(3), 321–354, 2003.
18. T. Katoh, H. Arimura and K. Hirata, Mining frequent k-partite episodes from event sequences, *Proc. Discovery Science 2009*, LNAI 5808, 136–151, 2009.
19. T. Katoh, H. Arimura and K. Hirata, A polynomial-delay polynomial-space algorithm for extracting frequent diamond episodes from event sequences, *Proc. PAKDD'09*, LNAI 5476, Springer, 172–183, 2009.
20. T. Katoh, K. Hirata, H. Arimura, S. Yokoyama and K. Matsuoka, Extracting sequential episodes representing replacements of bacteria from bacterial culture data, Proc. Complex Medical Engineering 2009, IEEE/ICME, 2009.
21. H. Mannila, H. Toivonen, A. I. Verkamo Discovery of frequent episodes in event sequences, *Data Mining and Knowledge Discovery* 1, 259.289, 1997.
22. S. Morinaga, H. Arimura, T. Ikeda, Y. Sakao, S. Akamine, Key Semantics Extraction by Dependency Tree Mining, Proc. KDD'05, ACM, 666-671, 2005.
23. Koji Tsuda, Taku Kudo, Clustering graphs by weighted substructure mining, ICML 2006, 953–960, 2006.
24. T. Uno, T. Asai, Y. Uchida, H. Arimura, An efficient algorithm for enumerating closed patterns in transaction databases, *Proc. Discovery Science 2004*, LNAI 3245, Springer, 16–30, 2004.
25. M. J. Zaki. Efficiently mining frequent trees in a forest, In *Proc. SIGKDD'02*, ACM, 2002.

Discrete Structure Manipulation for Discovery Science Problems

Shin-ichi Minato

Hokkaido University, Sapporo 060-0814, Japan
and
ERATO MINATO Discrete Structure Manipulation System Project,
Japan Science and Technology Agency

Abstract. Discovering useful knowledge from large-scale databases has attracted a considerable attention during the last decade. Recently, we have been working on decision diagram-based large-scale data processing for knowledge discovery. In most of our research work, we can observe that discrete structure manipulation is a key technique to solve many kind of real-life problems. This article presents our current and future work on discrete structure manipulation for discovery science problems.

1 Background

Discovering useful knowledge from large-scale databases has attracted a considerable attention during the last decade. Our research group have been working on decision diagram-based large-scale data processing for knowledge discovery. In most of our research work, we can observe that discrete structure manipulation is a key technique to solve many kind of real-life problems.

Discrete structures are foundational material for computer science and mathematics, which are related to set theory, symbolic logic, inductive proof, graph theory, combinatorics, probability theory, etc. Many problems solved by computers can be decomposed as a type of discrete structures using simple primitive operations. It is very important to compactly represent discrete structures and to efficiently execute the tasks such as equivalency/validity checking, analysis of models, optimization, etc. Those techniques are commonly used in many application areas in computer science, for example, hardware/ software system design, fault analysis of large-scale systems, constraint satisfaction problems, data mining, knowledge discovery, machine learning/classification, bioinformatics, web data analysis, etc.

In this article, we present our current and future work on discrete structure manipulation for discovery science problems.

2 BDDs/ZDDs for Discrete Structure Manipulation

Boolean function is one of the basic models of discrete structures. Systematic methods for Boolean function manipulation were started by Shannon in 1938,

E. Gelenbe et al. (eds.), *Computer and Information Sciences*, Lecture Notes
in Electrical Engineering 62, DOI 10.1007/978-90-481-9794-1_67,
© Springer Science+Business Media B.V. 2010

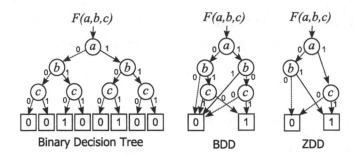

Fig. 1. Binary Decision Tree, BDDs and ZDDs

A Binary Decision Diagram (BDD) is a graph representation for a Boolean function, developed in VLSI design area. As illustrated in Fig. 1, It is derived by reducing a binary decision tree graph, which represents a decision making process by the input variables. If we fix the order of input variables, and apply the following two reduction rules, then we have a compact canonical form for a given Boolean function:

(1) Delete all redundant nodes whose two edges have the same destination, and
(2) Share all equivalent nodes having the same child nodes and the same variable.

The compression ratio by using a BDD depends on the property of Boolean function to be represented, but it can be 10 to 100 times in some practical cases. In addition, we can systematically construct a BDD as the result of a binary logic operation (i.e. AND, OR) for a given pair of operand BDDs. This algorithm is based on hash table techniques, and computation time is almost linear to the BDD size.

BDD is based on the on-memory data processing techniques, and it enjoys the advantage of using random access memories. Recently, commodity PCs are equipped with Giga-Bytes of main memory, and we can solve larger-scale problems which used to be impossible due to memory shortage. Thus, especially after 2000s, the BDD application areas are spreading.

applying Boolean algebra to logic network design, and then we have long history until today. As the data structure of Boolean functions, sum-of-products form (DNF/CNF) has been used for long time, however, after the epoch-making paper [2] by R. E. Bryant in 1986, BDD-based method becomes a hot topic and has been rapidly developed.

Zero-suppressed BDD (ZDD) is a variant of BDD, customized for manipulating combinatorial itemsets. This data structure was first introduced by Minato [6]. ZDDs are based on the special reduction rules different from ordinary ones. As shown in Fig. 2, we delete all nodes whose 1-edge directly points to the 0-terminal node, but do not delete the nodes which were deleted in ordinary BDDs. This new reduction rule is extremely effective if we handle a family of sparse sets. If the average appearance ratio of each item is 1%, ZDDs are possibly more compact than ordinary BDDs, up to 100 times. Such situations often appear in real-life problems, for example, in a supermarket, the number of items in a customer ' s basket is usually much less than all the items displayed there.

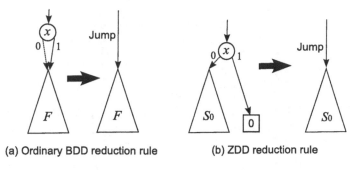

(a) Ordinary BDD reduction rule   (b) ZDD reduction rule

Fig. 2. ZDD reduction rule.

Because of such an advantage, ZDD is now widely recognized as the most important variant of BDD. Recently, D. Knuth presented a new fascicle of his famous
book series [5], which has a section of ZDDs discussed minutely in 30 pages with
70 exercises.

3   ZDD-based Data processing for Knowledge Discovery

Frequent itemset mining is one of the fundamental problems for data mining and
knowledge discovery. The task is to find all frequent itemsets that are itemsets
included in at least σ records of the database where σ is the user specified
threshold. Since the pioneering work by Agrawal *et al.*[1], various algorithms
have been proposed to solve the *frequent itemset mining problem* (cf., [3, 10]).

Recently, Minato et al. [8] proposed a fast algorithm "LCM over ZDDs" for
generating very large-scale frequent itemsets using ZDDs. This method is based
on *LCM algorithm* [9], one of the most efficient state-of-the-art techniques for
itemset mining, and directly generates compact output data structures on the
main memory, to be efficiently post-processed by using ZDD-based algebraic
operations.

The original LCM explores all the candidate itemsets in a backtracking (or
depth-first) manner, and the solutions are output to a sequential file one by
one during the backtracking search. Thus, time and space may be too large
if so large number of solutions are found. On the other hand, LCM over ZDDs
constructs a ZDD of all the itemsets found in the backtracking search, and finally
returns a pointer to the root node of the ZDD. This idea enables us to generate
billions of frequent itemsets in a small time and space when ZDD-based data
compression works well. Figure 3 shows our experimental results[8] to compare
the performances between LCM over ZDDs and the original LCM.

When using a conventional frequent itemset mining method, it may be mean-
ingless to generate billions of frequent itemsets because we cannot analyze so
large size of result in a practical time. However, by using LCM over ZDDs, a
huge number of itemsets can be stored and indexed compactly in main memory,

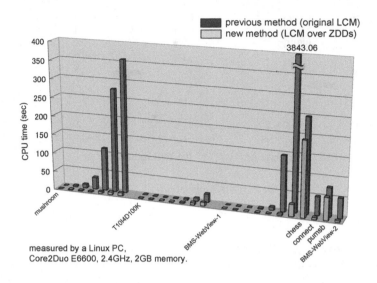

Fig. 3. Performance of LCM over ZDDs.

and then post-process them using algebraic ZDD operations. Figure 4 shows an example that our ZDD-based method can generate a pair of frequent itemsets for today's and yesterday's databases, and then compute a distinctive frequent itemsets such that the intersection or difference between the two databases. Our latest paper [7] presents a further extended idea for ZDD-based post-processing of frequent itemset mining, called frequentness-transitional pattern mining, for finding patterns with interesting sequential behavior from a time-segmented databases.

4   Conclusion and Future Work

In this article, we described our recent research activities on BDD/ZDD-based data processing for data mining and knowledge discovery. BDDs and ZDDs provide automatic compressed graph representations for a huge number of itemsets. The compressed representation can be post-processed and analyzed efficiently by using various set operations without decompression.

Since there are so many interesting and useful ideas using BDD/ZDD for knowledge discovery problems, we proposed to organize a new research project to focus on BDDs/ZDDs and their algebra as an integrated method for manipulating many types of discrete structures, to be utilized for various application areas. Fortunately our proposal has been accepted by JST (Japan Science and Technology Agency) as an ERATO (Exploratory Research for Advanced Technology) project [4], one of the nationwide projects in Japan. The main research activities started from April 2010 and will continue for five years.

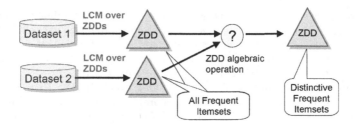

Fig. 4. Comparison of Two Frequent Itemsets

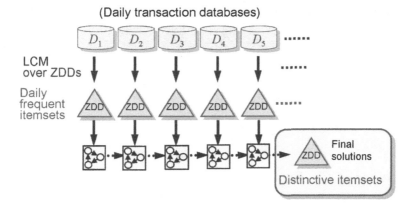

Fig. 5. frequentness-transitional pattern mining.

We expect that the discrete structure manipulation techniques will become more important and interesting in the field of discovery science, and now we can see some encouraging signs for applying to various real-life problems.

References

1. R. Agrawal, T. Imielinski, and A. N. Swami. Mining association rules between sets of items in large databases. In P. Buneman and S. Jajodia, editors, *Proc. of the 1993 ACM SIGMOD International Conference on Management of Data, Vol. 22(2) of SIGMOD Record*, pages 207–216, 1993.
2. R. E. Bryant. Graph-based algorithms for Boolean function manipulation. *IEEE Transactions on Computers*, C-35(8):677–691, 1986.
3. B. Goethals. Survey on frequent pattern mining, 2003. http://www.cs.helsinki.fi/u/goethals/publications/survey.ps.
4. Japan Science and Technology Agency. *ERATO MINATO Discrete Structure Manipulation System Project*, 10 2009. http://www.jst.go.jp/erato/project/mrk_P/mrk_P.html.
5. D. E. Knuth. *The Art of Computer Programming: Bitwise Tricks & Techniques; Binary Decision Diagrams*, volume 4, fascicle 1. Addison-Wesley, 2009.

6. S. Minato. Zero-suppressed BDDs for set manipulation in combinatorial problems. In *Proc. of 30th ACM/IEEE Design Automation Conference*, pages 272–277, 1993.
7. S. Minato and T. Uno. Frequentness-transition queries for distinctive pattern mining from time-segmented databases. In *Proc. of 2010 SIAM International Conference on Data Mining (SDM'2010)*, pages 339–349, 4 2010.
8. S. Minato, T. Uno, and H. Arimura. LCM over ZBDDs: Fast generation of very large-scale frequent itemsets using a compact graph-based representation. In *Proc. of 12-th Pacific-Asia Conference on Knowledge Discovery and Data Mining (PAKDD 2008), (LNAI 5012, Springer)*, pages 234–246, 5 2008.
9. T. Uno, Y. Uchida, T. Asai, and H. Arimura. LCM: an efficient algorithm for enumerating frequent closed item sets. In *Proc. Workshop on Frequent Itemset Mining Implementations (FIMI'03)*, 2003. http://fimi.cs.helsinki.fi/src/.
10. M. J. Zaki. Scalable algorithms for association mining. *IEEE Trans. Knowl. Data Eng.*, 12(2):372–390, 2000.

Recent Experiences in Parameter-Free Data Mining

Kimihito Ito[1], Thomas Zeugmann[2]* and Yu Zhu[2]

[1] Research Center for Zoonosis Control
Hokkaido University, N-20, W-10 Kita-ku, Sapporo 001-0020, Japan
itok@czc.hokudai.ac.jp
[2] Division of Computer Science
Hokkaido University, N-14, W-9, Sapporo 060-0814, Japan
{thomas,yuar}@mx-alg.ist.hokudai.ac.jp

Abstract. Recent results supporting the usefulness of the normalized compression distance for the task to classify genome sequences of virus data are reported. Specifically, the problem to cluster the hemagglutinin (HA) sequences of influenza virus data for the HA gene in dependence on the host and subtype of the virus, and the classification of dengue virus genome data with respect to their four serotypes are studied.
A comparison is made with respect to hierarchical and spectral clustering via the kLine algorithm by Fischer and Poland (2004), respectively, and with respect to the standard compressors bzlip, ppmd, and zlib.
Our results are very promising and show that one can obtain an (almost) perfect clustering for all the problems studied.

1 Introduction

In many data mining applications the similarity between objects is of fundamental importance. Quite frequently, domain knowledge is used to define a suitable domain-specific distance measure. As a consequence, many of the resulting algorithms tend to have many parameters which have to be tuned. This is not only difficult but also including the risk of being biased. Furthermore, it may make it hard to verify the results obtained.

Recently, as a radically different approach, the paradigm of parameter-free data mining has emerged (cf. Keogh *et al.* [12]). The main idea of parameter-free data mining is the design of algorithms that have no parameters and that are universally applicable in all areas. At first glance this may seem impossible. How can an algorithm perform well if it is not based on extracting the important features of the data and if we are not allowed to adjust these parameters? As pointed out by Vitányi *et al.* [17], parameter free data mining is aiming at scenarios where we are not interested in a certain similarity measure but in *the* similarity between the objects themselves.

---

* Supported by MEXT Grant-in-Aid for Scientific Research on Priority Areas under Grant No. 21013001.

The most promising approach to this paradigm uses Kolmogorov complexity theory [14] as its basis. The key ingredient is the so-called *normalized information distance* (*NID*) which was developed by various researchers during the past decade in a series of steps (cf., e.g., [2, 13, 8]). The intuitive idea behind it is as follows. If two objects are similar then there should be a simple description of how to transform each one of them into the other one. And conversely, if all descriptions for transforming each one of them into the other one are complex, then the objects should be dissimilar. Then, the *normalized information distance* between two strings x and y is defined as

$$NID(x,y) = \frac{\max\{K(x|y),\ K(y|x)\}}{\max\{K(x),\ K(y)\}}\ , \tag{1}$$

where $K(x|y)$ is the length of the shortest program that outputs x on input y, and $K(x)$ is the length of the shortest program that outputs x on the empty input. For the technical details of the *NID*, we refer the reader to Vitányi *et al.* [17].

To apply this idea to data mining tasks, standard compression algorithms have to be invoked to approximate the Kolmogorov complexity K. This yields the *normalized compression distance* (*NCD*) as approximation of the *NID* (cf. Definition 1). The *NCD* has been successfully applied to a variety of data mining problems (cf., e.g., [8, 12, 5, 6, 1]).

In this paper, we report the usefulness of the *NCD* for three classification problems for virus data. One task is to cluster the hemagglutinin (HA) sequences of influenza virus data for the HA gene in dependence on the subtype, where all data originate from the same host. The second task is the same classification but in dependence on the subtype *and* host of the virus. The third problem deals with the classification of dengue virus genome data with respect to their four serotypes.

2   Background and Theory

The definition of the *NID* depends on the function K which is *uncomputable*. Thus, the *NID* is *uncomputable*, too. Using a real-word compressor, one can approximate the *NID* by the *NCD* (cf. Definition 1). Again, we omit details and refer the reader to [17].

Definition 1. *The* normalized compression distance *between two strings* x *and* y *is defined as*

$$NCD(x,y) = \frac{C(xy) - \min\{C(x),\ C(y)\}}{\max\{C(x),\ C(y)\}}\ ,$$

where C *is any given data compressor.*

Common data compressors are `bzlib`, `ppmd`, `zlib`, etc[3]. Note that the compressor C has to be computable and *normal* in order to make the *NCD* a useful approximation. This can be stated as follows.

---

[3] We use here the same naming convention as in the CompLearn Toolkit [4]. Essentially, these compressors coincide with `bzip2`, `ppmz`, and `gzip`.

Definition 2 ([17]). *A compressor* C *is said to be* normal *if it satisfies the following axioms for all strings* x, y, z *and the empty string* λ.

(1) $C(xx) = C(x)$ *and* $C(\lambda) = 0$;	(identity)
(2) $C(xy) \geqslant C(x)$;	(monotonicity)
(3) $C(xy) = C(yx)$;	(symmetry)
(4) $C(xy) + C(z) \leqslant C(xz) + C(yz)$;	(distributivity)

up to an additive $O(\log n)$ *term, with* n *the maximal binary length of a string involved in the (in)equality concerned.*

Good real-world compressors like `bzlib`, `ppmd`, and `zlib` turned out to be normal for our data, and we used these compressors for our experiments. We used the `ncd` function from the CompLearn Toolkit (cf. [4]) to compute the distance matrix $D = \left(d^{ncd}(x,y)\right)_{x,y \in X}$, where $X = (x_1, \ldots, x_n)$ is the relevant data list.

To cluster the data we used hierarchical clustering and spectral clustering via kLines (cf. Fischer and Poland [9]). For a detailed description of the algorithms applied, we refer the reader to our paper [11].

3   Clustering Virus Data – Experiments and Results

The first paper using the *NCD* to analyze virus data was Cilibrasi and Vitányi [7]. In this paper the authors used the SARS TOR2 draft genome assembly 120403 from Canada's Michael Smith Genome Sciences Centre and compared it to other viruses by using the *NCD* and the `bzlib` compressor. After applying their quartet tree heuristic for hierarchical clustering, they obtained a ternary tree showing relations very similar to those shown in the definitive tree based on medical-macrobiological genomics analysis which was obtained later (see [7] for details).

Our first group of experiments dealt with influenza viruses, too. We have been interested in learning whether or not specific gene data for the hemagglutinin of influenza viruses are *correctly* classifiable by using the concept of the *NCD*. For any relevant background concerning the biological aspects of the influenza viruses we refer the reader to Palese and Shaw [16] and Wright *et al.* [18].

The family of *Orthomyxoviridae* is defined by viruses that have a negative-sense, single-stranded, and segmented RNA genome. There are five different genera in the family of *Orthomyxoviridae*: the influenza viruses A, B and C; *Thogotovirus*; and *Isavirus*. Influenza A viruses have a complex structure and possess a lipid membrane derived from the host cell.

We were only interested in their HA gene, since HA is the major target of antibodies that neutralize viral infectivity, and responsible for binding the virus to the cell it infects. In [11] we considered all 16 subtypes of the HA and collected a data set from the National Center for Biotechnology Information (NCBI) [15] containing a total of 106 sequences (all taken from viruses hosted by their the natural host) which could be (almost) successfully clustered into the relevant 16 subtypes of the HA. So, the HA subtype is *the* similarity between the different sequences.

Next, we shortly describe experiments dealing with influenza viruses hosted by duck and human. Note that H1N1 is a subtype of influenza A and the most common cause of influenza in humans. In June 2009, the World Health Organization declared that a new strain of swine origin H1N1 was responsible for the 2009 flu pandemic. Usually birds can pass avian influenza viruses to swines, where the viruses have to mutate so that they can circulate in the swine population. Then a new strain emerges which can be passed to humans or to other hosts. Of course, in order to become pandemic, the viruses may mutate again.

If one considers sequences for the HA gene originating from different hosts, it is only natural to ask which property is more "similar," the *host* or the *subtype*. For answering this question we chose 32 sequences having different HA subtypes that originated from both the duck and human host (again from NCBI). For a complete list of the data description we refer the reader to

http://www-alg.ist.hokudai.ac.jp/nhuman_vs_duck.html .

For the ease of presentation, below we use the following abbreviation for the data entries. Instead of giving the full description, e.g.,

>gi|218664152|gb|CY036815| /Human/4 (HA)/H2N2/South Korea/1968/// Influenza A virus (A/Korea/426/1968(H2N2)) segment 4, complete sequence

we refer to this datum as hH2N2CY036815 for short. The h stands for human here, and we use d if the host is the duck.

Each datum consists of a sequence of roughly 1800 letters from the alphabet {A, T, G, C}, e.g., looking such as

AAAAGCAGGGGAATTTCACAATTAAA...TGTATATAATTAGCAAA.

The results obtained by using the zlib and bzlib compressor and then applying hierarchical clustering are shown in Figure 1 and 2, respectively.

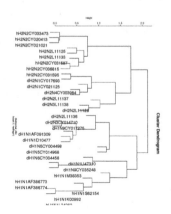 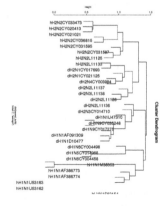

Fig. 1. Classification of HA sequences hosted by human and duck; compr.: zlib

Fig. 2. Classification of HA sequences hosted by human and duck; compr.: bzip

As these clustering results show, for this data set the similarity between subtypes is stronger than the similarity between the hosts. We could confirm this outcome by using spectral clustering, where we used two clusters.

3.1   Clustering the *NCD* for Dengue Virus Data

Dengue virus is an RNA virus that causes dengue fever, one of the most important emerging diseases, infecting 100 million people annually in more than one hundred countries around the world [3]. The genome of dengue virus consists of nucleotides approximately 11 KB long, and 10 viral proteins are encoded in the genome. Dengue virus exhibits extensive genetic diversity, and there exist four antigenically distinct serologic types (1 through 4). It is known that severe cases, called dengue hemorrhagic fever / dengue shock syndrome, occur in patients who have secondary infections by a different serotype from previous infections [10]. Around 250,000 cases of dengue hemorrhagic fever / dengue shock syndrome are annually reported. Nucleotide sequences of all four dengue virus groups have been determined, and the rapid development of molecular biology over the last two decades is accelerating the accumulation of genomic data on the pathogen.

So, it is only natural to ask whether or not we can correctly cluster dengue virus genome data with respect to their four serotypes. To answer this question, we used 80 sequences (20 for each serotype) from NCBI ([15]). For a complete description of the data used, please see

http://www-alg.ist.hokudai.ac.jp/Dengue-Data.html .

Then, we computed the distance matrix as described above by applying the standard compressors bzlib, ppmd, and zlib. It should be noted that the dengue virus genome data are much larger than the influenza virus data, i.e., 10.6 KB versus 1.7 KB. Our hierarchical clustering was perfect for the compressors ppmd, and zlib (see Figure 3 for an example), but not for bzlib. Hierarchically clustering the distance matrix computed via the bzlib compressor gave 11 errors. On the other hand, spectral clustering delivered correct results in all three cases.

Moreover, we repeated these experiments with a non-balanced data set, see

http://www-alg.ist.hokudai.ac.jp/imbalanced-dengue.html ,

where we used 44 sequences of type 1 and 20 sequences of type 2, 3, and 4.

The results have been almost the same, i.e., hierarchical clustering and spectral clustering have been correct for the compressors ppmd, and zlib.

Using the bzlib compressor and spectral clustering as described in [11] produced two errors. However, by using a different kernel width for transforming the distance matrix in a similarity matrix (i.e., 1.23), the clustering was again perfect. Moreover, in contrast to the experiments performed with the influenza virus data, the kernel width was much less influential.

To summarize, our results are very promising and show that one can obtain an (almost) perfect clustering for all the problems studied. Note that we do not have reported the running time here, since it was in the range of several seconds. The clustering algorithms used in our experiments will nicely scale up to the amount of data for for which we can efficiently compute the distance matrix.

References

[1] D. Benedetto, E. Caglioti, and V. Loreto. Language trees and zipping. *Phys. Rev. Lett.*, 88(4):048702-1–048702-4, 2002.

[2] C. H. Bennett, P. Gács, M. Li, P. M. B. Vitányi, and W. H. Zurek. Information distance. *IEEE Transactions on Information Theory*, 44(4):1407–1423, 1998.

[3] D. S. Burke, G. Kuno, and T. P. Monath. Flaviviruses. In D. M. Knipe and P. M. Howley et al., editors, *Fields' Virology*, pages 1153–1252. Lippincott Williams & Wilkins, Philadelphia, fifth edition, 2007.

[4] R. Cilibrasi. The CompLearn Toolkit, 2003-. http://www.complearn.org/.

[5] R. Cilibrasi and P. Vitányi. Automatic meaning discovery using Google. Manuscript, CWI, Amsterdam, 2006.

[6] R. Cilibrasi and P. Vitanyi. Similarity of objects and the meaning of words. In *Theory and Applications of Models of Computation, Third International Conference, TAMC 2006, Beijing, China, May 2006, Proceedings*, volume 3959 of *Lecture Notes in Computer Science*, pages 21–45, Berlin, 2006. Springer.

[7] R. Cilibrasi and P. M. Vitányi. A new quartet tree heuristic for hierarchical clustering. In D. V. Arnold, T. Jansen, M. D. Vose, and J. E. Rowe, editors, *Theory of Evolutionary Algorithms*, number 06061 in Dagstuhl Seminar Proceedings. Internationales Begegnungs- und Forschungszentrum für Informatik (IBFI), Schloss Dagstuhl, Germany, 2006.

[8] R. Cilibrasi and P. M. B. Vitányi. Clustering by compression. *IEEE Transactions on Information Theory*, 51(4):1523–1545, 2005.

[9] I. Fischer and J. Poland. New methods for spectral clustering. Technical Report IDSIA-12-04, IDSIA / USI-SUPSI, Manno, Switzerland, 2004.

[10] S. B. Halstead. Pathogenesis of dengue: Challenges to molecular biology. *Science*, 239 (4839):476–481, 1988.

[11] K. Ito, T. Zeugmann, and Y. Zhu. Clustering the normalized compression distance for influenza virus data. In T. Elomaa, H. Mannila, and P. Orponen, editors, *Algorithms and Applications, Essays Dedicated to Esko Ukkonen on the Occasion of His 60th Birthday*, volume 6060 of *Lecture Notes in Computer Science*, pages 130–146. Springer, Heidelberg, 2010.

[12] E. Keogh, S. Lonardi, and C. A. Ratanamahatana. Towards parameter-free data mining. In *Proceedings of the Tenth ACM SIGKDD International Conference on Knowledge Discovery and Data Mining*, pages 206–215. ACM Press, 2004.

[13] M. Li, X. Chen, X. Li, B. Ma, and P. M. Vitányi. The similarity metric. *IEEE Transactions on Information Theory*, 50(12):3250–3264, 2004.

[14] M. Li and P. Vitányi. *An Introduction to Kolmogorov Complexity and its Applications*. Springer, 3rd edition, 2008.

[15] National Center for Biotechnology Information. Influenza Virus Resource, information, search and analysis. http://www.ncbi.nlm.nih.gov/genomes/FLU/FLU.html.

[16] P. Palese and M. L. Shaw. Orthomyxoviridae: The viruses and their replication. In D. M. Knipe and P. M. Howley et al., editors, *Fields' Virology*, pages 1647–1689. Lippincott Williams & Wilkins, Philadelphia, fifth edition, 2007.

[17] P. M. B. Vitányi, F. J. Balbach, R. L. Cilibrasi, and M. Li. Normalized information distance. In *Information Theory and Statistical Learning*, pages 45–82. Springer, New York, 2008.

[18] P. F. Wright, G. Neumann, and Y. Kawaoka. Orthomyxoviruses. In D. M. Knipe and P. M. Howley et al., editors, *Fields' Virology*, pages 1691–1740. Lippincott Williams & Wilkins, Philadelphia, fifth edition, 2007.

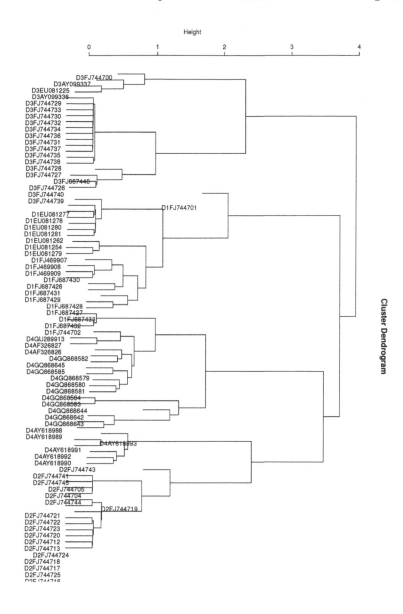

Fig. 3. Classification of dengue genome sequences; compr. `zlib`

Improving the Time Efficiency of ILP-based Multi-Relational Concept Discovery with Dynamic Programming Approach

Alev Mutlu[1], Mehmet Ali Berk[2], and Pinar Senkul[1]

[1] Middle East Technical University, Computer Engineering Department, Ankara
Turkey
{mutlu,senkul}@ceng.metu.edu.tr
[2] Aselsan Inc. Ankara, Turkey
maberk@aselsan.com.tr

Abstract. Large amount of relational data is stored in databases. Therefore, working directly on the data stored in database is an important
feature for multi-relational concept discovery systems. In addition to
concept rule quality, time efficiency is an important performance dimension for concept discovery since dealing with large amount of data is a
must. In this work, we present a dynamic programming based approach
for improving the time efficiency on an ILP-based concept discovery system, namely CRIS (Concept Rule Induction System), which combines
ILP and Apriori and directly works on databases.

Key words: Concept Discovery, ILP, MRDM, Dynamic Programming

1 Introduction

Concept discovery in relational databases is a predictive multi-relational learning
task[1]. The learning systems, which induce logical patterns valid for given background knowledge, have been investigated under a research area, called Inductive
Logic Programming (ILP) [2]. CRIS is a predictive concept learning ILP system
that employs relational association rule mining concepts and techniques to find
frequent and strong concept definitions for the given target relation under the
background knowledge [6, 7]. The system is integrated with relational database
and information necessary during concept discovery process is obtained through
SQL calls.

The size of the relational data is very large for most of the cases and the
concept definition is expected to be discovered in a feasible amount of time.
Searching the hypothesis space for repeating rules and calculating support, confidence values of the candidate rules constitute a significant part of the running
time. In order to improve the time efficiency for concept discovery on relational
databases, we adopted dynamic programming approach for reducing the time
spent during these tasks. Dynamic programming conventionally divides a complex problem into subparts and uses the previously calculated results of the

E. Gelenbe et al. (eds.), *Computer and Information Sciences*, Lecture Notes
in Electrical Engineering 62, DOI 10.1007/978-90-481-9794-1_69,
© Springer Science+Business Media B.V. 2010

subparts of the problem. It is basically a tabular approach in which sub-results are kept in a table for later look-ups. In a similar fashion, we employed hashing techniques, which provide efficient searching by transforming keys into table addresses [5], in order to keep the intermediate results and to reduce the time spent in these steps.

2   CRIS: Concept Rule Induction System

CRIS is a concept discovery system that uses first-order logic as the concept definition language and generates a set of definite clauses having the target concept in the head.

Two criteria are important in the evaluation of a candidate concept rule: how many of the concept instances are captured by the rule (coverage) and the proportions of the objects which truly belong to the target concept among all those that show the pattern of the rule (accuracy); support and confidence, respectively. Therefore, the system should assign a score to each candidate concept rule according to its support and confidence value. Support and confidence values can be obtained by the SQL queries given in [7].

Generalization step of the algorithm constructs the most general two-literal rules by considering all target instances together. By this way, the quality of the rule induction does not depend on the order of target instances. For a given target relation, $t(a, b)$, the induced rule has a head including either a constant or a variable for each argument of t. Each argument can be handled independently in order to find the feasible head relations for the hypothesis set. Support and confidence values for each clause are calculated and the infrequent clauses are eliminated. CRIS refines the two-literal concept descriptions with an Apriori-based [4] specialization operator that searches the definite clause space in a top-down manner. After the best clause is selected, based on f-score [3],concept instances covered by this clause are removed from the concept instances set. The main iteration continues until all concept instances are covered or no more feasible candidate clause can be found for the uncovered concept instances [3].

3   Using Dynamic Programming Approach in CRIS

The algorithm presented in Section 2 is modified by using the dynamic programming approach at two steps: specialization and filtering. The modification in specialization step is on the the search of repeating rules. In CRIS, a newly generated rule is added to the search lattice if it has not been already added. Although every rule is unique at level C_i, merging rules to generate level C_{i+1} rules may produce repeating rules, due to renamings of variables that have the same literals with different substitutions. Checking for repeating rules with the original implementation is of $O(n^2)$ compexity, while it is of linear complexity, $O(n)$, with the dynamic programming based approach.

---

[3] For the details of the algorithm, readers may refer to [7]

Experiment	SQL hits/All SQL queries	Repeating rules/ All Rules
Dunur	2002/3777	25/1850
Elti	946/3571	75/1832
Eastbound	9623/21868	0/7294
Mesh	141300/154015	323/57100
Mutagenesis	716/13500	25/6081
PTE (No Aggr.)	9328/25570	346/11008
PTE (5 Aggr.)	19684/131719	1843/61292
Same Gen.	400/996	9/397

Table 1. Hits on hash table

The modification in the filtering step involves the support and confidence value calculations. CRIS assigns a confidence and a support value for every rule and uses these values for pruning the infrequent and unstrong rules. However, different rules may have common queries, and this generally occurs when literals are substituted with different variables of the same type.

With the proposod modification, the results of queries are stored and used for common queries of different rules. To this aim, another hash table is built for storing the <SQL query, result> pairs. Before a query is sent to the database management system, it is first searched in the hash table. If the hash value of the query exists in the table, its results is returned and used without need for access to DBMS. Otherwise the query is sent to the query server and together with its result, the query is inserted into the hash table. On the basis of the number of common queries, this approach drops the execution time considerably.

In order to observe the improvement in execution time, we have conducted experiments on eight datasets[4].

Table 1 shows the hit ratio of SQL queries in the hash table over all SQL queries generated, and the number of repeating rules over the number of all rules generated. As seen in the results, the number of common queries (the number of hits) vary. However, even the smallest number of hits (716 for mutagenesis data set) provides an important gain. As seen on the second column of the same table, the number of repeating rules vary with the data sets, as well. However, the efficiency gain in finding repeating rules is more in this task, since the search complexity is improved even for small number of hits.

Table 2 summarizes the execution times of the original implementation and implementation with hash tables on the data tests. As shown in the table, the proposed approach decreases the execution times in important amounts. The highest gain appears on *Mesh* data set, where the number of query hits is 92%. The last column of the table presents the storage needed for hash tables. Hash tables constructed for repeating rule checking store only hash-key values. For the common queries, together with the hash-key, the query result, which is a single numeric value, is stored. For this reason the space requirement is quite limited.

---

[4] Readers may refer to [7], for more information on the datasets

Experiment	Original Implementation hh:mm:ss	Dynamic Prog Implementation hh:mm:ss	Memory Used for Hash Tables ≈ in KB
Dunur	00:00:26	00:00:01	28
Elti	00:00:35	00:00:02	41
Eastbound	00:11:36	00:00:01	2
Mesh	02:39:34	00:00:32	75
Mutagenesis	00:03:42	00:00:13	166
PTE (No Aggr.)	00:21:25	00:08:35	184
PTE (5 Aggr.)	05:17:00	01:37:16	1163
Same Gen.	00:00:12	00:00:01	8

Table 2. Running times and memory usage

4 Conclusion

In this work, we present the use of tabling for improving the execution time for concept discovery on relational databases. The approach is implemented on an ILP-based concept discovery system, CRIS, on two basic steps of the concept discovery process: detecting repeating rules in specialization and repeating queries in support and confidence value calculation in rule pruning. In both of these steps, hashing techniques are employed to construct look-up tables. Experimental results show that the proposed approach is effective and the execution time drops considerable. Independent of the nature of the data set and application, use of hash table improves the complexity of detecting repeating rules from polynomial time to linear time.

References

1. Džeroski, S.: Multi-relational data mining: an introduction. SIGKDD Explorations **5**(1) (2003) 1–16
2. Muggleton, S.: Inductive Logic Programming. In: The MIT Encyclopedia of the Cognitive Sciences (MITECS). MIT Press (1999)
3. Goutte, C., Gaussier, E.: newblock A probabilistic interpretation of precision, recall and f-score, with implication for evaluation. In: European Colloquium on IR Research (ECIR'05), Xerox Research Centre Europe 6, chemin de Maupertuis F-38240 Meylan, France, Springer (2005) 345–359
4. Agrawal, R., Mannila, H., Srikant, R., Toivonen, H., Verkamo, A.I.: Fast discovery of association rules. In: Advances in Knowledge Discovery and Data Mining. AAAI/MIT Press (1996) 307–328
5. Sedgewich R.: Algorithms, Second Edition Addison-Wesley Publishing Company (1988) 232–245
6. Kavurucu Y., Senkul P., Toroslu I.H.: ILP-based Concept Discovery in Multi-Relational Data Mining. Expert System with Applications, **36**(9) (2009) 11418–11428
7. Kavurucu Y., Senkul P., Toroslu I.H.: Concept Discovery on Relational Databases: New Techniques for Search Space Pruning and Rule Quality Improvement. In Press, Accepted Manuscript, Knowledge-Based Systems, doi:10.1016/j.knosys.2010.04.011

10 Distributed and Parallel Algorithms

16 Distributed and Parallel Algorithms

An Information Theory Based Behavioral Model for Agent-Based Crowd Simulations

Cagatay Turkay[1], Emre Koc[2], and Selim Balcisoy[2]

[1] University of Bergen, Bergen, Norway
[2] Sabanci University, Istanbul, Turkey
Cagatay.Turkay@ii.uib.no, emrekoc@su.sabanciuniv.edu,
balcisoy@sabanciuniv.edu

Abstract. In this paper, we propose a novel behavioral model which builds analytical maps to control agents' behavior adaptively with agent-crowd interaction formulations. We introduce information theoretical concepts to construct analytical maps automatically. Our model can be integrated into crowd simulators and enhance their behavioral complexity.

1 Introduction

In this paper, we are proposing an analytical agent-based behavioral model that integrates global knowledge about crowd formation into local, agent-based behavior control. We use analytical representations of crowd's activities, called *behavior maps* which are constructed with a statistical framework based on information theory. Our model proposes an agent definition responsive to behavior map values and agent-crowd interaction formulations. Agents behaving in realistic, variable and complex manners can be achieved with our behavioral model without the need for low-level scripting.

In our model, we utilize the notion of place-centered maps in crowd simulations and propose *behavior maps*. Behavior maps are automatically generated statistical analysis maps which record and represent both spatial and temporal dynamics of agents. Methods to construct behavior maps are derived from scene analysis methods introduced in [1]. Agents access behavior maps and modify their intrinsic properties. How agents respond and behave according to their intrinsic properties and behavior maps are defined with agent-crowd interaction formulations. Beneath all this high level structure, we utilize a multi-agent navigation system to solve agent-agent and agent-environment interactions through collision detection and path planning algorithms. Our model can extend any existing agent-based crowd simulator.

2 Related Work

There have been many studies on agent-based crowd models to create human-like behaviors. In [2], Pelechano et.al. assigned psychological roles and communication skills to agents to produce diverse and realistic behaviors. There are studies

E. Gelenbe et al. (eds.), *Computer and Information Sciences*, Lecture Notes
in Electrical Engineering 62, DOI 10.1007/978-90-481-9794-1_70,
© Springer Science+Business Media B.V. 2010

which model the virtual environment as maps to guide agents' behaviors. [3] used adaptive roadmaps, which evolve with the dynamic nature of the environment. In [4], Sung et.al. assign situations and behaviors directly to environment rather than the agents themselves. In our calculations, we employed quantities from information theory. In a recent study, Turkay et.al. [1] used information theory based formulations to automatically control the virtual camera in a crowded environment. In [5], they extended their information theory based model to control how agents behave in a crowd simulation. We improve the behavioral model proposed in [5] and develop concrete formulations and methods to use this behavioral model to extend any crowd simulator's variability and realism.

3   Analytical Behavioral Model

Our model provides global knowledge on crowd's activities and enables the crowd simulator to incorporate agent-crowd interactions to modify agents' behavior. Behavior maps constitute the foundation of our model. They record and analytically represent crowd's activities. The second element of our model is a generic agent representation to access behavior maps. The final element in our model is a set of formulations to link the underlying crowd simulator with behavior maps.

3.1   Crowd Representation With Behavior Maps

Behavior maps are analytical representations of the crowd which span over the whole virtual environment and monitor agents' locomotion during the simulation. A behavior map, B, is the convex combination of the values of *entropy* and *expectance* maps. Both of these maps address different aspects in the locomotion of crowd and each map has certain effects on agent's behavior. Readers can refer to [1] for technical details. In an entropy map, locations with smaller entropy values denote where agents move with similar velocities. Conversely, locations with higher entropy values represent disorder in agents' locomotion. In an expectance map, cells with high KL values denote *surprising* activities taking place at those locations. At cells with lower KL values the state of the crowd remain as *expected*. Behavior map can be formulated by;

$$B^t = \{w_1 e^t_{i,j} + w_2 kl^t_{i,j} : 0 \leq w_n < 1, w_1 + w_2 = 1, \ 0 \leq i < w, \ 0 \leq j < h\} \quad (1)$$

, where each w_i represents user-defined weight values to determine the contribution of each map. These user-defined weights provides a mechanism to control how a behavior map is constructed according to the simulation scenario. e and kl values are entropy and expectance map values respectively.

3.2   Agent Representation

In our behavioral model, we need a generic agent representation to fit into any type of agent based crowd engine. Our agent representation includes two properties, i) *behavior state* which enables interaction between agents and behavior maps and ii) *behavior constants* to determine agents' behaviors in combination with behavior state.

Behavior state, β, is the behavior map cell value assigned to an agent. Behavior constants, f, are agent specific values which are evaluated as personality attributes. The agent representation is extended to include these properties, in addition to physical properties, which are position, u, and velocity, v:

$$a_i = \{u, v, \beta, \langle f_0, p_0 \rangle, .., \langle f_n, p_n \rangle : \beta, f_n \in [0, 1] \forall\ n\} \tag{2}$$

p_n is a symbolic representation to indicate a feature associated with a_i. A single $\langle f_n, p_n \rangle$ pair represents p_n is controlled by f_n.

3.3   Extending a Crowd Simulator

Any crowd simulator can be extended with our behavioral model. Our model introduces agent-crowd interactions into agent based crowd simulators. In order to integrate our model, we first need to customize the agent definition given in Equation 2 according to the capabilities of the crowd simulator. This representation is then accompanied with formulations to define how agents handle behavior map values. In this study, we use extended Reciprocal Velocity Obstacles (RVO) multi-agent navigation system incorporating *composite agents* introduced in [6]. The agent representation proposed in Equation 2 is customized with respect to the features of the underlying simulator. For each feature an f value is associated. The next step is developing the formulations to include behavior state, β, and behavior constants, f, values to represent agent-crowd interactions for agent a_i.

4   Results & Test Case

In our test environment, agents can have aggressiveness and/or carefulness properties. To create certain agents which are aggressive and careful, we relate features of agents and formulations with f and β values. The interpretations of behavior maps are used to define how agents respond to them.

We perform a test to prove the validity of our approach by a comparison with a real world scenario. We used room evacuation videos and data produced in Research Center Jülich, Germany. These videos measure the flow of students while evacuating a room with a variable exit width. As the video incorporates students evacuating the room calmly, we set low aggressiveness to our agents. We observe that our results are consistent with the real world case (Figure 1). We made further studies with this scenario setting and instead of adding calm agents, we add aggressive agents into the room. Agents are competing more to get out quickly in this case, as a result clogging occurs through the exit.

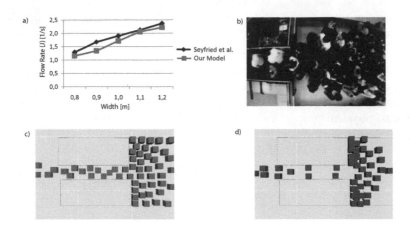

Fig. 1. a) Flow vs. width of exit b) Real-world scenario c) Our test environment with less aggressive agents d) Clogging occurs when agents are more aggressive

5   Conclusion

In this paper, we presented a novel analytical behavioral model which automatically builds behavior maps to control agents' behavior adaptively with agent-crowd interaction formulations. Probabilistic methods incorporating information theory quantities have been used to produce these behavior maps. The presented behavioral model can be integrated into existing agent-based crowd simulators and improve the complexity of resulting crowd behavior. In most of the crowd simulators, low-level scripts are developed to drive complex agent behaviors. The analytical maps produced in our model are utilized to control these behaviors automatically.

References

1. Cagatay Turkay, Emre Koc, and Selim Balcisoy. An information theoretic approach to camera control for crowded scenes. *The Visual Computer*, 25(5-7):451–459, 2009.
2. N. Pelechano, K. OBrien, B. Silverman, and N. Badler. Crowd simulation incorporating agent psychological models, roles and communication. In *First International Workshop on Crowd Simulation*, 2005.
3. R. Gayle, A. Sud, E. Andersen, S.J. Guy, M.C. Lin, and D. Manocha. Interactive Navigation of Heterogeneous Agents Using Adaptive Roadmaps. *Visualization and Computer Graphics, IEEE Transactions on*, 15(1):34–48, 2009.
4. M. Sung, M. Gleicher, and S. Chenney. Scalable behaviors for crowd simulation. In *Computer Graphics Forum*, volume 23, pages 519–528, 2004.
5. Cagatay Turkay, Emre Koc, Kamer Yuksel, and Selim Balcisoy. Adaptive behavioral modeling for crowd simulations. In *Proceedings of International Conference on Computer Animation and Social Agents (Short Papers)*, pages 65–68, 2009.
6. Yeh Hengchin, Curtis Sean, Patil Sachin, van den Berg Jur, Manocha Dinesh, and Lin Ming. Composite agents. In *Symposium on Computer Animation - SCA'08*, 2008.

Task-Parallel FP-Growth on Cluster Computers

Gülistan Özdemir Özdogan and Osman Abul *

Department of Computer Engineering,
TOBB University of Economics and Technology,
Ankara, Turkey.
e-mail: {gozdemir, osmanabul}@etu.edu.tr

Abstract. Frequent itemset mining (FIM) is one of the most deeply studied data mining task. A number of algorithms, employing different approaches and advanced data structures, have already been proposed to solve the task efficiently. Even the fastest serial FIM algorithms fail to scale up with the rapid growth of database sizes. Hence, parallel FIM algorithms are the only viable solutions in many domains as serial solutions have almost reached the physical barriers. To this end, parallel versions of a few serial FIM algorithms, including FP-Growth, have already been developed. In this study, we develop three different parallel FP-Growth implementations for cluster computers. They, all MPI based, are (i) Static Parallel FP-Growth, (ii) Dynamic Parallel FP-Growth, and (iii) (Tree-Sharing) Dynamic Parallel FP-Growth. All the three variants are task-parallel, i.e., not based on horizontal or vertical partitioning of database. The algorithms are experimentally evaluated on a 16-node cluster computer. Our results demonstrate the utility of the algorithms.

1 Introduction

Frequent itemset mining (FIM) is an established task in data mining, and a number of algorithms exploiting different approaches have been proposed as solutions [2, 8]. Apriori [2] is one of the earliest and also the most well known of them. Apriori algorithm, in essence, exploits the anti-monotonic property of support and requires multiple database scans. Since the database scanning is the main source of inefficiency, the performance of Apriori degrades considerably. Unlike Apriori, FP-Growth [3] scans the database twice, regardless of support threshold and database size. The success of FP-Growth lies in the compact representation of database in a specialized data structure called FP-tree.

With the rapid growth in database sizes and complexities, even the performance of fastest FIM algorithms are unacceptable. Not surprisingly, one promising direction in such cases is the parallel FIM algorithms. With a proper design, parallel FIM algorithms can scale up to very large databases. Regarding FP-Growth, different parallel approaches have been proposed in literature [7, 4, 9]. The approach taken by [7] is based on horizontal database partitioning. The

---

* Supported by TUBITAK, grant number 108E016.

database is divided horizontally and distributed to a set nodes for local FP-Growth execution. A parallel FP-tree construction algorithm, called PFPTC, is proposed in [4]. The algorithm produces the frequent pattern trees simultaneously on compute nodes. Then, these trees are combined into a single FP-tree with an algorithm called FP-merge. The same work has also developed an algorithm called QFP-Growth, to shrink the large amount of results of FP-Growth. Multiple local frequent pattern tree, MLFPT for short, algorithm is proposed in [9]. Like others, that work also generates the local frequent pattern trees too. Recently, a parallel FP-Growth algorithm working on distributed systems has been proposed in [5]. The objective with that study is to ease the significant communication overhead, previously confirmed by [9, 7]. Their method, called Map-Reduce, is more scalable and useful for web data mining.

In this study, three different approaches for parallel FP-Growth have been proposed: (i) Static Parallel (SP) FP-Growth, (ii) Dynamic Parallel (DP) FP-Growth, and (iii) (Tree-Sharing) Dynamic Parallel (TSDP) FP-Growth. In SP FP-Growth, every node has a copy of database, and performs the first scan. Frequent 1-items are statically partitioned and each partition is assigned to one node. So, the global task is divided into a number of local tasks, hence a task parallel processing. In DP FP-Growth, there is a copy of database on each node too. But, unlike SP FP-Growth, task parallelism is implemented dynamically. In TSDP FP-Growth, only one node owns the database, and others do not have their copy. The owner creates sub databases to be processed by next idle worker node. The sub database is sent online to worker nodes, and they run FP-Growth on the received sub database. The results are sent back to the owner for merging. The task parallelism is implemented dynamically like the second method. TSDP FP-Growth is designed in case the data owner does not want to disclose the whole database to worker nodes, *e.g.*, due to some privacy policy.

2   FP-Growth Algorithm

Let the set of items (itemset) be $\mathcal{I} = \{i_1, i_2, \ldots, i_d\}$, and the transaction database be $\mathcal{D} = \{t_1, t_2, \ldots, t_n\}$, where each t_i is a transaction. Each transaction consists of a subset of items from the itemset, i.e., $t_i \subseteq \mathcal{I}, \forall i$. An itemset X is called a k-itemset if $|X| = k$. Given the database $\mathcal{D}$, the support of an itemset X is:

$$sup_{\mathcal{D}}(X) = |\{t_i : X \subseteq t_i, t_i \in \mathcal{D}\}|/|\mathcal{D}| \qquad (1)$$

For a support threshold σ, the frequent itemsets are defined as given next.

$$F_{\mathcal{D}}(\sigma) = \{< X, sup_{\mathcal{D}}(X) >: X \subseteq \mathcal{I}, sup_{\mathcal{D}}(X) \geq \sigma\} \qquad (2)$$

The FIM problem [1] then is to compute the set $F_{\mathcal{D}}(\sigma)$ given $\mathcal{D}$ and σ. A number of algorithms have been proposed to FIM problem, where the main concern is the efficiency. To this end, FP-Growth is one of the prominent solutions [3]. It is an efficient algorithm since it scans the database only twice and uses compact data structures.

FP-Growth algorithm works as explained next. First, the support of each single item is calculated by scanning the database once. Frequent single items are sorted in descending order of support, and then they are put in a list L. On the other hand, all transactions in the database is sorted in the same order, and infrequent items are deleted from all transactions. Then, from the sorted transactions, the database is put in a specialized compact data structure called FP-tree, a special prefix tree. The construction of FP-tree (frequent pattern tree) starts with creating a root node, and then inserting each modified transaction into the tree by scanning the database second time. Each tree node also counts the absolute support of the prefix. The FP-tree is then input to the FP-Growth algorithm. The algorithm starts with the least frequent item in L, and identifies all the paths, originated from the root and ending in the respective node in the FP-tree. These paths create the conditional pattern base which are used to create conditional FP-tree on which FP-Growth algorithm recurses. Finally, the process is repeated for all items in L in turn.

3   Parallel FP-Growth

As discussed in the introduction section, there are a few parallel FP-Growth proposals. They mainly leverage data parallelism for parallel processing [6]. In this study, we take a task parallel approach, and propose three variants, (i) Static Parallel (SP) FP-Growth, (ii) Dynamic Parallel (DP) FP-Growth, and (iii) (Tree-Sharing) Dynamic Parallel (TSDP) FP-Growth. The former two are applicable when all the participating nodes have the same database (replica) to be mined. Since the database is replicated, the nodes only communicate to coordinate the mining process. Since no data is exchanged but only coordination information, the communication overhead is too small. The third algorithm is mainly developed for setting where privacy is a concern. Suppose the scenario that one of the nodes has a database to be mined, but sharing it with other nodes as a whole violates its privacy policy. So, it may decide to partially share the database with other nodes to exploit the parallelism. Since the database is not replicated, the communication requires both coordination information and data (conditional FP-tree) exchanges. Hence, the communication overhead is higher.

3.1   Static Parallel FP-Growth

In this method, every participating node finds the frequent itemsets from the database using the support threshold, and creates FP-tree independently. Since, all the nodes use the same database and the same support threshold, they all find the same FP-tree. During this stage, there is no message passing between the nodes. The parallelism is obtained by dividing the task into subtasks. Each subtask is mining conditional FP-tree of a frequent single item. To do so, each compute node is assigned a number, and using a modulo operator it easily identifies its subtasks and computes the local output. Each and every subtask is processed exclusively by one node. The global result is obtained by simply concatenating all the local results, since the subtasks are independent and collectively exhaustive.

An important feature of this method is the static distribution of subtasks. In doing so, something that must be taken into consideration is the load balancing. Our heuristic to this end is to assign frequent items to nodes in a circular fashion.

3.2   Dynamic Parallel FP-Growth

DP FP-Growth is essentially the same as SP FP-Growth except the subtask distribution is done in a dynamic manner for better load balancing. This way, the objective that every node finishes at the same time is targeted. To implement, we identify a node as the master which coordinates the subtask assignment. Its job is to generate subtasks and assign the next subtask to the next idle node. The worker node gets the subtask identifier from the master, and generates frequent itemsets from the respective subtask and saves the local result. On termination of the assigned subtask, the worker node notifies the master node about its availability for another subtask. Like SP FP-Growth algorithm, each subtask is finding frequent itemsets from a conditional FP-tree. Hence, on termination, simply merging the local patterns give the global frequent itemsets. Besides the role of coordinator, the master node also runs a worker thread to contribute subtask processing.

3.3   (Tree-sharing) Dynamic Parallel FP-Growth

In this method, unlike the other two, only one node (master) has access to the database, and the FP-tree construction is done by that node. The worker nodes are there to receive subtasks, process them and return its results to the master. Since the worker nodes have no access to the database, the subtask itself must be received from the master. The subtasks are the same as before, i.e., each subtask is a conditional FP-tree mining. To send subtasks, the master nodes serializes the tree into a stream, and sends it to a designated worker. The receiving worker node deserializes the stream to construct the respective FP-tree. The FP-tree is then input to FP-Growth and the patters are locally saved. On termination, the local patterns are concatenated as before.

4   Experimental Evaluation

The algorithms are developed in C using MPI library. Our test platform is a cluster computer having 16 compute nodes, each of which is equipped with 16 GB of memory, Intel Core Quad 2.83 GHz processors and fast Ethernet communication interface. Each node runs 64-bit Linux operating system, equipped with OpenMP.

We present experimental results on two databases: a real market-basket database `Retail` [1], and a synthetic database `T20.I5.500K`. Figures 1, 2, and

---

[1] http://fimi.cs.helsinki.fi/data

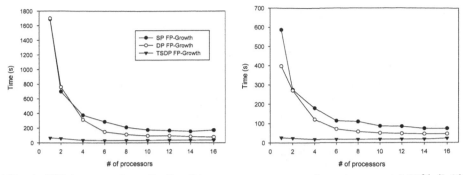

Fig. 1. Efficiency on `Retail`. Runtime vs. processor number at support 0.20% (left), and 0.40% (right).

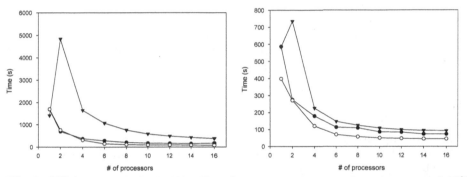

Fig. 2. Efficiency on `T20.I5.500K`. Runtime vs. processor number at support 0.20% (left), and 0.40% (right). The legends are the same as Fig. 1.

3 present the results. From Fig. 1 and 2, DP FP-Growth is better than SP FP-Growth for both databases. On the other hand, TSDP FP-Growth performs better than the others on `Retail` only. As another result, its relative performance on relatively larger `T20.I5.500K` suffers from too much communication overhead as anticipated. However, it should be kept in mind that this is the price paid for protecting the considered privacy. Nevertheless, it still has runtime improvements compared to the serial execution.

5   Conclusion

In this study, we developed a task parallel approach for parallel FP-Growth to run on cluster computers. To this end we developed three algorithms, SP FP-Growth, DP FP-Growth, and TSDP FP-Growth. The first two of them are designed for the cases where all the nodes have access to the database, while the third one is for the cases where only one node has access to the database. Due to the design, the first two has negligible communication cost, while the third

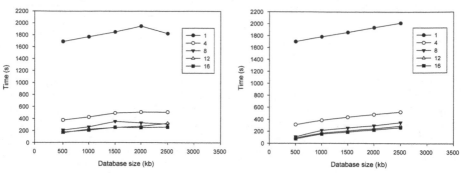

Fig. 3. Scalability: SP FP-Growth (left), and DP FP-Growth (right).

one may have considerable communication cost especially for large databases. Our experimental results show that all the three algorithms are scalable on cluster computers and achieve considerable speed up to make the mining process practical on relatively large databases.

References

1. R. Agrawal, T. Imielienski, and A. Swami. Mining association rules between sets of items in large databases. In *SIGMOD '93*, pages 207–216, 1993.
2. R. Agrawal and R. Srikant. Fast algorithms for mining association rules in large databases. In *VLDB'94*, pages 487–499, 1994.
3. J. Han, J. Pei, and Y. Yin. Mining frequent patterns without candidate generation. In *Proceedings of the 2000 ACM SIGMOD International Conference on Management of Data (SIGMOD 2000)*, pages 1–12, 2000.
4. Y-J. Lan and Y. Qiu. Parallel frequent itemsets mining algorithms without intermediate results. In *Proceedings of 2005 International Conference on Machine Learning and Cybernetics*, pages 2102–2107, 2005.
5. H. Li, Y. Wang, D. Zhang, M. Zhang, and E.Y. Chang. Pfp: Parallel fp-growth for query recommendation. In *Proceedings of the 2008 ACM Conference on Recommender Systems*, pages 107–114, 2008.
6. G.O. Ozdogan, O. Abul, and A. Yazici. Paralel veri madenciligi algoritmalari. In *Proceedings of the first National High-Performance and Grid Computing Conference*, pages 131–137, 2009 (in Turkish).
7. I. Pramudiono and M. Kitsuregawa. Parallel fp-growth on pc cluster. In *Proceedings of the 7th Pacific-Asia Conference of Knowledge Discovery and Data Mining*, pages 467–473, 2003.
8. A. Savasere, E. Omiecinski, and S. Navathe. An efficient algorithm for mining association rules in large databases. In *Proceedings of the 21st International Conference on Very Large Databases (VLDB'95)*, pages 432–444, 1995.
9. O.R. Zaiane, M. El-Hajj, and P. Lu. Fast parallel association rule mining without candidacy generation. In *Proceedings of the 2001 IEEE International Conference on Data Mining*, pages 665–668, 2001.

An Adaptive System for Movement Decision Support in Building Evacuation

Avgoustinos Filippoupolitis

afil@imperial.ac.uk
Imperial College London
Intelligent Systems and Networks
SW7 2BT, UK

Abstract. In this paper we propose the use of a system that provides movement decision support to evacuees. We first present a fully distributed system, which takes into account the spatial characteristics of hazard propagation. We also design and evaluate a system that is based on a decentralised architecture. We use a multi-agent simulation platform for building evacuation that we developed, in order to evaluate our proposed systems.

1 Introduction

There are various approaches regarding the problem of movement decision support during emergency situations. In [1] the authors propose a distributed algorithm for robot navigation using a sensor network and evaluate their approach using a robot and a sensor network composed of nine nodes. The authors in [2] propose an algorithm inspired by sensor network routing, in order to guide a flying robot. The evaluation scenario included only one human and twelve sensors positioned inside a building. In [3] a system based on sensor networks is proposed, for navigating the user to a goal location by avoiding hazardous areas. The path calculation algorithm is based on artificial potential fields.

Our goal is to design a system that operates during an emergency situation inside a building. The system should adapt to the changes of the environment and provide directions to the evacuees regarding the best available exit, in real time. We present a fully distributed system and a decentralised system that we have designed and compare their performance in various evacuation scenarios and different buildings architectures.

2 The Decision Support System

Our system is composed of a number of Decision Nodes(DNs) positioned in specific locations inside the building, whose role is to compute the best direction

This research was undertaken as part of the ALADDIN (Autonomous Learning Agents for Decentralised Data and Information Networks) project and is jointly funded by a BAE Systems and EPSRC (UK Engineering and Physical Research Council) strategic partnership (EP/C548051/1).

E. Gelenbe et al. (eds.), *Computer and Information Sciences*, Lecture Notes in Electrical Engineering 62, DOI 10.1007/978-90-481-9794-1_72,
© Springer Science+Business Media B.V. 2010

towards an exit. This is communicated to the evacuees via a dynamic panel or via a wireless device, such as a PDA, which is carried by the evacuees and receives the direction information from the DNs. We also assume that there is a network of sensor nodes installed in the building. Their role is to provide real-time information to the DNs regarding the conditions inside the building, such as the presence of fire or smoke. The known building layout is used to create a graph G. Each vertex of G represents a location where people can congregate, while a link between two vertices corresponds to a physical path that can be followed by the evacuees. The length $l(i, j)$ of a link (i, j) is the actual distance of the path between two neighbouring DNs. Each of the wireless sensors is associated to a link (i, j) and measures the intensity of the hazard $H(i, j)$ along the link. When there is not a hazard present, $H(i, j) = 1$ and its value increases along with the value of the observed hazard. We define the *effective length* of a link as: $L(i, j) = l(i, j) \cdot H(i, j)$. This metric expresses how hazardous a link is for a civilian that will traverse it. A DN is positioned at each of the vertices of the graph G, while a sensor node monitors the hazard intensity along a link between two DNs.

This paper extends the work that was presented in [4]. We let each sensor communicate with its neighbours and incorporate their readings into the "spatial" hazard value H_{sp} it reports. The number of neighbours with which a sensor can communicate is defined by a radius R. Let m be a sensor measuring the hazard level H_m on link (i, j). A sensor n measuring the hazard level H_n on a link (i', j'), belongs to the neighbours set $N(m)$ of m, if: $d(m, n) \leq R$, where $d(m, n)$ is the Euclidean distance of the sensors locations and R defines the radius of the neighbourhood area. The effective length $L_{sp}(i, j)$ that includes the spatial hazard information is given by $Lsp(i, j) = l(i, j) \cdot H_{sp}(i, j)$, where

$$H_{sp}(i, j) = H(i, j) + \frac{1}{|N(m)|} \sum_{k \in N(m)} H_k.$$

The distributed decision support algorithm that our system uses, is inspired by adaptive routing techniques such as the Cognitive Packet Network [5]. When the decision support system is in operation, each DN at u periodically executes Algorithm 1 and provides a suggestion to the evacuees that are in its vicinity. The suggestion is of the form **"go to v"**, where v is a neighbour of u.

Let us now present an algorithm that is based on a decentralised architecture. It uses a replicated data structure (i.e. the area graph), initially distributed to all the DNs. When a change in the environment occurs, due to the spreading of the fire, the DN that is close to the respective location detects this event. In order to inform the rest of the DNs regarding this change, the system must propagate this information to all the DNs. This process of updating the DNs can be achieved via flooding. Each DN compares the current value of the effective length $L(u, n)$, for each of its incident links, with the previous value $L_{old}(u, n)$. If a change is detected, it initiates the process of flooding so that the rest of the DNs can be informed. A message containing updated information information regarding the effective lengths is created and propagated inside the network. Such a message does not depend on the size of the area. Moreover, when a DN receives a metric

---

Algorithm 1 Distributed calculation for the effective length $L_{sp}(u, e)$

Send to every neighbour n of u, the effective length of the path from u to the exit
$e : L_{sp}(u, e)$
for each sensor node monitoring a link incident to u **do**
    Request hazard intensity H_{sp} from sensor node
    Calculate the effective length $L_{sp}(u, n)$,where n is a neighbour of u
end for
Update the effective length $L_{sp}(u, e)$ of the shortest path to the exit:
$L_{sp}(u, e) = \min \{L_{sp}(u, n) + L_{sp}(n, e): \forall$ neighbours n of $u\}$
Set the next suggested Decision Node v:
$v = \operatorname{argmin} \{L_{sp}(u, n) + L_{sp}(n, e): \forall$ neighbours n of $u\}$

---

update message, it only needs to update its local copy of the graph and forward the message to its neighbours (except the one from which it received it).No further processing of the message is necessary. Thus, in the implementation of the decentralised system we have made the assumption that the update in the graph of each DN, as a result of flooding, is performed rapidly. This way, each DN is able to have an up to date representation of the conditions inside the building when it locally executes the algorithm that calculates the safest path towards an exit. Each DN has locally available a global graph $G(V, E)$ of the area, where V is the set of DNs deployed in the building and E is the set of links between the DNs. Using the graph of the building, each DN executes a centralised version of the previous algorithm in order to provide a suggestion regarding the best direction towards an exit.

3 Simulation Results

We have implemented the proposed decision support system inside the Distributed Building Evacuation Simulator (DBES) [6]. When we use the decision support system during the evacuation procedure, the civilians move according to the directions of the DNs. When the evacuation procedure takes place without the use of the decision support system, each evacuee has full knowledge of the building's graph and decides his next destination by the use of Dijkstra's algorithm. When an evacuee reaches a hazardous area, he updates his representation of the building's graph and recalculates the shortest path. Between successive simulation runs, the civilians' initial locations and the spreading rate of the hazard are randomly chosen. The evacuation scenario takes place in a three storey building with three stair cases which provide access to the different floors and four exits located on the ground floor. A fire starts spreading on the ground floor of the building. The occupancy of the building is 60 civilians. The value of the radius of the sensor neighbourhood area is set to $R = 2m$. For each of these cases, we executed one hundred simulation runs. Figure 1 shows that when the system is in use, the civilians evacuate the building faster, avoiding exposure to the hazard. The decentralised system in some cases outperforms the fully distributed one, at the cost of limited scalability and increased memory requirements. Moreover, the use of spatial hazard information further improves the performance of the distributed algorithm.

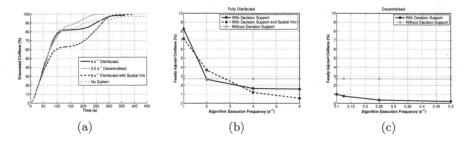

(a)   (b)   (c)

Fig. 1. Simulation results comparing the performance of the different algorithms

4   Conclusions

We designed and evaluated two algorithms used by a movement decision support system during an evacuation. The first is based on a fully distributed architecture while the second relies on a decentralised approach. We also compared our results against the case where a decision support system is not used. The overall evacuation outcome is improved by the use of the decision support system, since the civilians are able to reach an exit faster, by avoiding exposure to the hazard.

References

1. Batalin, M., Sukhatme, G.S., Hattig, M.: Mobile robot navigation using a sensor network. In: IEEE International Conference on Robotics and Automation. (April 2004) 636–642
2. Corke, P., Peterson, R., Rus, D.: Networked robots: Flying robot navigation using a sensor net. In: 11th International Symposium of Robotics Research (ISRR 2003), Springer-Verlag (October 2003) 234–243
3. Li, Q., Rosa, M.D., Rus, D.: Distributed algorithms for guiding navigation across a sensor network. In: MobiCom '03: Proceedings of the 9th annual international conference on Mobile computing and networking, New York, NY, USA, ACM (2003) 313–325
4. Filippoupolitis, A., Gelenbe, E.: A distributed decision support system for building evacuation. In: Proceedings of the 2nd IEEE International Conference on Human System Interaction, Catania, Italy, IEEE, New York, NY, USA (May 21-23 2009) 323–330
5. Gelenbe, E., Lent, R., Xu, Z.: Measurement and performance of a cognitive packet network. Journal of Computer Networks 37(6) (December 2001) 691–701
6. Dimakis, N., Filippoupolitis, A., Gelenbe, E.: Distributed building evacuation simulator for smart emergency management. Accepted for publication in The Computer Journal (2010)

A Maximum Degree Self-Stabilizing Spanning Tree Algorithm

Deniz Cokuslu[1,2,3]
denizcokuslu@iyte.edu.tr

Kayhan Erciyes[4]
kayhan.erciyes@izmir.edu.tr

Abdelkader Hameurlain[3]
hameur@irit.fr

[1]Izmir Institute of Technology, Department of Computer Engineering
Gulbahce, Urla, 35430 Izmir, Turkey
[2]International Computer Institute, Ege University
Bornova, 35100 Izmir, Turkey
[3]IRIT, Paul Sabatier University
118 Route de Narbonne, 31062 Toulouse, France
[4]Izmir University, Gursel Aksel Bulvari,
Uckuyular, 35350 Izmir, Turkey

Abstract. Spanning trees are fundamental topological structures in distributed environments which ease many applications that require frequent communication between nodes. In this paper, we examine and compare two spanning tree construction algorithms which rely on classical and self stabilization approach. Then, we propose a new self-stabilizing spanning tree construction algorithm which uses maximum degree heuristic while choosing the root node. We show experimentally that our new algorithm provides smaller tree diameters than the two existing approaches with favorable run-times.

1. Introduction

Spanning tree algorithms are widely used in many distributed applications. A spanning tree is a subset S of a graph G which contains every node in G without any cycles. Many algorithms have been developed to build different types of spanning trees [2,3]. Moreover, to cope up with the dynamicity of systems, self-stabilizing spanning tree algorithms have received attention recently [2]. Self-stabilizing paradigm ensures the validity of spanning tree structure without having the need to regenerate the spanning tree every time dynamicity occurs in the network. In this paper, we aim to show how self stabilization property affects the performance of a spanning tree construction algorithm. For this purpose, we select two spanning tree construction algorithms which do not consider any complex spanning tree property, a classical [3] and a self-stabilizing spanning tree construction algorithm [1]. We analyze, implement and test these two algorithms, and compare the test results in terms of runtime of the algorithms and resulting spanning tree diameters. We then

E. Gelenbe et al. (eds.), *Computer and Information Sciences*, Lecture Notes
in Electrical Engineering 62, DOI 10.1007/978-90-481-9794-1_73,
© Springer Science+Business Media B.V. 2010

propose a new self-stabilizing spanning tree construction algorithm based on [1] which considers degrees of nodes in determining the root node of the resulting spanning tree. The rest of this paper is organized as follows: Section 2 examines the two selected spanning tree algorithms by giving detailed analysis. The new self-stabilizing spanning tree algorithm is described in Section 3 and the implementation details of the three algorithms is given in Section 4. Finally in Conclusion, the tradeoffs and comparisons and advantages of the new algorithm are examined.

2. Main Algorithms

Classical distributed spanning tree construction approaches are excessively studied and many of them become the de facto standards in spanning tree construction such as Kshemkalyani and Singhal [3]. Besides classical approaches, there are also many studies which focus on self-stabilizing spanning tree construction [1,2]. In this section, we analyze, implement and compare the two spanning tree construction algorithms: memory-efficient self-stabilizing spanning tree algorithm (MEST) [1] and asynchronous concurrent initiator spanning tree algorithm (CIST) [3] and show the influence of the self stabilization on the performance of spanning tree construction algorithms.

2.1. Memory-efficient self-stabilizing spanning tree algorithm (MEST)

In [1], authors assume that nodes have unique identifiers and every node knows its neighbors. They also assume that nodes are aware of their neighbors' failures. In this model, every node runs the same algorithm. Each node i has local variables indicating its neighborhood (N_i), its parent node (P_i), its root node (R_i) and its distance to the root node (D_i). In the global legal state, each node has the same root with the biggest node id in the graph, parents of nodes are within their neighborhood and distance of each node is 1 bigger than its parent's distance ($D_i = D_{parent} + 1$). The root node has distance 0, and points to itself as its root and its parent. To achieve self stabilization, each node compares its neighbors' roots with its root node. If any neighbor has a bigger id root, then the node joins this tree.

2.2 Asynchronous Concurrent Initiator Spanning Tree Algorithm (CIST)

In the asynchronous concurrent initiator spanning tree algorithm [3], nodes only need to know their neighborhood information. The algorithm uses flooding in order to disseminate tree information to neighbors. Each node starts to build its own tree at the beginning. When a node wants to initiate the algorithm as a root, it sends a query message to its neighborhood indicating that it is a root node. When a node receives a query message it compares the id of the sender with the id of its root, if new root has a bigger id then the node changes its root to the new root, else sends a reject message.

3.   Maximum Degree Self-Stabilizing Spanning Tree (MDST) Algorithm

We propose an extended version of memory-efficient self-stabilizing spanning tree algorithm which considers degrees of nodes while selecting the root node. In [1], the algorithm constructs the spanning tree according to the id of the nodes by choosing the biggest id node as the root node. This heuristic may have some disadvantages in complex networks because it does not consider the suitability of the chosen node as a root node. For these reasons, we propose to modify the MEST algorithm so that it constructs a spanning tree rooted at the highest degree node. The assumption here is that the highest id node in the graph is a better candidate to be a root node than a randomly chosen root, because this choice may decrease the diameter of the resulting spanning tree by decreasing its height. To realize this, we first propose to use a simple hash function which combines degrees of nodes with their node ids. By using this function, each node generates a unique *tag* value which is sorted by nodes' degrees. The algorithm considers *tag* values in determining root of the spanning tree. At the end of the execution of the MDST algorithm, a spanning tree rooted at the highest degree node is constructed.

4. Implementation and Experiments

We implemented the three algorithms in the network simulator *ns2*. We generated 8 experiment scenarios by using randomly chosen wired network topologies ranging from 100 to 800 nodes. The runtime results of the algorithms can be seen in Fig.1.a. The difference between classical distributed approach and self-stabilizing approach is mainly caused by periodical updates in self-stabilizing algorithms. The effect of self stabilization property is magnified as the number of nodes is increased. While the runtime of asynchronous concurrent initiator spanning tree algorithm remains nearly constant, runtimes of self-stabilizing algorithms increase. But it is also seen that this increase is sub-linear with respect to the increase in the number of nodes which ensures the scalability of these algorithms. It can be observed that MDST performs much better than the original self-stabilizing spanning tree algorithm. The difference is more evident for greater number of nodes. Fig.1.b depicts the variation of diameters of resulting spanning trees by using three different algorithms. It may be seen that both MEST and CIST algorithms have resulted in similar results in terms of tree diameters, while MDST algorithm has resulted in smaller diameter spanning trees. This difference is caused by the heuristic which is used in choosing the root node.

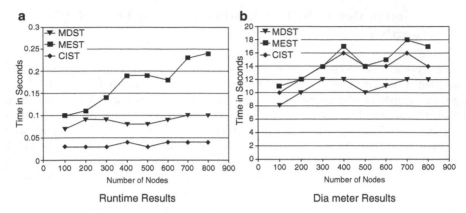

Fig.1 Results of spanning tree construction algorithms

5. Conclusions

In this paper, we described, implemented and compared simulation results of two basic existing spanning tree construction algorithms which rely on different paradigms and proposed a new self-stabilizing spanning tree algorithm which relies on choosing the maximum degree node as the root. We showed the differences and similarities between self-stabilizing and classical approaches and the new algorithm in terms of experiment results. According to the implementation results, we can say that both classical and self-stabilizing spanning tree algorithms behave similarly in terms of resulting spanning tree's degrees if the constraints are similar. In MDST algorithm, with the use of maximum degree heuristic, the diameter of the resulting spanning tree is decreased. According to the runtime results, we can say that self-stabilizing spanning tree algorithms are more sensible to the number of nodes than the classical approach. This difference is mainly caused by self stabilization property. Although runtime of the self-stabilizing spanning tree algorithms increase when the size of the network grows, this increase is sub-linear. This sub-linear increase proves the scalability of the self-stabilizing algorithms as investigated in this study. The benefit is the self stabilization property which can drastically decrease the maintenance costs of spanning trees in large networks.

References

[1]   Y. Afek, S. Kutten, and M. Yung. Memory-efficient self stabilizing protocols for general networks. In *WDAG90: Proceedings of the 4th International Workshop on Distributed Algorithms*, pages 15–28. Springer-Verlag, 1991.

[2]   Felix C. Gärtner. A survey of self-stabilizing spanning-tree construction algorithms. Technical report, 2003.

[3]   A. D. Kshemkalyani and M. Singhal. *Distributed Computing: Principles, Algorithms, and Systems*. Cambridge University Press, 2008.

11 Hardware Design

Defect-Tolerant Logic Mapping for Nanocrossbars Based on Two-Dimensional Sort

Sezer Gören, H. Fatih Ugurdag, Okan Palaz

Department of Computer Engineering
Bahçesehir University, Besiktas, Istanbul, Turkey
sgoren@bahcesehir.edu.tr

Abstract. High defect densities in self-assembled nanotechnology require defect tolerant design strategies. This article presents a heuristic that addresses the problem of mapping logic functions onto defective nanocrossbar structures. The heuristic is defect-aware, thus uses a defect map during the logic mapping process. The proposed algorithm involves a two-dimensional sort (2D-Sort) and is significantly faster than the previous works with defect-aware design flow approaches. This is mostly due to the fact that the search space in our case becomes smaller when a 2D-Sort is applied on both the logic function and crossbar tables.

1 Introduction

Nanoelectronic [4, 5] devices such as carbon nanotubes and silicon nanowires can be chemically self-assembled on a molecule-by-molecule basis due to their very regular structures. Since the regular and chemically self-assembled nature of these devices can support implementation of regular arrays similar to FPGAs, reprogrammable nanoarchitectures such as crossbars are currently being investigated.

Nanocrossbars consist of several perpendicular nanowires and two molecular diodes at the crosspoints. The horizontal nanowires are the inputs whereas the vertical nanowires are the outputs. The molecular diodes at the crosspoints act like programmable switches and contain only a few tens of atoms. Obviously, these devices exhibit higher defect rates, since with such small contact areas they can get damaged very easily and random breaks can occur during manufacturing. In the presence of defects, some nanowires or switches become unusable. Therefore, as opposed to a CMOS Programmable Logic Array (PLA), a nanocrossbar structure cannot offer full connectivity between every pair of perpendicular wires. Due to such topological constraints in nanocrossbars, logic synthesis process in a nanocrossbar-used-system becomes more difficult than that of a traditional PLA-based system. CMOS PLA based logic synthesis involves two steps: i) logic minimization and ii) logic mapping on to the underlying physical structure. On the other hand, for nanocrossbar based logic synthesis, two approaches have been proposed by researchers — defect-unaware [6] and defect-aware [2, 3, 7] design flows.

E. Gelenbe et al. (eds.), *Computer and Information Sciences*, Lecture Notes
in Electrical Engineering 62, DOI 10.1007/978-90-481-9794-1_74,
© Springer Science+Business Media B.V. 2010

Defect-aware design flow is the main focus of this paper and involves three steps: i) logic minimization (same as CMOS PLA-based), ii) identification of defect locations, and iii) logic mapping on to underlying physical structure by considering the defect map to avoid mapping logic variables and product terms on to the breaks.

In this paper, we represent a defect-aware logic mapping heuristic. Logic function (given in sum-of-products (product-of-sums) form) and the crossbar as tables of variables and product terms. 2D-Sort is applied on both the logic function and crossbar tables that are constructed from logic/crossbar variables and logic/crossbar products. Then a mapping from logic function table to crossbar table is performed afterwards. The intuition here is that 2D-Sort can make the tables look alike so that matching them row by row becomes trivial.

2   Preliminaries

In this paper, the process of embedding a logic function in a topologically constrained nanocrossbar is modeled by mapping the process to the problem of matching two tables. A *table* consists of an ordered arrangement of rows and columns.

Consider a two-level logic function in a sum-of-products form. The relationship between the logic variable set and the product set can be represented by a table $T(I,P,m)$, with the logic variable set I representing the rows, the product set P representing the columns, and the intersection of a row and a column, so-called a *cell*, is filled by the function $m(i,p): I \times P \to V_O$ where $V_O = \{0,1\}$. The function $m(i,p)$, where $i \in I$ and $p \in P$ is defined as

$$m(i,p) = \begin{cases} 1 & \text{if } p \text{ contains } i \\ 0 & \text{otherwise} \end{cases} \tag{1}$$

Both the logic function and crossbar can be represented as a table of products and variables. Each cell of the table is denoted as a "1" when the corresponding product term contains the corresponding variable; otherwise it is denoted as a "0".

Using a simple crosspoint defect model [10], a "0" assigned cell in a crossbar table corresponds to a *non-programmable* crosspoint, whereas a "1" assigned cell in a crossbar table corresponds to a *programmable* crosspoint. A programmable crosspoint can be in two states: open and closed. A nonprogrammable crosspoint cannot be programmed into closed state, but can be set into an open state. A "0" cell in a logic function table corresponds to a crosspoint required to be programmed into open state, whereas a "1" cell in a logic function table corresponds to a crosspoint required to be programmed into closed state. Note that every cell in a defect-free crossbar table is a "1" cell.

We define the problem of *table matching* as follows. Given a logic function table $T_L(I_L, P_L, m_L)$ and a crossbar table $T_X(I_X, P_X, m_X)$, find a subtable $T_C(I_C, P_C, m_X)$ in T_X where $|I_C| = |I_L|$, $|P_C| = |P_L|$, $I_C \subseteq I_X$, and $P_C \subseteq P_X$ such that $\forall (i_L \in I_L \text{ and } p_L \in P_L)$, $i_C \in I_C$, and $p_C \in P_C$ $m_L(i_L, p_L) \cong m_X(i_C, p_C)$ hold.

Compatibility is denoted as " $\cong$ " and defined as follows:

$$m_L(i_L, p_L) \cong m_X(i_X, p_X) \text{ if } (m_L(i_L, p_L) == m_x(i_X, p_X) \text{ or } m_x(i_X, p_X) == 1) \qquad (2)$$

The *degree of a variable* is defined as the total number of product terms which contain the variable. In other words, the degree of a variable is the sum of cells of the corresponding variable column. The *degree of a product term* is defined as the number of variables that the product term contains. Variable and product degrees are used to prune impossible mappings. A crossbar variable with degree k can only be mapped to a logic variable with degree less than or equal to k. Similarly, a crossbar product term with degree k can only be mapped to a logic product term with degree less than or equal to k.

Another property is that shuffling rows or columns of a table does not change the relationship between the variable and product sets. We apply this property during the process of matching the logic and crossbar tables.

In this paper, we define *2D-Sort* as ordering rows and columns of a table such that the numeric value of both the rows and columns are arranged in the binary array configuration: MSB and LSB of a row are taken as the left and right entries and rows are sorted in ascending order from top to bottom, whereas MSB and LSB of a column are taken as the top and bottom entries of the table and columns are sorted in ascending order from left to right. 2D-Sort is basically sorting rows first, after that sorting columns of the table which has its rows sorted recently and repeat this process – one after the other until the table is sorted in both directions. Note that each row of the logic function table is a $|I_L|$-digit binary number whereas each column is a $|P_L|$-digit binary number. To sort a d-digit number, *radix sort* algorithm is chosen. A d-digit number occupies a field of d columns. Radix sort solves the sorting problem by sorting on the least significant digit first, then on the second-least significant digit, and so on. The process continues until the "deck" of numbers has been sorted on all d digits.

We define *sorting by variable and product term degrees* (sort by *VD* and *PD*) as the ordering of rows and columns of a table in ascending variable and product degrees.

3   Logic Mapping Heuristic

Pseudocode of the logic mapping heuristic is presented in Fig. 1. In Fig. 1, the logic function table T_L and the crossbar table T_X are given as the inputs. In lines 1-2 of Fig. 1, the degrees of variables and product terms of the logic function table are calculated. In line 3 of Fig. 1, T_L is sorted by VD_L and PD_L. After that, T_L is 2D-sorted (line 4 in Fig. 1) as described in the previous section. Next step (shown in line 6) is to generate a subtable $T_C(I_C, P_C, m_X)$ that has the same number of logic

```
     /* Given  T_L(I_L,P_L,m_L)  and  T_X(I_X,P_X,m_X)  */
1    VD_L = VariableDegrees (T_L);
2    PD_L = ProductDegrees (T_L);
3    SortByVD&PD (T_L,VD_L,PD_L);
4    2DSort (T_L);
5    while (!TimeOut())
6       T_C = GenerateSubTable (T_X);
7       VD_C = VariableDegrees (T_C);
8       PD_C = ProductDegrees (T_C);
9       PruneImpossible (T_C);
10      if (CheckDegrees (T_C,T_L))
11         while (i < limit)
12            SortByVD&PD (T_C,VD_C,PD_C);
13            2DSort (T_C);
14            PerformExactRowMatch (T_L, T_C);
15            if (PerformCompatRowMatch (T_L, T_C))
16              return SUCCESS;
17            i++;
18         endwhile
19         if (MatchedCount)
20            if (ReplaceUnmatchedRows (T_C,T_X))
21               return SUCCESS;
22   endwhile
23   return FAIL;
```

Fig. 1. Pseudocode of the proposed algorithm.

variables and product terms ($|I_C| = |I_L|$ and $|P_C| = |P_L|$) as T_L. Sets I_C and P_C are randomly constructed from the crossbar variable and product sets I_X and P_X. After choosing subtable T_C, the degrees of variables and product terms are calculated in lines 7 and 8. As we described in the previous section before, the degrees of T_C are checked against the degrees of T_L. If any variable degree of T_C is lower than the minimum variable degree of T_L, then the corresponding column is replaced by another variable from I_X and a new T_C is built. Similarly, if any product term degree of T_C is lower than the minimum product term degree of T_L, then the corresponding row is replaced by another product term. This process is shown in lines 9 and 10. After pruning and checking degrees, T_C is sorted by VD_C and PD_C. After that, T_C is 2D-sorted (lines 12 and 13).

Once T_C is 2D-sorted, exact row match (shown in line 14 of Fig. 1) is performed by considering each row of T_L and looking for an exactly matching row in T_C. After this step, compatible row match is performed considering the rest of the unmatched rows of T_L and looking for compatible rows in T_C. Compatible rows are found using the " $\cong$ " relation defined in Table 1. If all the rows of T_L are mapped to rows of T_C, then the algorithm returns success, otherwise T_C is re-sorted by VD_C and PD_C. In lines 19-20 of the algorithm, the unmatched rows are replaced by the rows from T_X that have not been tried. Then, if all unmatched rows are replaced, the algorithm returns success. Note that if the unmatched row count is zero, then the all of the variables have to be replaced so a new T_C is constructed by using the variables that have not been tried, the while loop (in line 5) is repeated. If the timeout limit is reached, the algorithm decides that there is no solution for the given crossbar table.

3   Experimental Results

We have implemented the proposed heuristic in C, and the experiments have been performed on a laptop computer with an Intel Pentium 1.73GHz CPU and 1GB memory running Linux using LGSynth93 logic synthesis benchmarks [1].

Table 1. LGSynth93 Benchmarks Results

Circuit	$|I|/|O|/|P|$	5%		7%		10%	
		Time (s)	Row Match %	Time (s)	Row Match %	Time (s)	Row Match %
rd53	10/3/32	0.036	100	0.038	100	0.040	100
inc	14/9/34	0.158	100	0.168	100	0.160	100
misex2	50/18/29	0.088	100	0.088	100	0.094	100
sao2	20/4/58	0.262	100	0.304	100	0.298	100
bw	10/28/65	0.052	100	0.052	100	0.066	100
5xp1	14/10/75	0.104	100	0.106	100	0.112	100
9sym	18/1/87	1.038	100	1.106	100	1.180	100
rd73	14/3/141	0.598	100	0.686	100	0.708	100
table5	34/15/158	9.305	98	12.78	94	16.181	88
clip	18/5/167	0.838	100	0.961	99	0.989	99
t481	32/1/481	59.160	100	63.160	100	64.82	100

Same size crossbars are generated at various defect rates; 5%, 7%, and 10%. The results for LGSynth93 benchmarks are shown in Table 1. Except the benchmarks, *table5* (at 5%, 7%, and 10% cases) and *clip* (7% and 10% cases), the algorithm was able to match 100% of rows for all the defect rates in all of the experiments. The proposed technique is also compared to SAT-based technique [7] using larger crossbars with defect-rates 10%, 15% show as in Table 2.

Table 1. Compared with SAT-based Technique (50% redundancy)

Circuit	$|I|/|O|/|P|$	Defect-free (0%)		10%		15%	
		Time (s) [16]	Time (s) Ours	Time (s) [16]	Time (s) Ours	Time (s) [16]	Time (s) Ours
rd53	10/3/32	0.017	0.020	0.046	0.020	0.039	0.020
inc	14/9/34	0.018	0.048	0.054	0.080	0.063	0.090
misex2	50/18/29	0.068	0.046	0.146	0.047	0.483	0.046
sao2	20/4/58	0.087	0.116	0.176	0.164	0.214	0.165
bw	10/28/65	0.131	0.025	0.331	0.027	0.724	0.027
5xp1	14/10/75	0.179	0.052	0.411	0.056	0.488	0.058
9sym	18/1/87	0.297	0.157	0.738	0.590	0.630	0.576
rd73	14/3/141	1.463	0.198	2.219	0.354	2.288	0.364
table5	34/15/158	2.120	0.537	188.8	7.695	>1200	7.847
clip	18/5/167	2.380	0.301	4.107	0.499	6.582	0.526
t481	32/1/481	NA	1.539	NA	32.26	NA	35.092

4   Conclusion

In this paper, we have presented a heuristic for logic mapping on nanocrossbars based on 2D-Sort. This technique has a defect-aware design flow where it uses a defect map during the logic mapping process. The intuition behind the technique is that ordering rows and columns of two same size tables in the same way will make them look alike so that they can be compared row by row. The proposed algorithm has polynomial time complexity; it can efficiently solve large logic mapping problems.

References

1.   ACM/SIGDA benchmarks: 1993 LGSynth Benchmarks, http://www.cbl.ncsu.edu/benchmarks/LGSynth93/.
2.   NAEIMI, H. 2005. A Greedy Algorithm for Tolerating Defective Crosspoints in NanoPLA Design. M.S. Thesis, Calif. Inst. Of Technology.
3.   RAO, W., ORAILOGLU, A. AND KARRI, R. 2009. Logic Mapping in Crossbar-Based Nanoarchitectures. IEEE Design & Test of Computers, 26, 68-76.
4.   RATNER, M.A. AND RATNER, D. 2002. Nanotechnology: A Gentle Introduction to the Next Big Idea. Prentice Hall PTR.
5.   SHUKLA, S. K. AND BAHAR, R. I. 2004. Nano, Quantum and Molecular Computing: Implications to High Level Design and Validation, Kluwer Academic Publishers, Boston, MA.
6.   TAHOORI, M.B. 2005. A mapping algorithm for defect-tolerance of reconfigurable nano-architectures. In Proceedings of Int'l Conf. on Computer-Aided Design. 667-671.
7.   ZHENG, Y. AND HUANG, C. 2009. Defect-aware Logic Mapping for Nanowire-based Programmable Logic Arrays via Satisfiability. In *Proceedings of Conf. Design Automation and Test in Europe*.

Faster Montgomery Modular Multiplication without Pre-computational Phase For Some Classes of Finite Fields

Sedat Akleylek *, Murat Cenk, and Ferruh Özbudak **

Institute of Applied Mathematics, Middle East Technical University, Ankara, Turkey
{akleylek,mcenk,ozbudak}@metu.edu.tr

Abstract. In this paper, we give faster versions of Montgomery modular multiplication algorithm without pre-computational phase for $GF(p)$ and $GF(2^m)$ which can be considered as a generalization of [3], [4] and [5]. We propose sets of moduli different than [3], [4] and [5] which can be used in PKC applications. We show that one can obtain efficient Montgomery modular multiplication architecture in view of the number of AND gates and XOR gates by choosing proposed sets of moduli. We eliminate pre-computational phase with proposed sets of moduli. These methods are easy to implement for hardware.

Keywords: Montgomery modular multiplication, elliptic curve cryptography, public key cryptography, VLSI implementation

1 Introduction

Finite field arithmetic operations in $GF(p)$ or $GF(2^m)$ have many applications in coding theory, digital signal processing, pseudorandom number generation and cryptography [2], [7], [9]. It is important to have an efficient implementation of the underlying field arithmetic and this corresponds to the field arithmetic for $GF(p)$ or $GF(2^m)$. Scalar multiplication and modular exponentiation are the core operations of ECDSA and RSA, respectively. Montgomery modular multiplication algorithm is one of the most commonly used algorithm in hardware applications [1].

This note is organized as follows: Section 2 describes Montgomery modular multiplication algorithm for prime fields and presents the idea for prime case. In Section 3, we illustrate our method for certain finite fields of characteristic 2 and compare the complexities of original and our method. We conclude the paper in Section 4.

---

* Sedat Akleylek is also with the Department of Computer Engineering, Ondokuz Mayıs University

** Ferruh Özbudak is also with the Department of Mathematics, Middle East Technical University

E. Gelenbe et al. (eds.), *Computer and Information Sciences*, Lecture Notes in Electrical Engineering 62, DOI 10.1007/978-90-481-9794-1_75,
© Springer Science+Business Media B.V. 2010

2   Faster Montgomery Modular Multiplication Algorithm without Pre-computational Phase For Prime Fields

Let $w = 2^{w_1}$ be the word-size, where $w_1 > 2$ is an integer and $n_w = \lceil \frac{n}{w} \rceil$ be the number of words of n-bit moduli. Montgomery modular multiplication method proposed in 1985 in [8] is shown in Algorithm 1 for prime fields in short.

Algorithm 1 Montgomery Modular Multiplication Algorithm in $GF(p)$ [8]

Input: $A = \sum_{i=0}^{n-1} a_i r^i$, $B = \sum_{i=0}^{n-1} b_i r^i$, $M = \sum_{i=0}^{n-1} m_i r^i$, with $m_{n-1} \neq 0, 0 \leq A, B <$
    M, $gcd(r, M) = 1$, $r = 2^w$, $M' \equiv -M^{-1}$ (mod r) and $n_w = \lceil \frac{n}{w} \rceil$.
Output: $C = A \cdot B \cdot r^{-n_w}$ (mod M)
1: $C \leftarrow 0$
2: **for** $i = 0$ to $n_w - 1$ **do**
3:     $C \leftarrow C + A \cdot b_i$
4:     $q \leftarrow (C \pmod{r})M'$ (mod r)
5:     $C \leftarrow (C + q \cdot M)/r$
6: **end for**
7: **if** $C \geq M$ **then**
8:     $C \leftarrow C - M$
9: **end if**

Knezevic et.al. proposed two sets of moduli for speeding up Montgomery modular multiplication in [3] and [5]. The main idea presented in [3] and [5] is the following: Let M be the moduli, $M' \equiv -M^{-1}$ (mod 2^w) and Δ be an integer with $1 \leq \Delta < 2^{n-w}$. If M is of the form $\Delta 2^w + 1$, then $M' = -1$ and similarly, if M is of the form $\Delta 2^w - 1$, then $M' = 1$. By using these sets of moduli, one can eliminate multiplication by M' in Algorithm 1 in Step 4.

Now, we propose new sets of moduli for which pre-computational phase is eliminated and Step 4 of Algorithm 1 is simplified. Our starting point to obtain faster Montgomery modular multiplication without pre-computational phase is the following observation that extends the idea defined in [3] and [5]. We explain our contribution in Proposition 1 and Proposition 2 for prime fields.

Proposition 1. *Let M be an n-bit prime number, $k = 2^{w_1 - i}$, where $0 < i \leq w_1$, $M' \equiv -M^{-1}$ (mod 2^w) and Δ be an integer with $0 \leq \Delta < 2^{n-w}$.*

i) If $M = 2^n + \Delta \cdot 2^w + (2^k + 1)$, $M' = \frac{2^w - 1}{2^k + 1}$.
ii) If $M = 2^n + \Delta \cdot 2^w + (2^k - 1)$, $M' = \frac{2^w - 1}{2^k - 1}$.
iii) If $M = 2^n + \Delta \cdot 2^w - (2^k + 1)$, $M' = -\frac{2^w - 1}{2^k + 1}$.
iv) If $M = 2^n + \Delta \cdot 2^w - (2^k - 1)$, $M' = -\frac{2^w - 1}{2^k - 1}$.

Proof. We give the sketch of the proof of i). Other cases can be proved similarly.

$$2^w - 1 = (2^{2^{w_1-1}} - 1)(2^{2^{w_1-1}} + 1) = (2^{2^{w_1-2}} - 1)(2^{2^{w_1-2}} + 1)(2^{2^{w_1-1}} + 1)$$
$$= (2^{2^0} - 1)(2^{2^0} + 1) \cdots (2^{2^{w_1-3}} + 1)(2^{2^{w_1-2}} + 1)(2^{2^{w_1-1}} + 1)$$

Since $k = 2^{w_1-i}$, $2^k + 1$ is a factor of $2^w - 1$. Therefore, one can obtain $M' = \frac{(2^w-1)}{(2^k+1)}$.   □

Since the sets of moduli explained in Proposition 1 causes relatively small M''s, the multiplication with M' can be considered as a constant multiplication. Pre-computational phase and multiplication can be omitted. For example, let $w = 2^3$ and $M = 2^{285} + 2^4 + 1$. Then, $M' = \frac{2^8-1}{17} = 15$ and one can consider M' as a constant. One can obtain different sets of moduli by changing the range of k. This observation is given as a Proposition 2.

Proposition 2. *Let M be an n-bit prime number, $\frac{w}{2} \leq k < w$, $M' \equiv -M^{-1}$ (mod 2^w) and Δ be an integer with $0 \leq \Delta < 2^{n-w}$.*

i) If $M = 2^n + \Delta \cdot 2^w + (2^k + 1)$, $M' = 2^k - 1$.
ii) If $M = 2^n + \Delta \cdot 2^w + (2^k - 1)$, $M' = 2^k + 1$.
iii) If $M = 2^n + \Delta \cdot 2^w - (2^k + 1)$, $M' = -2^k + 1$.
iv) If $M = 2^n + \Delta \cdot 2^w - (2^k - 1)$, $M' = -2^k - 1$.

By using Proposition 1 and Proposition 2, one can define new sets of moduli for efficient Montgomery modular multiplication without pre-computational phase. These helps us to simplify Step 4 of the Algorithm 1. If one uses the sets of moduli defined in Proposition 1 and Proposition 2, the multiplication with M' is just shifting and addition operation. For example, if $M' = 2^k + 1$, then, multiplication with 2^k is k-times shifting. Therefore, Step 4 in Algorithm 1 can be considered as $q \leftarrow (C + C << k)$ (mod r).

3   Faster Montgomery Modular Multiplication Algorithm without Pre-computational Phase For Binary Fields

Let $A(x)$ and $B(x)$ be the elements in $GF(2^n) \cong GF(2)[x]/M(x)$ generated by an irreducible polynomial $M(x)$ of degree n. Let $\{1, x, x^2, ..., x^{n-1}\}$ be a polynomial basis for $GF(2^n)$. Montgomery modular multiplication method for binary fields is proposed in [6]. Now, we propose new sets of moduli for which pre-computational phase is eliminated. We explain our contribution in Proposition 3 that extends the idea defined in [4] for binary fields.

Proposition 3. *Let $GF(2^n) \cong GF(2)[x]/M(x)$ and $M(x) = x^n + x^w \cdot \Delta(x) + x^k + 1$ such that $\Delta(x) = \sum_{i=0}^{n-w-1} m_i x^i$, where $1 \leq w < n$, $m_i \in GF(2)$ and $k \geq 1$. Let $M'(x) \equiv M(x)^{-1}$ (mod x^w). Then,*

i) If $k = 1$, then $M'(x) = x^{w-1} + x^{w-2} + \cdots + x + 1$.
ii) If $\frac{w}{2} \leq k < w$, then $M'(x) = x^k + 1$.
iii) If $k \geq w$, then $M'(x) = 1$. The idea of this case is stated in [4].

Table 1 compares the original method with the method given in this study for binary fields in view of $\#AND$ gates, $\#XOR$ gates and pre-computational phase. According to Table 1, the proposed method gives better results in view of $\#AND$ gates and $\#XOR$ gates with the proposed sets of moduli.

Table 1. Comparison of Modular Multiplication Algorithms

	#AND	#XOR	Pre-computation
[6]	$3n^2$	$(n-1)(3n+5)$	Yes
Our Results	$2n^2$	$(n-1)(2n+5)$	No

4   Conclusion

In this paper, we extend the sets of moduli defined in [3], [4] and [5]. We give faster versions of Montgomery modular multiplication algorithm without pre-computational phase for $GF(p)$ and $GF(2^m)$ which can be considered as a generalization of [3], [4] and [5]. We eliminate pre-computational phase with the proposed sets of moduli which can be used in PKC applications. We show that one can obtain efficient Montgomery modular multiplication architecture in view of the number of AND gates and XOR gates by choosing proposed set of moduli. We show that these methods are easy to implement for hardware.

5   Acknowledgment

The second and third authors are partially supported by TÜBİTAK under Grant No.TBAG-107T826.

References

1. H. Cohen and G. Frey, *Handbook of Elliptic and Hyperelliptic Curve Cryptography*, Discrete Mathematics and Its Applications 34, ChapmanHall/CRC, 2005.
2. D. Hankerson, A. Menezes and S. Vanstone, *Guide to Elliptic Curve Cryptography*, Springer, 2004.
3. M. Knezevic, L. Batina and I. Verbauwhede, *Modular Reduction without Precomputational Phase*, IEEE International Symposium on Circuits and Systems (ISCAS 2009), IEEE, 4 pages, 2009.
4. M. Knezevic, J. Fan, K. Sakiyama, and I. Verbauwhede, *Modular Reduction in $GF(2^n)$ without Pre-Computational Phase*, International Workshop on the Arithmetic of Finite Fields (WAIFI 2008), LNCS 5130, pp. 77-87, 2008.
5. M. Knezevic, F. Vercauteren, and I. Verbauwhede, *Faster Interleaved Modular Multiplication Based on Barrett and Montgomery Reduction Methods*, COSIC internal report, 8 pages, 2009.
6. Ç.K. Koç and T. Acar, *Montgomery Multiplication in $GF(2^k)$*, Designs, Codes and Cryptography, vol. 14, pp. 57-69, 1998.
7. R.Lidl and H. Niederreiter, *Introduction to Finite Fields and Their Applications*, Cambridge University, 1997.
8. P. Montgomery, *Modular multiplication without trial division*, in Mathematics of Computation, vol. 44, pp. 519-521, April 1985.
9. G. Mullen and C. Mummert, *Finite Fields and Applications*, American Mathematical Society, 2007.

Hybrid Heuristics for Optimizing Energy Consumption in Embedded Systems

Maha IDRISSI AOUAD[1], René SCHOTT[2] and Olivier ZENDRA[1]

[1] INRIA Nancy - Grand Est / LORIA. 615, Rue du Jardin Botanique,
54600 Villers-Lès-Nancy, France
{Maha.IdrissiAouad, Olivier.Zendra}@inria.fr
[2] IECN - LORIA, Nancy-Université, Université Henri Poincaré.
54506 Vandoeuvre-Lès-Nancy, France
Rene.Schott@loria.fr

Abstract. In this paper, we propose new hybrid heuristics for memory management which outperform the best known existing heuristic (*BEH*). In fact, nearly from 76% up to 98% less energy consumption is recorded. Contrary to BEH, our hybrid heuristics do not require list sorting.

1 Introduction

Reducing memory energy consumption of embedded systems is crucial. To do so, various options exist. In this paper, we will focus on software techniques working on the memory management. Most authors rely on Scratch-Pad Memories (*SPMs*) rather than caches [6]. Although cache memory helps a lot with program speed, it is not the most appropriate for embedded systems. In fact, cache increases the system size and its energy cost (cache area plus managing logic). Like cache, SPM consists of small, fast SRAM. The main difference is that SPM is directly and explicitly managed at the software level, either by the developer or by the compiler which makes it more predictable. SPM requires up to 40% less energy and 34% less area than cache [1]. Additionally, manufacturing SPM cost is lower. In this paper, we will therefore use an SPM in our memory architecture. The rest of the paper is organized as follows. Section 2 describes BEH. Section 3 gives the energy model we used. Section 4 describes our optimization problem. Section 5 presents our hybrid heuristics. Section 6 shows the experimental results obtained. Finally, Section 7 concludes and gives some perspectives.

2 Best Known Existing Heuristic: BEH

BEH consists in allocating data memory into SPM by number of accesses and size. Data are sorted according to their ratio (access number/size) in descending order. The data with the highest ratio is allocated first into SPM as there is space available. Else it is allocated in DRAM. This heuristic uses a sorting method which can be computationally expensive for a large amount of data. Additionally, this sorting method will not work very well in a dynamic perspective where the SPM maximum capacity is not known in advance.

E. Gelenbe et al. (eds.), *Computer and Information Sciences*, Lecture Notes in Electrical Engineering 62, DOI 10.1007/978-90-481-9794-1_76,
© Springer Science+Business Media B.V. 2010

3   Memory Energy Estimation Model

We consider a memory architecture composed by an SPM, an instruction cache and a DRAM. Equation 1 gives the energy model where the terms refer to the total energy consumed respectively in SPM, in instruction cache and in DRAM.

$$E = E_{tspm} + E_{tic} + E_{tdram} \tag{1}$$

We distinguish between Write-Through (*WT*) and Write-Back (*WB*) cache policies [8]. Our aim is to minimize Equation 2 (terms are explained in Table 1).

$$
\begin{aligned}
E = {}& N_{spmr} * E_{spmr} + N_{spmw} * E_{spmw} \\
& + \sum_{k=1}^{N_{icr}} [h_{i_k} * E_{icr} + (1 - h_{i_k}) * [E_{dramr} + E_{icw} \\
& \quad + (1 - WP_i) * DB_{i_k} * (E_{icr} + E_{dramw})]] \\
& + \sum_{k=1}^{N_{icw}} [WP_i * E_{dramw} + h_{i_k} * E_{icw} + (1 - WP_i) * \\
& \quad (1 - h_{i_k}) * [E_{icw} + DB_{i_k} * (E_{icr} + E_{dramw})]] \\
& + N_{dramr} * E_{dramr} + N_{dramw} * E_{dramw}
\end{aligned}
\tag{2}
$$

Table 1. List of terms.

Term	Meaning
E_{spmr}	Energy consumed during a reading from SPM.
E_{spmw}	Energy consumed during a writing into SPM.
N_{spmr}	Reading access number to SPM.
N_{spmw}	Writing access number to SPM.
E_{icr}	Energy consumed during a reading from instruction cache.
E_{icw}	Energy consumed during a writing into instruction cache.
N_{icr}	Reading access number to instruction cache.
N_{icw}	Writing access number to instruction cache.
E_{dramr}	Energy consumed during a reading from DRAM.
E_{dramw}	Energy consumed during a writing into DRAM.
N_{dramr}	Reading access number to DRAM.
N_{dramw}	Writing access number to DRAM.
WP_i	The considered cache write policy: WT or WB. In case of WT, $WP_i = 1$ else, in case of WB then $WP_i = 0$.
DB_{i_k}	Dirty Bit used in case of WB to indicate during the access k if the instruction cache line has been modified before ($DB_i = 1$) or not ($DB_i = 0$).
h_{i_k}	Type of the access k to the instruction cache. In case of cache hit, $h_{i_k} = 1$. In case of cache miss, $h_{i_k} = 0$.

4   Optimization Problem

Our problem is a combinatorial optimization problem. It is a kind of knapsack problem. We want to fill SPM that can hold a maximum capacity of C with some combination of data from a list of N possible data each with $size_i$ and $access\ number_i$ so that the access number of the data allocated into SPM is maximized. if N is the total number of data, then a solution is just a finite sequence s of N terms such that $s[n]$ is either 0 or the size of the n_{th} data. $s[n] = 0$ iff the n_{th} data is not selected in the solution. This solution must satisfy the constraint of not exceeding the maximum SPM capacity (i.e. $\sum_{i=1}^{N} s[i] \leq C$).

5   Hybrid Heuristics

We have implemented Tabu Search (TS) [3] and Genetic algorithms (GAs) [7] as below:

TS: An initial solution is generated randomly. Initially, the optimal solution equals the initial solution, the optimal access number is the access number of the initial solution and the tabu list is empty. The eth neighborhood of the current solution is generated and a new matrix containing the neighboring vectors is computed. Based on this matrix, a vector of corresponding current size values and a vector of corresponding current access number values are calculated. Best solutions are kept from neighborhood. The tabu list is updated to make a transition back to the old solution impossible for a period. We update if this new access number is better than the existing optimal one. We repeat this, as long as the number of iterations is not exceeded.

GA: The initial population is chosen randomly. At each generation, the solution points are evaluated for fitness (according to how much of the SPM capacity they fill). Depending on a Crossover Probability (P_c), the best solution mates with a random (non-extreme) solution, and the offspring replaces the worst one. We used both the Single and the Two Points Crossover techniques [7]. To prevent the algorithm to be trapped in local optima, we set a Mutation Probability (P_m) where we turn a term to 0 if it is currently nonzero, and to the corresponding data size if it is currently zero. GA stops when a specified maximum number of generations is reached.

Each of our new hybrid heuristics is explained below:

TS - GA: We apply TS, then GA. For GA, we consider the best solution found by TS as the solution to improve.

GA - TS: We apply GA, then TS. For TS, we take the best solution found by GA as the initial solution of TS and then we try to improve it.

GA Hybrid: We consider the GA approach where we replace the mutation operator by TS. This heuristic is more elaborate than the two previous ones, in the sense that it does not implement a simple combination.

6 Experimental Results

Our energy model is based on OTAWA [2] to collect information about number of accesses and on CACTI [9] to collect information about energy per access. Due to the lack of space, only results concerning the WB mode are given. Our hybrid heuristics and BEH have been implemented with the C language on a PC Intel Core 2 Duo, with a 2.66 GHz processor and 3 Gbytes of memory running under Mandriva Linux 2008. We used benchmarks presented in Table 2. As these benchmarks contain uniform data leading to a big number of local minima, and in order to put some trouble in BEH we decided to modify slightly our benchmarks. Concretely, this modification consists in adding one variable to each benchmark. This variable performs an output (so did not change the benchmarks features) and is big enough to provide energy savings if it is chosen for an SPM allocation. We referred to a modified benchmark as benchmarkCE.

Table 2. List of Benchmarks.

Benchmark	Suite	Description
Sha	MiBench	The secure hash algorithm that produces a 160-bit message digest for a given input.
Bitcount	MiBench	Tests the bit manipulation abilities of a processor by counting the number of bits in an array of integers.
Fir	SNU-RT	Finite impulse response filter (signal processing algorithms) over a 700 items long sample.
Jfdctint	SNU-RT	Discrete-cosine transformation on 8x8 pixel block.
Adpcm	Mälardalen	Adaptive pulse code modulation algorithm.
Cnt	Mälardalen	Counts non-negative numbers in a matrix.
Compress	Mälardalen	Data compression using lzw.
Djpeg	Mediabenchs	JPEG decoding.
Gzip	Spec 2000	Compression.
Nsichneu	Wcet Benchs	Simulate an extended Petri net. Automatically generated code with more than 250 if-statements.
Statemate	Wcet Benchs	Automatically generated code.

In [4], we have shown that TS alone, performs as well as BEH on the standard benchmarks. But, with the modified benchmarks, both TS and BEH did not give the optimal solution. In contrast, in [5], we have shown that GA alone, outperforms BEH in terms of energy savings with the modified benchmarks but did not do as well as BEH with the standard benchmarks. With our hybrid heuristics, we look for optimizing energy nevertheless we are considering the standard and the modified benchmarks. In all experiments, 30 different executions for each heuristic are generated. *Heuristic Mean* refers to the average results obtained on 30 executions of the considered heuristic. In contrast, *Heuristic Best* refers to the best solution obtained from the 30 executions performed. For BEH, the solution found does not change from an execution to another one.

Standard Benchmarks: Due to the lack of space, we only give results obtained, figures will be plotted in the full version of this paper. *TSGA1*, *GATS3* and *GA_Hybrid5* represent the results obtained for $P_m = 0.1$, $P_c = 0.5$ and for a single point crossover. *TSGA2*, *GATS4* and *GA_Hybrid6* represent the results obtained for $P_m = 0.1$, $P_c = 0.5$ and for a two points crossover. *GA_Hybrid5* and *GA_Hybrid6* give similar results. We therefore call *GA_Hybrid (5,6)* the common value of their executions. On most of standard benchmarks, all methods achieve the same energy performance as BEH. In addition, results show that when we are looking for the optimization of the average results obtained through all the executions, it is better to consider the GATS Heuristic. In fact, at worst, *TSGA1 Mean* and *TSGA2 Mean* consume respectively 6,65% and 8,60% (Djpeg) more energy than BEH. When at worst, *GATS3 Mean* and *GATS4 Mean* consume respectively only 3,81% and 3,68% (Gzip) more energy than BEH. In contrast, when we are looking for a best solution it is better to consider the TSGA Heuristic. In fact, *GATS3 Best* and *GATS4 Best* consume respectively 2,20% and 2,07% (Gzip) more energy than BEH. When *TSGA1 Best* and *TSGA2 Best* consume respectively only 1,03% (Gzip) and 2,40% (Djpeg) more energy than BEH. *GA_Hybrid (5,6)* consumes, at worst, 7,67% (Djpeg) more energy than BEH which is worst than GATS and TSGA heuristics.

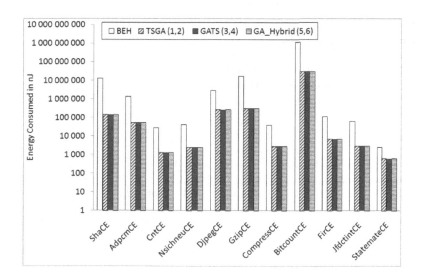

Fig. 1. Energy consumed by modified benchmarks with WB mode.

Modified Benchmarks: In this case, *TSGA1* and *TSGA2*, *GATS3* and *GATS4* give similar results. We therefore call respectively *TSGA (1,2)* and *GATS (3,4)* the common value of their executions. Figure 1 presents the results obtained. We see that all three methods achieve better energy savings than BEH on the modified benchmarks. In fact, these results show that *TSGA (1,2)*, *GATS (3,4)* and *GA_Hybrid (5,6)* consume from 76.23% (StatemateCE) up to

98.92% (ShaCE) less energy than BEH. However, the GA Hybrid is the faster approach as we reduce the number of generations. For BEH, although we used the modified benchmarks, we still obtain the same energy savings as before. The fact that BEH did not give the optimal solution for the modified benchmarks anymore is normal. This is due to the fact that BEH is a sort of access number/size of data. The variable we add in each benchmark has a given access number/size (this ratio depends on the data profiling of each benchmark) so that this variable is not a priority in the sorting made by BEH. This is done on purpose so that when it will be the turn of this variable to be treated by BEH, the SPM remaining space will not be enough to take this variable and hence it will be allocated in DRAM. In contrast, all our hybrid heuristics are robust enough to overcome this problem and find the optimal solution.

7   Conclusion and Perspectives

In this paper, nearly from 76% up to 98% less memory energy consumption is recorded with our hybrid heuristics when compared to BEH. In future work, we plan to investigate the same problem with relaxing the memory constraints by considering random memory sizes on one hand. On the other hand, we plan to explore other evolutionary heuristics.

8   Acknowledgments

The authors are grateful to anonymous referees for their comments and suggestions. This work is financed by the french national research agency (ANR) in the Future Architectures program.

References

1. H. Ben Fradj, A. El Ouardighi, C. Belleudy, and M. Auguin. Energy aware memory architecture configuration. ACM SIGARCH Computer Architecture News, 2005.
2. H. Cassé and C. Rochange. OTAWA, Open Tool for Adaptive WCET Analysis. In *DATE*, Nice, April 2007. Poster session.
3. M. Gendreau. *An introduction to tabu search*, volume 57. Kluwer Academic Publishers, Boston, MA, 2003.
4. M. Idrissi Aouad, R. Schott, and O. Zendra. A Tabu Search Heuristic for Scratch-Pad Memory Management. In *Proc. of WASET*, volume 64, April 2010.
5. M. Idrissi Aouad, R. Schott, and O. Zendra. Genetic Heuristics for Reducing Memory Energy Consumption in Embedded Systems. In *Proc. of ICSOFT*, July 2010. To appear.
6. M. Idrissi Aouad and O. Zendra. A Survey of Scratch-Pad Memory Management Techniques for low-power and -energy. In *Proc. of ICOOOLPS*, July 2007.
7. S. N. Sivanandam and S. N. Deepa. *Introduction to Genetic Algorithms*. Springer Publishing Company, Incorporated, 2007.
8. A. Tanenbaum. *Architecture de l'ordinateur 5e édition*. November 2005.
9. S.J.E. Wilton and N.P. Jouppi. Cacti: An enhanced cache access and cycle time model. *IEEE Journal of Solid-State Circuits*, 1996.

A Truly Random Number Generator Based on a Pulse Excited Cross Coupled Chaotic Oscillator

Salih Ergün

TÜBİTAK-National Research Institute of Electronics and Cryptology,
PO Box 74, 41470, Gebze, Kocaeli,Turkey
salih@uekae.tubitak.gov.tr

Abstract. Derivation mechanism of a non-autonomous cross-coupled chaotic circuit is presented. In order to guarantee robust chaotic behavior of the circuit against parameter variations, ideal set of parameters are determined by constructing bifurcation diagrams. A random number generator (RNG) based on this chaotic circuit is also introduced which relies on generating non-invertible binary sequences according to regional distributions of underlying chaotic signal. Experimental results verifying the feasibility of the circuit are given. Presented RNG features much higher and constant throughput rates, allows for offset compensation and fulfills the NIST-800-22 statistical test suite without further post-processing.

1 Introduction

In the last decade, the increasing demand of electronic official & financial transactions, the use of digital signature applications and the requirements of information secrecy have made the random number generators (RNGs) more popular. With this respect, RNGs, which have been generally used for military cryptographic applications in the past, have now an important role in the design of a typical digital communication equipment.

In spite of the fact that, the use of discrete-time chaotic maps in the realization of RNG is well-known for some time [1, 2], it was only recently shown that continuous-time chaotic oscillators can be used to realize RNGs also [3–5]. In particular, preliminary results of RNGs using a novel continuous-time chaotic oscillator have been reported in [4]. Although many chaotic oscillators exist in the literature, only a few of them are designed concerning high-performance integrated circuit (IC) design issues, such as low power consumption, high-frequency operation, operation capability at low voltage levels [6].

In this work we recall our previous paper [4] and further explain the derivation mechanism of the chaotic oscillator which is suitable for high-performance IC realization. Moreover, we further introduce the design of a RNG, which relies on generating non-invertible random binary bits according to regional distributions from one of the waveform of the chaotic oscillator. Presented RNG offers some considerable advantages over the existing ones [3, 4]. To guarantee robust chaotic behavior of the introduced design against parameter variations, ideal

E. Gelenbe et al. (eds.), *Computer and Information Sciences*, Lecture Notes
in Electrical Engineering 62, DOI 10.1007/978-90-481-9794-1_77,
© Springer Science+Business Media B.V. 2010

set of parameters are further determined in which the system is chaotic. For this purpose, bifurcation diagrams against all parameters are constructed. In comparison with the previous design [4], RNG introduced in this paper offers approximately sixfold rate expansion and constant output rate.

Furthermore, presented RNG have some other technical advantages. For instance, although the design is capable of passing randomness tests without compensation circuits [5], it allows for offset compensation for bias removal thus provide more robustness against external interference. Experimental results verifying the feasibility and the correct operation of the introduced RNG are presented such that numerically generated binary sequences fulfill FIPS-140-2 test suite [7] while RNG circuit fulfill the NIST-800-22 statistical test suite [8] without any further post-processing.

2   Chaotic Oscillator

Although many autonomous chaotic oscillators, which self-sustain chaos without need to excite, have been reported in the literature [9], there are relatively few non-autonomous chaotic oscillators [10]. In [10], a novel non-autonomous chaotic oscillator was reported and it was shown that an active second-order LC resonator can also exhibit chaos when excited by a periodic pulse-train.

In the reported chaotic oscillator [10], a comparator is employed to provide required nonlinearity and self feedback to the excited node where a bipolar periodic pulse-train voltage-source $V_P(t)$ is used to provide excitation. Pulse-excited LC resonator is activated through a linear negative resistor $-r$, which can be actively implemented using Op-Amp. Bipolar-transistor cross-coupled chaotic oscillator [4], which is used as the core of the RNG, is derived from pulse-excited LC resonator [10] by integrating two of them symmetrically and employing a differential-pair stage in order to realize two comparators.

The chaotic oscillator offers some considerable advantages over the existing one [10]. The circuit employs a differential pair to realize the required nonlinearity, which is the most widely used basic analog building block due to its high IC performance. The resistors employed in the circuit have very small values, so they can be effectively realized on IC. Moreover, the proposed chaotic oscillator is balanced; hence it offers better power supply rejection and noise immunity. Chaotic circuit is simple due to the absence of large blocks such as negative-resistor or comparator stages. Finally, the external source used to drive the circuit is a periodical pulse train, which can be very accurately and easily realized using the clock signal already available on chip.

When giving parameters for which the system is chaotic, appropriate intervals should be given rather than a single parameter set as it was reported in [4]. A practical circuit will always show parameter deviations and one should be sure that there is enough clearance for the latter. To guarantee robust chaotic behavior of the chaotic oscillator against parameter variations, ideal set of parameters are determined as the centers of the widest parameter intervals. For this purpose, bifurcation diagrams [11] against all parameters are constructed using a 4th-order Runge-Kutta algorithm with an adaptive step size.

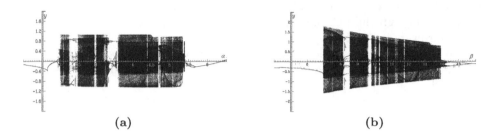

(a)   (b)

Fig. 1. Bifurcation diagram of y against a) α and b) β.

For example, bifurcation diagram of y against α and β are shown in Fig. 1. As a consequence, the ideal set of parameters are determined as $\alpha = 4$, $\beta = 12.85$, $\omega = 0.91$, $c_0 = 24.1$ and $\epsilon = 0.34$ which are the centers of the widest parameter intervals, in which the system is chaotic.

3 Random Number Generator Design

Due to having a positive Lyapunov exponent and a noise-like power spectrum, being extremely sensitive to initial conditions which make them unpredictable [12], chaotic systems lend themselves to be exploited for random number generation. In this paper, we further present a method for generating binary random bits which receives a chaotic waveform from the continuous time chaotic oscillator and which relies on generating non-invertible random binary bits according to regional distributions from the one of the state which corresponds to one of the waveform of the chaotic oscillator. It should be noted that non-invertibility is a key feature for generating random numbers [13].

In order to obtain a non-invertible map only the x variables of the Poincaré section was used. The voltage v_1, which corresponds to the variable x, was converted into binary sequences by using the circuit shown in Fig. 2a. In this circuit, the comparators were implemented from LM311 chips and the voltage levels V_{top}, V_{middle} and V_{bottom} were used to realize the thresholds in the equation given below:

$$
\begin{aligned}
S_{(top)i} &= sgn(v_{1i} - V_{top}) & when \ v_{1i} \geq V_{middle} \\
S_{(bottom)i} &= sgn(v_{1i} - V_{bottom}) & when \ v_{1i} < V_{middle} \\
S_{(xor)i} &= S_{(top)i} \bigotimes S_{(bottom)i}
\end{aligned}
\tag{1}
$$

An FPGA based hardware, which has a PCI interface was designed to upload the binary data to the computer. At an adjusted time inside a period of the external periodical pulse train, $v_p(t)$, output bit stream of the comparators was sampled and stored in binary format. Von Neumann processing (VNP) for S_{top} and S_{bottom} sequences and exclusive-or operation (XOR) for S_{xor} sequence were also implemented inside the FPGA. After Von Neumann processing and exclusive-or operation, the candidate random numbers were uploaded to the computer through the PCI interface. Maximum data storage rate of our FPGA based hardware is 62 Mbps.

We initially examined the distribution of v_1 along one period of $v_p(t)$. As a result, distribution of v_1 obtained $46\mu sec$ after the rising edges of $v_p(t)$ is shown in Fig. 2b.

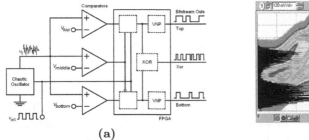 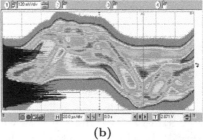

(a)   (b)

Fig. 2. a) Regional random number generation using pulse-excited cross-coupled chaotic oscillator b) Histogram of v_1 obtained $46\mu sec$ after the rising edges of $v_p(t)$.

To be able to determine the thresholds appropriately, we examined top and bottom distributions of the chaotic waveform. Then, V_{top} and V_{bottom} were determined as the medians of the top and bottom distributions which were $103mV$ and $-287mV$, respectively while V_{middle} was determined as $-107mV$. Then, S_{top}, S_{bottom} and S_{xor} bit streams of length 50MBytes were acquired for the given appropriate threshold values. The obtained bits were subjected to full NIST test suite.

As a result, we have experimentally verified that, bit sequences S_{top} and S_{bottom} thus obtained passed the tests of full NIST-800-22 test suite after Von Neumann processing and that bit sequence S_{xor} generated by S_{top} and S_{bottom} passed the tests of full NIST-800-22 test suite without any further post processing. Test results, which correspond to the uniformity of p-values and the proportion of passing sequences showing the correct operation of the RNG circuit are given in the Table 1. It is reported that, for a sample size of $419 \times 100000Bits$, the minimum pass rate for each statistical test with the exception of the random excursion (variant) test is approximately 0.975418.

Assuming that, top and bottom distributions have approximately the same density, bit rates of S_{top} and S_{bottom} are equal to the half of external periodical pulse train; hence throughput of S_{xor} is reduced by a factor of two and effectively becomes $\frac{14480}{2} = 7240bit/s$ when the frequency of $v_p(t)$ is 14.48 KHz. Maximum throughput data rate of RNG can be generalized as $f_{xor} = \frac{f_0\omega}{2}$, where

STATISTICAL TESTS	S_{xor} Bit Sequence	
	$P-Value$	$Proportion$
Frequency	0.561393	0.9857
Block Frequency	0.013779	0.9881
Cumulative Sums	0.289321	0.9857
Runs	0.556410	0.9809
Longest Run	0.095035	0.9833
Rank	0.502536	0.9905
FFT	0.663130	1.0000
Nonperiodic Templates	0.647276	1.0000
Overlapping Templates	0.632041	0.9928
Universal	0.227773	1.0000
Apen	0.051058	0.9905
Random Excursions	0.714660	1.0000
Random Excursions Variant	0.894201	1.0000
Serial	0.536606	0.9905
Linear Complexity	0.348514	0.9833

Table 1. Results of the NIST-800-22 test suite for S_{xor} Sequence.

$f_0 = \frac{1}{2\pi\sqrt{LC}}$. In our previous work [4], throughput rate of raw bit sequences which could not pass the randomness tests without Von Neumann post-processing decreased to $\frac{f_0\omega}{3}$. Considering that throughput rate of processed sequences after the Von Neumann post-processing approximately becomes $\frac{f_0\omega}{12}$, RNG introduced in this paper offers sixfold rate expansion in comparison with the previous design [4].

However note that, chaotic circuits operating at much higher frequencies are reported in the literature. For instance, simulation results of a non-autonomous chaotic circuit operating in the GHz range is presented in [14] which offers a throughput in the order of a few hundred Mbps. We can deduce that, such data rates which are substantially higher than the throughput of RNGs available in the literature, may render presented RNG exploiting continuous-time chaos attractive.

It should be noted that, since the chaotic oscillator utilized in this paper is non-autonomous, the available external clock signal was used to generate bit sequences. As a consequence of this clocking nature and fulfilling the randomness tests without post-processing, the introduced RNG is able to offer much higher and constant data rates in comparison with the previous designs [3, 4]. Moreover, on the contrary to [3, 4], the presented design allows for offset compensation [5] using the mono-bit test for bias removal thus provides more robustness against external interference, parameter variations and tampering and fulfills the NIST-800-22 statistical test suite without any further post-processing.

4   Conclusions

Derivation mechanism of a non-autonomous cross-coupled chaotic oscillator is presented along with ideal set of parameters. Several continuous-time chaotic oscillators may be designed by using the derivation mechanism described in this paper. A RNG based on this chaotic oscillator is also introduced which offers much higher and constant throughput rates, allows for offset compensation and fulfills the NIST-800-22 statistical test suite without any further post-processing. Experimental results presented in this paper not only verify the feasibility of the presented design, but also encourage its use as a high-performance IC RNG as well. In comparison with previous RNG designs available in the literature, it is seen that RNGs based on continuous-time chaotic oscillators can offer much higher and constant data rates without post-processing.

References

1. Stojanovski, T., Kocarev, L.: Chaos-Based Random Number Generators-Part I: Analysis. IEEE Trans. Circuits and Systems I, Vol. 48, 3 (2001) 281-288
2. Callegari, S., Rovatti, R., Setti, G.: Embeddable ADC-Based True Random Number Generator for Cryptographic Applications Exploiting Nonlinear Signal Processing and Chaos. IEEE Transactions on Signal Processing, Vol. 53, 2 (2005) 793-805
3. Yalcin, M.E., Suykens, J.A.K., Vandewalle, J.: True Random Bit Generation from a Double Scroll Attractor. IEEE Transactions on Circuits and Systems I: Fundamental Theory and Applications, Vol. 51(7). (2004) 1395-1404
4. Ergün, S., Özoğuz, S.:A Truly Random Number Generator Based on a Continuous-Time Chaotic Oscillator for Applications in Cryptography. LNCS 3733, (ISCIS). (2005) 205214
5. Ergün, S., Özoğuz, S.:Compensated True Random Number Generator Based On a Double-Scroll Attractor. Proc. International Symposium on Nonlinear Theory and its Applications (NOLTA). (2006) 391-394
6. Delgado-Restituto, M., Rodriguez-Vazquez, A.: Integrated Chaos Generators. Proc. of IEEE, Vol. 90(5). (2002) 747-767
7. National Institute of Standard and Technology, FIPS PUB 140-2, Security Requirements for Cryptographic Modules, NIST, Gaithersburg, MD 20899, (2001)
8. National Institute of Standard and Technology.: A Statistical Test Suite for Random and Pseudo Random Number Generators for Cryptographic Applications. NIST 800-22, http://csrc.nist.gov/rng/SP800-22b.pdf (2001)
9. Elwakil, A.S., and Kennedy, M.P.:Construction of classes of circuit independent chaotic oscillators using passive-only nonlinear devices. IEEE Trans. Circuits Syst. I, Vol. 48. (2001) 289-307
10. Elwakil, A.S., and Özoğuz, S.:Chaos in pulse-excited resonator with self feedback. Electron. Lett., 39, (11), (2003) 831-833
11. John, F., Marsden, J.E., and Sirovich L. Applied Mathematical Sciences. Ithaca, Fall Vol.42, (1985) 22-32
12. Devaney, R.: An introduction to Chaotic Dynamical Systems. 2nd ed. Reading, MA: Addison-Wesley, (1989)
13. Shamir, A.: On The Generation of Cryptographically Strong Pseudorandom Sequences. ACM Transactions on Computer systems, Vol. 1. (1983) 38-44
14. Ergün, S., Özoğuz, S.:Truly Random Number Generators Based on Non-Autonomous Continuous-time Chaos. Int. J. Circ. Theor. Appl. (2008) published online, DOI: 10.1002/cta.520

Author Index